The Transformation of EAST AFRICA

THE TRANSFORMATION OF EAST AFRICA

STUDIES IN POLITICAL ANTHROPOLOGY

Stanley Diamond & Fred G. Burke

EDITORS

BASIC BOOKS, INC., PUBLISHERS · New York, London

© 1966 by the Program of Eastern African Studies, Maxwell Graduate School
    of Citizenship and Public Affairs, Syracuse University
Library of Congress Catalog Card Number: 66–26211
Manufactured in the United States of America
Designed by Sophie Adler

FOREWORD

The hallmark of the program of Eastern African studies is its recognition of the dignity, the traditional cultures, and the future promise of the African. The task of a program of this kind in an American university is not to lecture at Africans nor to carp at their attempts to shape new political philosophies and institutions, but to understand and, when asked, to participate cooperatively in the pragmatic solution of pressing educational and technical problems.

It is in this spirit that the following essays were constructed for a faculty-student seminar on Problems of Nation-Building in East Africa. The Maxwell School is grateful to Professors Stanley Diamond and Fred Burke for their energies and efforts in soliciting and editing the papers which follow. It is hoped that they will make a fundamental contribution to a wider understanding of nation-building and modernization in a most important part of the world.

Syracuse, New York STEPHEN K. BAILEY
April 1966

ACKNOWLEDGMENTS

The editors are grateful to students and colleagues at the Maxwell Graduate School whose cooperation made their work feasible. Mr. Clyde Ingle, student of Africa, carried many burdens, contained many conflicts, and managed to do both gallantly.

S. D.
F. B.

THE AUTHORS

BRACK E. S. BROWN is a member of the Syracuse University team at the Kenya Institute of Administration. He is currently completing work for a certificate in Eastern African Studies at the Maxwell School, Syracuse University; his master's thesis is on East African Federation.

FRED G. BURKE is Professor of Political Science and Director of the Program of Eastern African Studies at Syracuse University. He has carried out fieldwork in East Africa over the past ten years and is the author of *Africa's Quest for Order* (1964), *Local Government and Politics in Uganda* (1964), and numerous contributions to scholarly journals.

ROBERT O. COLLINS has traveled widely in the Nile Valley and East Africa and has resided in the Sudan. He is the author of numerous scholarly articles on the Sudan and the *Southern Sudan 1883–1898* (1962). Currently an Associate Professor of History at the University of California, Santa Barbara, he has also taught at Williams College and the African Institute, Columbia University.

STANLEY DIAMOND, formerly Professor of Anthropology in the Maxwell Graduate School of Syracuse University, is now Professor of Anthropology in the Graduate Faculty of the New School for Social Research, and Senior Lecturer in Anthropology at Columbia University. He has done field work in Nigeria, Israel, and among the Iroquois. Professor Diamond has published widely in scholarly journals and is a contributing editor of *Africa Today* and *Dissent*. Among his works are *Culture in History: Essays in Honor of Paul Radin* (editor, 1960) and *The Anaguta of Nigeria: Suburban Primitives* (1966). He has been a fellow of the Social Science Research Council and a Wenner-Gren and Bollingen grantee.

CAROL FISHER, Assistant Professor of Citizenship and Anthropology at Syracuse University, received her Doctor of Social Science from that university with supporting work in sociology and social psychology. Among her publications is *The Middle East in Crisis* co-edited with Fred Krinsky, (1959). She is currently Field Coordinator of the Syracuse University Program of Eastern African Studies research project on village settlement in Tanzania.

WILLIAM H. FRIEDLAND, Associate Professor at the New York State School of Industrial and Labor Relations, Cornell University, conducted research in Tanganyika in 1958–1960 under a Ford Foundation Fellowship. His doctoral dissertation on Tanganyikan trade unions is currently being revised for publication. He is author of *Unions and Industrial Relations in Underdeveloped Areas* (1963), *Unions, Labor and Industrial Relations in Africa: An Annotated Bibliography* (1965), and edited (with Carl G. Rosberg, Jr.) *African Socialism* (1964) to which he contributed the chapter "Basic Social Trends."

CHARLES EDWARD FULLER is Professor of Anthropology, Scarritt College, Nashville, Tennessee. He was a missionary for the Methodist Church in Southeast Africa from 1938 to 1951. In addition to research during this period of residence in Africa, he conducted research in Africa in 1961–1962.

MARVIN HARRIS is Professor of Anthropology at Columbia University and a former chairman of that department. He did fieldwork in Mozambique in 1956–1957 as a Fellow of the Ford Foundation. One of the few American social scientists to have worked in both Brazil and Portuguese Africa, Professor Harris has devoted fifteen years of research to the problems of comparative race relations. *Minorities in the New World,* co-authored with Charles Wagley (1958), *Patterns of Race in the Americas* (1964), and *Portugal's African Wards* (1958) are some of his better known publications in the race relations field.

ELIZABETH HOPKINS received a master's degree in Anthropology from Columbia and is currently finishing work on the requirements for the doctorate at the same institution. She has engaged in research in Uganda under the auspices of the Social Science Research Council. She is at present an assistant professor at Smith College.

FRANCIS A. J. IANNI is a past Associate Commissioner for Research, United States Office of Education. He has published in the fields of education and anthropology and done field work under various grants in Ethiopia. He is currently Director, Division of Educational Institutions and Programs, Teachers College, Columbia University.

K. G. V. KRISHNA is a Senior Lecturer in Economics at University College, Nairobi. The author of numerous publications, Professor Krishna is currently doing a study, "The Role of Small Industry in the Industrial Development of Africa," for the United Nations. He was Visiting Lecturer, Syracuse University, in 1963–1964.

LARRY R. G. MARTIN prepared the maps for this volume. He has received a master's degree in Geography at Syracuse University and has contributed cartographic work to several publications.

GEORGE J. MOUTAFAKIS holds degrees from New York University where he was awarded a Fels Foundation grant for research overseas. He has taught at Lamar State College, College of the Holy Cross, New York University, and Syracuse University. While at Syracuse he received a grant under the auspices of the Maxwell Graduate School's East African Program to do research in Africa. He has written numerous articles on Africa for the publication *Report* of which he is a contributing editor. At present, Mr. Moutafakis is Assistant Professor of History at Williams College, Williamstown, Massachusetts.

ROBERT I. ROTBERG, Assistant Professor of History, Harvard University, is the author of *The Rise of Nationalism in Central Africa: The Making of Malawi and Zambia, 1873–1964* (1965), *Christian Missionaries and the Creation of Northern Rhodesia, 1880–1924* (1965), and numerous articles on Malawi and Zambia. His research has included four long visits to Africa.

ANTHONY H. RWEYEMAMU is Lecturer in Political Science, University of East Africa, University College, Dar es Salaam. A citizen of Tanzania, he holds a doctoral candidate in political science at the Maxwell Graduate School, Syracuse University.

GEORGE W. SHEPHERD, JR., is Associate Professor of International Relations in the Graduate School of International Studies, University of Denver. He is the author of *They Wait in Darkness* (1956), *Politics of African Nationalism* (1962), and numerous articles on the politics and international relations of Africa. Professor Shepherd spent the year 1964–1965 as Senior Lecturer at the University of Khartoum under Rockefeller Foundation auspices.

A. W. SOUTHALL is Professor of Anthropology at Syracuse University. Formerly Professor of Sociology and Social Anthropology, Makerere University College, University of East Africa and Chairman, East African Institute of Social Research (1957–1964), he is the author of numerous articles on Africa. Among his better known works are *Alur Society: A Study in Processes and Types of Domination* (1958), *Townsmen in the Making* with P. C. W. Gutkind (1957), and *Social Change in Modern Africa* (editor, 1961).

GORDON M. WILSON is the Chairman of Marco Surveys, Ltd., Nairobi. He is the author of *Luo Customary Law and Chik Gi Tim Luo* (1952).

CONTENTS

MAPS

THE PRE-COLONIAL
AND
COLONIAL SETTING

EASTERN
AFRICA

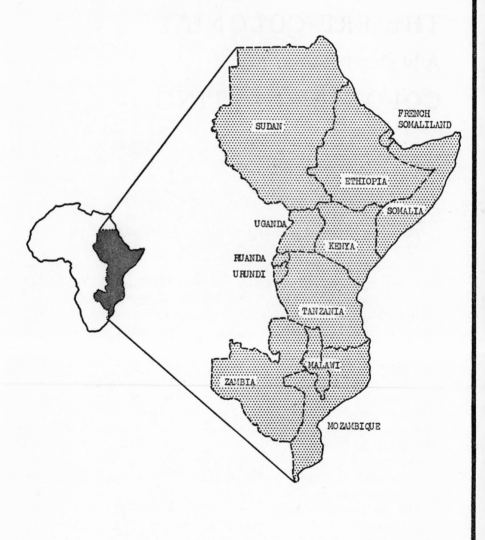

SUDAN

FRENCH
SOMALILAND

ETHIOPIA

SOMALIA

UGANDA

KENYA

RUANDA
URUNDI

TANZANIA

MALAWI

ZAMBIA

MOZAMBIQUE

LM

1

Introduction: Africa in the Perspective of Political Anthropology

Stanley Diamond

ETHNOCENTRISM AND HISTORY

No single discipline is adequate to cover the range of contemporary African phenomena, but this is not to say that individual scholars, broadly cultivated, well trained, and sensitive to African realities, could not create universal works of penetration and importance. Hopefully, that will happen eventually; however, it has not yet happened. Therefore, an effort such as the present volume must depend upon disciplinarians who bring specific points of view and more or less specialized training to a series of problems which have been worked out and, to a degree, coordinated in advance.

Orthodox anthropological inquiry, moving in space and holding time constant, or moving in time and holding space constant, has tended to emphasize the micro-social structure of "tribes" or "tribal groups"; the apparent self-sufficiency and isolation of African societies have strengthened this tendency. Even where culture areas were roughed out extensively, whether in the German or American ethnological traditions, and with proper regard for the differences between them, the criteria were more or less geographically continuous clusters of linked, presumably aboriginal traits, with certain patterns of spatial distributions assumed to be roughly translatable into temporal sequence. The scholarly significance of such studies can be considerable, but the approach is not adequate to a comprehension of modern Africa, the Africa that faces us fleshed out and alive, and which refuses to be reduced to a skeleton of abstractions. In that same Africa, it must be recognized, we are confronted with social and cultural wreckage, with what Lévi-Strauss has called, in a parallel context, junkheaps of

3

Western civilization, and not with societies that can be honestly analyzed as if they were pristine. Africa *is* the edge of *our* jungle. The use of the ethnological present is justifiable, but not at the expense of immediate realities.

As Africa underwent its forced march to modernization, the theoretical and practical problems involved attracted the attention of sociologists, economists, and political scientists. Each of these disciplines is represented here under the general rubric of political anthropology, for it is our contention that anthropological effort, embracing, as it presumes to, the ensemble of forms and relations in any given society, remains basic to an understanding of Africa. But the missing dimension, in orthodox anthropological work, has been political, in part because political factors increase in importance as societies shift from a traditional base, the main province of anthropology, to a modern one.

Anthropologists characteristically use the term "acculturation" to describe such historical shifts, and the political context has been slighted. The fact is that "acculturation," even where an exchange of traits is involved, is largely a matter of conquest and as used by anthropologists almost always implies the assault by civilized upon primitive or traditional societies. For example, the propagation of basic elements of ancient Egyptian culture along the eastern Mediterranean strip was a precipitant of political and economic conquest, that is, the less powerful, less technologically evolved peoples were confronted with a single set of alternatives, rooted in the Egyptian experience. Civilized peoples seem always to project their specific forms of development as the inevitably progressive destiny or fate of the human race. The political component has been largely replaced by deterministic arguments from natural law, natural history, and natural science. Anthropology as a civilized discipline has, despite dissent from many of its practitioners, tended, as a body of organized knowledge, to share these ethnocentric notions of historical inevitability. Political decisions are, however, rather more existential in their nature. They can be literally decisive; they are implicated with problems of will and authority. For politics is people in groups deciding to act in order to reject, create, or maintain the patterns of authority that legitimate their social behavior. Civilized peoples and civilized disciplines have therefore been particularly sensitive to political action on the part of "backward" peoples which created possibilities of alternative patterns of social evolution, patterns that the patron states thereby considered a potential threat to the integrity of their entire cultural spectrum. The fabric of world culture, our oral or inscribed literary, esthetic, and religious inheritance, may be, as we anthropologists are prone to put it, a multicolored fabric; but since the rise of civilization that fabric has been woven on a political loom.

Africa's struggle is, first and foremost, the struggle to consummate a political revolution, that is, a revolution to restore the dignity of enthralled peoples. Power and authority to command have been transferred, through the eastern and western segments of the continent, if not yet at its heart, from alien European to indigenous African hands. Even if that authority is no more than a symbol, a flag, a banner, a promise of a future reality in socioeconomic and cultural depath, Africans of all classes and statuses are committed to its meaning. Their nominal independence, occurring during what may well be the last phase of the era of the politically narcissistic state, has meant the transformation of far-flung colonial empires and obvious spheres of influence into a Balkan pattern of boundaries. That is to say, the political geography of the continent remains artificial, having its roots in conflicting metropolitan interests, and having been created in the image of nineteenth-century Europe. Yet, granted the economic subordination of Africa to the North Atlantic powers in a world in which the rich are getting richer and the poor poorer, granted the economic and social disparities within the new African states themselves, the African revolution is nevertheless real, and it is only beginning. If the political, economic, social, and cultural cleavages between the North Atlantic powers and Africa are further sharpened by a sense of racial distinction, we of the Western world are mainly at fault; it was, after all, commercial slavery that found it necessary to conceive blacks not only as culturally exotic but as inferior objects. Strangely, or is it strange, Europeans have rarely glorified the culturally alien or racially distinct as superior to themselves. Nor have they often acknowledged the right of such peoples to live undisturbed. Contact phenomena have been conquest phenomena. But the converse does not hold; how many traditional peoples have idolized the technological power of the Europeans, sought to join or emulate them; how many have innocently welcomed them as gods; how many have sought to evade that power by any means, fighting desperately to maintain their cultural breathing space? Black and white remain irrelevant and vulgar means of classifying human traits, but the practice is understandably gaining ground in sub-Saharan Africa, and should be understood as integral to the struggle for equal manhood. Indeed, the thrust toward pan-African unity, even if, at present, more formal than real in its manifestations, is in part a paradigmatic response to the convenient Western assumption that Africans were black but otherwise undifferentiated. However, pan-Africanism in both its ethnic and its political dimensions, is also an effort to bind up the wounds of arbitrary division inflicted by external force, to find a new unity across the barriers of gerrymandered states, and beyond the ancient boundaries of kin group or "tribe," which in themselves typically cross-cut district, regional, or "national" frontiers fixed by the colonial powers.

Since Portuguese slavers established their human factories along the eastern and western coasts of Africa, it has been typical, in the North Atlantic world, to stereotype the peoples and cultures of the continent, to regard them as a historyless, featureless, backward, and largely passive mass. These conventional rationalizations are familiar, as prophecies they can become self-fulfilling; that is the way masters are compelled to regard those whom they enslave. Actually, Africa is the planet's most diverse continent, rich with peoples on all levels of social organization and representing a splendid variety of cultural forms. The spectrum is wide, ranging from small, authentically primitive societies such as the Anaguta of the high Nigerian Plateau through the acephalous but populous Ibo or Kikuyu, to the complex proto-states of aboriginal Buganda or Dahomey. But this variety, this richness, lies like a mineral within its ore. The overburden of colonialism and slavery has blurred cultural outlines and, both grossly and subtly, shifted social functions even when the forms seem to have remained the same. Yet, as recently as 1963 Professor Trevor Roper, the distinguished British historian, pronounced from his well-fortified position as Chairman of the Faculty of History at Oxford University that British undergraduates, "seduced as always by the changing breath of journalistic fashion, demand that they should be taught African history. Perhaps in the future," he went on, "there will be some African history to teach. But at present there is none, there is only the history of the Europeans in Africa. The rest is darkness . . . and darkness is not a subject of history."

This can only be called intellectual imperialism, an inverted species of provincialism, for Africa has, of course, a prehistory, and a history written in the migrations of peoples, in the diffusion of cultural traits, in the artifacts found in its earth, in the connections traceable among its myriad languages, and in the great oral traditions of its societies. There are even documents available to us (and by "history" Trevor Roper probably meant *documentary* history)—conceived, for example, in Swahili and Hausa, but inscribed in Arabic, dating back several centuries. In Sudanic West Africa such documents as the Kano Chronicle give us a fairly clear picture of events ten centuries old. Of course, this kind of history is necessarily skewed by the attitudes of invading groups, notably, but not exclusively, Arabs, Arabic speakers, or upper-caste professors and confessors of Islam. But they provide, at least, a literature of pre-European conquest; the distortions are probably of the same order of magnitude as the information that has been filtered to us by the scribes, priests, and courtiers of eleventh-century England or, God save the mark, by the journalists and closet academicians of the twentieth. Historians who live by documents, and therefore consider documents sacrosanct, would deny authentic history to most of the human race for the greater period of time on this planet. Black Africa has a history, indeed a pre-European history, but what the subcontinent lacks is native historians, who must now begin to engage in a vast salvage operation to shore up the memory of a continent of people sinking under a tide of commercialism, a type of modernization which does not use, but obliterates, the past. Of course, within the past generation efforts to create archives and train indigenous African scholars have been undertaken at Ibadan, Accra, and elsewhere, and such efforts are being intensified as the dimensions of the problem become more obvious. It is of some historical interest that anthropologists as diverse and distinguished as A. L. Kroeber and L. H. Morgan discovered little in Africa to hold scholarly attention. The latter imagined that study of its peoples would be useless for our understanding of social evolution, and the former regarded them as constituting an inexplicable cultural backwater of limited relevance to world history, dominated by a few recurrent themes—two classic instances of civilized and disciplinary ethnocentrism.

Even though the popular image of Africa, ironically reported by Mark Twain as "that slab of a continent, burdened by jungles, wild animals and savages . . ." has faded away, the projection of the continent by the new masters of popular cant as a puzzle of inherently absurd quasi-modern principalities is equally unenlightened. Whereas Europeans, Asians, North Americans, and Latin Americans are referred to with a certain technical refinement, scholars have, on the whole, failed to honor fully the distinctions between African peoples. Correlatively, the similarities have not been adequately traced and clarified, whether in terms of geographical area, cultural trait, or level of sociopolitical integration; the latter classification is, in our judgment, critical, for reasons to be discussed below.

THE LIMITS OF EAST AFRICA

The apparent featurelessness of sub-Saharan Africa is a heritage of the phase of frank political colonialism. British West Africa, with its Slave, Ivory, and Gold Coasts, French West Africa, German East Africa, Portuguese East Africa, Portuguese West Africa, and so on—that robber's terminology which pooled or fragmented peoples and places with respect for the needs of conquest alone, and reflected in an alien arena the struggles of metropoles, continues to obscure a sensible historical or, for that matter, geographical definition of the continent. For example, the identity of the general area "East Africa" had, from 1918 on, been determined primarily by the British colonial sense of possession. Thus, Kenya, Uganda, Tanganyika, and Zanzibar, each territory in itself being a calculus of international rivalries and efforts at pacification, formed, in their ensemble, the image of East Africa, at least in the English-speaking world. In Portugal, of course, East Africa was somewhat more ambiguously defined; indeed, it was primarily confined to Mozambique. More scholarly definitions of people and places were not notably successful in penetrating these arbitrary political barriers.

The assumption that the "real" East Africa somehow represented the core British colonies and their descendant states died hard. For example, the Maxwell Graduate School East Africa Program found itself, because of historical inertia and the accessibility of the area, focused on the British-defined, imperially controlled territories. The seminar which served, during the academic year 1963–1964, as the basis for this book was, in part, a conscious effort to redefine the areal focus of the program. The result has been to substitute the term "Eastern" for "East" Africa, standing for a region which reveals certain geographical and cultural continuities, including, but not confined to, those imposed by colonialism. The map on page 2 indicates this still arbitrary, but rationalizable reach. Of course, such an effort at regional definition, whether undertaken geographically and/or culturally, is bound to be contradictory. Similarly, one must be content with an abstraction; each concrete cultural or geographical border poses a question, but at least we have tried to avoid the amorphous continental generalization, a micro-social focus, and the metropolitan-centered delineations. We have accepted the customary view that North Africa is part of the Mediterranean world despite certain shared traits, trade routes, and suggestive prehistoric associations; it is probably correct to consider the Sahara as, if not a barrier, at least a selective cultural filter. The Sudan *is,* as Robert Collins indicates, *one* link to the north. We have omitted Rhodesia and South Africa proper, although most of their native peoples are culturally continuous with those of the geographical east. The larger portion of our western border constitutes an ill-defined and irredentist series of frontiers—Uganda, Rwanda, Burundi, and Zambia—asymmetrically cut by the Great Rift Valley and the Great Lakes. If we attempt to give this area a formal ethnological definition by fitting cultural traits to geographical features, there is a reasonable continuity in the ideological and economic orientation to cattle. Migration patterns (cattle nomads), topography, and climate have contributed to a relative concentration on animal husbandry. With few notable exceptions—for example the Fulani of the Western Sudan—Africa's major cattle-herding peoples, both nomadic and sedentary, are found in the East.

Of course, the classic formulation of this region, extending from the plateaus of Ethiopia on the north through the Great Lakes to eastern South Africa, and fading into the forests of the Congo Basin on the west, contains within itself cultural and geographical contradictions, omissions, and exceptions. For example, the Ovimbundu are included in the eastern cattle complex area although they inhabit Angola. The Hottentots, who are also cattle nomads, are excluded, presumably on the arbitrary bases of their internally marginal habitat (Kalahari Desert), their Bushman affinities, certain of their attitudes toward and uses of cattle, and their distinctive language; yet such "irregularities" can be matched within the cattle complex proper. Languages, for example, other than "Bantu" (one division of "Niger-Congo," the dominant aboriginal tongue, probably originating on the Nigerian Plateau), exist in the area. Such difficulties are inherent in culture area classifications. Still, the cattle complex does provide a sturdier base for conceiving Eastern Africa than this or that shifting modern or indigenous political boundary. If we add to the general sense of formal cultural continuity in the area, the fact that Eastern Africa was, as a whole, settlers' Africa, as distinguished from the Africa of the West Coast, and that its aboriginal linguistic continuities have been strengthened by the development of Swahili as a *lingua franca,* the region begins to assume a fairly distinctive cultural-historical shape. Moreover, and this is probably the most critical factor, the reaction against colonialism has included a conscious search for cultural bridges uniting African peoples, part of the effort to put services and institutions imposed by metropoles to the uses of African union. In intra-African and international meetings, East Africans are inclined to close ranks and support one another. The founding of Tanzania was, of course, the most dramatic instance, but it may well be only the beginning of wider attempts in increasing depth.

However, culture area and/or geographical approaches, being inherently formal, and often arbitrary, help us, at best, to set the stage on which the historical drama unfolds. In Africa, as elsewhere, the drama is quickened by the clash, union, and evolution of peoples on different levels of sociopolitical integration. Eastern Africa, roughly coterminous with the plateaus and parklands supportive of cultures engaged with cattle, was, for example, the habitat of peoples quite distinct in social type; the latter circumstance determined the uses to which cattle were put. There were so-called "pure" pastoralists to the north who revered cattle, such as the Masai, Nandi, Dinka, Shilluk; sophisticated, relatively integrated native states such as Buganda, in which cattle were herded by a particular caste of pastoralists, and chiefs kept large herds, but the peasants remain disinterested. In another interlacustrine proto-state, Ankole, which reveals the dynamic of pastoralist conquest of peasants quite clearly, along with the remarkable fluidity and irredentism of these early states, only the Bahima ruling group, the conquerors, had the right to own cattle; among people to the southeast, the typical Bantu speakers, horticulture and herding were practiced by the same unit, and it is among such people that organized military federations in the pattern of the Zulu were formed.

The point is that once we begin to consider sociopolitical types in their historical dimension, that is, levels of sociopolitical integration—the ways in which specific traits function—the dynamic of any given area becomes of paramount importance. Moreover, we can then move from people to people, area to area, in order to refine our understanding of what Julian Steward has called "regularities" and, one should add, *alternatives* of change throughout widening segments of our increasingly constricted modern world.

Thus any heuristic focus on Africa must be calibrated through the lenses of social change. The critical angle of vision on social change involving traditional cultures is political; political anthropology is, we believe, the proper study of the (sometimes exotic) forms and processes through which aboriginal societies contemporaneously evolve. That is, in order to understand the development of polities in particular areas, whether colonial or post-colonial, it is necessary to understand the political character of the indigenes. Primitive democracies of limited population, whether simple horticulturists such as the pagans of the Jos Plateau, or Kung hunters of the Kalahari, understand nothing of political chieftainship, regularized taxation or tribute, codified laws or police, socioeconomic class. They tend to develop patterned means of evading such political claims until direct or indirect

resistance proves impossible and the culture, sometimes the people themselves, certainly their social identity, crumble. But this underlying strain of
primitive democracy in Africa grades subtly into more civilized (technically
defined) polities. The discontinuity is not abrupt. Therefore, we find a
similar resistance to civil imposition among primarily kin-organized local
groups within the loosely organized proto-states, which may be broadly
defined as societies in transition from kin to civil structure.

Although self-contained primitive democracies are on the verge of vanish-
ing in sub-Saharan Africa, the local groups in the native proto-states—
whether in Buganda, in Dahomey, in Hausaland, or in Ankole—more or less
persist, as a peasantry, a peasantry that faces the new challenges of an
utterly commercial market and the modern omnipresent state, after whatever indigenous military and bureaucratic controls may have existed have
been superseded by colonial and post-colonial structures. It is this peasantry,
containing within itself the remnants of primitive Africa, which remains to
be heard from. Ancient habits of resistance and of accommodation to civil
imposition endure. Under contemporary conditions of deprivation, basic
questions emerge—what kinds of government will the peasantry opt for, and
whom will they choose as their enemies?

One should note here that empathy with the subject of study is not only a
professional necessity, but a matter of prudence in an explosive world.
African peasants constitute the great majority of African people and they
have much in common with the vast peasantries of Asia. The peasantries of
the major local areas, whether still on the soil, partially displaced, or in
transition to cities, are, to use Frantz Franon's borrowed metaphor, the
"wretched of the earth." In seeking to study and understand them in anthropological—that is, historical—depth, we may, at least, help underscore
the need for less brutal means of change than have thus far characterized
the history of civilization.

SOCIOPOLITICAL LEVELS OF INTEGRATION —A PRELIMINARY SCHEME

It should be clear, then, that any inquiry into African political dynamics
must take into account the various strata of sociopolitical organization native
to any given area. These "levels of integration," moreover, cross-cut the
traditional ethnological culture areas, presenting what are, in effect, pan-
African base lines for studying social change from the time of initial European contact.

Such a scheme could be constructed along the lines shown in the table on
pages 11–13.

Until a more refined scheme of this sort is worked out, illustrating the
relations among the peoples on the various native levels of organization, and
until the colonial impact on, and shaping of, the pre-existent structures is

Table 1-1

Sociopolitical Level	Pertinent Characteristics[a]	Typical Peoples	Geographic Area	Culture Area	Language Family
Primitive nomadic bands (hunting and gathering)	Economically and socially egalitarian; particularistic status and rank via special skills and/or ordinary passage through life cycle; no classes or castes; no specialized political structure; no secular chiefs; decisions by adult band members; population magnitude: under one hundred per band	Bushmen	Kalahari Desert, South Africa	Khoisan	Click (Khoisan)
		Pygmies (Mbuti)	Ituri Forest, Congo	Congo	Niger-Congo (Central Branch or "Bantoid," Bantu)
Intensive primitive democracies (shifting horticulture, supplemented by hunting and gathering)	Economically and socially egalitarian; particularistic status and rank via special skills and/or ordinary passage through life cycle; no classes or castes; no specialized political structure; no secular chiefs; priest chiefs incarnating tradition; hierarchy of informal councils on familial analogue; "tribal-wide" kin, religious, ceremonial connections; population magnitude: hundreds to thousands	Anaguta, Nyango-Irigwe	Jos Plateau, Nigeria	Western Sudan–Guinea Coast border	Niger-Congo (Central Branch or "Bantoid")

[a] Characteristics are not intended to be exhaustive, only synoptic, and diagnostic, nor have I here pursued the functional relations among diagnostic traits, weighed them as relatively variant or invariant, or indicated dynamics of development between societies on different levels. Since we are dealing with a continuum, a series of types, traits overlap, and cut-off points between levels tend to be arbitrary. However, a qualitative distinction emerges between the first three and the succeeding groups on the basis of political structure and process. In terms of the abstract sequence of models, people such as the Masai are pivotal. A significant proportion of sub-Saharan Africa states were directly or indirectly catalyzed by pastoralists. It should be noted that no sub-Saharan African economy developed beyond an elaborate horticultural system, which certainly accounts for certain cultural similarities among cultivators on all levels. Political societies based on intensive agriculture, irrigation, or functional equivalents would probably, as a class, vary uniformly from the African proto-states. But the state-building processes and the reactions to them seem analogous; such a specifically comparative study in ethnographic depth needs to be done.

Table 1-1 (*Continued*)

Sociopolitical Level	Pertinent Characteristics[a]	Typical Peoples	Geographic Area	Culture Area	Language Family
Extensive primitive democratic "nationalities" (shifting horticulture)[b]	Economically and socially egalitarian; particularistic status and rank via special skills and/or ordinary passage through life cycle; no classes or castes; no specialized political structure; controls exercised through elders, age-grading systems, sodalities, religious chiefs, segmentary lineage systems, clans (or lineages) cross-cutting localities; large number of substantially autonomous local settlements, but recognition of cultural fellowship in language, religion, dress, art and ceremonial life; ordinarily no directly "tribal-wide" kin, religious, or ceremonial associations; population magnitude: tens of thousands to several million	Ibo	Southeastern Nigeria	Guinea Coast	Niger-Congo (Kwa, Ibo)
		Kikuyu	Kenya	East Africa cattle complex	Niger-Congo (Central Branch or "Bantoid")
		Tiv	Nigerian Middle Belt	Western Sudan–Guinea Coast border	Niger-Congo (Central Branch or "Bantoid")
Aristocratic, warrior-oriented pastoralists (cattle nomads)	Catalysts for state formation; vocationally and/or ethnically distinct castes, but no embracing state structure; egalitarian relationships among regular "tribesmen"; raid horticulturists; barter for produce	Masai	Kenya, Tanganyika	East Africa cattle complex	Macro-Sudanic (Eastern Sudanic, "Nilo-Hamitic")

Table 1–1 (*Continued*)

Sociopolitical Level	Pertinent Characteristics^a	Typical Peoples	Geographic Area	Culture Area	Language Family
Militaristic federations (shifting horticulture, and pastoralism)	Military bonds primary, regimental organization; beginnings of secular chieftainship; stratified lineages; incipient but transient political structures; external conquest; population magnitude shifts drastically with military success or failure; Zulu Federation at least 100,000 at its peak	Zulu	South Africa	East Africa cattle complex	Niger-Congo (Central Branch or "Bantoid," Bantu)
Conquest proto-states (basically horticultural, specialized crops, and labor service for civil power)	Emerging peasantry; emerging class and caste systems; rudimentary bureaucracy, including specialized legal apparatus and/or personnel; primary civil laws against homicide, suicide, etc.; census-tax conscription patterns; relative autonomy of local groups which pay tribute in goods and services, but politicization of kin relationships; degree of political integration function of economic resources, division of labor, and ethnic differentiation; incipient, politically stimulated nationality; population magnitude: hundreds of thousands to several million	Ankole	Uganda	East Africa cattle complex	Niger-Congo (Central Branch or "Bantoid," Bantu)
		Buganda	Uganda	East Africa cattle complex	Niger-Congo (Central Branch or "Bantoid," Bantu)
		Dahomey	Dahomey	Guinea Coast	Niger-Congo (Kwa, Twi)

b That is, aboriginal, apolitical nationalities, or cultural fellowships.

more fully and consistently documented, our understanding of African political dynamics will remain limited. What we need to study intensely, then, is the sequence from aboriginal and traditional through colonial to post- and neo-colonial forms. This is an undertaking in political anthropology; only such an undertaking, whether conceived by economists, sociologists, political scientists, geographers, or ethnologists, independently, or, as in this volume, cooperatively, can give us a sense of what is unique in Africa as it emerges into the modern world, how problems in various parts of Africa converge or differ, and how shallow, self-serving and dangerous generalizations about the course of African development can be when disseminated in the popular press, or proclaimed official policy—that is, the result of sectarian decisions covertly arrived at as part of some global, geopolitical strategy.

THE GENERAL RELEVANCE OF POLITICAL ANTHROPOLOGY

Political anthropology, then, seeks to understand and isolate the specific dynamics of social change in whatever historical depth proves pertinent. The approach alerts us to the dangers of ascribing contemporary conflicts to abstractions such as "tribalism," and helps us to avoid reifying processes such as "acculturation," in which we then locate difficulties and possibilities of change; moreover, it leads us to discriminate between peoples and their rulers. To illustrate, in northern Nigeria, a Fulani-Hausa quasi-feudal elite had been buttressed, streamlined, and used by the colonial power, an elite that had little connection with even the Hausa-speaking peasantry within its immediate orbit of rule. This peasantry remained largely unrepresented in appointive or elective office and suffered the most limited alternatives in the backward, monolithic electoral pattern. Yet the tendency remains to lump all Hausawa together, to manufacture an abstract unity which is then manipulated to account for apparently insoluble "ethnic" problems, indeed to serve as a model for such problems in Africa generally, despite the fact that under the ethnic epidermis there is always a political bone of contention.

Similarly, Ashanti opposition to the central government in Ghana was a function of the lingering desire of the bigger chiefs and the more substantial cocoa farmers to maintain regional power and profit. The litany of cultural symbols which such groups chant, groups whose traditional relations to the people at large have long since atrophied, too often diverts us from a clear understanding of either the aboriginal or the evolving modern character of social relations in any given polity.

Practical politicians have usually understood these matters better than the academicians. The British Colonial Office, as is well known, made use of anthropologists, or anthropological approaches, in order to locate sources of difficulty in administrating native areas. The problem of imposing rule upon essentially acephalous peoples such as the Ibo led, after the disturbances of 1929, to a thorough restructuring of provincial government, wherein the natural rulers supposedly assumed prominence. This, of course, was anthropology in the service of colonialism—applied political anthropology—but the same weaponry has been used in the cause of anti-colonialism.

The Mau Mau rebellion in Kenya, generated primarily by the Kikuyu, was a form of politico-military revivalism, using aspects of traditional ritual to bind a striking force among a democratically organized but broken and impoverished people. The purpose—as projected by the Europeans—to drive them into the sea and restore the land to the Africans could hardly have been realized, but it proved an important factor in Kenya's thrust to independence, although only a handful of whites, thirty-two by official count, were murdered. Mau Mau terrorism, the crude eclecticism of its symbols, must be viewed against the background of cultural breakdown and the less personally spectacular, institutionalized inhumanity of the white settlers. The point is that the Mau Mau movement was not authentically Messianic, not a reversion to previous modes of behavior; rather it manipulated the latter to modern ends. Even during the height of the disturbance in Kenya, essential public utilities and services including those easily accessible to the rebels, were hardly touched. Obviously, these modern installations were recognized as essential to the conception of an independent Kenya in which Africans would have their pride of place—the motive of the uprising. The rebellion itself evolved from an initial, relatively mild to a selectively brutal point, following the imprisonment of the acknowledged leaders of the independence movement.

It deserves note that in an uprising ancestral to the Mau Mau, the so-called Maji Maji* wars that broke out in 1905 in Tanganyika, tens of thousands of Africans were killed over a two- to three-year period. Here again, politico-military revivalism was the issue; originating in Makondeland, the central ritual was supposed to render persons immune to bullets, which were literally liquefied, turned into water. The fact that Africans kill Africans under these circumstances does not render them irrelevant to the colonial context in which they develop. That is, the colonial environment generates the reaction, native peoples may either turn upon each other in frustration or for real political motives, but the ultimate goal is to shake the grip of alien political rule.

The perspective of political anthropology, then, furthers our understanding of ways in which cultural forms function in varying contemporary situations of social change, and, moreover, how they may be equated among traditional peoples and areas. Confining ourselves to this latter problem, we

---

* Maji means "water" in Swahili.

find ourselves engaged in a type of inquiry which can be designated "political ethnography," that is, the setting of specific cultural forms peculiar to traditionalist societies in a political context, and the assimilation of these diverse forms among different peoples into similar or equivalent functions.

Such interpretations are not inherent in the description of the form; nor are they customarily forthcoming from informants who move within highly specific and closed cultural worlds, as do all primitive and most traditional peoples. Interpreting history is not, after all, the same as living an event or a pattern, certainly not since the rise of civilization; nor should it be confused with mere reportage. The difficulty is interesting—most primitive and traditional persons are probably too deeply imbedded in their usages to interpret them; moreover, they lack the comparative vantage point. When we speak of comparison, we are assuming observers who command the material of more than a single culture, and who are therefore foreign to at least one of the cultures under analysis. Most civilized persons suffer an obverse disadvantage. They are probably too alienated from their usages to interpret them deeply and in the round. This poses certain problems, since ultimately one lands on metaphysical or, better, meta-ethnological ground. But the very act of structurally systematic, functional comparison is clarifying, in somewhat the same way that recurring dream symbols and behavioral correlations give us more or less confidence in this or that psychoanalytic theory. In short, no interpretation can be ultimately proven in a social field, explanations are either better or worse, more or less illuminating, or instrumental. Human action, informed by understanding, not academic theory, constitutes the proofs of history.

COMPARATIVE POLITICAL ETHNOGRAPHY

Anarchy after the Death of a King

One of the more obvious and directly comparable cultural forms within the scope of political ethnography is social anarchy following the death of a king or paramount ruler in societies, otherwise divergent in form, that we have already designated as proto-states. Indeed, such anarchy is a symptom of proto-state formation. This phenomenon has a wide distribution in space and time—e.g., early Norman England, Carolingian and Merovingian France, Dahomey in West Africa, Ankole in East Africa—and is uniquely ritualized among Mongols in China. Confining ourselves to Africa, general civil lawlessness, including the stealing of livestock, personal or familial redress for unatoned wrongs, and highway robbery, lasted for an indeterminate period following the death of the paramount ruler. Now in fully developed civil societies, the death of a king, of any head of state, is an incident in the chain of rule; the state continues to function in its many-layered bureaucratic depth. The king is dead, we say of George V or VI, but then immediately *"Long live the king!"*

But in Dahomey, in the infancy of civil society, the death of the political ruler ruptured the fragile civil nexus binding the people. The feeble state structure, comprising the local communities, the bureaucracy, the royal and dynastic lineages, lost its linchpin. The structure collapsed until a new king was enstooled. In the interim, the people broke loose; they turned to their kinsmen for protection, incarnating the pre-state function of the kin groups; the imposed "peace" of the king no longer held. To the people, the king's death symbolized the lifting of onerous restrictions; to the royal clan and the dependent bureaucracy, it meant the extinction of the agency that enabled them to exploit the local communities, since the king was the ultimate sanction and source of the tributary network. On the death of each king the whole patriarchal fiction had to be renewed; the civil process, grinding to a halt, had to be reprimed. There are, therefore, two major aspects of this phenomenon, as evident in Dahomey. The first has already been implied— the suspension of the civil rule that was regarded as alien by the local communities which fed the tributary network; correlatively, the joint family and local sanctions for social behavior were being circumscribed by civil precedent, social anarchy being a logical result of the indeterminate cultural situation, no longer quite kin, and barely civil.

The second aspect was the dynastic struggle that occurred among the sons of the king, half-brothers to each through the commoner wives of their father. In Dahomey, the struggle was mediated by the two leading bureaucrats who formally selected the new king. But in order to get a fuller perspective on one possible form of the dynastic struggle, it is instructive to cross the continent to Ankole, where an actual war of accession raged among potential "crown princes."

In Ankole, each potential paramount ruler, following the death of the *mugabe,* or king, conventionally fought for the drum (the royal symbol) with the aid of cohorts drawn in significant part from his mother's clan. For if the child of one's clan sister became king, high appointment and special favor would accrue to one's clan. Indeed, the king's mother and sister held supreme positions in Ankole, equivalent in certain respects to that of the king himself, as did the king's mother's brothers. The ultimate battle in the war of accession was between the king's favorite son, until then hidden by his mother and sister, and the presumably last survivor among the half-brothers, who had defeated the others, and had mustered sufficient strength from cohorts and maternal relatives to challenge him.

The war of accession among the Bahima, a major cause of the anarchy following the death of the king, had the effect of enabling the clans contained in the cattle-herding upper class to compete roughly once every generation for the most rewarding positions in the state apparatus they themselves were building, while it stabilized the governmental structure for another generation. The convention that the king must not, and therefore did not, have any real brothers, paternal uncles, or nephews as a logical result of the war of accession, provided, of course, a rationale for the political prominence of his maternal kin. But more basically, the most effective means of dividing the spoils along lineage lines among the Bahima was to enable the clans of the mothers of the "crown princes" to contest the drum. It is likely that an analogous series of events unfolded in Dahomey, although in that polity each succeeding king was the son of a commoner mother; indeed, no offspring of female members of the royal clan could aspire to the stool, an alternative means of immobilizing possible dynastic rivals. In Ankole, kings were traditionally drawn only from the Bahima clans of the upper class. The relatively castelike quality of this class is symptomatic of a less complexly developed proto-state than Dahomey; the strata of conqueror and conquered, ethnically divided and representative of cattle pastoralists and horticulturists, stand out in sharper relief.

However, the functional similarities between these proto-states far outweigh formal distinctions. The role of the leading bureaucrats is pertinent here. The *enganzi,* Ankole's leading minister, was never a member of the king's paternal clan and thus could not compete for the royal position. But he played a leading part in the accession rites, and in the appointment of the new hierarchy of proto-bureaucrats; he incarnated the thin continuity of the early state. The role of the developing bureaucracy is further clarified by reference to the Baganda custom of enshrining the king's umbilical cord. In this East African proto-state, the leading minister is formally titled the Keeper of the Royal Umbilical Cord. The umbilical cord is a logical symbol of the bond between the generations; more precisely, it symbolizes the continuity of the ruling dynasty. By enshrining the umbilical cord, this continuity is sanctified; the umbilicus becomes one of the holiest of objects. The dynastic group thereby sanctifies its own position. And he who enjoys the honorific Keeper of the Royal Umbilical Cord is the chief minister, the mid-wife of the state; his position and that of the king are mutually dependent. By literally being the custodian or protector of the royal umbilicus, the dynastic succession, he not only pursues the king's interest but also his own. He is, to a considerable degree, manipulator of the king's ideologically exalted status, the emblem of the continuity of the state, as were the leading Dahomean ministers and the chief bureaucrat, the *enganzi,* in Ankole, in whose person state power resided during anarchic interregna.

Splitting the Image of the King

The complexity of the emerging forms of civil rule is suggested by another cluster of phenomena which can be set in a comparative context, again using Ankole and Dahomey as the locales. This process, which can be called "splitting the image of the king," has the effect of designating and symbolizing certain binding and divisive functions in emerging polities, while segregating each category from the other. In each indicated African proto-state, dual institutions were involved. On Ankole, they were the *mugabe,* the actual king, and *bagyendanwa,* the cult of the royal drum. The *mugabe* was always a member of the cattle-herding *Bahima* ruling class and, as such, personified the conqueror to the peasantry, despite his limited redistributive role as "giver." The exaction of tribute and service from the peasantry, the various civil restrictions upon their behavior, their general position as "serfs," regarded as racially inferior, were functions of the emerging state structure. The *mugabe,* as the pivot of the ruling Bahima clans, validated their paramountcy, justified, so to speak, the Bahima to the peasant Bairu. However, he, the actual king, whose many names were a series of martial and cosmically virile metaphors, was himself regarded as the servant of *bagyendanwa,* the royal drum. Logically enough, the anarchic interregnum that included the war of succession ended only when the new *mugabe*'s position was validated by possession of the drum.

Bagyendanwa was regarded as a real person, supplied with a female drum, protected at an offertory shrine, and was the subject of religious devotion from the Banyankole at large. The shrine was also a center for the accumulation and subsequent distribution of a certain portion of surplus wealth in times of economic distress. As the unifying agent in Ankole, the drum was believed to have the power to improve the social position of individuals, ensure success in acquiring material goods, right wrongs, punish evildoers, and increase the fertility of women and cattle. *Bagyendanwa* was unique in that it did these things for the people as a whole, whereas ancestral cults, for example, could not be such servitors, since they represented specific lineages. In this sense, the cult of the drum projected what Durkheim, taking a single aspect for the thing entire, considered the essence of religious belief—the necessary texture of social solidarity. Moreover, *bagyendanwa* served to differentiate Ankole from other kingdoms, thus helping to conceive an evolving national identity, despite the class and caste contradictions inherent in the state structure.

The critical issues here are twofold. First, the drum cult performed the functions of an *ideal king,* to use K. Oberg's apt phrase. This is most dramatically illustrated by the power of the drum to provide sanctuary for any *Munyankole,* cattle herder *or* peasant, who was condemned to death by the *mugabe.* If the person so judged could find his way to the sanctuary, he had to be pardoned, his former rights restored. Thus the shrine of *bagyendanwa* served as an asylum against the most extreme, oldest, and most vigorously guarded prerogative of civil power—that is, the exclusive and ultimate right of the state to the life of the person, and all the new legalities that were extensions of that right, as opposed to the former prerogatives of the kin groups. This function of the shrine, along wtih the economic assistance provided to the impoverished, further indicates how the cult of *bagyendanwa* acted not merely as the developing center for national unity on an ideological level, but was also concretely responsive to the needs of the people. Secondly, the existence of the *bagyendanwa* cult reveals a developing recognition of the injustices and displacements that flow from the process of state formation. The cult of *bagyendanwa* was a pressure valve easing some of the tensions generated by class and caste distinctions, although it did not radically alter the structure of social relations in the proto-state. It was not a revolutionary, but an integrative mechanism, a certain type of *king cult,* underscoring the social fact that neither the *Bairu* nor the *Bahima* could any longer be confined to an exclusively ethnic or otherwise segregated context. The cult confirmed the political structure, while making it somewhat more viable, and thereby helped to germinate the notion of an Ankole "citizenry."

In Ankole, therefore, the *mugabe,* the real king, primarily symbolizes the conquest process, whereas *bagyendanwa,* the ideal king, represents the beginnings of political integration and accommodation on a national level. The degree to which the integrative mechanisms worked to that end is, to repeat, problematical. There is no doubt, however, that it had the *symbolic value* of splitting the image of the king into relatively "coercive" and "protective" spheres of behavior.

In Dahomey, the dual institution was obversely defined. The real king pursued a patriarchal fiction. All Dahomey was viewed as his compound, and he was assumed to be the source of all benefactions. Although he was the ultimate legislator for the collection of tribute, he was also, on every conceivable public occasion, the dispenser of largess. This was perhaps a simpler undertaking than it would have been in Ankole, since ethnic and cultural distinctions between the ascendant royal clan and the local communities were hardly existent. Neither the Dahomean royal clan nor the dynastic lineage regarded the commoners as anything worse or more alien than politically subservient, whereas, Ankole, as we have seen, was a typical, ethnically stratified cattle conquest state. The bureaucracy in Dahomey was drawn, by kingly appointment, from the commoners; successful bureaucrats frequently married royal princesses, their offspring becoming members of the royal clan through a political inversion of the traditional principles of patrilineage. Of course, this bureaucratic privilege made it less likely that any commoner family would concentrate sufficient power to threaten the dynastic succession; at the same time membership in the royal clan honored the more important bureaucrats, ensured their children and their children's children lives of royal ease, and further diffused the ranks of the royal clan. Indeed, the prohibition against members of the royal clans becoming bureaucrats (although they did serve as spies for the dynastic lineages against the bureaucracy) provides an instructive instance of an alternative means for balancing power in an early civil milieu. Basically, this was accomplished by personalizing political relations as in the patriarchal fiction of the king—and by politicizing kinship relations, a transformation typical of the early growth of state power.

One aspect of this complementary process, the political transformation of kin usage, is apparent, both in Dahomey and Ankole, in that the paternal dynastic lines were, in fact, impersonal corporations. In Ankole, the king, theoretically, as we have seen, had no near collateral relatives in his own generation or in the first descendant or ascendant lines, since they, or their potential procreators, were supposedly killed in the war of accession. His link to his sons, only one of whom was favored, was a matter of political mediation through the kin groups of their mothers. In Dahomey, where the king's wives were drawn from the strata of commoners, the link was even more tenuous. The point is that these royal lineages have no substantial, only political and formal continuity and function.

The complementary process defined above is more fully exemplified in a Dahomean institution which can be called "civil mothering." In Dahomey, every important official in the emerging state structure had a female counterpart within the king's compound. This woman, termed his "mother," had precedence at "court," acting as a sort of buffer between the official and the king, personalizing the political relations involved. For example, the "mother" of the *miegan,* the royal executioner, chief judge, and primary bureaucrat, had charge of the king's wives in the royal enclosure, which— given the resident Amazons, other "wives" of the king, retainers and servants of varying degree—was, in itself, a political transformation of the local joint family compound. The "mother" of the *meu,* the custodian of the king's sons, and secondary bureaucrat, was charged with the king's daughters. The bureaucrats mustered from the local villages, the conquered and subordinate areas, had, of course, no original kin ties with royal clan or dynastic lineage. The system of "civil mothers" symbolized the new connections that had begun to develop in distinction to the web of relations in primary kin localities. Each important commoner-bureaucrat thus had a political mother in the governmental compound who mediated his relations with the patriarch; in such fashion, the real king in Dahomey was idealized as the father of all the people. And here we see the literal ancestry of the concepts of political parenthood—motherland, fatherland, and, collaterally, Uncle Sam.

However, as the Dahomean civil power developed, the patriarchal fiction of the king became increasingly insupportable. There appeared, during the reign of Gezu, the eighth head of the dynastic lineage, an institution known as the Bush King. The Bush King had a compound on the outskirts of Abomey, the indigenous capital, completely staffed with the usual retinue, and royal customs were held in his honor. He was represented as supervising the slave trade, organizing the manufacture of palm oil—in general, handling those exploitative activities which served as the material base for the perpetuation of the actual royal power. But the Bush King was, in the classic sense defined by Sir Henry Maine, a legal fiction; no such person existed, a fiction which had the effect of splitting the image of the Dahomean royal power into an ideal and a real aspect.

We therefore conclude that there are substantial functional equivalences between the Bush King in Dahomey and the *mugabe* in Ankole, each discharging exploitative activities which were nonetheless legitimate within the state structure. Correlatively, *bagyendanwa,* the cult of the royal drum in Ankole, symbolizes, as does the patriarchal kingship of Dahomey, a predominantly formal concern for the welfare and integrity of the people as a whole. It is particularly interesting to note that the negative aspects of the evolving civil power in Dahomey are fictionalized, the converse being the case in Ankole, still another category of formal inversion which increases the subtlety of political ethnographic analysis.

Such functionally equivalent forms are, then, symptomatic of an early phase of state formation in African societies. This implies a more general context in which the specific data of political ethnography can be fruitfully interpreted. In apolitically structured kinship societies, clans, extended families, and analogous kin or kin-patterned units discharge all significant economic, religious, and social functions; they therefore develop not only a practical communality but a tough *esprit*. The emerging civil power must, in one way or another, shrink the scope of kin control of persons and resources, while deflecting that *esprit* toward itself. That is to say, the radius of the state institutions constantly expands toward embracing the society as a whole. We must not imagine that this can happen without civil conflict, engaging not only material factors but the hearts and minds of men, conflict sometimes devious in the extreme, and often exotic in form. There were things happening in Dahomey that would have given Machiavelli pause and Rousseau, dare I say so, a certain dry satisfaction. The analysis of such conflicts, including the political transformation of tribal institutions, is a largely untapped historical route toward our understanding of the dynamics of those African societies in which political processes have begun to emerge. Such societies were not, as is frequently assumed, totalitarian, authoritarian, or despotic in any comprehensive sense. That is, they may be called *personal* despotisms because the reach of indigenous organs of the state was so limited, the bureaucracy so shallow, the effect of the civil power upon the profoundly autonomous local groups from which it drew support in goods and services, so relatively superficial. For this reason, the interpretation of the various personifications and fictions of civil power becomes critical. Africa has no tradition of aboriginal totalitarianism, a phrase which contains its own contradiction. Rather we are confronted historically by a great number of societies in transition from kin to civil structure.

If this is true historically, it is also true on a more sophisticated level contemporaneously. Current African societies are in either a colonial or a post-colonial condition; a realistic analysis of the common contexts of their particular situations, within the perspective of political anthropology, is useful and necessary. It corrects our inclination to interpret current African political forms, complicated by the recent impact of more developed, and alien, state structures, in self-centered political jargon. The envolving milieu of *African* politics is decisive, not our euphemisms, or misplaced analogies.

POLITICAL ANTHROPOLOGY IN A CONTEMPORARY CONTEXT

The Military Coups

Specific instances of political anthropological analyses of contemporary events and forms will sharpen the point. The military coups that have afflicted state after state are not necessarily sectarian, that is, representative of special interest groups. They may, of course, rapidly degenerate into mere Bonapartism if no more popular movement flowers in the military interlude. This or that military assumption of power may be revolutionary, counter-revolutionary, or, more narrowly, indicative of a struggle within the military for dominance, the warring factions buttressed by disappointed civilian elements, motivated, in their turn, by no specific political programs. But fundamentally the rule of the military, given the colonially inherited pattern of states in Africa, in many areas superimposed on the indigenous state structures, is generic to the very nature of state power. The military constitutes an interest group that have *as its interest* the annealing of the whole assemblage of state power, the setting of boundaries, the imposition of civil "peace," the elemental creation of a polity. The military, the army, is the instrument of the state; as such, it has an instinctive understanding of fundamental political processes. As E. B. Tylor, the pioneer British anthropologist, pointed out, in referring to the problem of state formation in the earliest civilizations, "political order came out of military order . . . the army served as [the] model on which to organize [the] nation." That is to say, state and army are interwoven structures; conquest and/or the growth of a new social establishment have thus far, in civilized history, been achieved by military instruments. Of course, the socioeconomic character of early states differs widely, but the military component has been essential to the stabilizing of whatever specific social or economic processes were at issue. A literal exemplar of the military factor is in the actual regimental organization of the Zulu, among whom incipient, but transient, political dynamisms were evident; less obviously, in Dahomey the people were divided into right and left wings to serve the twin purposes of conscription and mobilization.

Revolutionary conditions also reaffirm the military process. For when the basic structure of established states is radically changed, the military confirmation of territory and of new or reorganized internal systems becomes necessary. An interesting case in point is in the current struggle between those forces in China, presumably the Maoists, who are insisting upon a "people's" army, that is, an army which ostensibly has a mass base, a revolutionary army, and the "professionals" who are working toward a highly specialized, technically sophisticated corps, which, incorporating a whole new series of institutional interests and thus no longer being fundamentalist, is perceived as a potential threat to the interests of the people as a whole, as defined by the original revolutionary tribunal.

The fundamentalist element in the military coups in Africa should not be underestimated, although specific interests within, or outside, the army must and do quickly develop, overburdening the state-building function. The succession of military coups in Nigeria (Uganda is a less advanced parallel) is illuminating. During phase one, a group of young officers, mainly Ibo in origin (the Ibo identify themselves as the *Nigerian* nationalists *par excellence*), overthrew an unrepresentative coalition government that could not, moreover, resolve civil discord in the Western Region, the cockpit of the national struggle, or equably govern the country entire. In Nigeria, there were no other interest groups comprehensive enough to unite the four semi-autonomous regions, which were in fact becoming the principalities of increasingly bewildered and corrupt politicians. The weakness of the extant political parties had been exposed. Labor was insufficiently organized for a decisive national thrust; communication among workers, except for those in the civil services and utilities, was tenuous, and even in the latter cases, the regional differences in organization and patronage diffused their strength. Neither labor nor the peasantry had yet developed a national consciousness. Part of the heritage of colonialism had been the formal establishment (by military means) of the boundaries of an entity known as Nigeria, along with the apparatus of internal colonial rule, but the growth of self-determining Nigerian institutions, and the attendant social consciousness, could not and did not keep pace with the political fiction constructed by the metropole. The military took command, abolished the political parties, dissolved the swollen and redundant regional ministries, suspended the parliamentary organs, and announced its intention of cleansing Nigeria of corruption. But these were means; the primary goal was to clarify the political meaning of Nigeria by proposing the dissolution of the semi-autonomous federations and the reunion of the country as a modern, unitary state. This would have changed the nature of Nigerian citizenship; each Nigerian would, on the one hand, then have been juristically free to conceive of himself as, first and foremost, a citizen of the country at large; on the other hand, the central government would directly bear the responsibility for the welfare of all the people, including more rational planning, balancing, and distribution of resources than was possible under the Federation; and that responsibility would, in turn, substantiate further the juristic notion of Nigerian citizenship.

But the coup had apparently overshot the fundamentalist phase even before the smoke cleared. The younger officers who had taken the initiative were neutralized, and a more conservative figure rode into power on their actions. At first it appeared that the aim of the coup would nonetheless be realized, but Ironsi, the new head of state, found it increasingly difficult, and, perhaps, undesirable, to realize minimal reforms necessary for unification—the drafting of a new constitution, the simplifying of governmental machinery, and the moderation of northern vested interests, bringing them into phase with the needs of the people as a whole. The military government abolished, then reinstated, the northern House of Chiefs, which reflects the power of the old pre-colonial, and colonially supported, emirates. This kind of confusion led to government loss of initiative in plucking the reality from the colonial myth of Nigeria. Phase two, in what appears at this writing to be an accelerating cycle of coups, opened with the overthrow of General Ironsi, not by the more radical and fundamentalist elements that helped establish him, but by a more conservative—technically defined—a more reactionary military clique. A young Hausa-supported Angas officer from the north (Angas perhaps as a token effort to mollify the middle belt, the Northern irredenta, with its full complement of "pagan" and "near pagan" peoples) is at the moment Head of State, and has decreed the return to a Federation, along with the repeal of most of the ends proclaimed by Ironsi. This latest maneuver can be seen in a double context. First, it probably represents a struggle for power in the army, since such power, at this juncture in Nigerian history, cannot be confined to technical military matters alone or held in check as the last resort of a desperate state; those who control the army, or the most important faction within it, are likely to control the state. Second, the latest coup probably remains to some degree responsive to the actual political situation as it has developed historically. The alliance of reactionary elements in the North and West had, in the first instance, crippled Nigeria as a polity, leading to the initial coup. The successor coup was achieved by Hausa officers, in association with the more conservative Western elements, and was centered in the cities of the Western Region. It seems a military echo of the failed civilian coalition, and has, therefore, both an intra-military locus and a "counter-revolutionary" character.

The military instability in Nigeria is thus reflective of the need for primary decisions about the nature of the Nigerian state and immediately thereafter began to mirror more sectarian, and it would appear, discredited interests. Since the first fundamentalist coup was not able to achieve stated ends, the following seizure indicates a cyclic tendency. In the absence of any coherent national Nigerian popular movement, it is probable that this type of military point-counterpoint will persist. We can expect an end to it only when Nigerians have reconceived themselves as a unitary state, or dissolved into a series of regional principalities that eventually would be obliged to make their peace with West Africa at large, indeed could remake the map of West Africa along spectacular and unexpected lines, now that the colonial monuments are crumbling. But the fragmentation of the army which eventually results from politico-military behavior no longer symbolic of, nor any longer responsive to, popular will, but only to the sound of cabals, could lead to a tragic "Congo" period, a descent into mindless, unprincipled factionalism—the purgatory that follows the unfulfilled promises, the hollow national life of colonialism.

The Underlying Political Problem

This brings us to a synoptic consideration of the major *political problem* in contemporary Africa, namely, the relationship of the great mass of peasants, and urban workers, leavened by the few homeless intellectuals who identify with them, to the various types of elites established and emerging. There are, perhaps, three such categories. The first of these, referred to above, is the colonially supported chiefly elite, the so-called traditional rulers, who under systems of direct *and* indirect rule were gradually converted into both paid and ceremonial agents of the colonial power. These personages, their relatives and associates, are frequently the proponents of intra-national regionalism, which, in the name of tradition, comes to represent parochial economic and political interests.

The second elite consists of African private and public administrators and professionals, educated on various levels, either in the metropole or in the colonially established and operated primary and secondary schools and colleges. Such people range from high-class clerks to barristers, judges, and district commissioners. With the transition to political independence, many of them retained their roles via direct or indirect affiliation with a national political party. This second elite either strives to remain politically neutral, while shoring up its social and economic defenses, or divides its ranks, when pressed, between the first and third elite groups.

The third elite force is composed of the frank revolutionary nationalists who developed in contradiction to—that is, as a dialectical, not as a logical result of—colonial tutelage. They are the ideologues of the Africa that strives to be born. They supply the political leadership for national unitary parties, and they conceive themselves as being representative of the authentic interests of ordinary Africans. This latter leadership, which is the most dynamic of the three types, is also in the most ambiguous position. They are charged with the task of satisfying the economic expectations of the people and of uniting regions and groups in a new political context, groups which had existed traditionally, side by side, or hierarchically, in a more mechanical association. Moreover, this leadership is charged with transforming the rhetoric of independence into reality, while combating the newly emerging vested interests of the indigenous bourgeoisie, including former associates in the anti-colonial party, who are always willing to rest on their laurels. It is here that the dilemma of African socialism becomes evident. For the struggle for national unity is not merely territorial and, if at all, ethnic, it is basically social and economic. The distance between classes in the emerging polity must be kept from widening to the point at which national growth would be crippled, and unnecessary revolutions precipitated, for revolutions following so fast upon each other in polities so new and impoverished have nothing to win. This most dynamic elite is, therefore, in constant danger of capitulating to special interests generated in the post-independence turmoil and of losing its connection with the people at large.

Nor may these new leaders neglect the pull of tradition. As they seek to undermine the inherited colonial system, in which traditional forms were sometimes maintained, although their functions were shifted, as evidenced in the politicization of chiefs, they speak in terms of *negritude, the African personality, consciencism, ujaama*. Their purposes are simple in conception, most difficult in execution—namely, to forge a link between leader and people, a link that cuts through the colonial apparatus, and to do so in language that has a traditional echo. Beyond this symboling, they are obliged to hold the people to the task of contemporary redefinition in the face of the emerging vested interests which comprise only a fraction among them. If the semantics of popular leadership are not to degenerate into bombast, pragmatic results must be achieved. The fact that Ghana, for example, was the first African state to win independence, gave Nkrumah the foundation for his longevity as a popular leader. But his second most significant achievement, the Volta River project, with its multi-faceted potential for reconstruction, was completed too late to secure him the time necessary for future maneuvering against the colonial and neo-colonial forces remaining in his country and throughout the continent. In the interim between these two events, traditional symbolism, because it did not move beyond symbol to reality, failed.

Nkrumah—the Most Tragic Example

Nkrumah's efforts in Ghana were indicative of the problems of these new men in search not only of a political state but of a nation, a cultural fellowship. In the first place, he attempted to place himself above sectarian battles, to regard himself and to be regarded as the incarnation of Ghana. An aboriginal history was reconstructed which not only legitimated the contemporary unity of Ghana but served as a rationale for West African political integration. There is a very real parallel here with the position of de Gaulle in France, including the initial movement, designed to rally all of the French people, the publicizing of French national and cultural consciousness, and the insistence of de Gaulle that he could not and would not be compromised by sectarian concerns, that he represented, in his person, the French national interest, following on the deterioration of the Nazi occupation and the postwar republics. De Gaulle also charted an increasingly neutralist role for France, while intervening between the communist and capitalist powers in behalf of a "Third World" (the survival of the world was, after all, a condition for the survival of France), courses similarly, but hopelessly, pursued by Nkrumah. De Gaulle's success crystallized out of a series of initial failures of his own, and from the failure of other alternatives.

But Nkrumah, representing a new and poor state, not a disorganized but historically settled and advanced state, could not afford failure; and his tasks, given his resources, were far more complex, being progenerative, rather than regenerative. In dissociating himself from the interests of one emerging group after another—the specialized intellectuals, when they demanded the privileges and immunities of their training; labor, when it insisted upon higher wages and lower prices; traders and businessmen, when they solicited higher prices and lower taxes; bureaucrats, when they pursued their political privileges; the judiciary, sophisticated in English law, when their decisions seemed contrary to his conception of the national interest—he risked becoming, and then in fact became, his own unwitting executioner. Finally, he, who could not retire, as did de Gaulle, trusting in the people, compelled by their situation, to recall him, wrote his power, in the name of his political party, permanently into the constitution. Isolated at home, thwarted in his pan-African vision, frustrated at the lack of understanding of his situation on the part of the North Atlantic powers, he showed, we are told, symptoms of personal disintegration. But these are better understood as political tensions crystallized within the personality of a single man than the deeply rooted, paranoid constitution which was widely ascribed to him by contemptuous outsiders and internal enemies. The ubiquitous praise and portraiture of the popular leader is an aspect of popular mobilization, on the one hand, and an effort to reincarnate the role of the authentically traditional chief, on the other. All political polities generate similar constructs, and it is a sign of our own ethnocentrism that we venerate ours, while scoffing at theirs.

Nkrumah's steering of Ghana to political independence, which he perceived as only the scaffolding of socioeconomic viability, the trajectory of his efforts to keep special interests from dividing the state, while catalyzing a new sense of nationality, historically rooted, and his ultimate deposition by a military clique, presumably responsive to the immediate demands of ultimately incommensurable sectors of the populace, foreshadowed the political tragedies developing throughout the continent. Or better, pulls them together into a single tragedy, moving through equivalent acts, to the final dissolution. Only the military can hold these contradictions in suspension, as we have seen, but they cannot do so permanently and, *qua* military, they cannot resolve them.

CONCLUSION

In the perspective of political anthropology, the tremendous problem of modern Africa inheres in the tension between modernization, centralization, which are necessary political and economic processes, given the available technology, and the further growth of cultures and nationalities. This, of course, is not the same as the struggle between the proponents of unitary states, on the one side, and intra-state regionalists or federationists, on the other, for the latter represent socioeconomic interests, typically vulnerable and yielding to the metropole. Nor should that type of intra-national "statehood" which seeks to base itself on local cultural tradition, that is, ethnic statehood, while delegating primary social and economic responsibility to the center, be confused with socioeconomic and political regionalism. The forces arrayed against unitary states may speak in the name of cultural self-determination, but the voice is that of the discarded Africa, the world's servant.

Proliferation of cultural possibilities and of apolitical nationalities—that is, cultural fellowships—could and did occur under aboriginal conditions. But the colonizing powers stimulated the dynamics of modern state formation within arbitrarily defined areas, while constricting cultural usages in a European mold and fragmenting nationalities that cross-cut imposed internal and external boundaries. The exploitative character of colonialism consigned Africans to socially imitative and technologically inferior international status. The results were predictable—self-defeating conflict over slender resources and the four-hundred-year evolution of a continent of people into a mere reflection, occasionally a grotesquerie, of the Western experience, for that is the fate we hold *desirable,* and into which we have forced, are forcing them, as *inevitable.*

The full measure of our ethnocentrism is in our misunderstanding of African politics, our dismissal of African cultural potentialities. Above all, we suffer a failure of imagination, for we of the advanced industrial nations, owners of the most sophisticated technology in the world's history, consumers of the largest proportion of the world's resources, could disinterestedly help Africans convert their continent into a laboratory of applied, advanced technology, freeing, rather than impeding, cultural growth, dissolving political barriers, rather than erecting them. But we must first tend to our own political and economic inhibitions, prejudices, cruelties, and read the meaning of profit and loss, and of ideologies, as a calculus of the survival of the human race. However, that may prove one challenge too many for Western civilization.

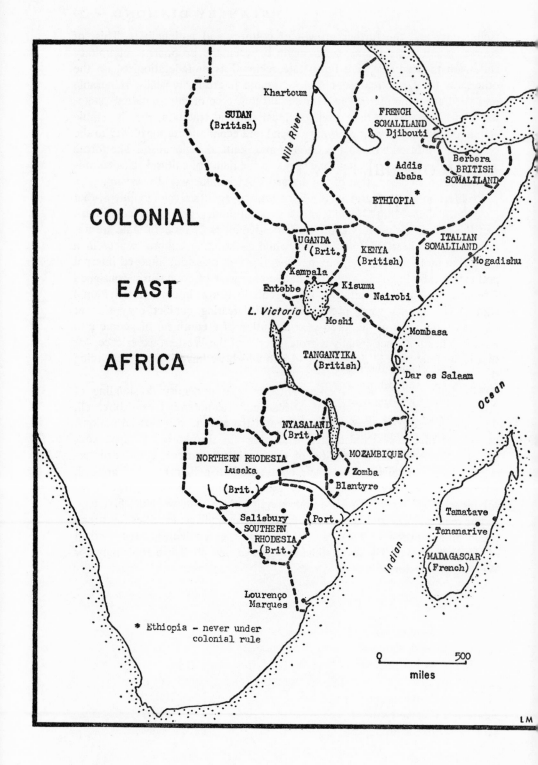

COLONIAL

EAST

AFRICA

SUDAN
(British)

Khartoum

Nile River

FRENCH
SOMALILAND
Djibouti

Addis
Ababa

Berbera
BRITISH
SOMALILAND

ETHIOPIA

UGANDA
(Brit.)

KENYA
(British)

ITALIAN
SOMALILAND

Kampala

Mogadishu

Entebbe

Kisumu

L. Victoria

Nairobi

Moshi

Mombasa

TANGANYIKA
(British)

Dar es Salaam

Ocean

NYASALAND
(Brit.)

MOZAMBIQUE

NORTHERN RHODESIA
Lusaka
(Brit.)

Zomba

Blantyre

Salisbury
SOUTHERN
RHODESIA
(Brit.)

(Port.)

Tamatave

Tananarive

Indian

MADAGASCAR
(French)

Lourenço
Marques

* Ethiopia — never under
colonial rule

0   500

miles

LM

2

The Colonial Heritage
of East Africa

George J. Moutafakis

IN ANALYZING THE COLONIAL HERITAGE of East Africa, careful attention must be given to the internal histories and power structures of the colonizing powers. These ingredients ultimately determined, at particular stages, the purposes for colonization and the kinds of settlers, missionaries, and administrators who constituted the European presence and contributed to the evolution of colonial policies and practices. The role of intellectual forces in apology for and in support or criticism of these practices must also be considered.

Most important is the effect that the European and Arab impact had on the indigenous peoples. The manner in which African social systems and colonial political and economic schemes were utilized to serve non-African interests caused a disillusionment with the promises of assimilation and association. A strong awareness of the exploitative practices and of the colonizing powers' weaknesses became evident during this century. When necessary reforms were rejected, violence developed which gradually removed the colonial influence—at least in the direct sense—from the East African scene.

PORTUGUESE POLICY AND PRACTICE

The Portuguese colonial heritage in East Africa has its origins in the profit-motivated sixteenth-century commercial revolution assisted by territorial exploration and the Iberian *reconquista* crusading zeal to disseminate Christianity. In this era, Portugal, with a population of 1,500,000, was a poor agricultural country whose main source of revenue was derived from the production and sale of port wine, cork, salt, and salted fish. The structure of society continued to have a medieval, feudal, corporative base, a

31

royal court, landed noble families and clergy, and the common folk consisting of merchant communities, craft guilds, laborers and peasants.[1]

Soon after Vasco da Gama's discoveries, the crown realized the strategic importance of East Africa in controlling the rich Indian trade and in eliminating the Islamic Middle East from competition. Commerce became a crown monopoly, and shares in colonial lands were acquired through court influence. The crown treated East African land like land at home and granted it as *donatorias* to courtiers in return for support and services against the powerful landlords. The *donatorias* plantation system, known as *prazos* after the sixteenth century, stemmed from the *reconquista* period when the crown gave victorious lords jurisdiction over conquered Moslem lands in Portugal. In the sixteenth century, the *prazos* enabled the crown to conquer lands in Mozambique by expelling the Arabs, to colonize and to exploit the gold and silver resources, and to evangelize by giving the missionaries free access—all at inconsequential costs for administration and protection. For the success of these schemes, the crown early declared a policy of protecting and respecting the rights of African rulers and of living in peace with them. Royal *regimentos* repeatedly urged humane treatment of the slaves.[2] Otherwise there were no further instructions to the traders and administrative captains. There was always confusion at court as to policy for the Mozambique colony.

This situation was aggravated by the corrupt competition of the large landed proprietors, constituting the military aristocracy, through gifts, bribes, and threats. Turbulent and treacherous, they sought gain through trade, profiteering, and graft by seeking positions as viceroys, captains of fortresses at Sofala and Mozambique, and as crown agents. In this manner, a few families realized large fortunes which were often squandered in luxurious living or munificent gifts to the Church. The crown could not resist the nobility and gentry since they included most of the important clergy. The Church, though lax, was in a strong position because of its role in the *reconquista* and as the leader of the Inquisition against the Moslems and Jews. Missionary orders, dominated by the Jesuits and Dominicans who went to Mozambique to Christianize the Africans, grafted a type of passivity and seclusion characteristic of the Moorish and Ibero-Catholic Portuguese women onto the indigenous women and made profits by engaging in the cotton textile trade and owning large properties.[3] The alliance of the great gentry and higher clergy did not oppose the Spanish occupation of Portugal

---

[1] George Young, *Portugal Old and Young: A Historical Study* (Oxford, Eng.: Clarendon Press, 1917), p. 115.

[2] A. Da Silva Rego, *Portuguese Colonization in the Sixteenth Century: A Study of the Royal Ordinances (Regimentos)* (Johannesburg, Aus.: Witwatersrand University Press, 1956), p. 67.

[3] Charles R. Boxer, *Four Centuries of Portuguese Expansion, 1415–1825: A Succinct Survey* (Johannesburg, Aus.: Witwatersrand University Press, 1961), p. 61.

from 1580 to 1640 because its class privileges and imperial prestige remained intact.

Beneath this hierarchy was a new generation of Lisbon and Oporto merchants who forsook the traditional northwest European commercial routes for the resources of the newly discovered territories. Influenced by the Renaissance, they wanted an urban, individualistic, and mechanized society and supported the crown by financing overseas voyages. However, the merchants were never a sufficiently large group to exert significant influence on Portuguese colonial policy and lacked large-scale capital to prevent foreign bankers from taking advantage of Portuguese commercial ineptitude. Antwerp bankers bought their way into the India fleets, often guaranteed their profits by taking first mortgages on returning cargoes, and dominated Lisbon despite the fact that its docks and warehouses were maintained by the Casa da India. The middle classes were not interested in settling in East Africa because of the climate, terrain, and disease, and their temperaments were repelled by the settlers' sensual customs, their tendency toward luxury, and their superficial adherence to religion.

It was from the lower classes that most pioneer colonizers and adventurers were drawn. With a gradual decline of agriculture in Portugal, there was a steady drift of tenacious, industrious peasantry from the land to the cities and the East. The landowners increasingly came to use Negro labor to till the soil. Other Portuguese elements which imposed themselves on African society were fishermen and town rabble, including artisans and laborers, transported criminals, political exiles, embittered beggars, thieves, assassins, incorrigible soldiers, sailors, and "wives" (girls from orphanages or reform schools). Because of the unhealthy climate, not many of them settled in Mozambique before modern medicine provided antidotes for malaria and other tropical diseases, but the few white and mulatto settlers did use African slaves as manual labor for mines and plantations.

Most crown-planned and supported expeditions in Mozambique were unsuccessful. Consequently, throughout the seventeenth century Lisbon was concerned about the small profits from the colony and attempted several times to open it to free trade. Mozambique settlers resisted these plans, however, and a free-trade decree of 1680 was reversed in 1688. To relieve itself of responsibility, the crown partly subsidized the East African Trading Company to control Mozambique; but, when the company failed, it resumed control of the colony. Lisbon could only hope for revenues from the small coastal commerce, Zambezi River trade, and the sale of colonial administrative posts.

Conditions did not change during the eighteenth century, despite the Marquis de Pombal's enlightened despotism from 1756 to 1777 supported by the urban gentry and intellectuals. He sought to curtail two traditional elements that were important in the formation of colonial policy. Pombal unsuccessfully encouraged the middle class to enter more vigorously into mercantile trade to undermine the nobility and to raise the popular educational level of the country. He suppressed the Jesuits at home and in Mozambique, removed them from public office, confiscated their property, and closed their schools. Actually his reform attempts further complicated the colonial scene, for the bureaucratic machine became more clogged than ever, so that decisions on colonial matters were delayed from two to ten years and many papers submitted for royal action were never acknowledged. The removal of the Jesuits left gaps in some local Mozambique education; did not remove the lax, simoniacal, and concupiscent clergy; nor did it weaken the power of the Church or gentry in Portugal. Though an imperialist, Pombal unsuccessfully sought to eliminate the color bar in the colony, anticipating the French revolutionary motto "liberty, equality and fraternity."

Pombal laid the basis for a liberal, anti-clerical sentiment, represented by the middle-class urban professional and artisan groups, which were pro-French during the revolutionary wars. During three occupations of Portugal, these groups assisted the French to overthrow the *ancien régime*. They were opposed, however, by the pro-British monarchical conservatives represented by most of the official bureaucrats, the landed aristocracy and the clergy, as well as by the peasantry and the Lisbon mob which depended on poor relief sponsored by religious orders. There was no reference to the Mozambicans during the revolutionary period, such as the French Jacobins' granting citizenship to the Senegalese in 1793. Nor was there any provision made for the colonies in the 1822 constitution. The liberals were confused, abolishing and re-creating the Ministry for Marine and Overseas several times. Parliament was content simply to apply metropolitan laws to Mozambique and declare an ineffective policy of "uniform assimilation" (legal status and protection as Portuguese citizens) for the African. The conservatives rejected this policy when they succeeded to power with the reactionary and absolutist Dom Miguel in 1826. Civil wars continued at staggering costs, resulting in the mortgaging of the nation's future finances, until a constitutional monarchy was restored with a charter in 1834. The old social structure of the nobility was shattered, while the masses and foreign financial cliques in Lisbon became stronger political influences.

Incredible chaos existed during the mid-nineteenth century in Portugal with the policy of *rotativismo,* whereby the government was alternately in the hands of the two major pro-constitutional monarchy parties which were supported by the better-educated upper and middle classes. The Regenerators who supported the moderate charter and the Progressives who supported the more radical 1822 constitution had no vitality and no interesting or differing political philosophies in the Parliament. Election consisted essentially of the parties' political bosses' bidding against each other to buy the public's votes by granting local favors.[4] This endless game continued without solid popular support.

---

4 Charles E. Nowell, *A History of Portugal* (New York: D. Van Nostrand Co., 1952), p. 209.

Despite these conditions there was some interest in overseas possessions as evinced by the 1832 decree that they were provinces of Portugal. In 1836 the prime minister of the liberal Progressive government, Viscount Sá da Bandeira, interested in the eventual emancipation, education, and enfranchisement of the African and in the maintenance and expansion of Portuguese territories amidst growing European interest in southern Africa, issued a decree prohibiting the export and sale of slaves from any Portuguese territory. Since the Mozambique European settlers complained that this would deprive them of their main source of revenue and a conservative segment of the Progressives ignored African culture, considering it infantile, the decree was not enforced. In 1858 Sá da Bandeira again issued a decree stating that by 1878 all slaves in Portuguese territories had to be freed. The twenty-year delay was to mollify the slave owners by permitting them to prepare for the final wrench. In 1869 the provision that all slaves considered *libertos* would be treated as workers until their freedom in 1878 planted in the colonial mind the long-enduring idea that a slave could be utilized as a worker in the absence of slavery. Since the 1878 law excluded vagrants from freedom, the Mozambique *prazeros* placed most Africans in that category, and the law's provision for contract labor further limited the Africans' opportunity for freedom. Actually, slavery in Mozambique persisted after 1878, and the local Portuguese opposition vitiated the liberal plan for a system of basic education.

Although the usual antipathy toward the African persisted in the last quarter of the nineteenth century, the Portuguese showed determined interest in maintaining, expanding, and further exploiting their African territories. This was the period of the intensive European imperialist scramble for colonies and the criticism of Portuguese rule by such travelers as David Livingstone. There was a background of imperial concern stemming from the founding of the Royal Academy of Sciences in 1780 and from the nineteenth-century conservative Miguelist intellectual, the Viscount da Santarém; both glorified the past of overseas discoveries. Such statesmen as Sá da Bandeira and such scholars as Lucian Cordeiro founded the Geographical Society in Lisbon in 1876, and ministers for the navy and colonies, such as João de Andrade Corvo, sponsored the society's scientific explorations. The society influenced the government to appropriate funds for engineering projects in Africa despite continuing treasury deficits and inadequate private capital, merchant marine, and industry.

These measures were not sufficient, however, to enable the Portuguese to reject the January 1890 British ultimatum requiring them to vacate the Shiré Highlands region, which was coveted by Cecil Rhodes's British South Africa Company. The Portuguese bowed to superior force, infuriated at the monarchy, which they believed had a private understanding with the British. The humiliation had at least two consequences. First, the monarchical and especially the growing republican parties were intent on preserving the empire as the remaining source of national pride against British and German imperial schemes regardless of cost. Second, there was a shift from a romantic to a practical positivist approach by various spokesmen who influenced colonial policy between 1890 and 1910. One of these was Antonio Enes, a hardheaded imperialist who blamed the liberal government's bureaucracy for all past colonial failures and asked that politics be excluded from colonial policies. He wanted colonial improvements by encouraging more European immigrants, free trade, and foreign capital investments, thereby changing the trading-post Mozambique economy into one of large-scale agriculture and mining.[5] With Moushinho de Albuquerque, a mystical nationalist who won popularity with the crown and populace for his military victories against the Mozambique indigenous rebels in 1895, Enes felt that lands had to be taken from the unproductive *senhores de terra,* but that the feudal *prazero* system was still indispensable. The *prazeros* were given to new renters, the *companhias majestaticas.* The Mozambique, Niassa, and Zambezi companies, supported by Portuguese, West European, and South African capital, received charters to explore for minerals and develop virgin lands. Both Enes and Albuquerque were racists who believed that the Africans were semibarbarous people obliged to labor as inferior *colonii* to develop a sense of dignity and to rise to a "superior" civilization. However, they were to be paid low wages, for the emphasis was to be on spiritual and not material benefits. This did not prevent Albuquerque from recommending the sale of Portuguese red wine to the Africans in place of foreign alcohols in order to reduce the metropolitan surpluses. Protestant missionaries were restricted, for it was believed that they incited African revolts. Roman Catholic missionaries, in turn, were limited to agricultural, trade, and health instruction for the Africans. Finally Enes, who hated the 1878 law, considering it a muddle-headed liberal idea, replaced it in 1899 with an obligatory native work law.

In 1888 Eduardo Costa, who like Enes and Albuquerque advocated colonial decentralization, permitted the colonies some control of financial matters and limited the traditional mercantilist Lisbon control over commerce and production. Nevertheless, the metropolitan area was always fearful of separatist agitation on the part of the settlers and of denationalization by a great influx of South African Boer immigrants. In 1910, the republican government increased local independence and, by 1914, permitted separate budgets and an embryonic legislature for Mozambique. There were to be fewer military and professional bureaucrats, but the African, who was considered unequal, was governed by an administrative statute, separate from the European. There was to be no indigenous tribal government, but gradually a pan-Portuguese community was to develop.

During the days of the republic, a Portuguese in the colonial service with

[5] James Duffy, *Portuguese Africa* (Cambridge, Mass.: Harvard University Press, 1959), p. 237.

a slightly different view was José Norton de Martos. A benevolent imperialist, he believed in paternalistic administration to assimilate the African into Portuguese culture by having him abandon his tribal customs, learn Portuguese, and become gainfully employed without forced labor. An Office of Native Affairs, which had been created in Lisbon, could set the policy toward this end. However, neither this nor Norton de Martos' later plan of a British Commonwealth type of relationship in the Portuguese empire materialized; nor did the expected profits from the adopted Enes, Albuquerque, or Costa plans. The shareholders in company stocks were disappointed, and financial interests did not invest unless they received monopolistic powers. Furthermore, few Portuguese peasants and workers emigrated to Mozambique. Nevertheless, those who did, with the few civil servants and professional businessmen, continued to keep the Africans in medieval ignorance.

The republic that was brought about by anarchists, Carbonari freethinkers, and other idealistic urban intellectuals did not change the traditional exploitive policies. It could not solve the chronic problem of chaotic finances nor aid the depressed workers who often struck and engaged in revolutionary outbreaks. The military, supported by the landlords, businessmen, underpaid and slowly paid civil servants, monarchical elements, and Church, suppressed the strikes. Finally, in 1926, the military, always opposed to the parliamentary system and concerned about rumors that Portugal would be deprived of its colonies, seized the government, ending the series of numerous short, weak ministries. Calling for a Greater Portugal, the military imitated the fascist seizures of power of Benito Mussolini in Italy in 1922 and of Primo de Rivera in Spain the following year.

By 1928, the military asked Antonio Salazar, an economics professor at Coimbra University, to undertake financial reforms and eventually full control of the government. Salazar, a nationalist authoritarian, believed the corporative character of church-controlled medieval society was superior to the individualism of the Enlightenment and the French Revolution. In his youth he had been a member of the Roman Catholic Centro Academico de Democracia Crista, which was inspired by the 1891 encyclical *Rerum Novarum* of Pope Leo XIII and by the 1931 encyclical *Quadrigesimo Anno* of Pope Pius XI, both of which sought to steer carefully between liberal individualism and socialist collectivism, and tended to support corporate fascism.[6] Salazar had also been influenced by the proto-fascist Charles Maurras' Action Française, which fought Protestants, Freemasons, Jews, and socialists; Frederic Le Play, who stressed the necessity of the family unit for a healthy society; and Albert Comte de Mun's conservative social Catholicism. In the 1933 constitution of the Estado Novo, only the heads of families were permitted to vote, workers were placed under national trade

---

[6] Antonio de Figueiredo, *Portugal and Its Empire: The Truth* (London, Eng.: Victor Gollancz, 1961), p. 31.

unions, strikes were declared illegal, and businessmen were placed under industrial guilds. The only party, the National Union, was influenced by German national socialism and Italian fascism.

Salazar's colonial policy evolved with the Colonial Act of 1930, which limited Mozambique's autonomy and placed stringent economic controls over the colony. Through speeches, colonial congresses, and the Agencia Geral do Ultramar, a colonial propaganda agency assisted by the Instituto Superior de Estudos Ultramarinos (formerly the Escola Colonial Superior) established in 1909 to train colonial officials, Salazar and his colonial spokesman, Marcelo Caetano, have concocted the concept of a Third Lusitan Empire.[7] This has served to distract attention from labor unrest at home because of low wages and agitation for political freedom as well as to convince Portuguese settlers (the *Herrenvolk*) that the government would help them in any emergency. There is a psychological assurance in the sentimental thought that their small country owns African territory equivalent in size to the area of Western Europe. More important is the fact that despite Portuguese reluctance to invest in Mozambique, British, American, Belgian, and West German capital does, thus enabling the metropolitan area to increase its prosperity by extracting valuable agricultural products and minerals, as well as continuing to use the area as a dumping ground for wine and cotton goods. One of the main reasons for the stability of this exploitive system has been the indirect support for the Salazar regime by its important North Atlantic Treaty Organization allies, the United States, Britain, and France.[8] Nothing, however, has changed for the African. The 1899 compulsory work law was replaced with one in 1926 which continued the practice while eliminating some obvious abuses. In 1930, Lisbon decreed that forced labor for private enterprise had to receive some compensation, but this was left to the interpretation of the local settlers.

According to Caetano, the roots of Portuguese policy are not ethnic pride and unabashed mercantilism alone, but faith in a total religious, social, and political culture, transcending territorial and racial boundaries. The instrument of this culture is the authoritarian corporative Portuguese state. The four principal objectives of colonial administration are political unity, spiritual assimilation, administrative differentiation, and economic solidarity.

Political unity stresses one government, people, and law with a strong legislating executive. The National Assembly and the Corporative Chamber act through the Council of Ministers, which establishes the broad outlines of policy for the Colonial Ministry (termed the Overseas Ministry after 1951 to thwart African nationalist and United Nations action). This body is the modern equivalent of the old Council of the Indies. According to the organic law of the overseas territories of 1953, the Overseas Minister consults and is advised by the Overseas Council, consisting of nominated

---

[7] Duffy, *op. cit.*, p. 276.
[8] Figueiredo, *op. cit.*, p. 145.

experts who serve as the highest administrative and judicial tribunal for overseas affairs, and the Conference of Overseas Governors. There are also colonial inspectors who report to the Mozambique governor and the metropolitan overseas minister and the Policia International e de Defensa do Estado (PIDE), the state security police.[9] The Mozambique Legislative Council, created in 1953 to express the opinions and interests of the European settlers, hardly strains the theme of political unity. Whether they are directly elected, chosen by corporative bodies of employers, by workers, or by cultural, religious, and administrative institutions, or nominated to speak for the Africans, the legislative councilors are mostly Europeans with a few *assimilados*.

Spiritual assimilation is another important unifying principle of Portuguese colonial practice. It stems from the early missionary zeal which rapidly dissipated itself into the Jesuit Inquisitorial control of African society from Goa and the Dominicans' desire for political and economic power. Liberal metropolitan governments in 1834 curtailed the Dominican slave economy and in 1910 completely banned missionary activity. Despite the continuous African hostility to the religious tutelage of the missionary which required him to abandon his indigenous culture for one relegated to a historical backwater, Salazar's 1930 colonial act supported the Roman Catholic missions as did the agreement appended to the Portuguese-Vatican concordat of 1940.

Administrative differentiation is the practical method of operating the theme of unity. Mozambique is divided into regions governed by provincial commissioners recruited from the Instituto Superior. The regions are divided into circumscriptions under administrators, and further into administrative posts staffed by locally recruited Europeans or *assimilados*. The *chefe do pôsto* who administers the latter has the effective administrative power. Actually, the modern administrative organization has replaced the old *prazo* system in name only, with some economic exploitive abuses removed. Since the *prazeros* keep order for the metropolitan government at their own expense, they receive administrative and fiscal authority over certain areas. The feudal *prazero,* a company *paterfamilias,* was simultaneously an administrative despot, judge, and military authority, just like the modern *chefe do pôsto*. Beneath the *chefe do pôsto* are the African chiefs, appointed by the Portuguese authorities, who have limited power to arbitrate disputes. The administrators apply the customary law of the tribes, which they consider wards, and stress their differences in order to prevent an indigenous sense of unity. There are no tribal courts, only Portuguese, and final appeals must go to Lisbon. The Africans are heavily taxed and must carry a *caderneta,* an identification book.[10] Only the *assimilados,* who must learn to read and

---

[9] *Ibid.,* p. 43.

[10] Lord Hailey, *An African Survey: Revised 1956* (London, Eng.: Oxford University Press, 1957), p. 563.

write Portuguese and attain a relatively high level of schooling and economic position, can escape these taxes and controls. They number less than 1 per cent of the Mozambique population.

Finally, economic solidarity is basic to the concept of unity and represents the older economic exploitation of the African by the corrupt local officials and *prazeros* who needed labor for their gold and silver mines and their maize, manioc, tobacco, and rubber plantations. They were assisted in this by the trade and financial prowess of both the Hindu Banian agents for Indo-British houses and the Goan half-castes. Despite legislation against forced labor for the benefit of European private interests, loopholes exist to permit the administrators and *chefes do pôstos* to send African laborers to private plantations as well as public works for an average of six months a year.[11] The Portuguese believe this personal economic servitude essential in their civilizing process and enforce it by passing laws whereby Africans cannot leave their employers.

As of 1966 the Africans continued to bear the burden of Portuguese rule. Supported by United States, West German, and French banking loans, the Portuguese government maintained a semblance of economic stability in Europe and, assisted by *assimilado* elements, military control over Mozambique. Claiming he will fight with all of Portugal's material and "spiritual" resources, Salazar has ignored protests from the Organization of African Unity (OAU) and the United Nations' Afro-Asian members and is training the white settlers in counter-insurgency tactics. These efforts are a financial strain even before the Mozambique Liberation Front effort exerts its full impact.

FRENCH POLICY AND PRACTICE

The French colonial heritage in East Africa is centered in Madagascar (the present Malagasy Republic) and French Somaliland. Although important policy toward these areas was not formulated until the nineteenth century, French influence in Madagascar stems from the venal *ancien régime* of the seventeenth-century period. The government was headed by cynical and incompetent despots who sporadically attempted reforms which were blocked by aristocratic resurgence and sabotaged by the self-seeking feudal *parlement* judges. The bourgeois merchants, shippers, and capitalists from Rouen, Marseille, Bordeaux, and Paris, who sought to establish trade with India via Madagascar, were content with domestic inequality as long as the upward channels of social mobility remained open for some of them to rise into the privileged class. When these channels were blocked, they turned to the egalitarian Enlightenment doctrines. However, despite the *philosophes'* defense of constitutional absolutism and free expression, they sought to pro-

---

[11] *Ibid.,* p. 1374.

tect their own privileged caste. Neither the bourgeoisie nor the neo-feudal reactionaries cared for the peasant masses which were enmeshed in cyclical periods of boom and slump aggravated by bad harvests.[12]

Despite Cardinal Richelieu's Compagnie de Madagascar ou des Indes Orientales of 1642 and Étienne de Flacourt's *Histoire de la grande île Madagascar* of 1658, both of which emphasized the island's importance for reasons of its strategic location and lucrative trade, most mercantile ventures failed.[13] The colonists spurned agricultural work and ill-used the Malagasy, whom they considered *sans ambition et sans luxe.* Moreover, the artisans quarreled with the military *gentilhommes,* who were often incompetent, tyrannical, and belligerent. Lazarist missionaries seized and burned Malagasy amulets, idols, and temples, thereby initiating an African reaction which was often violent, resulting in the destruction of supply posts and massacres of the settlers.[14]

During the eighteenth century, French ministers wavered between a renewed effort to establish colonies on Madagascar and its maintenance as a coffee and slave supply post for the Mascareigne Islands to the east. In 1750, the Betsimisaraka king granted the island of Ste. Marie off the east coast to the French, but a malaria epidemic forced the abandonment of many of the east-coast settlements. Meanwhile the Merina peoples living on the central plateau established a unified feudal state of nobles, freemen, and slaves which threatened the Betsimisaraka, who were French allies.[15] Although there was a brief period of friendship sparked by the French revolutionary ideas of *liberté, egalité,* and *fraternité* during the Jacobin period, the Merina, strengthened by British arms and subsidies, became a threat to the French. Napoleon Bonaparte had purely strategic designs when he asked his navy minister to submit a detailed report on the advisability of founding a colony on Madagascar. The revolution had now developed a conservative character, and the new urban-rural bourgeois alliance compromised with the peasants to keep the old landed autocratic *émigrés* out and to support the emperor in his imperial reorganization. The report suggested that the island be settled, its population won over by friendliness, united by stopping tribal wars, and eventually civilized under French rule. Its resources were to be used by Western technology for the mutual material benefit of the Malagasy and French. With this island base, France could always check rivals in the Indian Ocean. Napoleon accepted the report, and, in 1803, he divided the

---

[12] Gordon Wright, *France in Modern Times: 1760 to the Present* (Chicago, Ill.: Rand McNally, 1960), p. 111.

[13] Hubert Deschamps, *Histoire de Madagascar* (Paris, France: Berger-Levrault, 1960), p. 89.

[14] Herbert I. Priestley, *France Overseas through the Old Regime* (New York: D. Appleton-Century Company, 1939), p. 115.

[15] Pierre Boiteau, *Contribution à l'histoire de la nation malagache* (Paris, France: Éditions Sociales, 1958), pp. 76–78.

settlements into a northern and southern zone under Sylvain Roux, a French agent at Tamatave. However, the British intervened to seize the settlements in 1811 because they were supplying privateers which were causing considerable damage to British shipping.

During the first half of the nineteenth century, the French government showed little concern in expanding their influence in East Africa, with the exception of sporadic flashes of interest, such as those expressed by Louis Philippe for the Comoro Islands and the west coast of Madagascar. The 1814 restoration in France was followed by psychological lassitude. The autocratic playboys and skeptics of Versailles had become solid pillars of morality and religion and welcomed the marriage of the altar and the throne. The large landowners and bourgeoisie formed closely knit and entrenched business-banking family firms, such as Jacques Lafitte and Casimier Perier, which sought to imitate aristocratic manners and simultaneously chose either ultra-conservative or liberal political philosophies—not by conviction but by temperament.[16] Although they lobbied for protective tariffs for their textile and ironworks industries, they could not expand greatly because they lacked adequate coal and could not mobilize risk capital. Actually the established elements were critical of appropriations for the colonies and the navy.

Although the 1814 Treaty of Paris gave the British control of the Madagascar settlements, London did not press these claims lest they weaken Louis XVIII's insecure restoration government. The British governor of Mauritius, Sir Robert Farquhar, although interested in preventing the French from reestablishing their power from their Réunion base and engaging in the slave trade, was prevented from occupying Madagascar. However, the Merina ruler Radama I made an agreement with Farquhar to have the British educate his children. A British agent, James Hastie, resided at Radama's court, introduced Christianity through the London Missionary Society, and greatly influenced the monarch. In return for a promise to stop the slave trade, Farquhar provided the Merina ruler with an annual subsidy, trained the army, and provided it with military equipment. With these, Radama limited the French to the island of Ste. Marie, checked the Betsimisaraka, and, despite French protests, declared himself king of Madagascar.

When Ranavalona I, one of Radama's wives, seized power in 1828, both British and French interests were threatened. Suspicious of Europeans, she excluded their trade and declared Christian literature and worship illegal, imposing fines, imprisonment, and enslavement on those who disobeyed. The Roman Catholics kept the news of Christian persecutions alive in the French press and supported French claims to the island. Secular interest was aroused by Henri d'Escamps' *Histoire et géographie de Madagascar,* published in 1846, which greatly exaggerated the agricultural and mineral possibilities of the island. The French shifted their attention to the western

---

16 Wright, *op. cit.,* p. 199.

coast, where the Sakalava were resisting the Merina power, and established themselves at Nosy Bé Island.

The French Revolution of 1848 afforded a temporary though drastic change in the history of French colonialism. Slaves were freed, immediately made French citizens, and their owners compensated by small indemnities. But the republicans of that era were disinterested in colonies, ignored the radical intellectuals, and lacked a clear policy. They simply believed in assimilation which rested on the assumption that all men are free and equal and that overseas possessions ought to be integral self-governing parts of France. Though well-meaning, they were not influenced by class but by temperament in choosing between liberal rationalists, such as George Sand, and conservative reactionaries, such as Louis de Bonald. They naïvely permitted a bourgeois reaction based on the fear that property would be confiscated; a clerical reaction, such as that of the Comte de Falloux, which enabled the clergy to teach in the public schools; and finally the ambitious schemes of Louis Napoleon to destroy the Second Republic.[17]

Napoleon III, influenced by Le Play's conservative social reform concept which stressed the family rather than the individual as the ultimate unit in a healthy society, abandoned the liberal idea of assimilation, and stressed the governance of colonies from Paris as appendages in the interests of national prestige, economic and humanitarian motives. Spokesmen for the French Navy, powerful Bordeaux shipping interests, and the clergy all called for colonial expansion. The state, through such agencies as the Crédit Lyonnais, supplied public funds to encourage private investment among the Madagascar colonists.

After 1861, with the death of Ranavalona I, the French induced Radama II to accept a treaty extending their influence. When a new ruler refused to ratify this treaty in 1863, the French forced the Merina to pay 1,000,000 francs as compensation and to accept French and American consuls. Christian missionaries returned in force; and in 1868 Ranavalona II, recognized by the French as Queen of the island, declared Christianity the state religion, permitted foreign ownership of Merina lands, and granted Europeans extraterritorial jurisdiction through capitulations. Nevertheless, the French colonists complained of what they called the dictatorial nature of Merina rule and sought opportunities to further expand their influence.

During the Second Empire period, influence was also gained among the Danakil at Obok, an area which would become the Côte Française des Somalis. The Navy had been interested in the area since 1839, but by 1857, with the approaching completion of the Suez Canal and the British seizure of Perim Island, the need for a base at the southern entrance to the Red Sea became imperative. Napoleon III paid the chiefs 50,000 francs for Obok in 1862.

---

[17] *Ibid.*, p. 26.

With the fall of the Second Empire, the republican-socialist Commune of 1871, which had stirred anti-colonial opposition among the Kabylie in French Algeria, caused hysteria and fear among the bourgeois leadership. After it failed because of inadequate leadership, its leaders were exiled or executed, causing intense class conflict—a permanent rift between the embittered workers and the conservative middle classes and peasants. The Third Republic, which emerged as a compromise between right of center Orléanist monarchists and left of center republicans, did not change the colonial policies of the old order, for they were controlled by moderate libertarian republicans—not aggressive egalitarian property-seizing Jacobins. As Adolphe Thiers said, the Republic had to be conservative or it would not be at all. In fact, by 1875, the powerful upper bourgeoisie had placed their leading representatives in both the monarchist and republican movements in order to have control, no matter what form of government evolved. They administered the Third Republic, although the lower bourgeoisie operated and peasants dominated it. This closed system had the effect of corrupting many radical republican thinkers, averting them from solving economic and social problems and directing them toward routine and sterile positions, such as those against the Roman Catholic paternalist Louis Veuillot and the mystical-emotional fanaticism of the Assumptionists through nineteenth-century positivist restatements of eighteenth-century Enlightenment ideas. Two such leaders were Léon Gambetta, a leading spokesman for the position that politics is the art of the possible, and Jules Ferry, known as "Ferry-Massacre" for his efforts in suppressing the 1871 Commune, who was twice premier between 1880 and 1885. Though Ferry was originally an anti-colonial republican interested in domestic problems, such as education, he was persuaded by various interests to become an ardent champion of imperialist expansion—particularly in Madagascar.

The German imperial chancellor, Otto von Bismarck, believing that the French revenge attitude over the loss of Alsace-Lorraine after 1870 had to be satisfied outside continental Europe, encouraged Ferry in overseas adventures. In fact, various groups began to speak for French colonial expansion. These included the Geographical Society of France, Charles Maunoir and the Society of Paris which influenced chambers of commerce, and Paul Leroy-Beaulieu of the Academy of Moral and Political Science, who, in a work published in 1874, *De la colonisation chez les peuples modernes,* distinguished between colonies of settlement (which he considered outdated) and those of capital investment.[18] Another influential work was by the Abbé Raboison, *Des études sur les colonies et la colonisation au regard de la France,* published in 1877, emphasizing the grandeur of empires.

Career diplomats, army and navy officers, mainly from old aristocratic

---

[18] George H. Nadel and Perry Curtis (eds.), *Imperialism and Colonialism* (New York: The Macmillan Company, 1964), p. 118.

families, desiring excitement, promotions, pensions, and awards, often initiated colonial conquests *pour la gloire de la patrie*. Ferry, as a good bourgeois nationalist politician, took advantage of such opportunities to gain favor with pressure groups and to receive funds from Parliament. In addition to the standard reason that colonialism brought prestige and national honor, Ferry used the concept of a *mission civilisatrice* whereby France had a duty to bring the truths of its culture and Christianity to backward peoples, free them from barbarism and slavery, and ultimately assimilate them as French citizens. Ferry followed the beliefs of Louis Faidherbe, the French colonial expansionist in the Senegal, who described the indigenous African as naturally good and equal in intelligence to the European, but apathetic by reason of his environment and lacking force of character, perseverance, and foresight. At first he was unwilling to be influenced by the economic interests of the Réunion and Madagascar *colons,* but after the prolonged depression of 1877 had made an impact on France through the raising of protective tariffs, important trading, manufacturing, and investment associations encouraged Ferry in profitable colonial expansion. The general public and Parliament, not yet aroused by popular literature on archaeological and natural wonders overseas, were apathetic to colonial expansion, but retained the acquisitions even after defeating Ferry through parliamentary votes on his imperialistic actions.[19]

In 1883 Ferry sponsored French expansion in Somaliland and Madagascar. In addition to occupying Obok, the French annexed Djibouti, the future capital of French Somaliland, as a coaling station, purchased or exacted concessions from the Danakil and Isa Somali sultans, and established a protectorate. The Merina Hova government, because of its absolute feudal structure and its well-trained forces, resisted local French military claims for a protectorate over the Sakalava, believing that France had been reduced to a second-class power after 1871. An ultimatum was rejected, and French marines bombarded and seized Tamatave. In 1885, Queen Ranavalona III was forced to sign a treaty that, though recognizing Merina sovereignty, gave the French resident control of foreign affairs—which amounted to protectorate status even though the term was not used.[20] The Merina conceded further extraterritorial privileges; agreed to pay a 10,000,000 franc indemnity through a Comptoir Nationale d'Escompte de Paris loan, using the Malagasy customs duties as collateral; and made concessions to *colons,* including the use of 35,000 Malagasy as *corvée* laborers to construct roads. By 1890 the British, traditionally concerned about French activities on Madagascar, finally decided to recognize a complete French protectorate over the island in return for recognition of theirs over Zanzibar. However,

---

[19] Georges Bourgin *et al., Les Politiques d'expansion imperialiste* (Paris, France: Presses Universitaires de France, 1949), p. 18.

[20] Boiteau, *op. cit.,* p. 187.

the Merina again refused this, and various Malagasy, including the Sakalava, attacked *colons* and missionaries.[21]

In 1894, when the French National Assembly received notice of the Merina rejection of the protectorate ultimatum, 377 Conservative and Moderate deputies immediately voted 65,000,000 francs to send a 15,000-man army to Madagascar, while 143 Radicals and Socialists opposed the measure. The Radicals were motivated by a desire to embarrass the existing government—not because they had the interests of the Malagasy at heart.

By the 1890's, imperialism had won broader popular support, though it was not so widespread as in Great Britain. More vigorous pressure groups such as the Committee of French Africa and the Colonial Union emerged. Both were backed by textile exporters, shipowners, army contractors, and investment-banking groups, as well as older elements, such as the Roman Catholic hierarchy with Charles Maurras' Action Française, and *colon* deputies from Réunion.[22] The opportunist Moderates who held power for twenty years after 1879 were tied to the influential banking circles and therefore had to prepare the way for profitable investments by supporting colonial budgets for administrative and army salaries. Investments abroad increased sixfold by 1895, though investments in colonial areas did not exceed 10 per cent of the overseas total. The politicians also had to divert attention elsewhere from domestic political scandals such as the Boulanger, Panama Company, and Dreyfus affairs.

Some voices were raised against the imperialist expansion into East Africa, however. The great French novelist Anatole France described it as a new barbarism whereby the few rich made profits while flattering the ignorant mob at home. The Socialist politicians Jean Jaurès and Jules Guesde declared that the Africans wanted independence and not subjugation. But not being able to influence policy because of their political weakness, they broke with the Radicals after 1898.

By 1900 the Radicals had drifted away from their Jacobin-egalitarian backgrounds and had begun to lead governments with the moderates. Though still anti-clerical and anti-military, they based their strength on the rural elements and small shopkeepers. The Mascuraud Committee, which drew funds mainly from small businesses, had financed the election of Radical candidates since the late 1890's. Radical premiers, such as the banker Maurice Rouvier, and treasury officials, such as Joseph Caillaux, actually wanted to set aside ideas of revenge and reconcile and collaborate with Germany through financial investments in Africa and Asia.[23] During World War I, domestic political differences were further sublimated by the

---

[21] Deschamps, *op. cit.*, p. 188.

[22] Michael Curtis, *Three against the Third Republic: Sorel, Barrès and Maurras* (Princeton, N.J.: Princeton University Press, 1959), pp. 96, 187.

[23] Wright, *op. cit.*, p. 390.

spirit of the *union sacrée,* as the Cabinet was representative of every group from Guesde and his fellow Socialists, who voted unanimously for war credits, to Conservative representatives of Roman Catholic interests, such as Denys Cochin.

In 1895, the French occupied the Malagasy ports and, with Sakalava aid, penetrated, despite considerable losses mainly from fever and disease, to the Merina capital of Tananarive and bombarded and seized it. A protectorate was declared over the monarchy, but in 1896 an anti-European, anti-Christian rebellion broke out in the Merina-dominated central plateau provinces.[24] French troops suppressed the rebellion, and General Joseph S. Gallieni, a *dure* with experience in the Sudan and Indo-China, arrived as Governor-General to restore order. He immediately instituted martial law, abolished the Hova monarchy, and exiled Ranavalona III to Réunion and subsequently to Africa. Paris instructed Gallieni to establish a self-sustaining, rational, and inexpensive administration. His initial plan was to implement the *tâche d'huile* idea whereby peaceful civilian and orderly military penetration precede economic penetration. He sought to eliminate Merina feudal hegemony by heavily taxing the chiefs and confiscating property for public works and roads and by proclaiming the equality of all the tribes—the *politique des races*—in order to gain the confidence of all the Malagasy and to prevent any one people from dominating. Gallieni divided the island into military districts—*cercles*—in which small forces of French regular and Senegalese troops operated against rebellious Malagasy until 1905, forcing them to surrender since their leadership and villages were destroyed. French residents and numerous other officials administered under French officers, and both composed ruling advisory boards.

Gallieni wanted the Malagasy to construct roads to connect the civil and administrative centers on the island. However, he criticized the Malagasy as idle, content with only the basic necessities of life, and unable to understand the economic law of supply and demand. In order to get laborers, he abolished slavery in 1896 and declared that all unemployed males between sixteen and sixty had to pay a tax or, in lieu of it, serve fifty days each year on public works, including railroads, irrigation, drainage and mining projects, and ultimately on European-owned cash-crop rice, tea, and coffee plantations.[25] This "volunteer" labor system resembled the *corvée* of the feudal Hovas, but was more efficient and involved some compensation though strikes were forbidden. Nevertheless, in the early years there was a precarious labor supply which necessitated the importation of Chinese and Indian coolies to work and, according to Gallieni, to demonstrate industrious ways to the Malagasy. This project failed. The forced labor system, operated under labor offices which benefited the *colons* by protecting them from the

---

24 Deschamps, *op. cit.,* pp. 231–236.
25 Boiteau, *op. cit.,* p. 253.

hazards of a free labor market, evolved by 1926 into the *Service de la Main d'Oeuvre pour les Travaux d'Intérêt Général* (SMOTIG), which was similar to the Portuguese moral obligation to work and to labor as respect for the customary rights of the chiefs in the British East African colonies.[26] Although protests from international labor organizations charged that SMOTIG had claimed 1,000,000 victims, the French defended the system as a necessity for the improvement of communications and by calling attention to its provision of high wages and adequate care for the laborers. Furthermore, the Malagasy was liable for some military service, but he could serve in a second-class military contingent for public works and private enterprise. Nine-tenths of the labor necessary for European enterprises came from compulsory labor. In fact, the French politicians rejected general conscription for the Malagasy, using their manpower for public works instead. Although SMOTIG was abolished in 1936, World War II soon restored it in practice.

During the interwar years the Third Republic continued under the domination of France's 200 families which also controlled the Bank of France, the steelmakers Comité des Forges, and the coal industry's Comité des Houillières. Together in the Union of Economic Interests, they supplied slush funds for center and right-wing politicians and through a *mur d'argent* blocked leftist programs to soak the rich.[27] The extreme right continued to exert influence through semifascist organizations, such as the Action Française, Pierre Tattinger's Jeunesses Patriotes, and the veteran-supported Croix de Feu. Such moderate politicians as Aristide Briand, the franc-saving Raymond Poincaré, the champion of a new laissez-faire entrepreneurial zeal André Tardieu, and the bourgeois Pierre Laval could hardly have changed the trend of colonial policy. They believed that colonial peoples had no other ambition than to remain French subjects. During the 1920's, the politicians thought of using the Belgian Congolese policy of planned private investments for fair profitable returns by exploiting the tribes while simultaneously raising their living standards without political development. This was neither a different nor very effective policy because the world-wide depression intervened. Madagascar developed economically, however, and became a larger market for French goods. After 1918, French politicians sought to extend military conscription to overseas possessions which they believed had inexhaustible reservoirs of men to supplement dwindling French manpower and to shorten the conscription period, but did not permit racial integration of the French and Malagasy nor grant the latter citizenship in return for military service.

Nor could the Socialists, led by Léon Blum, an upper-class intellectual,

---

[26] Raymond K. Kent, *From Madagascar to the Malagasy Republic* (New York: Frederick A. Praeger, 1962), p. 77.

[27] Wright, *op. cit.,* p. 457.

effect much of a change in colonial policy. They were more concerned with opposing the Soviet Union's efforts to control the socialist movement than with domestic or imperial matters. However, during the Popular Front government, the Socialists did sponsor a change in the *mission civilisatrice* policy from mass assimilation to acculturating only a small native elite which would then share with Frenchmen the task of colonial government. This policy was first proposed by Jules Harmand in his *Domination et colonisation* of 1910 and was further defined by the Radical Colonial Minister Albert Sarraut in his two works, *La mise en valeur des colonies françaises* of 1923 and *Grandeur et servitude coloniales* of 1931. Although there was no thought of real decentralization toward autonomous decision-making for the colonial peoples, Parliament failed to enact the policy.

By the 1920's, in further implementation of their *mission civilisatrice,* French officials offered a few young Malagasy the opportunity to attend Parisian schools, even though most *colons* sought to prevent this, stating that the study of French in the secondary schools would expose them to subversive ideas. In fact, instead of becoming Frenchmen or pro-French, young Malagasy, particularly Merina who resented the loss of their independence, believed that they were just as educated and capable as their French comrades after reading law, history, and political science and assimilating new ideas from Socialists and Communists. They wanted French citizenship and effective representation in the local economic and financial delegations, which they characterized as debating societies. They felt that they were discriminated against in Paris because they were Malagasy and at home because they expressed opinions that differed from those of both the colonial officials and the European settlers.

The settlers did not come to Madagascar, like the missionaries, for religious motives; nor, like the officials, for professional, romantic, and patriotic reasons. Instead they committed themselves and their families to an unknown country and invested their lives, energies, and capital to what was often a speculative venture. Gallieni and succeeding governors-general wanted Paris to guarantee private investments and wrote to the Colonial Union to exert pressure on the usually reluctant Colonial Ministry to do so. The family-business *colons,* through their chambers of commerce, wanted the Malagasy to cooperate with them and to continue to work the plantations as share croppers or *corvée* laborers. However, the *colons* often attributed severe losses to what seemed their Malagasy servants' incredible neglect and stupidity. This is one of the basic reasons for the failure of the *mission civilisatrice*—the divergent views of the resident colonial officials and missionaries who believed they were civilizing and educating the Malagasy from those of the *colons* who considered the Malagasy almost hopelessly inferior and incapable of being civilized. This conflict eventually gave rise to the Malagasy independence and nationalist movement.

Although Governor-General Léon Cayla suppressed an independence movement in 1929, Malagasy organized themselves into student associations and, while still hoping for equality through assimilation or association with France, started some structure for future political action.[28] The French Communist and Socialist parties, traditionally strong in Paris among students and particularly so during the 1930's with the Popular Front against fascism and colonialism, encouraged these moves. Maurice Thorez and Jacques Duclos, working-class leaders of the Communist party, could see the premonitory signs of nationalist discontent which had developed since World War I in Madagascar.

The rightist-oriented "better Adolf Hitler than Blum" spirit of the 1930's led to the 1940 defeat of France and the rise of the benevolent autocrat Marshal Henri Pétain as head of the Vichy government. Supported by the upper-class big-business technocratic *attentisme,* the church hierarchy, and the semifascist Action Française, Croix de Feu, and Jeunesses Patriotes, Pétain called for the continuation of French national traditions and empire, replaced the Jacobin republican *liberté, égalité, fraternité* with the fascist *patrie, famille, travail,* and made France Germany's most important supplier of both goods and manpower during the war years. Vichy officials placed heavy food production quotas on the Malagasy and exhibited racist attitudes —both of which were resented. The British, fearing a Japanese seizure of the island, occupied it in 1942 and gave it to the Free French forces the following year. In 1944, General Charles de Gaulle rallied the Brazzaville conference in Equatorial Africa to consolidate the French colonies in the final struggle for victory. In order to hold the empire together and realizing the need for some colonial policy changes after the French defeat, which had really ruined the concept of European invincibility and infallibility, the French politicians and colonial officials with the support of Félix Eboué, the African Governor of Chad, promised the Malagasy citizenship a share in drafting the postwar constitution, parliamentary elections, and more local authority in representative assemblies in a French Union—not an empire.[29]

The first draft of a constitution for the Fourth Republic in May 1946 was representative of these promises and even granted the right of secession from the French Union. It was sponsored by a strong Socialist and Communist political ascendancy—a continuation of World War II's Resistance comradeship—which hoped for a *république pure et dure.*[30] Their hopes were quickly shattered. Conservatives, de Gaulle and his Rassemblement du Peuple Français (RPF), and Georges Bidault and his church-supported Christian democratic Mouvement Républican Populaire (MRP), all warned that the draft did not guarantee private property or the integrity of the

---

[28] Deschamps, *op. cit.,* p. 262.

[29] Hailey, *op. cit.,* p. 211.

[30] Alexander Werth, *France 1940–1955* (New York: Holt, Rinehart and Winston 1956), p. 223.

French empire. It was rejected in colonies where the franchise was restricted to Europeans, mostly *pétainistes,* and accepted where the indigenous voters were in the majority, as in Madagascar. When the June 1946 elections returned a heavier rightist Constitutional Assembly representation, a second draft was accepted which rejected secession. Actually the Malagasy found that their prewar conditions had not changed. Two Frenchmen and three Malagasy were sent to the National Assembly in Paris, and two Frenchmen and six Malagasy to the Council of the Republic. If the electoral procedures of metropolitan France had been applied to Madagascar, the Malagasy should have sent far more representatives. They were further limited in the Assembly of the French Union since half their representatives were chosen by the Chamber of Deputies. Domestically the Malagasy had two representative, though merely advisory and consultative, bodies—one for Europeans and one for Malagasy. The former had more powers, thereby perpetuating the discrimination between *citoyens* of French origin and *sujet* Malagasy, despite the abolition of the *code de l'indigènat.* Therefore the principle of territorial representation was only nominal—not actual. Reforms promised at Brazzaville—concerning forced labor, exploitive share-cropping and *déraciné* urban problems—were not enacted, nor was policy oriented in this direction by the system of rapidly changing though slow-moving ministries of the Fourth Republic. Despite some European egalitarian views, the bureaucratic colonial machine had its own laws, labored under a feeling of narcissistic self-importance, used Merina feudal functionaries, and was dominated and supported by the *petits blancs* and the Church.

On March 29, 1947, a Malagasy rebellion broke out resulting in the death of 200 Frenchmen. It was immediately suppressed as local French troops, aroused by the anger and panic of the settlers at what they called a Communist revolt, reacted with the utmost violence, killed many Malagasy, and destroyed villages. Martial law supported by Roman Catholic and Protestant missionaries was declared, and extralegal trials at Tananarive condemned hundreds. President Vincent Auriol, elder statesman of the Third Republic, refused mercy, and the Malagasy representatives in the French Parliament were expelled. With the anti-colonist revolt in Vietnam, the specter of communism in the French Union became part of the French Cold War psychosis. The MRP, representative of the influential bankers and the traditional Quai d'Orsay in France, conscious of the local planters and the concern of the United States for the strategic position of Madagascar, decided on a strong policy. It was able to control the weak Socialist ministers in the Cabinet and to expel the Communists, who vociferously denounced the government's reprisals which left 80,000 Malagasy dead.

After 1947, the Colonial Ministry, dominated by MRP members, did very little for Madagascar. There was insufficient social mobility in France to change the stagnant political system. Although the upper and middle bourgeoisie no longer monopolized the administration, they outnumbered the other groups. Even the Communists felt concern about their position in France if they continued their vociferous demands for complete independence of colonial peoples whose leadership was often bourgeois nationalist and anti-Communist. Another cause of political *immobilisme* was the dilemma over the continuous drain on French finances, manpower, and morale because of the continuing fight since late 1946 against anti-colonial rebellions in Asia and Africa. The system could not act independently of 1,000,000 *colons* in Algeria, particularly since they had the support of the Army. The latter's morale was low because of continuous defeats and the belief that weak scheming politicians and untrustworthy intellectuals in Paris had sacrificed the Army by giving it hopeless assignments without adequate support. One exception was the 1952 passage of a labor code in Paris that transplanted many of the rights of metropolitan workers overseas including the right to form unions and the requirement of equal pay for equal work regardless of race. The other exception was the seven-month ministry of Pierre Mendes-France in 1954 which showed dramatic vigor and forthright action on domestic and colonial problems, such as the ending of the Vietnamese war.

On the local level, the *colons'* severe policies alienated even the moderate upper-class Merina represented in the Mouvement Démocratique de la Rénovation Malagache (MDRM) which sought complete autonomy and equality within the French Union. The MDRM and its intellectual and youth branches won the majority of popular votes in elections, but the 50,000 settlers and colonial administrators rigged the electoral seats to support parties such as the Parti des Déshérités Malagaches (PADESM) representing church missionary interests and anti-Merina tribes. This was simply a continuation of Gallieni's *politique des races*. Funds from the Fond d'Investissement pour le Développement Economique et Sociale des Territoires d'Outre Mer (FIDES) were utilized for the benefit of European-owned agriculture in rice and coffee cash crops and coal, oil, and timber production. Only a few Malagasy benefited—most labored for very low wages. These conditions forced the nationalist leader Joseph Ravoahangy to seek Communist party support through graduate students abroad and organizers of the trade-union movement, and to form the Parti d'Union du Peuple Malagache (PUPM). The religious bodies opposed PUPM, but to prevent their identification with colonialism, supported moderate Christian Socialists such as Philibert Tsiranana.

In 1956, the Socialists rejoined government Cabinets after an absence of five years. There was a general realization that reprisals against nationalists were ineffective and that some administrative reform within the framework of the union had to materialize. The *loi cadre* was passed, abolishing the discriminatory double territorial assembly system, and a single Malagasy Assembly was given local budgetary, trade, police, and taxing powers. The body was still an advisory one, however, without decision-making rights.

A Government Council composed of members elected by the Assembly and appointed by the Governor-General assumed policy-making powers along executive lines. The Governor-General was president of the Council, receiving his orders from the Paris ministers, with ultimate executive control and reserve authority over both bodies. The change hardly pleased the progressive Malagasy nationalists, who considered it too little, too late.[31] Jean-Paul Sartre's existentialist descriptions of rootless intellectuals caught in doubt and despair, yet desiring freedom to choose and shape their lives through action, could well be applied to the nationalist leaders.

In 1958 the French Army High Command in Algeria seized control of the *colons'* Committee of Public Safety in Algiers and forced a change in the government to favor de Gaulle. One of the main purposes of the enlightened rightist-dominated new Fifth Republic was to provide a new, more flexible framework for the French Union—one which would, at least temporarily, halt the surge toward separatism. The overseas populations could vote against the new constitution and immediately receive independence like Guinea, or vote in favor of it with the choice of becoming an integral part of the French Republic, or a partially autonomous state, or a fully autonomous state in domestic matters within the French community with the control of foreign policy and defense in Paris. Both progressive and moderate, Malagasy chose the last option as merely transitional to complete independence. By 1960, the Malagasy Republic was politically independent within the French community under a moderate leadership. Tsiranana, its first President, entered on a program of agrarian reform through the redistribution of state-owned lands and the combating of illiteracy, unemployment, burdensome taxes, and debts. He also welcomed foreign investment through the French Fund for Aid and Cooperation (FAC), formerly known as FIDES. The progressives, however, do not want a capitalist democracy with social and economic injustices. The FAC favors primary production and a reduction in operating costs of foreign companies in Madagascar to permit them increased profits. Allocations for public health and education are small. But as of 1966 there appears to be little opportunity for a progressive opposition to exert political influence. Tsiranana's Parti Social Dêmocrate has overwhelming power, and the majority of its members want to continue a pro-Western foreign policy and strong ties with the French Community. They support Moishe Tshombe, former secessionist head of the Congolese province of Katanga and conservative prime minister of the Republic of the Congo, oppose the Third World policies of the Chinese Peoples Republic, and are critical of Kwame Nkrumah and his pan-African Socialist causes.

French Somaliland has remained under the *loi cadre* because of the almost equal distribution between the ethnically different Afar Danakil and Isa Somali. The Isa Somali, centered in the important port of Djibouti with its

---

[31] Kent, *op. cit.*, p. 139.

railroad connection to interior Addis Ababa, do not wish to take a secondary position to Mogadishu if they join a Greater Somalia. The French colonial officials exploit this whenever possible, but stirrings against them are evident. In 1965 they refused permission for the Liberation Committee of the OAU to enter the territory.

BRITISH POLICY AND PRACTICE

During the first half of the nineteenth century, the prevailing British colonial philosophy was based on Adam Smith's concept of free trade and manifested itself in the Manchester school's "Little Englandism," which wanted the government to refrain from undertaking expenses in acquiring and maintaining colonies. In 1870, Herman Merivale, the successor to the laissez-faire-minded Sir James Stephen, as permanent Under-Secretary at the Colonial Office, summed up Great Britain's colonial policy as one encouraging the colonies to prepare for independence. Both the Liberal William Gladstone and the Conservative Benjamin Disraeli believed that colonies were wretched millstones around their necks and withdrew troops from them. However, during this mid-Victorian period, the empire actually expanded through territorial acquisitions, strategic diplomacy, or extensions of informal rule through trade agreements.[32] As early as 1849, Thomas Carlyle wrote that the Anglo-Saxon had a moral duty to seize and civilize the world's backward regions. He even defended slavery, claiming that the white man must dominate the Negro. In 1868, Sir Charles Dilke declared that the Anglo-Saxons were destined to conquer the world and emphasized the economic and military value of tropical areas. The general public received these views enthusiastically.

By the last quarter of the nineteenth century, Great Britain's industries were producing more goods and meeting increasing competition from new technologically advanced tariff-conscious industrial powers like Germany and the United States. Although the British had lost their economic primacy, world-wide economic expansion increased their trade absolutely—not relatively. Invisible exports, such as shipping, banking, and insurance services, covered the difference and afforded a prosperity which improved some working-class wages and conditions. This attracted increasing numbers of industrial workers—given the franchise by the parliamentary Reform Acts of 1867 and 1884—not to the Marxist-oriented Social Democratic Federation, but to the moderate evolutionary and intellectual Fabian Society. Through thorough research and publication of social ills, the society made socialism respectable to the politicians of the major parties and was the basis for the parliamentary moderation of the future Labour party. Simultaneously, it attracted such wealthy industrialists and merchants as Joseph Chamberlain

---

[32] Nadel and Curtis, *op. cit.*, p. 100.

and William Booth as philanthropic contributors to its cause. The latter's work, *In Darkest London and the Way Out* of 1890, sought to elicit the same sympathy for the downtrodden in the London slums that Henry Stanley's earlier work, *In Darkest Africa,* sought to arouse for another part of the world. There was a skillful manipulation of the reaction against the Manchester school's exclusive employer emphasis on profits and neglect of human values at home where social reform was stressed, and abroad where a more humane public interest in colonies was asked. This paralleled a wider acceptance of the idea of a lofty moral mission rooted in the old humanitarian movement. Furthermore, the masses were instruments through which the irrational sentiment of nationalism against the post-1870 Continental varieties could be used for imperial expansion. Empire meant power, influence, and prestige.

Various sources were available to exploit the new opportunities to cultivate colonial expansion. In 1868 a select few officials and merchants founded the Royal Colonial Institute as a sort of club to demand that colonies be made markets for British goods instead of being forced toward independence. Disraeli, seeking to take advantage of the winds of change, declared, in his 1872 Crystal Palace speech, that the Liberals were responsible for the empire's dissolution. Three years later, in order to secure steam transportation and oceanic cable communication, he purchased controlling shares in the Suez Canal Company for England. While William E. Foster was proclaiming the need for imperial federation, in 1875 Colonial Secretary Lord Carnarvon was promoting it in South Africa by annexing the Transvaal and by fighting a preventive war against the Zulus. Although the Liberal William Gladstone returned to power in 1880, opposing what he termed Disraeli's immoral imperialism, he cautiously involved himself in South Africa. In 1881 British industrialists, concerned about the depression of the late 1870's and the increasing foreign tariffs, founded the National Fair Trade League to build support for empire and to channel a profitable outflow of capital, skill, and labor.

In 1883 the historian John R. Seeley's *The Expansion of England* popularized imperialism from the viewpoint of national energy and virtue—not from emotion. Regarding separatism as national degradation and ruin, he failed to understand the contemporary dominions' nationalism, nor did he envision a future commonwealth. The following year, the Imperial Federation League was formed as the core around which British imperialist agitation revolved during the 1880's and early 1890's. It had members in both parties, representatives in the press, numerous branches which held meetings and exhibitions, published a monthly review, *Imperial Federation,* and initiated the first colonial conference. Members, such as the Liberal imperialist Lord Rosebery, stressed Great Britain's civilizing influence; the journalist William T. Snead, the preservation of peace and the elimination of slavery among warlike peoples; and Chamberlain, markets for the British working-man's products. In 1886 the Anglo-Indian Rudyard Kipling's works and Rider Haggard's *King Solomon's Mines* aroused the public's romantic interests.

In addition to the general causes for late Victorian imperial involvement, there were particular reasons for concentration in East Africa. The Church and London missionary societies as well as the Universities Mission to Central Africa pressed the British as early as the 1850's to negotiate with African chiefs and the Zanzibar sultan to end the slave trade. The Scottish missionary-explorer David Livingstone called for the introduction of Christianity and legitimate trade. Actually such associations as the Livingstonia Central African Trading Company provided regular supplies for the missionaries and also exported ivory at a price that undersold the Arab merchants with their slave labor. Stanley, a strong economic imperialist, wrote accounts for the press, particularly *The Daily Telegraph* and *The Times,* channeling Livingstone's missionary fervor into an appeal for intervention to arrest persecutions of Christians in Buganda. By discussing the rich economic possibilities in Africa, he did much to incite the ensuing scramble to claim parts of the continent. This was laudable in the late nineteenth century, which believed that by removing stagnation it would raise the indigenous inhabitants' living standards. New medical knowledge made the continent less forbidding and engineering progress more exploitable.

Despite these incentives, the British government was cautious about expansion in East Africa. In 1882 it had intervened in Egypt to save financial investments and the canal, but soon withdrew from the Sudan because of the £200,000 annual loss to the Egyptian treasury. Both Disraeli and Gladstone rejected the Zanzibar sultan's offer to grant a seventy-year lease of all his mainland possessions to William Mackinnon, a shipowner and merchant, and not cede territory to any power but Great Britain, provided the sultan was given a protectorate status. However, in 1884 when Germans moved into the Kilimanjaro area where several Manchester merchants were trading, Foreign Secretary Lord Rosebery's stern protest gave the first indication that the British were ready to intervene. An Anglo-German agreement in October 1886 limited the sultan to the islands of Zanzibar and Pemba and divided his mainland dominions at the Umba River into spheres of influence—the Germans taking 600 miles of coastline to the south while the British took 400 miles to the north. The Germans were limited south of the first degree of north latitude crossing Lake Victoria. British foreign policy constantly stressed the theme that this chief reservoir of the Nile River and its upper waters should not fall into the hands of an important foreign power.

However, the British government hesitated taking responsibility for the area that later became the Kenya colony and was pleased when Mackinnon's royal-chartered Imperial British East Africa Company (IBEAC) undertook to administer the area in hopes of high profits through the ivory trade and the eventual development of the highlands. Meanwhile, Alexander Mackay of the Church Missionary Society (CMS), challenged by the Buganda *Kabaka* Mwanga, sought British assistance—even annexation—but since Conservative Prime Minister Lord Salisbury was reluctant, the CMS raised money in Great Britain to have IBEAC administer the area. Finally, Salisbury, in the Anglo-German Treaty of 1890, accepted a sphere of influence over Uganda in addition to a protectorate over Zanzibar. Again the cautious Salisbury, under constant pressure from the radical anti-imperialist wing of the Liberal party, refused to undertake the responsibility of administering Uganda and asked IBEAC as a government agent to do it and pay the expenses of a railroad survey from the coast to Uganda. He informed Mackinnon that the whole area would eventually be annexed and the company compensated for its expenditures. Not only did the company lack adequate funds for such a venture, but it was increasingly apprehensive that Gladstone and the radical Liberals in power in 1892 would withdraw British participation completely because they felt no obligation to the company and believed that the indigenous inhabitants were against the railroad and slavery nonexistent. The company agent, Frederick Lugard, waged a public campaign in Great Britain for retention. The CMS, the Anti-Slavery Society, Cecil Rhodes, and all leading newspapers except *The Manchester Guardian* and *Daily News* supported retention. Rosebery, after personally deciding to annex both Uganda and Kenya, despite the views of the Liberal leadership which was exhausted over the Home Rule for Ireland parliamentary battles, actually sent a retentionist, Sir Gerald Portal, to appraise the East African situation. In June 1894, a Liberal-Unionist and Conservative coalition accepted a protectorate over Uganda, the following year over Kenya, taking over IBEAC, and in 1896 Bunyoro, Toro, Ankole, and Busoga. However, the British government lacked a clear idea of how to administer the new protectorates—believing only that it had a little more responsibility.

Meanwhile Rhodes, interested in extending his scheme for a Cape-to-Cairo British sphere of influence and in limiting Boer expansion from the Transvaal, sought to exploit the rich agricultural and mineral resources of the Ndebele and Shona. He induced the Ndebele chief Lobengula to cede his mineral rights and then proceeded to London to acquire funds and a development organization. Rhodes was opposed by rivals, imperialists who wanted direct British rule, and the Aborigines Protection Society. However, Salisbury, with the encouragement of Protestant missionaries, sought to limit Portuguese claims to the region and, in 1889, permitted a royal charter forming the British South Africa Company. Although Rhodes had ultimate responsibility to the Colonial Office for the welfare of the indigenous inhabitants, this meant very little for their protection. In Northern Rhodesia (Zambia) and Nyasaland (Malawi), the company extended its influence relatively peacefully, largely with the consent of the native chiefs. Therefore tribal organization and the chiefs' prestige continued. In Southern Rhodesia (Zimbabwe), however, the company faced Ndebele opposition and rebellion, which it crushed only after blood conflicts that resulted in undermining the chiefs' authority.

At the turn of the century, the British government sought, through the Foreign and Colonial offices and often costly military campaigns, to maintain a dominant position in East Africa from the Gulf of Aden to the Limpopo River. Administrative policy was either nonexistent or differed from area to area. In British Somaliland, the Somali *mullah* Mohammed Abdallah Hasan fought to thwart the 1884 protectorate which was maintained by a platoon of troops and to prevent British control of the *qadi* interpreters of Moslem law.[33] To the west, a joint military and financial Anglo-Egyptian condominium took control of the Sudan after the Khalifa's defeat. Missionaries concerned about persecutions of Christians and the slave trade, as well as imperialists who sought to prevent the French from establishing a sphere of influence across North Africa from Dakar to Djibouti, had triumphed. The flag-waving *National Review* and the ha'penny *Daily Mail* owned by Alfred Harmsworth, later Lord Northcliffe, had intoxicated the masses with ideas of imperial grandeur. British army officials controlled from Khartoum, civilians were at the head of each *mudira* or province, and Egyptians filled lower administrative posts in the northern and central provinces. But the British moved to isolate the southern provinces and ruled them directly with a few British officials, since their non-Moslem traditional chiefs had been eliminated by chronic warfare. The British also introduced Christian missionaries for purposes of basic education and sought to prevent the exploitation of the peoples by more sophisticated northern riverine and urban inhabitants. To the south, the British were anxious to make the protectorates self-supporting and profitable. Sir Harry Johnson was sent to Uganda to establish an inexpensive administration. Seeking to make use of an established feudal administrative hierarchy in Buganda, he entered into the *mailo* agreement in 1900 with the *kabaka*'s chiefs, formerly his tenants, giving them half the land of Buganda in free-hold tenure and incorporating them as civil service chiefs in local government under British district officers.[34] This enabled the chiefs to be free of *kabaka* patronage and to exploit their cash-crop-producing, rent-paying peasantry. Buganda was a province-kingdom in Uganda, as was Toro, Bunyoro, and Ankole, and the laws of the protectorate applied to them unless specifically excepted. Although Lugard and Johnston hoped for European immigration and the establishment of cash-crop production of coffee, cocoa, and rubber, Hesketh Bell, who administered Uganda during the first decade of the century, believed that good-quality peasant-grown cotton was sufficient and advocated a policy of developing the protectorate primarily as an African country. A 1916 law actually prohibited

---

[33] Saadia Touval, *Somali Nationalism, International Politics and the Drive for Unity in the Horn of Africa* (Cambridge, Mass.: Harvard University Press, 1963), p. 56.

[34] Lord Hailey, *Native Administration in the British African Territories*, Part I. *East Africa: Uganda, Kenya, Tanganyika* (London: H.M.S.O., 1951), pp. 6–7.

the alienation of land to non-Africans. Actually European settlers were not attracted to the country because of the slow surveying of the *mailo* lands and the lack of adequate roads. However, Europeans and Asians did own the ginneries, means of transportation, finance, and export facilities.

Kenya lacked strong indigenous political structures and powerful chiefs which the British could use as in Uganda in their colonial policy of indirect rule. Since there were few British officials, the central colonial government decided to maintain the chiefly authority whenever possible, paying chiefs and elders to hold courts, and village headmen to administer locations and reserves. Their primary functions involved bringing wrongdoers to courts, helping collect head and hut taxes, and supplying laborers for public works —which the British interpreted as the chiefs' customary rights.[35] Nomadic peoples, such as the pastoral Masai and Nandi, were limited to reserves which often deprived them of adequate grazing lands and water. This and periodic European encroachments caused great distress, despite British government assurances that the reserves were crown lands and that the interests of their inhabitants would be protected.[36] Both Lord Elgin, a deadweight Colonial Secretary during the Liberal Sir Henry Campbell-Bannerman's government, and Sir Charles Eliot, an administrator of Kenya during the first decade of the century, agreed with Hugh Cholmondeley, the third Baron Delamere, on encouraging Europeans to settle in Kenya. The administrators proposed to give them fertile highlands as reserves, to the exclusion of the Indians who had remained in Kenya after completing work on the Mombasa-Kisumu railroad and the indigenous Kikuyu who originally inhabited the highlands. The latter had only temporarily abandoned the highlands because of a smallpox epidemic.[37] The railroad expenses had to be paid, but the African subsistence agriculture and nomadic pastoral pursuits could not provide the capital. In supplying the capital, the Europeans demanded and received African labor for the care of livestock and for their coffee, maize, and wheat cash-crop plantations. The settlers also wanted dominant political representation. Through their Convention of Associations, they demanded control of the colony's Legislative Council, considered legislation critically, summoned government officials to their meetings, and even had the Governor open their proceedings. Local colonial officialdom from the Governor down usually had close school ties or social friendships with the settlers and found itself persuaded to sell crown lands to the Europeans to enlarge plantations which they operated much more profitably than the Africans.

---

[35] Hailey, *An African Survey,* p. 450; Hailey, *Native Administration,* Part IV. *A General Survey of the System of Native Administration* (London: H.M.S.O., 1951), p. 12.

[36] Hailey, *Native Administration,* Part I, p. 90.

[37] George Bennett, *Kenya Political History: The Colonial Period* (London, Eng.: Oxford University Press, 1963), p. 11.

The Anti-Slavery Society influenced the Foreign Office to force the abolition of slavery in Zanzibar in 1897, but was unable to deprive the Arab owners of compensation. In 1914, Colonial Office indirect rule was established over the Arab and Indian civil servants in the local administrative and judicial systems. The British were unsuccessful, however, in modifying the Arab oligarchic, feudal economic and social systems which exploited the indigenous Shirazi peasants and traders and the African mainland laborers on the clove and coconut plantations.[38] In the Northern Rhodesia and Nyasaland protectorates, the Colonial Office established indirect rule whereby trained colonial civil servants maintained control but permitted the Africans a little participation in government through their chiefs.[39] The few white settlers often had to tolerate sympathetic treatment of the indigenous inhabitants by these officials.

In Southern Rhodesia, the European settlers established a system of direct rule. When the old company lease expired, the settlers in 1923 chose to associate themselves with Great Britain in a self-governing colony rather than with South Africa on their southern border. By this time the settlers owned the best farm lands, all the known mineral resources, and the transportation system. Because of this power, in 1923 Great Britain reserved the right to intervene and protect the 1,000,000 Africans from oppressive legislation passed by the 90,000 settlers. Despite this reservation, the settlers followed Rhodes' dictum of equal rights for all civilized men and considered themselves the only civilized people, with a duty to rule over ignorant Africans, while teaching them the habits of industry, discipline, and work. They implemented these views by further delimiting Southern Rhodesia into exclusive European and African areas, in part because of an underlying social Darwinist fear of miscegenation. Land ownership was prohibited to Africans so that a dependent wage-earning labor supply would always be available. By 1930 the settlers owned over 50 per cent of the land, Africans less than 30 per cent, and the crown 20 per cent (infested arid land). Pass laws were enacted to regulate native movements, and others to provide imprisonment and flogging penalties for those who left their jobs. In order to prevent competition, settler trade unions had legislation passed in 1934 which restricted Africans from learning skills and forming trade unions.

During the interwar period, there was hardly any leadership in Great Britain to modify colonial policy and alleviate these conditions. The Labour party, dominated by J. Ramsay MacDonald, was too moderate. After the final defeat of the Somali *mullah* in 1920, the Colonial Office established an orderly indirect-rule administration in British Somaliland with religious and

---

[38] Sir Reginald Coupland, *The Exploitation of East Africa, 1856–1890: The Slave Trade and the Scramble* (London, Eng.: Faber and Faber, 1939), p. 484; Lawrence W. Hollingsworth, *Zanzibar under the Foreign Office, 1890–1913* (London, Eng.: Macmillan & Co., 1953), p. 147.

[39] Hailey, *Native Administration,* Part IV, p. 20.

civil law courts. In the Sudan, the official emphasis was on creating an educated class of Sudanese that could be employed in indigenous agencies whenever possible. Decentralization was stressed, the authority of the sheikhs strengthened over the tribes, and a competent judicial system was established. An economic revival was evinced by irrigation schemes for cotton-growing. In Uganda, Colonial Secretary Lord Milner of Liberal David Lloyd-George's coalition government supported Governor Sir Robert Coryndon and Deputy-Governor Sir William W. Carter in encouraging European settlement and in favoring unofficial European dominance over the Asians in the Legislative Council. They were unsuccessful in the first endeavor, but successful in the second. Winston Churchill, who succeeded Milner at the Colonial Office, also supported a European majority; and the Secretary of State for India advised the Asians to cooperate. Actually no African sat on the Legislative Council for twenty years. In the early 1930's Governor Sir Bernard Bourdillon opposed advances in the literary education for Africans, but fortunately his successor Sir Philip Mitchell held the opposite view.

Milner and his Governor for Kenya, Sir Edward Northey, agreed that the railroad-development program had to continue, with each African contributing sixty days' labor every year. A 1912 law empowered the government, through interpretation of tribal custom, to require men to work on communal projects six days each yearly quarter. In 1920, the Chief Native Commissioner, John Ainsworth, in a circular informed the administrative officers in charge of the labor-supply districts that they should do all in their power to increase the supply for farms and plantations. He felt that young Africans should become wage-earners instead of remaining idle on reserves. Northey interpreted the circular as an order and, in a letter to the Convention of Associations, said that white supremacy was all-important and that the African should have an education only in technical, industrial, and agricultural fields. Through Parliament and the press, Protestant missionaries lodged accusations of forced labor against the colonial administration. Milner was not disturbed, and Churchill said that forced labor could be used only if absolutely necessary and if permission had been obtained from the Colonial Office. Milner and Northey also supported European dominance on the Legislative Council, which had the sole right to vote, as well as European rejection of a joint common roll of Europeans and Asians. Aware of the situation in Southern Rhodesia, the settlers even asked for self-rule status—something which Delamere, their outstanding spokesman, had asked for in 1913. Churchill refused, saying that there would be no question of self-rule until the 6,000,000 Africans and 200,000 Arab-Indians had equal citizenship rights with the 30,000 Europeans. Colonial Secretary Lord Devonshire, in Andrew Bonar Law's Conservative government, issued a white paper in 1923 stating that there were no immediate prospects for self-government, the Asians should have proper representation, and although the interests of the Africans were paramount, there would be no reversal or incumbrance on the European position.[40] The following year Kenya adopted the policy existing in Tanganyika, Northern Rhodesia, and Nyasaland of encouraging Africans as well as Europeans to produce cash crops. By 1937 the Europeans held 7,000,000 acres of cultivated land and the Africans nearly 2,000,000. The Kikuyu were particularly averse to raising merely subsistence crops on reserves which were often overgrazed by overstocking as well as to laboring on other men's farms and industries. However, there was no African representation on the Legislative Council until 1944.

During its two governments in the 1920's the Labour party was unable to enact a joint European and Asian common roll. This resulted in an Asian boycott of the Legislative Council until 1934 because they were under-represented in comparison with the Europeans. The Colonial Office, despite its official pronouncements and royal commissions of investigation, rarely interfered with European power in Kenya. In 1936 the settlers were per-suaded to accept a small income tax in return for increased influence on the Executive Council. Even Colonial Secretary Lord Passfield, the Fabian Sidney Webb, was unable to act against local repressive acts supported by the Convention of Associations and missionaries against the Kikuyu Central Association, prohibiting it from collecting dues and participating in tribal dancing and female circumcisions. Furthermore, many young Kikuyu did not want to cooperate with their British-appointed chiefs.

The Colonial Office assumed the administration of Tanganyika from the League of Nations as a Class B mandate. Sir Horace Byatt, the first Gover-nor, failed to ingratiate himself with the European settlers in 1923 when he issued an ordinance to secure the Africans' land rights. His successor, Sir Donald Cameron, reorganized the native administrative system and courts to strengthen the local traditional authorities' government.[41] He welcomed European settlers and in 1926 enabled them to secure an unofficial repre-sentative dominance in the Legislative Council. Cameron supported eco-nomic development schemes, labor improvements, and African primary education, but he opposed union with other East African territories.

Milner advocated close union—a view expressed by settlers during 1924 and 1925 at meetings held at various places from Kenya to Northern Rhodesia. They were concerned with the African majorities in their terri-tories and demanded the relaxation of imperial controls to favor the settlers. In 1924 a Conservative member of Commons, Sir Sidney Henn, asked the Colonial Office to investigate the possibilities of closer union from Kenya to Rhodesia, and the Labour Colonial Secretary J. H. Thomas appointed a commission to examine the possibility. Its chairman, William Ormsby-Gore, reported that the idea was unrealistic. However, in 1925 the imperialist-minded Leopold Amery, in Stanley Baldwin's second Conservative govern-ment, encouraged his friend the Governor of Kenya, pro-settler Sir Edward

---

[40] Bennett, *op. cit.*, p. 50.
[41] Hailey, *Native Administration*, Part I, p. 16.

Grigg, to press for closer union.[42] Cameron's concern that the scheme would adversely affect his native administrative organization and Buganda's fear that its privileged position in Uganda stemming from the 1900 agreement would be jeopardized played an important part in defeating the proposal. The 1927 Hilton Young commission found it impossible to accept the idea before the Africans were given more political responsibility, and by 1931 the scheme for a closer union was abandoned.

The proposal was not reconsidered until 1947, when the Clement Attlee Labour government proposed an East African High Commission (EAHC) for closer cooperation among the territories. It would have an executive consisting of the three governors and a central legislature based on racial equality, two each of Africans, Europeans, and Arab-Asians coming from each territory. The Tanganyika and Uganda settlers accepted the idea, but those in Kenya violently opposed it. Most Africans supported it, many were skeptical, but the Buganda hereditary landowners and hierarchy distrusted it. When Arthur Creech-Jones of the Colonial Office modified the EAHC structure, making it acceptable to the Kenya Europeans, the Africans opposed it. Nevertheless, it was enacted in 1948 because of the Colonial Official majorities in the territories. It ended eleven years later.

During World War II, the British defeats demonstrated to their colonial peoples that Great Britain was no longer an invincible power. In addition, the Labour party under Attlee's leadership officially declared in 1942 that it wanted a reform in colonial policy to emancipate exploited colonial peoples. It asked for the maintenance of indigenous land-tenure systems where they existed or their development for public use. In June 1948, a Labour party white paper outlined a program toward self-government for all dependent territories within the Commonwealth as soon as they were ready. However, Churchill, the Conservative leader, did not want to liquidate the empire. Nevertheless, there were international pressures against colonial rule from the socialist countries and from various international conferences, such as that at Bandung in 1955 and the 1958 All African Peoples Conference at Accra, which aroused the nationalists to action.

British Somaliland received its independence on June 26, 1960, and within four days joined the Somali Republic. Through the education of an elite in the government service and towns, the British developed the Sudanese for self-government. Sophisticated, exposed to a wide press and radio broadcasting, and encouraged by *tariqua* religious fraternities and British officials, the Sudanese were able successfully to challenge Egyptian claims to sovereignty by the time they received their independence on January 1, 1956. At the Juba conference in 1947, the exclusion of northern influence from the south was ended when a number of southern leaders were persuaded to accept the idea of union with the north. However, the British-imposed thirty-five-year isolation period had further widened the economic and cultural gap

---

[42] Bennett, *op. cit.*, p. 57.

between the two areas. When Khartoum instituted a policy of assimilation, the southern leaders, encouraged by Christian missionaries, became dissatisfied and opposition developed.

During the ten years since independence the situation in the southern Sudan has worsened perceptibly. The predominantly pagan and Christian populations continued to rebel against the central government's attempts to impose the Arabic language and Islamic culture on them. By October 1964, thousands were forced to flee as refugees because of the heavy-handed oppression by President Ibrahim Abboud. Although Clement Mboro, a southern Sudanese, was appointed Minister of the Interior as a reconciliation gesture after Abboud's fall, the civil disorders have intensified and increased the strain on the central government.

In Uganda the economic development for the African evolved more rapidly than the political. After the war, Governor Sir John Hall, encouraged by the Labour government, enabled African cooperative societies to purchase such European concessions as ginneries after they had been acquired from their former owners—by compulsion if necessary. Governor Sir Andrew Cohen in 1952 received the Conservative government's approval to put the scheme into effect, but the Africans' lack of sufficient collateral was a serious handicap. Young Baganda who had been educated abroad felt concern about the religious differences that divided their entrenched traditional chiefs and about the exploitation of the peasantry. They also resented exclusion from political life. In Buganda in 1952, Cohen embarked on constitutional reforms such as the creation of equal electoral constituencies that weakened the power of the traditional chiefs, instituted local government reforms, and increased the unofficial African representation on the protectorate's Legislative Council. The *kabaka* Mutesa II opposed any weakening of his power and was exiled, but was permitted to return with the reforms intact. He boycotted the Legislative Council, fought the creation of a popular unitary republican state such as that in Ghana, and wanted his traditional privileges that the British had fostered since the 1900 agreement. However, with independence in October 1962, the *kabaka* and his *lukiko* agreed to participate in a Ugandan state, provided they could nominate the Buganda delegates to the central legislature. Despite this concession, Buganda's institutions were being gradually democratized.

In Kenya, by World War II African land hunger, depressed wages, and urban restlessness caused increasing dissatisfaction. Meanwhile detribalized, uprooted Africans were exposed to missionary-sponsored education, and, during the 1940's, such Kenyans as the Luo Tom Mboya received secondary education in the coastal trade-union schools. The Labour government encouraged these schools and the trade-union movement in Kenya in order to improve Africans' living standards. In England, the Kikuyu Jomo Kenyatta was very active with William E. B. Du Bois and Kwame Nkrumah of the Pan-Africanist movement. Kenyatta even went to Moscow to study the Marxist interpretation of colonialism; he believed, however, that communism was too restrictive for the African scene. He returned to Kenya in 1950 convinced that the only way to eliminate the European economic and social controls was through a violent expulsion of all Europeans from Kenya. In 1952 the Mau Mau movement sought through surprise attacks on settlers to cause fear and hysteria. Kenyatta was imprisoned for allegedly leading the revolt, which was suppressed by 1955. Two developments followed. In 1954 Oliver Lyttelton, Colonial Secretary in the Churchill Conservative government, visited Kenya and proposed a multiracial policy for the country's development. Although the frightened settlers opposed this, they reluctantly began to consider the idea of permitting the Africans token representation on the legislative councils, entrance into the civil service, and admittance to hotels. The other development was Mboya's assumption of leadership for African rights. He was a moderate who called for majority, not token, representation on the Legislative Council. Mboya and other Kenyans were encouraged toward this goal by the practical and psychological support from Afro-Asian nations. The Africans wanted a single electoral roll for all voters, ministerial posts, African settlement in the highlands, universal compulsory education, and the release of Kenyatta.[43] Michael Blundell, the settler leader, though willing to accept multiracial education, was unwilling to permit an African majority on the Council. The Europeans hoped that some of the other African states which had tried the experiment of independence would prove it unworkable. But this was not the case—Ghana, Nigeria, and other areas were proving that African majorities could legislate effectively.

Because of the Africans' boycott of the Legislative Council, and other pressures, in 1960 the British government proposed that thirty-seven of the sixty-five elective seats on the Legislative Council be held by Africans and twenty-eight divided among Europeans, Indians, and Arabs. The confident Mboya objected to this suggestion because it did not give the Africans a clear procedural majority and furthermore required restrictive voting qualifications. Instead he demanded a popular "one man, one vote" plan which would truly represent the races in the population. All of Kenya's African parties, as well as the Arab-Asians who feared a boycott of their trade unless they cooperated, supported his new demand. Many of the Europeans opposed the popular vote, which they felt would end their domination of Kenya. They were further concerned by Mboya's statements that only a one-party system could work in Kenya; that capitalist democracy, though practicable in the United States and Great Britain, was unworkable in his country, and that Kenyatta would become Kenya's first prime minister. Though willing to tolerate a Mboya government, the settlers could not conceive suffering one led by Kenyatta. Some of them expressed the hope of marshaling their strength and forcing Kenya to join either the then European-dominated Central African Federation or the white supremacist Union of

---

[43] *Ibid.*, p. 141.

South Africa. But geography, African determination, and world conscience dashed this dream. By 1961 the popular common voter roll had been established, the Legislative Council had a clear African procedural majority, and even Europeans had begun to consider Kenyatta's release and national leadership practical. He assumed leadership when Kenya received its independence on December 12, 1963.

After World War II, Tanganyika was placed under United Nations Trusteeship control by the Labour government. Tanganyika's problems were less acute than Kenya's because land was not so scarce, there were relatively few settlers, and they were not so well established or vociferous. Actually, Africans, such as the Chagga coffee-growers on the Kilimanjaro slopes and those of Bukoba, and the diamond-miners of Shinyanga, earned relatively high incomes. However, the majority of Africans earned low wages, had few skills, and a meager education. Although there was local African government representation, no African sat on the Legislative Council until 1945. Meanwhile the trusteeship system operated through visiting missions which suggested administrative improvements or independence within twenty years —a suggestion condemned by both the Colonial Office and local officials as premature. Because of the nature of their responsibility, the British sought to fulfill their obligation to the indigenous peoples while simultaneously safeguarding the European settlers' interests. They tried various experimental devices during the 1950's to bring about a balanced system of representation on the Legislative Council. These included the equal system which gave the same numerical representation to each community and the balanced system of elections whereby each community elected three members from each race.[44] At the same time, restrictions limited African voters—they had to have either eight years of education, be a member of a chiefly hierarchy, or earn an annual income of about $420. However, by 1959, an African majority on the Legislative Council sought to Africanize the civil service, limit unchecked immigration and foreign investments, and end European privileges. Julius Nyerere, urging *uhuru na umoja,* moved the country uncompromisingly toward its independence and unity on December 9, 1960.

In Zanzibar, despite the social friction between the indigenous Shirazis and mainland African laborers which the Arab oligarchy sought to exploit, the two African peoples totaling 230,000 knew that they lacked the economic and educational resources of the 50,000 Arabs and 20,000 Asians whose representatives filled the more important positions during the seventy-three-year British protectorate.[45] The British had replaced the traditional Arab governing *liwalis,* modernized the courts, and permitted African representation on local district and urban councils, but these were small modifications. Zanzibari Arabs, realizing the potential danger to themselves of the African

[44] Hailey, *An African Survey,* p. 195.

[45] Hailey, *Native Adminsitration,* Part II. *Central Africa: Zanzibar, Nyasaland, Northern Rhodesia* (London: H.M.S.O., 1950), pp. 13–15.

nationalism rising on the continent during the 1950's, took advantage of the movement while they held power to perpetuate their privileged power structure over the Africans through political action calling for immediate self-government. Both African groups distrusted the Arabs and wanted to move slowly toward independence while they strengthened their economic position and, through education, developed their political and citizenship skills. Nyerere of Tanganyika urged the Africans to unite politically. They organized the Afro-Shirazi party, which won the majority of the popular vote in every election despite poor finances and factional strife. However, the well-integrated, well-disciplined, and well-financed Arab-Indian-supported political organizations, through coalitions and electoral districting under the protectorate constitutional framework, were able to form parliamentary majority governments until and beyond independence on December 10, 1963. Claiming that they tended to incite racial conflict, the Arab-dominated government tried to silence opposition Swahili newspapers which spoke for the deprived and impoverished African masses. Abeid Amani Karume, leader of the Afro-Shirazis, declared in August 1963 that not only British colonialism but Arab feudalism had to be overthrown. This was finally achieved on January 12, 1964, and within four months Karume and Nyerere signed an act of union establishing the United Republic of Tanzania. While hosting the African Liberation Committee of the OAU, whose headquarters is in Dar es Salaam, and violently criticizing the white supremacist governments south of the Zambezi River, Tanzania has steered a non-aligned course in foreign affairs accepting Western as well as East European and Chinese communist financial and technical aid.

The African nationalist reaction also manifested itself in central Africa, forcing Southern Rhodesia to pass a subversive activities act in 1950 which gave the settler government the powers to ban any organization. By 1953 the settlers were expressing concern and suspicion over what they considered Great Britain's and especially the Labour party's premature surrender of territories to black nationalism. In order to create a large self-governing European-dominated state, such as the Union of South Africa, and to expand their economic power by attracting more capital and settlers from Western Europe, the settlers decided to push for a federation of Southern Rhodesia and the British protectorates of Northern Rhodesia and Nyasaland. Southern Rhodesia's advanced industrial complex could effectively utilize Northern Rhodesia's mineral resources and Nyasaland's manpower. The question was whether federation would mean equal partnership between the settlers and Africans in the three states or an expansion of the Southern Rhodesian settler policy of trusteeship over and segregation of the Africans. The Churchill government, after hesitation and opposition from the Labour party, African tribal leaders, and detribalized missionary and British-university-trained African leaders, such as H. Kamazu Banda of Nyasaland and Kenneth Kaunda of Northern Rhodesia, permitted the federation. As soon as federation occurred, a special electoral system was enacted enabling the Europeans to vote for fifty-three of fifty-nine legislators from a common roll and the Africans for only six from a special roll to a single federation legislature. Banda and Kaunda proceeded to organize political parties—the African Congresses—demanding a dissolution of the federation. Sir Roy Welensky, the European trade-unionist leader and head of the federation, opposed this and called for independence of the whole federation from Great Britain. He even threatened Great Britain with a "Boston Tea Party" on the Zambezi River or Lake Nyasa. But the British government, gradually sensitive to African opposition and world opinion, refused the request and, after ten years, on January 1, 1964, dissolved the federation. The two former protectorates, Nyasaland (Malawi) and Northern Rhodesia (Zambia), were scheduled for independence during 1964. Malawi progressed with little friction toward independence; its Congress party remained unchallenged, and the European and Indian planters were assured that they would not face discrimination or expropriation of their properties. In Zambia there was a problem of leadership resulting from two African parties, Kaunda's more militant dominant one and Harry Nkumbula's more moderate group, and a European party representing the 77,000 settlers. In addition, the *Litunga* (paramount chief), Sir Mwanamina Lewanika III of Barotseland, wished to preserve a semifeudal chieftainship based on protectorate guarantees which his ancestors had contracted with Queen Victoria at the turn of the century.

Southern Rhodesia (Zimbabwe) remained under the rule of 250,000 settlers whose leadership became increasingly militant and refused the requests of European liberal leaders that the social and land *apartheid* policies end. The settlers' leadership, believing its rule would continue for another thirty years, even suggested the possibility of a unilateral declaration of independence, but the British government strongly hinted that it would not welcome such a move. Originally the African opposition, united under the leadership of Joshua Nkomo, rejected token reforms and used strikes, riots, intimidation, and violence to gain African popular majority rule. The government retaliated by banning the Zimbabwe African Peoples Union (ZAPU) in September 1962, arresting African leaders, and using troops, aircraft, tear gas, bayonets, and police dogs to quell the nationalist movement. In August 1963, a split occurred within ZAPU ranks as the Reverend Ndabaningi Sithole organized the Zimbabwe African National Union to carry out a more effective struggle. In turn Nkomo formed the Peoples Caretaker Council, and violence developed between the two. Nevertheless the government arrested and sentenced both leaders to imprisonment as bombing attacks against settlers increased and strikes and riots occurred in detention centers. The Southern Rhodesian government even issued grenades and tear gas bombs to settlers. White refugees from the Congo had alarmed the settlers who increasingly looked to South Africa for military and financial support and for advice in continuing the policy of separate race development.

By December 1962, all hope for a reversal of this trend was lost when the white supremacist Rhodesian Front came to power and immediately moved toward independence. Most whites considered this goal a moral right, even if constitutionally wrong, because of the lack of safeguards for the African population. The settlers believed that because they had ruled themselves since 1923 and the British government had never used its reserve power to intervene they were more than adequately prepared for independence. First with Winston Field and after April 1964 with Ian Smith, the Rhodesian Front spoke of a unilateral declaration of independence (UDI). British Prime Minister Harold Wilson made it clear in October of that year that such an action would amount to defiance and rebellion against Great Britain. Nevertheless, UDI occurred on November 11, 1965, and Wilson immediately applied economic sanctions and asked the United Nations Security Council to vote an oil and petroleum products embargo against Southern Rhodesia. This embargo was granted. Most Africans believed the sanctions were too little and too late and demanded military intervention. But Wilson lacked parliamentary support for stiffer action until after the April 1966 elections when a ninety-three-seat Laborite majority permitted stronger moves. The question of whether settler rule would continue forceful resistance to African majority rule or whether the two races would genuinely work together in a Zimbabwe state certainly would be answered in much less than thirty years. African nationalist success to the north was bound to have a decisive effect.

ITALIAN POLICY AND PRACTICE

Although free and united after 1870, Italy was neither prosperous nor powerful. The lucrative Renaissance commercial period no longer existed, and though there was some industry, especially in the sophisticated north, the high birth rate caused great strain on the country's meager resources. The majority of the people, especially in the south, were impoverished, illiterate, and heavily taxed to support the military and an establishment composed of antiquated aristocrats and a small grasping middle class. Politically there was little difference between the right and the left. Most politicians were opportunists who encouraged emigration in order that a return flow of money from abroad could balance the Italian budgets. Thus the Italian foreign policy was not aggressive until Francesco Crispi, an imperialist dreamer and visionary, came to power in 1887.

In 1869, the Rubbatino Navigation Company acquired land concessions from Somali sultans and later from IBEAC.[46] Crispi acquired these for the government and extended its influence along the Eritrean coast. The Somali areas had few resources of any value, and certainly few attractions for settlers. However, since Crispi had little parliamentary support in his im-

---

[46] Bourgin *et al., op. cit.,* p. 129; Denis M. Smith, *Italy: A Modern History* (Ann Arbor, Mich.: University of Michigan Press, 1959), p. 128.

perialist adventure and inadequate funds to administer Somaliland directly, he contracted with commercial companies to rule the area for him. Parliament soon criticized him for permitting the companies to enact racial laws and treat the indigenous inhabitants as slave laborers forced to work on Italian cotton, sugar, and banana plantations, and public works. The Somalis had a traditional culture and the Islamic faith, and resented the Italian introduction of Christianity and the use of Somali troops against fellow Somali.

Early in the twentieth century, Italian nationalists, seeking to revive an interest in the past, persuaded intellectuals and the middle class to support imperialism. Even the socialists accepted the idea, believing that, although it would increase the wealth of the bourgeoisie, the workers also would be given a chance to improve their living standards.[47] In any event, Italian colonial policy was always negative and remained subsidiary to foreign policy which sought to expand into the eastern Mediterranean against a weak Turkey. When the Fascists seized power in 1922, they found that the colonies had not absorbed much of the surplus Italian population and were a steady drain on the treasury. But they considered the few immigrants abroad as military *Fasci di combattimento* who could guard the areas against Somali tribal raids. The Fascists with a small staff of military-political officials re-organized the colonial structure, administered the area under Italian and Islamic law, improved trade facilities, and sought to increase Italian exports to the colony. They used the Somalis in the Ogaden area against Ethiopia and administered the area as part of Somalia, maintaining a nascent Somali consciousness without permitting the creation of a modern nationalism. After World War II, Somaliland was placed under United Nations trusteeship with Italy as the administering authority. During this trusteeship, the Italians accelerated Somali education for self-government. However, they continued to grant special concessions to Italian commercial companies and to emphasize Italian culture—aspects which remained after independence. Gradually a nationalist leadership arose, mainly under the Somali Youth League (SYL), which though appealing to Somali tradition was western educated and advocated a unitary centralized state to counteract tribal differences. The SYL succeeded in dominating the government after independence on July 1, 1960, and has campaigned for a greater Somalia to include the Somali inhabitants of northeast Kenya, southeast Ethiopia, and southern French Somaliland which were separated by arbitrary colonial boundary divisions.

ARAB POLICY AND PRACTICE

Arab colonialism in East Africa is best evinced in the former Zanzibar sultanate. Although policy was never specifically set, the Arab community through its sultan, landowning aristocracy, and newspaper *Al Falaq* ("The

---

[47] *Ibid.,* p. 276.

Dawn"), wished to maintain its supremacy over the indigenous Afro-Shirazi by emphasizing the two concepts—*desturi* (custom) and *heshima* (dignity). Similar attitudes evolved among the Arabs on the Swahili coast of the mainland and in the northern and central Sudan despite local conditions which fostered different manifestations.

As early as the tenth century, Arabs settled in East Africa as slavers and landowners. By the end of the nineteenth century, the most important Arabs on Zanzibar and Pemba were the Omani clans which had come with Seyyid Said a half century earlier. They seized the most fertile lands, mainly unoccupied, from the Shirazis, and with the financial aid of Banyan Indian merchants turned them into profitable slave-worked clove and coconut plantations.[48]

On the surface, the Arab community appeared to be enjoying splendid and prosperous times. After the two abortive attempts in 1893 and 1896 by Seyyid Khaled bin Barghash to seize power—his astrologers told him that the British naval guns could not fire—the foreign and colonial offices were able to control the sultanate family with regular annual stipends and moderate Western European advisors and teachers, reducing the sultanate to ceremonial functions. On numerous state occasions, the sultan had the Malindi harbor battery at Zanzibar Town fire salutes; and, at the electrically lighted Bet-el-Ajaib palace whose white interiors were hung with large mirrors and heavy festoons of crotons, the sultan held grand *barazas* (conferences) with the religious Aulad Imam and important Arab aristocrats.[49] He also entertained leading European administrative and diplomatic officials and the principal Indian merchants, but not the indigenous Shirazi until the 1940's. Until then, he met them only on visits to their areas when the Shirazi knelt and also performed *ngomas* (dances) before him. The Muscat-Omani sultans continued to send their annual gifts, and the Zanzibari sultana with her ladies in rich dresses, sparkling jewels, and golden bracelets and anklets, joined festivities with separate garden parties. The British supported the sultan's expensive taste for pomp and horse-drawn carriages, and the Scottish Caledonian Society, whose membership included most of the local colonial officials, regularly drank toasts to the sultan's health with encomiums and marveled at what they considered the lack of racial strife in the islands.[50]

All these activities emphasized the sultan's *heshima* (dignity), but the realization that political power emanated from the British residency to the palace escaped few. Any real power was limited to religious festivals, such as the Id-el-Fitr and the Id-el-Haj after Ramadan at the Hadith mosque, and conferring his Order of the Brilliant Star classes—the top of which went to

---

[48] Colonial Office (C.O.) 688/1, *Zanzibar Administrative Report* (*Z.A.R.*), 1912 (Zanzibar, 1913), p. 139.

[49] C.O. 689/2, *Zanzibar Gazette* (*Z.G.*) XXIII, No. 1160, 1914 (Zanzibar, 1914), p. 114.

[50] C.O. 688/1, *Z.A.R.*, 1911 (Zanzibar, 1912), p. 25; C.O. 689/17, *ZG*, XXXIV, No. 1759, 1925 (Zanzibar 1925), pp. 354–355.

Europeans and Arabs, then to Indians, and last to Shirazis. Gone were the days during the greater part of the nineteenth century when the sultan could collect his biannual *kodi* tax or exact *corvée* labor from the *mwenyi mkuu* (greatest land possessor), the accepted Hadimu and Tumbatu feudal hereditary ruler.[51] Perhaps a sign of the limited renown of the sultan can be evinced by an incident in October 1919. The steamer *Khalifa,* flying the sultan's red flag, put into Bombay with a leaking boiler. Port officials concerned about nationalist agitation and the Red Scare mistook it for a Bolshevik craft and searched it for arms and papers. Even the sultan's successful 1925 attempt to remove Zanzibar from the control of the Colonial Office's East African Protectorate Governor's High Commission based in Nairobi, as well as to abolish the resident select and secretive Protectorate Council's organization, and institute legislative and executive councils, was essentially the work of the planter Arab Association and the European and Indian mercantile communities. During the 1950's the Arabs sought to use the sultan as a symbol of a common Zanzibari Islamic religious and cultural tradition. Realizing the potential danger to their privileged power structure by indigenous African nationalist gains on the continent, the Arabs decided to take advantage of the movement while they could. By 1956 the Arab-dominated and Indian-supported Zanzibar Nationalist Party (ZNP) called for the patriotic union of all Zanzibaris under the sultan and immediate self-government.

By the end of the nineteenth century, the nucleus of Arab power was in the hands of the landowners who despised manual labor for themselves and their sons. Before the British Anti-Slavery Society imposed abolition of slavery in 1897, the Arabs as governing *liwalis* and as able-bodied *akidas,* commanding Baluchi troops, had displaced the weak *mwenyi mkuu,* demanded the loyalty of the *shehas* (Shirazi lords) in their districts, and sent domineering *jemandars* to collect tax revenues and *corvée* labor.[52] Although not part of a tribal system, the illiterate and backward Shirazi *wazee bwanas* (elderly knowledgeable lords), usually nominated by the *akidas* from local influential families on a hereditary basis and formally elected by the inhabitants, kept order through their *shekue-naibs* (overseers) by the use of stocks and whips, collected personal and hut taxes from poor farmers and coastal fishermen and forced communal labor, particularly on the reluctant and unfriendly Pemba, for road-making, planting, weeding, and harvesting. The Arabs despised the Shirazi as inferior and the mainland African slaves, particularly the Nyamwezi, as barbarian *shenzi,* and used both in gangs during the first, or *mwaka,* clove crop from August to November and the second, or *mvuli,* crop from January to March. The overseers, however, per-

---

51 C.O. 688/1, *Z.A.R.,* 1911 (Zanzibar, 1912), p. 165; C.O. 688/12, *Z.A.R.,* 1935 (Zanzibar, 1936), pp. 18–35.

52 C.O. 688/1, *Z.A.R.,* 1912 (Zanzibar, 1913), p. 40; C.O. 688/12, *Z.A.R.,* 1935 (Zanzibar, 1936), pp. 20–23.

mitted them to grow their own food crops for consumption and sale. In this manner most of the Shirazi communal lands were turned into freeholds interspersed with *waqf* lands for charitable-religious purposes, both governed by Islam law.

Despite this income-producing structure, the Arabs were generally disinterested in the business management of their estates or in successfully introducing new plants such as coffee, tea, spice and rubber.[53] Some Arabs lived on their *shambas* (plantations) and came to the towns only to dispose of their produce or settle boundary disputes before *gadis* (judges), but most lived in such towns as Zanzibar, and Mkoani, Chake-Chake, and Weti on Pemba. In Zanzibar Town, they lived among the Europeans and Indians particularly in the Shangani, Bhangani, and Vuga quarters. The closely-packed stone houses built increasingly higher to face the sea had their backs to the Afro-Shirazi huts on poorly drained lowlands separated from the town by a foul-smelling creek and a garbage incinerator.[54] The Arabs sought to maintain themselves in a traditional luxurious and leisurely life, including expensive weddings and funerals, and spent most of their time in their homes or on hotel terraces with iced sherbets and Turkish coffees, watching the harbor activity, chatting socially during the late afternoon before the sunset prayers and afterward into the night as the Afro-Shirazi crowded the beach to wash the dust of the go-downs from their bodies. Before 1897, the planters were borrowing increasing amounts of money from the wily Indians and more usurious Arabs.

The abolition of slavery caused a serious upheaval in the lives of the landowners. With the loss of slaves, their prestige declined and the cost of operating their *shambas* increased. One problem of *shamba* economics was that some of the freed slaves preferred to remain with their old masters as squatters, and in addition drifters increased the *maskini Muungu,* or God's poor, thereby abusing the classic Arab generosity.[55] Another problem was that under the Islamic law of inheritance, many of the properties were divided into many uneconomic parts.[56] Usually the estates were left in the hands of Arabs without means or of apparently trustworthy freed slaves who reported what would please the owners regardless of the actual facts. However, the planters insisted on continuing their customary life and borrowed from the Indians who charged interest rates averaging 15 per cent. Mortgaged at amounts often high as 60 per cent of assessed valuation, properties rapidly decreased in value, houses were sold at half-price, and—in cases of default—the Indians seized the properties but left the Arabs as overseers.

---

[53] C.O. 618/2, *Zanzibar Correspondence,* C.O. Memorandum, 3/9/1913.

[54] C.O. 688/3, *Z.A.R.,* 1916 (Zanzibar, 1917), pp. 76–79; C.O. 688/4, *Z.A.R.,* 1921 (Zanzibar, 1922), p. 81.; *Z.A.R.,* 1947 (Zanzibar, 1948), p. 9.

[55] C.O. 688/1, *Z.A.R.,* 1911 (Zanzibar, 1912), p. 165.

[56] *Ibid.,* p. 97.

The situation had become so desperate by World War I that planters claimed as theirs through inheritance lands formerly considered useless. In Pemba the planters had never, or not recently, controlled the desired lands which the Shirazi had cleared for *mohogo* (cassava) crops.

By 1920, the *shehas* had become apathetic and ineffective with the absence of the *mwenyi mkuu,* the abolition of slavery, and the supervisory presence of colonial officialdom. Troublesome Shirazis now openly opposed the *shehas,* refused to pay rents, and kept them busy with raids on *shambas,* committing acts of theft and violence. In 1929, 400 Afro-Shirazi tenants from the Zanzibar Town suburb of Kiwanja tried unsuccessfully to force their way into the sultan's palace to protest a ground-rent decree. The *wazees* (elders) now tried to keep order for officialdom with the aid of Indian *askaris* (troops), and—although they still could compel Afro-Shirazis to labor on public works including government-owned *shambas*—their functions had multiplied to include recording births and deaths, acting as auctioneers and brokers, and administering small estates. Workers now bargained directly with overseers and entered into regular contracts. Although master and servant decrees existed, they were difficult to enforce, for often the workers, particularly the Hadimu, broke contracts by not appearing for work either after receiving advance pay before Ramadan when they needed money most or before the *mvuli* crop harvest when they were anxious to return home to plant their own crops.[57] The Nyamwezi were most dependable, but also more expensive to retain. Although the Afro-Shirazis normally worked two or three days a week in uncomfortable positions until nightfall, the threat of force, taxes, and ground-rent payments made them work additional days. The Arabs insisted on controls over the weeders and pickers to avoid contract breaches.

British colonial officialdom in policy papers after 1914 considered the *akidas* as the best instruments of secondary political control. It retained and institutionalized them as *mudirs* heading subdistricts, gave them an apparent share in deciding how funds would be spent by representation on the Legislative Council, and invited them to sit on district courts as hopeful predecessors to district councils.[58] In Zanzibar most of the *mudirs* were literate, but not in Pemba. Although the Arabs appreciated this perpetuation of their power and recognition of their *heshima,* they rarely sat on the district courts. But the progressive landowners, such as the Ismaili at Wete, stressed plantation improvements which the Colonial Office believed were the main means to produce revenue. The British were concerned about labor recruitment, indebtedness to the Indian middlemen, and the increasing number of government-owned *shambas* (neither of which paid taxes). The anticolonialist agitation in India after World War I increased this concern. The British wanted the Arabs to become "typical English yeomen," better versed

[57] *Ibid.,* pp. 145–146.

[58] C.O. 688/9, *Z.A.R.,* 1931 (Zanzibar, 1932), p. 131.

in agricultural economic management and marketing practices. They formed a labor office to channel Afro-Shirazi laborers where needed, offered houses for new clove plantings, and storage space in government go-downs, as well as accepting stored goods as collateral for loans. Instead of paying high interest rates, the idea was for planters to save money for road and warehouse construction and marine-transportation facilities. The Arab Association and its newspaper, *Al Falaq,* and, after 1926, the New Generations Club supported these policies, which formed the basis for the Clove Growers Association.

Colonial officials believed that the association fitted both the individualist and collective character of the Arab. But many conservative Arabs, though accepting it, were suspicious of British designs, complaining that the latter had not fulfilled their compensation promises made before the abolition of slavery. These planters procrastinated in entering association agreements, constantly asked to see its accounts and profits, and preferred to control prices among themselves. By the late 1920's, financial stringency was evident as outside investors were reluctant to support the association. They were more interested in India and in the growing ports of Tanganyika and Kenya, did not believe that their investments could be easily recovered from the *shambas,* feared synthetic clove oil processing and increased production of Madagascar cloves and that copra would be sent direct from East African mainland ports to overseas markets without first being bulked with Zanzibar produce for re-export. Furthermore, in the 1930's, the Indian community, accused by the Arabs and Europeans of attempting to sabotage the association by contracting for Madagascar cloves for India, retaliated by accusing the Colonial Office of prejudice against it and suggested that the government leave the *shamba* business.[59] It reminded the Arabs of the Indian community's support on the Palestine question and of their common Islamic religious bond. The association survived and eliminated much financial waste, but did not enable the Arabs to gain economic independence or succeed generally as businessmen. Nevertheless, the Arabs wanted to appear successful even though many still signed for loans with thumbprints recorded on account books written in the Gujerati language.

The British were also intent on convincing the Arabs that primary education was an opportunity for competing with the Indian. The Arab children, with the abolition of slavery, suffered from a lack of early guidance, discipline, and education. However, any real educational progress was delayed by the Arab patriarchs' insistence on the teaching of the Arabic language, since they considered Zanzibar a center of Islamic culture in East Africa, and the method of instruction by *mualims* (teachers) to all boys before formal education of the Koran by *hitimu* (complete absorption).[60] The Arabs, emphasizing their *heshima* (dignity), wanted the use of Swahili limited—

---

[59] *Zanzibar Voice,* January 5, 1936, p. 5.

[60] C.O. 688/2, *Z.A.R.,* 1913 (Zanzibar, 1914), p. 2.

and certainly not used in explaining the Koran—even though Swahili was used in most of their homes, was the lingua franca of the islands, and was used in nine-tenths of the law cases. The colonial officials, supported by the *gadis* on these points, disagreed with the Arabs. The *gadis* were the best-educated Arabs—scholars in jurisprudence, very active, efficient, and well-traveled men who maintained regular contacts with Cairo and Ottoman Constantinople. They wanted to improve Arabic, but stressed that it had to begin at home where there was little encouragement. Although they urged Arabs to attend local agricultural schools on *shamba* management at Dunga and secondary schools, such as the ones at Dole for clerical work, they also encouraged students to go abroad to such centers as Cairo to receive training in government service, eventually to replace the European and Indian officials. They expressed concern when colonial officials, contrary to their expressed goals, withheld permission for Arabs to visit institutions abroad, such as Tuskegee and Hampton, for scientific agricultural knowledge. At the root of much disinterest or failure in education was the *desturi* (custom) of teaching young boys the Koran *hitimu* before formal education, often resulting in intellectual atrophy.[61] The parents were hostile to innovations in the practice and even preferred to keep their sons in schools near the plantations to retain home influences rather than expose them to the profligacy and *tembo* (local brew) drinking in the towns. Although a few students were able to attend the University of Makerere College in Uganda, the level of Arab education was lowest in the islands. In 1949, only 11.8 per cent of the Arab boys and 4.5 per cent of the girls attended school, compared with 72 per cent for the Indian boys and 62.5 for the girls.

A significant element in the Arabs' environment was their general health. Removed from their hot, dry, windswept southern former Arabian habitat, they found themselves on poorly drained tropical islands, living in crowded or unsanitary areas and contracting diseases, such as malaria and ankylostomiasis. Although they learned to accept vaccines, maternity care, and the surgeon's scalpel rather than the dirty village razor, the effects of chronic illness, such as anemia, asthma, bronchitis, and rheumatism, sapped their strength. They neglected the use of such medicines as quinine and cared little for the health of their Afro-Shirazi workers. Many habitually consumed opium to alleviate their misery, though they were not severely addicted.

During the 1930's and the 1940's, the Arabs maintained a semblance of power through the colonial administrative structure, but were under financial strain. Concerned about meager profits, they demanded that the Clove Growers Association and, later, during World War II, the Economic Control Board show their accounts and not touch reserved funds.[62] But they wanted

---

61 C.O. 688/4, *Z.A.R.*, 1924 (Zanzibar, 1925), pp. 46–48.

62 C.O. 689/26, *Zanzibar Legislative Council Proceedings* (*Z.L.C.P.*), December 16, 1932 (Zanzibar, 1933), p. 32.

aid from the Colonial Development and Welfare Fund to build roads to their *shambas* and to ensure their clove trees against sudden-death disease, bush growth, and fire. The Pemba Arabs particularly wanted hospitals, roads, schools, and the sending of young Arabs to study abroad in Egypt and in the Sudan.[63] They criticized what they considered to be a superfluous and expensive European-dominated bureaucracy and questioned why there were more Indians (whom they considered foreigners) than Arabs on the subordinate administrative staffs—particularly in the customs, port, and marine services. The Arabs protested that officials of East African domicile did not get the same allowances and vacations as Europeans. They did not want Arab debtors imprisoned and heavy deposits paid by Arab immigrants, even those infected with trachoma, and they opposed spending for Afro-Shirazi councils and municipal land courts to investigate small land titles as improper until normal economic conditions returned to the *shambas*. Seeking unrestricted African mainland labor to depress wages, they objected to accident or pension aid to uncontracted workers. The Arab planters attempted to curtail the Afro-Shirazis' planting of food crops. Before World War II, money was scarce, and, since the owners had a little to supply, people worked on the *shambas*. During the war, food had a high priority, the owners could supply it, and the *shambas* were worked. But with the large increase of food-crop plantings stimulated by the war effort for self-support and sale for cash, the Arabs found it difficult to draw the Afro-Shirazi workers to their *shambas*. With more attractive, unionized, higher-pay work in the town ports, the Afro-Shirazis were drawn to other work, such as on the docks.

The Arabs were economically doomed by 1950, and the political challenges were impending, despite their advocacy of a unified multiracial state stressing loyalty to the sultan and immediate independence. Though the Shirazis felt culturally superior to the African mainlanders and social friction existed between them, both knew that they did not have the economic and educational resources of the Arab minority, no matter how weak that was. Both African groups were suspicious of the Arabs and wanted to move slowly toward independence while they strengthened their economic position and mastered educational and political skills. Gone were the days when the Arabs could encourage or even take pleasure at strife between Nyamwezi and Hadimu or Nyamwezi and Digo, when they could be assured by the British resident that athletic contests were better than political propaganda in lessening race and class prejudices. Just before they departed from the dramatic historical scene on January 12, 1964, they found themselves with a sultan reduced to a ceremonial symbol, their absentee-landlord aristocracy undermined by social and administrative change, their brightest youths seeking permanent pensionable employment behind government typewriters, and

---

[63] *Z.L.C.P.*, December 4, 1945 (Zanzibar, 1946), p. 14.

their less-heralded youths living high in Zanzibar Town patronizing the local markets and coffee shops as their fathers had done a generation earlier.

COMPARISON AND CONTRAST

The historical ingredients that are a part of the colonial heritage of East Africa are similar in many ways. Despite the humanitarian causes which the European peoples expounded from the time of the Portuguese arrival during the Renaissance, they all believed that they possessed a superior civilization and were determined to increase their empires over the indigenous peoples, for this meant power, influence, and prestige. Though they advocated the abolition of foreign or indigenous slavery, the dissemination of Christianity as uplifting and the modification of feudal indigenous structures, the most important sustaining element in the European presence as well as in the Arab regardless of the cultural veneer of Islamic faith, was the possibility of economic gain. Since the sixteenth century, the commercial, industrial, and financial capitalist revolutions involved the European settlers in utilizing indigenous labor in a large-scale, cash-crop economy, extracting raw materials for export, and having a market for manufactured products.

The European economic and social structure in the metropolitan countries varied only according to the degree of their technological and economic change. Changing very little at home, Portugal maintained a feudal social structure supported by the aristocracy, church, and small middle class. Despite occasional attempts at domestic and colonial reform and republican governments, a medieval corporate structure survived which was grafted and entrenched in Mozambique through the *prazeros,* missionaries, and companies. In France, a greater economic impact gradually modified the old regime; however, the republican governments that succeeded it were maintained by the petty politicians and influenced their decisions on colonial policy. Great Britain and its Establishment, constituting the church, career officialdom in government service and the army in certain upper-class families, and the Press, was an important influence during the Liberal and Conservative governments, and parliamentary Fabianism modified the Labour party's socialist outlook on colonial questions. This outlook remained weak even after World War II. The Italian political scene was dominated by opportunists whether of the left or right who always lacked a clear policy in regard to Somaliland, and the Fascist government simply transferred its corporate system to the colony. The Arab concepts of *heshima* and *desturi* were merely degenerate trappings of rule fostered by British colonial officialdom.

All of these powers eventually dominated multitribal areas, which had no ethnic identity in the Western sense. They delimited boundaries and gradually formulated colonial policies—such as that of the Portuguese *assimilado,* the French *mission civilisatrice,* and the borrowed Belgian *mise en valeur,* and the British indirect rule—whenever possible, but with strong aspects of direct settler rule in Kenya and Southern Rhodesia. Often they made use of existing feudal regimes and divisive tactics to extend their rule. The Italian policy, though loosely defined, ultimately had one characteristic similar to the others—the use of forced labor for private enterprise and public works. The Catholic Church contributed to Italian policy, especially during the Fascist period, emphasizing the traditional conflict between the Cross and the Crescent. There was also discriminating legislation which prohibited the Africans' purchase of land and social contacts with the Europeans. These laws were, in great part, due to the power of the European settlers who were interested in exploiting the areas' human and material resources as well as in influencing their nations' colonial policy. The interaction of all these ingredients caused the uprooting and educating of young Africans who, seeing the discrimination against them and supported by the metropolitan Socialist and Communist parties, became aware of this exploitation. This awareness was usually manifested in demands for reform which were resisted by colonial officialdom influenced by European settlers. Only as a last resort were nominal reforms implemented. The interaction of all these ingredients brought forth African nationalist independence movements.

Often there were accelerating catalytic agents, such as the consciousness that European colonial powers were not invincible, manifested by their defeats during World War II. Also, world opinion and the success of other emergent African states, such as Ghana, tended to develop the independence movement more rapidly. On the other hand, there are also retarding factors, such as the ability of a settler minority in Southern Rhodesia to hold back self-determination and freedom for millions of Africans. This has been accomplished through the settlers' disciplined voting and loyalty to their segregationist leadership. Neo-colonialist ventures, such as financial assistance through the French FAC in Malagasy, also tend to retard social and economic reforms after political independence has been won. Recent reverberations in both areas, however, tend to show that African nationalism had made its impact there. When these movements will succeed and at what consequences to both the settlers and the Africans remain to be answered.

SELECTED BIBLIOGRAPHY

PORTUGUESE AFRICA

Axelson, Eric V. *South-east Africa, 1488–1530.* London, Eng.: Longmans, Green, and Company, 1940.

Duffy, James. *Portuguese Africa.* Cambridge, Mass.: Harvard University Press, 1959.

FRENCH AFRICA

Deschamps, H. *Histoire de Madagascar.* Paris, France: Berger-Levrault, 1960.

BRITISH SUDAN

Abbas, Mekki. *The Sudan Question*. New York: Frederick A. Praeger, 1952.

Duncan, J. R. S. *The Sudan: A Record of Achievement*. Edinburgh, Scot.: Blackwood, 1952.

Henderson, K. D. D. *Survey of the Anglo-Egyptian Sudan, 1898–1944*. London, Eng.: Longmans, Green, and Company, 1946.

UGANDA

Ingham, K. *The Making of Modern Uganda*. London, Eng.: Allen and Unwin, 1958.

Johnston, Sir Harry H. *The Uganda Protectorate*. New York: Dodd, Mead and Company, 1904. 2 vols.

Low, D. Anthony and R. Crawford Pratt. *Buganda and British Overrule, 1900–1955*. London, Eng.: Oxford University Press, 1960.

TANGANYIKA AND ZANZIBAR

Chidzero, B. T. G. *Tanganyika and International Trusteeship*. New York: Oxford University Press, 1961.

Coupland, Sir Reginald. *East Africa and Its Invaders from the Earliest Times to the Death of Seyyid Said in 1856*. Oxford, Eng.: The Clarendon Press, 1938.

————. *The Exploitation of East Africa, 1856–1890*. London, Eng.: Faber and Faber, 1939.

Hollingsworth, Lawrence W. *Zanzibar under the Foreign Office, 1890–1913*. London, Eng.: Macmillan & Co., 1953.

Leubuscher, Charlotte. *Tanganyika Territory: A Study of Economic Policy under the Mandate*. London, Eng.: Oxford University Press, 1944.

CENTRAL AFRICA

Gann, L. H. *A History of Northern Rhodesia: Early Days to 1953*. New York: Humanities Press, 1964.

Gray, R. *The Two Nations: Aspects of the Development of Race Relations in the Rhodesias and Nyasaland*. London, Eng.: Oxford University Press, 1960.

Jones, Griff. *Britain and Nyasaland*. London, Eng.: Allen and Unwin, 1964.

Mason, P. *Birth of a Dilemma: The Conquest and Settlement of Rhodesia*. London, Eng.: Oxford University Press, 1958.

Leys, Colin. *European Politics in Southern Rhodesia*. New York: Oxford University Press, 1959.

ARAB AFRICA

Freeman-Grenville, G. S. P. *The Medieval History of the Coast of Tanganyika*. London, Eng.: Oxford University Press, 1962.

Gray, Sir John. *History of Zanzibar from the Middle Ages to 1856*. London, Eng.: Oxford University Press, 1962.

SOMALILAND

Jardine, D. J. *The Mad Mullah of Somaliland*. London, Eng.: H. Jenkins, Ltd., 1923.

KENYA

Bennett, George. *Kenya: A Political History: The Colonial Period*. New York: Oxford University Press, 1963.

Dilley, Marjorie. *British Policy in Kenya Colony*. New York: Thomas Nelson and Sons, 1937.

Eliot, Sir Charles. *The British East African Protectorate*. London, Eng.: E. Arnold, 1905.

Kenyatta, Jomo. *Facing Mount Kenya*. London, Eng.: Secker and Warburg, 1938.

Leys, Norman. *Kenya*. London, Eng.: L. and V. Woolf, 1924.

Perham, Margery, and Elspeth Huxley. *Race and Politics in Kenya*. London, Eng.: Faber and Faber, 1956.

NON—AFRICAN SETTLEMENT

UGANDA

KENYA

Kitale (32)

Jinja (47)
Eldoret (34)
Kampala
(46)
Entebbe
(11)
Kisumu
(47)
Nakuru (27)

Lake

Victoria

Nairobi (46)

(61)
Lamu

Mwanza (21)

Moshi (31)

Arusha (45)

Mombasa
(50)

Lake

Tabora (16)

Tanga (28)

Ocean

TANZANIA

Dodoma (20)

Tanganyika

Morogoro (10)

Dar es Salaam
(27)

Iringa (16)

Indian

Lindi (13)

Percentage of urban population
which is non-African as of 1948
Nairobi (46)

Alienated Lands (in 1954)

LM

3

Racial Minorities in British East Africa

Elizabeth Hopkins

THE HISTORY OF RACE RELATIONS in the territories which constituted British East Africa provides a striking example of the way in which a colonial power can manipulate racial categories, whether consciously or implicitly, to sustain a colonial system of control.[1] Although the specific policy for each of the territories was to diverge in the degree to which the African was eventually to be accorded a position of political dominance, in all three the economic, political, and social institutions which supported the colonial authority structure exhibited a fundamental congruity of form. It is the articulation of these implicit mechanisms of control with the expressed policy toward minority relations which will be the concern of this chapter.

THE COMMON FRAMEWORK

Before examining the distinctive features of the minority situation in Kenya, Uganda, and Tanganyika, the elements which provided a common framework will briefly be reviewed.

Distributions of Population

Although there has been a general increase in population since British overrule was established in East Africa, the proportions of the major racial communities remained stable after World War I, reflecting both a comparable

---

[1] Although recent political developments would warrant the consideration of Zanzibar in the analysis, only the continental portion of British East Africa, that is, Kenya, Tanganyika, and Uganda, will be considered. Zanzibar differs too greatly in its history, its power structure under colonial administration, and in its racial and ethnic composition to permit inclusion in this article.

distribution of population in each of the three territories as well as certain significant variations. The most recent surveys place the population as shown in Table 3–1.

Table 3–1

	Tanganyika[a]	Kenya	Uganda
Indian/Pakistan	71,660	169,000	69,103
Goan	4,757	—	2,830
Arab	19,088	37,100	1,946
European	20,534	66,400	10,866
African	8,662,684	6,171,000	6,449,558
Colored[b]	2,257	964	1,334

[a] The figures given for Tanganyika and Uganda are from the 1957 and 1959 censuses respectively; those for Kenya, with the exception of the "Colored" category, are projected estimates for 1959 from the figures of the 1948 census. The figure given for the Colored population is from the 1948 census, since it is not represented separately in the projected figures.

[b] The category "Colored" includes all individuals of mixed blood; in each territory, however, persons of mixed Arab/African descent have been classified as Arab, "as the Arab race permits such children to be termed Arab."

Although territorial variations are evident, the basic ratio between the three major communities remained congruent, in each territory carrying connotations of class as well as racial affiliation, for the Asian community, as commercial middleman, assumed an intercalary position often assigned in other colonial areas to the half-caste.

Of the inter-territorial variations, the following were particularly relevant: the distribution of the Arab populations which reflected the traditional pattern of concentration on the coast; the higher proportion of both Asians and Europeans in Kenya relative to the total population, and, finally, the small size of the Uganda European community in relation to both the African and Indian populations. It is also critical to note the absence of any significant mixed population, for it meant that the half-caste never provided a serious alternative to the position assumed by the Asian.

INTRACOMMUNITY PATTERNS

Variations within each of the three major communities also proved revelant to the character of the race relations, for there was often a tendency in East Africa to identify individuals as members of racial subgroups rather than in terms of their major racial affiliation. Naturally these distinctions assumed their greatest importance in guiding intracommunity relations, but they could also be significant in interracial contacts. The literature is rife with facile statements on "the African" or "the Asian," but even the most impassioned European critic affirmed the uniqueness of certain tribes or carefully absolved the Goan or the Arab from his pronouncements on the Asian. The relevance of the subgrouping did, of course, vary. A Somali, Muganda, or Kikuyu normally found himself responded to as such, while a man from a smaller, less salient tribe in southern Tanganyika was defined with less specificity as an African. Similarly, an Englishman was perceived by Africans to be an Englishman, whereas a Norwegian or American remained more generically a *Mzungu* (European). In addition to ethnicity, other dimensions, such as religion or language were equally relevant cues in interracial contacts. A Hindu was not likely to be confused with an Ismaili, nor was an Italian whose linguistic skills went no further than a lilting Swahili to be perceived as English.

Within the European community, the values of the English middle class determined the ranking of members of the East African society. Language and nationality both served as barriers restricting interaction between the British—whether official or settler—and other Europeans, whereas, distinctions of class, occupation, and education provided the important criteria for establishing status within the British community. It was these factors and, more indirectly, their implications of intent that served to differentiate socially the administrator and the settler within the British community.

Major cleavages also existed within the Asian community. Although perceived as basically religious, they were ultimately ethnic and, in certain cases, racial in character. After 1947, with the partition of India, they acquired political implications as well. To accommodate these tensions, the Indo-Pakistani community was referred to both officially and informally as the "Asian" community, and, since 1950, the Pakistani segment has been tabulated separately in the East African census. The term "Asian" normally connoted the Indian population, although it did encompass the Arab in certain contexts as well. Here, however, no serious identification was intended, for the Arab is perceived by all racial communities to be distinctive in culture, language, and attitude and had, moreover, a distinctive tradition of political and commercial dominance in the coastal areas. The high degree of racial intermixture of the Arab population also served to distinguish them from the Indian, for the latter tended to remain aloof from the African, outside their commercial contacts. It was to prove politically expedient to consolidate these communities on legislative constitutional issues, however, for they shared common commercial interests and had some social coherence as recognized non-Christian, non-European British subjects, although the final distinction was somewhat undercut by the Arabs' status as "protected" subjects and by their primary political identification with the sultan of Zanzibar.

The Goan community also presented certain taxonomic problems, for although originally from India, they came from an area which was under

Portuguese, not British, control. In addition, in East Africa they have retained their Portuguese citizenship. To compound further their ambiguity of status, they were Catholic and normally of mixed Portuguese-Indian ancestry with singularly un-Asiatic surnames such as Dias, Fernandez and Sequiera. Marginal to the Indian community, they were the object of ambivalence for the European as well, for it was difficult to establish a behavioral correlate for such overlapping claims to both a European and Indian identity.

Within the African community, one critical ethnic division must be noted: that of Bantu/non-Bantu (Northerner). Although the latter encompassed several supra-tribal linguistic divisions such as Nilotic and Nilo-Hamitic, it was the "non-Bantuness" of these people that tended to be more significant than actual tribal or linguistic identifications. The distinction had ramifications on several levels, for it implied not only separate ethnic and linguistic traditions, but differences of race as well. For many tribes, particularly those which were not Bantu, the attitudes elicited by this distinction had all the accoutrements of racial bias: ridicule of physical features, fear of miscegenation, and the assumption of inferior intelligence and culture. Although the Bantu tribes predominate numerically in all three territories, in Kenya and Uganda where the Nilotic and Nilo-Hamitic tribes are less fragmented and of greater gross numerical importance, the attendant tensions were considerable. It must be remembered, however, that the salience of this distinction was largely relevant in inter-African relations. For the non-African, in contrast, levels of identification tended to be racial or tribal rather than in terms of these intermediate groups.

THE ASIAN COMMUNITY

Although the major subgroupings of the Asian community have already been discussed, the distribution in each territory may be briefly indicated by reviewing the census data for religion, occupation, and national status. Within the Asian community, the religious divisions were most recently tallied as shown in Table 3–2.

Table 3–2

	Tanganyika[a]	Kenya	Uganda
Hindu	29,035	45,238	47,469
Moslem	30,082	27,583	12,076
Arab	11,074	24,174	1,475
Sikh	4,232	10,621	3,047

[a] The statistics used in this and the following section on the European are derived from the 1948 census in Kenya, the 1957 census in Tanganyika, and the 1959 census in Uganda.

As there was little identification between Indian Moslems and the Arabs by virtue of ethnic, linguistic, and sectarian interests, the total number of Moslems had little relevance. What is critical is the varying ratio between the Hindu and Moslem communities of the Indo-Pakistani population, for these tended to be the politically active elements in the Asian community.

A second attribute which had political relevance was the percentage of the Asian population that held British citizenship, either by birth or naturalization, or as a protected subject. (See Table 3–3.)

Table 3–3

	Indian/Pakistan	Goan	Arab
Uganda			
British subject	48,037/4,457	672	602
British protected	15,009/1,506	778	1,238
alien	17/9	1,379	103
Kenya			
British subject	69,739	2,471	7,081
British protected	20,605	237	15,168
alien	67	4,400	1,883
naturalized	—	50	6
Tanganyika			
British subject	45,236/4,007	1,087	3,469
British protected	19,957/2,285	379	12,961
alien	151/2	3,291	2,654

It is important to note at this point that in each territory, the majority of the Indian-Pakistani community were British subjects with full status, not protected subjects; whereas, the Arab community was primarily one of protected subjects. In contrast, the majority of Goans retained their alien status as Portuguese.

One final comparison within the Asian community should be made: that of occupational distribution. For the Indian-Pakistani community the four leading sectors of employment are shown in Table 3–4.

Table 3–4

	Tanganyika	Uganda	Kenya
1.	trade	trade	trade
2.	manufacturing	manufacturing	manufacturing
3.	public service	agriculture	public service
4.	transport	public service	construction

In all three territories, wholesale and retail trade and various manufacturing occupations formed the major occupational commitments of the community.

For the Arab, the distribution is again similar in each territory (see Table 3–5).

Table 3–5

	Tanganyika	Uganda	Kenya
1.	trade	trade	trade
2.	agriculture	miscellaneous services	agriculture
3.	transport	manufacturing	manufacturing
4.	manufacturing	agriculture	transport

Here, however, the occupational bias toward trade was overwhelming, for the discrepancy between the first and second occupational preferences involves numerical drops from 4,287 to 295 in Tanganyika, from 544 to 57 in Uganda, and from 3,099 to 826 in Kenya. The Goan profile is shown in Table 3–6.

Table 3–6

	Tanganyika	Uganda	Kenya
1.	public service	public service	public service
2.	trade	trade	manufacturing
3.	transport	manufacturing	trade
4.	manufacturing	miscellaneous services	transport

Both the inter-territorial congruity and the prominence of public-service occupations are to be noted, the latter being a striking variant from the occupational pattern of the other Asian communities.

THE EUROPEAN COMMUNITY

Two features of the European community are relevant to our analysis: the proportion of British citizens to aliens and the occupational distribution of the community as a whole. To consider the first, the inter-territorial variations are shown in Table 3–7.

Table 3–7

	Tanganyika	Kenya	Uganda
British	14,177	26,347	9,213
aliens	6,170	2,391	1,563

The variations, it will be seen later, have been critical politically, for whereas the ratio in Tanganyika was no more than 2:1 in favor of the British, the proportion of alien Europeans in Uganda and Kenya was inconsequential. The occupational pattern again furnishes an index both of inter-territorial continuities and of politically relevant variations (see Table 3–8).

Table 3–8

	Tanganyika	Kenya	Uganda
1.	public service	public service	public service
2.	agriculture	agriculture	trade
3.	mining	trade	manufacturing
4.	trade/transport	manufacturing	construction

Here, the most striking inter-territorial features are (1) the importance of mining in Tanganyika, (2) the position of agriculture in Tanganyika and Kenya, and (3) the overwhelming preponderance of European employment in the civil service in each territory. The relative numbers involved in agriculture and government service are also important for this was a key area of intracommunity tensions. The ratios are, in fact, in many respects predictive (see Table 3–9).

Table 3–9

	Tanganyika	Kenya	Uganda
public service	2,140	4,764	1,677
agriculture	1,458	3,411	122

One final segment of the European community was of considerable importance in determining the character of race relations in each territory. Although numerically less significant than the public administrators or the Europeans engaged in agriculture or commerce, the missionaries, by virtue of their sustained contact with the African, had a position of far greater influence than their numbers would indicate. In terms of identification within the European community, it is also important to note the denominational correlates of national status, for the Protestant missionaries, particularly in Kenya and Uganda, were largely British, while the Catholics were recruited from various continental orders.

British Colonial Policy

A second major source of inter-territorial uniformity was the framework of a common colonial policy. Initially, British activity in East Africa was legitimized by a rationale which was altruistic in character: "England, the great chief of the commercial world, possesses a power that enforces a grave responsibility. She has the force to civilize."[2] The possible political or economic value of such operations was characteristically minimized or ignored by the British, for the ideological emphasis was on the patient tutelage of the "backward races." It was this mandate of moral and material progress that was to remain the major justification for British operations in East Africa. In the initial phase, however, there was no need to define the relationship between the African and the colonial power in terms of priorities, for the development of the commercial and indigenous sectors was regarded as complementary. It was only when the colonial situation not only encompassed the basic administrative relationship, but required the consideration of the demands of European settler and Indian populations as well, that British policy became explicit about the position and rights of the African.

Although the principle of paramountcy of African interests was to be a major policy commitment for the Colonial Office, in Kenya, the presence of large and permanent European and Asian communities inhibited the application of any simple or straightforward implementation of the economic and political advance of the African. In 1923, however, the relative claim to privilege of the non-African population was clarified in a White Paper which reviewed the status of the Asian in Kenya: "Primarily, Kenya is an African territory and His Majesty's Government thinks it necessary definitely to record their considered opinion that the interests of the African natives must be paramount, and that if, and when, those interests and the interest of the immigrant races should conflict, the former should prevail."[3] Distortions of the concept of African paramountcy to accommodate non-African interests in Kenya could already be found in 1925, however, in the Report of the East Africa Commission. There the policy of the trusteeship was construed as a tripartite responsibility, for it was extended to include commitments, not only to furthering the development of the "native inhabitants" and "humanity as a whole," but also to the "immigrant communities whose initiative, knowledge and material resources are necessary instruments in the fulfillment of the first two tasks."[4]

The White Paper of 1927 was to concede an even greater role to the European community, for although stressing that the Africans were not to be treated as instrumental to the needs of the immigrant population, the Paper emphasized that the European immigrant share as well in the exercise of the colonial mandate. This position was to be reversed two years later,

---

[2] Sir Samuel Baker, *The Albert Nyanza* (London: Macmillan & Company, 1867), Vol. I, xxii.

[3] Great Britain, Colonial Office, *Indians in Kenya,* Cmnd. 1922 (London: H.M.S.O., 1922), p. 10.

[4] Great Britain, Colonial Office, *Report of the Commission on Closer Union of the Dependencies in Eastern and Central Africa* (London: H.M.S.O., 1929), p. 36.

however, when the Hilton Young Commission Report of 1929 stressed the need to coordinate Kenya policy with the premises governing the political evolution of Tanganyika and Uganda.[5] Although conceding that "natives are at present incapable, not only of defending their interests effectively, but also of appreciating what those interests are," ultimately the African population must not only participate in the government, but participate "on equal terms."[6] Until such time, the control of Kenya was to remain in the hands of the colonial power. What was merely implied in 1929 was made explicit in the White Paper of 1930: ". . . the relation of His Majesty's Government to the native population of East Africa is one of trusteeship which cannot be devolved and from which they cannot be relieved. The ultimate responsibility for the exercise of this trusteeship must accordingly rest with them alone."[7] In Uganda and Tanganyika, where the European did not claim such preferential status, the premise of eventual self-government for the African population was an unambiguous commitment of colonial policy. In Tanganyika, this was to be a condition of the British mandate under the League of Nations, and, by 1920, land policy clearly defined Uganda as "an essentially African state."[8] Thus, in all three territories by 1930, the principle of African paramountcy and the subordinate status of the immigrant communities had been confirmed. The issue of the application of this common premise must be kept in mind as the political and economic history of each territory is reviewed.

The Colonial Officer

A second common feature of the inter-territorial colonial structure were the administrative officers, for these men exhibited both a similarity of background and a uniformity of attitude toward their professional self-image and toward the claims and needs of the nonofficial community. The segment of English society from which the colonial officer was recruited was strikingly homogeneous, for the administrator (as opposed to the technician) was selected almost exclusively from the upper and upper-middle classes and from those young men who had a public school if not a university education. Furthermore, those with university degrees were almost overwhelmingly from Oxford and Cambridge.[9] Although it was conceded that neither a public school nor a university education provided any specific preparation for the colonial service, they were felt to be essential for ". . . they have

---

[5] *Ibid.*, p. 86.

[6] *Ibid.*, pp. 84, 188.

[7] Marjorie Dilley, *British Policy in Kenya Colony* (New York: Thomas Nelson and Sons, 1937), p. 195.

[8] Sir Hesketh Bell, *Glimpses of a Governor's Life* (London: Sampson Low, Marston and Company, n.d.), pp. 121–122.

[9] W. M. Macmillan, *Africa Emergent* (London: Penguin, 1949), p. 194.

produced an English gentleman with an almost passionate conception of fair play, of protection of the weak, and of playing the game."[10] The emphasis in administration was to be on these virtues of the English gentleman, on a sympathy, a tolerance, and, above all, on a sense of justice.

Yet, however strong a professional sense of commitment to the welfare of the indigenous population, the actual relations of the colonial officer with the African remained carefully circumscribed. Whether on an isolated post, in a district center, or as a member of the central offices in the capital, both by inclination and by custom, informal social contacts outside of the European community were discouraged. British officers were expected to attend various official and semiofficial interracial events, but the norms of the administrative community were such as to deter the rare officer who might wish to associate privately with a local African or Asian. Although legitimized in terms of disparate interests, the practice of sharply restricting social activities to within the European community served to intensify racial sensitivity by reinforcing the differential status and social distance of the European segment.

As another dimension of this need to maintain a monolithic image of European solidarity, pressures for uniformity in dress and attitudes were strong among administrators as were pressures to participate in community activities such as the Saturday curry lunch, the weekend club dance, or sports tournaments.[11] Symbolic of this community solidarity throughout East Africa was "the Club." In the final years of the colonial period, it was to become more explicitly a symbol of racial exclusivity, but even when the European's status was not in jeopardy, it provided an important physical focus for community action. As one Englishman observed of Entebbe, the capital of Uganda, "by some happy chance all roads seem to lead to the Club."[12] One was expected to indulge in tea at four in one's home, then in "games" until dusk, to be followed by a drink at the Club before dinner. Tanner reports that until recent years junior officers could be formally censured for a failure to attend the Club or to participate with sufficient enthusiasm in the activities offered by the European community.

For the men assigned to outlying posts, there appeared to be no accepted alternative to isolation if there were no other Europeans in the area. Certainly there is no indication that companionship with Asian or African members of the staff was contemplated as a legitimate option. One officer reported that he did indulge in tennis with his Goan clerk, but his evenings were carefully spent in status-reinforcing isolation.[13]

---

[10] Sir F. D. Lugard, *The Dual Mandate in British Tropical Africa* (London: William Blackwood and Sons, Ltd., 1929), p. 132.

[11] Ralph Tanner, "Who Goes Home?" *Transition*, III, Nos. 8 and 9 (1963), 31, 34.

[12] Sir Frederick Treves, *Uganda for a Holiday* (London: John Murray, 1913), p. 206.

[13] R. O. Hennings, *African Morning* (London: Chatto and Windus, 1951), p. 66.

Whatever their fastidiousness about social distance, the welfare of the African community under their supervision was of the greatest concern to the British administrators. There can be no question of the sincerity of that commitment, nor of their frequent personal involvement with the tribe to which they were assigned. Yet, in spite of the warm, paternalistic relationship which often arose between the administrator and his people, he almost without exception operated with the same prejudices that distorted the perceptions of the nonofficial European. Frederick Lugard, however inspired and sympathetic his administrative innovations, or intimate and extensive his experience, could still assert: "we are dealing with the child races of the world."[14] The Bantu to him, temperamentally was a

> . . . happy, thriftless, excitable person, lacking in self-control, discipline, and foresight, naturally courageous, and naturally courteous and polite, full of personal vanity, with little sense of veracity . . . his thoughts are concentrated on the events and feelings of the moment, and he suffers little from apprehension for the future, or grief for the past . . . in brief, the virtues and defects of this race-type are those of attractive children.[15]

The attributes enumerated were to become part of the colonial stereotype of the African for, whether consciously or unconsciously, they provided a validation of the various features of the power structure.

Although this was the basic image of the African for the European community, differences in the response of the African to the colonial situation also led to the formation of certain tribal stereotypes. Given the British ideals for their own deportment, it is not surprising, however paradoxical, that they responded with genuine enthusiasm not to the docile peoples but to those pastoral tribes which regarded them with haughty indifference. Furthermore, these were tribes that had retained a strong commitment to their traditional way of life and, as such, offered no serious threat to the integrity of the pluralistic categories. That the Masai could serve as an object of romantic delight for their exotic appearance and indifference to European values only reinforced their identity as Africans.

While tribal distinctions were not seriously to challenge the basic social alignments of East African society, one division within the African community did have serious implications for interracial relations: that of the educated African. The colonial premise assumed a power relationship of fastidious isolation, of the suspension of European civilizing forces at some distance above the "child race." Certainly, to the early administrator, the principle of

---

[14] Lugard, *op. cit.*, p. 72.
[15] *Ibid.*, pp. 69–70.

segregation was patent, so obvious, in fact, that no explicit statement of policy or legislative restrictions was necessary.

With the emergence of a class of men who, through education, had acquired the same values and a command of the same body of knowledge, new tensions and hostilities arose, for now the position of the European and his monopoly on the esoteric knowledge of his society was at last challenged. Furthermore, the paternalistic values of the administrator were not such that they could be gracefully adjusted to accommodate the pressures of the educated African demanding recognition. The average British administrator's rationale for racial segregation was on grounds of common interest; but where in this scheme is there a place for the Cambridge-educated assistant district officer or medical officer who, although an African, ranks in status above most of the Europeans on the post? Within the administrative community, there was also a differential response to the educated African which reflected quite clearly the varying class origins of the colonial personnel. The ranking administrators were educated, "marketable." They were aware that they had serious professional options outside the colonial service and thus could approach the new African personnel, if not with enthusiasm, at least with *noblesse oblige*. In contrast, the zealots were those who would stand to lose most from the encroachment of the African into the central governmental structure. Untrained, accustomed to a standard of living and status far higher than his lower-middle-class origins or occupational skills would entitle him on his return to England, he perceived little recourse but to retrench and to demand an even more forceful expression of these values. In district after district, the European community refused to desegregate that symbol of British cohesiveness, the Club, and it was only in the year preceding independence, when the gesture was too late to be meaningful, that membership was opened to all races.

Officially, segregation by race was not a part of British colonial policy, yet such distinctions operated both residentially and in public facilities. In both cases, the legitimation was one of health and sanitation, for it was felt that only by isolating the European community could desirable standards be maintained. As a consequence, separate prison, school, and hospital facilities existed for each of the three communities in Tanganyika and Uganda, as well as in Kenya. In addition, government housing was allocated by race, and government and commercial buildings were careful to offer the European the option of separate locked lavatories. The government was also to sanction differential economic treatment of the three communities. Salary scales, both in the government and in commercial firms, were designed to vary with the race of the employee, with Africans, for example, receiving as little as one-fifth of the salary offered to a European for the position of sanitary inspector.[16] As there was no defense in law for such a system of wage differentials, ingenious systems of nomenclature and promotion channels arose to protect the

---

[16] Tom Mboya, *Freedom and After* (Boston: Little, Brown and Co., 1963), p. 22.

European. Marion W. Forrester cites, for example, the classification system of the railway where African stewards were paid less than Asian bartenders and Africans who examined tickets were designated "guards," while Asians and Europeans in the same job were known as "train conductors."[17] The government also sanctioned a system of public accommodations in transportation and in the theater which tended to factor out as ranked facilities for each of the communities. Here, however, there was not explicit legal or administrative support of segregation. Rather, the establishment of differential prices, reinforced by tacit conventions as to their significance, assured the European an inviolate isolation from the African or Indian.

PERCEPTIONS OF THE UNOFFICIAL EUROPEAN

In his relations with the European community, the British administrator had to deal with three major interest groups: the settler with agricultural interests, those engaged in the commercial or industrial sector, and the missionary. Of the three, the tensions were clearly least between the official and the commercial community, largely because the attitudes of these businessmen were moderate, and they were willing to accept the government's definition of their subsidiary position in East Africa. The settler, in contrast, whatever his periodic protestation of altruism, was not only dependent on the African for his labor supply, but interpreted any attempt to develop the indigenous sector of the economy as a direct threat to his interests. Given the commitment of the colonial administrator to the protection of African interests, it is understandable that tension would arise on issues such as cash crops, the regulation of the movement of native livestock, and the provision of adequate labor.

In addition, tension between settler and administrator in Kenya also polarized around the issue of competence. The settler felt infinitely more qualified, by virtue of his continuing residence, to assess the local situation and the needs of the African population and resented the fact that his experience and knowledge were often not utilized by the recently transferred officer. Settler hostility was also evoked in Kenya on the question of local commitment. The colonial officer was perceived, not as a man of serious aspirations with a healthy concern for his career, but rather as detached from the consequences of his decisions. It has been noted that ". . . however calamitous his errors of judgment, he would come safely to rest in the haven of pensioned ease. Not so the settler. He had to stay to reap the harvest sown by his departed rulers. He remained to pay the price of official blunders . . . and his children inherited the debt."[18] As a consequence of these tensions, there would appear to have been little social contact between the

---

[17] Marion W. Forrester, *Kenya Today* (The Hague: Mouton and Company, 1962), p. 131.

[18] Elspeth Huxley, *White Man's Country* (London: Chatto and Windus, 1935), p. 87.

two communities in Kenya. The development of two European clubs in Nairobi attested to the reluctance of the settler and, conversely, of the business and official communities to be in a situation of informal proximity to one another.

The relationship of the administrator to the missionary was also one of considerable tension, for the missionary felt that he was entitled to interfere actively in African affairs and to reinforce his professional interests through secular methods. Early friction was created by their insistence on proselytizing in politically unstable areas where the British could guarantee no protection and by their tendency, without authorization, to assume the role of government representative. Later, a recurring source of tension was the attempt of the major missions to manipulate the local power structure in their own interests. Also of concern to the administrator was the inflexibility with which the missionary denounced the traditional pattern of life as barbarous. Outraged particularly by such practices as polygyny, the levirate, and female circumcision in Kenya, the repressive actions of the missionary were to lead to profound social and political disruptions in some areas and more generally to the undermining of the authority of the older generation.

One final barrier to missionary-administrator relations, particularly with the more ascetic Protestant missionaries, might be designated temperamental. As Hesketh Bell, Governor of Uganda, noted, "most of us do the very things which the missionaries are always telling the natives not to do."[19] As the administrator was not averse to gambling, dancing, or other secular amusements, and certainly not averse to alcohol, there was a serious disparity between the demands of the missionary on his followers and the normative behavior of the colonial officer.

PERCEPTIONS OF THE ASIAN

The relationship of the official to the third community, the Asian, was again restricted by the structural need to maintain social distance. Though relations with men who worked in the British administration would be cordial during office hours, there was no informal contact after work. Contact with Asians involved in commerce was even more tenuous, for they were seen only in an official capacity or in a customer relationship. As a result, they tended to be perceived by the European, particularly for purposes of policy, as a homogeneous community, rather than as a series of competing subcommunities. The identity of the Asian as a single interest group served as well to reinforce the clarity of the East African class structure. By stressing their common identification as Asians and clearly differentiating them from the other subordinate group, the African, the British were able to manipulate more effectively minority group tensions and, by implication, to reinforce the

---

[19] Bell, *op. cit.*, p. 194.

dominance of the European's position. Unlike Great Britain where both groups are conventionally designated "Colored," the Asian and African in East Africa were made aware of their disparate status through differential treatment in the political and economic as well as in the social sphere. By virtue of their dominant commerical role, the Asians tacitly assumed the position of the "middle class" in the pluralistic hierarchy, although they failed outside the economic sector to serve as either a buffer or intermediary between the European and African as did the half-caste in other colonial contexts. In terms of their role in the maintenance of the system of ranked racial categories, however, the Asian community, at least implicitly, reinforced the subordinate position of the African by inhibiting his movement into the economic sector. The stability of the European position was also strengthened, for the Asian permitted the development of a ranked competitive structure, rather than a more monolithic ruler-ruled dichotomy. This was to prove particularly important in East Africa since at no time did the European form more than 1 per cent of the population.

The Asian

In addition to the colonial administrator, a second segment of the East African population can be regarded as basically uniform in each of the three territories. Numerically, occupationally, and in terms of national status and religion, the Asian community exhibited a striking consistency of profile. As constituted in East Africa today, the Asian population has three basic derivations: (1) descendants of the merchants who remained on the coast throughout the epoch of Arab rule; (2) the Hindus who opted to settle in East Africa after their term of service as indentured labor for the Uganda Railway; and (3) immigrants who, by virtue of contacts with resident Indians, have entered East Africa during the colonial period. Certain continuities may be seen in all these populations, for the majority, whether Moslem or Hindu, came from the Gujerati-speaking areas on the northwest coast of India.[20]

Throughout East Africa, the Indian tended to cluster in towns or, if in outlying areas, in the subdistrict trading centers. This pattern of settlement would seem to have been as much a matter of predilection as of law; for in Tanganyika, where no restrictive residential legislation existed, the same pattern emerged. In spite of their physical concentration in urban areas and their common political interest, the primary identification of the Indian was not with the inclusive Asian community, but rather to a specific ethnic or religious component. As Stephen Morris noted, "the Indian community as such was frequently a polite fiction."[21] Not only was there the basic

---

[20] Stephen Morris, "Indians in East Africa: A Study in Plural Society," *British Journal of Sociology*, VII (1956), 195.

[21] *Ibid.*, p. 197.

religious division between Moslem, Hindu, and Catholic, but caste or sectarian affiliation were often as important in defining social contacts or political interests. The proliferation of sectarian schools, the refusal of the Bohras to share mosques or cemeteries with other Moslems, and the elaborate devices to secure adequate representation for both Moslem and Hindu in the legislative assembly were all symptomatic of these intracommunity tensions. Relations outside the Asian community, insofar as they were differentiated, were largely the consequence of the degree of assimilation to British culture and values. Here, the basic cleavage was religious, for the Hindu communities tended to be more conservative, both culturally and in their continuing orientation toward India. In contrast, the Ismaili community made a conscious effort at the insistence of their leader, the Aga Khan, to assimilate. The late Aga Khan, perceiving that political and social disabilities in East Africa would be intensified if they retained a high degree of ethnic visibility, urged them to abandon their Indian customs and to adopt the culture and language of the colonial power. Their emphasis on education was one important factor in the implementation of this goal.

One final factor of relevance in defining the relations both within the Asian community and with the European and African was class. While little interracial interaction occurred on the middle- and lower-economic levels, the upper classes did have a certain degree of cross-cultural mobility. Indeed, status within the Asian community was often assessed in terms of access to interracial activities—with the ultimate goal, eligibility for functions at government house.[22] Considerable prestige was attached to being entertained by, or entertaining European officials, or by participation, if a woman, in various interracial women's associations. Until very recently, however, interracial contact remained for the Asian on this self-conscious, semiformal level.

KENYA

The Settler

"Every white man in Nairobi is a politician and most of them are leaders of parties."[23]

Tensions between the three racial communities in Kenya were expressed in an infinitely more baroque manner than in the other territories of East Africa, ranging as they did from the tragic brutalities of Mau Mau to settler protests which verged on a comic parody of race relations. Only one-tenth of the nonofficial European community could be defined in any social sense as

[22] *Ibid.*, p. 205.

[23] Winston S. Churchill, *My African Journey* (London: Hodder and Stoughton, 1908), p. 21.

settlers. Yet the history of Kenya was to be a history of the entrenchment of their privileged status and of the extension of their claims for further economic and political concessions. For this reason, their motives for settlement and self-image are critical to an understanding of developments in Kenya.

The actual composition of the Kenya settler community is somewhat controversial. Although they wished to perpetuate an image of a social elite, there was actually considerable variation both in terms of nationality and, if from Great Britain, of position in the class structure. The community was, however, basically homogeneous in terms of citizenship, for the majority of immigrants were from Great Britain or from other Commonwealth countries. The first settlers, the men who created the elite image, were from Great Britain. Although immigration implies mobility, the circumstances which motivated these men were such that the move could be done with considerably more *élan* than is normally found in immigrant populations. These were not the oppressed peasants or factory workers of Europe, but rather either younger sons of nobility whose opportunities in England or Ireland were constricted by the British institution of primogeniture, or the remnants of the British gentry who sought to continue a life in Kenya that was no longer possible in England. For these early settlers, men with independent incomes and an invulnerable position in British society, settlement was viewed as a high adventure which would hopefully be profitable, but, at the very least, would mean a life of excitement and liberation from the restraints of English society. Undeterred by lack of agricultural experience and happy to opt for a climatic explanation of their eccentricities, these settlers soon developed a cult of unconventionality which was to earn a reputation for Kenya throughout the Empire. Epitomized in Lord Delamere, who early affected shoulder-length hair and a Buffalo Bill costume, the Happy Valley crowd at Gilgil became renowned for reading Horace "lying under a tree with an iced champagne bottle handy," or for shooting "various members of its own set when sexual adventures became too complicated."[24]

With the acceleration of immigration in the period before World War I, however, the "distinctly *outré*" tone of the settler community was to change. Although backing or capital remained essential, these later immigrants were not men of wealth or even of independent income, but rather retired military officers or men from the middle or upper-middle class. Even more financially marginal were the veterans who were encouraged to settle in Kenya after World War I, but the elite image had been set by then. In consequence, there arose what W. R. Crocker has called the "fake gentry": "There are too many marks of the fake gentry; too much of the White Sahib who is white enough but not so Sahib."[25]

---

[24] Negley Farson, *Last Chance in Africa* (New York: Harcourt and Brace, 1950), p. 66.

[25] W. R. Crocker, *Self-Government for the Colonies* (London: Allen and Unwin, 1949), p. 77.

For immigrants who came from cultures which were not English in orientation, the pressure to assimilate was strong in Kenya. The high percentage of naturalized citizens was indicative of this, as was the proliferation of memoirs in English by French or Central European immigrants, whose very act of writing was, in part, an attempt to legitimate their status within the settler community. It was only the South African Boers who remained isolated and indifferent to the pressures of the British community, but this autonomy was facilitated by their decision to settle in enclaves such as Thomson's Falls or beyond the main highland area on the Uasin Gishu plateau.

In the subsequent discussion, it is therefore important to remember that the "settler," politically defined, constituted, for the most part, one specific segment of the resident European community: the British farmer. Although they presumed to represent all Europeans, regardless of occupation or nationality, their political emphasis, focusing as it did on issues such as land and labor, clearly reflected a specialized set of economic concerns.

PERCEPTIONS OF THE AFRICAN

In spite of contemporary biological and anthropological evidence, the settler was to retain the racial stereotype of the early colonial period, for the perception of the African as an irresponsible, semisocialized child race best served to validate his interests. J. F. Lipscomb could assert, as late as 1955, that African races are "all alike in being entirely devoid of any constructive ability" and that they have made "no moral, social or material advance from generation to generation," for in so doing he found legitimation for his right as a European to direct the development of political and economic events in Kenya.[26] Although there was a clear psychological and political need to perceive the African as inherently inferior, the way in which this racial premise manifested itself in European-African relations varied with both the nature and intensity of contact. The large plantation manager, the miner, the housewife, the storekeeper or businessman, the missionary, and the farmer all had different perceptions of the African, although all approached the relationship with basically the same assumptions of African potentiality and from a position of dominance in a power relationship.

Attitudinal variations within the nonofficial community were primarily based on occupation. Though both the commercial and agricultural sectors tended to view the African population as a labor pool existing largely for their convenience, it was only among the Highland settlers that racial tensions ran high. In contrast, the commercial class was far more moderate in its relations with both the African and Asian communities. This is not to imply that racial distinctions were not operative or that outside the commercial context there was not a strict segregation of the activities of each

---

[26] J. F. Lipscomb, *White Africans* (London: Faber and Faber, 1955), p. 17.

community, but merely that the tone of interracial relations, where contact was required, was muted and was characterized by a sense of *noblesse oblige* rather than by a strident reassertion of the authority structure.

For the settler, in contrast, there was a greater concern with the use of traditional stereotypes to validate the privileged status of the European. However, the stereotype was to undergo certain modifications: the capricious, undisciplined child became the clever child, mischievous and fully capable of holding his own against the European. "Although often they appear stupid, one is surprised how cunning and clever they are; when it comes to getting the better of their masters it is impossible to be up to all their tricks."[27] It was the household servant, by virtue of the greater intimacy of contact, who provided the model for this revised stereotype, yet many of the defining features of the stereotype were generated primarily by European expectations rather than by any inherent predilection or defect in the servants themselves. The European, for example, tended to be highly sensitive to any signs of incompetence, but as Macmillan notes, "It does seem as if an unnaturally high standard is set for African servants, sometimes by housewives who have never experienced service from their own kind."[28] In a similar manner, the housewife despaired of the proclivity of the African servant to steal, yet the atmosphere of the European home was hardly conducive to honesty for all the stores were placed behind locks and even the refrigerators distributed in East Africa were provided with the amenity of a lock and key.

In other respects, the attitude of the European to his house servant and farm laborer was also ambivalent, for the normative expectation was that of a paternalistic relationship in which loyalty and faithful devotion were rewarded by various attentions by the Bwana Mkubwa, notably of a medical or judicial nature. Evelyn Waugh noted the universality of this paternalism among the settlers in the early 1930's, observing that it "compared strikingly with the attitude of most European capitalists towards factory hands."[29] The zeal for the well-being of depressed employees exhibited a comparable lack of altruism in Kenya. A few daubs of iodine may have assuaged any misgivings the settler had about the legitimacy of his role in Africa, but certainly his fervor for the welfare of his particular charges stopped well short of increased wages, better housing, or adequate diet.

The stereotype of the African was also to prove useful in legitimating any discrepancies between the norms of the affectionate overseer and his actual behavior, for his actions could be defended as necessary measures to counter various deficiencies in the African character. Kindness or leniency, it was

---

27 Ethel Younghusband, *Glimpses of East Africa and Zanzibar* (London: John Long, Ltd., 1910), p. 31.

28 Mona Macmillan, *Introducing East Africa* (London: Faber and Faber, 1952), p. 94.

29 Evelyn Waugh, *They Were Still Dancing* (New York: Farrar and Rinehart, 1932), p. 245.

felt, would be construed by the African as weakness and would only lead to insubordination. Another versatile defense was the assumption that gratitude was beyond the comprehension of the African. Efforts in any way to make the conditions of the workers more pleasant could therefore be discountenanced, for improvements would not be perceived, let alone appreciated. Alternatively, proponents of authoritarian methods which ranged from vigorous to harsh could also legitimate them with the common defense that this was the "only language the African understands."

However useful these attitudes of the paternalistic colonial may have been in dealing with the tradition-oriented African, such patterns of behavior were to prove singularly inappropriate as a method of approaching the educated African. As D. H. Rawcliffe noted, "His habit of easy, superior, kindly patronage mixed with firmness cuts little ice with the educated African and he knows it."[30] The colonial perceived that, with a shift from dependency through education, the basic character of the relationship would be lost and his position threatened. Moreover, it meant as well that the cultural correlates which had previously supported the system of racial classification would be neutralized, undermining the legitimacy of the European's position in the structure and creating a situation in which race became the sole claim to preferential status. In consequence, the attributes of the African were once again reassessed. The traditional African was found not to be half-animal or a naughty child, but "an excellent fellow, as indeed the Negro unspoiled by civilization almost invariably is."[31] It was the urban African, both educated and uneducated, who became "degraded," while the tribesman was elevated to a state of ennobled savagery. Whereas, formerly, the social chasm was never in doubt, the issue became one of "keeping the black man in his place." In individual relations, as Julian Huxley observed, this primarily consisted of "snubbing educated natives on principle," if interaction was unavoidable, by addressing the African, although fluent in English, in Swahili.[32]

As in the other territories of East Africa, discrimination had its institutional aspects as well, but the defense of European solidarity and status against the encroachments of the educated African was felt with particular intensity in Kenya. As early as 1926, Delamere called for restrictions to ensure that the European community maintain a separate and superior status: "The civilized race has to protect its weaker members from lowering the standard if it is to raise the standard of anyone else."[33] Concern for the lower margins of the European community, always an issue where the power structure is contingent on a numerically small ruling caste, was to manifest itself in several

[30] D. H. Rawcliffe, *The Struggle for Kenya* (London: Victor Gollancz, 1954), p. 134.

[31] Ronald E. Wraith, *East African Citizen* (London: Oxford University Press, 1959), p. 99.

[32] Julian Huxley, *Africa View* (London: Chatto and Windus, 1931), p. 441.

[33] Archibald Church, *East Africa: A New Dominion* (London: H. F. and G. Witheby, 1927), p. 200.

ways: in the refusal to open immigration to skilled European labor; in the ideology of elite origins; and in the pressures exerted for legislative protections in land, labor, and political representation. The insistence on universal education of European children, particularly when complemented by inadequate African educational policies, was also, at least implicitly, an important mechanism for the maintenance of elite status. The principle of exclusivity was also used to legitimate restricted access to public facilities. Clearly sensitive to their numerical deficiencies vis-à-vis the other communities, many Europeans felt that racial restrictions were required to ensure the continuing availability of hotels and bars. As Rawcliffe observed, "They appear to envisage hordes of Africans of all classes rushing into all the hotels the moment the colour bar is lifted."[34]

Legitimation of the system of segregation was also sought by defining the issue as cultural rather than racial in character. "Some African and Asian social habits are repugnant to the European. I do not imply that these habits are wrong, only different. . . . If the European prefers to eat or view a movie without the proximity of a smelly, unclean native who may scratch himself and spit on the floor that is his privilege."[35] This poignant defense fails, however, to concern itself with the place of the educated African who had little tendency to indulge in these abhorrent activities. Even those who were willing to concede that a few Africans "have advanced to our standards" remained impassioned supporters of the system for it was felt that it would prove impossible to distinguish between the "truly civilized Africans and the many who merely ape our standards."[36]

It was not until 1960 when the London Constitutional Conference made the political course of Kenya clear that the color bar, out of political expediency if not personal inclination, was abandoned. In the Highlands, however, certain hotels resisted. When attention was called to their anachronistic policies, they sought refuge in a legal definition as clubs. When the central government made it obvious that such subterfuges were not to be tolerated, the response of the European was to retreat into the inviolate privacy of his home. By 1962, the famous settler hotels of the 1920's and 1930's, such as the Stag's Head at Nakuru, were notably devoid of all but the transient guest.

PERCEPTIONS OF THE ASIAN

The incessant pressure of the Kenya settlers to maintain a privileged position against the African was complemented by similar demands to receive differential treatment in respect to other immigrant communities. Although restrictions were envisioned as applicable to all non-European aliens, the

---

[34] Rawcliffe, op. cit., p. 179.

[35] William W. Baldwin, Mau Mau Man-Hunt (New York: E. P. Dutton and Company, 1957), p. 246.

[36] Lipscomb, op. cit., p. 118.

issue focused on the Indo-Pakistani population, for it was this segment of the Asian community that was economically of consequence and politically anxious to secure their position.

The settler encountered greater difficulties in his attempts to establish the Indian in an inferior rank, for claims of cultural and mental superiority which could so easily be advanced to constrict the privileges of the African were patently inappropriate here. The Indian heritage was not only one of unquestionable cultural sophistication, but one which had chronological priority to the development of the peoples of Europe. The tension was exacerbated by the Indian perception of the European. Here there was no trauma of contact with a technologically superior people or the concomitant response of docility, reverence, or fear, but rather a community which commanded considerable wealth and economic power and had, moreover, an independent claim to British status. The validation of the settler position, therefore, had to be expressed on a different dimension than the claims against the African. The issues that the settler turned to were moral degeneracy and economic exploitation. In both, the emphasis was placed not on restrictions vis-à-vis the European community, but in an unnecessarily solicitous manner, on the various detrimental effects of the Indian on the African. In considerable part, the successful projection of this image depended on a distorted identification of the current Asian community with the earlier coolie population, the "riff-raff" of a nation, rather than with the commercial class which had been established for centuries on the coast. Denunciation of the Indian on moral grounds focused on his commitment to the obvious depravities of the "oriental civilization." Considerable alarm, for example, was evoked by the possibility of common school facilities, for it suggested the "undesirable consequences of English children sitting beside Indian children who are in all probability married and initiated into the mysteries of sex."[37] In addition, the Indian was represented as a physical danger, for the English perceived his personal habits to be the source of numerous diseases and demanded residential segregation on these grounds.

The economic arguments of the settler focused on defining the role of the Indian in the East African economy as grossly parasitic and exploitative. Thus, any Asian profits were inevitably "sent straight to Bombay";[38] whereas, the British were represented as carefully reinvesting any profit "for the benefit of the population both black and white."[39] Such a dichotomy was not only simplistic but highly unfair, for a considerable amount of speculation and transfer of funds also characterized the European operations and most certainly was exaggerated as a feature of Indian commercial life. Even more threatening was the prominent position of the Asian in the commercial

[37] Dilley, op. cit., p. 156.

[38] Lady Evelyn Cobbold, Kenya: The Land of Illusion (London: John Murray, 1935), p. 73.

[39] Lord Cranworth, Profit and Sport in British East Africa (London: Macmillan & Company, 1919), p. 81.

sphere and the implicit threat of his monolithic concern with his work. For the Englishman who ritualistically concluded business at four to permit a round of tea and games and a drink at the club, the Indian work pattern would be cause for alarm. In addition, the Indian was willing to operate on a far more marginal level of profit and could depend for support in emergencies on a wide proliferation of family ties.

The European-Indian tensions in Kenya were to focus on five issues: (1) urban residential segregation, (2) property restrictions outside urban areas, (3) immigration regulations, (4) political representation, and (5) restricted access to public facilities. Of these, only the last was never to be defined as a political issue—a consequence, it would seem, of the Asian's acute sensitivity to the more informal areas of discrimination. European privilege was to be challenged on the first four points, however, provoking, in the mid-twenties, a sequence of events which, as an expression of minority group tensions, exceeded all other interracial conflicts in intensity during the colonial period except Mau Mau. The issue which was to precipitate the crisis was that of elective representation. In 1916, the claim of the European to representation had been acknowledged; yet, when the first elections were held in 1920, no attempt was made to extend similar privileges to the Asian community. Asian protest at the inequity of a system which permitted the European community eleven elected members, while conceding to them only one nominated representative, resulted six months later in the "wholly inadequate" offer that two Indians be elected on a special franchise.[40]

Under pressure from the Indian Office, in September 1923, the Colonial Office presented the Wood-Winterton proposals. The report, in an attempt to reconcile the conflicting claims of the two communities, recommended a common electoral roll, qualified only by educational and property tests which—it was calculated—would enfranchise no more than 10 per cent of the Asian population. Settler interests were reflected in the decision to retain the Highlands policy of exclusion of non-Europeans, while the suggested elimination of restrictions on urban accommodations and immigration were concessions to the Indian community. In effect, this meant that the Indian claims had been honored on three of the four points.

The settlers were outraged by the decision, for, throughout the preceding two decades, government statements of policy had unambiguously affirmed a position of economic and political primacy for their community. In an effort to force a repudiation of the Wood-Winterton proposals, the attempts of the Asian to secure equal rights were challenged as one phase of a sinister plot by India to gain political control in Kenya. Charges of imperial expansion against India were reinforced by settler appeals to Great Britain for protection against the "tentacles of this evil menace."[41] "Some panic-

---

[40] Kenneth Ingham, *A History of East Africa* (New York: Frederick A. Praeger, 1962), p. 271.

[41] George Delf, *Jomo Kenyatta* (London: Victor Gollancz, 1961), p. 66.

stricken women sent a cable to Queen Mary saying 'We, the women of Kenya, humbly implore your assistance to protect us and our children from the terrible Asiatic menace which threatens to overwhelm us,' " while on other occasions allusions were made to the ominous consequences for the "flower of Christian faith."[42] The settlers were not, however, to confine their activities to impassioned petitions to the British Crown, for it was felt that should any attempt be made actually to implement the proposals, it must be met with active resistance. Elaborate plans were devised to seize the transportation and communication systems, including a census of all available rifles, cars and horses, and ammunition and petrol supplies. As the culminating gesture, the governor was to be abducted and detained on an isolated farm which the settlers had courteously selected for its excellent fishing facilities. Perhaps the most striking feature about the proposed insurrection was the fact that no attempt was made to conceal either the intent to revolt or the nature of the plan. As Sir Philip Mitchell, a subsequent governor, noted: "Angry settlers in odd costumes, reminiscent of Buffalo Bill and his circus, plotted against the Government, in club and hotel bars mostly and at the tops of their voices."[43]

The publicity given to the rebellion would indicate that it was valued as much as a threat, perhaps more, than it was as a serious alternative to civil obedience. Certainly it was to function efficiently on that level, for the Colonial Office judiciously decided not to offer the settlers the option of revolt. In 1923, the recommendations of the Wood-Winterton Agreement were reversed. With the exception of a decision to abolish urban segregation, the other issues were resolved in favor of the settler community: the Highlands were to continue to be reserved for the European; the Asian was to have elective representation, but within a communal franchise; and "some further control over immigration in the interests of the African" was regarded as necessary.[44]

Although the Indian community continued throughout the remainder of the decade to reject elective representation on these terms with their decision to submit to a communal role in 1931, the Asians acknowledged the reality of their minority position in Kenya. No further attempts were to be made during the colonial period to claim a status equal to either the European or African.

The African: Initial Patterns of Political Activity

Although a more systematic review of the African political movements in Kenya will be found in Chapter 5, the issues and the course of the develop-

---

[42] *Ibid.*

[43] Sir Philip Mitchell, "Mau Mau," in C. Grove Haines (ed.), *Africa Today* (Baltimore: Johns Hopkins Press, 1955), p. 100.

[44] Lawrence W. Hollingsworth, *The Asians of East Africa* (London: Macmillan & Company, 1960), p. 99.

ment were, in large part, a response to interracial tensions. It is these aspects of the more general political problem that will be considered here.

From its inception with the formation of the Kikuyu Association in 1920, organized African opinion was to be fundamentally a response to European settler pressures. The grievances of the Association encompassed such issues as land, conditions of employment, and the demands of the settler for a stable labor force. Again, in the following year, it was the settler demand for reduced African wages which provoked the organization of the schismatic Young Kikuyu Association under Harry Thuku. These early attempts to consolidate African discontent within an organizational structure were regarded with considerable suspicion by the Kenya administration. The efforts of Harry Thuku, for example, to institute certain labor and taxation reforms were promptly defined by the government as "seditious" and designed solely to "stimulate enmity between black and white," and led to his deportation as a danger to public security in 1922.[45]

When the Young Kikuyu Association quietly re-emerged as the Kikuyu Central Association, the response of the chief native commissioner was to dismiss the leaders as "an indeterminate collection of malcontents with no constitution, no representative authority and no constructive programme of reform."[46] No attempt was made to consider seriously the legitimacy of their grievances, to treat them as representative of African interests, or, more fundamentally, to exhibit any concern with the African climate of opinion. The position of these early colonial officials set a pattern for subsequent official-African relations in Kenya, one in which the response of the administrator to the political leaders was to range from indifference to denunciation as self-seeking malcontents. Furthermore, the disparity between the government response to settler and African demands and grievances could only serve to increase the bitterness of the African, particularly when confronted with periodic reaffirmations of the Colonial Office of the primacy of his interests. Certainly the most dramatic example of this bias was the arrest and detention without trial of Thuku for organizing African opinion against forced labor, oppressive taxes, and low wages, while the well-publicized patently seditious activities of the settler vigilance committee were condoned.

LABOR

If political representation was the major focus for English-Asian tensions in Kenya, it was unquestionably in the economic sectors of land and labor that African-English hostilities were to polarize. It was here also that the power of the European settler as a pressure group was most clearly revealed, for government policy before World War II was strongly biased

---

[45] Raymond L. Buell, *The Native Problem in Africa* (New York: The Macmillan Company, 1928), Vol. I. 375.

[46] Ingham, *op. cit.,* p. 282.

toward the protection and extension of their interests. From the earliest period of settlement, in spite of the supremely equitable climate, the economy was defined as the plantation pattern. The immigrants were not colonists in the sense of the men who pioneered the opening of the United States or Canada with the labor of their own families, but men who came with the expectation that the basic labor requirements would be met by the indigenous African population. Labor emerged as a political issue as early as 1905 when assertions were made that it was "grossly unfair" to invite the Europeans to immigrate and then fail to supply them with labor.[47] Rather than consider possible inducements to attract labor, the settler position demanded the restriction of land available for native settlement so that the excess of population would be forced to seek European employment. By 1908, it was felt that a solution might be found in the institution of a poll tax, for this would force the African to seek a cash income and, in so doing, to leave the reserves. Within the next decade, the settler was to legitimate his needs with moralistic claims that no government should have to support communities "which were useless parasites doing nothing and paying little for protection."[48]

These sustained pressures for a stable labor supply were to have tangible results, for, in 1917, the settler demands were incorporated as an important aspect of the mandate for African development. Governor Belfield affirmed at that time: "I am prepared to state definitely that we desire to make of the native a useful citizen and that we consider the best means of doing so is to induce him to work for a period of his life for the European."[49] Moreover, should the native fail to respond voluntarily to the government definition of "useful citizen," "humane and properly regulated pressures" were to be exerted within the reserves.[50]

The legitimation used to justify such compulsion was characteristically altruistic: the European as an "unpaid teacher of civilization" provides a model toward which the African may strive. Moreover, as one governor was to note: "Nothing can be worse for the young native than to remain, according to his inclinations, in the reserve. Those that do are likely to become vicious and effete."[51] That such employment was also a validation of white settlement and European labor interests was an implication which both administrator and settler skillfully avoided.

During the 1920's, the labor issue shifted from a demand for a stable labor supply to the defense of substandard conditions of employment. It was asserted that an increase in wages would only aggravate the labor

---

[47] Dilley, *op. cit.*, p. 216.

[48] *Ibid.*, p. 222.

[49] Buell, *op. cit.*, p. 332.

[50] *Ibid.*

[51] Ingham, *op. cit.*, p. 344.

shortage, for the African would then amass his necessary tax money in a shorter time and return to the reserves sooner. Moreover, appallingly inadequate wages were reinforced by abuses in housing and diet. The settlers operated under the conviction that the "native does best on nothing but maize-meal," and any attempt to enforce a higher standard was bitterly opposed as an unnecessary indulgence.[52] As Archibald Church notes, "what is called pampering the native in Kenya is considered sound business in other parts of Africa."[53]

LAND

If the period prior to World War II was characterized by a consolidation of settler interests, certainly in no area was this more apparent than in the definition of African and European rights to land. The series of administrative decisions which led to the alienation of occupied land, the restriction of displaced Africans on tribal reserves, and the establishment of an exclusive European claim to the more attractive highland areas were clearly a betrayal of the British colonial mandate.

Although the events that marked the extension of settler control will not be dealt with in great detail here, it should be noted that they constituted the most serious abuse of the colonial ideology to occur during the British administration of East Africa. Under settler pressure and supported by a series of specious legitimations, the Kenya central government found it possible to institute a program of land alienation in which tribes were moved against their wishes, treaties rescinded, and reserve boundaries delineated to excise water supplies or contracted to provide additional land for European settlement. Although the British were later to protest that these abuses were inadvertent or the consequences of well-intentioned misconceptions, it cannot be doubted that the administrators were aware of the implications of their actions and of the disparity between the position of the Colonial Office and the local implementation of policy in Kenya. Sir Charles Eliot, in fact, as the first governor to encourage European settlement, was to defend his position as normative: "No doubt on platforms and in reports we declare we have no intention of depriving natives of their lands, but this has never prevented us from taking whatever land we want. . . ."[54]

In 1934, a serious attempt was made by the Kenya government through the Carter Land Commission to rectify some of the injustices of the early alienation policy. Recognizing that "a notable degree of mal-distribution exists," the Commission concluded that restitution of legitimate African claims would require the addition of 1,474 square miles or 3 per cent of the

[52] Julian Huxley, *op. cit.*, p. 159.

[53] Church, *op. cit.*, p. 184.

[54] Great Britain, Foreign Office, *Correspondence Relating to the Resignation of Sir Charles Eliot,* Cmnd. 2099 (London: H.M.S.O., 1904), p. 26.

total area of the existing reserves.[55] Although it is obvious that the Kenya government felt itself to be fully exonerated by this action, Lucy Mair and Margery Perham point to certain inequities in the investigation and assessment. Perham feels that the Commission "could not be accused of erring on the side of generosity" for they delineated the European Highlands "on the most generous scale while meticulously examining the legitimacy of each African claim and awarding land only if the evidence was incontrovertible."[56] Mair also calls attention to the basic bias of the Commission in that they chose to designate 53,000 square miles as African reserve and 16,700 square miles as White Highlands, an increase of 5 per cent and 60 per cent respectively over their previously recognized dimensions.[57] With the official delineation of the White Highlands in 1934, tensions over further alienation were alleviated considerably, for the settlers were denied any justification for challenging reserve boundaries and the Africans were, in turn, granted compensatory land against earlier claims. The resentment and suspicion were to remain, however, as a legacy of earlier abuses and were further compounded after World War II by an increasing disbalance in holdings, to become a key political issue for the African.

Minority Developments after World War II

"I have done my best and if all other people had done as I have done, Mau Mau would not be as it is now. You made it what it is, not Kenyatta."

Jomo Kenyatta.

Despite the official realignment toward the defense of African interests, during the 1930's, Kenya remained basically a white man's country. As the Asian community was by then politically passive, settler activity was to focus on a retrenchment of interests vis-à-vis the African. By the end of World War II, the returning African was faced with virtually the same economic and political situation and the same series of grievances that had provoked the earlier protests of the Kikuyu in the 1920's.

In regard to land, the European settler still retained exclusive control of the Highlands area, and the disparity between their numbers and the amount of potentially available land to which they had a monopoly of access had become an increasing source of tension. The conditions of tenure were also a major source of grievance: the African title to land was at the will of His Majesty, although European settlers were permitted to have clear title to the

---

[55] Great Britain, Colonial Office, *Report of the Kenya Land Commission* (London: H.M.S.O., 1934), p. 520.

[56] Elspeth Huxley and Margery Perham, *Race Relations in Kenya* (London: Faber and Faber, 1944), pp. 47–48.

[57] L. P. Mair, *Native Policies in Africa* (London: George Routledge and Sons, 1936), p. 88.

land as free hold or *de facto* title as leasehold on terms up to 999 years. By the late 1940's, the abuses of the system of alienation were patent: large areas were unoccupied, understocked, or badly farmed because of incompetence, absentee landlords, or the practice of land mining for quick cash returns.

In the area of education, little attempt had been made to alleviate the early settler bias in the educational system. For every shilling spent by the government in 1945 on an African child in school, 150 were allocated to each European child. If one were to compute on a per capita basis, the amount would be 500 times as great, for although education for the settler's child was compulsory, only a small percentage of the African population had access to schools.[58]

The inequities of political representation were also continued after World War II. In 1944, an African was appointed for the first time to the Legislative Council. Although this may have seemed a generous gesture from the point of view of the Kenya government, the African could hardly view it as any serious shift in the balance of power.

One final sector of political unrest involved discriminatory practices in employment, particularly salient issues being the wage scale and bias in the hiring of trained Africans. In 1939 and again in 1944, strikes in Mombasa revealed the deplorable labor and housing conditions in that area. Little improvement was to occur in the following decade, however, for, in 1955, the East African Royal Commission found that only 5 per cent of the African workers in urban areas had an income which could support a normal family.[59] Of far greater impact politically was the racial differential as it operated against the educated African. As L. S. B. Leakey noted,

Some of the most embittered leaders of anti-white propaganda are those who have university degrees and who never had any of their fees reduced on account of the colour of their skin, but who found, on returning to Kenya, that no matter what their qualifications, their colour and race precluded them from earning salaries even comparable to those of Europeans with lesser qualifications.[60]

Mboya reports, for example, that he was paid one-fifth of the salary that a European would receive as sanitary inspector.[61] It was discriminations such as these which led to the proud withdrawal of men such as Jomo Kenyatta and Mbiyu Koinange from conditions afforded the African within the employment structure.

---

[58] S. and K. Aaronovitch, *Crisis in Kenya* (London: Lawrence and Wishert, 1947), p. 139.

[59] Delf, *op. cit.*, p. 134.

[60] L. S. B. Leakey, *Mau Mau* (London: Methuen and Company, 1952), p. 115

[61] Mboya, *op. cit.*, p. 22.

The response of the administration to the alienation of the educated African during the 1940's was one of anger and denunciation. Seemingly unable to perceive that the African's bitterness and agitation for reform was a function of his rejection, officials tended to dismiss these men as vain, scheming megalomaniacs "with a pronounced dislike of honest work."[62] Furthermore, the denunciation of the alienated African was rapidly transmuted into a general condemnation of education for Africans, for such privileges were clearly unappreciated and only served to foster political malcontents.

Stimulated in the late 1940's by events in India and Ghana, the Kenya African Union (KAU) under Kenyatta pressed for political and economic reforms, particularly in respect to discriminatory practices restricting access to land and employment, and against oppressive labor conditions. The last had become increasingly an issue because the shortage of land in the Kikuyu Reserve was severe and forced greater numbers of young men into the urban and Highland labor markets.

Neither the settler nor the official was to regard the attempt of Kenyatta to mobilize African sentiment as an effort to correct political or social injustices. Rather, he was perceived to be acting only in self-interest, to be motivated solely by a "lust for personal power."[63] Professed concern for the welfare of the African was dismissed as no more than an expedient method for achieving a "profitable and very pleasant way of life"; whereas, attempts to proceed moderately and within constitutional limits were interpreted as a fear of deportation and the loss of the prerogatives of African leadership.[64] These perceptions were an important facet of the official ideology. They facilitated the rejection of the KAU leaders as fraudulent exploiters of African sentiments. It meant as well that KAU demands could be rejected as specious attempts at political agitation.

Continuing efforts were made by the leaders of KAU to proceed through constitutional channels, but by 1950 the organization had assumed overtly nationalistic aims: "the unification of the Africans of Kenya, freedom of speech, universal franchise and equal rights with Europeans."[65] Significantly, no mention was made of the land issue or of self-government. Rawcliffe feels that these were not included to avoid settler demands for the proscription of the society.[66] Even so, no attempt was made by the government to accommodate KAU on any of these issues.

In 1950, Kenyatta and Koinange attempted to reach some degree of rapport with the unofficial community by approaching several prominent

---

62 Sir Philip Mitchell, *African Afterthoughts* (London: Hutchinson, 1954), p. 255.

63 Mitchell, "Mau Mau," *op. cit.,* p. 488.

64 Farson, *op. cit.,* p. 114.

65 Rawcliffe, *op. cit.,* p. 43.

66 *Ibid.*

Europeans to form an interracial society, the Kenya Citizens Association, but this was to prove unsuccessful as well.[67] By the spring of the following year, no effort had yet been made to consider the legitimacy of African claims. If any one point may be cited at which the African leaders perceived a constitutional approach to be futile, it must be then, for from then until their arrest fifteen months later, their statements reveal not only their degree of alienation but a new militancy in which the use of force is advocated to achieve political domination.

Whatever Kenyatta's initial anticipation of his role in Kenya's society on his return from England in 1946, five years of frustration, indifference, and insult had turned his expectations to anger and bitterness. Here, again, the model of the early settler becomes relevant, for although the leaders of KAU could hardly expect the tolerance accorded the vigilance committees of the 1920's, they could appreciate the government's early sensitivity to threatened violence and its receptivity to reforms under such pressures. Faced with the same political and social inequalities that had characterized Kenya in the 1930's and with a government that was impassive in the face of repeated appeals for reform through constitutional channels, it is not surprising that the African, denied a legitimate expression of his need, would turn to more activist methods either to impress the government with the seriousness of the situation or as a withdrawal from a commitment to the system. In retrospect, the rejection by the Kenya government of the legitimacy of their demands and the stifling of all constitutional channels of political expression seems extraordinarily myopic. One can only assume that the British grossly misgauged both the degree of frustration and anger which their indifference would generate and the margin of tolerance of the Kikuyu to such apathy. As late as 1951, threats of action were dismissed by the administration as mere bravado, largely on the grounds of the "natural cowardice" of the Kikuyu.[68]

This basic misperception of the factors which were to lead to political unrest was reflected as well in the official explanation of the origins of Mau Mau. Again, we see an evasion of any direct responsibility for the movement. What is projected instead is the myth of the benign government, of an administration devoted to the welfare of the African suddenly confronted with an abuse of that trust. The possible validity of African grievances and the reality of their frustration as contributory factors are avoided in Official explanations because both would introduce the issue of administrative liability. Rather, Mau Mau was conveniently to become the product of the inherent fragility and barbarism of the African mind and its deterioration, when faced with the demands of "civilizing influences." "The failure of the Kikuyu to adjust themselves fully to the needs of this sudden change together

---

[67] *Ibid.*, p. 47.

[68] F. D. Corfield, *The Origins and Growth of Mau Mau*, Kenya Sessional Paper No. 5 of 1959/60.

with the planned exploitation of the attendant stresses and strains, were the primary causes and origin of Mau Mau."[69] One finds no acknowledgment in official documents that the European influence in itself may contain certain inherent deficiencies. Nor were any suggestions advanced to illuminate why the Kikuyu should wait some sixty years before reacting to the contact situation. One final area in which serious distortions occurred was in the European perception of the intent of the movement and of its organizational structure. Although Mau Mau was believed by both settler and official to be a general revolt dedicated to the expulsion or eradication of all Europeans, it was notably lacking in actions which could be construed to be specifically seditious in character. The terrorists had access to high explosives, yet none were used; nor were any attempts made to cut public telegraph or telephone lines. No efforts were made to derail the trains on the main line of the Uganda Railway, although the route traversed the Kikuyu Reserve; no roads were blocked; no bridges destroyed; and what is perhaps more striking, no attempt was made to interrupt or pollute the Nairobi water supply, which again was routed through the Reserve.[70] If Mau Mau had in any serious sense been a well-organized revolt rather than a protest, it is most unlikely that their activities would have been so strikingly free of sabotage.

The image of Mau Mau as a general uprising resulted in a serious distortion of the events that did occur. The impression created by the press and encouraged by both settler and official was one of the Highlands strewn with the eviscerated bodies of white settlers; yet the actual number of settlers killed by Mau Mau during the eight years of the Emergency was thirty-two. It is true that European livestock were killed or mutilated in the hundreds, and members of the Kikuyu tribe killed or mutilated in the thousands; but the official casualty figures do not evoke images of a Night of the Long Knives, let alone a series of organized if sporadic assaults on the European community. The figure thirty-two becomes even more impressive inasmuch as it is estimated by the Kenya government that fully 90 per cent of the adult Kikuyu, a tribe of over 1,000,000, had taken the oath. For an anti-colonial revolution, its methods were strikingly oblique.

The government response to early unrest, however, proceeded on the assumption that all violence was Mau Mau and that the activities of Mau Mau were undertaken under the direction of the KAU officials. This not only gave considerable license to the alienated and embittered veterans who had gravitated into a world of petty crime in Nairobi, but permitted the government, in its purge of Mau Mau, to sweep the upper strata of KAU with it. The men who were arrested on the second day of the Emergency in 1952 were not arrested because of any known involvement with Mau Mau,

---

[69] *Ibid.*

[70] Mitchell, *African Afterthoughts,* p. 264.

although this was the charge, but because they were ranking officers of KAU. The suppression of KAU was to have disastrous implications for the course Mau Mau was to take, for, by doing so, the government removed the more moderate leaders who could envision a *rapprochement* through negotiations. It is in this sense that Kenyatta's response to the Crown Council was to prove so prophetic: "You made it what it is, not Kenyatta." In addition, as Fenner Brockway notes, by detaining the very leaders who pressed for constitutional and administrative reforms as subversive, "the government encouraged many Africans to come to the conclusion that there was no alternative to Mau Mau."[71] Although the depravities associated with Mau Mau have been considerably exaggerated, the incidents that did occur had serious repercussions since they furnished the Security Forces with the legitimation for the use of considerable license in their treatment of Mau Mau suspects. For the first time in Kenya's history, the settler had a defense for his sadism against the African, for a man who had been through the abominations of the oath was regarded as no more than a depraved animal.

As a correlate, after the Emergency was declared in October 1952, the Security Forces operations became increasingly extralegal in character. As Baldwin, an American mercenary with the Security Forces suggests, "a number of concepts held dear in democratic societies (had to) be discarded."[72] Refinements such as judicial prosecution were soon abandoned: the Security Forces, impatient with the measured pace and uncertain results of court action, found it more efficient to execute Mau Mau suspects after interrogation, ostensibly while attempting to escape.[73] In addition, methods of interrogation were evolved which reflected considerable psychic and physical ingenuity. Certainly every European in the Security Forces knew about these tortures, and many had organized or participated in them.

Although it is probable that the government, in the sense of the professional administrator, was unaware initially of these abuses, it is clear that once the situation was called to the attention of the authorities, little effort was made to repress such practices. Only the most flagrant abuses were prosecuted, and then largely in response to protests from members of the British Parliament. The results of such prosecutions were not such to inspire confidence in the colonial judicial process. Prison sentences were imposed only for the most gross and well-publicized offenses. More commonly, charges were reduced to permit fines to be imposed. Two European officers, for example, who extorted incriminatory evidence under torture and then proceeded to beat the accused to death, were fined £50 and £100 for their patriotic excesses. In another case, a British officer who had the misfortune to attract the attention of the British press and Parliament was ac-

---

71 Fenner Brockway, *African Journeys* (London: Victor Gollancz, 1955), p. 130.

72 Baldwin, *op. cit.,* p. 178.

73 Rawcliffe, *op. cit.,* p. 108.

quitted of the charge of murder but sentenced by court martial to five years' imprisonment for disgraceful conduct. Of his several indiscretions, the most notable had been "ordering a soldier in his company to cut off the testicles" of a prisoner.[74]

Such disciplinary action was not likely to be initiated unless the incident had been given publicity outside of Kenya, for torture was regarded by both Security Forces and civilians alike as a legitimate technique of interrogation. The extent to which this attitude was to become overtly normative was reflected in the outraged response of the settler community on those rare occasions when prosecution was instituted, for considerable energy and publicity would be devoted by various patriots to the collection of a defense fund. The legitimacy of the particular charges was never at issue; rather, the situation was seized as an opportunity for the expression of community solidarity in the face of external criticism.

The abuses of the Security Forces were, in large measure, a consequence of its composition, for the men recruited came largely from the settler community. The Emergency operation was envisioned by these men as a big-game hunt, the Kikuyu as a particularly clever species. This ethos of the hunt was most flagrantly reflected in the incentive system set up in certain regiments where bounties were either established on a basis of five shillings per head or competitions were held between companies for the first kill of the day with the commanding officer supplying the requisite prize of £5.[75] To generate further competitive spirit, score boards of each company's record were kept in company messes.[76] The casualty statistics also reflect the ferocity with which the Security Forces applied themselves to their task. Between October 20, 1952, the beginning of the Emergency, and July 1953, 1,300 Africans were killed; 514 wounded; 2,673 captured; and 112,529 taken into custody. The disparity between the number killed and the number wounded indicates, as Montagu Slater observed, the ruthlessness of the operation.[77] The final figures are hardly more reassuring. Though Mau Mau was responsible for the loss of 2,356 African lives (1,832 civilians and 524 in the Security Forces) and the lives of 95 Europeans (32 civilians and 63 Security Forces), casualties among Mau Mau themselves are officially held to be 11,503, a figure four times as high as that of their victims. Furthermore, the figure pertains only to those Kikuyu killed by soldiers or police in active engagements and does not include those who were executed after trial or who died of maltreatment or torture in detention.

Although it was soon apparent that Mau Mau would not manifest itself in any operation that required the organizational coordination of a Night of

---

[74] Slater, *op. cit.,* p. 246.

[75] *Ibid.*

[76] Rawcliffe, *op. cit.,* p. 70.

[77] Slater, *op. cit.,* p. 245.

the Long Knives, the European civilian population in the Highland areas remained in constant fear of their personal safety. The fact that few murders had occurred, though statistically reassuring, made little difference to the individual, for the imminence of danger was perceived to be as real as if the movement had in fact been more widespread. The sporadic, unpredictable character of the attacks was certainly contributory to settler anxiety, which for many verged on the pathological. Women ventured into Nairobi with pistols strapped around their frocks, while Highland farmers barricaded themselves in their houses at night, admitting only trusted servants and then one at a time and at gun point.

One consequence of this inability to deal directly with the tensions of Mau Mau was the tendency to search for explanations for the disturbances outside of the local political and economic context. "Kenya's Europeans . . . blamed everyone and everything but themselves . . . the British Labour Party, Pandit Nehru, the United Nations and the Kremlin are the villains who have destroyed the 'utopian' peace of the colony."[78] Again, as with the administrator, there was no feeling that their actions may have been contributory factors. Perceiving themselves as innocent, they tended to define the disruptions of the Emergency solely in terms of the repercussions it was to have on their normal pattern of daily life. Certainly from statements such as Mrs. Huxley's, the impression arises that it was these disruptions, not the possibility of attack, that were the ultimate key to the settler's resentment of the Emergency.

> It was the farmers who bore the brunt of the Mau Mau revolt. . . . Not merely were the lives of the farmer and his family in constant danger, not merely was his valuable livestock stolen and mutilated, but, in many cases, his whole labor force either decamped or was removed, for security reasons, by the police, leaving him with no one to milk the cows.[79]

One finds no suggestion here that the irritations of an inadequate and unstable labor force may not be commensurate with the loss of over 14,000 Kikuyu.

The position of the Asian population during the Emergency was curiously ambiguous. Although there is no indication in the Mau Mau ideology that the Asian was a focus of resentment, Leakey states, "It was always understood that while the first object was to destroy European power in Kenya, once that was achieved, the problem of driving out Asians would be easy."[80] It would seem doubtful that the ideology was that developed, although it is true that, in the Nairobi area and in the isolated *dukas* of the Highlands,

---

[78] Rawcliffe, *op. cit.*, p. 96.

[79] Elspeth Huxley, *No Easy Way* (Nairobi: East African Standard, 1957), p. 194.

[80] L. S. B. Leakey, *Defeating Mau Mau* (London: Methuen and Company, 1954), p. 30.

Asian merchants were subject to a higher incidence of burglary during the Emergency—both as operations of Mau Mau and of the urban criminal element, which found it expedient to legitimate such actions as Mau Mau.

Politically, however, the Indians were to identify with the government, not with the African insurgents, for they felt their position would be threatened if the movement proved successful. In this commitment to the colonial superstructure, they were ironically to find themselves in opposition to New Delhi, for the latter supported Mau Mau as an independence movement. The ambiguity of their position was further increased by the restrictions placed on their role in the Emergency, for under settler pressure, recruitment of the Asian to the Security Forces was restricted to noncombatant duties. Even in the anxiety of this European-African crisis when concerted support of the government was essential, the settler was not about to concede privileges to the Asian which could later be cited as implying equality of status.

Factors in the Redefinition of Minority Status

A major shift in colonial policy occurred in 1954, one which conceded to the African the right to political expression and to a direct voice in the government of the country. It is ironic that this Colonial Office decision to acknowledge at last African representational demands in East Africa was first expressed in Kenya during the height of the Emergency when anti-African sentiments were high and the African had been deprived of all legitimate channels of pressure. The visit of the Colonial Secretary, Oliver Lyttelton, in 1954 presaged the first serious revision of policy in Kenya, for his proposed constitutional revisions provided for a multiracial representation on the Council of Ministers, albeit weighted to ensure European parity with African and Asian members. In addition, and perhaps more significantly, provision was also made for an African franchise.[81] The Lyttelton Constitution, with its implications of a multiracial power structure, unambiguously rejected white dominion as a serious political option for the Kenya settler. The reaction of the settler was muted, however, for although it was perceived that a major political adjustment would ultimately be necessary, the settler felt that for his generation, at least, some palatable compromise could be reached which would preserve the European position of dominance.

Although unified in their basic objectives of retaining economic and political privileges vis-à-vis the African, for the first time in Kenya's history serious conflicts of opinion were to divide the British community. These dissensions focused on the operational procedures through which the European position would be best maintained. One response was that of the United Country Party, which supported the multiracial propositions of the

---

[81] Carl G. Rosberg, Jr., "Political Conflict and Change in Kenya," in Gwendolyn M. Carter and William O. Brown (eds.), *Transition in Africa: Studies in Political Adaptation* (Boston: Boston University Press, 1958), p. 100.

Lyttelton Constitution, but clearly envisioned the development of a more representative government under the control of the benevolent but firm European leadership. If a multiracial partnership were conceded, it would be one in which the settlers were "very much the senior partner."[82]

For the settlers, however, the prospect of sharing a common political structure with incompetent, untrained, and possibly constitutionally incapable Africans was too unpalatable to concede graciously. Therefore, 1954 also saw the formation of the Federal Independent Party in which "provincial autonomy" was advanced as the mechanism to resolve Kenya's political tensions. Fundamentally a recommendation for *apartheid,* provincial boundaries were to be racially defined, and, within the area designated for European occupation, the cherished ideals of white supremacy were to reign.

In spite of these organized efforts to inhibit the extension of privilege to the non-European communities, in 1957, a second major concession was made to the African when it was proposed that African representation be increased to fourteen to achieve parity for the first time with the European unofficial members. By 1960, the final phase in the transfer of power was realized when the London Constitutional Conference suddenly and unambiguously affirmed the legitimacy of African political dominance by supporting universal adult suffrage in respect to fifty-three common roll seats. To ensure representation of the European, Asian, and Arab communities, twenty seats were reserved on a communal franchise, for it was assumed, by virtue of the overwhelming numerical preponderance of the African electorate, that the members elected on the larger common roll would be African.

Fully as significant as the redefinition of the role of the African was the abrupt relegation of the European community to the position of a political minority. No concessions were made, no affirmations of gradualism or shared trusteeship were offered to ease their acceptance of the power shift, and what was perhaps most striking, rather than expand African representation to make their position of dominance unambiguous, the Colonial Office chose rather to reduce perfunctorily European representation from fourteen to ten.

The reaction of the European community to the implications of the 1960 constitution was curiously oblique for a group whose history was rife with incidents of civil disobedience and venomous attacks on government policy. A few references were made to the possibility that Roy Welensky would supply them with arms,[83] but all overt expressions of hostility were curiously displaced from the offending British government to Michael Blundell who

---

[82] George W. Shepherd, Jr., *They Wait in Darkness* (New York: John Day and Company, 1955), p. 279.

[83] Mboya, *op. cit.,* p. 127.

had led the settler delegation at the conference. Thirty pieces of silver were cast at his feet as he emerged from a London plane, and settlers shouted lest there be any ambiguity in the symbolic gesture, "Judas Blundell, you have betrayed your people."[84]

The disaffection provoked by the 1960 constitution manifest itself as well in physical retreat or by preparations for such a withdrawal. The humiliation of a sudden relegation to minority status was compounded minimally with fears of economic depression, administrative inefficiency, and corruption, but fully as much with the possibility of gross abuses at the hands of an avenging African government after independence. Certainly, the events related by Belgian refugees from the Congo who fled into East Africa did little to assuage their fears. Furthermore, the Kenya settler found bitter irony in a situation in which the "child race," the race of depraved minds and doubtful capacities, was to be given political control of the country that he, the settler, had created.

The immediate response to the conference was a period of economic retrenchment, "No development was undertaken unless absolutely essential, very little buying of new articles took place, and replacement was cut down to a minimum."[85] During this period as well, the physical withdrawal began. In 1962, the *Standard* faithfully reported the exodus of each group of Afrikaners from the Eldoret area. Their departure was envisioned as a "trek" to their homeland, or at least to Southern Rhodesia, and as an affirmation of values held dear to every sane man. Few were to regard the possibility of staying as any serious option, in spite of reassurances by KANU that appropriations would only occur in the case of abuses or where there were absentee landlords, and that in such circumstances a fair compensation would be paid.[86] For those who wished to remain, the course was less clear. The fragmentation of parties in the 1961 election was an indication of the European's failure to conceive clearly his position under the new constitution or to reach a consensus on his new role in an African-dominated society.

In 1962, KANU opened its membership to non-Africans. Whatever misgivings the European might have had about African reassurances that they wanted all distinctions of race effaced, it was soon to be clear that any political influence the Europeans might salvage would have to be expressed organizationally through KANU and in the idiom of KANU values. Profound adjustments were required both politically and socially of those Europeans who opted to move into an independent Kenya. At the time of independence in December 1963, only the European's economic position had yet to be challenged.

---

[84] Susan Wood, *Kenya: The Tensions of Progress* (London: Oxford University Press, 1962), p. 73.

[85] *Ibid.,* p. 83.

[86] Forrester, *op. cit.,* p. 62.

The adjustment of the Asian community to the shift in political dominance in the postwar world was less traumatic, for although the power structure was redefined, their position was to remain that of a minority community. The movement into an African-oriented society did, however, imply certain fundamental changes for the Asian community. With the new emphasis on equality of privilege for all citizens, they were at last to have equal access to land, freedom from residential restrictions, protection against legislative discrimination of race, and the opportunity to vote in a common roll—although the last had ceased, by virtue of the African franchise, to have the implications for their status that it had in the 1920's.

The position of the Asian in Kenya was facilitated as well by a long history of sympathy and support for the African despite the risks of such cooperation. During the period before 1945 when direct representation was denied the African, the Indian representatives of the Legislative Council played an important role as spokesman for African opinion, often far more indeed than the European missionary nominated to ostensibly represent "native" interests. If one key tension was to emerge in African-Asian relations, it was the clear disparity in economic status between the two groups. In Kenya, as in the other areas of East Africa, the Indian approached independence with a virtual commercial monopoly and with a large share of the lower- and middle-level civil service posts. The Indian therefore saw a more personal threat to his security as a concomitant of the African's assumption of political power, with increasing African demands for entrance into these occupational sectors. For the businessman, there was also the additional fear, however irrational, of the confiscation of property or seizure of funds.

It was left for the Indian to balance these threats against his strong desire to remain in East Africa. For many families, Kenya represented a commitment of several generations, and for most there was little option. Lacking the mobility of the British European, the Indian was not free to emigrate to many Commonwealth countries, but had as his only alternative a reestablishment of ties in India, presumably under more marginal conditions. Given this alternative, it is understandable that the Asian was willing to make certain concessions to ensure his security of tenure. Recognizing that he could expect little sympathy as an interest group seeking privileges for the Asian community as such, he chose rather to seek political representation as an individual and within organizations that were not only African in composition but committed to the extension of African power. Symbolic of this was the decision of the Kenya Indian Congress in 1962 to withdraw from direct political action. "Let us now as Africans, as citizens of Kenya, have confidence in the African leaders."[87] Whatever the future envisioned by the Asians in independent Africa, it was clear that politically their role was

---

[87] George Delf, *Asians in East Africa* (London: Oxford University Press, 1963), p. 41.

to avoid any potentially provocative identification as an ethnic minority and to accept passively the policy decisions of the new power structure. By avoiding demands on that level, the issue of their economic position would be less salient in an area of possible reform.

UGANDA

The history of minority relations in Uganda exhibits none of the bitterness or drama which characterized Kenya's progression toward independence. Although the same ethno-racial elements are present in Uganda and in basically the same proportions, relations between the three communities have been, if aloof, surprisingly tranquil.

Interracial tensions were unquestionably present in Uganda, as the few rare expressions of overt hostility indicate, but unlike Kenya, the expectations of the non-African communities were congruent with the government's definition of their position in Uganda society. Critical to the course that race relations were to take was Uganda's avoidance of any definition as a "white man's country"; although there were early expectations of a plantation economy, by 1910, the British were committed to developing the country on the West African pattern of a peasant economy. The Europeans who opted for commercial or agricultural roles in the development of Uganda therefore did so, not with the expectation of ultimate political control, but because they felt it was to their immediate economic advantage. In a comparable manner, the Asian population accepted its minority position, although the Asians were to remain sensitive to securing non-discriminatory treatment vis-à-vis the European resident.

The tone of race relations was set initially by Sir Harry Johnston as Special Commissioner for Uganda. The uniform designed for the King's African Rifles, the official stationery, and the band of Johnston's straw boater all incorporated black, yellow, and white as a symbol of intercommunity cooperation.[88] In addition, Johnston was to redefine the character of economic development in Uganda. Though Lugard had earlier emphasized the need for a plantation economy under European management, Johnston stressed Uganda's potentialities as a peasant economy of the West African pattern. With this in mind, he was anxious to secure all unoccupied land as Crown Land, for in this way it would be "impossible for a greedy king or chief or collection of chiefs to sell large quantities of land to European speculators."[89] The personal commitment of Johnston to African interest was, of course, of pre-eminent importance in defining the course of Uganda's administrative policy, yet there were also certain political and physical factors which would suggest to him the appropriateness of his position. Climatically, Uganda was in large part considerably lower in

---

[88] Roland Oliver, *Sir Harry Johnston and the Scramble for Africa* (London: Victor Gollancz, 1954), p. 295.

[89] *Ibid.*, p. 303.

altitude than the Mau Plateau and, hence, less desirable for permanent white settlement. The inaccessibility of the Highlands areas to the west, particularly in terms of the Kenya coast, would also serve to inhibit European commercial development. The character of the indigenous political structure in many parts of Uganda was also relevant, for, in these areas, the British were dealing from the first with centralized kingdoms. Any attempts to alienate large tracts of land or to relocate inhabitants would have probably met with organized resistance of a scale and efficiency impossible for the decentralized tribes of Kenya. The sensitivity of these rulers to their rights under treaty would also suggest to the early administrator the expediency of avoiding any encroachment in such a sensitive sector as land. Certain demographic factors also served to inhibit a program of alienation in Uganda. The greater density of population, particularly in Buganda, discouraged any attempts to reserve large blocks of land for European settlement. Furthermore, patterns of tenure in Buganda were not ambiguous, as in pastoral areas, or even, for that matter, as among Kenya agriculturalists, where their crops and technology required large areas of fallow. The plantain was the staple of the Baganda, and there is little ambiguity in the dimensions of a *matoke* plantation.

Although no official action was taken to restrict European settlement until 1916, the implicit policy during the first decade of the twentieth century discouraged European immigration, while stressing the development of Uganda as an African state. Although Sir Hesketh Bell, governor during this period, placed no specific restrictions against alienation, it was apparent that a policy of inertia would, in its own way, be fully as effective, particularly when complemented by the extraordinary concessions offered to the prospective settler in Kenya.

In 1916, the ambiguities of the early land policy were unequivocally resolved with the publication of a notice that "pending receipt of further instructions from the Secretary of State, no more grants of freehold land would be made to non-Africans . . . and that no African-owned land could be transferred in freehold to a non-native of the Protectorate."[90] Although the Crown Lands Ordinance of 1922 included provisions for the alienation of land under lease for a maximum of ninety-nine years, few European immigrants were to opt for settlement in Uganda, for the conditions of alienation continued to be considerably less attractive than those offered in Kenya. One index of this is the total amount of land alienated throughout the colonial period to non-Africans both on lease and as free-hold. Accumulatively assessed at 731 square miles of which over 200 had fallen into disuse by 1962, the amount was inconsequential—given a total land area of 74,622 square miles.[91]

---

[90] Kenneth Ingham, *The Making of Modern Uganda* (London: Allen and Unwin, 1958), p. 142.

[91] Delf, *Asians in East Africa*, p. 26.

The gross amount of land in European hands was an important factor in minimizing land as a source of political tension. Also of significance was the high proportion of such land under mission control (120 of the 263 square miles of freehold), for it again muted the issue of commercial exploitation by non-Africans. Finally, the proportion of Europeans privately engaged in agriculture was such that agricultural interests would never become a serious issue. In 1959, the number of European males so employed was no more than ninety-nine, that is, less than 1 per cent of the European community. With such numerical marginality, it would be impossible to focus on land as a diagnostic sector of minority privilege.

The European

The occupational distribution of the European was one major index of the definition of Uganda as an African state, for, by 1959, fully 60 per cent of the European population was engaged in service occupations. Also indicative was the transient character of the European community: in 1959, over 82 per cent of the total population and 93 per cent of the population over fifteen years were born outside East Africa. Throughout the colonial period, the number of non-British subjects in Uganda remained small and hetereogeneous in origin. In the last census, the Italians with 632 constituted the largest number, followed by 297 Dutch, 117 French, and 166 Americans. The French and Americans were largely concentrated in service positions, such as education or missionary work, while the Dutch and Italians were more characteristically in the commercial sector. The large Italian population derives largely from those men who elected to remain in East Africa after their internment during World War II.

Though one would anticipate a politically passive role from these immigrants by virtue of their alien status, there was as well little expectation of privilege from the British segment of the European community. This was, in large part, a result of the transient character of their residence in East Africa. Those involved in commerce were primarily on contract with large international firms or banking operations, while those in service occupations were also subject to transfer both within and outside East Africa. Neither group would regard their position in Uganda as a permanent commitment and, as such, had little interest in establishing themselves as potential pressure groups. As their preoccupation with "home leave" indicated, their basic orientation remained toward England, and it was there, not in East Africa, that children were educated, houses purchased, and plans for retirement made.

The true European resident in Uganda tended to be the professional, the small businessman, the hotel keeper, the plantation owner, or the independent miner. It is not surprising, therefore, that involvement in political activity was confined primarily to the British representatives in these occupations. On an organizational level, the Chamber of Commerce and the Uganda

Planters Association were to serve as primary organs of European opinion; however, neither was exclusively European in membership. Whatever pressures they were to exert had, as a consequence, to be occupational rather than racial in character, and had to incorporate a consideration of Asian interests as well.

The pattern of European politics that emerged in Uganda was one of basic passivity. In this, Uganda presented a striking contrast to Kenya, for the relationship between official and nonofficial contained none of the elements of suspicion, hostility, or strident histrionics that defined relations between the administrator in Kenya and the Highlands settler. On the contrary, the British community in Uganda accepted without challenge the government definition of its position as marginal to African interests. On those rare occasions when reforms were suggested, they were both modest in scale and congruent with government policy. Once nominal representation had been established, even the Legislative Council failed to engage the interest of the Uganda European. Whereas the European communities in Tanganyika and Kenya were to have a continuing sensitivity to parity or dominance vis-à-vis the African and Asian or, for that matter, to the official, representation was not regarded in Uganda as a significant index of status.

The Asian

The occupational and ethnic patterns of the Asian community established in Uganda were analogous to those in Kenya and Tanganyika, although Uganda lacked the tradition of early Arab settlement which characterized the coastal areas. The Indian trader, with few exceptions, entered Uganda only after the Uganda Railway had been extended to Kisumu on Lake Victoria. Yet, by 1903, they had taken most of the retail trade in Kampala from the Arab and Swahili merchants.[92] Commercially, their role in the development of Uganda was clearly appreciated and encouraged by the British administration, for their numbers increased sharply from 1,904 in 1911 to 13,026 by 1931.[93]

Although early economic policies permitted them access to land, the Indian gravitated, presumably by preference, into basically commercial spheres. By the late 1920's, Buell estimates, the Indian community controlled 90 per cent of the Uganda trade and held a virtual monopoly on crafts.[94] At the time of the last census in 1959, the proportions remained basically the same, with 48.7 per cent of the Indian males engaged in wholesale and retail trade or banking; 8.6 per cent in manufacturing; and 9.4 per cent in agriculture, forestry, and fishing. Only 6.6 per cent were employed in public

[92] Hollingsworth, *op. cit.*, p. 52.
[93] *Ibid.*, p. 68.
[94] Buell, *op. cit.*, p. 560.

service. The Asian community thus differs strikingly in profile from the European population in Uganda where fully 66 per cent of the adult males were engaged in service occupations. In addition, the Asian population was considerably more stable, for 53.5 per cent were born in Uganda in contrast to a figure of 6 per cent for the European.

Politically, the Indians assumed a passive role throughout the history of Uganda. Administrative policy has, however, been cognizant of their interests where distinctions of racial status were drawn, the salient categories were African/non-African. As a consequence, there was little incentive for the Asian community to challenge government decisions, for any restrictions were to apply to the European resident as well.

On only one occasion during the colonial period was the Indian community openly to protest against government policy: when in 1919 R. T. Coryndon nominated two Europeans and one Asian as unofficial representatives of the newly formed Legislative Council. Though arguments for equal representation could be drawn both from their numerical superiority and from the importance of their commercial role, it was clearly the comparable tensions in Kenya at that time and the intensity of settler response there, not any existing disabilities in Uganda, that made the Indian so sensitive to the implied differential of status.

Although the issue was one of principle, not of power, it was not until 1926 that the Indian community agreed to accept the appointment of a single representative to the Council. During the subsequent years, they continued to press for a second seat and, when this had not been granted by 1929, refused to nominate a successor at the expiration of the incumbent's term of office.[95] In 1933, Governor Bourdillon agreed to increase the number of unofficial members by one, and, although he insisted that this would be a general appointment without implications of community representation, it was tacitly agreed that an Asian would be selected.[96] With the achievement of parity in 1933, representation ceased to be an issue for the Asian community, nor was it to become one again when African dominance was recognized.

On a statutory level, there was little cause for tension between Asian and European, for what discriminations existed had been instituted to ensure protection of African interests and, as such, were applicable to both as non-Africans. Access to land was restricted, but as a non-African not as an Indian; political representation was by nomination, but it was by nomination for the English as well. Where discrimination clearly lay was in areas which implied an intimacy of contact. School facilities were separate, hospital wards segregated, and lavatories in government and commercial buildings clearly marked.

---

[95] Ingham, *A History of East Africa*, p. 291.
[96] *Ibid.*

In addition, both the European official and resident defined his relationship to the Asian community as one of courteous avoidance. The Indian was thus to be found in a similar state of social isolation as in Kenya and Tanganyika: by option, aloof from the African community; by designation, excluded from informal contact with the European. Whatever bitterness the latter rejection may have elicited, and there is evidence that among the educated it was considerable, the grievance of the Indian was not publicly expressed.

Similarly, the Asian's belief in his superiority over the African was never advanced publicly to legitimate his interests. Nor was there any criticism of government policy in the 1950's when independence under African leadership was affirmed. Throughout Uganda's history, the Asian was resigned to his position as a minority community and to the vagaries of colonial policy. It was this passivity and ability to accept a fundamental redefinition of the political and social situation that was to ease the adjustment of the Indian to the changing demands of an independent Uganda.

The African

The position of the African in Uganda was not only ideologically favored, but, in the actual operation of the colonial government, considerable care was taken to protect his interests and to implement his movement into an international economy. Land was never a serious political issue in Uganda, for the amount of alienation was inconsequential (.08 per cent), nor did labor problems give rise to any significant interracial tensions. In contrast to Kenya, settler complaints about labor shortages were quickly countered by government assertions that the solution lay, not in legislative restrictions, but in providing sufficient inducement to make wage labor an attractive alternative to cash farming. Economic grievances for the African were thus confined to the more peripheral issue of central control of the marketing of commercial crops.

Representation, again, was not to be a serious tension in Uganda, primarily because the Baganda, as the most politically engaged tribe, felt they could exercise greater influence over the colonial administration by remaining outside the legislative structure.

> If we get a representative on the Legislative Council, it is quite possible, say, with one representative or two representatives, that we will be outvoted there by the majority, and when we have been outvoted in that way, it will be very difficult for us to reopen the questions . . . if you leave it as is, we have got every chance of complaining on anything which may be passed by the Legislative Council, and we can always approach the Secretary of State if nothing is allowed (Serwano Kkulbya, Treasurer of the Buganda Government).[97]

---

[97] *Ibid.,* p. 288.

Also relevant to African apathy was the political marginality of the other racial communities: all nonofficial members of the Legislative Council were selected by the government and, as the Assembly was constituted, had little hope of exerting any serious influence over a large and dedicated official majority.

The passivity of the African in Uganda was not to lead, however, to the retardation of constitutional developments. On the contrary, the dominant position of the African was recognized by 1950, almost a full decade before similar concessions were obtained in Tanganyika or Kenya. In 1945, as part of a major policy revision in East Africa, Africans were nominated to the Legislative Council for the first time in all three territories. Five years later, the membership of the Uganda Assembly was expanded to twenty-four, and, of the sixteen unofficials, eight were to be African, four European, and four Asian. In 1955, even this vestigial concession to non-African interests was abandoned, for African membership was increased to eighteen while the other communities agreed to a reduction of their representation to six.[98] The final phase of legislative development occurred in 1961, when elections were held in which the franchise was extended to a common roll.

If there was one serious tension for the African in colonial Uganda, it was in the differentiation of status, often subtle, sometimes explicit, when based on the criterion of race. Although there was unquestionably a greater option for mobility in Uganda than in Kenya and little discriminatory legislation, the distinction of color was clearly operative in many contexts. The position of the British official was to deny categorically that such a bias existed. Sir Andrew Cohen asserted "this evil thing will never be permitted in this country," yet it was he who organized the Uganda Club in the 1950's for the African elite who were denied access to suitable European facilities. Unquestionably, the issue was a sensitive one for the British resident, hence, the institutions and social patterns which reflected such bias were often defended on other nonracial grounds. The European Club was legitimated, for example, as an expression of British *esprit de corps,* although any person of European descent was eligible, and Cambridge-educated Africans were not.

Discrimination was also sanctioned on more official levels: government pay was scaled for European, Asian, and African employees, regardless of relevant educational qualifications; segregated lavatory facilities could still be found well into 1962 in government offices in Entebbe; and government housing was classified according to race, with age, size, and plumbing determining its allocation to European, Asian, or African personnel. Only in the area of public accommodation did the barriers against the African ease earlier than in Kenya, and, here, economic factors and informal pres-

---

[98] A. J. Hughes, *East Africa: The Search for Unity* (Baltimore: Penguin Books, 1963), p. 174.

sures continued to operate to restrict the access of Africans to hotels and restaurants. The tension of entering a social citadel of the European community, such as the hotel at Lake Victoria, was enough to deter many Africans who were financially able to do so.

On the level of informal social contacts, as in the other territories of East Africa, there was a tacit but sacrosanct agreement that community lines were not to be crossed by either African or European, unless required in a semiofficial context. Thus, an important African wedding or local government tea might be attended without jeopardizing the status of the European, but events that implied a greater degree of intimacy, such as a private drink or a dinner party, were regarded by the British community as a serious betrayal of white solidarity.

These various facets of racial discrimination were unquestionably resented, particularly by the educated African, but differential treatment was not to assume political importance until the late 1950's and, then, only as an implicit aspect of the nationalist's demand for independence. Unlike Kenya, where racial hostility was both overt and intense, European-African relations in Uganda were muted both by ideological protestations of good faith and by the absence of serious economic or legislative restrictions. Racial discrimination was never to be an open issue; rather, it was understood by both the resident European and the Ugandan that it would be corrected with a revision in the power structure.

PATTERNS OF POLITICAL ACTIVITY

Throughout the history of Uganda, the fight for political privilege had been tribal, not racial in character. Pivotal to this was the self-image of the largest and most politically salient tribe, the Baganda. By conceding to them certain prerogatives during the early administrative period, the Baganda were to enter the colonial period with the expectations of preferential treatment. The unrelenting pressure for special privilege of the Baganda was instrumental, not merely in defining the character of the relations with the colonial government, but, even more significantly, in defining the character of intertribal relations throughout Uganda. Buganda, not the Asian or European, was to be the primary reference group for other areas of Uganda. Each tribe, whether from the north, east, or west, assessed its position, not in terms of the alien communities, but in terms of the relative degree of privileges vis-à-vis the Baganda that it was able to secure from the central administration. This parochial focus of the Baganda was also an important factor in inhibiting any serious anti-colonial hostility on a national level, for potential political unrest outside Buganda tended to polarize around issues such as perceived areas of discrimination or the acquisition of concessions previously extended to Buganda.

The development of organized political activity also mirrored the pre-eminent position of the Baganda, for the political history of Uganda until the middle 1950's was an expression of the needs and discontents of the Baganda, not of the African. Early movements were, both in personnel and in intent, Bugandan, for they focused on local issues and pressed for concessions that would be specifically advantageous to the Baganda. Their dominant ideology displayed little concern with the general welfare of the African, but rather with the advancement and protection of a specific set of interests in opposition to other tribes, or with obtaining a greater degree of autonomy within the central structure.

The first of such expressions of political unrest was to occur in the 1930's as a direct response to a deteriorating international economic situation which manifested itself locally in lower prices and in an increase in the frequency of commercial failure. The anxiety and frustration produced by the instability of the period was polarized into a hostility toward the Europeans and Asians involved in marketing operations and toward government control of the ginning and marketing processes. As a correlated response, a renewed emphasis was also placed on the importance of adherence to various Kiganda traditions.[99] It was not until the postwar period, however, that the first overt expression of political discontent was to occur in Uganda. Manifest as a series of strikes and riots throughout Buganda, a key issue again was the perceived oppressiveness of government restrictions as a factor in commercial failure. Land was also at that time defined as a sensitive issue for the Baganda, for attempts by the Protectorate government to alienate plots within Kampala for educational and medical facilities were interpreted as "a most sinister plot to secure land in Buganda for European settlers."[100]

During the riots of 1945 and 1949, however, the focus for direct aggression was not the central government, but rather the Baganda chiefs who were charged with administrative abuses and with betraying the interests of the Baganda to the Europeans. Although the claims against the chief structure had considerable legitimacy in themselves, the riots would also seem to have served as an important mechanism for releasing displaced hostility against alien commercial interests.

The formation of the Uganda National Congress (UNC) in 1952 was to mark the first attempt to extend African political activity to areas outside Buganda. Although it drew its support largely from the Baganda, a serious appeal was made to recruit members from other sections of Uganda. The aims of the organization were to remain, however, in many respects a reflection of the specific concerns of the Baganda, for it opposed East African

---

[99] David E. Apter, *The Political Kingdom in Uganda* (Princeton: Princeton University Press, 1961), p. 194.

[100] D. Anthony Low and R. Cranford Pratt, *Buganda and British Overrule* (London: Oxford University Press, 1960), p. 274.

federation, supported a federal structure for independent Uganda, and emphasized the preservation of traditional political offices.[101]

On a less parochial level, the UNC was also to address the problem of minority status by affirming the right of "universal equality" for all residents who acquired Uganda citizenship after independence. Consistent with these aims, an initial attempt was made to attract European and Asian members, but, as none chose to register, the organization became exclusively African by default.

Two years later, Baganda sentiments were again polarized by the sudden deportation of their leader, the Kabaka, following his demands for autonomous status. Resentment at this action expressed itself, not as a direct protest against the government, but as a more diffuse rejection of all non-African elements in their society. Although ideologically defined as an anti-European measure, the mode of protest, a boycott of all non-African goods, was to affect most directly the Asian commercial community. Not unfortuitously, those who were to feel the full force of the boycott were the small Asian shopkeepers in the rural areas of Buganda who were in direct competition with the commercial elements of UNC. As a consequence of the boycott, many were permanently driven from these outlying sections of Buganda.

In 1959, Baganda hostility was again focused against the Asian, although phrased once more as a protest against certain government policies. The manifest issue as presented by the Buganda-based Uganda National Movement (UNM) was the decision of the government to ensure equal representation for all regions on the Legislative Council. As an expression of their displeasure at this proposed loss of Baganda privilege, UNM organized a boycott of goods of foreign origin as well as buses run by "non-Africans,"[102] There is no question that they were well aware that such an action, if sustained, would severely damage, if not destroy, the small Asian shopkeeper.

Although the Baganda petty trader would clearly profit from such a boycott, the motivations of the noncommercial class were more obscure. In part, they must be attributed to a resentment of Asian domination of the commercial sector, in part, to a more diffuse antagonism toward the alien intruder and his attempt to manipulate Baganda affairs. Anti-British elements were also evident, for the boycott involved a rejection of European goods and transportation and the reassertion of traditional values symbolized by the resumption of bark cloth.

Although hostility toward the Asian was to influence the character of Buganda political protest after World War II, resentment toward the resi-

---

[101] Harold Ingrams, Uganda: *A Crisis of Nationhood* (London: H.M.S.O., 1960), p. 311.

[102] Lloyd A. Fallers, *The King's Men* (London: Oxford University Press, 1964), p. 371.

dent nonofficial European never became a political issue. One factor may have been that the British, where commercially involved, were engaged in international operations or in retail trade to the local European community and did not impinge in any competitive sense on African trading ventures. Moreover, their political marginality had been made explicit by the government and was apparent to the African community as well.

The Asians, particularly those operating in economically marginal positions as petty traders, obviously elicited considerably more hostility, both because of common accusations of malpractices and because they presented an immediate economic obstacle to the African who wished to establish himself in trade on a small scale. In addition, there was resentment of their general monopoly of commercial control and of the wealth of the more successful, particularly as their operations had been contingent on African labor. Outside of Buganda, however, the hostility against the Asian remained latent, expressing itself largely in caution and mistrust in commercial contacts. Certainly, it was never to become the focus of political protest in other areas.

The commitment of the Indians to the national parties of the late 1950's, both as members and candidates and through considerable financial contributions, helped to alleviate such tensions, as did their acceptance without protest of their role as a political minority without special safeguards. The Wild Committee of 1959 reported: "There had been no request for any special representation on the Legislative Council for non-Africans, and indeed the Central Council of Indian Associations, the Central Council of Muslim Associations, and the Toro European Association have all expressed themselves as being opposed to any such special representation."[103] Both Indian and resident European had little desire to make their minority status more conspicuous through the retention of protective devices to ensure community representation.

If economic tensions and racial conflict were not really relevant, neither could political issues afford any serious catalyst for the mobilization of African opinion in Uganda. There was no ambiguity about the government's intention to grant independence. Certainly by 1957 there was every indication that such a decision would be imminent, for once independence was conceded to Ghana, it would be difficult to withhold it legitimately from Uganda. At best, the nationalist leaders could only urge a faster progression of events.

The one serious issue of independence, the one which was in fact responsible for the delay before self-government was granted, was the clarification of the role of Buganda within the national framework. Of concern fully as much to the non-Buganda as to the Buganda, it was this issue

---

[103] Uganda, *Report of the Constitutional Committee* (Entebbe, Government Printer, 1959), p. 21.

which was to dominate the negotiations at the London Constitutional Conference in 1961 and the content of the constitution itself. As Fred Burke notes, "The constitution . . . devotes considerably more space to describing the governing system of its constituent kingdoms and districts and their relationship to the central government than it does to the organization and powers of the central government."[104] It was this intracommunity focus that remained so distinctive a feature of Uganda's political development; for the politically critical minority structure in Uganda, unlike Kenya or Tanganyika, was tribal, not racial, in character.

TANGANYIKA [105]

The situation in Tanganyika under British rule has in many ways been the most paradoxical in East Africa. The structure of minority relations was analogous to Kenya, yet the expressed government policy was, like Uganda, an affirmation of the paramount role of the African. In Tanganyika, however, the character of the policy was determined less by the predilection of early governors than by its status as a mandate of the League of Nations and subsequently as a trust territory of the United Nations. As a condition of British overrule, both provided that the country be developed in the interests of the African inhabitants. Thus, although left with a German legacy of a settler community and expectations of a plantation economy, the British government was committed by Article 22 of the Versailles Treaty to the principle that "the well-being and development of such peoples form a sacred trust of civilization."[106] Implicit in this was a subordinate position for the immigrant communities: "First in importance come the interests of the natives; secondly the interests of the whites. The interests of the white should only be considered in relation to the direct or indirect exercise of protection over the natives."[107] The role of the mandatory power was conceived to be that of a temporary guide for the indigenous populations since British supervision was to continue only until they found themselves "able to stand by themselves under the strenuous conditions of the modern world."[108]

In December of 1946, jurisdiction over Tanganyika was transferred to a trusteeship administered under the United Nations. Again, the basic assumption was that the territory under the tutelage of the British was to be

---

[104] Fred G. Burke, *Local Government and Politics in Uganda* (Syracuse: Syracuse University Press, 1964), p. 43.

[105] For an explanation of why only Tanganyika and not the Republic of Tanzania in total is considered in this analysis, see footnote 1, *supra*.

[106] Buell, *op. cit.*, p. 545.

[107] *Ibid.*, p. 491.

[108] *Ibid.*, p. 490.

developed to the point where the supervisory control of the colonial power could be relinquished. In the actual implementation of the policy, however, the issue of the eventual transfer of power was not seriously considered until the decade immediately preceding independence. As Sir Donald Cameron stated in 1939, "It will take many years, many generations" before the Africans will be sufficiently advanced to assume a responsible position in the community.[109]

Although one condition of British control in Tanganyika was the development of African capabilities until ready for self-government, the political structure contemplated by the British for Tanganyika was not African, but multiracial in character. In this respect, Cameron was to stipulate that the European community would not be permitted to exercise control until the African was "sufficiently developed" to share in this role.[110] The mere act of inclusion was regarded as an adequate discharge of the requirements of the mandate. Certain concessions were also made to European settlement in the 1920's, but the international publicity and system of inspection ensured that the basic commitment of the British administration be, of necessity if not of personal inclination, to the African.

The protection of African interests was to be an even more sensitive issue after World War II, for the emphasis of the United Nations on the development of indigenous peoples was reinforced by a changing attitude toward the legitimacy of colonialism per se in the postwar world. Even among United Nations personnel, however, the issue of independence was not perceived to be of imminent concern until the end of the 1950's. In 1955, the Mission affirmed: (we) "look forward to self-government within twenty or twenty-five years"[111] while Julius Nyerere, although demanding a rapid progression toward independence, had similarly modest expectations of its realization: "By hard work, either in our own lifetime or that of our children, we shall achieve it."[112] Six years later, in December 1961, Tanganyika was to be granted independence. The rapidity of these developments can, in large part, be attributed to the response of the three racial communities to the 1954 Mission and to the sensitivity exhibited by the African leader, Julius Nyerere, in dealing with latent minority tensions.

The European

The European population of Tanganyika has always been heterogeneous, but the census figures suggest that the proportion of alien residents increased considerably under British administration, particularly in the period before

---

[109] Sir Donald Cameron, *My Tanganyika Service and Some Nigeria* (London: Allen and Unwin, 1939), p. 88.

[110] Mair, *op. cit.,* p. 265.

[111] Don Taylor, *The British in Africa* (London: Robert Hale, Ltd., 1962), p. 124.

[112] *Ibid.,* p. 134.

World War II. In 1912, the last German census indicated that of a population of 4,866 Europeans, 3,579 were German in nationality, with the Greeks and South Africans forming the two most significant alien communities. By 1929, the British government reported: "if officials and their families are left out the proportion of non-British to British is considerably more than two to one."[113] Although, in the postwar world, the British population assumed an unambiguous plurality, numbering 14,177 in 1957 against 6,170 alien residents, the proportion of aliens remained considerably higher than in Kenya or Uganda.

Occupationally, there were also some significant shifts in the composition of the European community after the transfer of German East Africa to Great Britain. Under German rule, the number engaged in plantation agriculture exceeded those in government service; in 1957, public service accounted for the largest occupational category (2,140), and agriculture (1,458) and missions (1,241) were next in importance.

Ethnic heterogeneity has characterized each occupational category, with the exception, of course, of the civil service. One fundamental reason for the development of this pattern was the provision of the mandate. In contrast to Kenya and Uganda, where the colonial government was to exercise considerable care in the admission of aliens, no discrimination could be shown in Tanganyika against any member of the League of Nations. It was this policy that permitted the return of the German population after World War I, for, although their plantations had been confiscated and sold and their entry initially forbidden, the British had no power to restrict their return once Germany had been admitted into the League of Nations in 1926.

The mission sector, for similar reasons, displayed a striking degree of heterogeneity which was not found in other areas of East Africa. By 1930, the fragmentation of both Protestant and Catholic interests was such as to provide for the African anxious to adopt Christianity the facilities of four branches of the German Lutheran Church, or Anglican, Congregational, Seventh-Day Adventist, African Inland, Moravian, and Bethel missions, if he chose to become Protestant. Catholicism was represented by the White Fathers, the Fathers of the Holy Ghost, Capucine, German Benedictine, and German-Swiss Benedictine orders.[114] However much this may have confused the image of Christianity, it would seem to have been politically advantageous, for the partisan intensity of religious feeling in Uganda was unquestionably facilitated by the duality of the issue.

The commercial class also exhibited considerable heterogeneity of origin, although, within this segment of the European community, there would appear to have been status differentials which served to segregate the British citizen from the alien. Small retail shops, such as tearooms, dress shops,

---

113 *Ibid.*, p. 28.

114 Gerald F. Sayers, *The Handbook of Tanganyika* (London: Macmillan and Company, 1930), p. 386.

bakeries, and hairdressers, tended to be operated by aliens rather than by Englishmen, for these, as G. L. Steer notes, were jobs "to which Britons do not descend in the tropics."[115] It was only in the agricultural sector that ethnic clusterings assumed an importance, and, even here, the regional pattern was one of considerable diversity. Arusha, for example, was regarded as the center of British settlement, yet Kathleen Stahl estimated that only 25 per cent of the agricultural population of the Northern Province was British.[116] Far more critical to the ethos of the area was the fact that 50 per cent were of South African origin. A similar concentration of German agricultural interests occurred in the Moshi and Tanga areas, though there was a certain degree of homogeneity in the European coastal population as well, for the German plantations were largely purchased by the British and Greeks. In contrast, the southern Highlands were more genuinely heterogeneous, for no single ethnic community predominated.

These distributional variations reflect major differences in attitude as well, for the settlers of the Northern Province, particularly those in the Arusha area, were clearly oriented in activity and attitude toward Kenya. Their produce was exported from Mombasa rather than from Dar es Salaam; their children were sent to Kenya schools; and shopping excursions were made to Nairobi rather than to the Tanganyikan capital. Politically, their sympathies and expectations lay with the white-settler community to the north. In contrast, the attitude of the settlers in other areas of Tanganyika was more analogous to the position of the European resident in Uganda, both in their fear of Kenya dominance and in their definition of their position as one of political marginality. Certainly the high proportion of non-British was an important factor in this passivity.

FACTORS IN THE DEFINITION OF EUROPEAN STATUS

Although the more militant attitudes of the northern settler communities were not representative and the European resident had few delusions about the character of ultimate political control, the European in Tanganyika did assume that he would be accorded a position of social privilege and isolation. The nature of the relationship of the European community with the African and Asian thus assumed a special character, for the premise persisted that true interracial harmony had been achieved, in spite of the handicap of a pluralistic structure.

Distinctions of race clearly existed, but the European felt little pressure to legitimate the implicit barriers through which informal social contacts with other communities were avoided. Although it is true that there were

---

[115] G. L. Steer, *Judgment on German Africa* (London: Hodder and Stoughton, Ltd., 1939), p. 294.

[116] Kathleen M. Stahl, *Tanganyika Sail in the Wilderness* (The Hague: Mouton and Company, 1961), p. 45.

few overt expressions of tensions during the colonial period and these were manifest only through oblique criticisms of government policy, the egalitarianism proclaimed by the administrative ideology operated only within the framework of occupational contacts or semiofficial activities. Within this context, there was the expectation that tact and courtesy would be exercised, but a polite conversation at a government tea party cannot be considered an adequate index of the absence of interracial tensions. Certainly there was no attempt to extend multiracial cordiality into more intimate or informal sectors, for the status of the European community was contingent on remaining autonomous and aloof.

The much-publicized interracial harmony of Tanganyika was not, as implied, the consequence of the absence of racial tensions, but rather the result of the failure of the African and Indian to challenge the European's privileged status. The Indians, particularly those of considerable wealth and education, were unquestionably hurt by the discriminatory policies in public facilities and by the implicit restrictions against informal interracial contacts, but chose, as in the other areas of East Africa, to accept the situation without protest.

The passivity of the Tanganyika African was even more striking, for the European readily conceded to them an ultimate role of political dominance. Perhaps, as Colin Legum suggests, this apathy was a consequence of the considerably lower proportion of educated Africans who would, by virtue of their expectations, be most sensitive to such discriminatory pressures.[117] The response would also seem, however, to be a function of the extreme ethnic fragmentation found in Tanganyika which inhibited a sensitivity to tribal status and of the fact that, for the largest tribes, status mobility could be achieved within the traditional chiefly system or through the local cash-crop economy.

Despite the patent disparities between the norm of racial harmony and the various discriminations which did exist, the image which the Tanganyika government carefully maintained was one of a model situation of interracial harmony. Certainly some extraordinary measures were taken to preserve Tanganyika's reputation for ethno-racial trust and camaraderie. Vernon Bartlett reports: "I once saw the Governor, at the Government House garden party, looking on with calm and confidence while an Indian schoolgirl, with a bow and arrow and unbelievable skill, shot apples off Lady Twining's head for the benefit of Red Cross Funds."[118] Yet it was not until political developments of the mid-1950's led to the formation of interracial parties that informal contacts between communities became an expected correlate of more formal organizational relations. Even here, however, Margaret Bates could

---

[117] Colin Legum, *Must We Lose Africa?* (London: W. H. Allen and Company, 1954), p. 174.

[118] Vernon Bartlett, *Struggle for Africa* (New York: Frederick A. Praeger, 1953), p. 205.

report, as late at 1962: "At first this interaction had its painful aspects and was undertaken as a matter of official duty; now it is becoming more natural."[119]

THE POLITICAL ROLE OF THE EUROPEAN

While perceptions of the Asian and African communities reflected a homogeneity of attitude within the European population, the degree to which the European sought to reinforce social privilege with political activity was to vary considerably. One major line of cleavage defining the degree of political engagement was national affiliation, for representation in the Legislative Council was limited to British citizens. The resident alien community, although larger, was thus denied access to channels of direct political representation and would perceive their interests as more marginal to the concerns of the colonial administration. In contrast, the British in Tanganyika were to acquire a different set of expectations, both by virtue of their common national and cultural identification with the officials of the colonial government and in response to the position accorded the British settler in Kenya.

The degree of identification with the settler community to the north was particularly strong during the first decade of British administration, for Delamere was then actively concerned with the incorporation of Tanganyika into a white dominion. These pressures from Kenya led the British settler in Tanganyika to expect similar concessions in the acquisition of land. Emphasizing that the development of European capital and industry was the appropriate way to advance native welfare, the government's commitment to African interests was dismissed by the settler in 1923 as the "outcome of a fanatical negro-philism."[120] Settler-official tension was subsequently aggravated by such practices as government support of cash crops for Africans, administrative indifference to European demands for a labor supply, and the restrictions placed on conditions for land alienation. All served to impress the British settler with the marginality of his position.

The issue was not defined merely as one of bias toward African interests, however. The British settler in Tanganyika also felt that the colonial government, in its zeal to adhere to the conditions of the mandate and to attain international approval, was also guilty of bias in favor of alien settlers. The restrictions placed on the transfer of land, for example, were interpreted as a devious conspiracy to make settlement unattractive to the English immigrant.

No bona fide settler . . . would sink his whole capital in property held on so short a lease and with no guarantee of compensation; but get-rich-quick landminers would accept such terms and are doing so. These people, as it so

---

[119] Margaret L. Bates, "Tanganyika," in Gwendolyn M. Carter (ed.), *African One-Party States* (Ithaca: Cornell University Press, 1962), p. 436.

[120] Buell, *op. cit.,* p. 492.

happens mainly Greeks and Indians, do not make the best citizens; meanwhile the young Englishman or Dominion citizen, fresh from the Forces, perhaps with a fine war record and wishing to build a home and raise a family, is turned away.[121]

Such invidious distinctions of intent and character on the part of the British would serve only to inhibit any serious coalition of settler interests.

One consequence of the failure of the European community in Tanganyika to consolidate itself as a single interest group was the differential response of the British and alien to the sudden transition to independence at the end of the 1950's. Whereas the alien had no misconceptions about his political marginality, the British resident had acquired, however implicitly, a position of political privilege. As in the other territories of East Africa, the British community had avoided the issue of ultimate African control by assuming that no such transfer could be realized within their lifetime. As one member of the Legislative Assembly was to state in 1951: "It would be quite unrealistic to imagine that anybody else could take the place of the European in the body politic of Tanganyika at the present time, or for a very considerable time to come."[122]

That a rapid redefinition of power could occur within the decade with so few repercussions can, in large part, be attributed to the foresight of certain politically prominent British residents who perceived the inevitability of such a development and were willing quietly to assume a more marginal role in an African-dominated society. In addition, the transition was eased by the general passivity of the entire European community, for, regardless of their personal misgivings, they were tactfully to refrain from public protest. To some extent, the historical circumstances were such that cooperation was inevitable. Even the British had no numerical claim to special attention, nor had they, as in Kenya, earlier administrative concessions to cite as precedent.

Whatever their motives, and clearly the demands of the newly formed Tanganyika African National Union (TANU) for African dominance were relevant, by 1956, the British community had sought refuge in the concept of a multiracial society. If the alternatives were to be parity or African control, the former was unquestionably more attractive to them. This pluralistic position was to receive formal expression in the United Tanganyika party (UTP), a government-sponsored organization which, although opposed to racial discrimination, validated the principle of pluralism by acknowledging the legitimacy of each racial group to protect its interests "as separate communities."[123] Political control under the guidance of a multiracial party

---

[121] Elspeth Huxley, *The Sorcerer's Apprentice* (London: Chatto and Windus, 1956), p. 94.

[122] Tanganyika, *The Constitutional Debate* (Dar es Salaam: Government Printer, 1951), p. 7.

[123] Hughes, *op. cit.*, p. 69.

ceased to be a viable alternative to African domination, however, with TANU's 1958 decision to support candidates from each racial community. After the overwhelming defeat of the candidates of UTP in the elections of 1958, the European community was to attempt no further political activity outside of the organizational context of TANU. The alternatives open to them, as Tanganyika approached independence, were to affirm the nationalistic goals of TANU or to withdraw from political participation. In either event, their position as a political minority with marginal influence was inevitable.

The Asian

The Asian community in Tanganyika exhibited basically the same occupational and ethno-religious profile as in Kenya and Uganda. In two respects, however, its composition differed from that of the other territories of East Africa: religiously, the Moslem section of the Indo-Pakistani community had a slight plurality over the Hindus; and, ethnically, the Arab community was more salient, for although numerically smaller than the Arab population of Kenya, it represented a higher proportion of the Asian community, and its ratio to the Tanganyikan European was almost 1:1. As in Kenya, however, the delimitation of the Arab population was somewhat arbitrary: there was a tradition of intermarriage with the African, and, as a consequence, the term "Arab" had little value as a racial category. As Stahl remarked of the coastal population: "For social purposes they call themselves Arab, and for taxation purposes where the change is beneficial to them, Africans."[124]

In both the Indian and Arab communities, trade was the overwhelming occupational commitment. For the Asian, manufacturing provides the next major category (a drop from 7,923 to 1,742), and transport and public service were also important. The occupational distribution of the Tanganyikan Arab reflects an even more dramatic specialization in commerce —from 4,287 engaged in that occupation, the statistics drop to 295 for the second largest category, agriculture.[125] One major distinction in the character of the two communities was the degree of urbanization. Although both were predominantly in trade, in 1952, 82.7 per cent of the Indian population lived in urban centers, while only 38.9 per cent of the Arabs were so located.[126] This may be primarily a reflection of the mixed racial origins of the Arab community and their degree of social identification with the African.

Considering the relative size of their community and its early political and economic importance, the Arabs in Tanganyika have been unusually passive

---

[124] Stahl, *op. cit.*, p. 64.

[125] Tanganyika, *Report on the Census of the Non-African Population Taken on the Night of 20th/21st February, 1957* (Dar es Salaam, 1958).

[126] Taylor, *op. cit.*, p. 35.

politically. Unlike the Kenya Arab, they displayed no interest in securing their position through minority safeguards either under British rule or after independence. Again, their degree of indifference must reflect the extent to which they have been assimilated into the African community.

In contrast, the Indian was highly conscious of his position relative to both the European and African. Particularly sensitive to ratios of representation in the Legislative Council, to discriminatory educational and medical facilities, and to biases within the civil service, the Asian focused on these as key grievances under British administration. The only occasion on which dissatisfaction was expressed as overt protest, however, was in 1925 when a recommendation was made that all commercial accounts be kept in English to facilitate the collection of the profits tax. When the Asian community responded by closing all the shops in Dar es Salaam, the government tactfully decided to defer a further consideration of the reform.[127] On other occasions, the discontent of the Indian population has confined itself to verbal protests through official and semiofficial channels such as the Legislative Council or the Indian Association.

Although the initial organized response of the Indian community to self-government supported a policy of multiracial leadership, by the 1950's, the Indian had clearly realigned himself in support of African interests. In contrast to the European who sought in UTP a serious alternative to African dominance, the Asian Association refused to endorse the government party because it was felt that an emphasis on legislative parity would only intensify racial tensions by making them organizationally salient.

As Tanganyika approached independence, the Asian chose to stress the nation as the primary level of political identification rather than his ethnic community. "We are Tanganyikans, not Asians" was their response to suggested minority safeguards, for they perceived that the stability of their position in an independent African state would depend on their success in assimilation and in the minimization of distinctions of ethnicity or race. In part an action of political expediency, an additional impetus was found in the predominance of the Ismaili community in Tanganyika, for the late Aga Khan stressed to his followers the importance of accepting culturally and politically the country of their adoption. Even without this sectarian pressure, however, the course of action taken by the Asian community might have been anticipated, since they had survived for centuries a succession of rulers in East Africa by adjusting their goals and expectations to conform to the ideology of the governing group.

The African: A Government Definition of Mandatory Responsibility

The position of the Tanganyikan African during the British colonial period was analogous to that of the African in Uganda, for although there was little claim to equality of status, particularly in the period before World War

---

[127] Cameron, *op. cit.*, p. 136.

II, government policy in such critical areas as land and labor was committed to the protection of their interests. Elsewhere discriminations clearly existed, but these lay largely in the area of tacit restrictions against social and occupational mobility, the most effective of these being an inadequate program of education and technical training.

Although labor conditions throughout the 1920's were conspicuously inadequate, particularly on the coastal plantations, the issue was one of government indifference, not of consciously oppressive policies. Reforms were later instituted to improve living conditions and transportation facilities as the government became more engaged in the active protection of African interests, but the general position of the Tanganyika administration, even in the early phase, was to refuse to define the demands of the white settler for labor as a legitimate responsibility of either the colonial power or of the African. Rather, the labor supply was regarded as a self-regulating mechanism. If the settlers complained of a shortage of labor, it was their responsibility to institute reforms to attract the African. "There had never been a time in Tanganyika when labor difficulties and shortages could not be met by offering adequate inducement either in pay, rations (or) housing."[128] Protection against conscription for labor was always accorded the African in Tanganyika, the agricultural policy explicitly encouraged a peasant economy as an alternative to wage labor. Furthermore, where government intervention did occur, it was to secure the interest of the African through restrictions on alienation of land or to improve facilities in transport or housing, not as in Kenya, to force the African into the labor market. Though such a commitment did not extend to the point where wages were regulated, the government was careful to disassociate itself from the process of labor recruitment, particularly when it was felt to be detrimental to the African. Through informal pressures on local levels, the government was frequently able to inhibit seasonal migrations, both by encouraging cash crops and by confining recruitment to periods that did not conflict with the local agricultural schedule.[129] In consequence, a pattern of plantation labor emerged that was analogous in character to that of Uganda, both in its failure to attract local labor, and in its dependence on migrant laborers from other territories, notably Rwanda and Burundi.

On the issue of land as well, government action was committed to the protection of African interests. Recognizing that a policy of African development would be difficult to reconcile with a settler-oriented economy, restrictions were imposed early on the alienation of land to avoid possible tensions or pressures from the European community. Land alienated during the German period was made available to non-Africans by auction after World War I,

---

[128] Mitchell, *African Afterthoughts*, p. 96.

[129] Buell, *op. cit.*, p. 492.

but the British administration was clearly adverse to any further transfer of African holdings. In 1923, a year after the mandate was declared, Governor Byatt prohibited any additional excision of land in areas already subject to intensive European settlement, and, in 1930, the four provinces where penetration had been light were closed to further European occupation. The explanation given at the time was not based on economic grounds, but rather expressed concern with the preservation of "racial homogeneity."[130]

Only in the sparsely populated southern highlands was European settlement encouraged, and there conditions of alienation were again to reflect the basic commitment of the British to the African, for land was transferred only as leasehold. In addition, the conditions of transfer were highly restrictive, particularly when contrasted to the concessions available in Kenya. Although the rates were low, twenty cents to one shilling per acre, the terms of alienation provided for a maximum of a thirty-three-year lease, and this was subject to repossession without compensation after fifteen years if it was felt that the land was needed by local Africans.[131]

In addition, the political ambiguity of Tanganyika's status was not conducive to European settlement. This was to be particularly true of the period between the world wars, for there was some question as to whether the control of the territory would revert to Germany. Such uncertainty was to be a major factor in inhibiting greater English immigration, for the insecurities and disadvantages would seem even more salient to the British, since they had the option, by virtue of their citizenship, of the considerable concessions offered by Kenya.

Following World War II, the reallocation of German farms as enemy property again occurred. The postwar policy was even more rigorous, for freehold rights were extinguished and the land was reallocated on a thirty-three-year lease with option of renewal. As a consequence, by the end of 1951, of the 2,284,434 acres of alienated land, 1,333,487 were held as leasehold, and only 950,947 remained freehold.[132]

Although the total amount of land alienated in Tanganyika represented no more than 1 per cent of the total land area, there was a certain amount of hostility on the part of the African toward British policy in areas where indigenous land pressure was severe. The Chagga of the Kilimanjaro area, for example, resented the failure of the government to return enemy property to tribal claimants after World War I, particularly as many of the large tracts of land transferred to Europeans remained undeveloped or, if occupied, were badly managed.[133]

---

130 Taylor, op. cit., p. 60.

131 Mair, op. cit., p. 141.

132 Taylor, op. cit., p. 116.

133 Great Britain, East African Royal Commission Report, Comnd. 9475 (London: H.M.S.O., 1955), p. 383.

Representation as an Index of Status

In Tanganyika, as in Kenya and Uganda, the patterns of political representation in the Legislative Council were diagnostic of the government's perception of each of the three racial communities. In Tanganyika, the National Assembly was first formed in 1926 with thirteen official and ten unofficial members. Although the racial composition of the Council was not specified by legislation, the accepted practise was to allocate seven seats to Europeans and three to Asians. Although provision had been made in 1926 for the nomination of an African, none were appointed until 1945, when similar concessions were also made in Uganda and Kenya. Two more were added in the following year, while, in 1948, the number of African representatives was increased to four to give them one member more than the Asian community. In terms of potential coalition, it meant that the Asian and African, when consolidated, would have representation equal to the European who numbered seven.

However progressive a gesture this may have seemed to the British government, in 1948, the United Nations Mission felt it appropriate to express its disapproval that the African and Asian communities "together about 99.9 per cent of the total population were accorded representation only equal to that of the European community."[134] The Colonial Office reassured the Mission that they intended to increase African representation, but felt that "such progress could only come with further educational advancement."[135] Three years later, in spite of the absence of any notable acceleration of the educational program, the Committee of Constitutional Development was to advocate representational parity for each of the three major communities. The decision was essentially a compromise to avoid evaluating the relative merits of the claims of each group: "We . . . found it impossible either on a basis of numbers, of financial interests or of political maturity to make any assessment of the relative claim to representation by the three races."[136] The equation of the "financial interests" of the Indian and the "political maturity" of the European with the importance of the numerical preponderance of the African represented, however, a basic evasion of the issue. As Ronald K. Wraith observed, "it cannot continue to be said indefinitely that 25,000, 72,000 and 8,000,000 people contribute equally to the national welfare."[137]

Although the first elections in 1958 reaffirmed this principle of parity through a common roll electorate in which each constituency was represented by three members, one from each race, Julius Nyerere, as leader of

---

[134] Taylor, *op. cit.*, p. 79.

[135] *Ibid.*, p. 81.

[136] Tanganyika, *The Constitutional Debate*, p. 19.

[137] Wraith, *op. cit.*, p. 172.

TANU, was to manipulate the system in such a way that a realignment of power was to be a *fait accompli* two years before parity was officially abandoned. The decision of Nyerere to participate in the elections was one of real tactical brilliance, for, by supporting European and Asian candidates, his party was able to secure seventy of the seventy-one seats in the Legislative Council. The high proportion of both Asian and European seats that remained uncontested indicated that both communities were aware that a TANU endorsement meant almost certain victory for any non-African candidate.

A year later, the principle of parity was unequivocally abandoned, for it was then announced that a general election would be held in September 1960, in which fifty of the seventy-one seats would be open and by implication, African. Representation for members of the Asian and European communities was assured by the reservation of eleven and ten seats, respectively. A major political realignment of the racial communities was thus to occur on two levels: the principle of African dominance had been established without transitional concessions, and the representation of the Asian community was to exceed for the first time that of the European. The rejection of parity also meant that the major African party, TANU, was to emerge more explicitly as the dominant political organization.

By July 1960, when the opportunity to file nominations for candidates had closed, TANU had already achieved an overwhelming victory—fifty of their seventy-one candidates were unopposed. The distribution of these uncontested seats in terms of racial representation is of particular significance, for they included forty of the fifty "open" or African seats, all eleven of the seats reserved for the Asian, and seven of the ten European constituencies.[138] This meant, in effect, that the majority of Europeans and all segments of the Asian community had committed themselves to political expression within the context of TANU.

In several respects, the course of political development in Tanganyika assumed a character that was distinctive for East Africa. One striking feature was the rapidity with which events moved once the African acquired an organized framework for the expression of political consciousness. In contrast to Kenya and Uganda, where certain segments of the population established political pressure groups in the early 1920's, TANU, as the first formal African organization, was not founded until July 1954. Yet within five years of the formation of TANU, the basic concessions were made, and, with some irony, Tanganyika was to be the first of the East African dependencies to achieve independence.

The sudden shift of government policy to the endorsement of African leadership was the consequence of several factors. First, the African political movement in Tanganyika had a monolithic character which was not found

---

[138] Hughes, *op. cit.*, p. 85.

in Kenya or Uganda. As a consequence of the high degree of tribal fragmentation and the uniform character of colonial policy, no one tribe was to assume a position of political salience, as did the Baganda in Uganda or the Kikuyu in Kenya. Organized African activity, when it was to occur, represented rather a trans-tribal claim for status, for the leaders sought identification as Tanganyikans not as representatives of particular tribes or ethnic divisions. In this respect, it is not fortuitous that the leader of the nationalist movement, Julius Nyerere, came from a tribe that numbered only 14,000.

Since political allegiances could not be based successfully on the activation of traditional tribal loyalties, the unifying factor for African sentiment was a common identification, as Africans, with the more general economic and political needs of their community. The legitimacy of this level of identification and the solidarity of the commitment of the individual Tanganyikan to a national rather than to a tribal identity was unquestionably facilitated by the existence of a single universally spoken language, Swahili, which could unify and underline the reality of a trans-territorial community of African interests. As a consequence of these various structural considerations, notably tribal fragmentation and linguistic homogeneity, TANU was able to assume a position as spokesmen for African opinion from its inception. Negotiations with the Tanganyikan administration could thus be conducted within the framework of a single nationalist organization, providing an image of solidarity lacking in comparable movements in Kenya and Uganda.

A third factor in British receptivity to a transfer of power was the conservative character of the African demands. Although clearly committed to seeking independence as an African state, the TANU leaders were claiming no more than what had been initially stipulated to be the goal of British tutelage. In addition, their active concern with independence was modestly phrased, if one is to consider that the first organized expression of these goals, TANU, was not to occur until 1954, three years after the government had conceded the legitimacy of racial parity. Their response to periodic harassments was such to encourage British confidence, for Nyerere decided to proceed at all times by constitutional means. In contrast to Kenya and Uganda, where boycotts were staged in protest against administrative failure to accede to African claims, Nyerere thought that more could be achieved by accepting and manipulating British policy, as in the 1958 elections, even when it represented a serious compromise on nationalist aspirations.

Finally, one also feels that the *de facto* demonstration of power of the 1958 election provided an important impetus for a prompt structural acknowledgment of the African position of dominance. In Tanganyika, however, as in Kenya and Uganda, the redefinition of minority status was confined during the colonial period to the political sector. As Tanganyika approached independence, the other areas of privilege and differential treatment established under British overrule remained weighted in favor of the European and Asian communities.

CONCLUSION

If a racial minority is defined as any group that is denied full social participation on the basis of genetically acquired physical traits, then, during the colonial period, the residential communities of East Africa constituted such self-conscious and restricted groups. Only the Kenya settlers approximated a privileged segment of the population, but even they attained politically no more than the position of a highly efficient pressure group. Members of the nonofficial European community were to hold, however, an advantageous position in other respects by virtue of their common racial identification with the administrative staff, for as "Europeans" they were eligible for the social and economic privileges that adhered to that status. This fusing of the official and nonofficial communities as a high-status class within the pluralistic structure was essential to the maintenance of the colonial system, for only by according all Europeans elite status could the criteria of race provide an unambiguous principle of alignment.

It was also necessary, once these racial categories were established, to provide a legitimation for their assignment in a ranked structure. As Raymond Kennedy notes, "colonialism, like other institutionalized systems, is supported by a set of rationalizations firmly held and fiercely defended."[139] Initially based on an ideology that affirmed the cultural superiority of the European and the propriety of the extension of European patterns of government, economy, and culture to the less privileged, the numerical ratio of the British staff to the subject peoples made it essential to the maintenance of power that these initial premises of cultural superiority be transmuted into distinctions of a more suitable and enduring nature, distinctions which would inhibit the movement of the subject population into sectors regarded as the monopoly of the European. In East Africa, as in other parts of the world, the emergence of a society based on ranked racial categories was to be a primary mechanism both for controlling the aspirations of the indigenous population and for legitimating and protecting the European position of privilege.

A key to the type of colonial system that was established lies in the distribution of population between the European and African communities. At no time in any territory numbering more than 1 per cent of the population, the Europeans, in order to maintain their dominant position, required an ideology which would not only rationalize their advantageous status but would also provide a justification for the structural isolation of the majority

---

[139] Raymond Kennedy, "The Colonial Crisis and the Future," in Ralph Linton (ed.), *The Science of Man in World Crisis* (New York: Columbia University, 1945), p. 312.

of the population as a subordinate group. Although logically, several alternatives are available to minority groups in a multi-ethnic society, in this particular context, it was essential to the survival of the structure that assimilation be inhibited, for only by maintaining the non-European elements of the population as discrete and subordinate communities could the clarity of a system of ranked privilege be preserved.

The basic distribution of population in East Africa was, in this respect, eminently suited for patterns of pluralism—for several communities were distinctive culturally, religiously, and linguistically, and were conscious of their distinct traditions. In addition and perhaps more significantly, these alignments had a racial dimension as well. Race, therefore, became the diagnostic feature for defining the categories of East African society, for, while these ethnic distinctions reinforced the legitimacy of the racial criterion, their relevance could be threatened and ultimately obliterated by a process of assimilation into the cultural patterns of the dominant colonial group. In contrast, race provided a mechanism for assigning members of the society to positions of restricted privilege which could not be negated by the process of acculturation. When this was complemented by the allocation of persons of mixed parentage to the subordinate group, the invulnerability of the European position was assured.

The assignment of various segments of the population by virtue of their racial affiliation to a series of ranked social categories is not, however, sufficient. For the system to sustain itself, an ideology must develop to justify the informal and structural mechanisms that define and support the patterns of differential privilege. As Marvin Harris suggests, "What we call prejudices are merely the rationalizations which we acquire in order to prove to ourselves that the human beings we harm are not worthy of better treatment."[140] The pluralistic system must have not only discrete boundaries, but content, in the sense of an ideological validation of the isolation of certain groups and the legitimation of their exploitation or of their authority. The definition of the Asian and African communities as respectively ineligible or biologically inferior was critical to the restriction and manipulation of these groups.

The colonial system in East Africa did not, however, rely solely on the ideological legitimations of the power structure; nor, as a consequence of the small number of administrators, could physical force provide an adequate sanction for the reinforcement of their authority. Rather, support for the system of dominance was sought in the creation of certain structural constraints and in certain symbolic techniques which reinforced both the ideology of dominance and the differential status of each community.

Although all territories of East Africa were ultimately to acknowledge the primacy of African interests during the colonial period, the structure of

---

140 Marvin Harris, *Patterns of Race in the Americas* (New York: Walker and Company, 1964), p. 68.

the colonial society was such as to inhibit any realization of a position of privilege by trained African personnel. On each institutional level, either implicitly or explicitly, the African was segregated for differential treatment, often with the implication of restricted participation. Though certain discriminatory regulations, particularly those relating to land and the marketing of produce, were defined as protective, they were based on the need to constrict the role of the African in East African society. More often, however, the institutionalized framework served to assign the African to a subordinate political and economic position.

In the political sector, for example, the representational patterns in the Legislative Council heightened the sensitivity of the African (or for that matter, of the Asian or European) to the relevance of race as a primary means of political identification. The indirect representation of the African by European missionaries until the mid-forties and the token representation thereafter until the major reforms of the late 1950's, clearly demonstrated the marginality of African participation. Africans did assume an active role in the administration of local government under the supervision of British district officers, but this level of responsibility in no way implied an intrusion into the central power structure, for the upper echelons of the civil service were the monopoly of the British administrator.

The policy toward the African in the economic sector also reinforced his low status in the pluralistic structure and his importance as an unskilled labor force. Occupationally, racial restrictions existed to deny access to positions of prestige or power to both the African and Asian, while differential pay scales reinforced the marginal position of both communities. Where middle-class occupations were made available to the African, they involved exclusively African facilities, such as churches, schools, or local administrative offices, and did not, in consequence, result in an encroachment of African personnel into positions of more generalized authority.

In Kenya, the restricted position of the African as a labor force was predictably more explicit. Access to land was limited to force the African into the labor market, the *kipande* (registration certificate) system imposed serious restrictions on his movements, and financial autonomy through cash crops was inhibited by various legislative restrictions. In all territories, however, the labor policies served to legitimate the very situation they had created, for, by denying the African of a serious system of incentives, they produced an inefficient, apathetic labor force which supported the European claims of inherent inferiority or incompetence.

The educational policy was again an important factor in ensuring the stability of the colonial structure. Although official expectations were ultimately of self-rule and it was felt that "proper training" was an essential precondition for the transfer of power, the educational policy did little to effect any such state. Discrimination on this level also provided tacit restrictions inhibiting social or occupational mobility by creating barriers of training or language for most Africans. The quality of instruction, the materials available, the failure to use English as the language of instruction until the secondary schools, and the proportionately far greater burden for the African family of school fees, boarding, and transportation expenses, all served to make advanced education an elite experience that only a small percentage of the young men of each generation could attain. It is not clear how conscious an inhibitory policy this was in East Africa, although certainly the implications of such an educational scheme were comprehended by the colonial authorities. Moreover, as Brewton Berry notes, "financial reasons are commonly offered as the excuse, although other social services, such as agriculture, veterinary, and public health programs, often receive a fair degree of support."[141]

The judicial system was to provide a final area of formal institutionalized constraints for the African community. Although race was not relevant in much of the East African legislation, certain laws were specifically drafted to define the prerogatives of the African. The registration, detention, and land laws of Kenya, or ordinances pertaining to liquor or firearms, were examples of restrictive legislation; whereas, the employment, marketing, and credit ordinances were designed to protect the African. In both cases, however, the applicability of the legislation was determined by race, for Europeans and Asians were not subject to such controls.

The structure of the court system was also explicitly delineated along racial lines, for jurisdiction was restricted in the lower courts to members of the African community. In addition to being denied jurisdiction over "non-natives" in all three territories, these lower courts also lacked the power to summon non-Africans as witnesses. The Kenya Criminal Procedure Code also required that Europeans charged with certain fairly serious offenses have trial by the Supreme Court with a jury of Europeans. In the lower courts of the central system in Kenya, all male residents "other than Baluchis and Africans" were also liable to serve as assessors. Racial distinctions in the legal system also operated on a more informal level, for a differential application of the Penal Code arose by convention. Though the Penal Code might be enforced with maximum effect against the African, charges would normally be reduced if a European were involved so that fines rather than imprisonment could be administered if convictions were necessary.

In addition to these formal institutionalized methods of defining and manipulating the three communities, certain informal constraints also functioned to delineate each racial group and to increase the sensitivity of each community to its specific interests. Traditions of social exclusiveness and the basic disparity of experience and expectations were in themselves important factors in reinforcing the self-consciousness of each group. Where interracial

---

[141] Brewton Berry, *Race and Ethnic Relations* (Boston: Houghton Mifflin, 1951), p. 434.

contact was required, particularly in situations demanding a certain degree of intimacy, the differential status of the individuals involved and the etiquette that arose to symbolize disparities in rank were sufficient to maintain patterns of social if not physical distance.

The salience of these distinctions of race and their clear implications of ranked status also provided an important mechanism of control, for both the Asian and European communities saw that their position was numerically insecure and subject to the potential threat of the African. These sentiments of anxiety, strengthened by the respective aggressions of the subordinate Asian and African groups, served to reinforce the isolation of each community within the pluralistic structure.

As the elite group, the Europeans were primarily concerned with maintaining a position of social distance, whether through formal or informal mechanisms, which would isolate them from both the Asian and African communities. The Indians, in contrast, defined by all groups as of an intermediate status, were more sensitive to their position in relation to the African, for their concern was largely with the entrenchment rather than with the extension of existing distinctions of privilege. In certain respects, their isolation from the European community was voluntary, for they wished to preserve their cultural identity and were by predilection a series of closely knit, endogamous, sectarian communities. If they pressed any claim against the European position, it was for equal status as a distinct segment of society, not for assimilation.

It was in regard to the African that serious tensions were to arise, for the Asian as well as the European had a vested interest in maintaining both the stereotype and the depressed status of the African. Many also felt that the African was in fact inferior culturally and intellectually and that his position in the colonial hierarchy was both natural and inevitable. Such attitudes would be reinforced by the normal patterns of interaction between Asian and African, for the Asian was generally in a position of authority as shopkeeper, master, or government clerk. There can be little doubt that initially the aggression exhibited in these contexts was a deflected response to their subordinate status vis-à-vis the European; but when the British, to preserve their own sectors of privilege, channeled African discontent into occupations which were traditionally the domain of the Asian, the threat of African encroachment became a more important impetus for Asian prejudice.

The African, with an unambiguously subordinate position in the colonial structure, had little option, short of rebellion or withdrawal, but to accept the colonial definition of his role in East African society. One major consequence of British policy was the emergence of a new level of identification for the African which superseded traditional tribal loyalties, for race, not tribe, was to be the primary determinant of status.

Within this framework, there was opportunity for covert aggression against both the European and Asian communities. Aggressive feelings toward the former were manifested in economic inefficiency and unreliability, in the petty thievery of the house servant, and in the malicious discussion or uncomplimentary nicknames bestowed on local Europeans. Deflection of hostility to a less powerful group, the Asian, also provided an important outlet for African discontent, for it could easily be legitimated by the discriminatory attitudes of the Asians and their favored economic position.

These tensions between communities, although the inevitable product of the ranked structure, were also to serve as an important factor in the maintenance of colonial control. The British, by reinforcing the distinct identity of each minority group, encouraged a sensitivity in the Asian and African of their disparate and competitive interests and of their subordinate position in the colonial structure. Divide and rule is, after all, as old as the very idea of Empire. It was only with the imminence of independence in the late 1950's and the inevitability of African political dominance that the British rejected the ideology which supported the existing pluralistic structure and affirmed, for an independent East Africa, the morality of democratic integration.

SELECTED BIBLIOGRAPHY

Apter, David E. *The Political Kingdom in Uganda.* Princeton: Princeton University Press, 1961.

Buell, Raymond L. *The Native Problem in Africa.* Vol. I. New York: The Macmillan Company, 1928.

Cameron, Sir Donald. *My Tanganyika Service and Some Nigeria.* London: Allen and Unwin, 1939.

Church, Archibald. *East Africa, A New Dominion.* London: H. F. and G. Witheby, 1927.

Cranworth, Lord. *Profit and Sport in British East Africa.* London: Macmillan & Company, 1919.

Datta, Ansu Kumar. *Tanganyika: A Government in a Plural Society.* University of Leiden, 1955.

Delf, George. *Asians in East Africa.* London: Oxford University Press, 1963.

———. *Jomo Kenyatta.* London: Victor Gollancz, 1961.

Dilley, Marjorie R. *British Policy in Kenya Colony.* New York: Thomas Nelson and Sons, 1947.

Eliot, Sir Charles. *The East Africa Protectorate.* London: Edward Arnold, 1905.

Fallers, Lloyd A. *The King's Men.* London: Oxford University Press, 1964.

Farson, Negley. *Last Chance in Africa.* New York: Harcourt and Brace, 1950.

Hollingsworth, Lawrence W. *The Asians of East Africa.* London: Macmillan & Company, 1960.

Hughes, A. J. *East Africa: The Search for Unity*. Baltimore: Penguin Books, 1963.

Huxley, Elspeth. *White Man's Country*. London: Chatto and Windus, 1935.

————, and Margery Perham. *Race and Politics in Kenya*. London: Faber and Faber, 1944.

Huxley, Julian. *Africa View*. London: Chatto and Windus, 1931.

Ingham, Kenneth. *A History of East Africa*. New York: Frederick A. Praeger, 1962.

————. *The Making of Modern Uganda*. London: Allen and Unwin, 1958.

Leys, Norman. *Kenya*. London: Hogarth Press, 1925.

Mair, Lucy P. *Native Policies in Africa*. London: George Routledge and Sons, 1936.

Mitchell, Sir Philip. *African Afterthoughts*. London: Hutchinson, 1954.

Morris, Stephen. "Indians in East Africa: A Study in Plural Society," *British Journal of Sociology*, VII (1956), 194–211.

Rawcliffe, D. H. *The Struggle for Kenya*. London: Victor Gollancz, 1954.

Rosberg, Carl G., Jr. "Political Conflict and Change in Kenya," in Gwendolyn M. Carter and William O. Brown, *Transition in Africa: Studies in Political Adaptation*. Boston: Boston University Press, 1958.

Shepherd, George W., Jr. *They Wait in Darkness*. New York: John Day and Company, 1955.

Stahl, Kathleen M. *Tanganyika Sail in the Wilderness*. The Hague: Mouton and Company, 1961.

Wood, Susan. *Kenya: The Tensions of Progress*. London: Oxford University Press, 1962.

I wish to acknowledge with gratitude the support of the Social Science Research Council during my two periods of field work in Uganda and of the National Institutes of Health during the period in which this manuscript was written.

I am also deeply indebted to Dr. Lucy Mair and Dr. John Middleton for their valuable comments on earlier versions of this manuscript.

PART II

THE EMERGING NATIONS

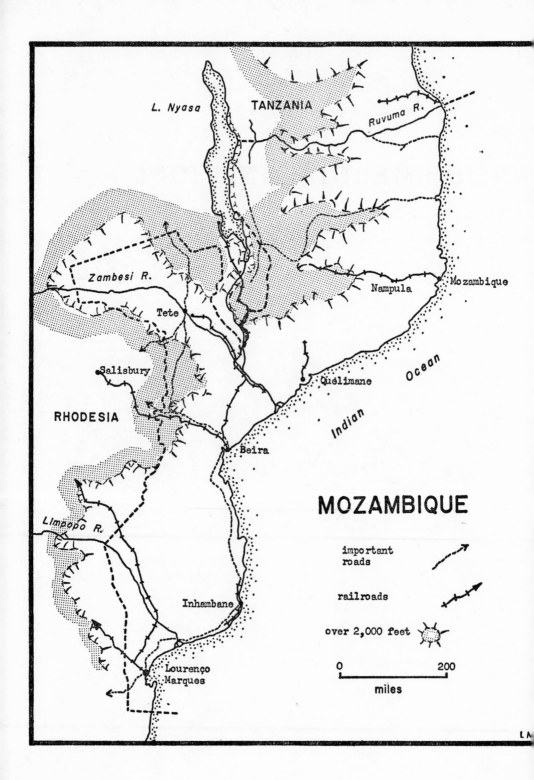

L. Nyasa

TANZANIA

Ruvuma R.

Zambesi R.

Tete

Nampula

Mozambique

Salisbury

Quélimane

Ocean

RHODESIA

Indian

Beira

MOZAMBIQUE

Limpopo R.

important
roads

railroads

Inhambane

over 2,000 feet

0   200

Lourenço
Marques

miles

4

Race, Conflict, and Reform
in Mozambique

Marvin Harris

I ATTEMPT HERE TO DESCRIBE the trajectory of race relations in Mozambique since the publication of my 1958 study, *Portugal's
African Wards*. Although the documentation for the conclusions reached in
that work consisted mostly of written sources, the general frame of analysis
was the product of fieldwork in southern Mozambique for the year June
1956 to June 1957. Fear of reprisal against my informants and the threat
of eviction by the Governor-General prevented me from gathering the kind
of systematic data which is accessible in more democratic political milieus.[1]
Social distance and social ranking tests, overt interviews, and statistically
valid opinion surveys could not then be used to help illuminate the nature of
race relations in Mozambique, nor can they be used now. The present review
suffers from an even greater handicap, for it has not been possible for me to
return to Mozambique since my departure seven years ago. Moreover, no
additional race-relations studies involving prolonged and intimate contact
by reasonably disinterested observers have been carried out by anyone else,
even on an impressionistic basis. Especially lacking are reliable first-hand
accounts of what has happened in Mozambique since the Angola uprising.
Portuguese East Africa continues to be, sociologically, one of the most
poorly known areas in Africa. This circumstance constitutes probably as
much of a threat to Portuguese sovereignty as the guerrillas who have
brought the independence movement to its fighting phase. If the Angolan
revolution demonstrated any truth about the character of the Portuguese

---

[1] In March 1956, then Governor-General Teixeira called me to his office and informed
me that I had violated the hospitality that his government extended to me. He
informed me that I had been asking questions which were none of my business and
that if I persisted I would be asked to leave the country.

157

colonialism, it is that no colonial system was ever based on a greater degree of self-deception and misinformation.[2]

Despite the lack of data about recent trends in Portuguese-African relations, much potentially enlightening evidence of an indirect sort is available for interpretation. Within the limits set by the nature of this material, a number of fairly probable conclusions can be reached concerning the past, present, and future of race relations in Mozambique.

RACE RELATIONS AS OF 1958

In 1958 the principal features of race relations in Mozambique appeared to me as follows:

Since the beginning of the century, the pattern of intergroup relations in Mozambique had been governed by a series of laws and decrees which constituted the administrative and juridical regimen known as the *Indigenato*. Under the *Indigenato*, 99 per cent of Mozambique's African population was legally designated as "natives," a status equivalent to that of a minor or ward. This status was established by a typical racial rule of descent, whose most recent version was stated in the *Estatuto Indígena das Províncias de Guiné, Angola, e Moçambique* of May 1954: "Individuals of the Negro race or their descendants who were born or habitually reside in the said Province and who do not yet possess the learning and the social and individual habits presupposed for the public and private law of Portuguese citizens are considered to be *indígenas*.[3]

To be an *indígena* was to be legally without citizenship and effectively without civil rights. *Indígenas* were subject to an elaborate complex of administrative procedures and controls that limited their freedom of movement; froze them to menial professions and minimum wages; relegated them to separate and inferior schools taught in a foreign language; exposed them to arbitrary beatings, to life-long banishment in penal colonies, and to forced labor on plantations, roads, railroads and docks. *Indígenas* had to carry a passbook, could not leave their district without specific authorization, and were confined in urban centers to their houses after 9:00 P.M. *Indígenas* could neither slaughter cattle, sell crops, nor buy machinery—anything from a power saw to an automobile—without official permission. They could establish bank accounts, but were permitted to withdraw their money only

---

[2] A somewhat poignant admission of this fact was contained in Adriano Moreira's 1961 address to the Lourenço Marques Municipal Council. Noting that hitherto genuine knowledge about African culture had been acquired only by lonely "autodidacts," he suggested that all those who tried to obtain exact knowledge of the past and present of African ethnic groups should be encouraged. It should be pointed out, however, that Portuguese Guinea is far more advanced as a center of ethnographic studies than either Angola or Mozambique.

[3] Marvin Harris, *Portugal's African Wards* (New York: American Committee on Africa, 1958), p. 7.

with special authorization. All legacies were subject to administration by public officials.

According to the Native Servant's Regulation, an *indígena* who was a household servant "must obey orders . . . zealously watch over his master's property . . . never leave the house without permission . . . and have the maximum respect for his master and the people who live with him."[4] This legally enshrined demand for respect was habitually extended to all contacts between whites and *indígenas,* whether legally defined or not. Africans in general, but especially *indígenas,* were expected to remain standing in the presence of whites; they were never addressed as *senhor,* but rather by their first names, and any display of impudence might lead to serious punishment. Signs declaring "The Right of Admission Is Reserved" barred *indígenas* from white hotels and restaurants; and administrative decree preserved the modern urban residential areas for exclusive white occupancy. By various *de facto* arrangements, *indígenas* were assigned separate sections at public stadiums and were confined to special movie houses which exhibited only specially censored films.

As a result of laws which in effect defined subsistence farming as vagrancy, approximately 400,000 Mozambique Africans were left with no choice but to seek employment as contract laborers in the mines and farms of the neighboring English-speaking territories. Approximately 100,000 *indígenas* from southern Mozambique were caught by their administrators and puppet chieftains and were turned over to European enterprises to become *shibalos* (the African's word for forced laborer). In the north, over 1,000,000 *indígenas* were subjected to the compulsory cotton-planting campaign, whereby African farmers were obliged to substitute cotton for subsistence crops for the benefit of monopolistic concessionaires who lost nothing if the cotton failed to grow, while the Africans starved by the thousands.

Portuguese spokesmen defended these discriminatory and exploitative practices by asserting that the status of *indígena* was not racial but cultural. They denied that the result of the *Indigenato* was the equivalent of a color bar. Following the lead offered by Brazilian sociologists, Gilberto Freyre's theory of the luso-tropical man, Portugal was alleged to be uniquely competent to lead the world toward racial democracy.[5] The intent and the effect of the *Indigenato,* it was repeatedly alleged, was to protect the Africans while they were conducted by gradual degrees toward Christian grace and Portuguese civilization. It was maintained that the Portuguese had no racial prejudices, and much was made of the provision in the *Estatuto Indígena*

---

[4] *Ibid.,* p. 11.

[5] Gilberto Freyre, *The Portuguese and the Tropics* (Lisbon, Port.: Executive Committee for the Commemoration of the Vth Centenary of the Death of Prince Henry the Navigator, 1961), and Gilberto Freyre, *Um Brasileiro em Terras Portuguesas* (Lisbon, Port.: Edicão Livros do Brazil, 1952). For a refutation of Freyre's theories on Brasil see Charles Boxer, *Race Relations in the Portuguese Colonial Empire, 1415–1825* (Oxford, Eng.: Clarendon Press, 1963) and Harris, *op. cit.*

for "assimilation," a process by which properly qualified Negroes could become "citizens." But this argument made little sense in Mozambique where, as late as 1960, only 10,000 out of 6,000,000 Africans had been permitted to change their legal identity. Moreover, the definition of *indígena* had another side to it. Although it is true that membership in the "civilized" group was for Negroes dependent partially on socioeconomic status and partially on descent, membership in the civilized group for whites depended exclusively on descent. Thus all Portuguese immigrants, no matter how illiterate or ignorant, were automatically assumed to be "civilized" and never came under the jurisdiction of the *Indigenato*. It was clear, in other words, that despite the official verbal denial of racial discrimination, the *Indigenato* was merely one of the varieties of southern Africa's systems of *apartheid*. The arbitrary beatings, the discriminatory wages, the forced labor, the curfews, the passbooks, the compulsory crops, the separate and unequal educational system, and the exercise of arbitrary justice left little room for any other conclusion.

Despite the mounting chorus of disapproval in the United Nations, the carefully documented corroborative testimony of James Duffy,[6] and the spread of African nationalism to adjoining territories, the Portuguese, led by Salazar, persisted in talking and acting as if the *Indigenato* was a benevolent and viable policy right up to the outbreak of the Angolan war. In the words of Castro Fernandes, President of the Executive Committee of the União Nacional (Portugal's only effective political party):

> In those primitive peoples, wholly given up to superstitions from the night of time with their atavism and ingenious cruelty, we saw brothers to be converted, souls to be saved, God's creatures that it was necessary to educate and to bring to the real dignity of man. Soon we began to feel affection for those to whom we had brought a higher, nobler life, to whom we revealed the value of peace and security, the virtues of authority and order. We became attached to them because of what we had done for them, the new prospects we opened up for them, the justice we taught them and also because we were the instruments of God to lead our black brothers out of moral chaos and to kindle in them that spark of the Spirit which has transfigured them.
>
> Our own way of life, the informal element in our temperament, a certain gift for relations which open the gates of our close friendship where others remain shut, our incapacity to measure and dole out our affection, and, above all, our complete lack of any racial concept have all contributed to link settlers and natives closely, to lead them to become allies and to mingle, even without crossbreeding, just because as whites we did not treat the Blacks humanely but because they found with us a family atmosphere . . .[7]

On March 15, 1961, the Africans in Angola replied to this bombast with the greatest massacre of whites in the history of Africa south of the Sahara.

---

[6] James Duffy, *Portuguese Africa* (Cambridge, Mass.: Harvard University Press, 1959).

[7] Castro Fernandes, "The Presence of Portugal in Africa," *Portugal,* IV (1960), 259

Within a short time over 1,000 Europeans, many of them women and children, were sliced and hacked to death.[8] Many of the dead Europeans were undoubtedly the counterparts of the Mozambican white settlers about whom I had observed in 1958 that they

> delude themselves into believing that the *indígena* likes the way he is treated, that he likes the Portuguese better than other whites, and that the high level of civil order . . . is proof of the amicable relations between white and African. All of the evidence, however, points in the opposite direction . . .[9]

Writing of the events of March 15, 1961, Len E. Addicott has remarked: "To many Portuguese, the happenings of that day were sudden and inexplicable. Weeks later they were asking over and over in shocked bewilderment, 'How could *our* Africans do this to us?' "[10] After this shock and disbelief, this sudden revelation of false premises and illusory security, vengeance was sought. The Portuguese civilizers proceeded to retaliate with the random massacre of some 30,000 of their African wards, including few, if any, of the originators of the attack. In Luanda, Africans were chased by screaming mobs, lynched, and thrown out of windows. In the countryside, village chiefs were killed and their heads stuck on poles, women and children were lured into ambush, and whole villages bombed and burned.[11] In the space of two short months,

> race relations passed from the paternalistic and accommodating phase into that of reciprocal genocidal war. . . . The Portuguese Army, under the command of the most rabid of the Fascist wing, engaged in an emotional campaign of retaliation, releasing on the defenseless peoples, the fury of their exalted ultranationalism. . . . Unused to this type of warfare, Portuguese soldiers in areas known to be occupied by rebels ruthlessly eliminated every African they spotted. . . . Troops went forth from village to village burning huts and slaying the innocent at random.[12]

It was in this tragic manner that the final bankruptcy of the *Indigenato* was announced to the world. The Portuguese government, has of course, never directly acknowledged that Galvão (1962), Davidson (1956), Duffy (1959), Figueiredo (1961) and many other critics had been, after all, fundamentally correct and its own defenders fundamentally wrong in their assessment of the extent to which the Africans accepted the Portuguese as

---

[8] James Duffy, *Portugal in Africa* (Cambridge, Mass.: Harvard University Press, 1962), p. 222, and Antonio Figueiredo, *Portugal and Its Empire: the Truth* (London, Eng.: V. Gollancz, 1961), p. 133.

[9] Harris, *op. cit.*, p. 35.

[10] Len E. Addicott, *Cry Angola* (London, Eng.: Student Christian Movement Press, 1962), p. 9.

[11] *Ibid.*, p. 33.

[12] Figueiredo, *op. cit.*, p. 133.

their benevolent masters. On the contrary, everything was officially blamed on foreign agitators and witch doctors who had poisoned the minds of the simple, happy *indígenas* with nationalism and racial hatred.

CONFLICT AND REFORM

Nevertheless, there can be no equivocation about the failure of the *Indigenato*. The Portuguese government has, in fact, all but proclaimed it in its recent legislation: for during the past five years almost the entire overt legal superstructure of the *Indigenato* has been repealed. This sweeping reform of colonial policy was in large part the work of Adriano Moreira, whose reputation for "liberalism" at the Advanced Institute for Overseas Studies earned him the post of Overseas Minister during the first years of the Angolan crisis.

It would not be correct, however, to associate the abolition of the *Indigenato* exclusively with the challenge of the Angolan War. Before the rebellion had begun, Moreira and other relatively enlightened elements in the Portuguese government had pushed for reforms. In particular, the new labor legislation has its origins in the late 1950's, especially with Portugal's belated acceptance of several important international labor agreements. Thus, in 1959 Portugal signed both the Internation Labor Convention of 1955 which provides for the abolition of penal sanctions in the enforcement of labor contracts and the Abolition of Forced Labor Convention of 1957.[13]

During 1960, the Overseas Ministry sought to bring existing administrative procedures into line with the terms of these conventions. In June of that year, by Decree 43,039, it repealed some of the most controversial sections of the 1928 Native Labor Code, including sections 351–355 and 359 which had conferred severe punitive powers on recruiters and administrative officials in order to prevent *indígenas* from breaking their labor contracts. In October 1960, the provincial government of Mozambique responded with a revision of the previously mentioned Native Servants Regulation. Even before this, in November 1959, the Mozambique Director of Public Works, anticipating ministerial instructions, promulgated a decision reversing the policy whereby administrative officials had acted directly to recruit forced laborers for public works. The provincial government went on, in 1960, to raise the minimum wage for unskilled contract workers, thereby stimulating the supply of free labor and correspondingly diminishing the need for *shibalos*.

It seems probable that these changes were intended to presage the eventual demise of the *Indigenato*. By the end of the last decade, the hoax of the *assimilado* system had been thoroughly exposed among Portugal's allies; it

---

[13] International Labor Organization, *Report of the Commission to Examine the Complaint Filed by the Government of Ghana Concerning the Observance by the Government of Portugal of the Abolition of Forced Labor Convention, 1957* (Geneva, Switz.: International Labor Office, 1962), pp. 94–95.

was of little use to argue in the United Nations that the handful of *assimilados* in Mozambique demonstrated the sincerity and effectiveness of Portugal's "civilizing mission." Even as early as 1957, this writer had taken part in discussions in Lourenço Marques, where it had been predicted that the *Indigenato* would soon be repealed to cut off foreign criticism. The effect of the Angolan crisis, if anything, was to hasten the Overseas Ministry along the path which it had taken at the signing of the Labor Convention. The war merely provided a good occasion for terminating the old system. As a result of the crisis, Portuguese settlers in both Mozambique and Angola were suddenly confronted with a situation which required them to draw closer to Lisbon, while at the same time military reinforcements were available for keeping not only the Africans but the anti-metropolitan settlers under control.

Thus, the 1961 decrees abolishing the legal basis for the concession system of compulsory cotton, rice, and castor bean planting and the decree establishing labor-inspection services were continuous with the labor legislation of the prewar years. All of these labor reforms were backed up in 1962 by a new Rural Labor Code (Decree 44,309, April 2). In the meantime, Moreira had succeeded, on September 6, 1961, in revoking the 1954 *Estatuto de Indígenas*. Henceforth, there was to be no legal distinction between natives and non-natives as far as political privileges were concerned. Since 1961, all native-born inhabitants of Angola and Mozambique have been Portuguese citizens, regardless of their ancestry.

Zealous protestations of good will toward the African population and a redoubled emphasis on the absence of color consciousness have accompanied these legislative innovations. In announcing the removal of central government support of the compulsory crop programs in a speech to the Mozambique Legislative Council, Moreira boldly called for economic sacrifices in order to defend the nation against its enemies. "Our policy which is binding on all, must be a permanent conquest of souls, a day-to-day demonstration of our will to help all racial groups."[14] In the preamble to the new rural labor code, the language of reform attained exalted heights.

All distinction between ethnic or cultural groups ceases to be made, and every worker, whatever the nature of his culture, has to comply with one sole kind of Law; no penal sanctions are prescribed for a [sic] workers who break their contracts; there is no longer any sort of paternalistic guardianship of workers; the Authorities do not intervene in the drawing up of work contracts; no discrimination is permitted between men and women as regards such contracts, save for the special rights the latter possess through the nature of their sex. It is hoped that once freedom and appropriate remuneration of work are assured, together with the best possible working conditions and social security, the workers will spontaneously seek employment; that the economy will prosper; that national income will increase; and that mutual trust and

---

[14] Adriano Moreira, "Velada de Armas," *Boletim Geral do Ultramar*, XXXVII (1961), 15–31.

understanding will reign between employers and employees. It is incumbent upon the State to inspect, to guide and to redress; to defend the law and guarantee Justice for all on equal terms.[15]

With Moreira's dismissal from the post of Overseas Minister in 1962 and his replacement by Antonio Augusto Peixoto, the policy of legal reform did not terminate. In 1963, a new Overseas Organic Law providing for greater provincial autonomy was instituted. One of Moreira's most significant proposals had involved the establishment of a university in Angola and another in Mozambique. The latter began to function on a limited basis in 1963 with 280 pupils taking courses in engineering, agriculture, veterinary science, and education.[16] These innovations, of course, cannot be properly assessed until the ratio between white and African students is published. According to FRELIMO sources in early 1965, only three or four Africans were attending the university in Mozambique.

Changes introduced in February 1964 have altered the three-year pre-primary rudimentary school requirement for *indígenas*. Provided he speaks Portuguese, it will now be possible for an African to begin his primary education in the regular first grade. In addition, for the first time, primary education for all children between six and twelve years of age has now become obligatory.[17] Finally, early in 1964, new legislation re-organizing the Overseas Health Services was announced, marking the first changes in this sector since 1945. Under the new plan, an ambitious development of hospitals, sanitary posts, health centers, maternity posts, and mobile units is envisaged.

It is impossible to dismiss the legal reforms that have been introduced in Mozambique since 1957 as if they were merely designed to quiet criticism without creating any real substantive changes in the status of the African minority. On the other hand, it would be equally incorrect to suppose that the mere promulgation of laws in Lisbon, by itself, fundamentally altered the racial situation in the colonies. In many respects, the abolition of the *Indigenato* invites comparison with the recent history of civil rights legislation and anti-segregation court decisions in the United States. These laws and decisions cannot by themselves compel an end to segregation, but they certainly do modify the context of behavior and bring actual changes closer to reality. In this analogy, the Lisbon government stands to its overseas provinces as Washington stands to Alabama or Mississippi. Even with the best of intentions, it cannot, without risk of insubordination by the whites,

---

[15] Adriano Moreira, "Betrayed Generation," *Boletim Geral do Ultramar*, XXXVIII (1962), 237.

[16] United Nations, *Working Paper of the Special Committee on the Situation with Regard to the Implementation of the Declaration on the Granting of Independence to the Colonial Countries and Peoples,* A/AC. 109/–126) (New York: United Nations, 1964), p. 34.

[17] *Ibid.,* p. 32.

abruptly change the traditional pattern of interracial accommodation. The question of the movement in both cases, therefore, is to determine the scope and pace of the actual changes which Moreira's reforms have produced. It is at this point that the analogy breaks down; reliable sources of information are abundantly available about the United States South, while events in Mozambique take place behind one of the world's more effective communication curtains.[18]

In order properly to interpret the significance of the repeal of the *Estatuto Indígena* and the other reforms, it should be noted, first of all, that the entire structure of "native" administration has been left intact. Under the new Overseas Organic Law, Mozambique and Angola remain divided into districts headed by district governors appointed by the provincial Governor-General, who is in turn an appointee of the Overseas Minister (and who is in turn an appointee of Salazar). The overseas provinces continue to be further distinguished from the metropolitan provinces by the fact that two kinds of local administrative units are found within the districts. On the one hand, there are the *concelhos* which are modeled after the metropolitan municipalities and are normally subdivided into *frequesías* (literally parishes, but actually a civil-religious unit). Such *concelhos* correspond to all heavily urbanized settlements and hence, by virtue of Mozambique and Angola's racial demography, to all communities containing a high percentage of white inhabitants. On the other hand, there are the *circunscricoës*. These are normally subdivided, not into parishes, but into traditional *regidorías,* or chiefdoms, under the care of a traditional African *regedor* or chieftain. The latter carries out the "functions delegated to him 'by his administrative su-superiors.' "[19] These superiors are none other than the familiar, invariably white, *administradores* and *chefes do pôsto.* Of very great significance is the provision that "parishes" rather than "chieftains" may sometimes be constituted wherever "groups of families developing a common social activity" are to be found.[20] This means that, in rural areas with appreciable white populations, the way remains open for the whites to maintain their own local political integrity without danger of subordination to African officials. By the same token, Decree 43,896 of September 6, 1961, provides that where "agglomerations of populations" come into existence which neither constitute traditional *regedorías* nor *frequesías,* the authorities may appoint *regedores.*[21] In other words, the provincial government can create artificial

---

[18] Even more than in Portugal, all media of communication in Mozambique are subject to heavy censorship. Thus, riots in Porto Amelia in 1960 are persistently rumored to have led to the death of some 500 Africans (James Skinner, "Portuguese Rule Is Harsh in Mozambique," New York *Herald Tribune,* February 8, 1961). Yet there were no press reports on the incident. Since the Angolan War, precautions against adverse publicity have been intensified.

[19] United Nations, *Working Paper* . . . , p. 16.

[20] *Ibid.,* p. 17.

[21] *Loc. cit.*

chiefdoms wherever there are a sufficient number of Africans to warrant special administrative measures. This provision supplies the key to the continued control of the urban African. In 1957, it was precisely by the maintenance of artificial urban chiefdoms that the notorious Feraz de Freitas, *adminis- trador* of Lourenço Marques, his *chefes do pôsto,* and puppet urban African chiefs maintained their iron-handed discipline over Lourenço Marques' 100,000 Africans. Nothing in the recent reforms seems to have altered this situation.

Despite the expanded provisions for local self-government in the new Overseas Organic Law, the political effectiveness of the African mass remains close to zero. The repeal of the *Estatuto Indígena,* whereby Africans had been refused "political rights with respect to non-indigenous institu- tions," has not been accompanied by any noticeable expansion of African suffrage. Literacy requirements, property ownership, and property tax quali- fications continue to bar the mass of Africans from voting for representatives to the provincial legislative councils and the National Assembly.[22] Moreover, since the great majority of Africans continue to reside in *regedorías* rather than parishes, their eligibility for suffrage in municipal-level elections re- mains rather academic. According to the report of the U.N. Special Com- mittee on the Implementation of the Declaration on the Granting of In- dependence to Colonial Countries and Peoples,

> . . . Neither the 1963 Overseas Organic Law nor the new political and administrative statutes of the territories have made any substantial changes in the dual form of local administration existing in Angola, Mozambique and Portuguese Guinea, which in 1962 led the Special Committee on Territories under Portuguese Administration to observe that "the great majority of the African population living in rural areas continue to be ruled as before by ad- ministrators approved by Portuguese authorities; their actual participation in the conduct of their own affairs remains limited."[23]

It would thus appear that each *administrador* continues to have well-nigh absolute authority over the affairs of tens of thousands of Africans. These appointed officials not only control the local constabulary, act as justice of the peace, tax collector, and district attorney, but they also command the African chiefs and headmen by their control over salaries and their power of appointment and dismissal. Although by Decree 43,898, September 6, 1961, provisions are made to reduce the magisterial authority of the *ad- ministradores,* the projected court system remains a paper façade. As the Special Committee on Territories under Portuguese Administration observed, "The committee has no indication that judges have been appointed to all the

---

[22] *Ibid.,* pp. 18–21. One must bear in mind that the provincial legislative council is itself a severely restricted body whose decisions are subject to the Governor-General's veto. The National Assembly is in turn subject to the control of the Portuguese dictator.

[23] *Ibid.,* p. 18.

courts established and it appears that there is no change in the wide powers of the administrators and *chefes de posto* over the lives of the indigenous inhabitants."[24]

The significance of this state of affairs arises from the fact that in 1957 the abuse of African labor, miscarriages of justice, arbitrary punishment, and throttling of economic incentive were products, not of any specific piece of legislation, but rather of the immense discretionary and interpretive authority which the system ceded to the *administradores* and *chefes de posto*. Forced labor, for example, except for criminals, had been illegal in Mozambique since the beginning of the century, yet that did not prevent the *administradores* from rounding up 100,000 *shibalos* per year. The *administradores* have always been charged with the duty of protecting the African's economic and social well-being, but the nature of the administrative system was such that *administradores* and white settlers connived in a thousand, sometimes subtle and sometimes blatant, ways to achieve the opposite effect. The abolition of the *Estatuto Indígena* does not affect these administrative powers, nor does it adequately combat the opportunities for connivance between administrators and white settlers.

In this connection, it should be pointed out that, in addition to the virtual maintenance of one set of local political institutions for the Africans and another for whites, most Africans and whites continue to possess different legal personalities. Although the population of Mozambique is no longer officially divided into civilized and "native" groupings, there remains the distinction between those Africans who have opted for being governed by written civil law as opposed to those who chose to remain under unwritten local customary law. By Article 5 of the Legal Reform Decree Law 43,897, September 6, 1961, written civil law is declared to obtain in all political divisions other than the *regedorías,* (i.e., rural and urban African neighborhoods). But provision has been made for those who reside within such *regedorías* to opt for ordinary civil law at any time by a "simple but irrevocable declaration" made before the administrator. In addition, Article 6 provides that "the act of marriage in the Catholic Church confers with it, upon appropriate entry being made in public records, the right to be governed by civil law." How many of Mozambique's Africans have opted for the Portuguese civil code is not known: presumably, all of the 10,000 *assimilados* automatically come under the written law; but, it is probable that 99 per cent of the African population is still governed by customary law. The significance of this fact is that no codification of the African customary law has ever been made, leaving it up to the *administrador* and his puppet African advisors to draw conclusions about its substance. From the ambiguities of customary law, there thus emanates an additional source of arbitrary power, unforeseen and unchecked by the recent reforms. Of course, the

---

[24] United Nations, *Report of the Special Committee on Territories under Portuguese Administration* (A/5160/Add 1 and 2) (New York, 1962), p. 135.

African who feels that the Portuguese *administrador* is not a fair judge of customary law could in theory choose the regular civil code. This, however, assumes that the African (1) knows about the options, (2) has an administrator who is willing to let him exercise it, (3) can obtain impartial legal counsel in pressing his civil and criminal claims after giving up his customary rights, and (4) can count on impartial judges. In the absence of bona fide research on this issue, such assumptions can scarcely be employed to evaluate the effects of the new options.

Even if large numbers of Africans opt for the regular civil code, there is not the slightest prospect that the *de facto* juridical and political distinctions between the former *indígenas* or their descendants and the former *civilizados* or their descendants are about to be abolished. This *de facto* survival of the *Indigenato* is betrayed in the process by which the new identity documents are issued. Now, as formerly, all of the "civilized" members of the population are registered with the local Civil Register (Arquivo de Identificacão Civil) and receive a booklet known as a *Bilhete de Identidade*. Under the *Indigenato,* the *indígenas,* not being Portuguese citizens, were not inscribed in the Civil Register nor were they issued a *Bilhete de Identidade*. Instead, they were registered at their respective administrative posts and were issued the hated *Caderneta Indígena,* or pass book.

With the repeal of the *Indigenato,* new *Cadernetas Indígenas* are no longer being issued. Holders of *Cadernetas Indígenas* have the option of turning in their pass books in exchange for the new identity booklet. Although the latter are now issued under the imprint of the Civil Register, it is the administrator rather than the Civil Register clerk who signs the new booklet. Moreover, as shown on page 169, the former *indígena*'s identity papers are clearly marked as such by the employment of a distinctive format and title. He receives a *Cartão de Identidade,* rather than a *Bilhete de Identidade*. The interior pages of the two booklets present additional differences of great significance. The African's *Cartão* calls for the bearer's place of birth to be designated in terms of an administrative post, and it specifies place of residence in terms of habitation site (*povoacão*), chieftaincy (*regedoría*), and administrative post. The European's *Bilhete* makes no reference to any of these parts of the system by which the Portuguese government continues to maintain its special dominion over the country's 6,000,000 Africans. In this respect, the salient result of the abolition of the *Indigenato* has been totally verbal; actual behavior continues much as before. The former *indígenas* continue to be identified as persons who are subject to the control of special government apparatuses. Since they cannot travel or change their residence without the administrator's permission, there is no chance that they may escape this special authority over them. If they flee to the cities clandestinely, they will be unable to obtain work without exposing themselves. As long as they reside within a *regedoría,* it is the appointed administrator who controls their civil and juridical destiny. It was in this fashion that under the former

REPÚBLICA PORTUGUESA

DIRECÇÃO DOS SERVIÇOS DE IDENTIFICAÇÃO

ARQUIVO DE IDENTIFICAÇÃO

BILHETE DE IDENTIDADE

DE

CIDADÃO NACIONAL

N.º ——————————

Nome: ————————————————
....

Filh.... de ————————————
....
....
....
....

Este bilhete leva o selo branco sobre a fotografia do portador e assinatura do director.

REPÚBLICA PORTUGUESA

PROVÍNCIA DE MOÇAMBIQUE

IDENTIFICAÇÃO CIVIL

(Portaria n.º 14331, de 29 de Setembro de 1960)

CARTÃO
DE
IDENTIDADE

system, Lourenço Marques' *assimilados* remained subject to the tutelage of Feraz de Freitas, despite the fact that they had ceased to be *indígenas*.

Despite the maintenance of administrative mechanisms capable of exercising almost unlimited control over many aspects of social and economic life, notice must now be taken of evidence bearing on the reduction of abuse in the wage-earning manpower sector. Shortly after the outbreak of the Angolan war, the Republic of Ghana accused Portugal of violating the Abolition of Forced Labor Convention. Ghana's complaint contained a series of obvious inaccuracies which inadvertently contributed heavily to Portugal's defense. Ghana's accusation that force was employed in the annual recruitment of 100,000 Mozambique Africans for work in the South African mines revealed a lack of comprehension of the basic historical processes underlying the development of the *shibalo* system.[25] This work force has never been obtained through *shibalo* capture; rather, mining on the Rand has figured as a dangerous but well-paid alternative to forced labor in Mozambique. At the same time, the attractiveness of the mines intensified the perennial domestic wage-labor manpower scarcity and helped to establish the need for forced labor among public and private employees in Mozambique. The Ghana complaint further misled the commission by emphasizing the forced labor of women. This again revealed a lack of historical and sociological understanding of the Mozambique labor situation. Historically, the *shibalo* system has depended entirely on assigning the major subsistence farming sectors to women, insulating them from the lure of wages and thereby freeing the men for migratory wage labor. Females have thus only sporadically and by exception been caught by the *shibalo*.

The Commission, which consisted of three jurists,[26] was perhaps professionally inclined to be overly impressed by legal façades and by the testimony of administrative officials and corporation executives whose motivations and rewards for lying were very high and against whom no punishment for perjury could be brought to bear.[27] Late in 1961, the Commisison

---

[25] The Commission would have been spared a great deal of trouble had Ghana's representatives been familiar with the lengthy exchange between the author and A. Rita-Ferreira in *Africa*. See Marvin Harris, "Labour Emigration among the Moçambique Thonga: Cultural and Political Factors," *Africa*, XXIX (1959), 50–66; Marvin Harris, "A Reply to Sr. Rita-Ferreira," *Africa*, XXX (1960), 243–245; A. Rita-Ferreira, "Labour Emigration among the Moçambique Thonga: Comments on a Study by Marvin Harris," *Africa*, XXX (1960), 141–152; and A. Rita-Ferreira, "Comments on Marvin Harris' Reply," *Africa*, XXXI (1961), 243–245.

[26] The Commission members were Paul Ruegger (Switzerland), chairman; Enrique Armand-Ugon (Uruguay); and Issac Forster (Senegal).

[27] One of the most blatant instances was the attempt by a witness to deny that the 1955 cotton legislation continued the policy of compulsory cotton-planting programs, despite the fact the decree contained the statement: "The establishment of compulsory programs is now permitted." The official tried, apparently with some success, to get the Commission to believe that this phrase was intended to compel the conces-

traveled for ten days in both Mozambique and Angola. Unfortunately, its itinerary was always known in advance, and its members were almost always accompanied by Portuguese officials (in Mozambique, by three labor inspectors).[28] The Commission was also accompanied by its secretariat, which apparently included at least one Portuguese-speaking member who could serve as an interpreter. The Commission believed that its investigations had not been hampered by linguistic difficulties and that it had been able to obtain spontaneous and uninhibited testimony from most of the African workers with whom it consulted. In this crucial matter, it exhibited a naïveté which will be self-evident to anyone who is familiar with the problem of protecting informants from the threat of reprisal in a society where the members of an oppressed minority have no practical defense against vengeful acts of brutality.

Despite the manifold tactical difficulties with which the Commission was confronted, its members did succeed, nonetheless, in identifying two flagrant instances of forced labor corresponding to cases which the writer had witnessed in 1956–1957. In Angola they visited the port facilities of Luanda and Lobito and discovered that

> All the recruited workers interviewed at these two ports and at Luanda Station stated that they had been ordered to come to work there by the local "chefe do pôsto" or administrator and their chief. They did not want to come, preferring to stay in their village. One of the men stated that he earned more at home. They had not been told what work they would have to do or how much they would earn. They did not leave their work because they had been ordered to stay for a certain time which appeared to be from 9 to 12 months. No very precise information could be obtained from the men about their wages . . . many of these workers appeared to have been brought from considerable distances, up to 650 km. away as the crow flies, considerable more in actual travel. . . .[29]

In Mozambique, traveling along the main road from the Union of South Africa, the Commission stopped to talk to a group of road workers at Umbeluzi, a scant twenty-five miles from the provincial capital.

> All four men questioned stated that they came from Inhambane district, that they had been sent to this work on orders of their respective "chefes do pôsto" and had not wanted to come, and that they were now about half way through a 12-month contract . . . . questions as to whether the men would

---

sionaires to implement their campaigns and that it did not apply to cultivation by the workers (International Labor Organization, *op. cit.,* p. 265). Several other witnesses undoubtedly lied about their knowledge of corporal punishment practices, forced labor, and compulsory crop systems.

[28] International Labor Organization, *op. cit.,* pp. 28–29.

[29] *Ibid.,* p. 250.

like to go home before completion of their contract did not elicit clear replies; none of them said he was anxious to leave at once.[30]

The commissioners' experience at the Cassequel Agricultural Company near Lobito in Angola surely helps to explain why they did not uncover a few more instances of the practice elsewhere:

> the workers questioned by the Commission stated that they had come there because they had wanted to do so, but none of them indicated clearly how he had been engaged. . . . The unskilled workers at the Cassequel Company, which is only about ten kilometers from Lobito and takes pride in receiving visitors, were more backward than any whom the Commission saw elsewhere and gave the impression of being intimidated. They certainly did not speak freely to the Commission, and, after the Commission and the representatives of the Company had moved on, some of them speaking only an African language, attempted to make contact with the Commission through its staff.[31]

These corroborative instances of the continued existence of a practice about whose generality scores of witnesses had given oral and written testimony failed to move the Commission to support Ghana's claims against Portugal. Instead, the Commission's report exonerated many of the specific companies and localities cited in Ghana's brief, accepted the negative instances as the inevitable result of individual human failings, and credited the metropolitan and provincial governments with a sincere desire to eliminate whatever abuses lingered on from a remote past when perhaps such practices might have been more widespread. In this connection, it should be stressed that the Commission was only interested in investigating labor practices since 1960, the year when Portugal began its obligation to the Abolition of Forced Labor Convention.

Those for whom it is difficult to disassociate the present Portuguese government from practices in the recent past will certainly find little of merit in the generally mildly reproachful and occasionally laudatory conclusions of the Commission.[32] It should be borne in mind, however, that the Commis-

---

[30] *Ibid.,* p. 252. The rather slow-thinking commissioners failed to point out that under the circumstances no *shibalo* would dream of breaking his contract until he found out whether he would receive the wages which had been withheld and unless he and his family were to receive perpetual protection against the *chefe de posto* whom they had accused.

[31] *Ibid.,* p. 288.

[32] The most favorable statement, based on the impressions of their twenty-day whirlwind tour, projects an image of the Commission members which will not inspire confidence among those who have lived in Angola and Mozambique for more extended periods and with an opportunity to be less obviously associated with Portuguese officials: "The commission . . . was favorably impressed by the degree of freedom exercised by a very large majority of those with whom it came in contact in both Angola and Mozambique (government officials, employers and workers alike, and Africans no less than Europeans) in expressing their views to it without constraint or inhibition; it has noted in its report the few exceptions which it feels it is necessary to make to this generalization" (*ibid.,* p. 358).

sion was called to its work at an especially inappropriate occasion. The Ghana complaint, already replete with gross inaccuracies, was brought forth at precisely the moment when the Overseas Ministry had begun to issue the many reforms which have signaled the end of the *Indigenato*. Both in its Geneva hearings and in its provincial tours, the members of the Commission were constantly confronted with testimony about the changes which these reforms were introducing. Everywhere, the impression was given that a new era of enlightenment had dawned and that criticism would only serve to undermine the reformist spirit. The satisfaction with which the Commission noted that the authorities had begun proceedings against the company responsible for the Umbeluzi *shibalos* and its willingness to believe that the port facilities of Luanda and Lobito had already ceased to acquire additional forced laborers shine through the laconic wording of the report. Nonetheless, it is difficult to dismiss the Commission's evidence indicating that a sharp reduction in the number of *shibalos* and compulsory crop workers had been achieved sometime after 1957, probably mainly between 1959 and 1961, for the following reasons:

In 1957, the port and railroad facilities of Lourenço Marques, like those of Lobito and Luanda in 1961, employed several thousand *shibalos*. This fact was known to every sea captain who brought cargo in or out of the provincial capital. Time and again during 1956–1957, this writer visited the dock area and conversed with the ragged, undernourished, and overworked captives who had earned for Lourenço Marques its reputation for reliable and rapid turnabouts based on twenty-four-hour-a-day stevedoring. The Commission failed to detect any signs of *shibalos* in its visit to the docks in 1961. Moreover, this is rendered credible by the fact that in FRELIMO's account of the recent disorders on the Lourenço Marques' docks, free workers rather than *shibalos* were implicated.[33] Indeed, such disorders were precisely what the former system was designed to prevent. Finally, the Commission reported that the dock workers whom it questioned earned between 240 and 280 *escudos* a month. These wages are competitive in the free labor market and 100 to 130 *escudos* above what the *shibalos* received in 1957.

The probable accuracy of the Commission's observations at the Lourenço Marques docks lends some credence to their failure to detect any evidence of forced labor at the Incomati Sugar Estates, another site where the author had the opportunity of verifying the existence of thousands of *shibalos* in 1957. Although there is no doubt that the plantation's management had ample opportunity to evacuate or to hide large numbers of *shibalos* prior to the appearance of the Commission, there is also no reason why, with competitive wages, sugar plantations in the Sul de Save could not obtain adequate numbers of voluntary workers. It must also be admitted that there is no reason to suppose that a majority of officials in the administrative

---

[33] Frente de Libertacão de Mozambique (FRELIMO), "The Stevedores Strike," in *Mozambican Revolution* (Dar es Salaam: 1963), p. 9. (Mimeographed.)

cadre are uninfluenced by changes in the law. Although cynicism and corruption undoubtedly prevent full compliance, the specific prohibition against labor recruitment by administrators cannot but result in a significant decrease in the incidence of the disputed practices.

Nonetheless, skepticism about the effectiveness of the new anti-forced-labor laws continues to be warranted. The preservation of the old system of administration, with its dictatorial local officials and the absence of any genuine channels of protest and expression for the submerged African mass, cannot inspire confidence in one who has seen and heard casual commands from *chefes de posto* result in severe beatings against which there was neither defense nor recourse. With this situation in mind, the author wrote in 1958: "All that is necessary in order for the *shibalo* system to function is for the administrator to have the power to indict Africans as malingerers without having to prove it in a court of law."[34] The recent reforms have not affected the pertinence of this observation. Despite the exalted language of the preamble to the new Rural Labor Code, local legislation contains the cynical refrain that, for hundreds of years, has provided the pretext for forced labor in the underdeveloped regions of the world.[35] The new legislation continues to imply that the subsistence farmer who refuses to work for wages is lazy and immoral and seeks to cure that condition by various intensities of government coercion. In repealing circular no. 566/D-7, which had defined the conditions that previously justified such coercion, Order 11 (September 1961) of the Governor-General of Mozambique did not fail to emphasize continuity with this principle:

5) The doctrine laid down in circular no. 566/D-7 of 5 May 1947, must therefore be revised, and the said circular is hereby revoked. However, there still remains the inevitable moral obligation of every *able-bodied male to work* in such a way as permanently to meet the needs which individual and family development impose if the people are to have better housing and a high standard of life. 6) Accordingly, the recourse to concentration for recruitment purposes must entirely cease, so that the workers may be enabled to take employment where the greatest advantages are offered to them. 7) It is also recommended that intensive action be continued, patiently and unremittingly, among the population so that they are induced to work with enthusiasm because they understand how much wealth is produced by effort and how much idleness brings hardship and impedes advancement. 8) Indeed, enjoyment of a high degree of well-being by all is not only an objective whose attainment we encourage but also a legitimate right for which the Government of this Province recognizes for all who engage in decent, persevering labor. Inversely, the Government recommends the *inexorable repression of vagrancy* as being extremely harmful to society.[36]

[34] Harris, *Portugal's African Wards*, p. 21.

[35] Cf. Marvin Harris, *Patterns of Race* (New York: Walker and Company, 1964), p. 20.

[36] International Labor Organization, *op. cit.*, p. 128. (Italics included.)

The recent legislation thus steadfastly ignores the fact that in a wage-labor system, the only method admitted by the laborers for increasing their willingness to work is for employers to raise wages or to offer additional benefits. The whole tragedy of African colonialism revolves around this point, for it has been the historical function of the colonial governments to force the Africans into European employment without paying the price which the Africans could have obtained had free market conditions prevailed. To call the Africans "vagrants" is only justified if it is recognized that, in the wage-labor frame of reference, the Europeans are "thieves." Note also that in clause 5, the wage-labor obligation continues to be restricted only to males. The fact that men and not women are morally bound to become wage workers exposes the sham morality in whose name the Portuguese actually intend nothing more elevated than the maintenance of low wages. The role reserved for African women continues to be that of subsistence farmers responsible for making up the gap between what the men can afford to buy with their wages and what is needed if their families are to avoid starvation.

Equally unconvincing is the method by which the government intends to ensure enforcement of its new legislation. As recognized in the report of the International Labor Organization Commission, "the most important single measure to ensure that the established policy of the Government is fully carried out in practice is a substantial reinforcement of the labor inspection service now in process of creation."[37] It is indicative of the Commission's frame of mind that it maintained its respectful composure while recounting the fact that the staff charged with labor inspection ". . . will be represented in the various administrative divisions and subdivisions by the local administrators and 'chefes de posto.' "[38] In this connection, it should also be pointed out that the legislation giving effect to the prohibition of penal sanctions to enforce labor contracts empowers the administration to enforce such contracts with civil sanctions. Among the civil sanctions mentioned is the following: "Native workers who, having concluded a contract of employment, refuse to present themselves at the workplace, shall be obliged to pay to the recruiters and employers compensation for the expenses incurred by them and to return to them anything received from them."[39] It would be interesting to know what has happened to contract wage workers who want to quit their work but are unable to pay the amounts which they are said to owe. Obviously, at a certain stage in pressing these claims, criminal charges would again be brought against Africans for refusing to obey court orders. Note in this connection that forced labor continues, of course, to be a punitive remedy sanctioned by the penal code. Moreover, Article 146 of the Portuguese Constitution continues to provide for labor conscription for public works.

---

[37] *Ibid.*, p. 311.

[38] *Ibid.*, p. 177.

[39] *Ibid.*, p. 174.

Numerous other legal loopholes continue to exist by which forced labor can be carried on despite reforms. But these loopholes are irrelevant. As long as local law enforcement remains in the hands of cadres that are not subject to representative local political bodies, there can be no confidence that any set of Lisbon-imposed laws will be interpreted in a manner favorable to those local populations. On this point, the ILO Commission expressed some further important opinions which were not consistent with the rest of its conclusions:

> In the case of territories in the stage of economic and social development of Portuguese Africa, the effective application of the laws and regulations implementing the provisions of an international labour convention presents certain further problems of a special character. Great distances and imperfect communications . . . mining and agricultural concessions covering large areas . . . a backwardness of certain parts of the population . . . which makes it difficult to gauge how clearly they understand their rights under law . . . or are in a position to exercise any real personal freedom in view of the constant pressure on them of habit and custom and an ingrained habit of obedience to both governmental and indigenous authorities; the barrier to intercourse represented by the lack of any considerable knowledge of African languages by either governmental officials or the senior or executive personnel in industry, transport, mining, and agriculture; the difficulty of having any real understanding of what is happening in the African mind in the absence of a substantial African administrative cadre in either government or industry . . . may well make it difficult for the Government to gauge with accuracy how completely its intentions are being implemented in practice.[40]

Skepticism about the effectiveness of the reform decrees is further warranted by the reports which filter out to the Mozambique Liberation Front (FRELIMO) headquarters in Dar es Salaam. The information bulletins published by FRELIMO are filled with notices of *shibalos,* sudden disappearances, unredressed assaults on persons and property, arbitrary imprisonments, expropriation of lands, beatings by *chefes de posto,* and unexplained deaths of persons held incommunicado in prisons. Although some of these accounts may be distorted by reasons of partisan zeal and difficulties inherent in maintaining lines of communication into Mozambique, one who has previously witnessed actual examples of these abuses finds it difficult to accept the proposal that they are now mere propaganda fabrication.

Indeed, there is reason to conclude that the mass of Mozambique Africans are now passing through a phase of colonialism which is characterized by unprecedented pressures for conformity. With the outbreak of the Angola campaign and the more recent hostilities in Mozambique, both countries have become armed camps. Military and paramilitary agencies now supplement the civil administration, and elaborate intelligence and propaganda networks attempt to reach down into the smallest hamlets and villages to

---

[40] *Ibid.,* p. 174.

head off the influence of FRELIMO's own agents who are known to be operating increasingly within Mozambique. Of special significance was the establishment of the Policia Internacional de Defesa do Estado (PIDE), in April 1961, as the agency primarily responsible for combating FRELIMO's underground activities. An African traveling beyond his *conselhos* and *circunscricoēs* must obtain permission from his administrator. Notification of the intended travel is sent ahead to the nearest PIDE headquarters, to which the African must report on his arrival. An additional countermeasure is the creation of a centralized intelligence bureau (Centralizacāo e Coordenacāo) headed by Feraz de Freitas, to ensure cooperation between PIDE and the older administrative networks of spies and informers. Before the reform, the Bureau of Native Affairs (Negócios Indígenas) exercised the function, among others, of disseminating and controlling information among the African population. By Decree 44,111, December 1961, this function was transferred to a newly created Bureau of Psycho-Social Action (Servico de Accāo Psico-Social) which has attempted to obtain the loyalty of the African mass through modern propaganda techniques.

In October 1964, FRELIMO began the military phase of its operations. FRELIMO's troops have repeatedly crossed over into Mozambique and engaged the Portuguese army, killing soldiers and capturing arms.[41] Thus far, white civilians have not been molested. Despite heavy censorship of the reports of these engagements, the whites are well aware that a war has begun on their northern border and that Africans all over the country are joining the FRELIMO underground. Unlike the whites in Angola, Mozambique's settlers are not going to be surprised by the violent hatred of their "tame" Africans. They have taken the probably well-advised precaution of arming themselves against the possibility of sudden attack and of refusing to believe that any African is beyond the point of "reverting to savagery." Despite what may be the best intentions of such men as Adriano Moreira to create a harmonious multi-racial partnership in Africa, it is clear that no moment in the history of Mozambique could have been less propitious for embarking on such a program.

In the midst of the avalanche of decrees which Moreira pushed through in 1961–1962, there is at least one which casts suspicion on either the sanity or sincerity of the technical staff of the Overseas Ministry. On the same day that the *Estatuto Indígena* was abolished, Decree-Law 43,895 declared the establishment of Provincial Settlement Boards in both Mozambique and Angola. These government agencies are empowered to plan and supervise all aspects of population movements, especially such as relate to stepped-up immigration from Portugal and the relocation of African villages and home-

---

[41] A report printed in FRELIMO's *Mozambican Revolution*, Vol. I (New York edition, March 25, 1965), pp. 9–10, lists engagements in which over 300 Portuguese soldiers are said to have been killed during December 1964.

steads. Incredibly, this legislation intends to promote peaceful multiracial adjustments in Portuguese Africa by rapidly increasing the size of the white settler group. According to J. P. Neto:

> The settlement boards are authentic indicators of a new era in our overseas policy, since it is through their intervention that a truly multi-racial society will be created, which will simultaneously promote the social development of the aborigines and the settlement of Portuguese from other Portuguese territories.[42]

Under Settlement Board aegis, the draftees now in Angola and Mozambique are being enticed to remain as permanent residents, with offers of ten to thirty-five hectares of free land per settler and additional heavy subsidies.[43] Presumably, there will be a multiplication of projects similar to the large Limpopo Valley Settlement Scheme.[44] Although Moreira had the reputation of being something of a scholar, it is obvious that his familiarity with the scientific literature on race relations in Africa and elsewhere is very deficient. Nothing is more obvious from the history of race relations in such widely dispersed areas as the United States, southern Brazil, England, Kenya, Java, and Trinidad, than that amicable interracial adjustments are inversely correlated with the intensity of competition for upward socioeconomic mobility. It is inevitable that the new contingents of Portuguese immigrants, endowed with what Charles Wagley (1958) and this writer have called a superior "adaptive capacity" for the colonial "arena of conflict," will interpose themselves between the African mass and most of the already severely limited opportunities for achieving modern economic standards.[45] These relatively small groups of whites, with their monopoly on managerial and technical positions, their automobiles, and luxury housing, could not possibly hope to win the good will and approval of the depressed African masses, even if Angola had never happened and even if each Portuguese immigrant remained perfectly color-blind. Already in 1957, interviewing African domestics and urban service workers had indicated fully conscious resentment against the whites stemming more from economic than from political frustration. Again and again, whenever it was possible to gain the confidence of shoemaker, carpenter, washboy, or other African menials, there would come the refrain, "They don't want us to get ahead." One carpenter who had spent two years abroad said, "If it wasn't for my family, I would go to

---

[42] João Pereira Neto, "Politica de Desenvolvimento Commitario," *Ultramar*, IX (1962), 35.

[43] *Ultramar*, XXXIX (1963), p. 114.

[44] Cf. A. F. A. Falção, "A Programacão do Desenvolvimento do Vale do Zambeze em Moçambique," *Fomento*, I (1963), 53–110; and Martius A. Alonso, "Provoamento Agrário no Ultramar Português. O Approveitamento Agri-social da Inhamissa em Moçambique," *Boletim Geral de Ultramar*, XXXIX (1963), 71–72.

[45] Charles Wagley and Marvin Harris, *Minorities in the New World* (New York: Columbia University Press, 1958).

Durban. There, if you work hard and know your trade, at least you get paid for it. But here, the administration won't let me buy a motor for my saw. It must be that the whites are jealous of us. Some of them, when they pass by and see me working in my shop, call me dirty names." An interpreter, aged twenty-five, who had already attained the highest administrative position open to Africans, was firmly convinced that "There is no chance to get ahead here because the government doesn't want us natives to get ahead. We don't have a chance here. They keep us down, but we have nobody to tell this to." The remarks of a fifty-five-year-old shoemaker in Lourenço Marques must be taken into account in judging the effectiveness of the repeal of the *Estatuto Indígena* in stimulating the development of racial democracy. Expressing his scorn of the *assimilado* policy, this man had noted:

> I'm just as civilized as an *assimilado* is, but it makes no difference whether you're civilized or not. When a white man, no matter where he comes from, goes into an office, the people there offer him a chair to sit down. They never offer a chair to an African. . . . Here there is no color bar, but there is a color bar. You never see any signs which say that you can't go in, but you can't go in just the same. Once my son and I got all dressed up in our best suits and went downtown to the Varieta (the worst of the white movie houses). I bought the tickets and we started to go in. But the man said we couldn't go in. I said, "Why not?" He said, "You know why." I said we had come here to see an important movie which we couldn't see at the Imperio (native quarter movie). We were lucky to get our money back. . . . The Portuguese are very smart. When the foreigner comes here and looks around he would never know there was any bar here.
>
> The reason for it is that they don't want us to make any money. They don't pay us any money here. They don't want us to get ahead in life. They want to keep us down forever. I don't know when things are going to get better. Maybe for my grandsons. A man came back from the Transvaal recently and tried to open up a store. They wouldn't let him. They took his money and closed his store.

Most of the Africans with whom the writer managed to speak frankly about economic opportunities had no illusions about their future prospects despite frequent promises by the administrator that better days were coming. During 1957, rumors about the possibility of partially or totally eliminating the *Indigenato* were already circulating among the local intellectuals. The Africans were not impressed:

> The administrator says that there is a law ready in Lisbon which is going to change everything here. All the members of the professional association who have never done anything wrong are going to become free citizens.
>
> Yes, we are going to have a lot of rich *indígenas*. And the administration is going to help us take care of our money. The administrator has told us that if we want to open a store we should come to him and he will take care of the

matter for us. Instead of having to pay a lawyer and pay for this paper and that paper—all these papers cost money—he will do it all for us. That's good because we couldn't do it without him. *No* native has enough money to pay for all those papers.

The people here must get better houses because if those foreigners from South Africa come and they ask whose house that is and go inside and see the bed and the radio, then they will say, "Hoo! The Portuguese people are good to their natives."

You must all work hard, learn how to spend your money properly, wear decent clothing, and keep your houses clean both inside and out. Then some day you will all become citizens. It used to be that no one owned cars. But there on a certain street you find all the people, very dark, with automobiles.

It used to be that the faucet was completely shut. Now it has been opened and the water is coming out: Ping . . ., ping . . ., ping . . .

The disparity between the simple but insightful view of Portuguese-African relations achieved by the Africans and the rococo opacity of mind with which the architects of the overseas reform are constitutionally afflicted, provides small hope that the "ping . . ., ping . . ., ping . . ." is about to change its pace.

Since rhetoric has always draped itself like a shroud over every glimmer of reality in Portuguese Africa, the cautious observer cannot help but impute opposite and sometimes quite ghastly meanings to the endless flowery phrases that emanate from the Overseas Ministry. Thus, returning to the remarkable decree that establshed the Provincial Settlement Boards, one might very well ask, what is the reality into which paragraph 15 of Article 3 is, at this very moment, being translated? Among the specially incumbent missions of the Boards, this paragraph enumerates, "To promote or encourage initiative tending to consolidate the bonds of solidarity and association of the different classes, or social or ethnic aggregates, particularly through sports, folklore, or cultural manifestations, youth labor camps, auto-construction of houses, etc." The actual event stimulated by the verbiage of this proposal appears to be the forced nucleation of African populations into more accessible and more easily controlled settlements. According to Neto, the first villages of 700 houses with populations of 3,000 "aborigines" each have already gone up in Angola. Even more extraordinary is the way in which these houses were built. Apparently the meaning of "auto-construction" is that once more the administration has found a way to control labor without having to pay for it. "Only skilled work is paid for . . ." and then (is the writer really serious?) "according to testimonies taken among the aborigines interested in these schemes, the populations which are going to benefit from them are overjoyed, and they give themselves with greatest satisfaction to the job to which they are summoned and speak proudly of their new *regedoria*."[46]

---

[46] João Pereira Neto, "Politica de Desenvolvimento Comunitário," *Ultramar*, IV (1962), 56.

Under Moreira's influence, Portuguese scholars have been devoting themselves with increasing narrowness to the task of proving Gilberto Freyre's tropical theory by finding historical roots for the multiracial society which the Settlement Boards are supposed to be creating.[47] Were there not drastic political consequences to pay for the kind of self-deception which these scholars are practicing on themselves, the evidence now being dredged up would be worthy of a musical comedy. One spokesman, Eduardo Freitas da Costa, recently had the inspiration to represent the Portuguese as the original abolitionists: "Portugal promulgated the first effective prohibition of slavery when D. José prohibited in 1755 slavery in Grão Para e Maranhão."[48] Of course, the slavery in question here was that of the American Indians and not of Africans; and even at that, the measure was not really effective until there were practically no Indians left after two centuries of war, enslavement, and mistreatment.[49] As for the Africans, this was the time when Angola and Mozambique had become the principal source of Negro slaves for Brazil's plantations and mines.

Recently, Moreira's familiarity with portions of the modern social sciences has stimulated his colleagues to propose that the Portuguese people have always been remarkable for their lack of ethnocentrism. The following proof of that fact is surely worth quoting in full for an English-speaking audience, since it would be difficult to find a more convincing demonstration of how thirty-five years of dictatorship in Portugal have destroyed the critical faculties of Portuguese historians and social scientists:

> Perhaps the document which best substantiates the attenuated ethnocentrism of the Portuguese is the Alvara Decree of April 21, 1761, whereby the king, in addition to commanding that all the natives of the Portuguese ought to enjoy, if they were baptized Christians, the same honors, titles, prerogatives and privileges which the naturals of Metropolitan Portugal enjoy, also imposed the severest penalties on any person of rank or condition who dispraises or discriminates against the native inhabitants of India, or against their children or descendants, *by calling them Negroes or Mesticos, or by labelling them with similar odious epithets,* or by trying by this means to deprive them of the honors, dignities, positions, etc.[50]

Even if we accept the premise that the recent reforms will be honestly and courageously enforced by the administration, and even if, by some

---

[47] Cf. Antonio Albertoa Banha de Andrade, "Um Caso Típico da Filosofia Política da História Portuguêsa," *Stúdia* (Lisbon), IX (1962), 7–27: A. da Silva Rego, A Cor-barreira, Argumento e Arma," *Ultramar*, IX (1961), 9–17; A. da Silva Rego, "Missoës," *Ultramar*, X (1962), 3–16; and Oscar Soares Barata, "O Sentido Humano do Pluri-racialismo Português," *Ultramar*, V (1961), 18–28.

[48] Eduardo Freitas da Costa, "Permanência de Portugal," *Ultramar*, V (1962), 88.

[49] Cf. Wagley and Harris, *op. cit.*, pp. 20–47.

[50] João Pereira Neto, "O Significado do Multirracialismo Português," *Ultramar*, IV (1963), 83. Italics mine—M. H.

miracle, the influx of white immigrants to Mozambique does not intensify interracial hostility, it still remains unlikely that the trend toward armed conflict along racial lines can now be reversed. While Lisbon's inept notions of racial fraternity may soothe the consciences of men like da Costa and Neto, the leaders of the FRELIMO are in no mood to be swayed by a fumbling courtship. It is true that in Eduardo Mondlane, President of the Liberation Front, the Portuguese face an opponent whose Ph.D. in Sociology from Northwestern University and professorship at Syracuse University scarcely incline him toward racial vendettas. Moreover, Mondlane's wife is an American Caucasoid. Nonetheless, FRELIMO's military and para-military operations have already taken the form typical of revolutionary movements which have arisen in the bitterest currents of interracial hate and violence. There is only one thing wrong with Portugal's plan for an interracial paradise in Portuguese Africa: the Portuguese have never taken the trouble to find out if the Africans agree to it.

SELECTED BIBLIOGRAPHY

BOOKS

Addicott, Len. *Cry Angola*. London: Student Christian Movement Press, 1962.

Boxer, Charles R. *Race Relations in the Portuguese Colonial Empire, 1415–1825*. Oxford, Eng.: Clarendon Press, 1963.

Davidson, Basil. *The African Awakening*. London, Eng.: Macmillan & Co., 1955.

Duffy, James. *Portuguese Africa*. Cambridge, Mass.: Harvard University Press, 1959.

——. *Portugal in Africa*. Cambridge, Mass.: Harvard University Press, 1962.

Figueiredo, Antonio de. *Portugal and Its Empire: The Truth*. London, Eng.: Victor Gollancz, 1961.

Freyre, Gilberto. *The Portuguese and the Tropics*. Lisbon, Port.: Executive Committee for the Commemoration of the Vth Century of the Death of Prince Henry the Navigator, 1961.

——. *Um Brasileiro em Terras Portuguêsos*. Lisbon, Port.: Edicão Livros do Brasil, 1952.

Galvão, Henrique. *Santa Maria: My Crusade for Portugal*. Cleveland, Ohio: World Publishing Company, 1962.

Harris, Marvin. *Patterns of Race*. New York: Walker and Company, 1962.

——. *Portugal's African Wards*. New York: American Committee on Africa, 1958.

Rodrigues, José H. *Africa e Brasil*. Rio de Janeiro, Arg.: Editôra Civilização Brasileira, 1961.

Wagley, Charles, and Marvin Harris. *Minorities in the New World*. New York: Columbia University Press.

ARTICLES

Alfonso, A. Martius. "Povoamento Agrário no Ultramar Português. O Aproveitamento Agri-social da Inhamissa em Moçambique," *Boletim Geral do Ultramar*, XXXIX (1963) (454/455), 71–92.

Andrade, Antonio Alberto Banha de. "Um Caso típico da Filosofia Politíca da Historia Portuguêsa," *Stúdia* (Lisbon), IX (1962), 7–27.

Barata, Oscar Soares. "O Sentido Humano do Pluri-racialismo Português," *Ultramar*, V (1961), 18–28.

Blumenfeld, F. Yorick. "Portuguese Dictatorship," *Editorial Reports*, I (March 8, 1961).

Costa, Eduardo Freitas da. "Permanencia de Portugal," *Ultramar*, V (1962), 85–98.

Falcão, A. F. A. "A programacão do Desenvolvimento do Vale do Zambeze em Moçambique," *Fomento*, I (1963), 53–110.

Fernandes, Castro. "The Presence of Portugal in Africa," *Portugal*, IV (1960), 256–265.

Harris, Marvin, "Labour Emigration among the Moçambique Thonga: Cultural and Political Factors," *Africa*, XXIX (1959), 50–66.

———. "A Reply to Sr. Rita-Ferreira," *Africa*, XXX (1960), 243–245.

Moreira, Adriano. "Velada de Armas," *Boletim Geral do Ultramar*, XXXVII (1961), 15–31.

———. "Betrayed Generation," *Boletim Geral do Ultramar*, XXXVIII (1962), 226–241.

Neto, João Baptista Pereira. "O Significado do Multirracialismo Português," *Ultramar*, IV (1963), 54–68.

———. "Politica de Desenvolvimento Communitário," *Ultramar*, IX (1962), 40–57.

Rego, A. da Silva. "A Cor-barreira, Argumento e Arma," *Ultramar*, V (1961), 9–17.

———. "Missoes," *Ultramar*, X (1962), 3–16.

OTHERS

Frente de Libertacão de Moçambique (FRELIMO). "The Stevedores Strike," in *Mozambican Revolution,* mimeographed, Dar es Salaam: 1963.

International Labor Organization, *Report of the Commission to Examine the Complaint Filed by the Government of Ghana Concerning the Observance by the Government of Portugal of the Abolition of Forced Labor Convention, 1957.* Geneva: International Labor Office, 1962.

United Nations, *Working Paper of the Special Committee on the Situation with Regard to the Implementation of the Declaration on the Granting of Independence to Colonial Countries and Peoples,* A/AC, 109/1. 126. New York: United Nations, 1964.

United Nations. *Report of the Special Committee on Territories under Portuguese Administration,* A/5160. New York: United Nations, 1962.

KENYA

SUDAN

ETHIOPIA

UGANDA

L. Rudolf

Moyale

Soroti

SOMALIA

Kitale

Maralal

Kisumu

Bura

Nairobi

L. Victoria

TANZANIA

Voi

Indian Ocean

railroads

roads

national
boundaries

provincial
boundaries

Mombasa

Tanga

0   100

miles

LM

5

Political Evolution
in Kenya

Fred G. Burke

> At many places and times, tribes have merged to form peoples; and
> peoples have grown into nations. Some nations have founded empires;
> and empires have broken up into fragments where populations later
> attempted again to form larger units. Such recurrent patterns of
> integration . . . raise the problem of the comparability or uniqueness
> of historical events.
>
> —KARL W. DEUTSCH, "The Growth of Nations,"
> *World Politics,* V (January 1953), 168.

INTRODUCTION

Although economists are concerned with economies and sociologists with
societies, political scientists do not, to a similar extent, speak of polities.
However, this concept is useful for purposes of tracing the political evolution of new nations. Rather than regard political behavior as an aspect of
a single manifestation of social organization, it is here proposed to regard
the "polity" as the society viewed from the perspective of the organized
allocation and exercise of authority. Cultural objectivity is as difficult to
obtain as personal or ideological objectivity. Western analysis of political
transition in Africa, and particularly in what was once settler Africa, is
peculiarly culture-bound, even when explicit attempts are made to overcome
this recognized tendency. This cultural subjectivity expresses itself most pro-
nouncedly in a tendency toward discontinuity. The political history of Kenya,
for example, is most often thought to have commenced with the activities
of the British East Africa Company in 1888 or the establishment of the East
African Protectorate in 1895. None would deny the fact that, before 1888,
the lands now collectively termed Kenya were the homeland of hundreds of
thousands of men, women, and children who—as those who were to follow—
required, not merely food, shelter, and love, but also an organized means of

reconciling inevitable interpersonal and intergroup conflict, of waging war on one's enemies, of protecting the life and property of those who perceived themselves as belonging to a single society, or, for our purposes, a polity. Since it appears possible that Homo sapiens may have had his origin in Kenya, the necessity to view political organization as continuous is all the more obvious.[1]

It is not denied that the political systems of the indigenous peoples of Kenya were found to be quite unlike those to which political scientists and administrators from the West were accustomed. However, it is suggested that the analytic discontinuity between what are often termed primitive and modern political systems is misleading and not always conducive to a comprehensive understanding of the nature of contemporary government and politics. It is with this observation firmly in mind that an attempt is made in this study to regard the political evolution of Kenya as a continuous process, as a process of conflict incurred in the gradual amalgamation of many polities into a few—and, on December 12, 1963, into a single, independent Kenyan state.

Invariably this approach requires a disciplinary amalgamation as well, and it is our intention that this chapter be, in fact, a study in political anthropology. Taking this view of political continuity, we must acknowledge the assumption that the present entity called Kenya is not an end in the developmental process, but simply one stage in the political evolution of that portion of the world. Kenya, it is here prophesized, will contribute its essence to a more inclusive future polity as the Kamba and Kikuyu—now rapidly fading as polities—have done in the past.[2] Our purpose then is to trace selectively the formation and dissolution of polities in that portion of the world now labeled Kenya. This is done with a view toward showing that the present is composed of ideas, values, and behaviors which are, in fact, a product of a continuous past and that a more distant future can be perceived if the here and now is regarded in this fashion.

ORIGINS OF EARLY KENYAN POLITIES

For our purposes, Kenya is an artificial category, relevant only to a description of politics and government at the time of writing. The innumerable political communities that have inhabited the 225,000 square miles in East Africa to which this discourse is confined had their origins in far distant lands.

---

[1] L. S. B. Leakey's discovery of human fossil remains in the Kavirondo region of Kenya dating to the lower Pleistocene suggest that Homo sapiens may have had its origins in this region. See also Sonia Cole, *The Pre-History of East Africa* (London: Penguin Books, 1954).

[2] That one chapter in this book is devoted to the question of East African federation lends weight to our prediction, as does the existence of the Organization of African Unity.

Early Nilotic and Bantu Polities

Negroid peoples probably entered East Africa relatively late, as archeological evidence indicates that they were not present in the area in any numbers until the Iron Age.

The scholarly distinctions among Nilotic, Nilo-Hamitic, and Bantu peoples are controversial ones. Though the author is neither an anthropologist nor an African, he has spent a number of years among peoples of each of the three ethnic strains in Kenya and Uganda. He is inclined to go along with the view that the Bantu, basically Negroid peoples, entered East Africa from the Congo Basin.[3] The Nilotes, a sub-Negroid race, entered the lake region of East Africa from the north somewhat later than the Bantu intrusion from the south and west. The degree of Cushitic (Hamitic) cultural and linguistic influence has largely determined whether a modern people is classified as Nilotic or Nilo-Hamitic. Groups experiencing greater contact with a Cushitic-speaking people, whom they gradually absorbed, are termed Nilo-Hamites and include the following major Kenyan tribes: Masai, Nandi, and Kipsigis. As the early Bantu peoples of Kenya were essentially agriculturalists, they tended to occupy only the well-watered plateaus and hill slopes.

As they moved southward out of their Sudanese homeland and approached the great lakes, the Nilotes encountered powerful Bantu kingdoms, which shunted their migratory path farther to the east along the Rift Valley and Lake Rudolf route. Here early Nilotes likely came into contact with remnants of Cushitic-speaking peoples whom they absorbed. Subsequently, they carried southward elements of Cushitic cultures.[4] These essentially Nilotic peoples, significantly Cushiticized as they moved south and west, moved out of their Sudanic homeland and penetrated into modern Kenya from the northeast along the Rift Valley trajectory, in such a manner as to drive a wedge between the agricultural Bantu of the Kilimanjaro-Meru highlands and the related Bantu of the Mt. Kenya-Nyeri region farther to the north. The most aggressive of these Cushiticized Nilotes were the Masai, who rapidly expanded their influence and domain southward nearly to the Indian Ocean.[5] The impact of these Cushiticized Nilotes on their Bantu neighbors was significant and greater than that of the Nilotic peoples who

---

[3] The question of Bantu origin is a fascinating one. However, as the writer is incapable of shedding any light on the subject, it is fortunate that the question is not relevant to this paper.

[4] George Peter Murdock, *Africa: Its People and Their Culture History* (New York: McGraw-Hill, 1959), p. 333.

[5] The Kenya Nandi and the Uganda Iteso both trace their origins to present-day Karamoja in northeastern Uganda. The Iteso relate that *Karamajong* refers to "those who stayed behind." See G. W. B. Huntingford, *The Southern Nilo-Hamites* (London: International African Institute, 1953). See also the author's *Local Government and Politics in Uganda* (Syracuse: Syracuse University Press, 1964), Ch. 6.

were to arrive considerably later.[6] Among the Bantu peoples most influenced by their Nilo-Hamitic neighbors were the Kikuyu and the Kamba, who, for example, adopted from their invaders such customs as initiation rites, age-grade organization, patrilineal inheritance, circumcision, and clitoridectory. Had the migration of the Nilo-Hamitic peoples flowed through the areas of the interlacustrine kingdoms to the north of Lake Victoria, it is conceivable that the politics of paramount chieftaincy and hierarchical bureaucracy would have penetrated into Kenya. Instead, the Nilo-Hamites carried with them a diffuse, small-scale sociopolitical system based on age grades and kinship lineage. Thus, unlike much of Uganda, there did not evolve in traditional Kenya a pattern of protostate formation, centralized decision-making, and sophisticated bureaucracy.

Political organization based on a division of responsibility and function according to a systematic relationship of age grades not only characterizes the numerous Nilo-Hamitic peoples of Kenya (the Kipsigis, Iteso, Masai, Turkana, Nandi, and Suk), but also some of the large Bantu tribes as well. For such peoples as the Kikuyu, Meru, Taveta, and Taita have absorbed numerous social and political institutions from their Nilo-Hamitic neighbors. Thus, essentially Nilo-Hamitic sociopolitical structures gradually came to predominate over the greater of modern Kenya. As contemporary Kenya is composed of Bantu, Nilotic, and Nilo-Hamitic peoples, the significance of the prevalence of such widely shared institutions as age-grade organization and patrilineal inheritance is apparent. Later in this analysis, it will be suggested that such modern Kenya political institutions as competitive "youth-wings" are a modern-day manifestation of earlier reliance on age-grade organization. The fact that Kenya politics are characterized by a high degree of personal loyalty, which, on occasion, operates independently of party ideology or faction, is consistent with traditional institutionalized, interpersonal solidarity common to many (but not all) Kenya tribes.[7]

It is also important to note that both Nilotic and Nilo-Hamitic societies were fundamentally egalitarian. Status distinctions tended to be few and situationally related to war, games, land inheritance, etc. For example, the position of women and children is considerably less subservient than among the interlacustrine Bantu, where Nilo-Hamitic influence has been considerably less.[8]

Neither slavery nor hereditary rule was common among the Nilotic or Nilo-Hamitic Kenya peoples. Such small-scale, diffuse, egalitarian polities

---

[6] Roland Oliver and Gervase Mathew (eds.), *A History of East Africa* (London: Oxford University Press, 1963), Vol. I, 199.

[7] The Nandi, for example, established a blood-brotherhood relationship which significantly affects political obligation even into the present.

[8] We are aware of the Hima component of the interlacustrine states, but take the view that this status distinction is more a product of Nilotic adaptation to a prior existing hierarchical system than the reverse.

frustrated the extension of the British principle of indirect rule to Kenya. More importantly, they required that the British institute novel forms of administration, which also have contributed to the unique style of government and politics in modern Kenya. And, although tribalism is certainly a factor in modern political conflict, it is less so than in Uganda, for example, where the cultural lines separating the major indigenous polities are sharply drawn.

Impact of the Bantu

Whereas the Nilo-Hamitic peoples entered Kenya from the north, the greater part of the Kenya Bantu (southern and central highland Bantu) peoples entered the country from the south. It is thought that the Bantu migration into East Africa from the Congo Basin moved around the west side of Lake Victoria, then south, and east to the coast, where it dispersed both to the north and farther south. One segment of the Bantu peoples migrating northward turned inland and gave rise to such Bantu speaking groups as the Chagga, Kamba, Kikuyu, Meru, Embu, Pare-Taveta, Shambala, and Taita.[9] Our findings support the view that these highland Bantu share an affinity and common legacy, and are, indeed, a relatively homogeneous cultural group.[10]

Although possessed of a polity slightly more specialized and extensive than the Nilo-Hamites with whom they subsequently came into intimate contact, it should be recalled that the highland Bantu had earlier absorbed and been affected by the early inhabitants of the coast and interior. When added to the fact that the Bantu were essentially an agricultural people inhabiting relatively isolated slopes and homesteads, this factor appears to be partially responsible for the absence of indigenous protostate polities which characterize the interlacustrine Bantu.[11]

In contrast to the Nilo-Hamitic peoples, the Nilotic peoples in Kenya resemble the Bantu in respect to the rapidity of their transition toward modernity. There would seem to be a much closer indigenous relationship between Bantu and Nilo-Hamitic peoples than between Bantu and Nilotic. (The persistence of a sense of antipathy toward the Nilotic Luo on the part

[9] Murdock, *op. cit.*, p. 342.

[10] *Ibid.*, p. 343. See also Fred G. Burke, "Some Grass-Roots Attitudes Affecting Political and Social Integration in East Africa" (paper delivered to the African Studies Association, San Francisco, October 26, 1963).

[11] Murdock suggests that the egalitarianism of the Bantu peoples is partly a product of their association and absorption of Cushitic-speaking cultures. In his opinion, the Bantu (save for the Shambala and the Taita peoples) adapted, from the same Cushitic source, the age-grade organization which entrusted political authority to a council of elders. It may be that the relative similarity of the Kenyan Bantu and Nilo-Hamitic politics is partially explained by the fact that both groups underwent prolonged association with—and subsequently absorbed—Cushitic-speaking peoples.

of the Bantu peoples of Kenya—their present political alliance in KANU notwithstanding—is illustrative.) The attitudes of various Kenya tribes toward one another is discussed in greater detail below.

To complete this early picture, it is necessary to trace briefly the arrival in East Africa of the Nilotic peoples. In contrast to Bantu or Nilo-Hamitic penetrations into what is now Kenya, the Nilotic migrations came considerably later in time. Yet today, numbering nearly 1,000,000 persons, Luo is Kenya's second largest tribe. This extraordinary migration of Nilotic peoples from the Sudan into Uganda and Kenya probably occurred during the fifteenth through the seventeenth centuries. However, this Nilotic movement was still under way when the British arrived on the scene to establish suzerainty over the area. In fact, this migration is a continuing process.

The recent expansion of Kenya Luo along the south of Lake Victoria may be regarded as a modern expression of this pattern. Luo-speaking peoples inhabit much of the southern Sudan, northern Uganda, and the central Nyanza district of Kenya.[12] Luo migration and penetration took a particular form which is reflected in the indigenous political system of the Kenya Luo. The basic Luo political unit is the dynastic ruling clan. Attached to the ruling clan are a number of other clans composed of commoners.[13] In most instances, these "commoners" are descendants of peoples whom the Luo conquered and absorbed along their route of penetration. Among the Luo-speaking Padhola of Uganda, for example, we discovered that the Nyapolo clan is regarded as the founding unit and that it is composed of relatively pure Nilotic Padhola. The majority of the tribe's clans consisted of alien peoples who had been absorbed through an elaborate form of adoption on conquest.[14]

The entrance of relatively politically sophisticated Nilotes into diffuse, small-scale Nilo-Hamitic and Bantu polities is considered by one eminent historian as "the outstanding event that marked the beginning of a new age."[15] However, the extraordinary impact of the Nilotic political institutions was limited primarily to the interlacustrine Bantu kingdoms, where a Nilotic royal clan, the Batio, was superimposed over a polity composed of a subservient Bantu peasantry and a basically Hima (Hamitic) aristocracy.

The Kenya Luo are separated from their nearest Luo-speaking "relatives," the Uganda Padhola, by the Bantu Abaluhya and the Nilo-Hamitic Iteso. The Padhola themselves are but a small Luo enclave surrounded by Bantu and Nilo-Hamitic peoples. Although representing the southernmost penetration of the Nilotes and separated from the primary root in northern Uganda and the southern Sudan by nearly 1,000 miles, the Kenya Luo are the single largest Nilotic tribe in East Africa.

---

12 Robert O. Collins, "Sudan Link to the North," Ch. 8 in this volume.

13 Since the advent of British rule, this distinction has tended to disappear.

14 Burke, *Local Government and Politics in Uganda, op. cit.,* Ch. 6.

15 Oliver and Mathew, *op. cit.,* p. 180.

The Luo did not traditionally possess a paramount chieftaincy system comparable to that of the interlacustrine Bantu kingdoms. On the other hand, their relatively elaborate hierarchical clan structure, exercising precise authority over a significant area, stood in marked contrast to the diffuse, small-scale polities of the Bantu and Nilo-Hamitic polities inhabiting neighboring areas. The twenty original administrative locations established by the British administration in central Nyanza paralleled approximately the same territory which existed under the suzerainty of a single, quasi-royal, exogamous clan. The principle of indirect rule was thereby applicable in some small degree to the Luo.

In Padhola land in Uganda, the British, at one stage in the political and administrative development of the country, recognized the indigenous polity and appointed the leader of the embryonic royal Nyapolo clan as chief. Likewise, in central Nyanza, until 1912, the British tended to appoint hereditary leaders of the major clans as chiefs in charge of locations. Interestingly enough, the identification of a clan possessed of some traditional authority and the subsequent elevation of this clan's elders as headmen or chiefs frequently served to exaggerate their traditional authority. Lord Hailey wrote in 1949 that: "Out of the existing fifteen headmen, seven are members of families recognized as holding a leading position while eight have been selected on other grounds."[16]

It is important to note that whereas the Nilotic peoples generally practiced a mixed herding and agricultural economy, the Kenya Luo are predominantly an agricultural people and, in this respect, differ substantially from their cousins to the north. This difference may not be without significance, for it is evident that a cattle economy tends to place certain universal demands on the political system, and herding societies—be they Nilotic or Nilo-Hamitic—tend to reveal a number of common characteristics. However, the Luo, in contrast to the Acholi and most other Nilotic peoples, are not socially or politically organized in age grades. Authority is allocated more in terms of a recognition that some clans and their elders are paramount to others and deserving of special trans-clan recognition and obedience. Lucy Mair has perceptively ventured that "the less a people are dependent on herding, the less significant is the connection between their pattern of settlement and their political system."[17]

For our purposes in this analysis, this introduction must suffice as a sweeping description of the origin and evolution of early indigenous polities in that section of the African continent now called Kenya. Bearing in mind that the presentation is a general introduction, we may proceed to study the evolution of contemporary Kenya, in terms of the interplay of its indigenous polities, and to delineate the manner in which various political structures

---

[16] Lord Hailey, *Native Administration in the British Territories* (London: H.M.S.O., 1950), Vol. I, 152.

[17] Lucy Mair, *Primitive Government* (Baltimore: Penguin Books, 1962), p. 29.

acquired over the centuries have influenced the form of the emergent Kenya nation.

AN EMERGENT POLITY

Prior to the involvement in the penetration of East Africa by Arabs, Indians, and Europeans, the indigenous polities of Kenya consisted of a number of small-scale, diffuse Bantu peoples in what is now North Nyanza; an expanding Nilotic peoples, the Luo, in central South Nyanza; the Nilo-Hamitic pastoral Masai herding their cattle in an area extending from the Rift Valley to nearly central Tanganyika; the related Nandi peoples growing in power and influence south of Victoria-Nyanza; and the Kikuyu, an expanding forest-highland Bantu peoples, gradually moving southward from the central plateau. To the south and east resided the related Kamba, who had been quick to establish a *quid pro quo* relationship with Arab traders and caravans moving north up the Tana River.

It was not until the latter part of the nineteenth century that these numerous small-scale polities were required to cope with still another migration—the Europeans and Arabs from the north and south. However, from this time on, polities that evolved were largely shaped by these external forces. During the early days of the scramble, a near pathological fascination with the source of the Nile; a knowledge of the existence of the extensive interlacustrine kingdom-states; the intransigence of the Masai whose *moran* (warriors) rendered passage from Mombasa to the lakes a most risky venture; and the confluence of British, French, and German interests to the region of Victoria-Nyanza served to distract attention away from Kenya and its constituent polities. During the exploratory period, Kenya was little more than an inhospitable land and peoples, hindering access to the lake region to the north. About 1840, the penetration of Arab traders and slavers into the lake region of East Africa began to gather momentum. By 1870, traders from Zanzibar and from Khartoum were familiar figures at the court of the Kabaka of Buganda and the Omukama of Bunyoro. Even the missionaries—who initially sought to spread the gospel inland from the coast to the lakes—were forced to give up their early attempts at establishing mission stations in Kenya. Soon they joined the explorers and Arab traders on the distant, but more hospitable, northern shores of Lake Victoria-Nyanza.

Pastoralists and European Penetration

At this precise point in time, the Masai military tide, which had carried this virile people from the highlands and Rift Valley of Kenya to the territory of the Wogogo in central Tanganyika—had begun to recede. The cause of the Masai decline, however, did not so much result from the emergence of a competing polity as from a prolonged civil war which sapped the strength of the constituent tribes of the Masai nation for more than half a century. So bitter was this feud that early explorers, such as Krapf, assumed that the warring Masai groups were distinct peoples.[18] Had the Masai been united and had they evolved a centralized polity enabling them to field a single large army, it is conceivable that European and Arab penetration would have been systematically repelled and the subsequent history of Kenya significantly different. Krapf, one of the first Europeans to come into contact with the Masai (in the 1840s), spoke of them as "dreaded as warriors laying all waste with fire and sword, so that the weaker tribes do not venture to resist them in the field, but leave them in possession of their herds, and seek only to save themselves by the quickest possible flight."[19]

Among the Masai, authority was invested in the age-grade units. However, considerable authority was also exercised by the *laibon,* a ritual prophet and mystical expert who was particularly influential in matters of warfare. There was no single Masai chief or, for that matter, any figure of authority, claiming allegiance over a sizable group or area. Each age set had its assigned responsibility, and, as Lucy Mair correctly noted, "Of all the political systems which have come under European rule, this type is least capable of adaptation to the purposes of the ruler."[20] There was considerable and politically significant variation between East African pastoral tribes as to the organization of their age grades. For example, among the Nandi (whom we will discuss further later), the transfer of political responsibility from one age set to another brought the entire tribe together and thereby contributed to the evolution of a homogeneous Nandi polity. Among the Masai, however, this was not the case. The allocation of authority occurred among relatively small sections independently. While Masai power in central East Africa declined, that of the Nandi to the north was increasing. And, when the East African Protectorate was declared in 1895, the Nandi were firmly established as the dominant power in the west.[21]

At about the middle of the nineteenth century, the Nandi adopted the institution of *laibon* from their Masai neighbors. Termed *orkoiyot* by the Nandi, this figure exercised considerable influence. Though hardly an all-powerful chief, the *orkoiyot's* sanction was nonetheless required in matters of war, circumcision, and agriculture.[22] Perhaps more importantly, the *orkoiyot* served as the symbol of tribal unity and solidarity. This institution was a curi-

---

[18] Reginald Coupland, *East Africa and Its Invaders* (Oxford: Clarendon Press, 1938), p. 343.

[19] *Ibid.,* p. 344.

[20] Mair, *op. cit.,* p. 80.

[21] Oliver and Mathew, *op. cit.,* p. 418.

[22] George W. B. Huntingford, *The Nandi of Kenya* (London: Routledge and Kegan Paul, 1953), p. 3.

ous one and may be revealing of subsequent political behavior. It is not un-common in East Africa to find the intrusion into a relatively homogeneous peoples of a single leader, or group of leaders, or ritual specialists from an-other, sometimes radically different peoples. Nilotic leaders, for example, were established in the interlacustrine kingdoms as a third and superordinate ele-ment in those protostate polities. G. W. B. Huntingford, an authority on the Nandi, remarks that:

> The situation is curious. A group of medicine men come as refugees to a tribe which has been their enemy for many years. In a short time these men establish themselves in a position of influence, if not of actual authority, which they have retained to this day, in spite of the fact that they are con-sidered even now to be foreigners, and that the tribe as a whole dislikes them.[23]

An indigenous heritage which provides for the involvement of an external factor within the organization of the polity is, conceivably, conducive to the amalgamation of Kenya's multiple, competing polities into a single na-tion.

The Masai have never existed as a single unified tribe, but are better compared to a nation composed of similar and related peoples. However, the Nandi were a single polity, albeit one characterized by diffuse and small-scale political systems. It was this relative unity which permitted the Nandi first to repulse the more numerous Masai and subsequently to expand their own holdings. Nandi territory was divided into six regions (*emotin-wek*). However, the subdivisions of the *emet* (singular of *emotinwek*), termed *pororiet*, were politically more significant. At first, the *pororiet* served to identify a single age set or group which fought together (a regi-ment) and subsequently came to include the area or region inhabited by such a group.[24] It is important to note that these regimental units did not coincide with clearly demarcated regions; on the contrary, frequently the *pororiet* had branches located quite a distance from the territory of origin.

When the British finally subdued the Nandi in 1905, the country was divided, for administrative purposes, into "locations." However, the twenty-five locations "followed as far as possible the distributions of the *pororiet*.[25] The fundamental political unit among the Nandi, however, was the *koret* (parish). The *koret* consisted of from twenty to one hundred adjoining homesteads, the number depending on topography and other related fac-tors.[26] The *koret* council, termed "*kokwek*," was "the most important of the Nandi councils because all the men of the *koret* . . . (could) attend it."[27]

---

[23] *Ibid.*, p. 40.

[24] *Ibid.*, p. 8.

[25] *Ibid.*, p. 13.

[26] *Ibid.*, p. 6.

[27] *Ibid.*, p. 23.

This assembly is significant, for it reflected the egalitarian and democratic nature of Nandi political behavior. Each *kokwek* had its leader (*poiyot*). This leader's election to office and his performance while in office is reminiscent of the Quaker-meeting style of decision-making. Nandi culture, as reflected in the indigenous political institutions, was characteristic of Kenya's Nilo-Hamites. Aspects of this political style have been carried over into the present and contribute an important element to the polities of modern Kenya. "The Nandi considers himself the equal of any man, and superior to all who are not Nandi. He respects no chief (for he has none to respect) and gives in to old age only."[28]

The Kikuyu and European Penetration

While the Nandi and their neighbors were shaping the political future of the Nyanza region, the Kikuyu (an essentially agricultural peoples constantly under attack by the marauding Masai) were moving southward into the Kiambu area where they purchased land from the Dorobo, a primitive forest peoples thought to be the descendants of an earlier Negroid-Bushmanoid stock. Wary of the Masai, the Kikuyu kept to the hills and forests which offered them the necessary protection. We noted earlier that the Kikuyu had adopted the age-grade system and other institutions from the Nilo-Hamitic peoples with whom they came into contact. In fact, much of the Kikuyu culture, generally, and their political institutions, in particular, were, in essence, a reaction to, or an emulation of, the institutions of the Masai. A polity based essentially on age grades had its origins in the necessity to organize a defensive system in the face of Masai raids.

Like the Masai, the Kikuyu were a nation composed of constituent tribal polities, with political authority residing in the hands of the elders of one generation and handed down to the succeeding generation at regular intervals. This ritual transfer of authority from one elite to another *ituiko* occurred when the firstborn grandson of the generation in power reached the age of circumcision—a span of about thirty years.[29] The military was distinct from the governing age set, except for a limited control exercised by the elders over the warriors. In a fashion remarkably similar to the manner in which a segment of the KANU (Kenya African National Union) youth wing functions today, the age set just beneath the ruling group served as the elders' police force and bodyguard.[30]

The mass base of KANU among the Kikuyu people and its relatively highly organized system of tributary membership categories (youth, women,

---

[28] *Ibid.*, p. 22.

[29] H. E. Lambert, *Kikuyu Social and Political Institutions* (New York: Oxford University Press, 1956), pp. 40–42.

[30] *Ibid.*, p. 69.

etc.), in conjunction with a ritual and the paraphernalia of membership, including regular payment of dues, is consistent with an indigenous age-grade system which required ceremonial demonstration of acceptance and the payment of established fees for entrance into each succeedingly more important status unit. For example, payments required for entering the elder class were spread over approximately a six-year period.

The tendency for secrecy and cliques within the Kikuyu-dominated KANU is in conformity with the function of Kima (plural, Biama), the major political institution among the Kikuyu. The Kima was, at the same time, a court, a legislative council, and a private and secret club. Council-club secret initiations were common to nearly every unit of each age set. For example, the warrior council was responsible for decision on military operations, maintenance of internal order and discipline, education of the younger warrior set, provision of police protection for the elders, and public punishment, including execution. The women, too, had their council. They discussed and decided on matters for which they were primarily responsible. The important role of women in traditional Kikuyu polities has been noted by many observers, as has the important position of women in Mau Mau. All observers of Kikuyu-KANU political rallies and meetings have been impressed by the role played by the Kikuyu women. The leader of the council (*muthamaki*) was not hereditarily appointed, but was chosen on the basis of qualities of leadership and judgment demonstrated over a long period of time. Nonetheless, as Lambert notes, there were "certain clans and subclans associated in the minds of others with qualities which are regarded as hereditary and likely to appear in every generation."[31]

A more significant aspect of indigenous Kikuyu political behavior that would seem to contribute to the style of contemporary politics is the attitude toward justice. Although the Kikuyu had a relatively highly developed sense of legislation, justice was determined more on the basis of *ad hoc* equity than on precedent or what we would call "law."[32] Furthermore, the law that was legislated and promulgated by the senior rank of elders did not bind the succeeding age set when it assumed power. "Law passed and promulgated by the ruling age grade would have the force of law during its rule, but not a moment longer."[33] Lambert adds that it was customary for the succeeding age set to repeal deliberately the legislation of its predecessors. The frame of mind—a regard of the law as temporary and having an enforcement span coterminous with the existing political power structure—is much in evidence today in Kikuyu (and other Kenyan peoples') attitudes toward the constitution. Whereas KADU spokesmen regard the independence constitution as inviolable, KANU leaders have demonstrated in word and in action that, as they are now in power, the constitution is subject to

[31] *Ibid.*, p. 102.
[32] *Ibid.*, p. 118.
[33] *Ibid.*, p. 131.

change and, in fact, should be drastically altered. For example, following the May 1963 elections, the victorious KANU leaders immediately declared that the "*majimbo*" (regionalism) constitution was unworkable and demanded that the regional governments be "little more than local authorities."[34]

Like the Nandi and the Masai, the Kikuyu did not regard with favor the efforts of immigrant Europeans and resident Arabs to run caravans through their country from the sea to the lakes. Zanzibar's Sultan Barghash, fearful that he would lose all rights to the mainland, urged the British to establish an East Africa Company.[35] A charter for the Imperial British East Africa Company was obtained in 1888. From the Sultan, the IBEA soon acquired responsibility for ruling his ill-defined mainland domains. The company's commercial interests were centered in the lake region, and Kenya was perceived merely as an obstacle to be overcome on the road to Uganda. However, the obstacle proved so serious that eventually it led to the withdrawal of the IBEA and the assumption of administrative responsibility in East Africa by Her Majesty's Government. Captain Frederick Lugard was engaged to construct a series of inland forts which would protect the company's caravans. Lugard was impressed by the Kikuyu, "a fine intelligent-looking race."[36]

However, relations between the company officials and the Kikuyu in the vicinity of present-day Nairobi were poor. The Kikuyu were among the first East African people to appreciate the fact that European penetration would result in the employment of Africans to further European enrichment and power. The caravans on the way to Uganda depended heavily on obtaining food and other provisions from the Kikuyu, as Kikuyuland was one of the few fertile regions between the coast and the lake. The journey from Mombasa to Kikuyuland took about six weeks. Another approximately six-week period was needed to travel to Kampala in Uganda. As the cost of portage was enormous, nearly £250 per ton, only ivory or gold could be profitably exported from the interior. The need for a railroad was apparent.[37]

Early contact between the Kikuyu and the caravans of the IBEA did very little to establish a foundation for understanding between these two peoples. "While passing though Kikuyu land they would indulge in systematic pillaging of the crops so that very naturally the local tribes would turn hostile."[38] The Kikuyu retaliated by murdering company personnel and by burning company forts. These demonstrations elicited one British punitive

---

[34] *Reporter* (Nairobi), October 5, 1963, p. 9.

[35] E. R. Verge-Hodge, *Imperial British East Africa Company* (London: Macmillan & Company, 1960), p. 18.

[36] Frederick John Dealtry Lugard, *East Africa: November 1889 to December 1890*, Vol. 1. *The Diaries of Lord Lugard* (Evanston, Illinois: Northwestern University Press, 1959–1963).

[37] Oliver and Mathew, *op. cit.,* p. 410.

[38] Verge-Hodge, *op. cit.,* p. 75.

expedition after another. Soil in which the seeds of Mau Mau would grow was being prepared at this early date. The Kikuyu residing in the Kiambu areas destroyed the British fort at Bagoretti. In 1892, the leader of the Kikuyu raiding party was captured and taken prisoner. Waiyaki Hinja is today regarded as one of Kenya's earliest patriots.[39] Thus, while amiable relations were established with the Baganda and other Uganda peoples at the western terminus of the route to the lakes, the British and their Arab cohorts were systematically alienating nearly every Kenya tribe. That Uganda and Kenya took quite different routes toward independence is, in part, a consequence of these early relationships.

Other Bantu-British Relations

Here and there, the relationship between the European caravans and certain polities assumed major significance. For example, in the Kavirondo region, the small Wanga tribe of the Baluhya cluster cooperated closely with the Europeans. The leader of this group, one Chief Mumia, provided supplies and shelter for the caravans on the way to the lake.[40] This association served to augment rapidly the influence of this petty chieftain. After British government suzerainty was established, Mumia emerged as a major chief with substantially expanded authority. To a significant degree, the relationship of Mumia and the European caravans contributed to an emergent unity of the numerous tiny Bantu polities in the Nyanza area. Today these small Bantu tribes conceive of themselves as Abaluhya, possess their own political association, and have attempted, with limited success, to designate a single paramount chief—the grandson of Mumia.

Our purpose here is not to trace the history of Kenya, but to abstract selective eras and places which demonstrate our thesis of political continuity. Significant events, but relatively unimportant from our point of view, are passed over lightly. However, to ensure a sense of chronological continuity, they must be noted.

The fortunes of the IBEA went from bad to worse. Sultan Khalifa, who succeeded Barghash in 1888, was highly unstable and created considerable trouble for the company before he died in 1890. The Germans, too, were increasingly active in the area, and the resources of this undercapitalized and understaffed British company had to be diverted to cope with German inroads. In 1891, the IBEA announced plans to withdraw from Uganda and, necessarily, from Kenya as well. Shortly thereafter, plans for a railway from Mombasa to the lakes were announced. The Uganda protectorate was declared in 1894, and the East African Protectorate came into being a year later. However, few Nandi, Masai, or Kikuyu were aware of these changes.

---

[39] P. Kibaara Kabutu, "The First Freedom Fighters," *Pan Africa,* December 12, 1963.

[40] Oliver and Mathew, *op. cit.,* p. 414.

As one historian has noted, "A map of British influence drawn in 1894 would show a thin red line stretching through the area of the East African Protectorate (Kenya), and a much heavier coloring from a center in Buganda. . . ."[41]

Although the evolution of indigenous polities at this particular juncture in history was influenced by this "thin red line" (some more than others), the decline of Masai power was of far greater significance. But there was a sign of times to come in the guise of one James Watt, an Englishman who was the first of thousands to settle permanently in Kenya. In 1894, this adventurous Englishman, along with his wife and children, established a store in the interior. In 1897, construction of the Uganda Railway was begun. Four years later, at the cost of £9,500 per mile and hundreds of lives, the 572-mile railway line from Mombasa to the terminus in Kisumu on the lake was completed. Now the way was clear for alien settlement and commerce. The construction of the railroad was directly responsible for bringing more than 32,000 Indians to Kenya, an element that has since grown to 120,000. This Asian minority, which monopolizes the commercial life of the country, poses a major contemporary political issue, as we shall see.

As settlers moved along the railway line, some perceptive and anxious British administrators foresaw a struggle over land, a form of conflict which has characterized Kenya's politics ever since. The Kikuyu, residing in the most desirable highland regions, were themselves expanding southward and taking up new lands. Because they believed that the conquest of Dorobo lands—in the area of present-day Kiambu—was alien to their gods, they negotiated and purchased the land. However, the outbreak of an epidemic of human and animal diseases, plus an infestation of locusts and a severe drought, decimated the peoples of this region of Kenya. The newly purchased lands in Kiambu were deserted as the stricken Kikuyu temporarily migrated toward their Nyeri land of origin. In part, it was their seemingly deserted lands that the early European settler coveted and claimed, unaware that but a few years earlier the Kikuyu had purchased the same land from its original Dorobo owners.

Land

Thus, abolition of the slave trade and a demand for easy access to the lake region called forth the railway; the economics of the railway demanded commerce, taxation, and development. These factors required settlers; and, beginning with Sir Charles Eliot (the Commissioner for the East African Protectorate), British policy was to bring as many settlers as possible to the highlands. In 1901, the East African (lands) Order in Council was passed. This order gave the Crown control over the allocation of lands; but there is

---

41 Marie de Kiewiet Hemphill, in Oliver and Mathew, *op. cit.,* p. 430.

evidence that the British were aware, as early as 1896, that the Kiambu area of the highlands was held in distinctive plots of individual freehold tenure by the Kikuyu, and it has been suggested that the British elected to suppress this knowledge.[42] Sorrenson maintains that the fact that the Church of Scotland Mission purchased land, as early as 1896, that was definitely held in freehold by Kikuyu is indicative of British knowledge and understanding of Kikuyu freehold land tenure. Ironically, knowledge of Kikuyu freehold title was suppressed because Sir Arthur Hardinge-Ainsworth and other officials feared that if the Asian and European settlers became aware that the Kikuyu held the land in freehold title, they would take advantage of the Kikuyu's ignorance and poverty to purchase the entire region.[43]

Given this information, the British government initially decided to grant settlers certificates of occupancy limited to twenty-one years; however, few settlers were to be attracted to East Africa under these terms. In 1899, the Foreign Office appealed to the courts to decide on the legality of the Crown's title to land in a "protectorate." There then followed a series of land ordinances which gave legal credence to the myth that the Kikuyu had no claim to land that they no longer happened to be cultivating or occupying. "European settlers began to select land in the midst of African settled areas as African occupation was a sign of good land."[44]

If the desired land was occupied, the would-be settler had but to offer the Kikuyu a small compensation for "occupier's rights." In this fashion, approximately 11,000 Kikuyu lost 60,000 acres of their patrimony in the choice Kiambu-Limuru areas. Kikuyu land tenure is complex, and, for our purposes, only a brief description is possible. In essence, the Kikuyu believe that, in the Kiambu and Limuru areas, they purchased their holdings (*ithaka*) from the Dorobo. The original Kikuyu owner of a ridge, which is the characteristic feature of the terrain, propagated and expanded his family into a unit of considerable size. On occasion, such a lineage evolved into a distinct clan. On the death of the original owner, the land was subdivided among his heirs. In each case the boundaries were precisely marked off, and the smaller units of land were held in freehold by the heirs.

In 1912, the district commissioner of Kiambu recommended that the government pay the Kikuyu £50,000 in compensation for alienation of their holdings. But Governor Dottfield preferred not to recognize either *ithaka* or the history of the Dorobo purchases. The juxtaposition of white settler and African holdings and the steadily growing pressure from the Kikuyu to recover their land required that the system of land occupation and tenure be

---

42 Much of what follows concerning the early relationship—with respect to land—of the British administration and the Kikuyu draws heavily on the work of M. Sorrenson, "The Official Mind and Kikuyu Land Tenure," a paper delivered at the East African Institute of Social Research Conference at Kivukoni College, January 1963.

43 *Ibid.*, p. 3.

44 *Ibid.*, p. 4.

institutionalized. Thus, agreements were reached with the Masai to bring the two major sections of that tribal nation together into a delineated area termed "a reserve," and in the process freed—perhaps only incidentally—the Likipia area for white settlement.[45]

The European settlers were always quick to establish organizations to demand and defend their interests. The Kenya Planters and Farmers Association was founded in 1903. This group was shortly renamed the Colonialists Association; somewhat later it became the Kenya Farmers Association.[46]

In 1901, there were but thirteen English settlers in Kenya. But, by the end of 1904, they had claimed 220,000 acres of land. Companies were also involved in the rush for land. In the early days, the East African Syndicate Ltd. took 350,000. Grogan Forest Concessions claimed 200,000, and Lord Delamere—a name that we will not be able to ignore from this point on—laid claim to 100,000 acres for a lease period of ninety-nine years at a price of ½ cent per acre.[47] The trend toward European domination continued and was given impetus in 1932, when the Carter Land Commission defined the boundaries of the white highlands. "African rights to settlement on European farms, guaranteed them in 1902, and 1915 Crown Land Ordinances were abrogated."[48] After 1933 and the report of the Carter Commission, Europeans held 10,000 square miles of which only 12 per cent was cultivated.

Lord Hailey writes that European settlement had four major consequences with respect to the development of administration in Kenya: (1) it significantly affected the composition of political and local government institutions; (2) it served to reserve lands for European settlement; (3) it was responsible for relatively large expenditures of public monies on the "settled" areas; and (4) it gave rise to differential legislation, such as the infamous Kipande system of fingerprinting and registering of all Africans and the prohibition on African planting of certain cash crops. For our purposes, the first consequence is the most significant. Settler influence, plus the nature of the indigenous polities described above, gave rise to a form of administration and local government quite different from those evolved elsewhere in British Africa. The European settlers sought to structure the political system to preserve and enhance their control and to further their economic development of the country.[49]

The "location" system of local administration lent itself well to the needs for cheap farm labor. The absence of centralized protostates of chieftaincies

---

[45] Lord Cranworth, *Kenya Chronicles* (London: Macmillan & Company, 1939), p. 63.

[46] *Ibid.*, p. 65.

[47] Jack Woodis, *Africa: The Roots of Revolt* (New York: Citadel Press, 1962), p. 4.

[48] Sorrenson, *op. cit.*, p. 11.

[49] Including attempts to federate Uganda, Tanganyika, Kenya, and Nyasaland as early as 1923 in order to extend their white man's domain.

favored this bureaucratic arrangement since it permitted the appointment of headmen (sometimes styled chiefs) suited to implement means that would lead to European ends. The Village Headmen's Ordinance of 1902 is revealing. At this early date, before much of the country was pacified, reference was made not to chiefs, as was the case in Uganda and even in Tanganyika, but to official headmen for villages or groups of villages.

The European Polity

The European polity developed quite independently of administrative arrangements in the reserves. The first Legislative Council was established in 1907. Two men, one Kikuyu, the other British, dominated the politics of their respective communities. Jomo Kenyatta's career and the growth of modern African political consciousness is described below. A description of Lord Delamere belongs to this earlier era. A. G. Church wrote of his friend, "Kenya, and to a lesser extent lately, the neighboring territory of Tanganyika, are to him a vast stage . . . he is their Moses . . . no Joshua has yet arisen to challenge his supreme authority."[50]

Faced with a government dominated by first the Foreign and later the Colonial Office, the settlers, led by Lord Delamere, sought to seize control of the powers of government in order to pursue their own end unhampered by London. They felt that the Colonial Office did not comprehend either their situation or their problems. In 1905, the central government was little more than an executive council of heads of departments presided over by the Governor. Kenya's first Legislative Council, established in 1907, consisted of eight persons nominated by the Governor. It is not surprising that Lord Delamere was one of the two unofficial members appointed. Delamere discovered, however, that the position of the unofficial European carried little weight. In 1908, in frustration and protest, he resigned. It is unlikely that Delamere could have foreseen that, half a century later, African members, similarly frustrated and angered, would refuse, for similar reasons, to sit in the same Legislature.

World War I, though not as significant, vis-à-vis the political development of Kenya, as World War I, was not without its effects. The German forces in Tanganyika were numerous; moreover, they possessed an extremely able commander. Estimates have placed German forces of the period at 3,000 white troops (or potential troops) and 8,000 highly trained African soldiers. Of equal importance was the fact that the Germans possessed seventy machine guns and forty artillery pieces. Against this, the British could muster but 700 African troops and two machine guns.[51] There was considerable anxiety in Kenya that the German commander, Paul von Lettow-Vorbeck,

---

[50] A. G. Church, *East Africa, A New Dominion* (London: Witherby, 1927), p. 276.

[51] Cranworth, *op. cit.*, p. 181.

would lead his relatively well-equipped army across the frontier into Kenya in an attempt to capture the railway. Indicative of this anxiety was the fact that of Kenya's European population of 3,000, nearly 2,000 volunteered for military service.[52] The consequences to many partially developed or half-cleared farms and plantations were enormous. In many instances, years of work and sacrifice slipped gradually back into the bush. In 1916, the British forces took the offensive, crossed the frontier, fought, and defeated the Germans on the slopes of Kilimanjaro, and took possession of Moshi, the main town in northeastern Tanganyika.

More Africans were involved in this strange war than is sometimes realized. Lord Cranworth, in his *Kenya Chronicles,* reports that Mr. Ainsworth, one of Kenya's first able administrators, reluctantly "undertook the vast organization required to recruit and maintain such a body (porters) which numbered at one time upwards of 200,000 men."[53] The loss of life through disease and disorganization was appalling. Though relatively few in this vast army ever carried a weapon or saw the enemy, "The porters died in tens of thousands."[54] Although there is little data available, we do know that the British military and supporting forces in East Africa eventually included not only thousands of Kenyans and other East Africans, but African troops from Nyasaland, the Gold Coast, Nigeria, and the Belgian Congo as well. It is not inconceivable that a few seeds of pan-Africanism were sown during this strange interlude.

It is difficult to measure the impact of the war on the hundreds of thousands of East Africans caught up in the struggle, but it became evident that the relationship between black and white would never again be the same. Charles W. Hobley, an early and particularly astute scholar, observed in 1922 that:

> The black troops soon came to realize the physical disabilities of the Europeans and their vulnerability. They saw the European shot down and even bayonetted by enemy black soldiers. They realized that very few Europeans were crack shots. They noted the inferior marching capacity of the white man, his inability to find his way about in the bush ... and in some cases they even saw that the courage of the white was not greater than that of the black ... it is not surprising that the attitude of many of the blacks to the white man has altered.[55]

The war seriously dislocated Kenya's economy. More important, it brought Tanganyika into the British sphere. Land that the German Colonial Office had alienated was recognized by the British. The office of the Custodian of

---

[52] Zoe Marsh and G. W. Kingsworth, *Introduction to the History of East Africa,* (Cambridge, Eng.: Cambridge University Press, 1957), p. 186.

[53] Cranworth, *op. cit.,* p. 73.

[54] G. W. Hobley, *Bantu Beliefs and Magic* (London: Witherby, 1922), p. 287.

[55] *Ibid.,* p. 287.

Enemy Property was established to reallocate these choice highland holdings to deserving Englishmen and to a few Greeks and Indians. With Lord
Delamere providing the initiative, Kenya settlers speculated on the opportunity of linking their holdings with British whites in Tanganyika and Nyasaland in a manner which would eventually extend the political influence of
the settlers from Nairobi to Capetown. The politics of closer union between
Kenya, Uganda, Tanganyika, and Nyasaland is treated in Chapter 10 in this
book, and no attempt is made to comprehensively cover this important
subject here. Nonetheless, it must be pointed out that the politics of the
dominant European community between the two wars revolved around this
controversial issue. Fearful that the wartime experiences of thousands of
Africans would constitute a security problem, attempts were made to rapidly
increase the number of Europeans and white South Africans inhabiting lands
in Kenya. Thus, the postwar period witnessed a dramatic increase in the
settler population.[56]

In order to further stabilize the situation, the East African Protectorate
was dissolved in 1920. Under terms of the Kenya Annexation Order in
Council, the area became Kenya Colony (Kenya Colony Order in Council,
1921) and was declared to be a British settlement within the terms of the
British Settlements Act. In response to an increasingly more vociferous
settler position and in recognition of their contributions to the war, the
Colonial Office agreed to liberalize the political system and permit a greater
role for European settlers. In 1920, eleven Europeans were elected from as
many constituencies to sit in a reconstituted Legislative Council. Just as
important was the inclusion of two settlers on the previously completely ex
officio Executive Council. The struggle of the Indian community for political
power is treated elsewhere in this chapter. Here we have only to note that
the dynamic European settler community was not inclined to share its rising
political influence with a larger Asian minority. As early as 1906, the settlers
had successfully precluded the Indian community from taking up land in
the white highlands. The following year, the tone of settler and official
attitudes to Indian participation in the emerging, restrictive polity was set
by the Governor in a letter to the Secretary of State for the Colonies: "There
is a growing tendency amongst the white settlers in the uplands to keep the
Indian not only out of the uplands but out of the country altogether."[57]

In 1909, A. M. Jivanjee, the remarkable Indian leader who had built a
personal fortune in providing materials and contracting for the building of
the Uganda railway, was appointed the first Indian member of the Legislative
Council. The Indian community, aware that it outnumbered the European
community by nearly four to one, demanded a common electoral roll. The

---

56 It is worth noting that in their efforts to attract white settlers to Kenya, the British
government at one time offered land to the Finns and also to the Zionists in the hope
that the Jews would make Kenya their national home.

57 George Delf, *Asians in East Africa* (London: Oxford University Press, Institute
of Race Relations, 1963).

Indian Association, led by Jivanjee, sent deputations to London and Delhi and successfully elicited the support of the Indian government for its position. The Delamere-led settlers resisted mightily and sent a deputation to London to present their case to an undecided Colonial Office. That the settler position eventually won out is not surprising.

Later efforts of the Indian community in 1923 succeeded only in winning them five seats on a communal roll (the system in which each major racial community elects representatives separately, as opposed to the common roll, wherein all qualified voters—regardless of race—constitute the electorate). The Devonshire Paper of 1923 reaffirmed the reservation of the white highlands for Europeans and severely restricted Indian immigration into Kenya. Stunned by this blow, the Indian community refused for seven years to accept the communal roll principle and boycotted the Assembly. However, in 1931, they reluctantly accepted this basis of representation and took their place in the Legislative Assembly. During the 1920's, the principle of a common European-Indian electoral roll was nearly realized. Had the Indian position been a bit stronger, had the forces of Delamere been somewhat weaker, and had the common roll been accepted by the Colonial Office, it is likely that the incorporation of Africans into the polity at a later date would have been accompanied with considerably less bitterness and violence. In part, Sir Winston Churchill must bear some responsibility for the perpetuation of the communal philosophy and for the subsequent racial antagonism which came to characterize this country. While Secretary of State for the Colonies in 1921, Churchill reaffirmed the exclusive rights of settlers to the highlands. Churchill also advocated a limit on Indian immigration.

Two European unofficial members were nominated to the council to represent the interests of the Africans. Martin Wight, a scholar who has studied the evolution of colonial legislative assemblies, has noted, "It is likely that the Africans were better represented by the official members such as the Secretary for Native Affairs and the Provincial Commissioners than by the settlers."[58] Though they did not regard the Assembly as unimportant, the settler and Indian communities were more concerned with representation on the Executive than on the Legislative Council. Two unofficial Europeans were appointed in 1917, and an Indian was added in 1921. In 1923, an unofficial European was appointed to represent African interests.[59] In 1938, ex officio membership on the Executive Council was decreased from eight to four—the same number as the unofficial element.[60]

At the governmental level, the interwar years witnessed a relatively successful series of attempts on the part of the European-settler community: (1) to achieve a degree of internal self-government; (2) to manipulate the

---

[58] Martin Wight, *Development of the Legislative Council* (London: Faber and Faber, 1957), p. 90.

[59] The first African was not appointed until 1952.

[60] Wight, *op. cit.*, p. 132.

political system to their economic advantage; and (3) to employ political power to check the rising demands of the Indian community for participation in the polity. There was only incidental thought given to African participation during this period. The policy of separate communal development—not unlike the system of *apartheid* which was to emerge later in South Africa—contributed to distinct and separate governmental and political development of the various racial communities during this important formative period.

THE EMERGENCE OF AFRICAN POLITICS

Emergence of Kikuyu Political Organization

It is not surprising that initial African political agitation should have commenced among the Kikuyu. The Kikuyu Association, led by Harry Thuku, a government-employed telephone operator, was formed in 1920 and, the following year, was renamed the Young Kikuyu Association.[61] Among its members was a meter-reader for the Nairobi Town Council—a certain Johnstone Kenyatta. This embryonic political organization protested the increase in poll taxes and the Kipande registration system. In 1922, Thuku was arrested and deported—setting a precedent often followed in years to come—and his organization was proscribed. When Thuku was temporarily held in a Nairobi jail, thousands of his supporters gathered on the street and threatened to set him free by force. The British opened fire, Kikuyu fell dead, and Kenya had its first nationalist martyrs.

Three years later, the Young Kikuyu Association was revived under the name of the Kikuyu Central Association. This regrouping was led by Joseph Kangethe and Jesse Kariuki. However, the issues had not changed: demands for the return of the land, an end to the color bar, and representation in the Legislative Assembly were heard once more. Added to these were the further demands that the government establish the office of Kikuyu Paramount Chief and allow Harry Thuku to end his exile and re-enter the country.

The attitude of the era was reflected by A. G. Church, following his tour of the territory: "Wherever we went in East Africa we were made conscious of the increasing desire of the natives to be represented by members of their own race on all councils where their interests were affected and to have the right of choice of these representatives."[62]

At this early date, the first efforts were made to link the protest movements of the Kikuyu and the Luo. For example, before Harry Thuku was arrested, he had traveled to Kavirondo in an abortive attempt to establish a large Kenya-wide organization. However, tribal differences prevailed; and not

---

[61] In 1919, Thuku had established the East Africa Association, but it was quickly superseded by the Kikuyu associates.

[62] Wight, *op. cit.,* p. 205.

only was it found to be impossible to join the separate movements of the north and the south, but friction between the Nilotic Luo and the Bantu Abaluhya in the Kavirondo Taxpayers Association split the KTA into respective tribal wings.

A year before he left for the United Kingdom, Jomo Kenyatta was serving as secretary of the Kikuyu Central Association (KCA) and editor of its journal *Mwigwithania*. In 1929, he left for England, carrying with him a petition on behalf of the KCA urging the direct election of Africans to the Legislative Council. It was to be seventeen years before Kenyatta was to return for any length of time. In London, he joined the now famous "first generation" of African and Negro nationalists. Kenyatta's political biography is well known, and it is not necessary to repeat it at length here. He returned to Kenya in 1946, to a country which, from an African point of view, was only slightly altered from that which he had left seventeen years earlier. There had been some progress in the development and reorganization of local government, and, in 1944, the first African had been appointed to the Legislative Council. However, settler control of the polity was—if anything —more secure than it had been in 1929 when he had left. True, Harry Thuku had been allowed to return from exile and had defeated the incumbent Joseph Kangethe for the presidency of KCA. However, the incipient Kikuyu nationalist movement was badly split into moderate and radical wings. In 1935, the unhappy Thuku, now leader of the moderate forces, withdrew from KCA and attempted to establish a rival group, the Kikuyu Political Association. It could not compete, however, successfully with the more radical KCA.

The Kamba were the third Kenya people to organize a scheme of political agitation in response to their grievances. In July 1938, fifteen hundred Kamba tribesmen, led by Muinde, marched on Nairobi protesting the government's policies of destocking and confiscation of the cattle. The following year, they formed the Kamba Members Association which rapidly affiliated with the KCA. A comparable situation provoked action in the Taita district and led to the Taita Hills Association, which also allied itself with the KCA.

This early pattern of separate, tribally oriented organization was important, for it established a precedent that has characterized Kenya politics ever since. Although two major parties, KANU and KADU, eventually emerged, the persistence (latent as well as manifest) of tribal political associations has served both as a check on central party authority and as an obstacle to political unity.

The Emergence of KAU

In 1940, the British suspected the KCA of supporting the enemy and the organization was declared illegal. Twenty members, including representatives of the Kamba Association and the Taita Hills Association, were arrested. In a prelude to what was to come, the KCA went underground and re-emerged in the guise of the Kenya Farmers and Traders Association.

While the war was still on, Peter Mbiyu Koinange, son of the famous senior chief Koinange, returned from studies in the United States but was denied an opportunity to employ his education in the existing school system. Greatly concerned with education, and in particular with teacher training in Kenya, Koinange quickly established the independent Kenya Teachers Training College at Githunguri in the Kiambu area of Kikuyuland. It was this teacher-training college that was subsequently to become a political issue of great importance and the center of early nationalist agitation and organization.

In an attempt to win the support of increasingly disaffected African nationalists, the colonial government agreed in 1944 to appoint the first African to the Legislative Council. Although, at the time, there was no legal political movement, the leaders of the Kenya Farmers and Traders Association strongly supported the candidacy of Peter Koinange. However, the Governor nominated Eliud Mathu, a man the British felt to be more moderate. Although Mathu was careful not to overstep the line in the legislature, his subsequent public speeches made it quite clear that his nationalist credentials were in order; nonetheless, he subsequently proved to be too moderate for Kenyatta and was gradually moved aside.[63]

The postwar period, replete with the Atlantic Charter, returning servicemen, the coming to power in England of the Labour government, and the independence of India and Burma, gave rise to a set of expectations among Kenya's political activities. The extent of these expectations was not immediately realized in official circles. Instead of the British compensating African troops for service during the war—as the Kikuyu had some reason to anticipate—3,300,000 acres of Kenyan land was offered to the Zionists as a home for the Jews. Furthermore, Kenyan land was offered to British ex-servicemen but not to their African comrades. Frustration of this nature, the acquisition of organizational skill acquired during the war, and the coming of age of an important leadership group all contributed to a movement to establish a Kenya-wide political organization. By 1946, the unique Kikuyu Independence School System was educating 60,000 children in 300 schools.[64]

When Kenyatta returned and informed the Governor that he intended to enter active political life, he was advised to seek a seat on the newly formed district councils and gradually work his way into more widespread public life. For one who had spent seventeen years abroad awaiting an opportunity for action, participation in the relative boredom and bureaucracy of local

---

[63] George Delf, *Jomo Kenyatta: Towards the Truth about the Light of Kenya* (London: Victor Gollancz, 1961), p. 144.

[64] *Ibid.,* p. 137; G. P. Pinto, in "Glimpses of Kenya's Nationalist Struggle," *Pan Africa,* December 12, 1963, p. 28, states that at the time of the emergency in October 1962, over 175,000 children were being educated in the independent schools.

government was not particularly appealing. Just prior to Kenyatta's return in 1946, the Kenya African Union—an outgrowth of the two-year-old Kenya African Study Union founded by Mathu—was established with James Gichuru, now Minister of Finance, as its first president.[65] In June 1947, Jomo Kenyatta became the KAU's first president. It is possible to date to this point the emergence of the continuous, concentrated, political action which finally led to independence on December 11, 1963. George Delf, who has carefully traced Kenyatta's political career, has noted that "by the end of 1947, African nationalism was set on a course which must lead inexorably either to the end of white rule or to an explosion."[66] At this point in time, Jomo Kenyatta began to take an increasing interest in the Kenya Independence School System and moved to Githunguri Teacher Training College. This location became the command post of the pre-Mau Mau nationalist movement.

African resistance to the administration and increasing racial hostility were characteristic of the immediate postwar period. A land-terracing scheme in the Fort Hall region was sabotaged. Kenyatta was blamed. It is more than likely that this was the work of the "forty"—a group of disaffected young men who had come of age at the same time and many of whom had spent a year or more in military service. This group was reminiscent of an indigenous age-grade with intense solidarity. The "forty" roamed the countryside and eventually emerged as the extremist wing of Mau Mau. Government headmen and chiefs who, it will be recalled, were without a traditional base, were increasingly subjected to attack and intimidation. Intelligence reports from the district officers throughout Kikuyuland ominously warned of growing disaffection and a spreading unease. For the few who cared or who dared to look, the clouds of Mau Mau were gathering. The more radical leaders of the outlawed KCA were found to be infiltrating the squatter population on European farms, seeking their support, and promising that in return they would fall heir to the Europeans' land. In the following years, the infamous oathing commenced, and the countdown began. It was in 1949 that the term Mau Mau was first used; by 1950, it had been officially banned. However, it is important to note that it was not until 1952—just prior to Kenyatta's arrest—that the "killing oaths" first appeared.[67]

Following the Nairobi general strike of 1950, the Trade Union Congress was suppressed, and the leaders, Makkan Singh and Fred Kubai, were arrested. Makkan Singh was convicted of sedition and exiled to the northern frontier where he remained for ten years. Fred Kubai, the TUC general secretary, was charged with murder but found not guilty. He subsequently

---

[65] Others important in the early organization were Peter Mbiyu, Albert Owino, Tom Mbotela, Fred Kubai, Jesse Kariuki, and Francis Khamisi.

[66] Delf, *Jomo Kenyatta*, p. 145.

[67] *Ibid.*, p. 153.

became the vice-president of KAU and was later charged and imprisoned with Jomo Kenyatta.

On his return to Kenya, Kenyatta sought to revive KAU as a truly national party. He toured the country seeking converts. And as Thuku had done earlier, he turned to Nyanza for a larger base of support. Oginga Odinga, director of the Luo Cooperative and Thrift Corporation, joined KAU. In September 1952, just prior to KAU's prosecution, he was deputized by Kenyatta as chairman of the Central Committee.

The material factors of discontent were apparent for all to see. For example, a United Nations survey in 1953 showed that the average annual income of Kenya's Africans was £27. Asians averaged £280, while the average European income was £660. Nearly £50 per year per child was spent on the education of European children; approximately three shillings per pupil was appropriated for African education.

Emergence of Luo Political Organization

To the west, the Luo (future political allies of the Kikuyu) had also begun to agitate for alterations in the distribution of resources and of the loci of power. One observer writing in 1927 stated that he had noted signs of political unrest as early as 1921, with the founding of the Young Kavirondo Association.[68]

In the Nyanza region of Kenya, the geographical, historical, and cultural association with Uganda affected the emergence of political organization. By the 1920's, missionary activities were already largely in the hands of trained Africans. Although the attempts of the Kikuyu to participate in the modern society and economy were frustrated, the Luo were encouraged to organize. In 1923, the activities of the Kavirondo Association were regarded with some anxiety by the colonial government. In the same year, two days before Christmas, the YKA held a mass meeting. The district officers who attempted to attend the meeting were ejected. The British, now alarmed by the spread of dissension, called a mass meeting of the Luo to air grievances. At a baraza (meeting) of 4,000 Luo, the British discovered beyond doubt that the Luo—like the Kikuyu—were politically restive. It is worth noting that this meeting occurred within a month of the deportation of Harry Thuku and the death of twenty-one Kikuyu rioters outside the Nairobi police station.[69]

The underlying grievances which led the Luo to coalesce in opposition to government policy in a fashion quite out of keeping with their traditional diffuse political system were remarkably similar to the issues which were

---

[68] Church, op. cit., p. 205.

[69] For an excellent treatment of this subject, see John Lonsdale, "Archdeacon Owen and the Kavirondo Taxpayers Welfare Association" (an unpublished paper, East African Institute of Social Research, January 1963).

bringing unity among the Kikuyu, taxation and a fear of land alienation. The transformation of Kenya from protectorate to colony in 1920 led many partially educated Luo to fear that the alienation of land to the Europeans would consequently spread to Nyanza.

By 1923 the situation was deemed critical, and the Provincial Commissioner turned to Archdeacon Owen for assistance in dealing with the growing racial bitterness of the Luo. Through his personal influence and the extraordinary respect with which he was regarded by the Luo, Owen was able to transform the KYA into the Kavirondo Taxpayers Association. However, even Owen could not counter the ground swell of anti-Europeanism; the missionaries were white and their close association with the colonial government was apparent to all. The Luo responded by forming independent churches—with the result that the missionaries found themselves squeezed ever more tightly between the dictates of a settler-dominated government in Nairobi and growing African antagonism in Nyanza.[70] The KTA, beset by a revival of Luo clan parochialism, dissension between its predominantly Luo and Abaluhya wings and Catholic-religious factions, and the emergence of a competing system of government-sponsored local government councils, gradually declined in importance.

The Mau Mau Interlude

The May 1951 visit of James Griffiths, the Labour Colonial Secretary, to Kenya was seen by some as a last-hour reprieve. KAU demanded twelve elected African seats instead of the four nominated seats which the Africans held at that time. It also demanded that the color bar be abolished, that the government provide financial assistance to African farmers, and that labor unions be given freedom to organize.[71] Unfortunately, Griffiths failed to rise to the challenge, and little was done to relieve the growing pressure for reform. The Kenya government insisted on regarding the KAU as a front organization for Mau Mau. Further, the government viewed Kenyatta as the leader of both organizations. However, after three years of close surveillance, there was no proof or evidence that Kenyatta was leading, or even connected with, Mau Mau activities.[72]

In September 1952, ex-senior Chief Koinange was arrested on the charge of murder and, though found not guilty, was confined, along wtih his son Peter Koinange. In October, the colonial government proclaimed a state of emergency, and troops were flown in from the Suez Canal zone. Kenyatta and 182 other Africans were arrested and detained. It was not until a week after the Emergency was declared that a European settler was killed—the first white victim of Mau Mau. On October 20, Kenyatta, along with five

[70] *Ibid.,* p. 10.

[71] Delf, *Jomo Kenyatta,* p. 168.

[72] *Ibid.,* p. 172.

leaders of the KAU, was charged with directing the activities of Mau Mau. The trial was held in the remote western border town of Kapengeusia, 300 miles from Nairobi. Delf reports that this village was so remote that when a resident magistrate was chosen to hear Kenyatta's case, he was in error appointed to the wrong province.[73] The trial began late in November with Kenyatta entering a plea of not guilty. After a session which lasted five months, Kenyatta was found guilty and sentenced to seven years' hard labor to be followed by an indefinite period of restrictions. There then commenced four years of vicious fighting in which thirty-two European civilians and sixty-three members of the security forces were killed. On the opposite side, 11,500 Mau Mau died at the hands of the Kenya military forces, and nearly 2,000 Africans were killed by Mau Mau.[74]

Emergence of Kenya Nationalism

The postwar period was also one of considerable political agitation outside of Kikuyuland. Numerous associations of a political nature were established in many areas. George Bennett writes that, by the end of 1947, "the administration knew of 63 such (organizations) in Mombasa, of which 28 had been formed in that year. Many of these there and elsewhere were tribal in character. They were even formed among the pastoral tribes. . . ."[75]

It was the goal of the Kenya African Union to attempt to bring these various organizations together into a single, Kenya-wide association. It is important to note that in 1947, at KAU's first congress, delegates representing every main tribal group in Kenya were present. It was at this meeting that the KAU elected Kenyatta as president. The Corfield Report accurately notes that:

In Jomo Kenyatta and the Kenya African Union, all the Kikuyu organization strains eventually met—Independence Schools; the Teacher Training College at Githunguri; age-group organizations; and lastly, the Kikuyu Central Association. But in the earlier days they were often reported on and treated as separate entities or manifestations of political unrest.[76]

Concurrent with the attempt to establish KAU as a nationwide political movement were the first movements toward pan-African association. In 1950, for example, the African League invited KAU to send delegates to a Conference on Democratic Rights for Africans which was scheduled to be held in the United Kingdom. Also in 1950, the secretary of the Tanganyika African

---

[73] *Ibid.*, p. 184.

[74] *Ibid.*, p. 194.

[75] George Bennett, *The Development of Political Organization in Kenya, Political Studies* (New York: Clarendon Press, 1957), p. 26.

[76] The Corfield Report, *Origins and Growth of Mau Mau* (Nairobi, Kenya: The Government Printer, 1960), p. 51.

Association visited Kenyatta in Kiambu where, possibly for the first time, representatives of Kenya and Tanganyika discussed the questions of East African nationalism and, conceivably, the possibilities of eventual closer union.

From the very outset, there existed a close relationship between KAU and the emerging labor organizations. In 1951, Fred Kubai, general secretary of the East African Trade Union Congress, was elected chairman of the Nairobi branch of the Kenya African Union. Though a predominantly Kikuyu party, by 1951, KAU had extended its membership over much of Kenya and listed some 150,000 members. Significantly, however, its executive committee was almost solely composed of Kikuyu.

The arrest of Kenyatta, the proclamation of the Emergency, and the banning of KAU brought a halt to organized political activity and substituted violence in its place. All nationwide political organizations were proscribed; among the Kikuyu, meetings of more than three people were prohibited. In the non-Kikuyu Embu-Meru areas, political organization was permitted only at the district level. Thus, the Emergency itself gave rise to a revival of tribal-district nationalism and political organization which served as a brake on the evolution of national politics and unity in the post Mau Mau, pre-independence period. Expressions of discontent and articulation of interests were voiced through organizations, such as the labor movement, that were not proscribed. This incidentally provided an opportunity for the emergence of a new leadership which was to play an important part in subsequent events. As one Kenyan graduate student at Syracuse University has written: "In short, the Emergency operations had arrested the trend and evolution of mass political activities. It froze what political activity remained at the district level. It wrested the torch of political leadership from the Kikuyu, and this was handed over to other tribal groups, particularly the Luo."[77]

In October 1953, Tom Mboya was named general secretary of the Kenya Federation of Registered Trade Unions (subsequently, the Kenya Federation of Labor). Mboya's successful handling of the potentially dangerous Mombasa dock strike, in March 1955, catapulted him to pre-eminence in the Kenya political environment which, prior to this event, had been characterized by a relative leadership vacuum. Up to 1955, all African political organizations had been forbidden; after this time, organizations were permitted on a district basis. In addition to the tribal-based associations and organizations that emerged at the district level, political organizations also formed in Nairobi and in Mombasa. For example, a Luo lawyer, C. M. G. Argwings-Kodhek, who had established a reputation for defending Kikuyu Mau Mau detainees in Nairobi, was the founder of the Nairobi District African Congress.[78]

---

[77] Kamau Mwangi (draft of an unpublished paper, Syracuse University, 1963), p. 65.

[78] This organization was initially termed the Kenya African Congress and was denied registration because it sought to organize on a district-wide basis.

In 1956, elections were permitted on a district level, and the Nairobi District African Congress, along with Mboya's Nairobi Peoples Convention party, became a major political force. The emergence of a multi-party system and the bitterness and scope of the Mau Mau Emergency brought the realization to the Kenya government and to the Colonial Office that a new era had dawned. In 1954, Oliver Lyttelton, Secretary of State for the Colonies, advanced some significant constitutional changes which provided for the election of African representatives to the Kenya Legislative Council. The Lyttelton Constitution also provided for one African minister and decreased the number of European ministers to three and the number of Asians to two. Eliud Mathu, the transitional spokesman of African nationalism, led the opposition to Lyttelton's proposals. As Susan Wood, in her timely work, *Kenya: The Tensions of Progress,* noted, "Their main objection was not that executive power was passing into the hands of the people in the country, but that it was into European and Asian hands that it was passing and not African. This they considered a dangerous precedent."[79] It is possible to note here an important contradiction between the movement for self-government and the struggle for African representation. At this period, self-government implied the transfer of authority from a relatively sympathetic Colonial Office to settler and/or Asian hands; in this respect, the movement could be construed as detrimental to African nationalism.

There could be no doubt but that the Mau Mau episode wakened many considerate Kenyans—black, brown, and white—to the seriousness of the impasse they had reached. In July 1954, Michael Blundell, a liberal white settler, formed the United Country party, which was based essentially on a multiracial principle. In reaction to this and drawing a different lesson from the Emergency, those Europeans of the far right established the Federal Independence party to advance a form af *apartheid* or autonomy for the essentially white regions of Kenya. The African counterpart to the settlers' United Country party was the multiracial Kenya National party formed by Masinde Muliro. This party's position was generally moderate and favored the gradual acquisition of self-government. However, racial pressure was so great that, in November 1958, the Asian members were dropped from its executive committee.

In June 1955, when the government permitted Africans to re-establish political organizations on a local basis, C. M. G. Argwings-Kodhek was required to restyle the Nairobi Kenya African National Congress. This party, with its slogan of "Africa for the Africans," was possibly the most racially and radically oriented faction during this important transitional period. The political biography of Argwings-Kodhek is extremely interesting, for, in many respects, he was the first of a group of Kenyans to attract transtribal support. Though a Luo, he was highly regarded among the Kikuyu for, as

---

[79] Susan Wood, *Kenya: The Tensions of Progress* (London: Oxford University Press, 1960), p. 36.

noted before, he had provided legal assistance to Kikuyu convicted as Mau Mau under the laws during the Emergency. Because the Kikuyu were prohibited from taking part in any political activity at this time, the 1956 election in Nairobi was essentially a contest between two Luo candidates—Tom Mboya and Argwings-Kodhek. The vote was surprisingly close, with Kodhek receiving 1,746 votes to Mboya's 2,138.[80]

Midway between the more radical Nairobi African National Congress and the multiracial Kenya National party was Mboya's Peoples Convention party (PCP). Although it advocated immediate independence, had a relatively smooth organization, and was supported in large part by the financial assistance of American friends and labor organizations, it was not as anti-European as the Congress. Because Mboya was highly regarded as a union leader, his party drew most of its support from the workers in the Nairobi region. The style of campaigning initiated at this time—involving the use of mass rallies and newspapers—was a preview of the effective techniques which were to be employed by KANU at a later date.

The 1956 Election

The European phase of the 1956 election was essentially a struggle between Blundell's "liberal" New Kenya party, which advocated a multiracial policy, and the United party of Captain Lewelleyn Briggs. The Briggs faction, possibly more realistic than the New Kenya party, correctly interpreted the trend of events and sought—while the Europeans still retained power—to dissolve the existing political system and to establish, in *apartheid* fashion, separate black and white polities. The election resulted in a defeat for Blundell's New Kenya party and for the policy of cooperation among the races. Briggs' group won eight of the fourteen seats, leaving only six to Blundell and his supporters.

The African part of the election, the first in history, took place late in 1956 and was based on eight constituencies: North Nyanza, Central Nyanza, South Nyanza, Nairobi, Central Province, Rift Valley, Coast Province, and Akamba. It is important to note that in the Central Province only those Kikuyu, Meru, and Embu who had been designated as "loyalists" were allowed to participate in the election. The candidates elected in this important contest, their tribe of origin, and their constituencies are shown in Table 5–1.

Tom Mboya and Oginga Odinga rapidly assumed leadership positions in the African Elected Members Association that emerged. They proceeded to shock their moderate European friends by immediately demanding that the number of African seats be increased to fifteen. Under Mboya's leadership, all of the newly elected members refused to accept ministerial portfolios in the government. As Mboya had anticipated, the Lyttelton Constitution was rendered inoperative.

---

[80] George Bennett and Carl Rosberg, Jr., *The Kenyatta Election* (New York: Oxford University Press, 1961), p. 12.

Table 5–1

1956 Kenya Election Results

Constituency	Dominant Group	Total Votes	Winner's Votes	Winner's Name	Winner's Ethnic Group
North Nyanza	Luyia	19,869	6,728	Mulira	Luyia
Central Nyanza	Luo	11,750	9,316	Oginga Odinga	Luo
South Nyanza	Luo, including other such groups as Kisii, Kipsigis, Nandis	26,177	13,882	Lawrence Oguda	Luo
Nairobi	Kikuyu	2,348	2,138	Tom Mboya	Luo
Central Province	Kikuyu	35,644	24,758	Bernard Mate	Meru
Rift Valley	Nandi and Masai	5,030	4,773	Daniel Arap Moi	Nandi
Coast Province	Amali, Digo, Giriama and others	5,912	3,406	Ronald Ngala	Giriama
Akamba	Kamba	17,778	8,851	J. Nzau Muimu	Kamba

SOURCES: *East African Student Newsletter*, III (March 1957), No. 1; II (February 1957), No. 12.

In October 1957, the newly installed Colonial Secretary, Alan Lennox-Boyd, came to Nairobi to resolve the impasse. The compromise that emerged granted six additional representative seats to the African community. This gave them parity with the European-elected members.[81] The Lennox-Boyd solution also provided for the addition of twelve special seats, four for each major racial group, to be elected by the Legislative Council sitting as an electoral college. It is not surprising—given the rapid rate at which events were moving—that the African leaders, flushed with victory, rejected this compromise and refused to accept the principle of the specially elected seats. The African leadership was further angered by Lennox-Boyd's statement that the proposed racial balance in the reconstituted legislature should stand at fourteen Africans, fourteen Europeans, and eight Asians for ten years. To the Africans, riding the winds of change, this was too little and too late. To the Europeans, their refusal to accept the offer was a final indication of the dissipation of their own power and a sharp reminder that their hopes for extended political domination were doomed. For the first time, the long sacred principle that European membership in the Legislative Assembly should at least be equal that of all other racial groups combined was denied.

However, despite African objections, the Legislature proceeded to elect twelve new members (four Asians, four Africans, and four Europeans). The African boycott was not completely successful for, at the last moment, Musa Amalemba, the moderate spokesman of the Abaluhya, agreed to stand as a candidate; this opened the door to others. It is somewhat ironic that possibly the most liberal of the European candidates, Ernest Vasey, who had long supported the common roll in Kenya, was defeated because his liberal views did not elicit the support of the European members of the Legislative Assembly, whereas those Africans who might have supported him boycotted the election.[82] Mr. Vasey received the same number of votes as Mr. Humphrey Slade, but lost the seat in a draw of names.

After some confusion, the African members decided to boycott the newly constituted Legislative Council. In the meantime, the name of Jomo Kenyatta was again heard with frequency and emotion. In 1958, Oginga Odinga spoke in the Legislative Council about the obligations of the country to those leaders still in prison. In September 1958, Mboya's Nairobi Peoples Convention party called for an observance of the October anniversary of Kenyatta's arrest as a day of fasting.[83]

Pre-Independence Politics and Government

Contemporary Kenya politics might well have commenced with the release of Jomo Kenyatta from prison, on April 14, 1959, and his detention at

---

[81] *Ibid.*, p. 14.

[82] Wood, *op. cit.*, p. 41.

[83] Bennett and Rosberg, *op. cit.*, p. 15.

Maralal. Although the colonial government, supported by certain elements in Great Britain, felt strongly that Kenyatta should not be freed, it is worth noting that a *Times* editorial, in April 1959, tended to support his unconditional release.[84] At about the same time that Kenyatta was moved to Maralal, Michael Blundell resigned his seat in the Legislative Assembly and his position as Minister of Agriculture in order to establish the New Kenya Group. This new political party—established in April 1959 and composed of forty-six members of the Legislative Assembly—proved again to be too little and too late. The appointment of Bruce MacKenzie as Minister of Agriculture to replace Blundell elicited considerable opposition on the part of the African Elected Members Organization. Led by Oginga Odinga, the African legislators vehemently opposed the principle that a European settler should occupy the Ministry of Agriculture, regardless of how liberal he might be, largely because this sensitive portfolio significantly affected land tenure and ownership, still the most critical issue of all.

In July 1959, the government lifted its ban on countrywide political organization, but only as long as the parties seeking registration were prepared to declare themselves multiracial. As soon as the announcement was made, Arvind B. Jamidar, as Asian member of the Legislative Assembly, proclaimed the formation of the Kenya National party, composed of seventeen elected members—ten of whom were African, six Asian, and one European. The KNP—supported by Ronald Ngala, T. Towett, and Daniel Arap Moi —was essentially a rural faction advocating racial harmony and not adverse to a moderate march toward independence. More important, however, was the decision of Oginga Odinga, Tom Mboya, and Dr. Julius Kiano to forego membership in the KNP. It was obvious that the more astute African political leaders had correctly gauged the velocity and direction of the winds of change and were not about to involve themselves, at this critical stage, in a multiracial political undertaking. The more radical African legislators coalesced in the Kenya Independence Movement (KIM) and, from the very outset, demanded *Uhuru* in the very near future, a responsible government based on a common roll, and an end to reservation of the white highlands for Europeans.

The question of land, land tenure, and land holding—always at the crux of Kenya politics—broke into the open again in October 1959. The European members of the Legislative Assembly had organized themselves into an Elected Members Organization and generally supported the New Kenya Group. The Kenya government White Paper, which opened the previously restricted white highlands to African settlement, was vigorously opposed by the Kenya United party. Group Captain Briggs initiated an informal referendum to determine the attitude of the European settlers to the government's policy.

---

[84] *The Times,* April 15, 1959.

Finally on November 11, 1959, after seven years of anxiety and conflict, the Mau Mau Emergency was declared to be at an end. Approximately 2,500 prisoners were released, much to the worry and chagrin of the settler community. By the end of 1959, the relations among black, white, and brown had reached a point of no return. The Asian-elected members of the Legislative Assembly who, up to this time, had sought to identify themselves with African nationalism were asked by Muliro to resign from the KNP executive board. The handwriting was on the wall. There was to be no middle ground. Kenya was to be independent—a new nation of, for, and by Africans. In retaliation, the Asian legislators elected to disassociate themselves from the demands of the African-elected members, who were demanding responsible government in 1960, general elections on a common roll, an African prime minister, and a division of the country into eighty single-member constituencies. In a pattern already well-established by his predecessor, Ian Mac-Leod rushed to Kenya, in December 1959, in an effort to resolve the crisis. He was met by a group of angry European settlers who clearly informed the Colonial Secretary that they were not prepared to stand still for the implementation of a Tanganyika-type constitution in their Kenya.

Under the leadership of the more liberal Ian MacLeod, the 1960 Lancaster House Conference, which emerged as Britain's solution to the impasse, dealt, in the words of Group Captain Briggs, "a death blow to the European community in Kenya."[85] Although it sought to provide protection for property and other rights, the MacLeod constitutional compromise generally supported the African position. This fact, however, did not restrain Tom Mboya from saying, on his return to Nairobi, that even this victory was temporary and that the new and liberal MacLeod Constitution would not last more than five years.

Reactions to the Lancaster Conference and the MacLeod Constitution were electric. Ferdinand Cavendish-Bentnick, the Speaker of the Legislative Council and a fixture in Kenya politics for more than a quarter of a century, resigned; in March 1960, he announced the formation of the "Kenya Coalition." The African leaders, just returned from the Lancaster Conference, refused to accept ministries in the existing government and demanded that the MacLeod provisions be implemented even before the proposed elections. The nationalist leaders, flushed with the Lancaster triumph, refused to sit in the same government with Musa Amalemba—the "imperialist turncoat" —whom they regarded as an "Uncle Tom." In addition, they demanded their choice of ministerial portfolios; they were particularly interested in obtaining control of Education and Agriculture—the two portfolios critical to the realization of their political interests.

By the spring of 1960, the country once again faced a serious political crisis; the Africans refused to take part in the government despite the fact

---

[85] *Ibid.*, February 22, 1960.

that they had won a major victory at the Lancaster House Conference. More important, however, were the stepped-up demands that Jomo Kenyatta be released from detention so that he might assume leadership of the nationalist movement. African political leaders, in general, and Tom Mboya and Oginga Odinga, in particular, began to compete with one another as to who was the most devoted supporter of Jomo Kenyatta. The 1960 Lancaster House Conference, which set Kenya on the road to independence, gave notice to the tribal, regional, and racial factions that the struggle for power had commenced. Thus, the spring of 1960, which saw the formation of KANU and KADU, was one of maneuver and countermaneuver, of conflict between parties, between races, and between tribes. The youth wings of the respective parties and factions emerged as quasi-party instruments, employed by party elders to intimidate the opposition and to protect the faithful. The KANU youth wing in Central Nyanza, for example, had its own police force. Also present in this predominantly Luo district was an institution termed "Uhuru Chiefs"—a cadre of party elders whose positions and influence ran parallel to that of the official government headmen.

It should be recalled that age-grade organization is unknown among the Luo; it would seem likely that the failure of the party elders, or Uhuru Chiefs as they are termed in Central Nyanza, to control the irresponsibility and violence of the youth wings is, in part, a consequence of the absence of traditional structures regulating generational relationships among the Luo. During the summer of 1962, it was common in Central Nyanza for roving bands of KANU youth-wing members to arrest people for not possessing a party membership card, to assault persons who opposed them, and even, on occasion, to arrest and torture people in order to force them to confess political unorthodoxy.

In May 1960, Mboya warned the government that time was running out and that violence would ensue if Kenyatta were not quickly released. The situation had reached such a state that, also in May, the government supported the opening of an office in Nairobi for those Europeans wishing to emigrate to South Africa. Africans who had joined Dr. Kiano, the American-educated Minister of Commerce and Industry; J. Nzan Muimi, a former member of the Legislative Council; and James Gichuru, the Minister of Finance (leaders of the proposed new Kenya African National Union) threatened to resign unless Kenyatta were released. The government maintained that Kenyatta represented all that was evil and savage in the past; but Oginga Odinga, leader of the African Elected Members Organization, spoke for all when he said, "I think it is for the African people to decide what type of life they are going to live . . . if they decide savagery is the most fitting thing, then they will decide upon it."[86] The incipient Kenya African National Union added fuel to the flames when it proceeded to elect Jomo

---

86 *Ibid.*, May 11, 1960.

Kenyatta President. Tom Mboya, astutely aware that politics had coalesced to a point where a national party was about to emerge, agreed, in May, to merge his Nairobi Peoples Convention party with the new KANU.

However, the ever latent fear of Kikuyu domination, which had characterized transtribal relations even before Mau Mau, broke into the open. On June 26, 1960, the leaders of five essentially tribal-party associations met at Ngong—a town physically and symbolically separating Bantu Kikuyu from Nilo-Hamitic Masai country—to jointly face up to the *fait accompli* of Kikuyu-Luo domination of KANU. Present at this meeting were the leaders of the Kalenjin Political Alliance, the Masai United Front, the Kenya African Peoples party, the Coast African Political Union, and the Somali National Association. A decision was made to establish a new party; and Muliro, chairman of the Kenya African Peoples party, was chosen President, while John Keen, then head of the Masai United Front, was elected Secretary.[87] The pattern of Kenya politics and political organization that was to persist through independence and beyond crystallized. Kenya's two largest tribes, the Kikuyu and the Luo, tended to dominate the KANU, while the remaining smaller tribes, fearful of Kikuyu-Luo domination, banded together in a close federation in an attempt to maintain the tribal balance of power.

KANU's parliamentary leaders took the initiative and, in June, threatened to resign in retaliation to the government's stand that only those elected members who were also ministers would be permitted to visit Kenyatta. An obvious purpose of this maneuver was to preclude Oginga Odinga, who had received, evidence indicated, financial support from communist sources, from visiting Mzee Kenyatta, Kenya's most famous detainee.

The vacuum caused by Kenyatta's absence encouraged competition between Oginga Odinga and Tom Mboya. The labor movement, which Mboya ably led, plus the ban on the participation of Kikuyu in the political life of Kenya provided an opportunity for Mboya (a Luo) to rise quickly to positions of political influence. Oginga Odinga, leader of the Luo Union and an early supporter of KAU, saw a threat in the meteoric ascendancy of Mboya to his political stature as Kenya's most important non-Kikuyu politician. With the aid of not a few Kikuyu politicians in the Nairobi area, Odinga sought to destroy Mboya's urban political support. One tactic used with considerable effectiveness was labeling Mboya an American lackey. He was also accused of secretly plotting with the British to keep Kenyatta in prison. In late January 1961, Mboya sought Odinga's expulsion from the party. In the ensuing struggle, both tried to secure the support of the earlier generation of leaders and particularly those leaders who had been intimately associated with KAU. Oginga Odinga received the backing of KANU's Nairobi branch chairman, Dr. Waiyaki Hinji, who was seeking to displace Mboya as the

---

[87] John Keen subsequently defected to KANU and, in fact, became its Organizing Secretary.

major political personage in the Nairobi urban area. Waiyaki and Odinga publicly claimed that Peter Koinange, a former leader in KAU and a patron saint of the nationalist movement, had written from Accra indicating that it was acknowledged there that Mboya was selling out to the United States. Of course, Mboya asked for and obtained a letter from Koinange denying this and similar allegations. Friction between the two KANU factions grew more intense in direct proportion to the increasing likelihood of Kenyatta's release from detention.

The fact that national elections were scheduled for early 1961 added fuel to the flames. The 1960 Lancaster House Proposals provided for election of a Legislative Council of fifty-three common roll seats, twenty of which would be reserved seats, plus twelve special seats for "national members." The reserved seats were to be divided among ten Europeans, eight Asians, and two Arabs. Separate constituencies for open and reserved seats were demarcated, with the electorate of each race required to vote on a common roll for candidates from other than their own communities. It was necessary, therefore, to hold a primary election for the special seats to determine whether or not candidates had substantial support within their own communities. The primary elections in the ten European constituencies, held on January 24, brought 165,000 Europeans to the polls. The results were a further indication of the hardening of race relations. In every constituency, a heavy majority supported the Kenya Coalition party and voted against Michael Blundell's New Kenya party. Only Blundell himself succeeded in obtaining the necessary 25 per cent of the total votes cast in his constituency, enabling him to stand in the general election. As the African election drew near, the split within KANU grew wider. Dr. Waiyaki Hinji, who had decided to contest the Nairobi constituency against Mboya, claimed that a secret agreement existed among James Gichuru, the chairman of the party; Tom Mboya; and the "imperialists."[88]

Joseph Murumbi, another patron saint and former Secretary General of KAU who could not return to Kenya for fear of being placed in restriction, wrote from London that, in his estimation, KANU was a legitimate successor of KAU. As KAU was regarded by the European community as synonymous with Mau Mau, his statement did little to dissipate their fears.

The union of Kikuyu and Luo leaders in KANU, despite the two peoples' being separated by hundreds of miles, endowed KANU with a highly nationalistic and radical profile, which was in sharp contrast to KADU. The fact that both Kikuyu and Luo peoples were characterized by a relatively high degree of urbanization and education emphasized this contrast. Musa Amalemba, a political independent, flirted with both major factions, but eventually allied his movement with KADU. Amalemba defended tribalism as a necessary component of nationalism: "If I have no tribe, I am a

---

[88] *Kenya Daily Nation,* February 1, 1961.

bastard."[89] Amalemba spoke for other supporters of KADU when he maintained that true national unity could only be built on the pluralistic association of succeedingly larger unities, beginning with the family.

Although both warring factions within KANU were headed by Luo, the conflict reflected, in part, long-standing differences between the Luo and Kikuyu peoples. Although Odinga and Mboya perceived the struggle primarily as a personal feud to determine who should prevail, Kikuyu political leaders regarded the split as an opportunity to further Kikuyu control over the party. There was, for example, little opposition on the part of major Kikuyu leaders to Dr. Waiyaki Hinji's contesting the Nairobi constituency, despite the fact that Mboya had been designated the official party candidate.

The February 1961 election was a tremendous victory for Mboya. In the predominantly Kikuyu Nairobi East constituency, he polled 31,000 votes as compared with 2,600 votes for Dr. Waiyaki, his Kikuyu opponent. Running on the common roll, Michael Blundell of the National Kenya party drew African support and won handily over Cavendish-Bentnick, his conservative opponent. Blundell received 20,000 votes to Bentnick's 2,000 in the Rift Valley constituency. KANU emerged from the election as the dominant party, winning sixteen seats to KADU's nine, while four seats were taken by independents.

After the election, the governor agreed that James Gichuru and Tom Mboya from KANU and Ronald Ngala and Muliro from KADU—leaders representing the two major parties—could visit Jomo Kenyatta in a joint attempt to win his support for a program of national unity. That the 1961 election, despite numerous ominous warnings, had been peaceful and orderly gave impetus to the demand that Kenyatta be released. It seemed unlikely that his freedom and presence would pose a threat to security. On July 19, 1961, Governor Sir Patrick Rension—who earlier had referred to Kenyatta as a "leader into darkness and death"—indicated that in August he was prepared to authorize Kenyatta's release from detention and his removal to a house near Nairobi.[90] On August 17, Jomo Kenyatta returned to his native Kiambu for the first time in seven years and to a house which had been built for him at Gatundu. For three days and nights, Kikuyuland, if not all Kenya, celebrated the end of one era and the commencement of another.

Though it had received a majority of seats in the May 1961 election, KANU had refused to accept ministries until Kenyatta was set free. The resultant impasse had been resolved only when KADU agreed, despite its

---

[89] *Kenya Daily Nation*, February 6, 1961.

[90] The author visited Mr. Kenyatta at Maralal during the last week of his detention. It was interesting to note how his obvious good health, vigor, and alertness contrasted with the rumors current among the Europeans that he had deteriorated and was only a shell of his former self. The subsequent quality of his leadership bears out the impression that the author carried away from the meeting.

electoral and parliamentary minority position, to form a government. However, Kenyatta's release in August opened the way for KANU's renewed participation in the government. Thus, it is not surprising that in less than three months from his release, Jomo Kenyatta was once again in London, but this time as head of a KANU delegation to discuss the preparation of a constitution for an independent Kenya with the very same government that had arrested and imprisoned him. Kenyatta's position as leader of KANU was formalized, in January 1962, when he was elected to fill a deliberately vacated seat in the Legislative Assembly; he was subsequently designated leader of the opposition. The presence of Kenyatta on the political scene as leader of the majority party rendered a continuation of minority KADU government inappropriate.

In response to these circumstances, the second Lancaster House Conference was held in February 1962. The party lines were sharply drawn, and the stakes were high, as it was obvious that Kenya's independence constitution would emerge from this conference. KADU proposed and vigorously supported a federal type of constitution, including a number of fundamental reserved powers for what were essentially tribal regions (*majimbo*); whereas, KANU advocated a highly centralized unitary state. Also at issue was the emotion-laden question of constitutional safeguards for minority rights and properties. The question of land ownership and control—perennial issues in Kenya politics—once again came to the fore.

The Lancaster House Conference provided for a federal form of government, a 117-member lower house based on population, an upper house representing the constituent districts, and seven regional governments. Having accepted this interim constitution, the two major parties agreed to man a coalition government until national elections could be held. Jomo Kenyatta and Ronald Ngala became, respectively, Minister of State for Constitutional Affairs and Administration and Minister of State for Constitutional Affairs and Economic Planning. Each party also received six additional portfolios.[91]

No sooner was the new government functioning than the two parties began to prepare for the forthcoming elections. The question of race loomed large, as it was inevitably linked with the questions of political power and control over land. KANU sought to discredit KADU by insisting that it was essentially European-supported. Kenyatta's words are indicative: "The time is now ripe for us to tell KADU men, who are the settlers' bootlickers, that we are fed up with them."[92] Although Kenyatta provided a degree of unity to the party, the struggle for pre-eminence of position between Mboya and Odinga continued.

---

[91] The British government refused to accept Oginga Odinga as Minister of Finance despite Kenyatta's wish to appoint him.

[92] Jomo Kenyatta at Nairobi Stadium on October 20, 1962 (as quoted in the *East African Reporter*, October 27, 1962, p. 10).

Elections were held in May 1963, and, to the surprise of few, KANU won a majority of the crucial lower-house seats and even captured control of the Senate from the KADU-APP (African Peoples party) alliance. Thus, in two short years, Kenyatta moved from detention to become Kenya's first Prime Minister. In the election for the regional assemblies, KANU won a majority of seats in the Eastern, Central, and Nyanza regions; KADU won control of the remaining three: the Rift Valley, Coast, and Western regions. (Elections were not held in the Northeastern region due to a failure of the Somali to put forth candidates.)

Competition between the two parties continued with independence although the forces supporting KADU gradually declined and the trend toward a one-party system became readily apparent. In September 1963, Paul Ngei, leader of the APP (an essentially Kamba party which had earlier allied itself with KADU), left KADU and, along with his supporters, returned to KANU.

The Kenya constitution that emerged from the February 1962 Lancaster House Conference was a compromise between the wishes of KADU for a decentralized, loose federation and KANU's desire for a strong unitary state. Although the trappings of a federal system are apparent, it is evident that the preponderate interests of KANU in conjunction with the British antipathy toward a federal structure won the day. The central government is supreme and, given the emergence of a single-party state, it seems inevitable that even the trappings of regional autonomy will eventually wither away—hopefully without violence or irreparable bitterness. The constitution includes a bill of rights essentially based on that of Nigeria. Of direct significance to the settler community are those provisions in the bill of rights emphasizing safeguards on an individual's life and property.

The National Assembly consists of a Senate of forty-one seats (one from each district) and a House of Representatives drawn from 117 single-member constituencies, plus twelve seats specially elected by the lower house sitting as an electoral college. The Senate can only delay legislation for a short period of time; its real power lies in its relationship to the amending process. Extraordinary majorities of both houses are required to make fundamental changes in the constitution affecting the most sensitive issues in Kenya politics—namely, the rights of individuals and the rights of various constituent regions, including their boundaries. Constitutional amendment requires a 75 per cent majority of the House of Representatives and a 90 per cent majority of the Senate, which is representative of regional, as opposed to popular, interests.

Kenya is divided into seven regions: Coast, Eastern, Central, Rift Valley, Western, Nyanza, and Northeastern. The power to govern is divided between the central and regional legislatures. Responsibility for health, education, and, to some extent, roads is reserved for the regions. In contrast to the central government, the regions have a unicameral legislature of approximately thirty members, including eight specially elected seats for each constituency member. Although the regional assemblies are more powerful than the former district councils, the central government nonetheless retains ultimate control. Residual powers rest, not with the regional authorities, but with the central government; and the latter retains the important prerogative of declaring an emergency in a given region. It can suspend the regional government and, if necessary, send in its own police. Furthermore, the regions' revenues are severely limited. The constitution specifies that 35 per cent of the revenue from custom and excise duties be divided among the regions, depending on respective populations. The regions all receive excise and consumption taxes on motor fuels consumed within their respective boundaries. Land is now largely the responsibility of the regional assemblies and their constituent local governments. Alienated lands not held in individual titles have become the responsibility of the regional assemblies; whereas, "native," or "trust," lands now fall under the control of the county councils.

The Politics of Independence

The split within KANU was reflected in, as well as augmented by, a division within the KANU youth wing. Pitched battles between rival youth groups supporting one faction or another were common. In the city, too, where customary control over the younger generation was impossible to exercise, the youth wings tended toward irresponsibility and often acted independently of, even in opposition to, the commands of the party elders. That there exists a connection between elements of the KANU youth wing and a revival of oath-taking in parts of Kenya has long been evident. Duplicate membership in the Land Freedom Army—a modern-day revival of Mau Mau—and in youth-wing organizations has been apparent. The mystique of interpersonal solidarity, characteristic of the LFA, is not unlike the association of youths in blood-brotherhood.

Unemployment, urban dislocation, the failure of Uhuru to meet psychic needs or land and job expectations have added fuel to the disaffection of the youth. The traditional customs of secret oathing and intense solidarity among young men are providing the organization and impetus for youth wings, and even for the LFA. In August 1963, one government official said that the situation in the Rift Valley had reached such a state that "The KANU youth wing virtually rules the place."[93]

Since independence, the situation has improved, although white farmers complain that the growing number of unemployed farm laborers squatting on European-owned plantations are being infiltrated and led by youth-wing

[93] East African Standard, August 14, 1963.

leaders who are frequently acting independently of the party hierarchy. Early in 1964, the now independent Kenya government announced plans to establish a national youth service, initially to be composed of 3,000 youths. The national leaders of the youth wings have endorsed this policy, though it is difficult to say how many will come forth to join its ranks. One can be quite sure that this domestic Peace Corps will be led and staffed by loyal KANU youth-wing leaders and will seek to further a policy of national integration, even within those regions supporting a KADU regional government and espousing regional autonomy.

The difficulty in controlling the unruly youth wings is a modern manifestation of the indigenous problem of intergenerational conflict. The pre-Mau Mau leaders of KAU, KCA, and related organizations were predominantly Kikuyu, and, though out of circulation during the Emergency, they now hold the major political and governmental positions. Because the number-two position in the Luo-Kikuyu KANU coalition must necessarily be held by a Luo, the conflict for the heir apparent's role between the two Luo—Mboya and Odinga—tends to confuse the political picture. It must be recalled that, though a Luo, Odinga was an early supporter of KAU and is closely identified with the pre-Mau Mau nationalist movement. At the same time, he also served as President of the Luo Union and has retained much of his tribal support. On the other hand, Mboya is a product of the Emergency (that period when organized political activity was proscribed), which placed a premium on non-political party organizations such as the labor movement. He has elicited the support of the urban workers and the growing white-collar class, who are relatively less influenced by tribal tradition and obligation. Ironically, competition between Mboya and Odinga is in the best interest of KANU and of national unity as well as of the party.

This complex tribal-personal-generational conflict is reflected in related institutions as well. For example, the struggle for control of the labor movements between the ICFTU-oriented KFL and the Eastern-bloc-supported Trade Union Congress is indicative. In 1953, Mboya was elected general secretary of the Regional Trade Union—subsequently the Kenya Federation of Labor. As one graduate student in Syracuse University's Program of East African Studies has astutely noted, "After the ban was placed on KAU, Mboya's work and that of the KFL became as much political as trade unionist."[94] Mboya himself has said, "The KFL became the voice of the African people, in the absence of any other African organization remaining to speak for them."[95]

In the post-Emergency period, Mboya moved from labor unions to national politics, never, however, completely severing his modern urban power

---

[94] Laurie Bruns, "Trade Unions: Function, Structure, and Style in East Africa," (unpublished paper, Syracuse University, 1964).

[95] Tom Mboya, *Freedom and After* (Boston: Little, Brown and Co., 1963).

base. Leadership of the KFL went to a young Mboya designate, Peter Kibisu, who has occasionally been critical of the Kikuyu leaders and even of Mzee Kenyatta. The emergence of the rival Trade Union Congress led by Fred Kubai—a former leader of KAU and holder of the detainee certificate, as well as a friend of Jomo Kenyatta—demonstrates the continuity of the traditional-ideological-generational gap separating the two major factions of KANU.

The election campaign in the spring and early summer of 1963 did little to provide the unity and harmony that the country needed so badly in the wake of a long armed struggle and a series of indeterminate constitutional arrangements. KADU campaigned on the preservation of *majimbo* (regional autonomy). Momentarily submerging its conflicts, KANU—with the assistance of a revitalized secretariat—closed ranks for the campaign and embarked on a strategy to increase the substantial plurality it won in 1960. Fearful of a Kikuyu-Luo victory, KADU warned of the dire consequences of a KANU triumph to the non-Kikuyu and non-Luo peoples. At the same time, the leaders of KANU made it clear in their campaign speeches that, after victory, they would demand that the constitution be altered to eliminate such provisions as the requirement of an extraordinary 75 per cent majority of the house seats and 90 per cent of the Senate for constitutional amendment.

The May 1963 election, which brought nearly 2,000,000 Kenyans to the polls, was vitally important, for it determined which faction and philosophy would control the powers of government and thus interpret the 1962 Lancaster House constitution. Although both parties agreed that a final conference before independence would be necessary, KADU held that such a meeting should only be concerned with minor questions of technique and that the existing constitution should become the fundamental instrument of independence. On the other hand, KANU maintained that the crucial questions of central versus regional powers and of safeguards for minorities must be reopened. In June 1963, the Cabinet, with Jomo Kenyatta as Prime Minister, was sworn in while 50,000 cheering Africans watched. Oginga Odinga, previously denied a portfolio by the British colonial government, became Kenya's first Minister for Home Affairs; and Tom Mboya assumed the Ministry of Constitutional Affairs and Justice. The first session of the self-governing Kenyan Parliament was called to order on July 11.

The struggle over the relative autonomy of the seven regions increased in intensity after the election and the inauguration of the KANU government. The tribal and regional factions that had coalesced in KADU in order to oppose KANU began to disintegrate. Ronald Ngala retired to Mombasa, where he sought to convert the coastal region into a single polity. The nationalist leaders, generally, and Tom Mboya in particular, as he had a special responsibility for constitutional interpretation, belittled regional power and warned Ronald Ngala against attempting to turn what was essentially a local authority into an independent state. Musa Amalemba, President of the Abaluhya Political Association, blamed KADU for his humiliating electoral defeat. He claimed that his failure to win was caused by KADU's refusal to accept him as a party candidate. M. Muliro, spokesman for the Western region, tended to withdraw from the national scene and return to his parochial base of power, despite his responsibilities as KADU Vice-President. The disaffection of Paul Ngei's Kamba African Peoples party from KADU and its subsequent reassociation with KANU further strengthened the latter's growing political pre-eminence.

On July 2, 1963, Jomo Kenyatta announced that Kenya would receive its independence on December 12 and that one last London conference would be held to settle the final constitutional arrangements. The period between the inauguration of the KANU government in July and independence in December was characterized by desperate maneuvers by the remnants of KADU to preserve regional autonomy from what they feared would be, after independence, a period of vindictive domination by the Luo-Kikuyu coalition. The Kamba, whose differences with the Kikuyu were minor and non-traditional, tended to move back into the KANU fold. The Nilo-Hamitic pastoral peoples of the Rift Valley and Northeastern provinces sharpened their spears and threatened secession.

KANU's representatives to the September 1963 London conference dominated the scene and were generally successful in achieving a favorable hearing for most of the twenty constitutional issues that they sought to alter. Jomo Kenyatta, now speaking from strength, demanded fundamental alterations in the constitution. In response, KADU leaders—fearful of the emergence of a Luo-Kikuyu-dominated unitary state—proposed that the country be divided and that the essentially KADU areas become a separate state. This proposed new state was to consist of a U-shaped block including the Rift Valley, the Western, the Northeastern, and the Coastal regions. The center of the U was to be excluded and supposedly would constitute a KANU-Kenya state. It is interesting that a map of the two proposed states reflects not only the existing geology and geography of the country, but its historical and ethnic settlement and agricultural-pastoral dichotomy as well.

In the post-independence period, threats of secession abated. The realization grew that the KANU government was prepared to maintain the union by force if necessary and was not inclined to violate parochial, ethnic, or racial rights arbitrarily. Nonetheless, the central government was deliberately slow in transferring powers and functions to the new regional governments. Complaints to this effect by the KADU regional presidents were met by counter-accusations that the regions had not fulfilled prerequisite obligations and were therefore ineligible for new responsibilities. In the desire to establish a single-party hegemony, KANU sought to extend its support into the

Rift Valley region, but met with little success, despite the fact that some Rift Valley and Western region legislators had crossed the aisle and joined KANU.

Along with a legacy of tribal antagonisms, the British bequeathed the new government an unhealthy economy and a potential irredentist war with Somalia over the vast northeastern region of the country. Growing unemployment reached endemic proportions and was seen by some as a serious threat to the stability of what had proved to be an effective and dynamic government. The land issue was still paramount, with frustrated and angry squatters defying the government and refusing to leave. The process of acquisition and compensation for European farms in the highlands and its subsequent allocation to African peasants proved to be a thorny political issue and an administrative problem. In response, the government struck an agreement (the Tripartite Agreement) with the Federation of Kenya Employers and the Kenya Federation of Labour whereby the government would increase its employment by 15 per cent and private business by 10 per cent, while the trade unions agreed to a moratorium on strikes and demands for wage increases. Nonetheless, the number of unemployed was estimated to have passed the 100,000 mark—about one-sixth of the employed labor force. Since 1960, total employment had decreased about 20,000 and was only 100,000 higher than in 1950. The seriousness of the situation was revealed when it was noted that about 80,000 young Kenyans were leaving and entering the labor market every year. As unemployment and disaffection over land increased, potential recruits for the radical and irresponsible youth wings became more numerous.

Kenya Becomes a One-Party State

One of the most significant features of African political developments over the last decade is the emergence of one-party states, irrespective of the ideological complexion of the governments in power in the various countries. In line with this development, the Kenya government announced in mid-August 1964, that on December 12, Kenya was to become a one-party republic. In announcing his desire to establish a one-party state in Kenya, Kenyatta told the House of Representatives that one-party states were an expression of Africanism and offered the best machinery for fighting aggression emanating from the nation's enemies and subversion originating from some of Kenya's self-appointed friends, both within and without. In addition, Kenyatta stated that the necessity for a one-party system in most parts of Africa stemmed from two predominant factors. First, traditional African society revolved around the family, the wider pattern of blood-brotherhood, and the even wider network of clans and tribes, all of which acted in concert in times of emergency. Second, to the African, the supreme authority was the tribal council which was at once a government and the expression of every citizen's personality. African leaders were advised by the elders, and the people maintained that by obeying the tribal councils they obeyed themselves and their true will. Constructive opposition from within was therefore not alien to traditional African society. Thus, Kenyatta claimed there was no need to create leaders of opposition, to maintain them from public funds, and to tolerate their insatiable desire for agitation merely because they want to oppose for opposition's sake.

Although the reaction of the opposition to the proposed one-party state was half-hearted, the government sought to ease fear of a one-man one-party dictatorship by contending that Kenya's proposed republican constitution would differ from that of Tanzania in that decisions would be made in the Cabinet as opposed to the party and that the Cabinet would be answerable to Parliament.

On October 21, 1964, the government published a bill setting forth proposed amendments to the constitution designed to transform Kenya into a one-party republic. The following day, Ronald Ngala, leader of the opposition, described the proposed amendments to the constitution as the "climax of KANU's tricks and schemes to reduce the country to the status of a mere totalitarian regime in which the reality of regional and local responsibilities are eliminated."[96] He pledged that KADU would fight tooth and nail in Parliament and in the country to prevent the passing of the amendments. In early November 1964, the House of Representatives passed the second and third readings of the constitutional amendment bill to make Kenya a republic, but Ngala predicted that his party would defeat the government in the Senate. During the next few days, however, it became apparent to him and his followers that theirs was a losing battle. Ngala's support crumbled when the Masai, Samburu, and Kalenjin opted out of his party and thereby destroyed part of the core of the minority tribes that constituted the source of KADU strength. It may be noted, at this point, that although in the preceding discussion it has been said that traditional Masai society was not characterized by strong single tribal leadership, such as was the case with the Kikuyu, it was largely through Masai chiefs and elders that Kenyatta sought to win the Masai and Kalenjin support which resulted in defeat for the opposition. A series of meetings of these chiefs and elders was held with Kenyatta at his residence at Gatungu and in their tribal areas. Only two days before the Senate was due to vote on the Republic bill, two Masai and one Samburu senators crossed the floor in the upper house. This provided the government with the over-all 75 per cent Senate majority needed to push the bill through. The final result of all the KANU maneuvers and KADU countermaneuvers was that on December 10 Kenya became a one-party state by consent as the opposition gave up their last ditch fight and Ngala announced in the House of Representatives the voluntary dissolution of KADU. His decision to

---

[96] *Africa Report,* December, 1964, p. 20.

dissolve KADU came as a surprise to most people, in view of the fact tl
did so only five days after a party executive meeting during which it had
decided to stand firm. It is important to note, however, that unlik
practice in most of the one-party African states, the Kenya opposition
not legislated out of existence and the machinery for launching new pa
still remains.

At this point, it is appropriate to comment on the position of the ex
opposition leadership in the new government. Briefly, when the new government was being formed, there were hopes in many quarters that Ngala would
rank high in the ministerial ranks. These hopes were ill-founded. On
January 6, however, President Kenyatta announced that the former opposition leader was to become the new chairman of the Kenya Marketing Board,
a post held from 1963 by Paul Ngeli, who was subsequently appointed
Minister for Cooperatives and Marketing. To some, Ronald Ngala appeared
to be on his way out of the Kenya political scene, but as Edward Rodwell
wrote one month later, "My feeling is that we have not seen the last of Mr.
Ngala in spite of what some regard as a shrewd move to whisk him away
from a position of potential strength in his home constituency.[97] And how
right he was. Politics makes strange bedfellows. By June 1965, R. Ngala was
again in the news, not as leader of an opposition party or group, but as one
of the staunchest supporters of the government side in a conflict over matters
of economic policy.

One last point should be made. On the establishment of Kenya's republican
status, Mr. Kenyatta became executive Head of State, with a Cabinet responsible to Parliament. The President is leader of the majority party and
appoints his own Cabinet, his full term of office being related to the life
of the Parliament.

Party and Tribe

In the foregoing discussion, we have attempted to outline the process of
polity formation and dissolution in Kenya with special reference to the importance of continuity. The process of polity formation and dissolution did
not cease with independence. It is currently manifest in the movement
toward East African federation and pan-African unity and, on the other
hand, in the movement toward regional autonomy and secession. The abortive mutiny of the military in January 1964 and subsequent fears of subversion testify to the inherently fluid nature of present arrangements.

With the assistance of the Marco Surveys Ltd., a research company in
East Africa, the author undertook in 1963 a study of attitudes of 7,000
randomly selected East Africans toward one another and toward issues
bearing on political integration. Some of this data is particularly revealing
and supports the thesis put forth here.

---

[97] *Kenya Weekly News,* January 15, 1965.

Unfortunately, the high cost of sampling the relatively pastoral Nilo-Hamitic peoples has effectively eliminated them from our sample. The 2,400 Kenya interviewees were portioned as indicated in Table 5–2. The 2,400 respondents were asked this question: "Of the following tribes shown on the

Table 5–2

Tribe	Number	Percentage
Kikuyu/Embu/Meru	863	36
Abaluhya	336	14
Luo	333	14
Kamba	328	14
Coast	310	13
other	230	9
	2,400	100

card (Coast Kenya, Kikuyu, Luo, Baganda, Iteso, Acholi, Sukuma, Chagga, and Coast Tanganyika) which tribe—other than your own—would you most like to live amongst if you had to leave your present tribal area?" The respondents were asked to give first, second, and third choices. The weighted results are shown in Table 5–3. The findings reveal that modern politics

Table 5–3

Affinities of Selected Kenyan Tribes

Tribe[a]	Kikuyu Cluster	Abaluhya	Luo	Kamba	Coast	Others
not stated	14	23	28	20	30	22
Coast Kenya	9	12	6	12	—	10
Kikuyu	—	7	14	18	5	15
Luo	25	9	—	14	6	9
Baganda	22	26	17	12	14	20
Iteso	1	8	5	1	5	3
Acholi	2	2	16	1	2	3
Sukuma	2	3	2	4	5	3
Chagga	14	6	8	11	13	7
Coast Tanganyika	11	4	4	7	20	8

NOTE: Weighted scores are arrived at by giving 3 to each first choice, 2 to each second choice, and 1 to each third choice. Percentage by tribe is calculated from total weighted score of choices by tribe.

[a] Tribes named across the chart were the interviewees; tribes named in the left-hand column were the responses given.

is a major factor influencing political integration. Though the Kikuyu and the Luo, in contrast to many other tribal combinations in Kenya, do not possess a legacy of conflict, neither do they possess a history of association or contact. More important still is the fact that they are possibly more culturally dissimilar than any two other Kenyan peoples. Yet most Kikuyu maintained that they would prefer to live among Luo than any other people. Note also, however, that two non-Kenyan Bantu peoples were selected nearly as frequently.

A similar, though less pronounced, pattern evolves in the identification with the distant coastal peoples made by the Abaluhya located just south and east of Victoria-Nyanza. The fact that KANU's major tribes, the Luo and Kikuyu, are more closely unified than KADU's major centers reflects the important differences in party unity and solidarity characteristic of the two parties.

A pattern simultaneously revealing the attraction of modern politics and the traditional indigenous factors in the identification of tribal affinity is also evident in the Abaluhya preferences. On the one hand, there is a marked tendency to identify with a physically and culturally distant Kenyan Coastal people who are allied with them in opposing KANU. On the other hand, there exists an even stronger tendency to identify with the Bantu Baganda in neighboring Uganda, with whom they share certain historical and cultural ties.

Other patterns emerge. For example, the existence of a sizable pocket of Iteso-speaking people in the Abaluhya region of North Nyanza no doubt accounts for the slight tendency toward identification with the Uganda Iteso. The Luo pattern is the most revealing of all. It sharply highlights the dichotomy of traditional indigenous association and modern nationalism. Although the Nilotic Luo do not regard life among the Bantu Kikuyu to be as desirable as the Kikuyu do among the Luo, the tendency is still remarkable, given their cultural, physical, and historical separation. Note, however, the greater affinity of the Luo for the Uganda Acholi—a Nilotic people far to the north, but regarded by the Luo as a country and people of their origin. Given the marked identification of two of Kenya's major peoples (the Luo and the Abaluhya—comprising more than a third of the total population) with Uganda peoples, it is interesting to ponder the future possibility of their seeking political destiny in association with Uganda rather than with Kenya. Had the Luo and Abaluhya found themselves political allies rather than enemies—not an improbability—such an orientation could have conceivably emerged. The predominantly Bantu coastal people are precluded by modern party politics from identifying too closely with the Kikuyu; interestingly enough, they have shown a marked affinity to the Chagga. Given the historical migratory route of the Chagga and Kikuyu noted earlier, this is not surprising, though any generalizations require additional research.

The response to a reverse question, concerning the people with whom a tribe would least like to live, is shown in Table 5–4. The Kikuyu tendency to monopolize modern political activity in Kenya has consistently elicited antagonism and suspicion from other Kenya tribes and has contributed to their relative unpopularity. Interestingly enough, the chart reveals a low Kikuyu affinity for non-Bantu peoples, except, of course, for their political allies, the Luo. Note the tendency to displace the antipathy which otherwise

Table 5–4

Antipathies of Selected Kenya Peoples

Tribe[a]	Kikuyu Cluster	Abaluhya	Luo	Kamba	Coast	Others
not stated	34	33	42	36	35	32
Coast Kenya	6	2	4	3	—	4
Kikuyu	—	15	9	11	2	14
Luo	3	11	—	5	19	10
Baganda	2	2	3	3	3	2
Iteso	18	8	10	12	5	10
Acholi	14	11	5	12	5	11
Sukuma	13	9	14	9	5	9
Chagga	5	5	8	5	5	4
Coast Tanganyika	5	4	5	4	2	4

[a] Tribes named across the chart were the interviewees; tribes named in the left-hand column were the responses given.

would likely have fallen on the Nilotic Luo to their Acholic brethren in Uganda and to the Nilo-Hamitic Iteso of Uganda. In fact, the Bantu aversion to the Nilotic peoples, which renders the Luo-Kikuyu alliance so remarkable and so important, is a constant finding. Note the Bantu Abaluhya's antipathy toward the Kikuyu for predominantly political reasons and toward the Iteso Acholi for traditional ethnic reasons. The Kamba reveal a pattern similar to that of the Kikuyu and Abaluhya, although when this survey was carried out, the Kamba—under the leadership of Paul Ngei—had broken away from the Kikuyu-dominated KANU and had founded their own African Peoples party (APP). This accounts for the relatively high antipathy to the Kikuyu, their physical and cultural neighbors.[98] The marked antipathy of the predominantly Bantu coastal people for the Luo is indicative of the powerful confluence of indigenous and modern attitudes. The Luo are not well re-

[98] Bear in mind, however, that though the relationship between the Kikuyu and the Kamba has been intimate, it has also—on occasion—been violent. Ngei's defection in 1963 was not the first time that this Wakamba leader has split with Kenyatta.

garded because they are Nilotic, because they are KANU, and because they have infiltrated the coast and have come to monopolize many of the better positions on the waterfront.

CONCLUSION

The quantitative data, selective historical survey, hunches, and hypotheses ventured here have been presented to verify the utility of a "continuity" approach to the emergence and dissolution of polities, in general, and Kenyan polities, in particular. The very nature of this continuity approach to political evolution in Kenya implies further questions and fields of research. For example, are there fundamental differences in contemporary political behavior of peoples possessed of radically different traditional, sociopolitical systems which are capable of precise analysis? Such Nilo-Hamitic peoples as the Jie and Turkana possess little organization of significance beyond the family, age set, and stock (cattle) association. As Gulliver has noted, there is little effort to recollect one's ancestry beyond the grandfather, and "they cannot link together two or more families in one rational system."[99] The age set and stock association are the predominant forms of solidarity. This is in marked contrast to the Kikuyu, for example, where a relatively elaborate and extensive set of obligations exist. How are these radically different organizational frames of reference reflected in the respective postures of these two peoples toward modern political participation and behavior?

Is there a fundamental difference with respect to the political attitudes and predispositions of matrilineal and patrilineal kinship systems? Is this reflected in the ease, scope, and complexity of party organization and affiliation—in attitudes toward individual liberties, in the role of women in government and politics? In those tribes where it is customary for the wife to be incorporated into the extended family of the husband, as is the case among the Masai, what is the political significance of such institutions as the taking of Kikuyu wives by Masai males? Do traditional societies characterized by large tightly-knit extended families have an advantage in modern politics? Are they maneuvered by party leaders and organizations, as were the heads of patrilineal Irish, Polish, and Italian clans in American politics during the early part of the century?

We have attempted to show a relationship between age-grade organization, which is characteristic of most major Kenya peoples, and the activities of youth wings. This fascinating subject demands intensive research. How are variations in age-grade organizations reflected in contemporary politics and government? Obviously, differences in points of eligibility to participate are significant. Among the Nandi, for example, circumcision occurs between the

---

[99] P. H. Gulliver, *The Family Herds* (London: Routledge and Kegan Paul, 1955), p. 76.

ages of fourteen and eighteen, and the warrior is eligible to enter the elder class at about the age of thirty. Among the Kikuyu, the process is different with respect to age as well as to time. Circumcision, which among most Kenyan tribes denotes entry into manhood, is not practiced by the Luo. How is the attitude of the non-Luo affected by this failure to acquire this most important symbol of eligibility for political participation? During the height of the 1963 political campaign, the Nandi threatened to circumcise any Jaluo-KANU spokesman who had the audacity to venture into their territory.

Does the fact that some peoples possess a high degree of intra-personal solidarity, institutionalized in the form of blood-brotherhood and related associations, affect the style of their politics? Are they, for example, more prone to charisma and less to ideology?

What are the implications of the use of traditional terms for modern party and government organization? When party leaders are referred to as elders and youth wingers as warriors in the vernacular, is a set of rights and obligations quite unlike those associated with such roles in the West implied?

Is the modern and real problem of generational transference of political power complicated or eased by the various indigenous institutions that traditionally cope with this universal problem? Is a conflict imminent because of the contemporary generational bunching of leadership? What will be the reaction of the would-be elite, who through custom expect entry into the higher ranks of government and party, but whose paths are blocked by a uniformly aging elite?

These and many more questions remain to be posed and to be answered.

SELECTED BIBLIOGRAPHY

Bennett, George. *The Development of Political Organization in Kenya: Political Studies.* New York: Clarendon Press, 1957.

Bennett, George, and Carl Rosberg, Jr. *The Kenyatta Election.* New York: Oxford University Press, 1961.

Burke, Fred G. *Local Government and Politics in Uganda.* Syracuse: Syracuse University Press, 1964.

Church, A. G. *East Africa, A New Dominion.* London: Witherby, 1927.

Cole, Sonia. *The Pre-History of East Africa.* London: Penguin Books, 1954.

Coupland, Reginald. *East Africa and Its Invaders.* Oxford: Clarendon Press, 1938.

Cranworth, Lord. *Kenya Chronicles.* London: Macmillan & Company, 1939.

Delf, George. *Asians in East Africa.* London: Oxford University Press, 1963.

―――. *Jomo Kenyatta: Towards the Truth about the Light of Kenya.* London: Victor Gollancz, 1961.

Gulliver, P. H. *The Family Herds*. London: Routledge and Kegan Paul, 1955.

Hailey, Lord. *Native Administration in the British Territories*. London: H.M.S.O., 1950.

Hobley, Charles W. *Bantu Beliefs and Magic*. London: Witherby, 1922.

Hughes, Anthony J. *East Africa: the Search for Unity*. Baltimore: Penguin Books, 1963.

Huntingford, George W. B. *The Southern Nilo-Hamites*. London: International African Institute, 1953.

Huxley, Elspeth, and Margery Perham. *Race and Politics in Kenya*. London: Faber and Faber, 1956.

Ingham, Kenneth. *A History of East Africa*. London: Longmans, Green, and Company, 1962.

Kenyatta, Jomo. *Facing Mount Kenya*. London: Secker and Warburg, 1959.

Lambert, H. E. *Kikuyu Social and Political Institutions*. New York: Oxford University Press, 1956.

Lugard, Frederick John Dealtry. *East Africa: November 1889 to December 1890, The Diaries of Lord Lugard. Vol. I*. Evanston, Ill.: Northwestern University Press, 1959–1963.

Mair, Lucy. *Primitive Government*. Baltimore: Penguin Books, 1962.

Marsh, Zoe, and G. W. Kingsnorth. *Introduction to the History of East Africa*. Cambridge, Eng.: Cambridge University Press, 1957.

Mboya, Tom. *Freedom and After*. Boston: Little, Brown and Co., 1963.

Murdock, George Peter. *Africa: Its People and Their Culture History*. New York: McGraw-Hill, 1959.

Oliver, Ronald, and Gervase Mathew (eds.). *A History of East Africa*. Vol. I, London: Oxford University Press, 1963.

Verge-Hodge, E. R. *Imperial British East Africa Company*. London: Macmillan & Company, 1960.

Wight, Martin. *Development of the Legislative Council*. London: Faber and Faber, 1957.

Wood, Susan. *Kenya, The Tensions of Progress*. London: Oxford University Press, 1960.

Wooddis, Jack. *Africa: The Roots of Revolt*. New York: Citadel Press, 1962.

OTHERS

Bruns, Laurie. "Trade Unions: Functions, Structure, and Style in East Africa," Unpublished paper, Syracuse University, 1964.

Burke, Fred G. "Some Grass-Roots Attitudes Affecting Political and Social Integration in East Africa." Unpublished paper delivered to the African Studies Association, San Francisco, October 26, 1963.

Corfield Report, *Origins and Growth of Mau Mau*. Nairobi, Kenya: The Government Printer, 1960.

Lonsdale, John. "Archdeacon Owen and the Kavirondo Taxpayers Welfare Association." Unpublished papers, East African Institute of Social Research,
January 1963.

Sorrenson, M. "The Official Mind and Kikuyu Land Tenure," a paper delivered
at the East African Institute of Social Research Conference at Kivukoni College, January 1963.

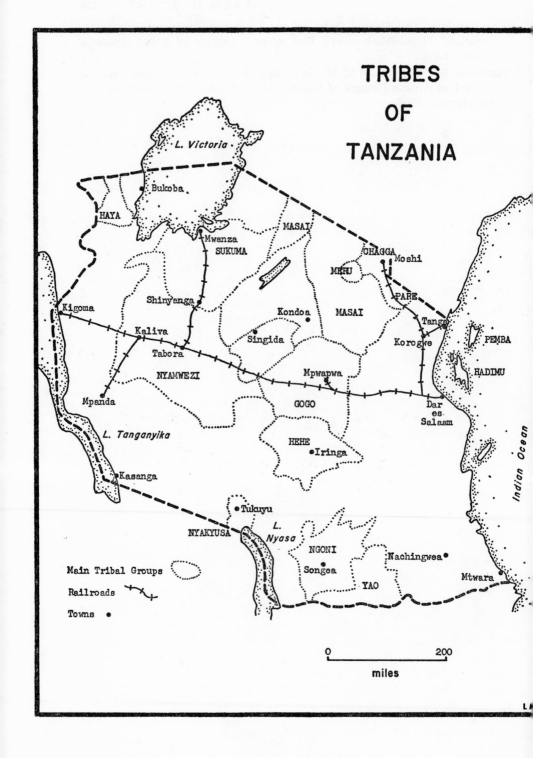

TRIBES
OF
TANZANIA

L. Victoria

Bukoba

HAYA

Mwanza

MASAI

CHAGGA   Moshi

SUKUMA

MERU

PARE

Shinyanga

Kigoma

Kaliva

Tabora

Kondoa

MASAI

Tanga

Korogwe

PEMBA

Singida

HADIMU

NYAMWEZI

Mpwapwa

Mpanda

L. Tanganyika

GOGO

Dar
es.
Salaam

Indian Ocean

HEHE
Iringa

Kasanga

Tukuyu

L.
Nyasa

NYAKYUSA

NGONI

Nachingwea

Main Tribal Groups

Songea

Railroads

YAO

Mtwara

Towns

0   200

miles

6

The Evolution of
Tanganyika's Political System

William H. Friedland

INTRODUCTION

This chapter examines the force—broadly defined—that conditioned and affected the development of Tanganyika's[1] political system. No political system appears by accident: all are the product of forces—conscious and unconscious—that can be elucidated by historical analysis. The dilemma of examining the development of political systems in "older" (for example, European) societies is that their evolution has been influenced by so many complex forces that delineation of variables affecting the system becomes extremely difficult. The advantage of studying more recently developed political systems is that the specification of factors contributing to their evolution is *relatively* simple. Accordingly, this chapter will deal with a society whose history, as a single polity, is very recent.

The term "political system" can encompass a variety of phenomena. Accordingly, it should be made clear that this paper deals with government and political administration, on the one hand, and politics on the other. As shall be noted, politics have become significant in Tanganyika only relatively recently. Tanganyika's political system has centered largely around government and administration. Only since World War II has politics begun to involve more than a tiny elite of European administrators, although the response of the indigenous population to external political control has provided an undercurrent to political developments since the 1930's.

Tanganyika's system is the product of three distinct forces: the metropolitan powers, the representatives of the metropolitan powers, and the indigenous population. A fourth force consisting of non-African settlers played a somewhat significant role for a period of time. However, Tanganyika was

---

[1] The chapter deals only with Tanganyika and does not encompass recent developments out of which emerged the United Republic of Tanzania.

never dominated by settler politics or interests as was the case with many of its neighbors. Although the role of settlers could be examined in considering Tanganyika's political evolution, it does not warrant an extensive treatment and, accordingly, will be dealt with only briefly.

Of the three major forces which influenced the development of the political system, the metropolitan powers require consideration first. The emergence of Tanganyika had its origin in European exigencies: political development began with the scramble for Africa that sent European nations in quest of pieces of the world. Not only did the exigencies of European politics give rise to modern-day Tanganyika, but political evolution was significantly directed and/or redirected in terms of the domestic politics of the dominating metropolitan power.

The second significant force consists of the representatives of the metropolitan powers: the governors, administrators, and experts who constituted the government of the country. These agents, first of the German East Africa Company, later of the German Colonial Office, and finally of the British Colonial Office, were directed to a considerable degree by the politics of their home countries. Domestic politics enforced certain general policies, but enormous areas were left undefined for colonial governors and their administrations to "fill in." Thus, the agents of the colonial power, at once an instrument of that power, also constituted an independent force, interpreting and dealing with the indigenous population.

The third force consists of the indigenous population. Tanganyika, as has been often noted, has a large number of ethnic groupings—"tribes"—frequently estimated at between 100–120. Although few of these groupings had coherent political systems, their responses to the imposition of external control produced changes in the system of control. Thus political evolution had to accommodate the response of the indigenous population. This original indigenous response was neither coherent nor systematic; it was protonationalist and marked by spontaneous violence, traditionalism, and messianism. It was not until the 1930's that a more coherent pattern began to become evident that reached its fullness in 1954 with the creation of the Tanganyika African National Union. From 1954 on, political development is largely the product of the initiative of the indigenous population.

These are the forces at work in producing political evolution. The major political institutions which were produced can be summarized as follows:

1. A political-administrative apparatus for the control of the country—originally of crucial significance, provincial administration became relatively unimportant in the recent past.

2. Central government—at first there was a governor with several advisors who later became heads of departments. This originally simple structure later proliferated into a full-scale ministerial system and cabinet.

3. Local government—given life in 1925 by Sir Donald Cameron, these political units developed and ramified considerably. As shall be seen, however, they remained insignificant compared to the previously mentioned

institutions and have shown little significance in independent Tanganyika.

4. A nationalist party—most recent of the political institutions—has become most significant. Originating in the changing social structure created by the establishment of a colonial system, nationalism saw its first feeble manifestations prior to World War II. Following the war, nationalist sentiments became increasingly significant until the party, the Tanganyika African National Union (TANU), was created in 1954. TANU moved the country toward independence rapidly as it built a mass base in the African population. Ultimately, the party has proved to be the most significant of all political institutions in becoming the *focal institution* of the country, permeating all other institutions.

In examining political development in Tanganyika, historical data will be used to examine the various factors producing change and evolution in the political system.[2]

---

[2] A methodological footnote is unfortunately necessary. A number of gaps will be found in this chapter, and, at the same time, a certain amount of "distortion" has taken place, as trends which proved to be ultimately of small significance have been given considerable space. There are various reasons for this.

For one thing, the paper could not be prepared in Tanganyika where additional materials might have been available that would have permitted a more balanced development. In the United States, literature dealing with the period of Zanzibar hegemony and German control are limited. Both periods warrant additional research. A second reason for some of the imbalances is that some aspects of Tanganyika's political development have been adequately treated by other writers and it was thought desirable to avoid repetition. For a good study of recent political development concentrating mainly on nationalism, see Margaret L. Bates, "Tanganyika," in Gwendolen M. Carter (ed.), *African One-Party States* (Ithaca: Cornell University Press, 1962), pp. 395–483. See also J. Clagett Taylor, *The Political Development of Tanganyika* (Stanford: Stanford University Press, 1963). Other relevant sources are cited in the bibliography.

Other imbalances have developed because the material available is oriented to a particular viewpoint. Thus, while there are many articles on African administration, almost all reflect the viewpoint of the British. It is unfortunate that, while a substantial amount of anthropological research has been conducted in Tanganyika, the political illiteracy of most anthropologists and their fascination with pots or kinship has precluded their paying much attention to the changes wrought in traditional societies by European control. The work of the political scientist, J. Gus Liebenow, however, has been invaluable in this respect. Parenthetically, it might be noted that the pioneering study edited by Meyer Fortes and E. E. Evans-Pritchard and subsequent work by Max Gluckman and his students seems to have sensitized some to the value of political anthropology. This book is one of the most encouraging signs of this trend.

A most significant gap exists in literature dealing with the interwar period, particularly in the 1930's, when the first stirrings of nationalism began to take form. All too frequently, studies of the development of nationalism in Tanganyika assume that the Tanganyika African National Union sprang almost full-blown on the scene in 1954. Most writers mention its predecessor, the Tanganyika African Association, but little data are available on this organization or on other pre-nationalist organizations. The present paper attempts to examine both the social bases for the development of nationalism and some of the early attempts that provided the later basis for TANU's emergence.

THE ZANZIBAR PERIOD

Prior to the period of Zanzibar "control," there were few developments that left any impact relevant to Tanganyika's future development. While there is now some slight knowledge of this early period in East Africa's history,[3] it has little significance for our analysis. Arab contact and settlement on the coast had already taken place prior to the growth of Islam,[4] but it was only later that significant establishments were put down along the coast by the Arabs, the Persians, and, much later, by the Portuguese. These were all coastal settlements, and their influence on the interior of the continent was slight until the nineteenth century. At the beginning of the nineteenth century, Arab domination of the eastern coast of Africa became increasingly significant. While the coast was claimed by the sheiks of Oman, little centralized control was maintained, and, indeed, the suzerainty of Oman was continually overthrown as Arab families established independent small-scale kingdoms based on the coastal towns. The "opening" of the coast awaited the movement in 1840 of the court of Seyyid Said, the ruler of Oman, to Zanzibar. The shift was only in part motivated by political reasons; more significantly, as Coupland has shown, the move occurred because of a realization of the economic potential of the African mainland.[5] Said was concerned with controlling the trade between East Africa and the rest of the world by collecting duties through control of the ports and entrepôts along the coast and by trading into the interior as an entrepreneur in his own right.

Said proceeded to develop the economy of the area rapidly through three policies: (1) increasing the volume of exports from the East African mainland—ivory, slaves, copra, palm oil, etc.; (2) exploiting Zanzibar itself through the large-scale planting of cloves; finally, (3) opening new markets for the products of his territories by welcoming European and American traders who were beginning to enter the area.

It is with the first of these policies that this chapter is concerned since it required control over ports and a means of maintaining amicable relations with inland tribes to facilitate the passage of trading caravans. Thus, it led to the rudiments of a political system. The ports were controlled through "tax farming," wherein the right to collect customs was leased to a contractor, usually on a five-year basis, for a lump sum. Taxing was normally farmed out by Said to a member of the Indian community. Although subject

---

[3] See, especially, Roland Oliver and Gervase Mathew (eds.), *History of East Africa* (Oxford: The Clarendon Press, 1963), Vol. 1, Chs. 3–9.

[4] Gervase Mathew, "The East African Coast until the Coming of the Portuguese," Ch. 4 in Oliver and Mathew, *op. cit.*, p. 102. See also Reginald Coupland, *East Africa and Its Invaders* (Oxford: Clarendon Press, 1936), Ch. 2.

[5] *Loc. cit.* Much of the material that follows on Said is based on Ch. 10 which discusses Said's activities in detail.

to considerable variation, Said's control of the coastal ports was clear although the degree of control varied: it was relatively light along the northern portion of the coast (the area of the Horn of Africa), but there was much closer control between Mombasa and Cape Delgoa. Control inland was very thin except directly opposite Zanzibar; even there, Zanzibar's control was tenuous. The area from the Pare Mountains to Tanga and south was a condominium of Kimweri, the king of Usambaa, and Said. Kimweri was completely independent of Zanzibar and appointed headmen (*diwans*) in the coastal strip. The *diwans* were, in turn, confirmed by Said who made a present to them. South of Usambaa, there was no centralized kingdom, such as that of Kimweri, and Said was ostensibly the ruler over the whole area. He had little desire to establish direct control over the hinterland. Students of the period are fond of quoting him to the effect that "I am nothing but a merchant."[6] Distinctions must be made, therefore, between *the coastal areas,* where Said (and his successors) exercised relatively direct control and were concerned with the collection of custom duties, and *the inland areas.*

The Coastal Towns

The towns were primarily entrepôts for the transshipment of commercial articles, slaves, ivory, copra, etc., being exported and manufactured goods being imported. The towns extended from Mogadishu in the north to Kilwa in the south. In the area of what is now Tanganyika, the important centers included Tanga, Pangani, Saadani, Bagamoyo, Mboamaji (rather than Dar es Salaam), and Kilwa. Even in many of these towns, control from Zanzibar was often tenuous.

> . . . the primary, almost the only, direct administrative function of his (the sultan's) overlordship was to secure the customs dues payable to him at every port.
>
> In each of the towns he installed a Governor, sometimes a local Sheikh, sometimes a man of his own from Zanzibar or Muscat, and furnished him with a show, but only a show, of military force. Along the coast there were only about four hundred of his "Baluchis" in 1846; and of these some hundred and fifty were then in occupation of Fort Jesus (at Mombasa). At Lamu there were about thirty, at Pate twenty-five, at Kilwa half a dozen, and at the other places two or three apiece . . . it is clear that Said's Governors, with only a handful of poor soldiers at their call, did little governing. On Said's behalf they may have heard appeals from the judicial decisions of the local Sheikhs; but, in general, though Said was in theory the overlord and the Sheikhs his vassals, they were in practice and in the normal course of events the almost unchecked masters of their own little parcels of the coast. They paid their feudal "tribute"

---

[6] *Ibid.,* p. 299; see also John M. Gray, "Zanzibar and the Coastal Belt, 1840–1884," in Oliver and Mathew, *op. cit.,* pp. 223–224.

in the shape of the dues on their trade; and that was practically all that Said and his deputies required of them.[7]

Said and his successors were almost entirely concerned with their ability to control customs collections, a responsibility regarded as too important to be handled by Arabs and was therefore farmed out to Indians. Thus, Zanzibar's sultans maintained a small military force mainly to ensure the ability of the tax farmer to collect duties and not to maintain direct political control.

The Inland Areas

Here control was even more tenuous. Coupland points out that Arab settlements took place in Tabora, Ujiji, and Masana (Msene). Along the caravan routes, the most important of which was between Bagamoyo and Tabora, Arab trading posts could be found but they were hardly settlements.[8] There were two groups to be "controlled" in the inland areas, the Arabs and the Africans. The Arabs who passed through the various tribal lands, established trading posts and centers at Tabora and elsewhere, were Said's subjects. Communications with them from Zanzibar were fragile, and they were, to all intents and purposes, free of Zanzibar control once they went inland. Yet they respected the sultan and considered him their ruler.

> All those traders were nominally Said's subjects. They acknowledged his overlordship no less than their kinsmen of the coast. At Tabora, as at the coast towns, Said seems to have appointed a leading Sheikh as his personal representative or governor. . . . It was impossible . . . for Said to make his power felt there (at Tabora) as he could by means of his fleet along the coast. None the less the Arabs of the interior . . . seem generally to have obeyed their overlord. It was only in small matters, after all, that he was likely as a rule to require obedience. . . . The inland Arabs, it appears, professed a deep respect for their distant sovereign's wishes and did all they could to help a stranger commended to their care.[9]

Said appointed one Arab as his representative—the "governor"—but since instructions were rarely forthcoming, the hand of Zanzibar did not lie too heavily on its subjects at Tabora, Ujiji, or further inland.

As far as relations with the African tribes were concerned, Zanzibar represented a far-distant and vague authority. Relationships with the inland areas were regularized to facilitate the movement of large caravans in relative

---

[7] Coupland, *op. cit.*, p. 33. See also Gray, *op. cit.*, p. 224, and Lawrence W. Hollingsworth, *Zanzibar under the Foreign Office 1890–1913* (London: Macmillan & Company, 1953) p. 10.

[8] Coupland, *op. cit.*, pp. 309–311.

[9] *Ibid.*, p. 358.

safety while the inland tribes retained their autonomy. This "live-and-let-live" pattern permitted the growth of an enormous trade in goods in both directions. Regular routes of travel were established to the interior: the route via Mpwapwa and Tabora led to Ujiji and the sources of ivory beyond Lake Tanganyika; the route via Kilwa led to the sources of slaves in the Lake Nyasa area. Throughout the area, the red flag of the sultan meant a peaceful passage for a caravan as did a *firman* (passport) obtained from the sultan by many of the early European explorers. A common feature was the payment of *hongo* (tribute for the right of passage) by caravans to the chiefs/headmen of the tribes through whose lands the caravans passed. Care was taken to avoid some tribes such as the Masai. On the whole, the sultan's attitude was to avoid trouble if at all possible.

> Said's attitude to the African chiefs and the tribes inland was much the same as his attitude to the Arab coast towns. He would have no trouble with them if he could help it. Peace, not war, was the condition of good trade . . . he had no appetite for conquest, no desire to impose his rule. He would no more interfere with the affairs of an African chief than with those of a sultan of an Arab seaport—unless his claim to a general and loose, *but exclusive,* over-lordship were seriously threatened from within or without.[10]

Later in the century, the Arabs were to become increasingly involved in tribal politics in the areas where they had important settlements. At Tabora, the Arabs drove out Manua Sera, the chief of Unyanyembe (near Tabora), when he sought to impose *his* duties on incoming merchandise. The Arabs ". . . replaced him with a series of more compliant puppets. . . ."[11] The Arabs were less successful in dealing with Mirambo, a Nyamwezi chief who emerged at Urambo, forty miles west of Tabora. Mirambo engaged in continual conflict with the Arabs at Tabora until peace was concluded in 1876.

Zanzibar policy with respect to Mirambo is revealing. While Zanzibar had used the Arab colony at Unyanyembe as a "cornerstone for political influence," the sultan was prepared to turn to Mirambo and support him after he had proved his ability to control the behavior of "the unruly and predatory forces on which he depended."[12]

Arab policy was concentrated on facilitating commerce, but keeping external forces off the continent. Thus, when the French naval officer Maizen was murdered inland in 1845, Said responded to French threats to mount a punitive expedition by burning the village where Maizen was killed.[13]

---

[10] *Ibid.*, p. 356. (Emphasis in original.)

[11] Alison Smith, "The Southern Section of the Interior, 1940–1984," in Oliver and Mathew, *op. cit.*, pp. 278–279.

[12] *Ibid.*, p. 291.

[13] Coupland, *op. cit.*, pp. 353–356.

Similarly, in 1860, when the German explorer Roscher was killed near Lake Nyasa, the offenders were brought to Zanzibar for punishment.[14] The same pattern can be seen at a later date when the Germans had begun their work on the continent. Zanzibar's sultans had never gone to the trouble of raising their red flag over the continent. It was only after Carl Peters began his treaty-signing expeditions inland in 1884 that Sultan Bargash sent an expedition to the Kilimanjaro area, an area he had long claimed, to raise his flag.[15]

In the period after 1840, European penetration accelerated. Missionaries arrived in increasing numbers and mission stations began to appear throughout the area following the travels of the great explorers: Livingstone, Stanley, Burton, Speke, and others. This, plus the growing nationalism and competitiveness of the European powers, produced sharp changes in Africa. Whereas, Zanzibar had had few challenges either internally or externally to its "authority" in the past, it was now to be confronted by a series of crises. The attempt to keep the Europeans off the continent was futile, however, since the changes that were being wrought in Europe were beyond the scope of Zanzibar's sultans. A more extensive trade had developed, including considerable traffic in firearms and gunpowder, which gave rise to war lords of the interior (such as Mirambo) who threatened Arab commerce. Even more significantly, Europeans were beginning the "scramble for Africa." Even if Zanzibar had had greater control over the interior, it is unlikely that it could have resisted the pressures of the European powers. With so little effective control, the question of who would dominate the mainland was only a matter of time, but it was certain that the Arabs of Zanzibar would not.

Although Zanzibar rule did not establish any pattern of political control or any enduring political institutions, the period has some significance for future developments. For one thing, the somewhat loose patterns utilized by Zanzibar in the coastal towns, where an *akida* (a military figure) had political control over an area, were taken over by the Germans. More will be said about this later. More significantly, as a result of Arab commerce, a lingua franca was spread throughout the breadth of East Africa. Though tribal languages continued to play an important role in everyday life, the linguistic basis for a future nation was successfully established.[16]

THE GERMAN PERIOD

German interest in East Africa began much before 1884 when Carl Peters won a series of "treaties" with inland chiefs on behalf of the German East Africa Company (GEAC) and 1888 when the sultan's ports on the Tan-

---

14 J. P. Moffett (ed.), *Handbook of Tanganyika* (Dar es Salaam: Government Printer, 1958) p. 39.

15 Coupland, *op. cit.,* p. 409.

16 G. S. P. Freeman-Grenville, "The German Sphere 1884–1898," in Oliver and Mathew, *op. cit.,* p. 448.

ganyika mainland were taken over. Although much that transpired during the establishment of German control does not concern this essay, a brief description of these events is useful.

German concern with East Africa and other non-European areas was the product of two major tendencies that became marked in the middle of the nineteenth century. On the one hand, there was the growth of nationalism in Europe. Germany itself was a product of this nationalism growing out of the Franco-Prussian War (1870–1871). Nationalism expressed itself, not only in tension between the European nations in Europe, but also in the form of expansion into undeveloped areas of the world. Thus, the major European powers were beginning the scramble not only for Africa but for Asia and Oceania as well. The second factor was the considerable emigration from Germany to the New World. Emigration represented a loss of its population to Germany. If opportunities could be found for Germans in German territories abroad, it was felt that this loss would be minimized; indeed, emigration under these circumstances would strengthen the home country.

German interest in the East African area began with the explorations of Johannes Rebmann and Johann Krapf in the Kilimanjaro and Usambara areas in 1848. German commercial houses were established at Zanzibar by the middle of the century, and, by 1871, one-quarter of Zanzibar's trade was with Germans.[17] German missions were also moving into the area during this time. German activities accelerated rapidly after Carl Peters made a trip through Uzigua, Usagara, Ukami, and Nguru in 1884, signing treaties with the local chiefs. As a result of Peters' trip and because it suited Bismarck's policies vis-à-vis the British at the moment,[18] Bismarck issued a charter to the German East African Company (GEAC) in March 1885, giving the Company the right to manage the territories. From 1885 on, the GEAC sent out expeditions to collect information relevant to immigration and the development of the area. Subcompanies, such as the East African Plantation Company and the German Planters Company, were formed which established branches on the Pangani and Umba rivers. By 1888, there were thirty such stations, and tobacco was being exported to Germany.[19]

The issuance of the charter to the GEAC aroused Zanzibar which claimed these territories. The issue was "resolved" by the arrival of German naval vessels at Zanzibar with decks cleared for action in August 1885; thus, Zanzibar "admitted" Germany to the hinterland. On August 19th, Bargash conceded Dar es Salaam to the Germans as a port with "control of customs, on condition that it should not be fortified or garrisoned . . ." by the

---

[17] *Ibid.*, p. 434.

[18] John Flint, "The Wider Background to Partition and Colonial Occupation," in Oliver and Mathew, *op. cit.*, pp. 364–366.

[19] J. Scott Keltie, *The Partition of Africa* (London: Edward Stanford, 1893), pp. 245–246. For a list of the expeditions, see Fritz Ferdinand Müller, *Deutschland-Zanzibar-Ostafrika* (Berlin: Rütten & Loenig, 1959), pp. 228–229.

Germans. Occupation took place on May 25, 1887. In the meantime, in 1886, as a result of tensions between the European powers, a commission came to East Africa to delimit the sultan's realms and German and British spheres of influence. The commission left Bargash with a coastal belt ten miles in width, but stripped him of the entire interior.[20] In 1888, the new sultan, Sayyid Khalifa, signed an agreement with the Germans leasing them the coastal territories between the Umba (just north of present-day Moa, near the current border with Kenya) and Ruvumu rivers. This included seven ports and three roadsteads.[21] The Germans were to operate this territory in the name of the sultan, flying his flag, and subject to his sovereign rights.[22] This marked the end of Zanzibar's "legal" control over the mainland.

The Response to German Rule

The establishment of German rule on the mainland initiated a variety of responses that can be called proto-nationalist or pre-nationalist.[23] The significance of this early response is that (1) a new sense of solidarity was created in a variety of indigenous groups which had previously shown little cohesion; (2) the response was largely violent and sought physically to repel the foreign invader; (3) the reaction was characterized by considerable messianism, but was also strongly traditionalist in outlook. It is for this reason that the response is designated as proto-nationalist; it was not until Africans were able to work within the *same frame of reference* (constitutionalism, written law, bureaucratic procedures, etc.) as Europeans that the response became truly nationalist. In the case of Tanganyika, the initial response to the Germans along the coast in 1888–1894 and the later Maji Maji rebellion of 1905–1906 were clearly proto-nationalist. Many of the other responses were purely and simply traditionalist in that established societies were seeking to maintain the status quo.

The first reaction to European control came as soon as Hauptmann Leue arrived in Dar es Salaam, on May 25, 1887. The chilly reception that he received soon "warmed" as the entire coast rose against German control. In taking over the rest of the coastal towns following the agreement of April 28, 1888, the Germans moved rapidly and often tactlessly to establish their presence. The entry of German dogs into the Tanga mosque during Ramadan hardly augured well for the future peace of the country. When the com-

---

20 Freeman-Grenville, *op. cit.,* pp. 437–438.

21 Keltie, *op. cit.,* p. 247.

22 Freeman-Grenville, *op. cit.,* p. 438.

23 For a discussion of proto-nationalist movements in similar circumstances, but involving an entirely different set of cultures, see the literature on cargo cults in Melanesia. Cf., Peter Lawrence, *Road Belong Cargo* (Manchester: Manchester University Press, 1964), p. 7.

mander of the German military forces arrived at Pangani in August 1888, he tore down the sultan's flag and raised the GEAC flag. The reaction was so strong locally that a German gunboat had to withdraw from the port. Similar flag incidents occurred at Bagamoyo, Tanga, and Kilwa.[24]

The hostility at Pangani was so intense that Abushiri ibn Salim al-Harthi (generally referred to as Bushiri), a local notable, initiated a revolt that took a heavy toll in lives and eventually brought an end to the rule of the GEAC and the establishment of a German crown colony in its stead. Bushiri's revolt threatened German control along the entire coast, and a number of towns were actually captured from the Germans.

The Company, requesting help from the German government, was, in effect, taken over by Bismarck who dispatched the explorer Hermann von Wissmann as Imperial Commissioner to re-establish control. The thirty-odd Germans representing the GEAC were put under Wissmann's direction. He was also given a small army consisting of German officers and noncommissioned officers, Sudanese, and Zulus.[25] The revolt was finally put down and Bushiri hanged in December 1889. Shortly afterward, Mkwawa, chief of the Hehe, led a rebellion in the south that lasted intermittently from 1891 to 1898. Still later came the celebrated Maji Maji rebellion of 1905–1906 which began on a cotton plantation at Kibata, forty miles from Kilwa. The African workers, forced to labor on the plantation by the Germans, revolted and sparked a rebellion that spread throughout the south, took some 120,000 lives and left parts of the country permanently devastated.[26] These were the

---

[24] Freeman-Grenville, op. cit., pp. 438–439.

[25] Evans Lewin, The Germans and Africa (London: Cassell, 1915), p. 189; see also Keltie, op. cit., p. 249. The confusion in the literature dealing with Tanganyika is illustrated by the description of the force given to von Wissmann. Keltie, writing just after the events, states: "The Commissioner had at his service sixty German officers and soldiers, and about two hundred sailors from the German navy." p. 250. Freeman-Grenville writes that von Wissmann had ". . . a hastily recruited army of 600 Sudanese recruited in Egypt, 50 Somalis, and 350 Zulus from Mozambique." p. 440. Later, Freeman-Grenville states that "1500 German officers volunteered, but he was only permitted to select twenty-five," p. 447. Hans Schmiedel says: "He recruited Sudanese soldiers in Egypt and Zulus from Portuguese East Africa. They were under the command of German officers and N.C.O.'s Instead of only twenty-five officers, fifteen hundred who wanted to escape the drill of the barrack-yard at home reported for duty." See "Bwana Sakkarani: Captain Tom von Prince and His Times," Tanganyika Notes and Records, No. 52 (March 1959), p. 36. With these conflicting figures, it is difficult to come to any conclusion about the size of von Wissmann's force. This point is not raised simply to indicate difficulties in research; the size of the force might provide some indication as to the size of the German administration in Tanganyika following the suppression of Bushiri.

[26] Margaret Bates, "Historical Introduction" to Abdul Karim bin Jamaliddini, Utensi wa Vita vya Maji-Maji, Supplement to the East African Swahili Committee Journal, No. 27 (June 1957), 8–9. See also David F. Clyde, History of the Medical Services in Tanganyika (Dar es Salaam: Government Printer, 1962), p. 35.

Table 6–1

Responses to German Control in Tanganyika, 1888–1906

1888[a]	Arab revolt at Pangani against German East Africa Company. Ignites "Bushiri rebellion" from Pangani to Kilwa. Revolt put down by Imperial German force led by von Wissmann in October 1889.
1889–1894[b]	Siki, chief of Unyamwezi, expresses hostility to Germans in 1889. Closes the caravan routes at Tabora, 1892. His son attacks German forces. Defeated by Germans; Tabora occupied in 1894.
1890[c]	Gogo raids in Tabora area. Punitive expeditions sent out to put an end to the raids.
1890[d]	Kalmera, chief at Usambiro, bars Stuhlmann's passage in 1890. German troops destroy two bomas; 163 Africans killed and wounded.
1890–1898[e]	Ngoni rebellion at Unyanyembe and Urambo. Not subdued until 1897–1898.
1891[f]	Sinna of Kibosho (West Kilimanjaro) tears down German flag. Subdued by von Wissmann.
1894–1898[g]	Mkwawa rebellion. Destroyed Zelewski's column in 1891. Although seriously defeated in 1894, he continued to be an irritant until he committed suicide in 1898.
1892[h]	Meli, successor of Mandara, chief of Chagga, collides with Germans and kills Baron von Bülow. Punitive expeditions sent.
1894[i]	Sultan Hassan bin Omari tries to take Kilwa from west in order to re-establish slave trade. Captured in punitive expedition.
1895[j]	Machembo, Yao chief southwest of Lindi, refuses to pay hut tax. Persists until 1899 when a punitive expedition imprisons his followers and he flees to Portuguese territory.
1905–1906[k]	Maji Maji rebellion. Begins on cotton plantation and spreads throughout southeast. Suppressed at estimated cost of 120,000 lives.

[a] J. P. Moffett (ed.), *Handbook of Tanganyika* (Dar es Salaam: Government Printer, 1958), pp. 56–59; also Richard Reusch, *History of East Africa* (New York: Frederick Ungar, 1961), pp. 306–308.

[b] Reusch, *op. cit.,* p. 316; also G. S. P. Freeman-Grenville, "The German Sphere," in Roland Oliver and Gervase Mathew (eds.), *History of East Africa* (Oxford: Clarendon Press, 1963), p. 442.

[c] Moffett, *op. cit.,* p. 66.

[d] Reusch, *op. cit.,* p. 310.

[e] Freeman-Grenville, *op. cit.,* p. 443; Moffett, *op. cit.,* p. 678.

[f] Reusch, *op. cit.,* p. 314.

[g] *Ibid.,* p. 315.

[h] Moffett, *op. cit.,* p. 65.

[i] Reusch, *op. cit.,* p. 316; Moffett, *op. cit.,* p. 63.

[j] Freeman-Grenville, *op. cit.,* p. 446; Moffett, *op. cit.,* p. 63.

[k] Reusch, *op. cit.,* pp. 322–26.

large rebellions. Table 6–1 summarizes what can be gleaned about the more significant violent reactions to the establishment of German hegemony.

The causes of these reactions were manifold. Bushiri's revolt was largely a coastal response that was in part patriotic (to Zanzibar), in part a cultural reaction to unclean infidels who did not respect local customs and sensibilities. It was also a reaction to German interference with the important slave trade, by this time illegal, but still an important element in the coastal economy. Mkwawa's revolt represented the attempt of a traditional chief to retain his hard-earned prerogatives. Mkwawa had created a considerable kingdom stretching from the area near what is now the Central Line to 100 miles south of Iringa, his capital. Mkwawa wanted to control caravan travel as had been customary in the past. When Mkwawa wiped out a German column in 1891, a war was initiated that ended only after his death in 1898. The Maji Maji rebellion was, in contrast, a revitalization movement[27] uniting the southeastern tribes that were increasingly being subjected to forced labor by the Germans. It was the last of the major proto-nationalist rebellions.[28]

The Establishment of Control and Administration

Von Wissmann's immediate problem on arrival in East Africa was to suppress Bushiri. Once accomplished, his task was to establish a permanent administration to maintain control, facilitate the growth of the economy, and encourage immigration and settlement. During the next decade, a number of German centers of administration were strategically located in terms of many often overlapping considerations. Among these considerations were the following:

1. The control of trade and communication. These included the coastal centers taken over from Zanzibar—Tanga, Pangani, Saadani, Dar es Salaam, Kilwa, and Lindi. Later, German control over Tabora, Mpwapwa, and Ujiji became crucial for communication, and these became centers of administration.

2. The control of real or potential rebellion. Concern with Mkwaya's revolt in the Iringa area led to its becoming a center of administration.

3. The concentration of existing population. Major population concentrations existed in Usambaa, Upare, Kilimanjaro, and the present-day Rungwe district, all of which became administrative centers.

4. The possibility of economic expansion and/or immigration. Kilimanjaro and the Lushoto area became administrative centers for this reason.

---

[27] See Anthony F. C. Wallace, "Revitalization Movements," *American Anthropologist*, LVIII (1956), 264–281.

[28] Julius Nyerere, first president of Tanganyika and now president of Tanzania, has called Maji Maji the action which initiated Tanganyikan unity. *Uganda Argus,* April 10, 1962, as quoted by John Iliffe, "Reflections on the Maji Maji Rebellion," *Spearhead,* I (November 1962), p. 21.

Table 6–2

German Stations and Personnel, 1896

Town	Germans	Colored
Dar es Salaam	37	118
Kilwa Kivinji	6	106
Moshi	5	100
Marangu	1	21
Iringa	12	257
Kilimatinde	7	84
Mpwapwa	4	60
Perondo	1	?
Pangani	6	87
Lindi	7	121
Ujiji	8	133
Tabora	7	119
Bukoba	8	122
Mwanza	5	72
Kilosa	5	48
Others	7	112
Total 14	126	1,560

SOURCE: G. S. P. Freeman-Grenville, "The German Sphere 1884–1898" in Roland Oliver and Gervase Mathew, *History of East Africa,* Vol. I (Oxford: Clarendon Press, 1963), pp. 447–448.

NOTE: There is some question about the accuracy of the data in Table 6–2 since some of the former centers of administration, Tanga, Saadani, and Bagamoyo, for example, seem to have disappeared. It is possible that the personnel in these towns were included in the complements assigned to Dar es Salaam and Pangani. Heinreich Schnee, in *German Colonization Past and Future* (London: Allen and Unwin, 1926), p. 79, provides some additional figures for military and police forces in 1896. Schnee gives a total military establishment of 2,760 persons including 152 officers or subofficers, 2,500 native soldiers and 108 German Red Cross personnel. The police force, he claims, consisted of 4 German officers, 61 subofficers (probably German) and 2,140 "colored natives."

In addition to these considerations, two centers were created to mount a possible offensive into the British "controlled" area north of Tanganyika. Largely because of Emin Pasha's work, a station was created at Bukoba with a supporting station at Mwanza. Bukoba was also a center of population and an area of eventual economic exploitation, but the prime motive in creating this station was to have a base for expansion into Buganda. Bukoba and Mwanza were created in the last stages of the scramble for Africa, and although they lost their function immediately, they were maintained because of the rule of "effective occupation" which had become a predominating theme in colonial expansion.

Although evidence of the early pattern of administrative settlement is sparse, some data exist through which it is possible to develop a picture of the size and shape of early administration. In 1888, GEAC apparently had thirty officials located at eight stations which included Tanga, Pangani, Saadani, Bagamoyo, Lindi, and Mikindani. In August 1888, sixty German officers were sent to run the administration, and, when the territory passed into the hands of the German government, a civil governor was placed at the head of the administration. By 1892, there is a record of twelve stations plus four subsidiary stations. The twelve stations were at eight coastal towns: Tanga, Pangani, Saadani, Bagamoyo, Dar es Salaam, Kilwa, Lindi, and Mikindani; and four inland towns: Mpwapwa, Moshi, Mwanza, and Bukoba.[29] By 1896, the number of stations had grown to at least fifteen. These, with their complements of German and colored personnel, are listed in Table 6–2 and illustrate how thinly the German administration was spread throughout the country.

The few details that can be found on the pattern of administration in the period 1890–1906 indicate that the administration was weak and attenuated.

> Each station was commanded by a semi-military commissioner known as a *Bezirksamtmann*, to whom were directly responsible *liwalis* and *akidas*, with village headmen, *jumbes*, as the lowest stratum, or, in certain areas, hereditary chiefs . . . in the areas where hereditary rulers had not been the custom and where the tribe was no more than a headless mass of clans, the Germans had perforce to adapt the system which Zanzibar had employed in the coastal region before their advent. This was hardly a matter of choice, for the Swahili were the only literates available for employment in any trusted capacity. This local government was responsible for the maintenance of law and order with the assistance of the small bodies of troops under the *Bezirksamtmann*, and later for the provision of labour for public works, and, after 1896, for the collection of the hut tax.[30]

The revenue of the colony in 1891–1892 was 1,458,000 marks or £73,000. Revenue rose to £310,780 in 1895–1896. Expenditure in 1891–1892 was £170,680; this rose in 1895–1896 to £1,616,350.[31] Although revenue was considerably less than expenditure, and grants-in-aid had to be made by the German government, the increase in revenue indicates a considerable growth of the economy in spite of the troubles the colony experienced. J. P. Moffett's summary of the period probably best indicates the shape of the administrative apparatus:

---

[29] See Lewin, *op. cit.*, p. 189, and Keltie, *op. cit.*, pp. 247, 251.

[30] Freeman-Grenville, *op. cit.*, p. 448.

[31] *Ibid.*, p. 449.

Germany . . . had to depend . . . upon personnel who were very often completely incapable of adapting themselves to local circumstances. The great majority of her early colonial officials, including medical officers and officials employed upon technical work, were army officers largely imbued with the traditional militarism of the service in which they had been trained. Certain of the senior officers, such as Hermann von Wissmann, fully realised that there were fresh lessons to be learned in East Africa and that the regimentation prevailing in Germany was not necessarily suitable to conditions existing in their colony. But the great majority of the officers were subalterns with two or three years' experience of regimental duty, many of whom were quite incapable or else quite unwilling to learn anything outside the ordinary scope of their military duties. Still more unsatisfactory were the German non-commissioned officers, who had been brought up in a hide-bound militarism, in which most of their time had been spent in licking conscripts into shape. . . .

It was equally unfortunate for the reputation of the German administration that they almost entirely depended for the recruitment of their rank and file upon Africans who belonged to races which were alien to German East Africa, such as Zulus, Sudanese, and Swahilis from the coast. These mercenaries took full advantage of the protection of the German uniform to prey upon the inhabitants of the countries in which they were stationed and through which they passed. Their superiors very often turned a blind eye to their depredations and rarely took any measures to see that justice was done to their victims.[32]

"Scientific Colonization": The Rationalization of Colonial Administration

The early violent reactions by Africans to German rule were not limited to Tanganyika. In the Kamerun (Cameroon), Southwest Africa, and Togo, a series of scandals had plagued the colonial section of the Foreign Office and aroused groups within Germany. Carl Peters, who was largely responsible for the creation of German East Africa, was brought to trial in 1896 for unjustly condemning to death a native servant and was found guilty and discharged from the colonial service. Similar outrages, as well as the rebellions by the Hereros in Southwest Africa and Mkwawa in East Africa, precipitated a major controversy in Germany. Though the debate was triggered by revolts in the colonies, it was primarily abetted by considerations of German internal politics.

In 1906, two groups in the Reichstag began to create opposition to the government of Chancellor von Bülow: the Socialists on the grounds of economic exploitation by capitalists at the expense of the German people and the Catholic Center because of discrimination in the colonial department and claims of "murder, robbery, and lust" in the colonies. The Catholics began to block colonial appropriations and grew especially vocif-

---

[32] Moffett, op. cit., pp. 70–71.

erous in response to news of the uprisings. Von Bülow defended his colonial policy on the basis of its economic value. This argument was answered by the Socialist, August Bebel, who showed that the colonies were not only a financial liability but a failure in regard to emigration. The government fell in 1906 when supplementary estimates for Southwest Africa were rejected by the Reichstag. In the ensuing election, the campaign of the government forces was directed by Dr. Bernhard Dernburg, newly designated Colonial Director, and colonial policy played an important role among the campaign issues. Dr. Dernburg, who had been manager of a bank and was selected for his business abilities, led an effective campaign for the government, which won on January 25, 1907. Dernburg subsequently became Germany's first Colonial Secretary.[33] Following the election, Dernburg made a tour of the colonies and returned appalled by what he had seen.[34] As a result, a major overhaul took place in the Colonial Office (which had become a separate ministry in 1907) and in the colonial governments. In the application of the new policies in East Africa, there were two important developments which must be underscored. These were the regularization of central government and administration and the creation of an advisory council.

Central Government and Administration

Although the governor was retained as the head of the civil and military administration, a new policy emphasizing the civilian approach to problems was established. This was accomplished by appointing civilians rather than military men to the governorship. To assist him in his task, the governor had a *referent* who was the equivalent of a chief councillor. Other *referente,* fourteen in total, were placed in charge of twenty functional departments.[35] Leaving out Ruanda, Urundi, and Bukoba where indigenous chiefs were established and the Germans created Residencies to control these existing political mechanisms, the rest of German East Africa was divided into nineteen civil and two military districts.[36] Each of the former was directed by a district commissioner (*Bezirksamtmann*) responsible to the governor for maintaining order and collecting taxes. Below the *Bezirksamtmann,* the

---

[33] This summary of Germany's political crisis of 1906 is based on Mary E. Townsend, *The Rise and Fall of Germany's Colonial Empire 1884–1918* (New York: The Macmillan Company, 1930), pp. 225–245.

[34] Moffett, *op. cit.,* p. 77.

[35] H. William Rodemann, *Tanganyika: 1890–1914—Selected Aspects of German Administration* (Unpublished Ph.D. dissertation, University of Chicago, 1961), p. 72. Ansu Kamar Datta, *Tanganyika: A Government in a Plural Society* (The Hague: 1955), pp. 2–3.

[36] The nineteen civil districts were Wilhelmstal (later Lushoto), Tanga, Pangani, Bagamoyo, Morogoro, Dar es Salaam, Kilwa, Lindi, Rufiji, Songea, Langenburg (later Tukuyu), Bismarckburg (later Kasanga), Ujiji, Dodoma, Moshi, Mwanza, Tabora,

structure of administration followed that of Zanzibar, but control was more direct and immediate, even if thin. Control was exercised through *akidas* who were responsible to the *Bezirksamtmann* for groups of villages. The *akidas* continued to be of Swahili or Arab extraction and had no roots in the areas they administered. Under the *akidas* came the *jumbes,* the village headmen, who were responsible to the *akida* for the maintenance of order and the collection of taxes, and had magisterial power over their villages.[37]

The system can be characterized as "direct rule" in that the *Bezirksamt-mann* was directly responsible to the governor and his subordinates were directly responsible to him. In particular, the *akida's* position reflects the "directness" of rule since no attempt was made (except in Ruanda and Urundi) to utilize indigenous political mechanisms. No data are available on the methods used to select the *jumbes;* it may be that the *akidas* consciously or unconsciously utilized, to some degree, indigenous political systems in order to facilitate control. However, this was not a matter of German administrative policy. German administration was very thin. In 1914, the European administrative staff consisted of seventy-nine persons[38] which, considering the size of the territory and the state of communications,[39] meant that enormous discretion remained with the *akidas* and *jumbes* because of

---

Arusha, and Kondoa-Irangi. The military districts were Iringa and Mahenge. The only residency in what later became Tanganyika was at Bukoba. See United Kingdom Foreign Office, *Tanganyika (German East Africa)* Handbooks Prepared under the Direction of the Historical Section of the Foreign Office, No. 113 (London: H.M.S.O., 1920), pp. 37–38.

[37] Based on Lord Hailey, *Native Administration in the British African Territories,* Part I (London: H.M.S.O., 1950), pp. 212–213; Moffett, *op. cit.,* p. 78. The language used by Moffett is almost identical to that of Hailey. No data are available on the number of *akidas* or *jumbes* or on the numbers of *akidas* responsible to a *Bezirksamt-mann.*

[38] Moffett, *op. cit.,* p. 78. However, if German data were made consistent with British personnel statistics, there were 551 officials in the German administration in 1914. See Rodemann, *op. cit.,* pp. 71 ff.

[39] While roads along the coast were relatively good, communications inland were exceedingly poor, especially during the rainy season. For a description of some of the hazards of a regular caravan traveler in the pre-railroad days see Marius Fortie, *The Black and the Beautiful* (New York: Bobbs Merrill, 1938), *passim.* The construction of the Tanga and Central railways facilitated communication and trade considerably. The Tanga Line was begun by a private company in 1893, but did not reach terminus in Moshi until 1912 when it was completed by the government. The Central Line, a government operation from the beginning, was begun in 1907 and reached terminus on Lake Tanganyika in 1914. See Moffett, *op. cit.,* p. 81. Telegraphic communication along the railroads was good once the railroads were actually built. In 1914, there were thirty-four telegraph offices, 2,537 kilometers of land lines and three main lines of telegraphic communication. These were (1) the Central Line system from Dar es Salaam to Ujiji-Kigoma with branch telegraphs from Kilosa to Iringa, Tabora to Mwanza, and Ujiji to Bismarckburg (Kasanga); (2) Dar es Salaam to Tanga in the

the inability of German administrative officers to cover the ground effectively.

The Advisory Council

One innovation introduced as a result of Dernburg's direction of the Colonial Office was modeled on the British legislative council system: this was an advisory council which the governor consulted at regular intervals. This reform was introduced in 1911. The council consisted of three officials and between five and twelve unofficial members, all of whom had to be German-born. The council met three times a year to provide opinions on the draft budget and proposed legislation. Unofficial members were nominated by the governor out of thirty nominees chosen by the German residents of the various areas of the colony.[40] Although there is no information available about the operation of the advisory council, its creation emphasizes the change that took place as a result of Dernburg's visit to the colonies.

It is not possible to detail the many accomplishments of the Germans in sharply accelerating economic growth during this period. Not only were plantations begun, but stations for agricultural research were founded. The school system developed rapidly. Land policy was stabilized, and, while immigration continued to be encouraged, alienation of lands was stopped and areas were set aside for exclusive African occupancy. Direct taxation in the form of a poll tax of three rupees (five shillings) was begun in 1905, not only as a source of revenue, but to encourage the development of a labor force.[41] This was a period of steady growth. The heart had been cut out of any indigenous response through brutal repression (the so-called policy of *Schreklichkeit,* "frightfulness")[42]: now, under Dernburg's more enlightened

---

north and Mikindani in the south; (3) the Tanga Line system from Tanga to Arusha via Wilhelmstal (Lushoto) and Moshi. There was also a heliograph signalling system connecting Dodoma with Kondoa-Irangi, Singida, and Kilimatinde as well as Mahenge with a number of smaller towns. See United Kingdom Foreign Office, *Tanganyika (German East Africa)* (London: H.M.S.O., 1920), pp. 50–51. There was also an unreliable heliograph system between Iringa and Langenburg (Tukuyu). The only reliable communication between Dar es Salaam and Langenburg was via British lines to South Africa and then northward. See Paul von Lettow-Vorbeck, *East African Campaigns* (New York: Robert Speller & Sons, 1957), pp. 12, 26.

[40] United Kingdom, Foreign Office, *Tanganyika (German East Africa)*, p. 38; Rodemann, *op. cit.,* p. 72.

[41] P. H. C. Clarke, *A Short History of Tanganyika* (London: Longmans, Green, and Company, 1960), p. 105.

[42] The Swahili number *hamsa ishirini* (25) is synonymous with "arbitrary authority." This stems from the German period when arbitrary judgments by the *Bezirksamtmann* often imposed twenty-five lashes with a rhinoceros-hide whip. See Margaret Bates, "Tanganyika," in Gwendolyn Carter (ed.), *African One-Party States* (Ithaca: Cornell University Press, 1962), p. 402.

direction, colonial advance took place at a rapid pace. This was shortly to be interrupted and destroyed by the rolling battle fought by von Lettow-Vorbeck to keep the allies occupied during World War I.

An Assessment of the German Period

For purposes of the present study, the important aspects of German rule can be summarized as follows:

1. The Germans permanently established in the minds of the indigenous population that an external force was in control of the country and that political direction would come from this force. This was accomplished by the brutal policy followed by the Germans up until 1907.

2. A weakly articulated administrative organization was created, consisting of twenty-one districts run by the Germans with *akidas* and *jumbes* responsible to them.

3. An advisory council was organized which provided some local involvement in the determination of political decisions.

4. The colony was developed economically to a considerable degree. The creation of roads and railroads led to increased agricultural productivity and to the gradual development of commercial crops. This process was aided by the establishment of the poll tax which helped to create a labor force for the German-owned plantations.

By 1914, the basis for an expanding colonial political organization had been established. It is fruitless to speculate as to its future course had there not been a major war; however, the basis for a future political system was installed by the Germans and was taken over relatively intact by the British.

THE BRITISH PERIOD

The main development of Tanganyika's political system took place during the course of British rule. It was in the period from 1918 to 1961 (when independence was achieved) that the political system evolved and became fully developed. In considering political evolution during the British era, attention will be concentrated on three areas crucial for the political system: (1) the installation and evolution of indirect rule; (2) the creation of a legislature, an executive, and a ministerial system; and (3) the growth of nationalism and the emergence of the Tanganyika African National Union. All of these developments must be considered within the framework of a government which was characteristic of British colonial policy, highly centralized by virtue of the crucial power of the governor and his provincial administration. This key administrative-political structure was initiated as the British fought with the Germans for Tanganyika. Immediately after the war, it was given a firm structure which remained intact with small variations throughout the period of British rule and constituted a primary political legacy to independent Tanganyika.

The Governor and the Provincial Administration

As the territorial agent of Britain's Colonial Office, the governor was the chief authority responsible for executing general policies formulated by the Colonial Office. Because of the centrality of power of the governorship, a discussion of this position is necessary to understand not only the centralized nature of colonial administration, but also the reasons for the orientation of African nationalists to the national scene.

The powers of the governor were very broad. As the trustee of public lands, he had the right to alter boundaries and names of provinces and districts. As the highest executive officer, he could appoint public officials, prescribe their duties, and suspend them given due cause. As chief legislative officer, he presided over the Legislative Council until 1953 and had the power to determine the rules and orders for legislative procedures. "It is lawful for the governor with the advice and consent of the council to make laws for the administration of justice, the raising of revenue and generally for the peace, order and good government of the territory."[43] In his legislative capacity, the governor controlled the enactment of all bills and could, in fact, enact a bill blocked by the Council. Moreover, the governor possessed judicial power to remit sentences.

The first governor, Sir Horace Byatt, in the period immediately following the dislocations of the war, introduced few administrative changes. Byatt retained the basic structure created by the Germans, utilizing the twenty-two districts and the *akida* system.[44] This initial period is marked by a gradual re-establishment of centralized control and a reawakening of the economy which had become moribund. It was not until the arrival of Sir Donald Cameron in 1925 that fundamental changes were undertaken in the political-administrative system. Cameron introduced a number of innovations but the three most significant of these were (1) the establishment of a system of "indirect rule," (2) the revamping of provincial administration by the creation of eleven provinces with districts within the provinces, (3) and the formation of a Legislative Council (Legco) out of which emerged the present parliamentary system. In addition, under Cameron's administration, the government establishment began an expansion that was to continue throughout the British period. This growth is indicated in Tables 6–3 and 6–4.

---

[43] Tanganyika (Legislative Council) Order in Council, *Statutory Rules and Orders* (1926), p. 579. Quoted in Datta, *op. cit.,* p. 29. The list of governor's powers is extracted from a more detailed discussion in Datta, *op. cit.,* pp. 26–37.

[44] Moffett, *op. cit.,* p. 94. The discrepancy between this figure and the figure for the Germans is probably explained by the fact that the Germans maintained a structure of nineteen civil and two military districts and three residencies, or a total of twenty-four administrative units. In the division of German East Africa after the war, the Belgians won Ruanda and Urundi, while the Bukoba residency remained attached to Tanganyika.

Table 6–3

Civil List—Tanganyika

	Europeans	Asians	Africans
1919	356		
1924	575		
1930	950		
1933	795		
1937[a]	896	706	6,248
1938[b]	940	758	6,642
1943	940 (141 absent in the forces)		
1945	982 (on duty; includes railway personnel)		
1954	2,485		

SOURCE: J. P. Moffett (ed.), *Handbook of Tanganyika* (Dar es Salaam: Government Printer, 1958), pp. 92, 96, 108, 121, 144.

[a] *Report to the Council of the League of Nations on the Administration of Tanganyika Territory*, Colonial Office Report No. 148, 1937.

[b] Colonial Office Report No. 165, 1938.

Table 6–4

Provincial Administration—Tanganyika, Selected Years

Year	Total
1921	104
1926	119
1929	167
1931	184
1936	169
1940	176
1946	169
1951	192

SOURCE: *The Dominions Office and Colonial Office List* (London: Waterlow & Sons, Ltd., 1953).

NOTE: Categories of offices changed from time to time. The totals given include First-, Second-, Third-Grade Officers, and Cadets for 1921; Senior Commissioners, First- and Second-Grade Officers and Cadets for 1926; Senior Provincial Commissioners, Provincial Commissioners, Deputy Provincial Commissioners, District Officers, Assistant District Officers, Supernumerary District Officers, and Cadets for the succeeding years.

With his introduction of these new political institutions, Cameron left an indelible mark on Tanganyika. While there was to be gradual political evolution after his departure, little of significance transpired until the growth of the nationalist movement during the administration of Governor Twining.

This lack of development was, in part, due to lack of continuity. Between the administrations of Cameron and Twining, no governor remained in office for more than four years.

Provincial administration during the British period was directly controlled by the governor. As the representatives of the governor "on the ground," the provincial and district commissioners were responsible for implementing the policies at the local level which had been centrally determined by the governor. Thus, the provincial administration served as a link between the native authorities and central government.

While the provincial commissioner directed the district staffs, it was the district commissioner who had key responsibility for the actual operation of government and control over the implementation of indirect rule policies. His power, varying considerably according to the competence of the native authority, included supervision of the courts, safeguarding native land rights, and administering local development and education. Moreover, a substantial means of control existed through management of the native treasuries. Annual budgets were handled and approved by administrative officers in the provincial administration. Although ostensibly expanded by Cameron for the purpose of building up indirect rule, the provincial administration served in many cases to undermine the native authority as it was realized that ultimate authority rested at the level of central government.

Indirect Rule

In establishing a policy of indirect rule—or, as he preferred to call it, "indirect administration"—Cameron initiated vast amounts of activity by British administrative officers and many indigenous elements. In retrospect, it is clear that this effort ultimately produced a set of institutions of local government that was relatively insignificant for the main stream of political growth. This contention is made in the light of the ultimate importance of the nationalist movement and the fact that its sources are mainly found in areas outside of "native administration." In spite of its relative unimportance, native administration represents an area within which enormous energies were directed on the part of the administration and through which a great many of the small but important problems of the country were handled. In addition, the very fact that the political units created by indirect rule failed to become viable currents in the ultimate evolution of the political system is itself worthy of analysis.

THE BACKGROUND OF INDIRECT RULE

On his arrival to take up the governorship, Sir Donald Cameron found that much of the basic postwar reconstruction had been completed. In the area of administration, however, he found that the German *akida* system was still in force although Governor Byatt had defined a native authority system in

1923. Cameron was impressed by the fact that, despite the existence of direct rule, many traditional patterns, particularly in the native courts, still functioned though often *sub rosa*,[45] ". . . survival under such adverse conditions being a truly striking token of the deep roots that native institutions do strike among African natives."[46] Indirect rule was an established part of British colonial policy. Cameron had an intimate knowledge of indirect rule from his experience with Frederick Lugard in Nigeria. He claimed "not to belong to the group in Nigeria which blindly worshipped indirect rule" and did not start with the intention of instituting the system in Tanganyika.[47] He was firmly opposed to instituting any administration resembling British constitutional government.

There is evidence to indicate that Cameron utilized Tanganyika's status as a mandated territory to implement the liberal views he personally held. This was certainly true in his active rejection, at a later stage, of the idea of closer union of the East African territories.[48] Cameron's view of indirect rule indicates deep concern for the maintenance of indigenous institutions and the construction of a base from which they might evolve toward modernity. Cameron felt that it was his responsibility as governor of a mandated territory to train people for eventual self-government. Since the League of Nations as the mandator lacked powers of enforcement, the application of the mandate, in the long run, depended on political expediency. Cameron found indirect rule expedient both in view of the small size of the administration,

---

[45] Sir Donald Cameron, *My Tanganyika Experience and Some Nigeria* (London: Allen and Unwin, 1939), p. 82.

[46] Cameron, *Principles of Native Administration and Their Application*, Memorandum No. 1 (Dar es Salaam: 1930), p. 7.

[47] Cameron, *My Tanganyika Experience*, p. 34. The evidence as to the degree to which Cameron came to Tanganyika with preconceptions about installing indirect rule is mixed. Cameron indicates that he arrived with no firmly fixed plans to install indirect rule. *Ibid.*, pp. 32–33. Dundas, at the time Assistant Chief Secretary, states in contrast that even ". . . before the arrival of Sir Donald Cameron a conference of senior officers . . . [had] recommended that the system of native administration should be on the general lines of Indirect Rule. It transpired that this was precisely the policy Sir Donald had decided upon even before he set foot in East Africa." Sir Charles Dundas, *African Crossroads* (London: Macmillan & Company, 1955), p. 132. Hailey puts the date of the idea of indirect rule even earlier. ". . . the Administration indicated in 1922 its intention to base the system of local rules on the use of indigenous institutions of the country . . ." Lord Hailey, *op. cit.*, Part IV, p. 16.

[48] See the discussion of closer union in Sir Donald Cameron, *My Tanganyika Experience*. For additional material on closer union, see Margery Perham, *Lugard: The Years of Authority 1898–1945* (London: Collins, 1960), Ch. XXXII. This presents the question from the viewpoint of Lugard. See also Robert Gregory, *Sidney Webb and East Africa: Labour's Experiment with the Doctrine of Native Paramountcy, University of California Publications in History*, Vol. 72 (Berkeley and Los Angeles: University of California Press, 1962).

and in terms of his own ideas of the "material and moral advantage of this kind of rule."[49] The expediency of indirect rule was later acknowledged by the Hilton-Young Commission which regarded it as an "outlet for the natural desire to participate in the management of their own affairs. . . . There can never be a complete absence of political agitators, but if a practical outlet is provided for the natives in the management of their own affairs, . . . agitators against British rule are likely to receive little general support."[50]

Cameron's personal views may have also played a strong role in his formulation of indirect rule policies. It is significant, for example, that Cameron acknowledged that he owed his appointments as governor in Tanganyika and Nigeria to Labour ministers.[51] Although there is no evidence that Cameron was himself much inclined toward the Labour party, the pattern of his activities is quite different from that of more conservative civil servants, such as Lugard.

Cameron had to take up the problem of local government two weeks after his arrival in Tanganyika because of a taxation problem. The chiefs, unable to get their traditional tribute from the people because of the tax system, had been complaining for some time. Taxes had been raised to incorporate within them the traditional tribute due the chiefs. The administrative question arose about how to handle these sums. This was resolved by granting the chiefs a temporary stipend with the understanding that they were to be incorporated into the governmental structure. It was this administrative decision that laid the basis for the elaboration of the native authorities.

THE NATIVE AUTHORITY ORDINANCE AND ITS IMPLEMENTATION

The Ordinance, the administrative embodiment of indirect rule, was a flexible document allowing for the variety in traditional authority patterns. There were four recognized categories of native authorities: (1) the paramount chief as the native authority having under him a group of subordinate chiefs; (2) a federation of chiefs, pooled for financial stability, each chief having authority over his own area but sitting as a council for common purposes; (3) a tribal council composed of petty chiefs or headmen, all of the same tribe, where a paramount chief does not exist; (4) a small chief or village headman of an isolated portion of a tribe. Since the native authority was supposed, in so far as possible, to derive from the traditional leadership of the tribe, Cameron expected that the traditional safeguards against abuse would be built into the system. As a further safeguard, although the govern-

---

[49] Cameron, *My Tanganyika Experience*, p. 81.

[50] *Report of the Commission on Closer Union of the Dependencies in Eastern and Central Africa*, Cmnd. 3234 (London: H.M.S.O., 1929), p. 76. Cited by Datta, *op. cit.*, pp. 74–75.

[51] Cameron, *My Tanganyika Experience*, p. 18.

ment could not choose a chief, it could exercise veto power by refusing to accept a chief and requiring the tribe to make an alternate selection.[52]

Three kinds of problems developed in the implementation of the Ordinance: (1) problems of "discovering" traditional authorities where none existed, (2) problems of sustaining traditional authorities when they were forced into new molds, and (3) problems of administrative abuses.

1. There are a great many so-called "tribes" in Tanganyika.[53] Many of Tanganyika's tribes always were acephalous, e.g., having no political system, no chiefs or headmen. Such political authority as existed was vested in clan heads. In some cases, because of wars, the slave trade, and the *Schreklichkeit* of the Germans, tribal social organization had been shattered, leaving acephalous groupings scattered very thinly in many areas. In cases such as these, the British administrators had to search for chiefs where none existed. "Inquiries were instituted at once to ascertain to what extent similar authorities still existed in other tribal units where the position was not so clearly defined and there the matter remained until I had seen something of the country. . . ."[54] There followed a search for "traditional authorities" by many administrative officers about which comparatively little information is available. The indications are that many gave up the task as a bad job within a short period of time. In some cases, there is reason to believe that chiefs were simply "created," where none existed before, to fulfill the demands of a well-meant administrative policy that had no relationship to reality.[55] In such cases, it was natural for these "rulers" to be considered and to consider themselves agents or employees of the British rather than rulers with genuine authority among their people. This controverted the aim of the entire policy which was based on an explicit commitment to utilize indigenous people whose authority was *already* established.

2. There were a number of situations (among the Haya, the Chagga, the Nyamwezi, etc.) where genuine chiefs existed with legitimate authority based on traditional rule. The dilemma was how to give these chiefs modern responsibilities, making them ultimately responsible to the British adminis-

---

[52] Cameron, *Memo I, op. cit.,* pp. 7–13. Hailey, in discussing the three types of native authorities, groups the second and third categories set by Cameron, *op. cit.,* Part I, p. 218.

[53] This is not the place to discuss some of the scientific problems revealed in the usage of the term "tribe" in Tanganyika. Suffice it to say that many groups exist in Tanganyika with some degree of cultural and linguistic identity but without any political coherence. For a discussion of aspects of the problem, see P. H. Gulliver, "A Tribal Map of Tanganyika," *Tanganyika Notes and Records,* No. 52 (March 1959), pp. 61–65.

[54] Cameron, *My Tanganyika Experience,* p. 33.

[55] Cf., the case of Mgeni bin Hema, appointed Paramount Chief of the Nyaturu, whose apparent claim to fame was that he had been an interpreter for the Germans. J. Gus Liebenow, "Legitimacy of Alien Relationship: The Nyaturu of Tanganyika," *Western Political Science Quarterly,* XIV (March 1961), 64–86.

tration, while expecting them to retain traditional authority. It is obvious that the demands of traditionalism stand in contrast to the impersonal objectivity required of modern political administration. The kinship-based system of chieftaincy was not an easily manipulated institution adaptive to changing political circumstances. As shall be seen, the institution of chieftaincy largely became ossified within the pattern of native administration as it evolved. This was because of structural difficulties involved in using a system based on ascribed factors such as kinship when the evolving political system required the selection of personnel based on talent and ability.

3. The entire system was also subject to many administrative deficiencies. The fact that the British reserved the ultimate right to veto appointments or to remove chiefs opened the system to all kinds of possible abuses. Thus, a Sukuma chief states: "I was elected by the *banang'oma,* but the people wanted my elder brother. So the district commissioner came and arrested some of the citizens and they came to normal."[56] As Liebenow summarizes the Sukuma situation:

> It is readily admitted that a district commissioner may take a direct hand in the nominating and election of a chief on occasion. If it appears that one of the claimants has served a term in prison, has a notoriously bad reputation or lacks the education and training . . ., the commissioner will let it be known that such an individual would never secure recognition from the Governor.[57]

Similarly, the removal of chiefs from office was entirely a prerogative of the British administration. Although it was formally difficult to remove a chief without good cause, there was, as is usual in most administrative organizations, much leeway for abuses in discretion often having inadvertent results. Thus, in 1946, the Chagga native authority was reorganized, and the former nineteen chiefdoms were reduced to three major divisions, each governed by a superior chief as the recognized native authority.[58] Though the other chiefs retained a limited degree of influence, their power was effectively reduced. While the British may have been attempting, quite creditably, to remake the Chagga native authority into a somewhat more wieldy apparatus, the ease of manipulation and experimentation meant that the indigenous systems of authority could be continually disrupted.

These abuses can be seen at their worst in the changes undertaken in Usukuma.[59] Between 1919 and 1926, *akidas* from the coast replaced many

---

[56] Quoted by J. Gus Liebenow, "A Tanganyika Federation: The Sukuma," in Audrey I. Richards (ed.), *East African Chiefs* (London: Faber and Faber, 1960), p. 245.

[57] *Ibid.*

[58] Hailey, *op. cit.,* Part I, pp. 282–285.

[59] The subsequent discussion of Sukumaland is based on Liebenow, in *East African Chiefs,* pp. 238–240.

of the traditional chiefs. Later, the chiefs were re-installed, and more than sixty native authorities emerged in Usukuma. Because this was too difficult to manage, consolidations were undertaken at various times until, around 1958, there were about forty-seven chiefdoms. Even more intricate were the developments aimed at creating a federation of the chiefs. In 1932, the Federation of Iganiko was created, but foundered almost immediately. The idea of federation was resurrected in 1947, but, after proving unwieldy, most of its power was given over to federation councils created in each district. Some of the federation's powers were also given over to the South-East Lake County Council, which was, at the time, a multiracial geographically based political unit.

Several other examples of the problems confronted in the implementation of the policy of indirect rule indicate its difficulties. In the Mikindani and Lindi districts, the members of the tribal council were appointed in 1927 from the *Wakulungwa*. These were not heads of clans, but descendants of the first immigrant families to clear portions of the bush. This "shadow of a claim" led them to be appointed as members of the Makonde Tribal Council, but their authority proved to be ineffective. The system was changed in 1937 when the area was redivided into five units and a *liwali* selected by the people in each unit at public meetings.[60]

In Uluguru, the chiefs who were appointed "exhibited laziness and apathy . . . and had to be visited continually by the District Officer and his Assistants."[61] In the Rufiji area, no traditional authority was found. Africans divided their loyalties between chiefs and *waalim* who were Moslem teachers owing allegiance to a sheikh. "The natives prefer to follow, singing, their *Mwalim* . . . than attend their Chiefs' tax meetings." The district administration was required to support those Africans designated as chiefs in this area. The Mafia island group was still under direct control in 1935. This was exercised through the *khadi,* two *akidas* and twelve headmen paid directly by the central government. In this area problems of drunkenness existed due to drinking cashew gin. In the Mahenge area, the *watua* were the native authority. They were the sons of the men who had authority in the days of direct rule and considered themselves nominees of the government rather than leaders of the people. These examples can be multiplied. The few that have been chosen indicate the magnitude of the problem that confronted

---

[60] "Report to the Council of the League of Nations on the Administration of Tanganyika Territory for 1937," *Colonial Office Report No. 148* (Dar es Salaam: 1937), pp. 14 ff.

[61] The examples that follow are from *Annual Reports of the Provincial Commissioners on Native Administration* (London: H.M.S.O., 1934). See the report of the Provincial Commissioner, Eastern Province, pp. 7–9. The Waluguru chiefs were not, in fact, hereditary rulers, but rainmakers with supernatural rather than political powers. Though they had traditional authority in a ceremonial sense, the nonpolitical nature of their authority lay at the root of their problems. See Roland Young and Henry Fosbrooke, *Smoke in the Hills* (Evanston: Northwestern University Press, 1960), pp. 84 ff.

Cameron, his successors, and the subordinate officers of the administration as they sought to make indirect rule a viable political reality.

THE FORMAL OBJECTS OF INDIRECT RULE

As created by Cameron, the native authorities were intended to engage in three kinds of activities. Firstly, "It involved . . . the recognition of the status of chiefs, and an authorization to enact local by-laws. . . . Secondly it involved the establishment everywhere of Native Courts. . . . Thirdly it involved the establishment of Native Treasuries which were in effect embryonic Local Government treasuries."[62]

As the native authority, a chief could issue orders for the "peace, good order and welfare" of the African population within his jurisdiction. Such orders were enforceable in the native courts. Thus, the first type of activities was executive in character. The amendments to the original ordinance in 1930, 1935, 1941, 1942, and 1946 were largely directed to increasing the autonomy of local units by broadening the activities of the native authority. In the original ordinance, the administrative officer was the executive authority, expected to issue orders. The amendment of 1930 stated that the administrative officer was expected to issue orders directly only if the native authority neglected to do so. It also increased powers of subsidiary legislation. The 1935 amendment recognized an additional category of native authority, and, in 1942, additional power in financial matters was granted.

The second major activity of the native authorities was concerned with the administration of justice. In 1920, the basic Penal Code of India had been applied to Tanganyika with modifications. Under the 1920 code, native authority courts were organized prior to the implementation of the policy of indirect rule. The Ordinance of 1929, however, linked the native courts directly to the native authority and provided for a self-contained system of native courts under administrative supervision. The courts were removed from the control of the Supreme Court and, thus, from a judicial authority to an executive authority. The reasons for this were that the judicial authorities were less acquainted with everyday details of native life and thus less able to supervise local courts than local administrators. In addition, Africans were unable to understand the separation of judicial from executive functions.[63] All cases had the right of appeal to the High Court of Tanganyika and then to the Court of Appeal for Eastern Africa. The usual procedure in resolving disputes was for the local headman or family head to litigate informally as the first step. The cases came to a native court only if one party was dissatisfied with the solution. Although some districts saw an increase in the use of the courts, this was not the case in every area, due to differences in local customs

---

[62] Moffett, *op. cit.*, p. 100; see also Hailey, *op. cit.*, Part I, pp. 219–220.

[63] C. L. Upthegrove, *Empire by Mandate* (New York: Bookman Assoc., 1954), p. 107.

and accessibility. Minor courts and mobile courts were instituted to resolve the problem of inaccessibility.

The third activity of the native authorities was the development of native treasuries. The treasuries were, on the whole, less successful than other aspects of the native authorities. British control in this area was more stringent, although it was believed that self-administration of finances was most important as "experience teaches that it (the native authority) soon becomes of little account if no funds are placed at its disposal out of which it can pay the salaries of its personnel, build court houses, and schools, etc."[64] The revenue of the native treasuries was derived from a share of the hut- and poll-tax, from native court fees and fines, from salt royalties and sales of produce, and from grants-in-aid in poorer areas. The hut tax continued until 1955 as a flat (i.e., ungraded) rate. In 1955, an ordinance replaced it with a personal, graduated tax. Expenditures were made for public works (including medicine, sanitation, education, construction, and tsetse reclamation) and tribal administration, which included the maintenance of the sons of chiefs at government or native administration schools.[65] Because of the variety of forms of native authorities, the provincial commissioner made arrangements for the supervision of each treasury in his area.

As the native authorities took over more responsibility for financial matters, changes occurred affecting the tribal structure. In 1934, the chiefs of Iringa, Sandawe, and Burungi formed a council with a central treasury in order to pool their resources.[66] The Chagga, Kahe, and Arusha also amalgamated their treasuries at this time. Thus, the treasury became a substitute for some of the power traditionally held by the chief. Earlier, the system of tribute had served as a provision against famine, and food was given to the chief to redistribute in times of need. By remitting to the treasury a percentage of the tax equivalent to this tribute, an abstract institution acquired the important chiefly function of alleviating famine.

Taxation policy in Tanganyika differed from that of other British colonies. In Nigeria, the native administration collected the tax and remitted a percentage to the central government. In Tanganyika, the government made the remission to the native authority.

THE EVOLUTION OF THE NATIVE AUTHORITIES

The prevailing emphasis in the initial application of the indirect-rule policy was to find individuals who were, as chiefs, to embody within their persons the native authority. In the initial enthusiasm of this effort (and probably

---

[64] "Native Administration Memoranda, The Native Treasuries," *Memorandum III* (3rd ed.; Dar es Salaam: Colonial Office, 1938), p. 3.

[65] *Ibid.*, p. 38.

[66] *Annual Report of the Provincial Commissioners . . ., op. cit.*, p. 4.

before all of the problems had been fully appreciated), some 679 tribal chiefs were officially gazetted by 1927.[67] The Haya had nine chiefs; the Masai had a religious leader; the tribes in the Southern Province recognized only clan heads and, as a result, in the Mikindani District alone, a total of 156 authorities were recognized. By 1947–1948, when Lord Hailey resurveyed British administration, the situation in Tanganyika had become somewhat more rationalized. Hailey distinguished three types of native authorities: those where chiefs or headmen are individually gazetted as native authorities (i.e., embody authority within their own persons), where tribal councils or councils of headmen exercise power as the native authority, and where persons have been directly appointed by government having no traditional authority whatsoever. Hailey's survey revealed 329 chiefs or headmen, 34 councils and 44 nontraditional *liwalis* or *akidas*.[68]

Prior to World War II, some tentative experiments were undertaken in shifting toward council types of organization in the native authorities. This was manifested by a tendency to create federations of chiefs. It became more pronounced because of the increasing number of Westernized Africans being turned out through the educational system. Although relatively small in number, the presence of a group of somewhat educated Africans, articulate but without access to the political system as then constituted, began to create increasing pressure on the traditional chiefs. The first significant developments along these lines can be noted among the Haya and the Chagga.[69]

No effective action was taken during the war, but the British began to anticipate difficulties at its conclusion when they expected that the veterans would return home and demand access to the political system. Although these expectations were not fulfilled, demands for political access continued with the increasing number of modernized Africans. As a result, the British sought to democratize the tribal councils by making changes that provided for representation within the councils of nonchiefly elements, and a considerable number of experiments were gotten underway.[70] The experiments

---

[67] Cameron, *Memo I, op. cit.*

[68] Hailey, *op. cit.*, Part I, "East Africa: Uganda, Kenya, Tanganyika," p. 218. In his concluding chapter in Part IV, Hailey uses a different threefold typology to describe native administration in Tanganyika. The first is represented by the coastal areas where there were no traditional authorities and where rulers were appointed having no traditional status. The second type consists of genuine authorities that are unadaptive to modern circumstances. The third type consists of native authorities that are efficient and adaptive to modern circumstances. See Part IV, pp. 17–18.

[69] *Ibid.*, Part I, p. 227, for reference to Haya. No separate reference has been found to such difficulties with the Chagga. Various commentators indicate difficulties with the Chagga over a number of problems relating to the growth of the cash-crop economy and the marketing of coffee. See Cameron, *My Tanganyika Experience, passim,* and Dundas, *op. cit.*

[70] Many of these experiments are described in the *Journal of African Administration.* See, for example, C. Winnington-Ingram, "Reforming Local Government in a Tanganyika District" (April 1950), pp. 10–15. C. I. Meek, "A Practical Experiment in

consisted of setting up councils on four levels: the province, district, county, and the town or municipality. Table 6–5 summarizes the various experiments, showing how they moved slowly and frequently failed.

The experiments with the councils failed, largely because these bodies were not genuinely representative. This was particularly the case with the provincial and county councils whose members were drawn largely from the native authorities. Indeed, the councils had no statutory powers; they were dominated by the provincial commissioners who had full power to act without consulting them. The creation of the councils represented, in effect, a decentralization of central government activities without a concomitant decentralization of power. Their only real function was to provide a slight check on local government.[71] In addition, all councils were hampered by their lack of executive power and by shortages in technical staffs.

At any rate, it was a case of too little and too late. As the pace of nationalism grew, attempts were made to democratize the councils: elections were introduced, the powers of the chiefs reduced, etc. The attempt was in vain, however, since the main thrust of activities shifted entirely to the area of national politics, and the emergent local governments were left largely untouched. Indeed, as independence drew near, the British permitted local governments to emerge from the now-outmoded husks of the native authorities. But the nationalist leaders looked on these local governments in the same manner as had their British predecessors, as instrumentalities to be controlled from the center.

AN ASSESSMENT OF INDIRECT RULE[72]

Considering the vast energies invested in the development of the system of native administration; the sheer quantity of man-hours on the part of British

Local Government," II (July 1950), 21–28; F. A. Montague and F. H. Page-Jones, "Some Difficulties in the Democratization of Native Authorities in Tanganyika," III (January 1951), 21–27; Z. E. Kingdon, "The Initiation of a System of Local Government by African Rural Councils in the Rungwe District of Tanganyika," III (October 1951), 186–191. This list is not intended to be exhaustive, only indicative. The democratization of the native authority system was, in all likelihood, the subject of the Colonial Office's Summer School of 1947. Hailey, too, makes oblique references to the question of democratization and increasing the adaptiveness of the native authorities: ". . . the absence of any regular system of Councils attached to the chiefdoms is a symptom of the weakness of the indigenous organizations in Tanganyika . . ." Hailey, op. cit., Part I, p. 219.

71 "A Survey of the Development of Local Government in the African Territories since 1947—Tanganyika," Journal of African Administration IV, II (Supplement) (April 1952), 13.

72 A full and comparative examination of the application of the policy of indirect rule in Africa (and elsewhere) is much needed. The assessment undertaken here is limited to Tanganyika, but has been illuminated by discussion of indirect rule con-

Table 6–5

Experiments with Local Government Structures, 1948–1959

1948	Conference of provincial commissioners asked for policy statement on broadening local government.
1949	Policy statement to expand local government by establishing councils based on existing native authorities.
1949–1951	Creation of district councils following three major patterns:
	1. Kisarawe pattern (in areas of low tribal identity or cohesion). Councils consisted of the gazetted native authority, village headmen, one commoner from each division, members nominated by the district commissioner.
	2. Usambara/Chagga pattern (where traditional political leadership existed). Councils consisted of chiefs or councils of chiefs, members nominated by chiefs because of personal merit, commoners from the subchiefdoms, and in the case of Usambara, of subchiefs. These councils were advisory and deliberative, not legislative or executive.
	3. Masai pattern (acephalous groups with age-grade systems). Area councils and members chosen for the district councils existed here from the area councils by tribesmen in proportion to population. These councils had advisory, deliberative, and legislative powers.
1949	First municipality created in Dar es Salaam with a 15-member council.
1949	Provincial Council formed for Lake Province.
1950	Formation of Southern Highlands Provincial Council.
1953[a]	Special Commissioner for Commission on Constitutional Development recommends renaming provincial councils "Provincial Commissioners Councils," recognizing the ultimate power of the provincial commissioner.
1953	Local government ordinance.
1953	Southeast Lake County Council created. (Dissolved 1959.)
1954	First town council established in Tanga. Twenty-four members with racial party.
1955	Town councils established in Lindi, Arusha, and Mwanza.
1956	Local government election ordinance providing for elections where there was public demand.
1958	First election of town council members in Arusha.
1958	Municipalities amendments. Ward councils established with executive power.
1959	Ten town councils created plus Dar es Salaam municipal council.

SOURCES: Data through 1950 extracted from "A Survey of the Development of Local Government in the African Territories since 1947—Tanganyika," *Journal of African Administration*, IV (supplement) (April 1952), pp. 13–24. Data from 1953–1959 from J. Clagett Taylor, *The Political Development of Tanganyika* (Stanford: Stanford University Press, 1963), pp. 204–210.

[a] A. K. Datta, *Tanganyika: A Government in a Plural Society* (The Hague, 1955), p. 86.

administrators, African chiefs and subchiefs, and others, the contribution that native administration made to political evolution in Tanganyika was almost negligible. This does not mean that local government has no significance; rather, this writer contends that, of all Tanganyika's modern political institutions, local government is probably the least significant.

There were many reasons why the native authorities failed to develop into viable political units. For one thing, the indigenous political systems of the country were largely acephalous. Accordingly, the bulk of the authorities appointed did not have legitimate authority in their own right. A political system was imposed that was esoteric to most of the indigenous population. Even where there were legitimate traditional rulers, the responsibilities assigned to them as native authorities weakened their traditional authority. The British, as good civil servants, increasingly bureaucratized and impersonalized the procedures of government at the local level. Though this was a creditable activity, it nevertheless undermined the traditional basis of authority. In addition, the pattern of indirect rule reinforced the chief in his position, but removed him almost entirely from the system of checks and balances that had existed within the tribe traditionally. It made the chief accountable to the district commissioner rather than to the traditional councils, age groups, and the other units that had, in the past, controlled his actions.

Thus, the basic failure of indirect rule lay in the fact that the policy sought to utilize traditionalism for modern purposes. This represented, in effect, a structural contradiction that could not be overcome. For modern purposes, modernized personnel had to be found, and, although individual chiefs were often educated and Westernized, this very fact undermined the ostensible source of their authority. The case is, perhaps, tragically illustrated by Thomas Marealle, a Westernized Chagga who became the first paramount

---

centrated on Nigeria. Perham, *op. cit.,* for example, has examined the application of indirect rule in the three different regions of Nigeria, the North, the East, and the West, showing the enormous discrepancies that developed when the policies were applied to widely variant cultures. See Vol. II, Chs. 12–14. Mary Bull, "Indirect Rule in Northern Nigeria, 1906–1911," in Kenneth Robinson and Frederick Madden (eds.), *Essays in Imperial Government* (Oxford: Basil Blackwell, 1963), pp. 47–87 has provided detail on the implementation of indirect rule after Lugard left the governorship of Northern Nigeria. Michael Crowder, "Indirect Rule—French and British Style," *Africa,* XXXIV (July 1964), 197–205, provides additional material on indirect rule in Nigeria. This article constitutes a reply to Hubert Deschanns, "Et maintenant, Lord Lugard," *Africa,* XXXIII (October 1963), 293–306, who argues that Lugard's ideas were not unique to him and that the French also practiced the policy from an early period. D. Anthony Low and R. Cranford Pratt, *Buganda and British Overrule 1900–1955* (London: Oxford University Press, 1960) have dealt with the application of indirect rule in Uganda. An examination of the application of indirect rule in the Lake region of Tanganyika is being undertaken by Ralph Austen. See "The Study of Indirect Rule in a Tanganyika Province," *Proceedings of the EAISR Conference Held at Kivukoni College, Dar es Salaam, Tanganyika, July 1963,* Part A, "History and Political Science Papers." For additional materials on Tanganyika, see Liebenow, *op. cit.*

chief of the Chagga. Urbane, sophisticated, knowledgeable in the ways of modern British life, he sought to marry the symbols of traditionalism with modernity. In carrying out his functions as a chief, however, Marealle came into conflict with the Chagga Council, the group which represented the Chagga population in a more representative fashion. Marealle had to resolve three basic elements, Chagga traditionalism, Chagga modernism, and Tanganyika nationalism within his own person. His failure to do so culminated in his being sacked as paramount chief.

The British system of indirect rule, though elaborately developed, failed to accomplish its role as a mechanism for political evolution. Instead, change took place *outside* the framework of native administration, within a host of modern associations. The failure of the British to develop a *viable modern* pattern of local government meant, not only that nationalism was focused on national problems, but that as independence was attained, local government remained weak and continued to be dominated by the central government. By the time action was undertaken to strengthen the local authority, the main thrust of African political activities had been translated to the national scene. When the British opened opportunities for the burgeoning African politician to enter the local councils, this was considered a blind alley by most modernized Africans who turned exclusively to national politics.

The Legislative Council (Legco)

Cameron created the basis for a modern legislature because he recognized that unofficials would be useful in helping to govern a complex society. He was firmly opposed to creating an advisory council—one in which discussion alone would take place—and created instead a council with voting procedures so that the unofficial members of the council would have responsibility for the passage of legislation.

Here, a word is necessary on legislative councils generally. Most legislative councils, particularly in Africa, contained two groups and represented in miniature the parliamentary system of Westminster. The majority in the early stages of evolution were composed of "officials" or members who held positions within the civil service of the colony. The "unofficials" were not civil servants and frequently were selected by the governor for membership because of their representative character. Thus, governors generally sought to obtain a broad representation of the local population. In the African territories, this initially consisted mainly of Europeans; in West Africa, however, African representation in the legislative councils began at a fairly early period.[73] Both official and unofficial members of the councils had the right

---

[73] For a general discussion of legislative councils appropriate to African circumstance, see Martin Wight, *The Development of the Legislative Council 1606–1945* (London: Faber & Faber, 1947), Ch. 4. In the case of Sierra Leone, African repre-

to discuss legislation; the legislative councils never, in their early periods, had the right to initiate or adopt legislation, that power being reserved to the governor. Some councils were given voting rights (as was the case in Tanganyika), but the vote was advisory to the governor. All members of the councils, official and unofficial, were originally appointed ("nominated") by the governors, and it was not until relatively late that the principle of election to the legislative councils in Africa was introduced.

Table 6–6

Evolution of Tanganyika's Legislative Council

	Membership			Racial Divisions		
Year	Total	Officials	Unofficials	European	Asian	African
1926	23	13	7 (10 allowed)	5	2	—
1935	23	13	10	7	3	—
1945	27	15	12	7	3	2
1947	28	15	13	7	3	3
1954	29	15	14	7	3	4
1955	61	31	30	10	10	10
1957	67	34	33	11	11	11
1959[a]	53	28	25	—	—	—
1960[b]	81	71 (elected)	10 (nominated)	16	13[c]	52

SOURCES: J. P. Moffett (ed.), *Handbook of Tanganyika* (Dar es Salaam: Government Printer, 1958); *Tanganyika's Parliament* (Dar es Salaam: Government Printer, 1961); J. Clagett Taylor, *The Political Development of Tanganyika* (Stanford: Stanford University Press, 1963).

[a] First general election.

[b] In 1960, 71 elected, 10 appointed.

[c] Includes 1 Arab and 1 Goan.

In the case of Tanganyika, the first Legco, appointed in 1926, had thirteen official and seven unofficial members. Although ten unofficial members were allowed by the Order-in-Council creating Legco, the full complement was not named until 1935. These were divided between Europeans and Asians with Europeans in the majority. Table 6–6 summarizes the changes that took place in the Legislative Council between 1926 and 1960. According to Cameron, there was not a single African representative of the African population capable of functioning in Legco (e.g., able to speak English). The Secretary for Native Affairs, Sir Charles Dundas, therefore, represented

---

sentation dates from 1798, but this was an exceptional case. See pp. 42–43. Wight is unable to name the first African to serve in a legislative council, although the first African appointed in the Gold Coast was named in 1889, p. 75.

African interests in the early Legcos. In 1945, the first Africans were appointed. Significantly, both of these, Kidaha Makwaia and Abdiel Shangali, were chiefs whose source of authority was traditional. Two years later, they were joined by a third chief, Adam Sapi. In 1948, the first commoner, Juma Mwindadi, a school master from Dar es Salaam, was appointed. It was not until August 1957 that recognition was given to Africans having a popular social base by the appointment of Julius Nyerere, leader of TANU, and Rashidi Kawawa, general secretary of the Tanganyika Federation of Labor.[74]

The growth of Legco in size and significance came during 1955 and 1957 when its representation more than doubled. This was in response to the growing pressures created by the mushrooming nationalist movement— pressures which were explicitly recognized by the United Nations Visiting Missions of 1948 and 1951. The Visiting Missions, confronted by petitions from the Tanganyika African Association (TAA) and the Chagga Cultural Association demanding the right to vote, recommended that opportunities be created in the national government[75] and that legislation be introduced "to stimulate the participation of the indigenous inhabitants in the legislative and executive bodies . . . on the basis of a democratic election system."[76]

However, European concerns about the increasing influence of Africans found expression in the form of the Tanganyika European Council (TEC), established in 1949 with a British and Greek constituency. The emergence of the Mau Mau in Kenya and other indications of incipient violence in the colonies were contributing, however, to a redefinition of colonial policy. Governor Twining responded to the various pressures by seeking to introduce the principle of multiracialism into Tanganyika's legislative process by establishing provincial representation within Legco based on racial parity. Tanganyika's eight provinces were each given three representatives in Legco plus one representative of each racial group from Dar es Salaam and one of each group to represent general interests. The principle of multiracialism represented the working-out in Tanganyika of the "non-racial" views of the Capricorn Society in the Rhodesias. The basic idea in Tanganyika was to obtain racial parity in the legislature, thus denying the principle of "one man, one vote."

The approach of the Tanganyika African National Union (TANU) to the question of multiracial parity presented one of the most delicate tactical

---

[74] Julius Nyerere had been appointed to Legco in 1954 as a temporary member. It was around this time that he was converting the Tanganyika African Association into a political party, TANU. It is not clear if Nyerere was appointed by Governor Twining to Legco because of a desire to obtain representation of the modernized Africans or in spite of it. Nyerere was, at the time, recently returned from Edinburgh with a master's degree and was outstanding among Africans for the extent of his education.

[75] U.N. Trusteeship Council, *Report of the Visiting Mission to the Trust Territory of Tanganyika under British Administration*, T/218 (November 8, 1948), p. 33.

[76] U.N., *Yearbook* (1947–1948), p. 759.

problems confronted by a still inexperienced leadership. Accepted by Africans as an interim measure, the enlarged Legco held its first meeting in April 1955. All unofficial representation continued, of course, to be appointed by the governor. The period following 1955 was one in which TANU's growth was remarkable, and considerable tension was experienced in Tanganyikan politics. A slight change in representation in Legco took place in 1957 when the Lake Province constituency was divided, raising the number of unofficials to thirty-three. At the opening of the new Legco, Twining announced that the franchise was to be broadened, and election of unofficial members to Legco was introduced. This was implemented in general elections held in September 1958 and February 1959, when TANU swept the elections and effectively demolished all political opposition.

There was considerable political maneuvering prior to the actual election. In 1956, Twining had promulgated an electoral law providing that all eligible electors had to vote for one candidate from each of Tanganyika's main racial communities. Nyerere, in December 1957, moved that the requirement be dropped, but the motion failed to pass Legco, and Nyerere resigned. In 1958, TANU's leadership accepted the challenge of the election, while denouncing the parity principle in multiracial representation. TANU found a number of Asian and European candidates willing to accept TANU support and run against the government-inspired candidates of the United Tanganyika party (UTP). Because it had a majority of all electors supporting it, all TANU candidates were swept into office in the first set of elections held in September 1958. By the time the subsequent set of elections was held in February 1959, the UTP had completely collapsed. TANU's leadership thereby indicated its commitment to accept the basic structure of political evolution laid down by the British, even while pressing for changes. This commitment was further underscored in the period following the election when, as most of the country joined in the rush to TANU, the major thrust of political activities was focused on Legco. As shall be indicated, five TANU representatives joined the government bench and became the first elected ministers.

Much of 1959 and 1960 was devoted to broadening the franchise as constitutional discussions began to shape Tanganyika's political organization for the move toward independence. The principle of multiracial parity was abandoned although, under pressure of the British, sixteen seats in an eighty-one member assembly were reserved for Europeans, and thirteen seats were set aside for Asians. It was this particular structure that carried Tanganyika to its ultimate independence in December 1961.

The Executive Council and the Ministerial System

Just as the Legislative Council evolved into the National Assembly of independent Tanganyika, the Executive Council (Exco) evolved into Tanganyika's Cabinet. Exco, with top-level civil servants responsible for departments of central government, was created in 1920. It was essentially an administrative body created to assist the governor in the increasingly complex work of administration. It remained largely untouched until 1948, when political changes began to take place more rapidly. At that time, a "Member" system was introduced in which "Members" were designated for various services of government, answerable ultimately to the governor, but having the obligation to defend their work within Legco. Therefore, Members became incipient future ministers.[77]

Although recommended by the 1948 Visiting Mission of the United Nations, no Africans were represented in Exco until 1951, when Chief Kidaha became one of the five unofficial members. Adam Sapi, a second African, was added in 1954 when the principle of racial parity was introduced.[78] The next significant change took place in 1957 when six assistant ministers were designated from the ranks of Legco unofficials. This included four Africans, one Asian, and one European.

The most significant changes, preliminary to accelerated movement toward independence, came after the first general elections of 1958–1959. Under TANU's leadership, the elected members of Legco created TEMO (Tanganyika Elected Members Organization) which became, in effect, the official opposition to the government. An agreement was reached between TEMO and the government that five elected members would switch sides and join the government bench as ministers. These included three Africans, one Asian, and one European. It did not include Julius Nyerere, leader of TANU and TEMO, who continued to lead the opposition, but a number of key leaders were "surrendered" to the government side and began their ministerial training. This pattern of ministerial responsibility was maintained until the election of September 1960. After this, a Cabinet of ten elected members of the newly-renamed National Assembly and two civil servants was created. At this time, the Executive Council was abolished. The leader of business in the National Assembly became the Chief Minister who was now assisted by a Cabinet consisting of various ministers. With the achievement of independence, the Chief Minister became the Prime Minister and shortly afterward, representation within the Cabinet by civil servants was reduced to one.

Since that time, there has been a proliferation of the posts of Parliamentary Secretary as large numbers of members of the National Assembly have been appointed to these positions. This rapid increase in the number of sub-ministerial positions has probably had two functions. It provides a base of administrative experience for future ministers. The demands for experienced personnel continue to be heavy, and the parliamentary secretaryship repre-

---

[77] Datta, *op. cit.,* p. 32; J. Clagett Taylor, *The Political Development of Tanganyika* (Stanford: Stanford University Press, 1963), p. 80.

[78] B. T. G. Chidzero, *Tanganyika and International Trusteeship* (London: Oxford University Press, 1961), p. 144; Taylor, *op cit.,* p. 92.

sents a mechanism for the development of administrative talents. The post may be regarded as a political "payoff" to loyal and/or talented members of the National Assembly. It is significant that a number of trade unionists, formerly in the militant wing of the Tanganyika Federation of Labor, and a number of the more militant TANU leaders have emerged as parliamentary secretaries. Their appointments coincide with a marked reduction in their militancy.

In summary, evolution of the legislative council was relatively slow after Cameron had created the basic pattern. It was not until the nationalist movement began to grow that the council began to evolve rapidly. In this respect, it can be said that the British utilized the system of parliamentary representation to respond to growing nationalist consciousness and that the legislative council proved its basic adaptiveness. Unlike the pattern of native administration, the legislative system proved to be far more flexible to the rapid changes that took place.

THE SOCIAL BASES OF NATIONALISM

Nationalism, the most significant force in the evolution of the political system, culminates the development of the political system during the period of British control. Though some changes took place under the British following the period of Cameron's governorship, political evolution was relatively slow. Commonly referred to as a "Cinderella colony," Tanganyika's uncertain future had long precluded significant investment of capital or manpower.[79] To the extent that development took place in the political arena, it had largely been a response to nonindigenous forces: Zanzibar established a nominal hegemony to facilitate trade; Germany established control because of nationalist feelings and the desire to have a place for migrants to settle and to retail German culture; the British established a modern administrative apparatus and created the skeleton of a legislature.

It is not *until* African nationalism developed that significant political evolution began as a reaction primarily to internal demands. From 1947 on, events must be interpreted in terms of the response of the British to the first significant, modern, indigenous forces. A variety of factors contributed to the spread of nationalism after World War II.

1. The growth of a Westernized elite. Small in numbers prior to the war, the Westernized elite grew rapidly after the war. This group of educated Africans, in the parlance of the time, was "detribalized" and occupied a marginal position between the European population and the traditional African society. Their guides to the world were provided by the Europeans who, at the same time, imposed discriminatory practices and impeded their social mobility.

---

[79] For some time during the interwar years, there was much uncertainty because of the continuous rumors that Tanganyika might become a pawn to Hitler with the resurgence of German nationalism. See Moffett, *op. cit.*, pp. 113–114.

2. The growth of a proletariat and peasantry. Because the elite was small in size, it required a mass base on which to operate. This had been created in the form of a working class of increasingly stabilized workers and a peasantry which was increasingly involved, in production of cash crops. These groups provided the mass following for the elite.

Contributing, in particular, to the growth of the proletariat was the major economic event that resuscitated Tanganyika's moribund economy, the so-called "groundnut scheme," a plan initiated after the war by Britain's Labour government to alleviate an expected world shortage in edible fats. Although the plan turned into a fiasco,[80] it brought thousands of Africans into the labor market and gave the economy an enormous boost.

3. The impact of the war and of postwar nationalism in Asia and Africa. Although it is somewhat difficult to assess the changes wrought by the war and by the growth of nationalism in the underdeveloped areas, both probably played a key role in supporting the formulation of Tanganyikan nationalism.

The war was probably a broadening experience to many Tanganyikans. During the war, more than twice as many Africans were drawn from traditional pursuits than usual. In addition, many were exposed to ideas about democracy. Although the British anticipated that this group, in particular, would have to be accommodated by changes in the political system after the war, veterans did not play an important role in the formation of the nationalist cadres, although they may have made an important, if as yet unascertained, contribution at the grass-roots level.[81]

The Roots of Nationalism

The colonial system introduced, albeit inadvertently, a new basis for social structure. It must be recalled that there existed no such entity as Tanganyika prior to the arrival of the Europeans. The creation of a European colony provided geographical boundaries within which political and other forms of action had to take place. Where there were once a considerable number of autonomous tribes and/or kinship groups of varying culture and language, the Europeans introduced a single political unit and began to stimulate the growth of an economic system.

It is, therefore, somewhat meaningless to talk about "Tanganyika's social structure" prior to the arrival of the Europeans. After European hegemony was established, a territorial social structure began to develop. Its basic

[80] Alan Wood, *The Groundnut Affair* (London: The Bodley Head, 1950); S. Herbert Frankel, *The Economic Impact on Under-Developed Societies* (Cambridge: Harvard University Press, 1953), pp. 141–153.

[81] There is a belief among a number of students of Tanganyika politics that the veterans became important grass-roots leaders of TANU when it began to grow in 1954. A nonrandom study of the background of national-level TANU leaders does not support this hypothesis. It is possible, however, that many TANU branch chairmen or committee members had military experience.

constituents, from the viewpoint of the development of nationalism, were the Westernized elite, a proletariat, and a peasantry. These three strata began to form slowly after the 1880's, interrupted by the dislocations of German pacification, World War I, and the economic catastrophe of the 1930's. It was not until each new stratum was substantially established that a nexus took place between the three, which culminated in the creation of the nationalist party.

The Westernized Elite

Two basic forces are responsible for the creation of a substantial stratum of Westernized Africans. On the one hand, there were the Christian missionaries searching for new souls. Secondly, there were the burgeoning needs of government and commerce as the political and economic infrastructure developed. Each served to increase the number of Africans who, in their understanding of European ways, were increasingly alienated from traditional society.

Missionary settlement in Tanganyika began as early as 1844.[82] Although the first missions experienced considerable difficulties in becoming established, by the time that the Germans took over the area, a number of missions had become permanent. Over the years, missionary groups increased in number in spite of the political instability of the colony.[83] Christian missionary endeavors are distinguished by two characteristics. On the one hand, the universalism of Christian doctrine—the notion of the equality of all men in the eyes of God—underlies the efforts of all successful missionary work. A further characteristic of Christian missionary endeavor is an emphasis on the need of communicants to read the word of God directly. This has given rise to two distinct strategies: to train communicants in the word of God as understood by the missionaries (in the case of Tanganyika, German originally and later English), and to reduce indigenous languages to writing in which to translate the word of God.

In Tanganyika as elsewhere, missionaries systematically trained Africans to read and, at the same time, instilled in them ideas about the equality of men before God. To accomplish this task, it was necessary to isolate children and communicants in a Christian environment. Because of the relatively low population densities, mission enclaves were required where education could

---

[82] Krapf was probably the first of the missionaries to begin work in Tanganyika. Zoe Marsh and G. W. Kingsworth, *An Introduction to the History of East Africa* (Cambridge: The University Press, 1957), p. 79.

[83] Roland Oliver, *Missionary Factor in East Africa* (London: Longmans, Green, and Company, 1952), p. 236, illustrates the increase. The German Lutheran churches, in Tanganyika, for example, increased "from about 20,000 in 1914 to 92,000 in 1938 and to 150,000 in 1949."

be carried on without children having to walk impossibly long distances to school. In addition, home environments were hardly adequate to support serious endeavors at study. Thus, education was carried on almost entirely within the missionary enclave.[84] Over the years, as the missions grew in size, more and more children entered them to obtain the only formal education then available in Tanganyika. Prior to the 1950's, it was the missionary schools that had the greatest impact on the educational system.[85]

Government support was originally handled through subventions to the missions to support their work. However, government activities were increasingly, over time, oriented toward the creation of a system of government schools. This was, in part, a response to widespread European beliefs that the mission system of education was spoiling Africans. As labor shortages developed with the growing economy, European ideas about education began to concentrate on the idea that Africans should be trained for specific occupational roles at the lower levels of the occupational hierarchy. A second aspect of the problem was that it was believed that many mission-trained students adapted badly to the colonial environment which insisted that Africans "know their place" in the subordinate ranks of society and provide deference to their superiors. Over a period of time, the term "mission boy" became one of opprobrium, symbolizing the inadequately-trained, semi-Westernized African whose tendency toward theft, irresponsibility, and alcoholism soon became enshrined in local European mythology. Government emphasis in education after 1955 increasingly concentrated on the development of trade schools.[86]

As in most African territories, Tanganyika's educational system experienced considerable strain as more and more African parents realized that formal education was exigent for mobility. Further pressures were created as the expanding economy and government required increasing numbers of educated Africans to staff various structures to help reduce the exorbitant costs required to maintain European staffs. The government planned to handle the bulk of expansion of the educational system immediately after World War II. In 1947, a ten-year plan was initiated with the expectation that 36 per cent of African children would be educated. By 1951, 12 per cent of all students were enrolled in government schools.[87] Table 6–7 shows the accelerated development of education in Tanganyika in recent years. The

---

[84] *Ibid.,* p. 63.

[85] In 1947, for example, there were 40 government schools, 219 native authority schools, 294 Christian missionary schools (with government standing), 3,850 bush missionary schools. U.N. Trusteeship Council, *op. cit.,* T/218, p. 152.

[86] Tanganyika Department of Education, *Triennial Survey for the Years 1955–1957* (Dar es Salaam: Government Printer, 1958), pp. 12–13.

[87] Datta, *op. cit.,* p. 124.

Table 6–7

Growth of African Education

type of school	1947	1949	1954	1955	1956	1957	1958	1959	1960	1961
primary and middle	115,025	132,490	294,435	340,574	358,924	391,143	403,301	414,879	431,056	506,260
secondary	2031		2956	1893	2409	2989	3499	4132	4645	6031
teacher-training	1543		2122	2442	2381	2216	1784	1467	1441	1698
vocational and technical	235		667	929	696	1204	2035	1836	2075	1386
Makerere University College			112	150	167	181	206			

SOURCES: *United Nations Visiting Mission Report* T/218, pp. 152 ff; Tanganyika, *Statistical Abstract* (Dar es Salaam: Government Printer, 1959), p. 140; J. P. Moffett (ed.), *Handbook of Tanganyika* (Dar es Salaam: Government Printer, 1962), p. 158.

NOTE: In 1936, there were only 36,668 Africans enrolled in all government schools. Although data for intermediate years are not accessible, the U.N. Visiting Mission of 1951 (T/946, p. 104) notes that between 1947 and 1950, there was a 50 per cent increase in the number of pupils in primary schools and greater than 50 per cent in secondary schools.

growing educational turnout not only increased the numbers of Westernized and educated Africans but created substantial expectations with respect to social mobility, expectations that shall be seen to have been somewhat unrealistic.

This growing group of educated Africans was to be confronted by frustrations that laid the basis for the creation of an alienated social stratum. On the one hand, in the immediate postwar period, under the impact of the groundnut scheme, Tanganyika's economy began to develop very rapidly, which indicated growing opportunities as new jobs requiring administrative abilities were being created. Tables 6–8 to 6–10 summarize, from available data, some indices of the expansion of the economy. At the same time, however, the bulk of movement into upper-echelon positions in the growing economy was reserved for non-Africans. Table 6–11 provides a crude indication of the blockage in mobility of Westernized Africans into upper-level occupations.

Table 6–8

Tanganyika Government Expenditures, 1953–1960/61

1953	18,045
1955/6	22,575
1956/7	23,129
1958/9	24,686
1959/60	25,095
1960/61	26,689

s o u r c e : Tanganyika, *Statistical Abstracts 1962* (Dar es Salaam: Government Printer, 1962), p. 110.

n o t e : These figures are given in thousand £'s.

Table 6–9

Number of Registered Companies, Tanganyika, 1953–1961

1953	1278
1955	1487
1957	1626
1958	1764
1959	1882
1960	1947
1961	2096

s o u r c e : Tanganyika, *Statistical Abstracts 1962* (Dar es Salaam: Government Printer, 1962), p. 91.

Table 6–10

Total Volume of Trade (Imports and Exports)

1946	17,500
1949	52,500
1952	84,908
1953	64,037
1954	69,736
1955	80,945
1956	82,192
1957	80,320
1958	77,396
1959	81,673
1960	94,418
1961	90,286

SOURCE: Tanganyika, *Statistical Abstracts 1962* (Dar es Salaam: Government Printer, 1962), p. 33; J. P. Moffett (ed.), *Handbook of Tanganyika* (Dar es Salaam: Government Printer, 1958), p. 126.

NOTE: These figures are given in thousand £'s.

Table 6–11

African School Enrollment and Occupational Opportunities— 1955 and 1959 Compared

	1955	1959	Percentage Increase
primary school enrollment	340,574	414,879	22%
secondary school enrollment	1,893	4,132	117%
Africans employed in clerical positions	10,413	11,395	10%
Africans employed in office and store positions	9,058	9,125	1%

SOURCES: Tanganyika, *Statistical Abstracts 1962* (Dar es Salaam: Government Printer, 1962), pp. 157–158; Tanganyika, *Annual Report of the Labour Department* (Dar es Salaam: Government Printer, 1955), p. 46; *Ibid.* (1959), p. 44..

Thus, the combination of three factors, increased turnout of educated Africans, opening of employment opportunities, and the bulk of advancement in employment being reserved for non-Africans, produced a situation in which dissatisfaction began to increase substantially within the Westernized elite.

The Disaffected Elite

In the past, most educated Africans had adapted to the colonial system by accepting, by and large, their subordinate role in the social system. Mobility was possible in the lower levels of the administrative ranks for a small number of talented and educated Africans. The number of Africans at this level was so small, however, that no listing appeared for administrative workers in government reports until 1959, when 2,750 Africans were mentioned.[88] What limited mobility was possible in the early days was dependent not only on education and talent but also on the ability to provide proper deference to Europeans. Those Africans unable to do so found themselves excluded from government service.

Interviews conducted by this writer with early trade unionists indicate that many occupied relatively marginal positions in the employment market, shifting from job to job with considerable frequency. Some apparently became discouraged and returned to their homes, disappearing, in effect, from the employed labor force. Others remained, sometimes finding a sympathetic employer or occasionally maintaining a simple existence by engaging in retail trade. Such interviews also provide a graphic picture of the indignities and the social slights of the colonial period. It is unfortunate that this type of data cannot be subsumed with ease; nor is this the place to develop an ethnographic picture of the experiences of Africans who sought to live within a Western milieu. However, the contribution which the colonial situation made to creating a disaffected elite must not be overlooked.

Initially, the number of Africans who were unwilling to accept the colonial situation was very small. As the numbers of educated Africans increased faster than job opportunities, disaffection or alienation began to grow. And as the numbers of alienated Africans increased, each was in a position to obtain social support from other disaffected elements. Individual Africans found that, although expressions of hostility to the colonial system might produce economic sanctions from government or the employer, there were many Africans who were willing to support those expressing hostility to the system. As this group grew, a small number of "entrepreneurs" undertook to manage this dissatisfaction by working to build organizations which would express the discontent of Africans. This entrepreneurial undertaking can, perhaps, be best exemplified by Julius Nyerere who left a promising career to undertake the task of building a political party.[89]

---

[88] Tanganyika, *Annual Report of the Labour Department 1959* (Dar es Salaam: Government Printer, 1960), p. 44.

[89] Taylor, *op. cit.,* p. 96. While conducting field research in Tanganyikan trade unionism in 1959–1960, this writer found strong elements of entrepreneurialism still present among trade-union leaders. The subject will be given detailed treatment in a forthcoming book. The use of the term "entrepreneurial" is not intended to be invidious; there is no intent to imply that political and/or trade-union "entrepreneurs" were

The disaffected elite soon found or created different types of organizations within which they could function, win social esteem for the expression of sentiments hostile to the colonial system, and gain experience in the operation of modern associations. These included tribal associations, modern national associations (such as the Tanganyika African Association), trade unions, cooperatives, old boys' clubs (alumni associations), and other kinds of voluntary associations. To indicate how these organizations became precursors of TANU, the cooperatives, the tribal associations, and the Tanganyika African Association (TAA) will be examined.

The Cooperatives

Initiated by the British as agencies to control the agricultural economy, cooperatives were to become an early focus of dissatisfaction. By virtue of their organization and their aggregation of informed and educated participants, the cooperatives contributed substantially to the emergence of a nationalist movement. It is notable that three of the nine Africans holding ministries when Tanganyika became independent had their roots in the cooperative movement.[90]

The first law for the registration of cooperative societies, enacted in 1932, was a product of the cooperatives encouraged by Dundas among the Chagga on Kilimanjaro. Moshi was, indeed, the center for cooperative activity, but the movement soon spread to other areas of the country. Table 6–12 illustrates the growth of cooperative organization. With the appointment of a Commissioner for Cooperative Development in 1951, the cooperatives began to expand the range of their activities. Besides their primary work as marketing organizations, they became increasingly involved with transport, banking, education, and other social services. Several unions later became purchasing as well as marketing agents. By 1954, the U.N. Visiting Mission noted that the movement was beginning to break the hold of non-Africans on internal trade.[91]

Perhaps the best way to summarize the growth of the cooperatives is to consider the example of the Kilimanjaro Native Cooperative Union (KNCU). Created in 1932, KNCU was a union of primary cooperative societies of Chagga coffee growers. By 1959–1960, it had grown to the point where it had 43,000 members. The KNCU also became sufficiently strong financially

---

concerned with moneymaking. The action of such individuals was "entrepreneurial" in the sense that many undertook definite risks to follow their convictions. There was a financial aspect to this entrepreneurial activity in that such risk-takers had to find some economic base in order to sustain their activities on a full-time basis.

90 Paul Bomani, George Kahama, and Nsilo Swai.

91 U.N., *op. cit.*, T/1142, p. 234.

Table 6–12

Cooperative Growth in Tanganyika

Year	Number of Registered Societies	Number of Cooperative Unions	Total Membership
1933	12	1	—
1940	48	—	—
1949	79	—	60,445
1950	127	—	—
1955	243	7	—
1957	474	22	304,786
1958	546	—	318,900
1959	617	—	324,994
1960	691	—	326,211
1961	763	34	327,000
1963[a]	1,045	45	500,000

SOURCE: *The Cooperative Movement in Tanganyika* (Dar es Salaam: *Tanganyika Standard, Ltd.*, n.d.), passim.

[a] International Labor Organization, Expanded Program of Technical Assistance, *Report to the Government of Tanganyika on the Development of Industrial and Transport Cooperatives* (Geneva: International Labor Organization, 1964), p. 1.

to create its own training school and build impressive hotel-headquarters in Moshi.

The manner in which KNCU disperses skills necessary to sustain modern organizations can be seen by examination of the structure of the organization. When an area on the mountain is interested in forming a primary society, a meeting is called and a chairman is elected. Each village elects a representative to attend the monthly meetings of the primary societies. Attendance has been remarkably successful, and an estimated 75 per cent of these representatives attend meetings. Each primary society is responsible for collecting and pooling the output of its members. It must also maintain records of meetings and of quantities of coffee collected. The KNCU, as a union of primary societies, maintains control over the primary societies by reviewing minutes and inspecting budgets. KNCU also publishes a monthly bulletin to disperse information among members and to ventilate public opinion.[92] Although KNCU was one of the more conservative of the cooperative organizations during the growth of the independence movement, it served as a training ground for many young Tanganyikans who later became active in TANU.

[92] A. L. W. Bennett, "A Short Account of the Work of the KNCU Ltd.," *East African Agricultural Journal*, I (September 1935), 169–174.

The Tribal Associations

Associations based on ethnicity are a common feature of all migratory groups. In Tanganyika, such urban-based organizations are widely found. More significant for the early formation of nationalism, however, were the tribally based voluntary associations found in the area of traditional settlement of the tribe but based on the nearest town. Among these were the Chagga Association, the Bahaya Association, and others. These tribal associations developed in response to various irritants experienced by the rural population as they moved into production of cash crops. Among these were concerns about the alienation of land which, though minimal as compared to Kenya, continually underlined the ineffectuality of the traditional authorities. There were other irritants when, as a result of government control over production and marketing of crops, many African growers believed that they were being cheated in pricing arrangements.

Considering the nature of their indigenous political and economic organization, it is not surprising that the Chagga were among the first to experiment with a response outside the native authority system. They had a history of political unity and increasing consolidation of political control dictated largely by the extensive irrigation system used on Kilimanjaro. In addition, there was early and continuous contact with Europeans; the missions found Kilimanjaro's climate salubrious, and it became an early place of concentration of European farmers as well. The Chagga were already familiar with money and were experienced in trade from Arab times.[93]

Experimentation with modern associations began in the early 1930's as a result of dissatisfaction with the incumbent chiefs. Much of Chagga dissatisfaction was channeled by the administration into the cooperative movement, and KNCU provided a vehicle for resolving many problems. Because of this, a full-fledged *political* association did not emerge until 1949, when the Kilimanjaro Citizens Union was formed. Although the KNCU was relatively non-political, it did become involved in hot political issues such as the Meru land case.

Perhaps the earliest of the tribal associations formed on a modern basis was the Bahaya Association. Organized in 1937 and based in Bukoba, it was initiated to protest the regulations (imposed by the Native Authority at the behest of the government) requiring sanitation on coffee farms of Bahaya growers.[94] During the prewar period, the association was involved in a great variety of activities, some of them reflecting concern about the reputation of the tribe. One early action sought to suppress the movement of women to the cities where, according to local folklore, Bahaya women had an inordinate proclivity to become prostitutes. This action indicates a growing

---

[93] G. Liebenow, "Tribalism, Traditionalism, Modernism in Chagga Local Government," *Journal of African Administration*, X (April 1958), 73.

[94] Tanganyika, *Annual Reports of the Provincial Commissioners*, 1945.

concern with a wider world and not simply with tribal interests. Again, much activity was channeled into the development of cooperative societies and the Bukoba Cooperative Union, formed as a secondary society in 1950, became an active focus of early nationalist activity.

On the whole, it was not until after World War II that more coherent political movements began to emerge. The alienation of Meru lands[95] gave rise to the creation of the Meru Citizens Union in 1948. This organization took on an increasingly political complexion and expressed its hostility to the British continually. Under the leadership of Kirilo Japhet, the organization was created to collect funds to send a tribal representative to protest to the U.N. This action took place outside of the established Native Authority; although the traditional authorities had opposed alienation, they were ineffectual. The Meru Citizens Union solicited a high degree of support from the Meru and ultimately was responsible for bringing prominent Union members into the Native Authority.

The rural tribal associations tended to be largely concerned with local affairs and did not exhibit special preoccupation with territorial problems. According to the 1951 U.N. Visiting Mission, "Their activities tend to be local in character, but because they attract the most educated element in the tribal society, they can act as useful instruments for developing a wider outlook."[96] However, though largely concerned with local problems, the content of petitions filed by these associations with U.N. Visiting Missions in 1948 and 1951 indicates an increasing degree of consciousness of territorial problems.

This brief treatment of modern associations indicates two important points. Serious experimentation was taking place, beginning in the 1930's, with the formation of new organizations *outside of the structure created by the British,* to express the sense of dissatisfaction of the African population. The new organizations provided important areas within which Africans could obtain organizational skills relevant to functioning in the bureaucratic society created by the British. Of equal or perhaps more significance were a variety of other types of organizations such as the Tanganyika African Association and the trade unions. These organizations transcended the tribe, operating at the territorial level. These will be dealt with at this point.

The Proletariat

No proletariat existed in Tanganyika prior to the arrival of the Europeans. It was the establishment of a taxation system, more than any other single factor, that gave rise to enormous changes in behavior of subsistence agriculturists. Initially forced to work by the Germans, a complex of migratory patterns emerged over the years as taxation brought increasing numbers into

---

[95] For a discussion of the Meru land case, see Chidzero, *op. cit.,* pp. 236–245.

[96] U.N. Visiting Mission, *op. cit.,* T/946, p. 43.

the labor force. Migratory laborers constituted the bulk of the labor force until well after World War II. Over a period of decades, however, more workers began to spend longer periods of time in the towns, and the significance of migratory labor as the base for the employed labor force began to decline. Data concerning the numbers of workers committed to long-range, full-time wage employment over the years are unavailable in Tanganyika. However, Table 6–13 provides a rough index of the tendency for increased

Table 6–13

Indicators of the Decline in Migratory Labor in Tanganyika

Year	All Africans in Employment	Africans Accommodated in Government Transit Centers	Africans Recruited through Recruitment Organizations
1951	455,398	225,949	38,300
1952	443,597	282,878	34,393
1953	448,271	269,241	32,388
1954	439,094	243,975	30,610
1955	413,100	224,240	27,777
1956	424,209	265,950	26,472
1957	430,470	199,106	23,930
1958	430,547	173,601	32,840
1959	428,268	177,795	22,740
1960	387,475	135,288	11,614
1961	442,092	76,771	3,967
1962	398,816	45,328	5,693

SOURCE: Tanganyika, *Annual Report of the Labour Department* (Dar es Salaam: Government Printer, 1951–1962).

stabilization. The data must be treated tentatively because the numbers of Africans accommodated in transit centers is only a rough index of the numbers of migrants moving to and from centers of employment. Data on the number of laborers recruited through recruitment organizations are included to show that this number has also declined substantially.

It was this increased commitment toward employment that gave rise to a proletariat—a new stratum that would become significant in effecting social change. As more workers spent longer periods of time in employment, they came into contact with other Africans from a variety of ethnic groups. This fact, plus the tendency of Europeans to treat all Africans as Africans and not to differentiate between them on the basis of ethnicity, led to a growing sense of identity.

Early strikes were spontaneous, unorganized, and frequently encompassed only tribal brethren. By 1939, a strike took place in Tanga which indicated some growth of African consciousness. But it was not until 1947 that the territory had its first major strike.[97] It was as a result of this strike that the first significant African trade union was created. This was a premature effort. Largely dominated by illiterate traditionalists, the union perished in a disastrous strike in 1950. By 1952, however, new tendencies toward union organization were noted; this time, significantly, organization was undertaken by literate and Westernized Africans. Although discouraged by the British initially, an attempt was made to contain the growth of unionism within small, localized craft unions. This program collapsed after a visit to Tanganyika in 1955 of Tom Mboya, then rising to power within the Kenya unions. Mboya recommended that the unionists create a central federation of labor and amalgamate the growing number of tiny unions into a small number of national industrial unions. Within several months, the TFL was created, and the amalgamation process had changed the structure of the nascent unions beyond recognition. Table 6–14 provides data on the growth

Table 6–14

Growth of African Trade Unionism in Tanganyika

Year	Total Number of Unions	Total Estimated Members[a]
1952	2	301
1953	5	687
1954	6	291+
1955	19	2,349+
1956	24	12,912+
1957	15	33,986
1958	18	44,600
1959	17	78,100
1960	16	91,770
1961	14	199,915
1962	12[b]	182,153

SOURCE: Calculated from *Annual Report of the Labour Department* (Dar es Salaam: Government Printer, 1952–1962).

[a] Membership estimated by Labour Department; "+" means that the Department's estimated membership is in excess of given figure.

[b] The TFL, registered as a union, is not included in the figure.

of trade unionism. Despite enormous difficulties because of the inexperienced leadership and the total novelty of ideas of unionism among the largely illiterate workers, the test of a general strike in Dar es Salaam, in December 1956, was survived. From that point on, the unions began to spread their net

[97] A discussion of the changing strike patterns will be found in my article, "The Institutionalization of Labor Protest in Tanganyika and Some Resultant Problems," *Sociologus*, XI (1961), 133–147.

into the rest of the country. By 1958, organization was successfully under-taken among plantation workers, the largest single category in Tanganyika's labor force.

A crucial decision by the unionists was taken in July 1957, when the TFL adopted a resolution that endorsed, in effect, TANU's program. The resolu-tion argued that independence and development could not be separated and that a date for the establishment of independence should be fixed "without delay"; the restrictions on the franchise were identified as discriminatory, and an open franchise was called for; finally, the unions argued that while they were not political organizations, it was necessary for them to express views on the "progress of the country" and that unions should therefore be repre-sented in the legislature.[98] Although TFL did not formally endorse TANU at this time, its resolution roused a storm of criticism in UTP and government circles. In spite of this, liaison with TANU developed continuously, and TFL was given formal representation at TANU's annual conference and in the National Executive Committee by two delegates. In 1960, Rashidi Kawawa, leader of the unions, became TANU's Vice President, and later served as Prime Minister, and is, at the time of writing, the second Vice President of Tanzania.

For the early trade unionists, the distinction between TANU and the unions was enforced only by the power of the British: both were seen as engaging in the same struggle against colonialism, although the unions were more limited in their approach since they directed their activities against employers instead of against the entire colonial system. Early relationships between TANU and the unions were complementary. The unions frequently obtained vigorous TANU support when broad-based boycotts of products were required to back strikes. At a later stage, beginning in 1960, strains began to develop between the unions and TANU, as TANU began to take over the reins of government and thereby became one of the major employers in Tanganyika. The development of this conflict will be treated briefly in this chapter.

The growth of the unions symbolizes the creation of a proletariat, stabilized and amenable to mobilization for political/economic purposes. From the point of view of the development of nationalism, a growing social stratum was created, concentrated in the urban areas where the disaffected elites were mainly to be found. The working class therefore provided TANU with its earliest base.

The Peasantry

The gradual and accretive process whereby increasing numbers of subsistence agriculturists and nomads begin to produce small quantities of products for sale on a market is not one which lends itself to the presentation of any

---

[98] Resolution adopted by the TFL General Council, July 4–6, 1957.

dramatic data. Over a period of years, as the Germans established a communications network and the British expanded it, an economic infrastructure was slowly created. Asians scattered throughout much of the country, opening up small retail shops that also served as purchasing and bulking agencies for cotton, coffee, and other crops. The growth of the cooperatives also facilitated the movement of subsistence agriculturists into small-scale cash-crop production. This spread gradually to other areas and, at the same time, the awakening of demands for manufactured goods led pioneer cash-crop growers to increase their output where it was feasible to get crops to a local bulking agent.

It is possible to present only crude indices of the shift of agriculturists from subsistence to cash-cropping. In Maswa district, for example, African cotton production increased from 10,300 tons in 1955 to 25,000 tons in 1957.[99] Table 6–15 shows the increase in coffee grown in Bukoba between 1924 and 1934.

Table 6–15

African Coffee Output, Bukoba, 1924–1934

Year	Plantation	Native
1924	662	2,869
1926	1,020	3,579
1928	2,582	5,254
1930	2,708	4,660
1932	1,401	5,706
1934	3,331	6,898

SOURCE: T. S. Jervis, "Bukoba Coffee," *East Africa Agricultural Journal,* I (March 1936), 368.

NOTE: The figures are given in tons.

The tendency toward cash agriculture was sufficiently marked that the Department of Agriculture became concerned about its consequences in various places in Tanganyika. "The tendency to swing from food crops (i.e., subsistence agriculture) has to be continually watched and sustained propaganda is necessary to prevent this swing from going too far."[100] As subsistence agriculturists became peasants, they were concerned with a wider world than that to which they had been accustomed. The workings of the world market affected the prices they received for their crops as they sold them as well as the prices they paid for the manufactured goods they wanted to buy. As their

[99] Tanganyika, *Annual Report of the Department of Agriculture* (London: H.M.S.O., 1957), Part I, p. 25.

[100] Tanganyika, *Annual Report of the Department of Agriculture* (London: H.M.S.O., 1950), p. 4.

world broadened, the peasants became a group potentially mobilizable by the disaffected elites. Although dispersed over the land, the spread of cooperatives facilitated the dispersal of information which often fostered dissatisfaction. They became the primary organization for mobilization of the peasantry, and, like the unions, were formally represented by two delegates at the TANU annual conference and within the National Executive Committee. TANU carefully nurtured its base in the rural areas. By 1959, a network of village organizations had been created which encompassed the entire country. The effectiveness of this development was made possible only by virtue of the integration of the bulk of the rural population by their participation in the cash economy. It was the nexus of the proletariat and the peasantry with the disaffected elite—capable of working within the limits of a bureaucratic-legal system and able to manipulate symbols which were legitimate in the mother country—that provided the necessary ingredients for the creation of mass movement.

The Organizational Expression of Nationalism

The Tanganyika African Association (TAA) was probably the first of the associations to group modernized Africans on a territorial rather than a tribal basis. Organized in 1929, its constituency probably consisted almost entirely of urbanized Africans in government service.[101] TAA was founded as an educational and social organization concerned with social welfare and civil service conditions and was initially encouraged by the government. In the years before the war, the organization's activities were so innocuous that no mention of them can be found in official government reports, a sure sign that TAA was hardly involved in "trouble-making" or political activities. After the war, membership of TAA grew as it began to establish relations with the tribally based organizations of modernized Africans. During this period, it also began to develop increasingly political attitudes. These became manifest through the presentation of petitions to the Visiting Mission of the United Nations in 1948. Four members of TAA presented a petition which discussed wages, working conditions, the need for cooperative development, cultural and social conditions of Africans, and, most important, the need for their education for self-government.[102] According to the Visiting Mission, TAA membership included 1,780 members in thirty-nine branches.[103]

By the time the second Visiting Mission came to Tanganyika in 1951, TAA

---

[101] The origins of TAA are somewhat shrouded, and little hard data exist on its membership. Some discussions with TANU leaders and the existing literature indicate a membership that was entirely Westernized, educated, and largely employed by government. However, until additional research is conducted on TAA, it will not be possible to make definitive statements about the membership.

[102] U. N. Visiting Mission, *op. cit.*, T/218, pet. 2.61, 1948.

[103] *Ibid.*, T/218/add. 1, p. 17.

had expanded its membership to 5,000. The tone of its petitions was increasingly critical of the government. In addition, various branches presented petitions to the Mission. The lack of coordination between the branches showed that, whereas the organization was growing, it lacked coherence since different arguments were made, some of them contradictory. Beyond that, however, the significance of the political complexion of TAA was recognized by the Mission.[104]

TAA continued to grow. Late in 1953, having returned, in October 1952, from Edinburgh where he had taken a master's degree, Julius Nyerere was elected its President. Under his stimulus, TAA was converted, in July 1954, into a conscious political movement and began to grow more rapidly. It was not until March 1955, however, that Nyerere decided to surrender his career as a teacher and devote himself fulltime to building TANU. This was a fateful decision. Bringing enormous talent, organizational abilities, and political insights to his work, Nyerere built a nationwide network of branches, obtained direct and indirect affiliates within the burgeoning network of modern associations, and laid down the basic strategy for the attainment of independence.[105]

Thus, the years after 1947 were marked by an increasing shift of political initiative from the European administrators to the Westernized Africans. The growth of nationalism did not go unnoticed by the British who began to change their attitudes in an attempt to contain and control the developing trends. It was during this time that the creation of councils within the native authorities was accelerated in the hope that the emerging forces would be diverted from the national level into local politics. Legislation was also introduced in an attempt to allay discontent. For example, the educational plan of 1947 sought to meet the complaints about the disproportionate share of the budget being devoted to non-African education. Also, an ordinance restricting immigration was adopted in 1947 in order to avoid added competition for skilled occupations.

With the groundwork laid by TAA and with Nyerere devoting his career to its development, TANU grew rapidly. Its early membership consisted of the TAA affiliates and tribally based associations largely in the Lake, Northern, Tanga, and Southern Provinces, as well as in Dar es Salaam. A year of increasing activity, 1955 was marked by efforts to arouse nationalist feeling in rural areas by actively denouncing tribal institutions and other divisive tendencies. As a result, in the process of expanding, TANU lost many of the original group of TAA members which included some traditionalists. However, it was rapidly becoming a mass movement. In 1956, a women's section was formed, followed, in 1958, by a youth league, created

---

104 *Ibid.*, T/946/1951, p. 13.

105 Details of the growth of TANU and the elections of 1958, 1959, and 1960 are well covered in Bates, *op. cit.*, and Taylor, *op. cit.* The following discussion only indicates the general trend of events.

to assist in gaining mass support. Table 6–16 provides some data on TANU's growth.

Table 6–16

The Growth of TANU

	Number of Branches	Members (estimated)
1955	20	100,000
1956	25	150,000
1957	48	200,000
December 1959		1,000,000[a]

SOURCE: J. Clagett Taylor, *The Political Development of Tanganyika* (Stanford: Stanford University Press, 1963), pp. 136, 151.

[a] Margaret Bates, "Tanganyika," in Gwendolyn Carter (ed.), *African One-Party States* (Ithaca: Cornell University Press, 1962), p. 430.

In the period of TANU's early growth, the administration sought to impede its development. The government insisted on the registration of all political parties[106] and restricted the political activities of civil servants by banning participation in political parties for officials in the senior and junior services. This was particularly damaging since TANU's new leadership and much of its membership were heavily based on the civil service, and this left many Africans in a position of either surrendering their jobs or their party attachments. The main thrust of the government's counterstrategy came in two directions. One was to sponsor a political party to compete with TANU, and the second was to seek to strengthen the power of the traditional authorities.

Governor Twining, in seeking to create a multiracial society, was heavily committed to the principle of racial parity which would have denied Africans political power concomitant to their population. The United Tanganyika party (UTP) was created in February 1956 to support the principle of racial parity and opposed TANU in the 1958 election. Its annihilation in the 1958 election and the subsequent agreement by Governor Turnbull to establish a common roll system instead of racial parity left TANU essentially in control of the formal instrumentalities of government. The second counterstrategy was doomed to similar failure. The Convention of Chiefs, organized in 1957, was urged by Twining to oppose TANU in order to preserve chiefly offices. The chiefs, however, reassured by Nyerere's indication that there was no conflict between the chief's role and TANU[107] and seeing support of nationalism as the best way to protect themselves, sided with

---

[106] U. N. Visiting Mission, *op. cit.*, T/1142/206.

[107] Young and Fosbrooke, *op. cit.*, p. 180.

TANU in the election of March 1959. A representative of the Convention, Chief Abdullah Fundikira, ran for election on the TANU ticket and became Minister for Lands and Surveys. Held in esteem by Europeans for his gradualism, his affiliation to TANU helped work a moderate transition once the government's strategy with respect to multiracialism was defeated.

INDEPENDENCE: THE FOCALIZATION OF TANGANYIKAN SOCIETY

Since the attainment of independence, rapid political evolution has taken place in which TANU[108] has emerged as a crucial organization dominating all sectors and institutions of society. The process wherein a single organization or institution becomes dominant shall be referred to as *focalization;* societies of this type shall be referred to as *focal-institutional* societies. I have elsewhere[109] sought to describe focal-institutional societies as one key aspect of African socialism. The remaining section of this chapter will examine the manner in which focalization has taken place in Tanganyika. There are, however, a number of methodological difficulties. It is difficult to examine the interpenetration of a complex institutional network by a single institution, except by examination of behavior at the microlevel. In lieu of this type of analysis which is not possible because of the paucity of finely detailed research in Tanganyika, it is possible only to examine focalization macroscopically. This will be attempted by a survey of developments in the main institutions of Tanganyika since the attainment of independence. Before doing so, however, it is necessary to note that two kinds of forces have encouraged the development of a focal-institutional society in Tanganyika. On the one hand, there was a legacy of British colonialism, a legacy which was, in a sense, focal-institutional. The colonial regime tended to dominate and divert the significant developments of this society. Colonialism was considerably different, however, from the present tendencies toward focalization. For one thing, many aspects of life were left untouched by the colonial government. Independence has seen, in contrast, a systematic endeavor by TANU to mobilize the entire population in an effort to develop a sense of nationhood.

The requirements of political mobilization constitute a second imperative for a focal-institutional society. The problems of the post-independence period: the need to make good on promises made during the struggle to

---

[108] Additional documentation of the subject of TANU's penetration of Tanganyika's institutions can be found in a recent article by Harvey Glickman, "One-Party System in Tanganyika," *Annals of the American Academy of Political and Social Science,* CCCLVIII (March 1965), 136–149.

[109] See my chapter, "Basic Social Trends," in William H. Friedland and Carl G. Rosberg, Jr. (eds.), *African Socialism* (Stanford: Stanford University Press, 1964), pp. 26–30.

obtain independence; to cope with problems of economic development, the formation of conflicting interest groups, the maintenance of social control, etc., all pose dilemmas for the new nations of Africa. To hold things together, TANU has found it necessary to integrate various institutional sectors and to extend its controls.

Taking advantage of its considerable popularity as the party that won independence, TANU has used a variety of techniques to permeate most of the key institutions of Tanganyikan society. The locus of power within TANU itself is not, however, institutionalized. Though the organization has clearly permeated most institutions of society, it is not possible to actually designate where the center of decision-making lies within TANU. Not only is it difficult to assess the political power of individuals within the party, but also, there is no single political unit that is clearly the locus of power. Decision-making shifts from the Cabinet to the National Executive to individual leaders, no one of which is consistently responsible for the formulation of TANU policy. Partly because of this, it is clear that there has been no conscious, thought-out attitude toward focalization. It is the contention of this writer that the political leadership of TANU has sought to deal with political problems in a piece-meal fashion, as is characteristic of political leaders everywhere. However, the consequence of TANU's political activities has been to undermine competing centers of power everywhere—within the TANU leadership, within Parliament, within the unions, within the cooperatives, and in a great variety of social units. We shall examine this process in three institutional sectors: the political, the economic, and the social.

The Political Institutions

Although TANU has frequently presented a visage of almost monolithic unity, the party has been continuously divided among a number of different orientations. Though there is little evidence that *organized* factions exist within TANU, at various times, leaders have expressed themselves in ways that indicate considerable disagreement within the party. In the elections of August 1960, TANU won fifty-eight seats by default since there was no opposition. Of the thirteen contested seats, TANU candidates won every seat but one. Yet the magnitude of the victory did not present the country with a single voice within the National Assembly. Various forces were soon pressing for more radical action with respect to undermining the power of the Europeans and the Asians against a more conservative orientation embodied by Nyerere. The expressions of views in Parliament indicated that many members of the government benches were critical of the policies of the leadership. It soon became clear that an informal policy of cooptation was at work as a large number of parliamentary secretaryships were created and were filled by members of the assembly who had been expressing critical views.

By January 1962, ten parliamentary secretaries had been named. Of these, it is instructive to note that three had been top-level party leaders with militant reputations. The fourth was a trade unionist who was one of two leaders of the militant and increasingly anti-TANU wing of the Federation of Labor. While it is true that the position of parliamentary secretary can provide its occupant with considerable pre-ministerial experience, it was also convenient to place people who were publicly critical within Parliament into positions of responsibility where they could no longer criticize government policies. Slowly and subtly, the character of Parliament began to change.

It changed even more when the government undertook to politicize the provincial administration in February 1962. In the colonial period, provincial administration had been the embodiment of government in the rural areas. After independence, while the Africanization of provincial administration began, this was a slow process. This meant that, for the bulk of Africans in the country, government continued to be embodied by the British provincial and district commissioners. This administrative structure was politicized by retitling the political units and making the commissioners in charge political appointees. The British civil servants in the now eliminated positions were assigned as administrative secretaries/advisors to the political appointees designated by the TANU government. The appointment of a number of members of the National Assembly as Area and Regional Commissioners meant that these persons now became responsible members of government and were no longer in a position to offer criticism of government policies within the assembly. There were, of course, perfectly legitimate reasons for politicizing the civil service. It was pointed out, for example, that "enthusiasm (for development plans) could be kindled by a politician more effectively than by a civil servant."[110] Yet there could be little doubt that the outcome of the policy was to mute criticism within Parliament from the government benches. From time to time, complaints were heard that many of the politicians holding important positions in the administrative structure were not qualified and were "there simply to spread TANU policy."[111] However, these complaints won few supporters.

Focalization also took place in the form of expanding the control over local government bodies. The chiefs were officially removed from power within local government structures. In June 1962, Mr. Lusinde, the Minister for Local Government, announced that nontraditional chiefs were to be replaced by elected council chairmen, whereas traditional chiefs were to be gradually replaced on retirement.[112] Local governments were to be run by elected councils. This creditable goal meant, in most cases, that local TANU branches designated the candidates to stand for election. Since there was a

---

110 *Journal of Local Administration Overseas.* II (October 1963), 163.

111 *Tanganyika Standard,* Oct. 22, 1963.

112 *Sunday News,* June 17, 1962, p. 7.

paucity of political opposition, designation as a candidate was tantamount to election.

There was some small political opposition within the country, however. Although not illegal until 1963, it was so effectively discouraged that opposition parties found themselves completely unable to function.[113] In 1961, for example, Zuberi Mtemvu, president of the opposition African National Congress (ANC), complained that the Minister for Home Affairs forbade his organization to hold public meetings. The All Moslem National Union of Tanganyika (AMNUT), an even more minuscule organization, was persecuted and warned to keep religion out of politics. C. S. K Tumbo, a union leader who had been coopted as High Commissioner to London and returned to take up opposition politics, found it impossible to function in Tanganyika and went into voluntary exile in Kenya.[114] The end to overt political opposition came, in January 1963, when the one-party state was announced. Although it was not given legal form at the time, all political opposition collapsed. Mtemvu rejoined TANU individually. The ANC was formally integrated into TANU in April. The last ANC hold-out, J. Saileni, who openly opposed the one-party state, was imprisoned and was committed, in August 1963, to a mental institution.[115] These cases illustrating the focalization of Tanganyika's political institutions should suffice to provide some idea of the manner in which all aspects of political life became interpenetrated and controlled by the policies of TANU's leadership.[116]

Economic Institutions

Several examples of the permeation of economic institutions of Tanganyika show a similar type of development. The most prominent of the economic organizations which had to be brought under control after independence were

---

[113] Bates, *op. cit.*, pp. 470–474, discusses the political opposition and the problem of national unity.

[114] In 1963, after Kenya obtained its independence, Tumbo was turned over to the Tanganyikans by the Kenya police and detained. At the time of writing (April 1965), Tumbo is still in detention and has never been tried for any violation of law.

[115] This writer has no idea about Saileni's mental condition. However, the mortality rate in Tanganyika's single mental institution has always been exceedingly high. No knowledge is available, at the time of writing, as to Saileni's condition.

[116] In the interim between the writing of this chapter and its going to press, Tanganyika has formally become a one-party state. TANU continues to dominate the entire political system and society, but has recognized that mechanisms are necessary to permit some expression of dissatisfaction. This has been embodied in an electoral procedure which, while permitting only TANU candidates for the National Assembly, does permit contests *between* TANU candidates. In the elections of September 1965, 16 of 31 members of Parliament standing for election were defeated and 6 ministers and subministers also failed to be reelected. TANU's political control remains as strong as ever; indeed, it has been reinforced, but political focalization has not meant that there do not exist some alternatives in the political system.

the trade unions.[117] There had been complete cooperation between the unions and TANU in the pre-independence period. As independence drew closer, latent strains became increasingly manifest. Strain became evident after two long strikes of postal and railroad workers in late 1959 and early 1960. The strikes posed the essential dilemma of unions in multiracial societies: though the African response to the strikes was almost unanimous, services were maintained because the work was performed by Asians and Europeans. Accordingly, the strikes taught the unionists that *political* access and control would be crucial in the future and that sheer dependence on economic weapons would be inadequate.

Following the strike, a split developed within the unions, with one wing supporting TANU and the government and an opposition wing becoming increasingly hostile to TANU. Significantly, the split was between those unions of workers employed by various governmental organizations (anti-TANU) and those of workers employed by private employers (pro-TANU). The split was hastily covered over in March 1962 when the leaders of the contending factions were coopted into government. Michael Kamaliza, leader of the pro-TANU group, became Minister of Labour; C. S. K. Tumbo, the major leader of the anti-TANU group, was sent to London as High Commissioner; Jacob Namfua, the other leader of the anti-TANU group, became a parliamentary secretary.

For the moment, the matter was quiet. Shortly, however, matters came to a head over a number of issues, but the precipitating factor was the resignation of Tumbo and his return to Tanganyika to take up oppositionist politics. The leader of the TFL, then John Magongo, was expelled from the unions by the president of TFL, Victor Mkello. Mkello was, however, to be rusticated shortly afterward for having encouraged a series of wildcat strikes in 1962. The removal of Magongo and the detention of Mkello left the TFL in weak hands; but even then, proposals made by Kamaliza to absorb the TFL into the Ministry of Labour were rejected by TFL. Immediately after the mutiny of January 1964, the bulk of the trade-union leaders were arrested and detained. The removal of most of the full-time leaders of the unions (some 200 are believed to have been detained) permitted new legislation to be introduced consolidating all unions into a single new union whose key officers were appointed by the President of the Republic. The designation of the Minister of Labour, Michael Kamaliza, as general secretary of the new organization meant that the new union, the National Union of Tanganyika Workers (NUTA), was effectively controlled by the Ministry of Labor.

The situation with respect to the cooperatives was quite different. Although

---

[117] For an expanded discussion of the relations between the unions and government, see my chapter, "Cooperation, Conflict, and Enforced Conscription: TANU-TFL Relations, 1955–1964," in A. A. Castagno and Jeffrey Butler (eds.), *Boston University Papers in African Politics* (Boston: Boston University Press, 1964).

the cooperatives did not offer any overt opposition, they had the potentiality of serving as an independent center of power. The focalization of agriculture was well developed during colonial times through the encouragement of cooperatives *and* the passage of legislation that effectively required Africans in many sections of the country to market their produce through these co-ops. The British favored focalization in agriculture because it was an effective way to facilitate capital accumulation. By the creation of a network of cooperatives, marketing facilities could be developed more rapidly. In addition, the cooperative unions could become, in effect, banking institutions by reserving a portion of the sale price of the crop for future expansion. If marketing had been handled with less government restriction, it is likely that it would have fallen to the Asians, i.e., a foreign minority; it would have been less efficient since competition between Asians for the trade was unlikely, and capital accumulation would have been slow. Finally, the British would have had less control over quality and future investment and expansion. For these reasons, a legal structure was erected that enforced marketing of African produce through the cooperative organizations while Cameron was still governor. From the beginning, the cooperatives were therefore not voluntary associations as is connoted by the term "cooperative" in the normal Western context. They were also involuntary by virtue of the degree of operational control and direction which was exercised by the British.

Accordingly, well before the development of the nationalist movement, the cooperative "movement" in Tanganyika was well focalized in the sense that the entire operation was directed and controlled by government. The inheritance of this system by the TANU government was, therefore, natural. Just prior to independence, an experiment with a new organization, which would have competed with the established cooperative, was formed. Its experiences provide an opportunity to examine TANU's insistence on focalization and its rejection of tendencies toward plural growth of organizations in agriculture. The particular case involved the creation of an organization called "Saidia Waafrika" (Help the Africans) in the Lake Victoria area, an organization which sought to compete with the Victoria Federation of Cooperative Unions (VFCU). Relatively little is known about Saidia Waafrika except that it emerged publicly in late July 1960 when the newspapers briefly reported its activities in seeking to purchase cotton in competition with VFCU, offering to pay higher prices. The activities of the organization were denounced publicly by Mr. Nyerere and the TANU-oriented newspapers, and, after a meeting in Dar es Salaam with Mr. Nyerere, the organization "disappeared." It seems likely that the disappearance was not entirely fortuitous.

Another means to focalize the cooperatives was through the creation of higher level cooperative organizations that would control the hitherto relatively autonomous secondary unions such as the KNCU, the VFCU, etc. In the spring of 1962, a new organization, the Cooperative Union of Tanganyika, was formed embracing thirty-four cooperative unions and 850 primary societies. Since these organizations handled one-fourth of all of Tanganyika's exports and one-third of agricultural exports, the move established centralized control over a significant segment of the national economy. The national organization also announced its intention to move into banking and insurance. The National Cooperative Bank was established in 1962 to provide financial services for all cooperatives, and banking with the new organization became obligatory. In 1963, a national cooperative insurance company was formed. Further standardization and control were instituted, in March 1964, with the passage of legislation providing for the formation of a unified cooperative staff service.

One technique for maintaining control over the cooperatives is through overlapping leadership. Although there are, again, perfectly valid reasons for this by virtue of the shortage of effective leaders, the consequences produce centralized controls over a large segment of the economy. As an example of overlapping leadership, O. M. J. Lema, the president of KNCU, was, in 1963, also regional chairman of TANU for Kilimanjaro, a member of the TANU National Executive Committee, and member of the controlling group of the Cooperative Union and the Cooperative Bank.

In April 1962, the government moved into the arena of consumer cooperatives, an area of retailing which had hitherto been left largely to the Asian population. The Cooperative Supply Association of Tanganyika (COSATA) was formed for this purpose.[118] To support its growth, government bodies were required to purchase their supplies through COSATA. Later COSATA became a tool to exert pressure on retail shops. Thus, in January 1963, when the retail shops refused to sell *sembe* (meal) because of its low price, Vice President Kawawa ordered the centralization of its sale through COSATA shops. In November 1963, the government announced its intention to expand COSATA to "a fair percentage of national wholesale and retail trade."[119] The continuous expansion of existing cooperatives as well as the spread of cooperative activities to new areas is planned by the government. In the second five-year development plan projected for 1964–1969, it is envisioned that cooperatives will undertake significant work in the processing of agricultural produce and livestock; in the timber industry where cooperatives are to be given a monopoly of forestry concessions but will work with private enterprises; in the manufacturing of building materials, farm supplies, clothing; as well as in building, construction, and transport.[120] The extension of the cooperative network has, more than anything else, under-

---

[118] For a brief discussion of COSATA, see Fred G. Burke, "Tanganyika: The Search for Ujamaa," in Friedland and Rosberg, *op. cit.*, p. 211.

[119] *Tanganyika Standard,* November 5, 1963.

[120] International Labor Office, Expanded Program of Technical Assistance, *Report to the Government of Tanganyika on the Development of Industrial and Transport Cooperatives* (Geneva: International Labor Office, 1964), pp. 4–6.

mined the degree of control exerted over the economy by Asians who had been largely responsible for the extension of the modern economy into the rural areas. And, while the cooperative program has never been presented as an anti-Asian activity, its consequences have been to erode the economic base of this formerly significant group.

Social Institutions

The penetration of the party apparatus into organizations which are neither political nor economic indicates the all-inclusive extent to which Tanganyika has moved in the direction of creating a focal-institutional society. In examining social institutions (defined here as institutions which are neither economic nor political), it will again be necessary to be selective.

One potential source of opposition rests with the various tribal associations. Many of these organizations were discouraged or were merged into TANU. Thus, the Meru Citizens Union, one of the first of the prenationalist organizations, was incorporated into TANU in 1961. Other tribal associations met a similar fate, such as the Wazaramo, a coastal tribe centered in the Eastern Province, who sought to create a tribal association and obtain registration. This was refused by the government, which rejected the need for any new associations based on traditional attachments.

The mobilization of groups of elders also became a way of spreading control at the village level. Because of the considerable respect given to elders in most Tanganyikan tribes, they represented a potential threat to TANU effectiveness at the local level. Instead, the elders were organized into groups at the village level and became, in effect, a primary communications mechanism to spread government plans.

The youth were mobilized by TANU at an early stage through the creation of the TANU Youth League (TYL). Originally forming a militant subsection of TANU and at times somewhat obdurate at the conservatism of the TANU leaders, the TYL was integrated, in 1963, into a National Council of Youth which was controlled by the Ministry of National Culture and Youth. Women were mobilized at the village levels through the creation of a women's section of TANU. Led by Bibi Titi Mohammed, a TANU stalwart, the women were organized to provide ululating sections at public meetings and also to goad their men into participation in local development schemes. Parents were brought into the network of controls that were created to bring pressures on the schools to instill a curriculum in keeping with the new Tanganyika. The primary organization for mobilization was the Tanganyika African Parents Association (TAPA) which was integrated closely with the Ministry of Education.

The major vehicle of mobilization in the rural areas became the community self-help programs. Initiated largely by TANU leaders at the local levels, but controlled from the center through a requirement that all materials provided by government had to be approved by a centralized agency, community self-help programs involved building community centers, roads, wells, etc. The entire local population of villages would be mobilized through the TANU branch.

Religious groups have remained one of the major groups unpermeated thus far, as long as they keep completely out of politics. In October 1963, two leaders of a religious society, Dawat el Islamia, were rusticated for "exploiting religious differences for political purposes."[121] The issue involved a somewhat broad definition of "political purposes," since the group was concerned with raising Moslem educational standards. The action of government undoubtedly must have served as a warning to all religious communities involved in education, even though President Nyerere promised the right of freedom of religion as long as religion remained distinct from politics.

The mutiny of the army, in January 1964, also had the inadvertent consequence of producing a permeation of that crucial institution. Because of their political unreliability, most soldiers were dismissed from the army, and a new army was recruited largely from the TYL in the hope that it would be more politically committed to TANU and the government. At the same time, the army, which had been regarded as immune from politics, was politicized by a conscious introduction of political indoctrination..

In terms of control of the elections, of the national assembly, and of the machinery of government, and of the economic and social institutions, TANU thus remains all-powerful, and no significant force has threatened this power. The mutiny in January 1964, although crucial in its consequences, must be considered an aberration since it did not represent the action of a coherent force struggling for power, but that of a protest group concerned with specific issues of wages and Africanization.

CONCLUSION

In many respects, the heritage of British colonialism continues to be manifest in Tanganyika's political system. Certain comparisons between British and African control are compelling: the central position of a single political figure, political decision-making lost in hidden mazes and emerging from time to time as government edicts, the effective control over political life. In addition the continuation of much of the formal structure of government: Parliament, the provincial administration reconstructed as a regional administration, local government, etc., leave impressions of continuity.

These surface similarities should not be permitted to obscure the revolution in political organization that has occurred in just a few years. Most important is the fact that the politics are now determined by a local force and by events in Africa, not by some external force. Second and unlike

---

[121] *Tanganyika Standard,* October 12, 14, 15, 1963.

British times, the government has a broad and popular base, even if this is somewhat unstable. Third, while political decision-making rested with the governor and civil service in British times, its location in present-day Tanganyika is more difficult to locate. It is not possible to state definitively that President Nyerere "controls" political decision-making or that there is a clique or a cabal within TANU that does. While the party interpenetrates and permeates the network of institutions that have developed, this does not automatically mean any single agency within TANU has authoritarian control. It is possible to have a focal-institutional society without totalitarian domination, if only because the institutional network is only incipiently developed.

Thus, Tanganyika's political system is neither fully developed nor well institutionalized. Nor have tendencies toward focalization continued unabated since the events in Zanzibar in January 1964. These events, culminating in the creation of a United Republic of Tanzania, created serious problems of integrating Zanzibar into the newly merged nation. This appears to have provided a considerable amount of "political indigestion" for the Tanganyikans, and problems involved with Zanzibar have caught them up for the moment.

But even more important than specific political events, it is the low degree of institutionalization of modern institutions that will continue to create problems. The cold, hard fact is that the formal structure of government inherited from the British is not yet institutionalized, in the sociological sense, in the population. Most of the people do not understand the network of roles in the modern political system, nor do they understand how to interact with that system. The takeover of a complex administrative structure by a tiny elite of Africans who understand what is going on does not mean that the overwhelming bulk of the population grasp the meaning of this structure. Until the population can be drawn into regular interaction with the political structure and understand it normatively, the stability of the political system remains in some jeopardy.

The low degree of institutionalization exacerbates the problems of any modernizing society; but problems are also intensified by the variety of tendencies leading toward pluralism and the development of conflict of interests that occur with modernization. This has been seen in the conflict between the unions and TANU. The conflict was "resolved' in effect by a takeover; it is unlikely, however, that this administrative solution has eliminated the basic forces giving rise to the dispute.

And other conflicts also exist. It is possible, for example, to see serious strains developing between the educated intellectuals and many of the uneducated party leaders; between Africans in the civil service, demanding to be upgraded into positions still held by expatriates, and ministers, responding to a general restraining influence exercised by Mr. Nyerere; between the new returnees, educated abroad and coming back to Tanganyika, and the older generation that was moved up rapidly in the civil service in response to cries for Africanization. There are also incipient conflicts between Africans desiring to take over the entrepreneurial roles held largely by the Asians and the TANU government which wishes to channel the bulk of economic development into cooperatives and other organizational forms more amenable to control.

The mutiny of the army, in January 1964, was symptomatic of many of these strains; it was more dramatic because it showed what a handful of men with rifles could do. The mutiny was open and above board; many of the other strains that have been mentioned are buried within the privacy of the party apparatus and hidden in the private actions of individuals. All too frequently, the tendency for political leaders in Tanganyika (as elsewhere) has been to eliminate criticism and opposition by creating a façade of unity. The imprisonment of individuals, such as Tumbo, Saileni, the trade unionists and others, has produced a public silence in Tanganyika that could be interpreted as indicative of total national unity. However, the mutterings of civil servants heard privately in hotel corridors and elsewhere belie this unity.

It is impossible for any sympathetic observer of the struggle of Africa, initially for independence and now for dignity in the comity of nations and a better life for its peoples, not to feel compassion for the problems of its political leaders. Being relatively withdrawn from the realities of minute-by-minute decision-making, the observer can afford the luxury of "Monday morning quarterbacking." Political leaders are too caught up in events to have the same withdrawn and critical facility. Yet the detached outsider must recognize the dilemmas facing a new leadership, must understand the realities of attempting to deal with a population that does not yet have a full understanding of the complexities of modern society or the mechanics of modern government. The present historical and critical analysis has been undertaken in the hope that it may illuminate some of the dilemmas confronting a new nation as it seeks to effect a compromise between the needs for a centralized and unified government and the pluralistic demands of a modernizing society.

SELECTED BIBLIOGRAPHY

WORKS ON TANGANYIKA AND EAST AFRICA

Bates, Margaret L. "Tanganyika," in Gwendolen M. Carter (ed.), *African One-Party States*. Ithaca: Cornell University Press, 1962.

Datta, Ansu Kamar. *Tanganyika: A Government in a Plural Society*. The Hague: 1955.

Moffett, J. P. (ed.). *Handbook of Tanganyika*. Dar es Salaam: Government Printer, 1958.

Moffett, J. P. (ed.). *Tanganyika, A Review of Its Resources and Their Development*. Dar es Salaam: Government Printer, 1955.

Oliver, Roland. *The Missionary Factor in East Africa*. London: Longmans, Green and Company, 1952.

Oliver, Roland, and Gervase Mathew (eds.). *History of East Africa*. Oxford: The Clarendon Press, 1963.

Singleton, Carey B., Jr. *The Agricultural Economy of Tanganyika*. Washington, D.C.: Foreign Regional Analysis Division, Economic Research Service, U.S. Dept. of Agriculture, 1964.

Taylor, J. Clagett. *The Political Development of Tanganyika*. Stanford: Stanford University Press, 1963.

THE ZANZIBAR PERIOD

Coupland, Reginald. *East Africa and Its Invaders*. Oxford: Clarendon Press, 1939.

Hollingsworth, Lawrence W. *Zanzibar under the Foreign Office 1890–1913*. London: Macmillan, 1953.

THE GERMAN PERIOD

Bell, R. M. "The Maji-Maji Rebellion in the Liwale District," in *Tanganyika Notes and Records*, No. 28 (January 1950).

Lettow-Vorbeck, Paul von. *East African Campaigns*. New York: Robert Speller & Sons, 1957.

Müller, Fritz Ferdinand. *Deutschland—Zanzibar—Ostafrika*. Berlin: Rütten and Loenig, 1959.

Rodemann, H. William. *Tanganyika: 1890–1914—Selected Aspects of German Administration*. Unpublished Ph.D. dissertation. University of Chicago, 1961.

United Kingdom Foreign Office. *Tanganyika (German East Africa)*. Handbooks Prepared under the Direction of the Historical Section of the Foreign Office, No. 113, London: H.M.S.O., 1920.

THE BRITISH PERIOD

Cameron, Sir Donald. *My Tanganyika Experience and Some Nigeria*. London: Allen and Unwin, 1939.

Chidzero, B. T. G. *Tanganyika and International Trusteeship*. London: Oxford University Press, 1961.

Gregory, Robert G. *Sidney Webb and East Africa: Labour's Experiment with the Doctrine of Native Paramountcy, University of California Publications in History*, Vol. 72, Berkeley and Los Angeles: University of California Press, 1962.

Lord Hailey. *Native Administration in the British African Territories*. Part I, London: H.M.S.O., 1950.

Leubuscher, Charlotte. *Tanganyika Territory: A Study of Economic Policy under the Mandate*. London: Oxford University Press, 1944.

United Nations Trusteeship Council. *Report of the Visiting Mission to the Trust Territory of Tanganyika under British Administration.* T/218, 1948, T/1142, 1954, T/946, 1951.

Wood, Alan. *The Groundnut Affair.* London: The Bodley Head, 1950.

NATIONALISM AND INDEPENDENCE

Burke, Fred G. "Tanganyika: The Search for Ujamaa," in William H. Friedland and Carl G. Rosberg, Jr. (eds.), *African Socialism.* Stanford: Stanford University Press, 1964.

Glickman, Harvey. "One-Party System in Tanganyika," in *Annals of the American Academy of Political and Social Science,* CCCLVIII (March 1965).

Liebenow, J. Gus. "Tribalism, Traditionalism, Modernism in Chagga Local Government," *Journal of African Administration,* X (April 1958), 71–82.

Nyerere, Julius. "Ujamaa—Speech at TANU Conference on Socialism," in William Friedland and Carl Rosberg, Jr. (eds.), *African Socialism.* Stanford: Stanford University Press, 1964.

Nyerere, Julius. *Democracy and the Party System.* Dar es Salaam: Tanganyika Standard Ltd., n.d.

"A Survey of the Development of Local Government in the African Territories since 1947—Tanganyika," *Journal of African Administration,* IV, 2 (Supplement) (April 1952), 13.

Young, Roland, and Henry Fosbrooke. *Smoke in the Hills.* Evanston: Northwestern University Press, 1960.

For books and articles on labor and trade unions, see entries under "Tanganyika" in William Friedland, *Unions, Labor and Industrial Relations in Africa: An Annotated Bibliography.* Ithaca: Center for International Studies, Cornell University, 1965.

I am indebted to Dorothy Nelkin for research assistance. This chapter has also benefited from a critical reading by James Brain. All views expressed are, of course, those of the writer.

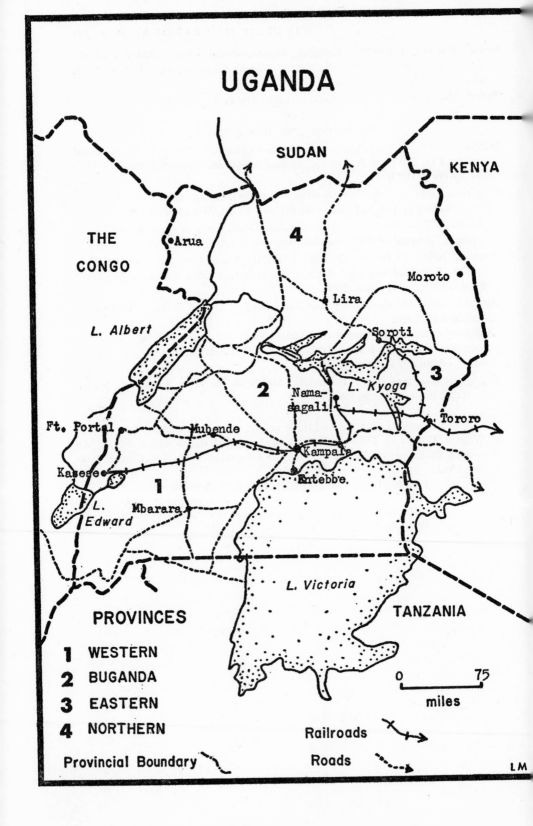

UGANDA

SUDAN

KENYA

THE
CONGO

•Arua

4

Moroto •

L. Albert

Lira•

Soroti•

2

Namasagali

L. Kyoga

3

Ft. Portal

Mubende

Kampala

Tororo

Kasese

Entebbe

1

L.
Edward

Mbarara

L. Victoria

TANZANIA

PROVINCES

1 WESTERN

2 BUGANDA

3 EASTERN

4 NORTHERN

Provincial Boundary

0   75
miles

Railroads

Roads

LM

7

Modernization in Uganda: The Struggle for Unity

George W. Shepherd, Jr.

UGANDA'S RISE TO NATIONHOOD offers an excellent example of a conflict between modern and traditional African social forces. Prof. Lloyd Fallers describes the implications of this clash in speaking of the Kingdom of Buganda: "She exemplifies a fascinating and intellectually challenging phenomenon, relatively rare in Africa: a society which has enthusiastically and successfully accepted many elements of modernization and has confined these within and adapted them to traditional culture and social structure."[1] The nature and direction of the nationalist movement has been determined by the struggle between modern and traditional forces, and the important political alignments after independence (1962) grew out of this conflict. National unity has been imperiled by this conflict, and the future success or failure of the young state of Uganda hinges on the extent of its resolution.[2]

In general, it can be said that modernization forces in Uganda have been centered in the new national government, where the prime minister, the majority party (the United Peoples Congress, known as the UPC), and the central bureaucracy possess a high level of initiative, growing prestige, and a definite capacity for action. Traditionalism, in the main, has been centered in the conservatives in the several rival kingdoms, the district and local councils, and particularly in the most populous province of Buganda, where Buganda separatism has long been an explosive political force. Traditionalism was given political impetus by the Kabaka Yekka movement. Further, the traditional-modern movement is formally represented in the constitutional structure of the society, as Uganda is one of the few federal

---

[1] Lloyd Fallers (ed.), *The King's Men* (New York: Oxford University Press, 1964), p. 3.

[2] This chapter was written before the crisis of 1966.

political systems in Africa. However, this interpretation must not be carried too far, as forces of modernization and tradition have penetrated both the central and regional governments. The conflict, therefore, takes place on many fronts, as will be demonstrated. The important question concerns the nature of the origins of these contending forces, and whether or not they can —allowing for some diversity—coexist within a country like Uganda.

This analysis uses the concepts of modernization and traditionalism in the framework of the widely employed functional method, while avoiding technical terminology. Functionalism emphasizes the role of individuals and the interests of groups as contrasted with the description of a formal structure. From this standpoint, traditionalism has been well defined by Talcott Parsons and his followers[3] as a social system in which individuals and groups behave according to their "ascribed" status, caste, and kinship positions. A modernizing society is one in which behavior is increasingly determined by "achievement" or the ability to fill new needs and roles. Modernization is egalitarian, breaking down the hierarchy of status in tribal mores, and it requires services to be performed by the capable and the educated. The conflict that arises is symbolized by the replacement of traditional hereditary chiefs by "modernized," educated servants of common origin.

The major stimulant to modernization is technical innovation and the gradual spreading of new desires and needs in a widening circle of the population. These desires and needs are functionally met by a reorganization of the political and economic structure. The process of change may be gradual and peaceful, or it may result in revolutionary upheaval. Once the process of change begins, it cannot be stopped; and the essential issue for every awakening society similar to Uganda is, Can unity and a new national consensus be built within the modern framework without separatist violence, civil war, and chaos?

Modernization in the African context may be dissected as follows. It is characterized by three basic stages of development with various gradations in between: (1) the traditional stage, (2) the Western-modern stage, and (3) the African-modern stage.[4] Steps toward the second stage are precipitated by the introduction of Western values and technological advances. Under the leadership of a Westernized elite, an independence movement is formed, and a new national consensus that transcends traditional loyalties is propagated. In the third stage, the desire to imitate Western values and institutions is replaced gradually by a neo-traditionalism that attempts to mobilize the emotional force of indigenous values and symbols while retaining the

---

[3] See Talcott Parsons, *Essays in Sociological Theory* (revised ed.; Glencoe: Free Press, 1958), pp. 386–439.

[4] This is a modification of my conception of the evolution of nationalism presented in *The Politics of African Nationalism* (New York: Frederick A. Praeger, 1962), p. 244.

egalitarian and functionally specific character of Western institutions. This is the ideological phase of development, and two basic patterns emerge within it—the plural pattern and the mobilizational pattern (with variations of emphasis according to conditions). The plural pattern is less centralistic and authoritarian than the mobilizational. While both appeal to neo-traditionalist sentiment, the application of what are called "African values" and "indigenous institutions" is doctrinaire in the case of the mobilizational pattern and pragmatic under the plural pattern.

Uganda is nearing the end of the second and approaching the third stage of African modernism, while retaining extensive pockets of traditionalism in both the more remote areas and—more importantly—in the Buganda kingdom. Uganda's lack of a national modernizing consensus has created a variegated political pattern giving rise to a great deal of internal stress. This is in contrast to a neighboring country like Tanzania, where traditionalism has had less power and modernization has proceeded more rapidly.

HISTORICAL SETTING

There was no nation of Uganda prior to the effective British establishment of the Protectorate under the agreements of 1895 and 1900. However, early explorers such as Speke, Baker, and Stanley were much impressed with the centralized authority systems of the Baganda and the Banyoro, who had created highly specialized and powerful social systems.[5] In particular, Buganda was admired by the British for its extensive communication systems, efficient government administration, and considerable agricultural development. According to European standards of the day, these kingdoms were "primitive," but they were not physically weak. If they had not been at war with one another and internally divided between rival tribal and religious factions, they would not have been easily subjugated by invading European interests.

In addition to these two large kingdoms, there were several smaller kingdoms and many less-centralized tribes. These groupings now make up the new nation of Uganda with 7,190,000 people, as of 1963. Most important among the smaller kingdoms were Toro and Ankole, both tributary states to Bunyoro. To the east of Buganda, Busoga had become, by the early nineteenth century, a tributary state to Buganda. Other tribal groupings, important to distinguish from the kingdoms because of their different social organization, are the Karagwe and Madi in the west and the Lango, Teso, Acholi, and Karamoja in the east.

Thus over a period of thirty years, many disparate groups were pulled

---

[5] See Kenneth Ingham, *The Making of Modern Uganda* (London: Allen and Unwin, 1958), pp. 16–17.

together into a colonial crucible from which emerged a nation roughly the size of Britain.[6] One of the broadest and most important differences between these groups, and one the subject of much social scientific interest, was (in the terminology of Fortes and Evans-Pritchard) the "centralized" versus the "decentralized" social systems.[7] The cohesive and controlling force among the tribal groups such as the Lango was the clan and lineage system. In these societies, authority was pyramided among clan and lineage heads, and virtually no centralized authority existed to direct the autonomous units of the tribe. This contrasted with the perpendicular authority system of the kingdoms—particularly Buganda—which did not even possess a royal clan and, therefore, had a system of personalized and centralized leadership. The difficulties of adapting the two different systems to the requirements of modernization have been well set forth in the studies of Lloyd Fallers, David Apter, Fred G. Burke, and Audrey Isabel Richards. Conclusions vary as to which of the two is the more adaptable to modern systems, but there is agreement that various methods and rates of adaption emerge and conflict with one another, creating political differences in the modern Uganda political arena.[8]

Ancient rivalries between kingdoms, especially those that revolve around the ascendency of Buganda, are more significant in current politics than traditional social and structural differences. Buganda was at one time a part of the Bunyoro Empire; but in the eighteenth century it split off and began a period of rapid imperialist expansion. This expansion was immediately successful in the east against the Basoga; but in the west, an almost continuous state of war existed between the Banyoro and the Baganda, with Buganda achieving some control in Ankole. When the British and the Egyptians arrived on the scene in the nineteenth century, they found the two kingdoms consolidated under powerful rulers engaged in a widening conflict.[9]

A third major influence on the Uganda political system was the influence of alien Moslems and Christians. This religious factor has contributed to political rivalries for more than half a century. Such rulers as Kabaka Mutesa I, Mwanga of Buganda, and Kabareka of Bunyoro sought to play a subtle game of politics, using the Moslems and Christians (Protestant and Catholic)

---

6 From 1901 to 1926, the Uganda Protectorate was roughly halved in size by concessions to Kenya and the Anglo-Egyptian Sudan. See Zoe A. Marsh and G. W. Kingsnorth, *An Introduction to the History of East Africa* (2nd ed.; Cambridge: Cambridge University Press, 1961), p. 211.

7 Meyer Fortes and E. E. Evans-Pritchard, *African Political Systems* (London: Oxford University Press, 1949), p. 5.

8 There are twenty-one major ethnic groups in Uganda.

9 Ingham, *op. cit.*, p. 19.

against each other. But as these faiths gathered support from among Ugandans, this new force was utilized against the *kabakas* (the kings of Buganda) by their rivals. The Church of England played a critical role in the British decision to intervene with force in Buganda and establish the Protectorate.[10] While the Protestants thus gained a dominant political position, they also created the opportunity for Catholicism and Islam to flourish and spread throughout the Protectorate. Serious religious strife, leading occasionally to civil war, characterized the early years of the Uganda Protectorate. On a smaller scale, these struggles were reflective of the same bitter conflicts that beset Europe during the Reformation. Some men who participated as young warriors in these civil wars are alive today and attest to the animosity that still grows from the fire of past religious conflict.

BUGANDA'S PREDOMINANCE

Buganda would probably have remained simply one among many of the stronger kingdoms, rather than the ascendent one, had it not been for the alliance formed between the British and the Baganda. The British selected the Baganda as the major indigenous administrative force to assist them in the integration of the diverse tribal groups of Uganda. They elected this course of action for its Machiavellian, divisive results and also because such men as Captain F. D. Lugard and Sir Harry Johnston had a genuine respect for the Baganda's administrative ability. Moreover, they thought that the comparatively secular character of Buganda life offered the prospect of greater adaptation to Western culture. The *kabaka,* for example, was not regarded as a god by his followers, but rather as a secular autocrat. This institution resembled somewhat the European tradition, and it was thought, therefore, that the *kabaka* and his government would be a more pliable instrument—in comparison to the other kingdoms—for the infusion of Western values. Thus, the British and Baganda military forces joined in the conquest of Bunyoro, Busoga, and other areas. In districts where the British found that they could not rely on local traditional leadership, they appointed Baganda to chieftainships and new administrative posts. This policy cut into traditional patterns of leadership selection from royal clans and kinship systems and created considerable resentment. The Baganda, backed by British arms, were only too willing to extend their authority to new areas.

Utilizing Baganda and Sudanese soldiers, able British officers such as Colonel Henry Edward Colville and Major Owens extended the authority of the emerging Protectorate. First, protracted war was carried on against the powerful Kabaka of Bunyoro, Kabareka, who—though defeated in open battles—carried on guerrilla warfare resistance over a wide area. Buganda

---

10 The Church Missionary Society raised enough money to enable the Imperial British East Africa Company and its representative, Lord Lugard, to stay in Uganda after the Company had decided to withdraw.

chiefs then demanded all of Bunyoro, claiming it as a former vassal state. After careful consideration, the British decided these claims were not fully substantiated, but they permitted Buganda to assimilate a portion of Bunyoro (eight counties). On assuming administration of the territory, Buganda chiefs attempted to compel the people to remain as laborers, thereby inciting a struggle that broke the peace periodically up through the time of independence. Still a major issue today, this conflict is known as "the lost counties dispute."

Baganda then succeeded in incorporating the kingdom of Koki as a (saza) and attained great influence in Busoga, Ancholi, Lango, and Teso. Particularly significant was the conquest of Lango and Teso by a Kiganda officer, Semei Kakunguru. Kakunguru established a line of forts and set up a Baganda-style administration in these regions. Further, Baganda were established as chiefs at the Saza, Gombolola, and Miruka levels.

Despite their alliance, the Baganda were not docile tools of the British. At times, they revolted under the leadership of their erratic king, Kabaka Mwanga. Mwanga, a master of intrigue, was finally deposed by a group of his own chiefs acting in cooperation with the Protectorate government in 1897. His fall initiated a period of complete Baganda-British cooperation.

A further indication of the primacy of Buganda under British rule was the nature of the relationship established between the Kabaka's government of Buganda and the Protectorate government. While Buganda was officially regarded as a province under British administration, complete with a provincial British administrator, relations were much more direct between Buganda and the Protectorate government than, for example, in Bunyoro, where the *mukama* was forced to deal through a Western Province commissioner, whose jurisdiction included Toro and Ankoli as well. This situation was partly geographical in origin since the Protectorate government was based in Buganda at Entebbe. In practice, however, the Protectorate governors from Sir Harry Johnston on gave precedence to the *kabaka* of Buganda.[11]

This deference to the *kabaka* pointed up one of the early major errors of the Protectorate, the failure to establish a territorial council to bring together the traditional chiefs as well as newly appointed heads of provinces. British colonial administration generally favored separatist development and thus hindered the emergence of a sense of national unity. The reason for the slow development of a national consciousness in Uganda, however, lies more in the British reliance on the Baganda for support than in a deliberate "divide and rule" policy.

A major innovation in Uganda, and indeed in Africa, was the Land Free-

---

[11] Johnston conceded the title of "Highness" to the Kabaka as a symbol of his importance, placing him on the same level of importance as the Sultan of Zanzibar. See D. Anthony Low and R. Cranford Pratt, *Buganda and British Overrule, 1900–1955* (London: Oxford University Press, 1960), p. 82.

hold Program instituted by the first governor of Uganda, Sir Harry Johnston. This program was a part of the famous Protectorate Agreement. The program grew directly out of the British-Buganda alliance and had far-reaching consequences on the sociopolitical structure of Buganda specifically and the politics of Uganda in general.

As a reward to the Baganda chiefs and as an incentive to further the emergence of a loyal and industrious middle class, the Protectorate government inaugurated the allocation of 9,000 square miles of Buganda land as freehold. Previously, all land was regarded as belonging to the *kabaka,* and considerable portions were directly under the administration of clan heads, known as *bataka.* The freehold innovation shifted land control from the *kabaka* and the *bataka* to a second group of chiefs. As the redistribution of the land was put in the hands of the *lukiko*—the governing council of Buganda, which was composed of traditional chiefs—the allocation went in favor of those chiefs and families represented therein.

At the time of the redistribution, a regency existed for the infant Kabaka Daudi Chwa. The three regents received between forty-five and sixty square miles each. Twenty chiefs were granted twelve square miles or more, and 150 became entitled to between eight and twelve square miles. Many were added to the original 1,000 specified allottees, but at the same time many others who considered themselves eligible—and who had traditional authority—were given nothing.[12] Large domains were, of course, reserved for the *kabaka,* and the Protectorate government retained certain forest and other areas as Crown Land. This system of freehold land was not instituted on any significant scale elsewhere in the protectorate, although the *mukama* of Bunyoro did receive some freehold as a part of land reorganization in his district.

Of all steps taken by the British administration during its entire period of rule, the freehold innovation in Buganda has had the most important impact on African political and social development. With this act, the Buganda political system was transformed from an autocracy dominated by the central authority of the *kabaka* into an oligarchy of chiefs.[13] While the *kabaka* retained his power of appointment and the symbols of rule, he lost his control of the land in this fast-developing agricultural country where land *was* wealth. The chiefs under the Regency were not slow in consolidating their new power, centered in the legislative branch, the *lukiko.* The large landholders became the real rulers of the country. Such men as Sir Apolo Kagwa and Stanislaus Magwanya served as early prime ministers and ran the

---

[12] David Apter, *The Political Kingdom in Uganda* (London: Oxford University Press, 1960), pp. 123–124.

[13] C. C. Wrigley states: "The old structure of a pyramidal hierarchy culminating in the Kabaka was retained intact, but in reality the government was now a corporate oligarchy which culminated in the collective leadership of a small group of chiefs." "The Changing Economic Structure of Buganda," in Fallers, *op. cit.,* p. 26.

new Baganda bureaucracy. Their influence extended far beyond the boundaries of their own province. This land program sowed the seeds of discontent among those who had not shared in these spoils or who found their previous power challenged.

By way of summary, the historical bases of Buganda separatism can be found in the ancient rivalries between the kingdoms and tribes of Uganda. This situation was only temporarily resolved by Buganda's predominance under the British Protectorate. With the freehold land program in Buganda, the Protectorate transformed what might have been a highly integrative, progressive political force of Ganda leadership into a semi-feudal system of privilege. This had the paradoxical result of the most advanced area of the country becoming a stronghold of traditionalism in politics, set against the modernizing centralizing forces growing up in the surrounding provinces.

MODERNIZATION FORCES

Modernization, as had been previously observed, is fundamentally concerned with a change in value orientation and consequently with institutional change. The beginning of modernization in Uganda predates European influences and really begins with the influence of Moslem traders seeking slaves and ivory. These traders came up from the east coast and down from the Sudan (then the Equatorial Province of Egypt). Islam contained new religious concepts, among them a latent egalitarian idea of the brotherhood of man, as well as functionally specific roles in production and trade. When the British arrived, they found that Buganda was already a well-organized, agriculturally productive trading society, exchanging ivory and slaves for cotton goods, brass wire, and cowrie shells. Strategically located, Buganda controlled most of the market northwest, north, and east of its own territory.[14]

However, the alien entry into East Africa in the late nineteenth century and European colonization of the area introduced massive and rapid social change. For example, Christianity presented a new view of equality and dignity of the individual. The new religion found fertile soil for growth in Uganda, especially in Buganda. The Protectorate government introduced a new legal system protecting the rights of the person and defining the responsibilities of ruling authorities in new and non-traditional ways. For example, life could not be taken capriciously and arbitrarily by despotic monarchs as had been the case so often in the past. But of all the instruments of modernization, the educational system and the new methods of production in agriculture stand out as most important.

During the early years of the Protectorate, education was the primary

---

[14] C. C. Wrigley, *Buganda: An Outline of Economic History* (London: Reprint Series No. 1, Institute of Commonwealth Studies, University of London, 1962), p. 74.

responsibility of the missionaries. The relatively extensive amount and high quality of education in Uganda grew out of the success of the missionaries. These early churchmen gained many followers and rapidly converted them not only to Christianity, but also to the pursuit of education. Vigorous competition between Catholics and Protestants in the building of schools probably had the effect of spreading education more widely in Uganda than would have been the case had a single sect dominated the mission field. In the development of good secondary schools for Africans, Uganda far surpassed her East African neighbors. In 1922, with the founding of Makerere College, Uganda became the site of an institution that grew into the first East African University College.

Several studies have shown that this system created an "educated elite" and that this elite has formed the leadership for the new political, economic, and educational institutions of modern development. Apter demonstrates that, by the 1950's, the leadership in the Buganda bureaucracy and the *lukiko* was drawn from the graduates of secondary and junior secondary schools and, in particular, from King's College Budo (Protestant), St. Mary's (Catholic), and Makerere College. Generally, these leaders were landowners, especially the *saza* chiefs.[15]

In Buganda the traditional elite did not oppose education, but accepted it very quickly. Most of the Buganda landowners were converts to Christianity and, therefore, to mission education. Thus, most of the younger generation of the Westernized elite in Buganda tend to have traditionalist, landowning ties. The *bakopi* (peasants) also took to education easily, but were less able to educate their offspring in the best schools. This is one example of the fusion of modernization and traditionalism in Buganda that has produced the dominant conservative temperament among Buganda's "establishment."

In other parts of the Protectorate a stronger clash developed between education and traditionalism. Fred G. Burke points out how considerable resistance developed in Bunyoro to the appointment of younger educated men to chieftainships and positions of responsibility in the bureaucracy.[16] In Bunyoro, not only was Christianity weaker, but stronger traditions concerning lineage and ethnic authority existed. Under such situations, those persons outside the "establishment" have tended to become the best educated. They are, therefore, in a strong position to claim political responsibility under a modernizing system. Thus, while the central political leadership in Uganda is predominantly Christian, it is drawn more from the middle class and peasants than from the aristocratic leadership of Buganda.

Powerful forces of social change were introduced by the British Protec-

---

[15] David Apter, *op. cit.*, p. 369.

[16] Fred G. Burke, *Local Government and Politics in Uganda* (Syracuse: Syracuse University Press, 1964), p. 113.

torate with the transformation of subsistence agriculture into a cash-crop economy. In Uganda's fertile soil and humid climate, cotton very quickly proved to be a suitable crop for wide development. Later, coffee became successful and surpassed cotton as the major cash crop. The energetic Baganda were the first to plant cotton on an extensive scale, and the commercialization of Buganda forged far ahead of the other areas of Uganda. Kampala soon emerged as the major processing and trading center. However, by 1914, the center of cotton production moved to the Eastern Province. As the landowning class was easily content with its income from rents, the freehold system did not prove to be the incentive its proponents had expected. Much of the actual labor was performed by immigrant labor from the East and the North, and this labor grew gradually more expensive. By the 1950's, coffee proved to be a more lucrative and less laborious source of income for the Baganda. The economist C. C. Wrigley commented on this rather sluggish adaptation to modern production:

> Though habits of deference died hard, the Ganda masses were incomparably freer under the new dispensation than under the old—freer in fact than the people of the surrounding tribes, some of which had had a much more "democratic" social structure but now enjoyed a much more restricted range of economic opportunities. And whatever its ultimate effects, their freedom meant that in the short run the productive impulse tended to slacken, since the multiplication of wants proceeded more sluggishly among the masses than among their leaders, and since the hoe-cultivation of cotton is a laborious and boring process. Life can be easy in a fertile country under the British peace, and the Ganda on the whole took it easily once the first excitements of contact with civilization had died down. For their part, the revolutionary leaders of the 1890's had become a satisfied, even a conservative class. In the main, they treated their estates not as a field for productive enterprise, but as a routine source of tribute income or as a capital asset which could at need be converted directly into cash (*op. cit.*, p. 77).

The over-all impact of these new production changes brought (1) shifts in population and (2) changes in occupation and status with profound ultimate effects on the social structure and political system. Foreign immigration was very significant. With the coming of the railway to transport crops, Indians from other parts of East Africa entered Uganda in large numbers. This distinctive group, with their capacity for commercial organization, technical skill, and available capital soon monopolized the exchange of goods, the minor processing industries, such as the ginning of cotton; and external trade. A number of Europeans, mostly English, established themselves in manufacturing and finance as well as in the processing of agricultural goods and the export trade. However, both of these foreign groups were excluded from large-scale farming enterprises by the land policy of the government. Uganda's colonial administration never permitted the emergence of a large, foreign, landowning class that gave such a different character to the economic and political system of Kenya. Deliberate limitation of foreign influx was one of the major achievements of the Protectorate government, since it prevented the growth of a serious settler problem. In part, this policy was undoubtedly a response to the very determined opposition of the Baganda and other ethnic groups to the alienation of their land for development by non-Africans. Any suggestion that this policy might be altered at any time led to severe political reactions in Uganda.[17] The small non-African commercial minority did, however, produce strains within Uganda's social structure. They brought with them a racial arrogance particularly distasteful to the African people who were prepared to accept the technical competence of non-Africans but did not view them as superior beings. In addition, a considerable amount of exploitation of the unsophisticated African took place. Members of the rising middle class who had attained education and technical competence found that this non-African minority was inclined to resort to the power of finance and the government to preserve its monopolistic privileges.[18] Bitterness arising from this experience has carried on into the period of independence and has continued to weaken the progressive influence the non-African minority has had on the modernization process. The contribution the expatriate has made in setting an example, training Africans, and providing numerous means for rapid economic growth is undeniable. Yet the relations between Africans and non-Africans would be much more productive and warmer today if the non-Africans had acted with greater humanity and foresight during the period when they held the predominant position in commercial enterprise and government.

An African commercial and professional class emerged very slowly in Uganda, as has been the case elsewhere in East and Central Africa. It is from this group that most of the leadership for modernization and political change must come. Its retardation in Uganda delayed independence and has greatly effected post-independence development. African lawyers were a significant group in West African countries twenty-five years before the first lawyers, such as Apolo Kironde and Davod Lobogo, returned to Uganda from study abroad. Very few successful African businessmen were to be found in Kampala prior to 1960. On the lowest rungs of the commercial ladder, there was a rash of African activity from the 1940's on, but much of this was inept and unsuccessful. The most conspicuous and successful middle class among Africans arose in the government bureaucracies of the Protectorate and in the regional and local administrations. The explanation lies in a number of coordinate circumstances. Predominance of non-Africans, particularly Indians, in those positions which Africans were qualified to pursue,

---

[17] The *kabaka* debacle of 1953 was a direct outgrowth of these fears.

[18] See my previous comments in *They Wait in Darkness* (New York: John Day, Inc., 1955), p. 303.

unquestionably hindered African commercial emergence. But equally important was the traditional distaste of the Baganda elite for commercial life. Their land incomes were sufficient to allow them to acquire the few luxuries of modern life they desired. Moreover, the modern educational system was not aimed primarily at technical and commercial training. The Church missions, especially the CMS, carried on the classical educational system of the upper classes of Europe and extolled the virtues of the country gentleman rather than the tradesman and entrepreneur.[19]

Somewhat surprisingly, the most dynamic forces for social and political change emerged among the peasantry, the small landholders, tenant farmers, and petty shopkeepers in the rural villages. Aligned with these groups were the clerks, teachers, and semi-entrepreneurial units, such as lorry drivers in the major centers. Katwe, a teeming slum area on the outskirts of Kampala containing a wide variety of illicit activities ranging from prostitution to underground political associations, became the center for the operation of these groups. Out of the struggle between rival factions within these groups—and the temporary alliances they formed with each other against the chiefs, the Indian and European businesses, and the Protectorate government—came the political and social organizations that created and now control modern Uganda.

PRE-INDEPENDENCE POLITICAL MOVEMENTS

The character of present-day political parties and the nature of Uganda's most basic political problems can be best understood by tracing the struggle and programs of these earlier movements.

Political parties in Uganda really begin with the spread of the world religions (Christianity and Islam) in the late nineteenth century. Religious allegiance became a primary base of interest integration. This attitude did not die out with the end of the civil wars. However, these religious factions were primarily parties of factions of rival chiefs who fought one another for political control in the *lukiko* and other legislative councils.[20] Mass movements and parties arose only after the strains caused by economic change had created popular discontent.

Land, the source of life and wealth in Uganda, became very early the key

---

19 Allan Rawick comments in "Makerere and Uganda's Elite," *Africa Today*, (December 1963), p. 11: "Makerere University students returned to the soil and became either farmers or chiefs. In more recent times there has been a shift to the professional field, which has held a key position for African advancement. However, the younger elite has acquired neither a class consciousness nor a class culture. In fact, the student is still linked to his tribal heritage in thought and speech, with a restricted and parochial outlook."

20 See D. Anthony Low, *Political Parties in Uganda, 1949–1962* (London: Commonwealth Papers No. 8, Institute of Commonwealth Studies, University of London, 1962), pp. 10–11.

political issue. The freehold land policy in Buganda not only created an oligarchy of chiefs, but also led to both a traditionalist and modernist opposition to the chiefs. The "modernist" opposition arose among the peasants (the *bakopi*), the tenant farmers, and the small landowners, and chiefs. Since land is relatively cheap and life is easy under Uganda's lush conditions, serious political difficulties might not have arisen had not a powerful traditionalist group also been opposed to the large landholders. This group, the *bataka,* was composed of the clan heads who held certain rights respecting disposal of clan lands and authority over burial grounds, as well as the adjudication of disputes. They also enjoyed the privilege of sending their sons to the *kabaka's* court as pages where they might gain positions of favor and privilege. The *bataka* were thus the Baganda aristocracy that provided the rulers and future *kabakas*. Further, they were the prime local authority for the settlement of disputes and the protectors of the rights of their members. The *bataka* viewed new chiefs and landowners as a major challenge to their authority. Apter describes well the political antagonism that ensued:

> This conflict, represented by the chiefs and the Bataka, was an old struggle which now took a new tact. With land settlement and political power backed up by British power, the chiefs appeared to have won the day and established themselves for all times as the dominant political force in Buganda. Meanwhile, the Bataka, aggrieved and angered by the consequences of the Agreement, sought to speak in the name of the peasantry, the Bakopi, or the ordinary man. The importance of the Bataka struggle was that it identified economic grievance with social status, or the lack of it, and paved the way for the formation of the first political and economic organizations of modern Buganda.[21]

It should be noted that under the new system some of the *bataka* did receive land. However, even those who received land were inclined to believe that the new system so challenged their position that they must oppose it.

The *kabaka* had the title of Sabataka, head of the clans. Although the *bataka* held their authority independently of the *kabaka,* they regarded him as their head. This fact is very important, as the antagonism of the *bataka* became directed at the new chiefs and not the *kabaka,* although he himself had become the principal landowner. Moreover, the rise of the oligarchial power of the chiefs had deprived the *kabaka* of the autocratic authority he once possessed. Thus, in the initial stages of the dispute, the interests of the *kabaka* and the *bataka* seemed to be parallel. In the later stages this was not to be the case, although the emotional grip of the *kabaka* on the loyalty of his subjects long delayed such a realization.

This was demonstrated with the first fully organized campaign of the *bataka* through the Bataka Association, led by the *mugema* and James Miti, a senior *mutaka* who had become a Buganda chief in Bunyoro. This associa-

---

[21] David Apter, *op. cit.,* p. 115.

tion petitioned the *kabaka* concerning (1) the return of *bataka* estates, (2) the recognition of clan institutions, and (3) the authority of the chiefs in the *lukiko*. On the latter point, the authority of the Prime Minister, Sir Apolo Kagwa, was specifically challenged. The Kabaka eventually sided with the Bataka Association in this dispute and offered a moderate compromise, but the *lukiko*—supported by the Protectorate government—rejected the *kabaka's* proposals.[22]

Thus the initial attempt of the Bataka Association was defeated by the combination of chiefs backed up by British power. The protest continued to grow, however, creating new and stronger movements of peasants and clan leaders. In the late 1930's, the Sons of Kintu organization was founded, based on a combination of the traditionalist *bataka* leaders and the very new peasant cooperative and trade-union associations. James Miti, the *bataka* leader, was now joined by the first important modernist political leader to emerge in Uganda, Ignatius Musazi. Musazi was a son of a landowner and former chief, but he was educated at Budo College and in England. He was interested initially in peasant cooperative organization. Later his attention was to turn to the formation of a Uganda nationalist political movement. The Sons of Kintu, together with the Baganda Cooperative Association and a loosely organized Lorry Drivers Association, again presented a petition to the *kabaka* for land reorganization. This time, they added the more modern request for popular elections in the *lukiko*. Over a period of years, a protracted debate ensued in which the Sons of Kintu won some support in the *lukiko* but not with the young *kabaka*, Mutesa II. When the tone of the protest grew too strident, Musazi and other leaders were jailed for a short period. On Musazi's release in 1945, the issue came to a head over a dispute concerning the acquisition of land for Makerere College. The Prime Minister was shot, serious rioting resulted, and the Protectorate government moved to restore order. The organizations of protest were once again banned. Some moderate reform in representation was introduced in the *lukiko*, but the status quo was generally maintained.

Inevitably the same coalition of forces under new organizations returned to the attack in 1949. The result was widespread rioting and bloodshed. The organizations of the protest, the Bataka party and the Uganda African Farmers Union, were again banned and the leaders sent into exile. By 1949, the demands of the protesting *bataka* and *bakopi* had shifted in emphasis from issues of land discontent to economic grievances concerning the price of cotton and marketing facilities. The *kabaka* continued to ignore the grievances of these people, in part for lack of sympathy, but mainly because the matters they raised, such as the price of cotton, were beyond his control.

This protest movement had been, in the main, provincial in extent, traditional in motivation, and politically unsophisticated. But by the 1950's, Musazi had been to England and was receiving tactical advice elsewhere in

---

[22] *Ibid.*, pp. 147–149.

Africa. Musazi therefore undertook a major shift in tactics and launched the first genuine nationalist movement in Uganda, the Federation of Partnerships of Uganda African Farmers. This organization was modernist in orientation and aimed at improving marketing conditions for the farmer's cotton and coffee. While the center of the organization was in Katwe in Buganda, it drew wide support from the Eastern and Western provinces, with very active branches in Acholi, Lango, and Busoga.[23] Musazi severed most of his connections with the Bataka movements and directed the pressures of the new organization on the Protectorate government. Fortunately this activity coincided with the arrival on the scene of Uganda's most enlightened colonial governor, Sir Andrew Cohen, who took office in 1952. During Sir Andrew's administration, a considerable amount of reform of the marketing conditions and political system, especially of the central government, was introduced.

Despite all reforms, Musazi's economic enterprises failed completely, but others were able to take advantage of the changes he had suggested, especially in the coffee-marketing sector. The veteran spokesman of the *bakopi* then turned directly to politics. In 1952, Musazi launched the Uganda National Congress. The UNC is the parent organization of the now-governing Uganda Peoples Congress (and several other less-successful political parties). Much of the leadership and early following of the UNC came from Musazi's old Federation of Partnerships, and the new group quickly attracted to its ranks younger, educated professional men, such as Apolo Kironde, Abu Mayanja, Godfrey Benaisa, and Dr. Muwazi. Prime Minister Milton Obote, on his return from Kenya, began his career as a branch leader of the UNC in Lango.

The failure of the Uganda African Congress to lead Uganda to independence cannot be attributed so much to faulty leadership as to a curious combination of circumstances that led to a resurgence of Buganda separatism. This separatism divided the Congress' Baganda leadership and antagonized the non-Baganda in the movement. The Congress lost its initiative, and its leaders were plunged into confusion.

Intimation by the British Colonial Office in 1953 that it might consider an East African Federation aroused the latent anti-white settler feeling in Buganda. The *lukiko* presented the Protectorate government with a demand for separate independence for Buganda. A very complicated series of negotiations took place, ending in the forced exile of the *kabaka*.[24] This immediately aroused all the traditional ties of sentiment in Buganda for their king. Chiefs, *bakopi, bataka,* and the Baganda within the UNC swept together in a remarkable and unanimous outburst of loyalty. Although Musazi and many of his Baganda associates had long been opposed to Baganda separatism, they found it impossible to stand against the tides of passion sweeping the country. The chiefs took full advantage of this situation and whipped up the

---

[23] The author was associated in an advisory role for two years with this organization.

[24] See Great Britain, *Uganda Protectorate*, Cmnd. 9028, 1953, "Withdrawal of Recognition from Kabaka Mutesa II of Buganda 1953–1954."

pro-*kabaka* sentiment. Events that led to an early return of the *kabaka* played completely into the chiefs' hands, and out of resurgent traditionalism emerged the present neo-traditionalist mass movement headed by the chiefs of the *lukiko* which stands primarily for Baganda separatism.[25]

Non-Baganda nationalist leadership found it impossible to accept Baganda separatism within their concept of a united Uganda and therefore split off from the UNC. The consequences for Uganda nationalism were severe. Most of the more able leadership was lost in the reedy marshes of Kabaka Yekka (or "*kabaka* only," the new party of Buganda separatism) sentiment for several years and the non-Baganda were set against Baganda, reviving the ancient hostilities of the kingdoms of the past. These events set back Uganda's progress toward self-government by at least two years, and the division of Uganda into Baganda and non-Baganda political parties became the most difficult issue of independence.

POLITICS OF TRANSITION

Several important political groups emerged from the break-up of the UNC and aided in the extension of self-rule and the transition to independence. Not all of these can be mentioned, but among the most important was the United Congress party. The UCP was led by a number of "Young Turks," younger professional men such as Godfrey Benaisa, Erisa Kironde, Joseph Zake, Dr. Muwazi, and David Lobogo, who were dissatisfied with the lack of ideology and direction in the UNC. These young intellectuals drafted an intelligent program for independence; but they had no following among the *bakopi*, and they failed to gain national representation, although Muwazi won a seat in the *lukiko*. David Lobogo of Busoga became President General, but the UCP did not attempt to oppose the *kabaka* on an all-Uganda program and failed to gain any following in other provinces. Nevertheless, this group constituted an important group of Baganda leaders who were sufficiently modernized to be skeptical of the traditionalism of the Baganda chiefs and therefore quick to join forces with Milton Obote and the UCP after its formation in 1959.

The Democratic party was far more successful than the UCP and remained as one of the most important post-independence political parties. Its resilience was partially explained by the confessional charatcer of its origin, although this has changed substantially through the years. An important group of Catholic leaders created the party in 1956 with a program opposed to Buganda separatism and aimed at the achievement of an independent, united Uganda. Its first president was Matayo Mugwanya, who was then the leader of the Catholic group within the *lukiko*. A significant group of politically active *bakopi* and *bataka* who were dissatisfied with Masazi's

---

[25] As late as 1961, the *lukiko* passed a resolution calling for Buganda independence.

leadership supported the Democratic party.[26] This economic and traditional base enabled the Catholic leaders to form a significant anti-chiefs party in Buganda. Moreover, the confessional link enabled the Democratic party to win an important following in other provinces, thereby emerging as the first all-Uganda political force since the collapse of the UNC. The Democratic party provided a link between Buganda and the rest of Uganda during a very critical phase of transition to self-rule. In the first country-wide elections to the Uganda Legislative Council, in 1958, the Democratic party won only one seat. But in the 1961 elections, it won a majority of the seats, and its leader, Benedicto Kiwanuka, became Leader of Government Business. The Democrats were clearly a minority party at the time, yet they were able to take advantage of the attempt of the Baganda chiefs to boycott the elections. Only a few thousand Baganda registered for the elections in the face of the *kabaka's* opposition, and these were Democratic party supporters. Therefore, the Democrats took twenty seats in Buganda with little opposition. These, combined with the twenty-three seats they won in other provinces, topped the UPC's thirty-four. The effect of this was to force Buganda into the constitutional talks in London in 1961 where the basic framework of the new constitution was hammered out.

The Uganda Peoples Congress emerged in 1959 out of a complex merger between a discontented remnant group of Musazi's Uganda National Congress and an alliance of the legislative faction led by Milton Obote (an articulate Lango legislative representative) with the non-Baganda Uganda Peoples Union. The ostensible issue that produced the new group was the status of a United Congress party Foreign Mission in Cairo; the real reason was the confusion of the Baganda leadership and their inability to accept the necessity of a centralized united Uganda. Following the 1958 elections, a number of non-Buganda representatives in the Legislative Council had disaffiliated from the United Congress party and formed the Uganda Peoples Union. Obote was able to bring this group together with his wing of the old UNC and established the UPC. Thus the UPC was initially a non-Buganda movement and aroused great alarm among the chiefs of Buganda concerning their future in a united Uganda. However, a number of the "Young Turks" among the Baganda, such as Godfrey Binaisa and Joseph Zake, soon threw in their lot with Obote and were joined by an increasing number of modern Baganda who found the courage to break with the neo-traditionalists. This was particularly important since the UPC became the largest party in the 1961 elections. Its leader, Obote, became the first Prime Minister of Uganda.

Kabaka Yekka began first as a popular movement and only later transformed itself into what could be properly called a political party. It was the

---

26 This group was centered in Masaka, a stronghold of Catholicism. Some authorities dispute the confessional character of this party, but both Apter and Low agree that, though it was not restricted to Catholics, its initial leadership was comprised overwhelmingly of this group.

last of the pre-independence parties to be formed and was set up by the Baganda chiefs to contest the 1962 elections in Buganda. The chiefs were very bitter over the representation of Baganda in the Central Legislature by the Democratic party. They succeeded in forcing the London Constitutional Conference to adopt a unique form of representation for Buganda wherein the *lukiko* might determine whether (1) to appoint the representatives to the Central Legislature or (2) to have them elected at large. The UPC supported the Buganda request, and it was adopted. Thus, the *lukiko* retained control of the Assembly representatives in Buganda, and the Kabaka Yekka swept the February 1962 elections to the *lukiko* (sixty-five Kabaka Yekka to three Democrats), with the cry that the Democratic party wished to destroy the Kabakaship.

The 1962 National Assembly was composed of twenty-two Democrats, twenty-one Kabaka Yekka, and thirty-seven UPC. Since the Democratic party was the chief opponent of both the UPC and the Kabaka Yekka, it was only natural that a coalition should be formed between the latter two in order to create the first independence government of Uganda. Nevertheless, this was a very uneasy alliance of neo-traditionalists and modernists and probably would not have worked well at all if the Kabaka Yekka had not sent to the Assembly several younger, modernist types, such as Joseph Zake, who became a cabinet member as Minister of Education. (Zake soon crossed the floor to UPC membership.) The coalition worked well enough for the transition to independence and had great significance in settling—temporarily—the issue of Buganda separatism, as the *kabaka* and his chiefs had come to accept the necessity of a unified central government for Uganda. Symbolic of this step was the election of the *kabaka* to the Presidency of Uganda in 1963. Prime Minister Obote successfully overcame the opposition of other traditional monarchs as he saw the necessity of conceding at least symbolic power to the Baganda. What remained to be settled was the extent to which the special interests of Buganda could be preserved within the new nation without destroying the delicate fabric of federal unity.

The final result of this maneuvering was that Uganda gained independence as a federation. At first only the status of the Buganda kingdom was defined, but soon four other kingdoms were granted similar recognition and autonomy of local government wtihin the federation.[27]

POLITICS OF INDEPENDENCE

The first two years of independence have shown a continuing struggle between the modernists, centered in the government, and the neo-traditionalist chiefs of Buganda, who have sought to align with other traditionalist interests, outside of Buganda. The initial coalition has gradually dissolved, and by mid-1964 a thorny *rapprochement* between Kabaka Yekka and the

---

[27] For details, see Fred G. Burke's *Local Government and Politics in Uganda,* op. cit.

Democratic party was in the making, since this was the only basis on which the opposition could hope to defeat the spreading power of the UPC.

One of the most serious disputes that the new government has handled with great skill is that of the "lost counties." Six counties claimed jointly by Bunyoro and Buganda were the subject of the dispute. A commission under the Protectorate government carefully investigated the conflicting claims and present loyalties of the residents of these counties. It concluded that four should remain with Buganda and two should go to Bunyoro, a decision at first unacceptable to both kingdoms. However, a compromise formula was found providing for temporary central government administration of the two counties awarded to Bunyoro, pending a referendum. The *kabaka* forced acceptance of this formula on his reluctant followers[28] and then attempted to ensure that the Baganda would win the referendum. Thousands of Baganda were offered land in these areas, and the *kabaka* personally directed a campaign of settlement. Much hostility and some fighting resulted from these activities, because the Banyoro chiefs resisted this Baganda invasion.[29]

The central government decided against a further delay on the "lost counties" referendum; and, in November 1964, residents of these two counties voted on whether to join Buganda or Busoga or to form a separate district.[30] By a substantial margin, they elected to leave Buganda and join Busoga, despite all the strenuous efforts of the *kabaka*'s government to produce a different vote. The actual results in Bugangadzi were 2,253 for Buganda and 3,275 for Busoga with 67 for separate status. In Buyaga, 1,289 voted for Buganda; whereas, 8,327 chose Busoga and 50 desired separate status.

The effect of this result on Buganda was to produce serious rioting and the downfall of the Michael Kintu government, which had failed to preserve Buganda's position. Both traditionalist groups and progressives were aroused to action against the ineffectual Kintu government, and, in the ensuing shuffle, a young progressive, Abu Mayanja-Nkanji, was appointed leader and *katikiro* (prime minister) of a new government that reflected the growing power of the elected members and educated young men within the *lukiko*. One of the side effects of this dispute benefiting Prime Minister Obote's party has been the crossing over to the UPC of the Democratic party representatives from Bunyoro, as it was felt that the Democratic party was moving toward an alignment with the Kabaka Yekka.

Other ethnic separatist and aggressive interests have plagued the new government. Karamojong tribesmen have undertaken extensive cattle raids on neighboring peoples. The Bamba and Bahonjo have agitated for separate administration by the central government. Thousands of Batusi refugees

---

28 *Reporter* (Nairobi), July 7, 1962, p. 11.

29 *Ibid.*, April 6, 1963, p. 13. Finance Minister of Buganda, Nelson Lebugwawo, pledged to lead the army "to fight to the last drop of blood" and similar hostile statements came from Bunyoro. *Ibid.*, May 12, 1963, p. 11.

30 See: *Uganda Argus*, November 6, 9, 1964, and January 2, 1965.

from Ruanda have strained facilities. All of these events have compelled the government to spend more on a stronger police force and army than was originally deemed necessary.

A general drift toward the strengthening of the position of the UPC appears to have taken place. In part, this is because rival groups find the central government the most useful arbitrator.[31] Another reason for UPC growth has been the extension of the power of the central administration. Local government has been modernized and centralized under the Local Administration Ordinance of 1962. Despite the heredity system, this has given the UPC control over appointments in local governments in most districts.[32] Thus, the UPC has not been slow to take advantage of opportunities to appoint its own supporters to office, thereby promoting the feeling among the ambitious non-UPC that they were "missing the bandwagon."[33] In Ankole, the Democratic party has collapsed and has been completely replaced by the UPC. With all these defections, the UPC became a majority party in the Assembly by the summer of 1963—without an election.

Even in Buganda, the pull of the UPC was strong among the Kabaka Yekka representatives in the Central Assembly. Several, such as Abu Myonja and E. Mk. Muliva, crossed over, and most of their twenty-one representatives sought permission to join the UPC. However, they were firmly told by Mengo authorities that this would be against party policy.[34] The alliance of the UPC and the Kabaka Yekka broke down completely by 1965. UPC officials opened an office in Katwe and put up candidates against the Kabaka Yekka in local Buganda elections. To date, they have not won any elections in Buganda, but they have shown considerable strength, especially in Kampala, where they have the support of organized labor.

At the top, the neo-traditionalist Kabaka Yekka has splintered with many modernists crossing over to the UPC. Its leadership has seen the Kabaka Yekka losing both its roles as the balancing force in the Assembly and as the rallying point of the Buganda tradition. Although the solid front of popular support for the *kabaka* and chiefs has held with surprising firmness, a large crack has opened with the revival of *bakopi* discontent in what is called "The Common Man Movement" or "Bawejere." Its attack on the chiefs is reminiscent of the Bataka party with a modern twist. Instead of requesting that the Milo land be returned to them, the Bawejere has called on the *lukiko* to see that the rents from these lands go into the Buganda treasury rather than the pockets of the chiefs.[35] The association is clearly

---

[31] The six members of the Toro Democratic party crossed over to the UPC. *Reporter* (Nairobi), June 15, 1963, p. 13.

[32] Fred G. Burke, *op. cit.,* p. 46.

[33] *Reporter* (Nairobi), June 15, 1963, p. 13.

[34] *Reporter* (Nairobi), June 22, 1963, p. 12.

[35] This movement is also vigorously for East African Federation in contrast to Kabaka Yekka opposition. See *Reporter* (Nairobi), January 26, 1963 and August 31, 1963.

pro-UPC, while using a militant socialist phraseology of slogans more familiar in West African politics than in Uganda. Although the organization won some sympathy from the elected members of the *lukiko,* the Kabaka Yekka government declared the movement subversive and arrested its leader, Eriyabu Lwebuga. However, he was soon released by the Acting Director of Public Prosecutions of the Central Government. This time the *bakopi* protest had the powerful support of the Uganda government, in comparison to the complicity of the Protectorate government with the chiefs in their suppression of Bataka protests. Old peasant protest leaders, such as Musazi, have broken with the Kabaka Yekka and are taking up the cause of the *bakopi* once again. Thus there are strong indications that a modernist, mass-based political movement is finally under way in Buganda. The task facing such a movement is to gather together the traditional grievances of the *bataka* and the modern discontent of the farmers in a challenge to the power of the chiefs and the *kabaka.* As Apter so well observed in speaking of the embers of the Bataka movement still smoldering in Ganda society, ". . . whichever political party serves to attract them in large number will have captured the popular movement in Buganda—a movement which has as its last stronghold rural populism" (*op. cit.,* p. 250).

There are indications that the Kabaka himself has seen the writing on the wall and is dissatisfied with the limited vision of the Kabaka Yekka leadership. As President of Uganda, he has a modernizing role and is in a strong position to be the catalytic agent, preserving Buganda regional authority while bringing it fully within the structure of the modern nation.[36]

Some leaders of the UPC have urged that the party move from the position of majority party to that of the single party, a direction taken in so many of the new African states.[37] This has happened elsewhere, not always because of conscious design of the party in power, but rather because the traditionalist groups in control of the opposition either became subversive in their activity (as in Ghana), or simply collapsed, leaving no basis for opposition (as in Tanzania). The opposition in Uganda is built primarily on traditionalism in Buganda and confessionalism on a broader basis. Although Uganda regionalism with historic roots might well be a solid base on which to build national opposition to the UPC, the reactionary self-interest of the chiefs cannot adequately lead such an opposition under the pressures of *bakopi* protest. In addition, religious differences are a rather shallow basis for political choices, and already the majority of the Democratic party sup-

---

[36] The events of 1966 show this to have been too generous an estimate of the compromising ability of Buganda separatism and UPC centralism. The suspension of the constitution by Obote, backed by the army, and the deposition of the *Kabaka* have plunged the country into a crisis of unity that will continue for some time.

[37] Milton Obote hinted at this in addressing a local rally in Lango early in 1964. The militant UPC youth wing is strongly in favor of such a move. But many UPC leaders are against it, especially those from Buganda who fear any such suggestion would arouse tribal sentiments against them.

porters do not vote for the party on these grounds. What other consistent principles distinguish the Democratic party from the UPC have yet to be demonstrated. If the Democratic party could become a modernist voice for regionalism and respect for individual rights against the centralistic and occasionally authoritarian directions of the UPC, it might find a solid ground for continued opposition.

CONCLUSION

Uganda appears to be passing successfully through the second stage of national development with a new Westernized elite controlling the major central forces of government and economic growth. Most significantly, a new national consensus has crystallized among this group and is being rapidly accepted throughout the population. Traditionalism is still strong, especially in Buganda, though it is losing its leaders and its overwhelming popularity. In giving recognition to ethnic diversity, the federal form of government is a solid instrument, if it is honored in practice as well as in form. It would be a mistake for the UPC to try to achieve a single-party system at this stage because it would disturb this balance. Yet, if traditionalism collapses completely in Buganda, this may be the end result. The Kabaka has often been called a "modernizing monarch." Many of his past actions are directly contrary to this designation, yet his assumption of the presidency reflects an acceptance of the reality of a greater Uganda. Already both he and his government have left the possibility of Buganda separation behind. The remaining issue of unity is whether the economic strength and tremendous energetic leadership of the Baganda will remain confused and obstructive or will turn to become a vital new force for modernization.

Uganda demonstrates very well how a modernized elite that has gained control of central authority can take advantage of the modernizing forces at work in a society and gradually—with a minimum of coercion—achieve a consensus for unity.

The gravest problems still lie ahead as Uganda enters the third stage of African modernization. In this stage, certain long-postponed ideological issues will have to be settled. These issues include the nature of her party system, i.e., whether it will maintain a plural-party system similar to Nigeria or move toward the mobilization form of Guinea and Ghana. Secondly, the character of her economic development will have to be decided in terms of the rate of Africanization, the degree of public control, and the extent of popular participation through cooperatives as opposed to state-controlled farms and industries. Most significant will be her decision regarding the extent of Uganda's integration within an East African Federation.[38] All of

---

[38] The attitude of the *lukiko* has been the major obstacle to acceptance of East African Federation by Uganda.

these issues have been postponed pending the outcome of the struggle for unity. Now that a basis of unity and consensus has been found, there are good reasons to expect that Uganda will move rapidly into the third stage. As in the second stage, Uganda's ethnic diversity and historic rivalries will play a major part in the directions taken. However, under modernization, the economic forces have moved to the forefront, and the new instruments of social organization—political parties, cooperatives, trade unions, and educational systems—have begun to play a more vital role. There are good prospects that Uganda can maintain the balance of a plural society that lends itself more fully to democratic development. Yet the dangers of authoritarianism are always present as the temptations grow to regard opposition to national progress as subversive. The finding of a national consensus, the recovery of lost arts, the discovery of a new human dignity, and the creation of new wealth all make for a recognition of the immense importance of this new state and its leadership. If Uganda Africans can, at the same time, preserve their inherent respect for the individual and his rights within the community, they may avoid some of the worst excesses of modern nationalism.

SELECTED BIBLIOGRAPHY

Apter, David. *The Political Kingdom in Uganda.* London: Oxford University Press, 1960.

Burke, Fred G. *Local Government and Politics in Uganda.* Syracuse: Syracuse University Press, 1964.

Fallers, Lloyd (ed.). *The King's Men.* New York: Oxford University Press, 1964.

Fortes, Meyer, and E. E. Evans-Pritchard. *African Political Systems.* London: Oxford University Press, 1949.

Ingham, Kenneth. *The Making of Modern Uganda.* London: Allen and Unwin, 1958.

Low, D. Anthony. *Political Parties in Uganda, 1949–1962.* London: Commonwealth Papers No. 8, Institute of Commonwealth Studies. University of London, 1962.

————, and R. Cranford Pratt. *Buganda and British Overrule, 1900–1955.* London: Oxford University Press, 1960.

Marsh, Zoe A., and G. W. Kingsnorth. *An Introduction to the History of East Africa.* 2d ed.; Cambridge: Cambridge University Press, 1961.

Shepherd, George W., Jr. *The Politics of African Nationalism.* New York: Frederick A. Praeger, 1962.

————. *They Wait in Darkness.* New York: John Day, Inc., 1955.

Wrigley, C. C. *Buganda: An Outline of Economic History.* London: Reprint Series No. 1, Institute of Commonwealth Studies, University of London, 1962.

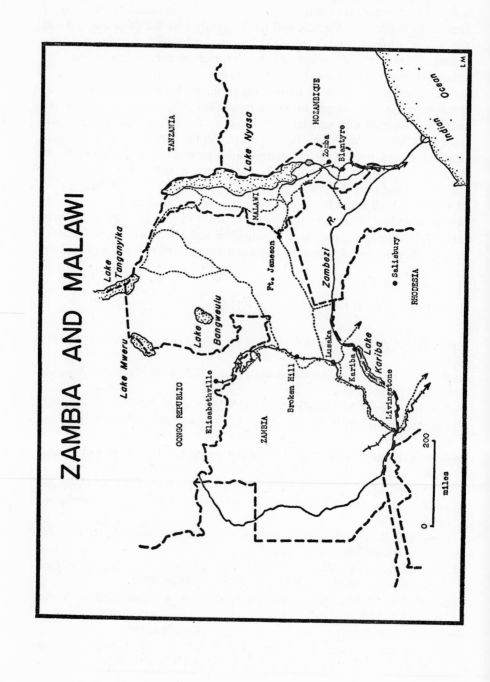

ZAMBIA AND MALAWI

8

The Modern Emergence
of Malawi and Zambia

Robert I. Rotberg

> The sun of righteousness, it seems to me is rapidly springing upon the
> sons and daughters of Africa and who knows that sooner or later we
> may hail the dawn of freedom. To accomplish this fact we must act
> in unionism, breaking all our tribal prejudices. . . .
> —CLEMENTS KADALIE TO ISA MACDONALD LAWRENCE
> April 4, 1925

IN 1964, BOTH NYASALAND and Northern Rhodesia—respectively Malawi and Zambia—achieved their independence from British
colonial oversight. *Kwacha,* Kadalie's "dawn of freedom," burst on the
Central African scene with an incandescent light that well rewarded those
who had devoted themselves to the pursuit of a political New Jerusalem.
For them, independence and the creation of new states constituted a beginning. Yet, at their birth, both Malawi and Zambia owed the orientation of
their leaders and parties to the nature of their long struggle for independence.

BEFORE THE EUROPEANS

Sometime during the sixteenth and seventeenth centuries, pastoralists from
the northeast and agriculturists from the northwest entered the upland region
that lies between the headwaters of the Zambezi River and the shores of
Lake Nyasa. The former, who may have been descended from groups owing
loyalties to the interlacustrine Cwezi dynasty, settled for the most part between Lakes Tanganyika and Nyasa. Apparently they intermarried with the
indigenous inhabitants and may have gradually influenced peoples living
beyond the zone of their immediate penetration. The agriculturalists recall
intimate connections with the Lunda-Luba empire of Katanga. Perhaps in
the seventeenth century, this empire began to disintegrate, and, under a

337

number of leaders, segments entered Bulozi, the heartland of Barotseland, and the Kafue basin, while others crossed the Luapula River and then fragmented again to form the eastern Lunda, Bemba, and Bisa states. Still another émigré section, that of the Malawi under their leader Karonga, continued across the Chambezi and Luangwa rivers into modern Nyasaland. They gave their name to the lake only later called Nyasa. In time, fissiparous pressures brought about further tribal divisions.

On the eve of the nineteenth century, trans-Zambezia contained an amalgam of very different Bantu-speaking Africans and a few Arab and Indian traders who had already begun to transport copper ingots, wax, salt, and slaves to entrepôts on both coasts. In the far west, in Bulozi along the upper Zambezi, the Luyana governed a number of subject tribes. To the north, the Eastern Lunda dominated a fairly large region between the Lufira and Chambezi rivers. The Bemba raided on the eastern flank of the Lunda, but, as yet, had failed to usurp the Lunda paramountcy. In the southeast, meanwhile, the Yao raided for slaves, and apparently the various Malawi peoples prospered from the products of their lands. There were rivalries and wars, but ordered government and an atmosphere of calm apparently prevailed until the Nguni irrupted into trans-Zambezia from the south.[1]

In the early nineteenth century, the most important of the Nguni chiefdoms of eastern South Africa began to compete energetically among themselves. Out of this struggle for power, the Zulu, led by Shaka, emerged victorious after overwhelming a warrior group loyal to Zwide. A section of this latter group soon followed Zwangendaba, a subordinate of Zwide, out of Zululand. Zwangendaba and his followers penetrated the hinterland of what became the colonies of Mozambique and Southern Rhodesia, everywhere gathering adherents, and then, in 1835, crossed the Zambezi near its confluence with the Luangwa River. They settled for a time along the Nsenga and the Cewa and then moved north, through the western marches of Malawi country. In Ufipa, near Lake Tanganyika, they paused again until Zwangendaba died. Dissident segments then separated from the main Ngoni group. One segment continued north to Unyamwezi, where it later helped Chief Mirambo control the trade routes to Tanganyika. Another faction went east to attack the inhabitants of the Bagamoyo before finally conquering and settling in the Songea district. The majority, however, followed Mpezeni, a chief who seems to have been the legitimate heir of Zwangendaba. He and most of the

---

[1] For the early period in trans-Zambezia see, *inter alia*, Jan Vansina, "The Foundation of the Kingdom of Kasanje," *The Journal of African History*, IV (1963), 355–366; Max Marwick, "History and Tradition in East Central Africa through the Eyes of the Northern Rhodesia Cêwa," *ibid.*, pp. 378–379; Ian Cunnison (trans. and ed.), *Central Bantu Historical Texts II: Historical Traditions of the Eastern Lunda* (Lusaka: 1961), pp. 3–4; Ann Tweedie, "Towards a History of the Bemba from Oral Tradition," *Conference of the History of the Central African Peoples* (Lusaka: 1963), n.p.; Lishoma S. Muuka, "The Colonisation of Barotseland in the Seventeenth Century," *ibid.*

members of the main section of the Ngoni circled back through the country then dominated by the Bemba and the Bisa.

The wanderings of the segments loyal to Mpezeni finally ended when the Ngoni crossed the Luangwa River into what became the eastern districts of Northern Rhodesia. Lastly, even before these segments had penetrated into Bembaland, Mwambera, a rival claimant, had led a number of Mpezeni's erstwhile supporters onto the plateau lands west of Lake Nyasa. Another breakaway group followed a similar route down the west side of the lake into the Dowa district. In this process of finding homes for themselves, the various Ngoni segments had thrown the previous inhabitants of trans-Zambezi into turmoil. They had raided the lakeside Tonga, battled with the Tumbuka, and attacked the various Malawi peoples. The Ngoni had pillaged, ravaged, and generally helped to disrupt the pre-existing social equilibrium. By sundering the various tribal loyalties of the people of Nyasaland, they may well have smoothed the path for its eventual conquest by Europeans.[2]

To the west, an invading group similarly imposed its rule on the inhabitants of Barotseland. In about 1833–1835, the Kololo, a people who had fled Basutoland in the face of Shaka's hostility, plundered their way northward—under the leadership of Sebitwane—through Bechuanaland to the Zambezi, finally settling forcibly among the Tonga or Toka who grazed cattle on the northern shores of that river. Soon the Kololo moved westward to Bulozi where the soldiers of Sebitwane defeated a Lozi army. Sebitwane thereafter ruled Barotseland while several of the defeated *indunas,* or princes, governed independent chiefdoms beyond the northern limits of Kololo power.

Evidently Sebitwane ruled harshly and successfully. His son Sikeletu, however, and Mbololu, who soon succeeded Sikeletu, lost the confidence of their supporters as well as their subjects. In 1863–1864, conditions proved conducive to revolt. Njakwa, a leading Lozi commander, gathered a large following, obtained the support of Sipopa, a Lozi prince, and freed Barotseland from Kololo domination. Thereafter, Sipopa enlarged the size and effective power of the Lozi state. During his reign and the reigns of his successors Mwanawina and Lewanika, peoples living as far from the center of the kingdom as the Kafue and Chobe rivers acknowledged the might of the Lozi. Only Europeans proved the undoing of Lewanika.[3]

---

[2] For the Ngoni, see A. T. Bryant, *Olden Times in Zululand and Natal* (London, Eng.: Longmans, Green, and Company, 1929), pp. 206–208, 459–461; Yesaya Mlonyeni Chibambo, *My Ngoni of Nyasaland* (London, Eng.: Lutterworth Press, 1942), pp. 8–10; J. A. Barnes, *Politics in a Changing Society: A Political History of the Fort Jameson Ngoni* (Capetown: Oxford University Press, 1954), pp. 7 ff.

[3] For the Lozi, see Adolpha Jalla, *Litaba za Sicaba sa Ma-Lozi* (Capetown: 1909 and 1951), pp. 32–53; Gervas Clay, "Barotseland between 1801 and 1864," *Conference of the History of the Central African Peoples*, n.p.

THE COLONIAL EXPERIENCE

Europe intruded into trans-Zambezia during the last years of the nineteenth century. The British government gave that region the unity of colonial rule and the integrity of artificial borders. It offered a focus for the loyalties of disparate peoples, channeled the aspirations of a subject population along new paths, and provided a necessary framework within which "nationalism" could eventually transform itself into African self-government.

The explorations of David Livingstone and the presence of English-speaking missionaries provided a historical excuse for the British diplomatic and military conquest of what became Nyasaland and Northern Rhodesia. Successive British foreign ministers had at first refused to interest themselves in the affairs of such distant peoples. In about 1887, however, the agitation of the missions and their influential supporters coincided with an imperial attempt to prevent either Portugal or the Transvaal from occupying Matabeleland and Mashonaland.

The alliance of Cecil John Rhodes and Henry Hamilton (later Sir Harry) Johnston finally persuaded Lord Salisbury, then British Prime Minister, to act decisively in Central Africa. In 1889, Rhodes, a thirty-six-year-old imperialist, personally worth millions, came to London from South Africa. He requested the support and the sanction of Her Majesty's Government for the annexation of Matabeleland. In return, he offered to pay for the colonization and administration of Matabeleland and the Bechuanaland Protectorate, to extend the existing rail and telegraph lines to the Zambezi River, and to obtain for the Crown all of trans-Zambezia. With that abundant resolution of which Livingstone would have approved, Rhodes simply proposed to paint the heart of Africa British red without cost to the imperial Exchequer. By a few, swift strokes of Salisbury's pen, Rhodes promised to forestall the Transvaal and Portugal, to obviate any disastrous entanglements with African warriors, and to discharge all the responsibilities of a government.

The British government authorized the British South Africa Company, a creation of Rhodes's, to rule and administer lands lying between the Limpopo and Zambezi rivers. In addition, Salisbury declared that the Northern Rhodesian portion of trans-Zambezia, in which the Prime Minister was essentially uninterested and which he had purposely excluded from the first draft of the charter, would—probably because Rhodes suspected the existence of copper there—henceforth form a part of the British sphere. In concert with Johnston, Rhodes also made possible the inclusion of Nyasaland within this domain. He offered at once to provide funds for future treaty-making expeditions and promised to absorb the expenses of other activities in the future.[4] For more than three decades, practical sovereignty

---

[4] FO 2/55: Johnston to Rhodes, 8 October 1893. Much of what follows parallels the argument in Robert I. Rotberg, *The Rise of Nationalism in Central Africa* (Cambridge, Mass.: Harvard University Press, 1965).

in much of Central Africa thereby passed to a chartered undertaking, the activities of which remained effectively beyond the control of the British government.

Johnston became Queen Victoria's representative in the Nyasa regions. He quickly forestalled the forceful assertion of Portuguese sovereignty over trans-Zambezia by unilaterally declaring a protectorate over the Shire Highlands which Salisbury, in his turn, secured by threatening the Portuguese with war. At the same time, Johnston's representatives concluded a series of agreements with indigenous chiefs throughout a vast unpartitioned land stretching from the Ruo River west to Lake Mweru and north toward Lake Tanganyika. These treaties simply bound the chiefs in question to seek British approval before ceding any territory or sovereignty to another European power. They testified to the existence of peace between a tribe and the Queen of England and promised to accord Her Majesty's representatives consular jurisdiction over all disputes that arose between the indigenous inhabitants and Britons. These treaties did not, however, confer or promise protection, and, when Johnston later "protected" the environs of Lake Nyasa, his action bore no juridical similarity to the original understandings between the Queen's consuls and the chiefs. Nevertheless, in May 1891, after the British government and Rhodes had settled on a financial allowance for the new protectorates, the Foreign Office formally declared that "under and by virtue of Agreements with the native Chiefs, and by other lawful means, the territories in Africa, hereinafter referred to as the Nyasaland Districts, are under the Protectorate of Her Majesty the Queen."[5]

In western trans-Zambezia, Rhodes sought minerals and territory. There, with the help of the French missionary François Coillard, a representative of his chartered company persuaded Lewanika, chief of the Lozi, to sign away his lands and subsoil rights.[6] This treaty, however unscrupulously obtained, later proved the basis for the British South Africa Company's assumption of direct rule in northwestern Rhodesia and, certainly wrongly, for its rights to the lucrative ores that have since allowed Zambia to become the world's second largest producer of copper. In 1891, it and the treaties obtained by Johnston and his representatives also permitted the chartered company formally to include these regions within its sphere.

But treaties meant little. During the next eight years, soldiers forcibly imposed British rule throughout what became Nyasaland and northeastern Rhodesia. They deposed difficult or troublesome chiefs and fought a number of bloody wars with Africans. "The history of Sir Harry Johnston's Administration," a colleague wrote, ". . . while it records many notable civil achievements, is yet in its more salient features a history of successive mili-

---

[5] Edward S. Hertslet (ed.), *The Map of Africa by Treaty* (London, Eng.: Harrison and Sons, 1896), i, p. 286.

[6] A copy of the treaty is contained in *Africa South*, CCCCXIV, no. 245 (encl.).

tary expeditions."[7] Indeed, Johnston and his compatriots destroyed the power of the principal Yao, Cewa, and Arab rulers, and then turned their attentions first to the Ngoni and the eastern Lunda, both of whom fought unsuccessfully to forestall a British conquest.

Henceforth, Nyasas and Northern Rhodesians found themselves "protected." In practice, however, Her Majesty's Government and its local representatives tended to ignore the legal limitations presumably inherent in a "protectorate" and treated these new dependencies of the Crown as conquered colonies. Johnston and later commissioners, administrators, and governors thus derived their legal authority to rule Africans not from the consent of their subjects, but from the British Order-in-Council of 1889, as amended. Empowered thereby, they made so-called Queen's Regulations in order to promote "peace, order, and good government." They established courts wherein Africans could be tried and sentenced for transgressing the Queen's Regulations. Thus, after 1891 in Nyasaland and after about 1901 in Northern Rhodesia, the subordinate imperial pro-consuls (variously styled Collectors of Revenue, Resident Magistrates, and Native Commissioners) each supervised particularly circumscribed districts. They became super-chiefs and, as agents of the governor or administrator, their word constituted local law. They settled disputes between chiefs, decided where roads should be constructed, conscripted labor, organized a postal service, raised revenue, and acted as a combination overseer of and handyman for the public weal.

Under such a system, the authority of the chiefs in Nyasaland soon became merely nominal, and, by 1904, they played "no real part in the affairs of their country."[8] Eight years later, the government once again congratulated itself on the success of its policy of direct rule. "The decay of the power of native chiefs and the tendency all over the Protectorate to the splitting up of villages into small family groups continues: this tendency is to some extent gratifying in that it originates in the native's sense of his complete security under the existing Government. . . ."[9]

Across the territorial boundary, the two protectorates of Northeastern and Northwestern Rhodesia led separate administrative lives until 1911. In that year, the British South Africa Company fused them in order to form a united Northern Rhodesia. Most of the few thousand settlers who had been attracted to the territory after the South African War then lived on either side of the single railway. Some farmed, others mined lead and zinc at Broken Hill, and, in a small way, copper at Bwana Mkuba and a number of smaller centers.

---

[7] Hector L. Duff, *Nyasaland under the Foreign Office* (London, Eng.: George Bell and Sons, 1906), p. 17.

[8] Quoted in S. S. Murray (ed.), *A Handbook of Nyasaland* (London: Nyasaland Government, 1932), p. 126.

[9] *Ibid.*, p. 128.

These settlers exerted an influence out of all proportion to their number (in 1921, fewer than 4,000 whites resided in Northern Rhodesia), and the Company listened carefully to their grievances. The white farmers and miners of Northern Rhodesia grew increasingly more powerful than their counterparts in the neighboring protectorate. As a result, the government of Northern Rhodesia never really attempted to safeguard African rights to the same extent as the government in Nyasaland. Northern Rhodesia, as its name implied, furthermore, was ideologically no more than an extension of the commercially-controlled colonial system of Southern Rhodesia.

In both Nyasaland and Northern Rhodesia, the character of white rule disillusioned Africans. Sanctioned by their governments, settlers occupied choice terrain in the productive Shire Highlands, along the Rhodesian railway, or in the eastern districts of Northern Rhodesia. In Nyasaland, admittedly, whites early purchased a proportion of their large estates. But Africans knew nothing of Western ideas about property. They sold much of what later became the municipality of Blantyre-Limbe for trifling amounts; a coffee planter purchased more than 3,000 acres for a gun, thirty-two yards of calico, two red caps, "and several other things." A missionary obtained more than 26,000 acres for seven trusses of calico measuring about 1,750 yards.[10] A district officer later analyzed the problem: "They could not possibly have understood the meaning or functions of a commercial firm and they could not have realized that the agreement they made was a sale and that by this act they disinherited their tribe and deprived posterity of the rights to their land. I submit that this is tantamount to false pretence. . . ."[11] Nevertheless, by 1900, the ownership of more than half of the best part of the densely populated Shire Highlands had passed into European hands. Over all, whites controlled about 15 per cent of the total land and water area of the protectorate.

On these large estates, Africans became tenants at will without security of tenure.[12] Other abuses followed. White planters monopolized the labor of their tenants, paid Africans only nominally for their labor, and prevented them from selling the produce of their own gardens without first offering it to the estate. Moreover, despite the claims advanced by the local Chamber of Agriculture and Commerce, Africans had no option. Cultivable acreage for gardens was available only on the vast European-owned estates. Near Blantyre, the government earmarked all unused Crown land for railway development or official construction. Then too, Africans saw that the more

---

[10] W. H. J. Rangeley, "Early Blantyre," *The Nyasaland Journal*, VII (1954), 37–42.

[11] S 1/1519a/28, J. J. O'Brien to the Provincial Commissioner (Northern Province), May 7, 1930, Zomba archives.

[12] See Judge John Joseph Nunan, judgment of April 28, 1903, in Supervisor of Native Affairs v. Blantyre and East African Company.

important landholding companies refused to develop the bulk of their extensive holdings. By 1903, Europeans had developed less than 1 per cent of the total alienated acreage of the country. On the British Central Africa Company estate, for example, the owners had cultivated only 5,000 of its 367,000 acres. On the Bruce estates, against which John Chilembwe later directed his ire, all but 500 of its 160,000 acres lay fallow.[13]

The lack of rights of Africans on alienated estates in Nyasaland remained a source of indigenous grievance for fifty years. Settlers successfully opposed administrative attempts to alleviate some of the main causes of African distress. The European planter simply wanted cheap labor and disliked policies that tended to raise Africans above the level "at which they would be content to work for a pittance."[14] In 1928, an ordinance even enshrined custom. Thereafter, the government officially excused Africans residing on tea and coffee plantations from the obligation to pay rent so long as they worked for their proprietor whenever he called. If Africans refused to work, they either paid rent in cash or subjected themselves to eviction. Further, landlords told their tenants what and when they should plant and purchased the resultant crops from them at arbitrarily contrived prices.[15] From the settler's point of view, the estates were private property that had been purchased with hard-earned money. Africans, on the other hand, claimed that they had been arbitrarily deprived of their lands and, in the process, unconscionably abused. When they exhausted one piece of land, estate owners refused to allot them new ones. If they moved onto fallow land, the owner uprooted their crops. They could not cut down trees in order to build huts in the traditional manner. In an area where the customary pattern of settlement was matrilocal, Europeans forbade young men to settle on the lands of the family of their prospective spouse. Proprietors often compelled youths to leave the estates when they came of age. In short, if Africans distrusted white rule, they need only to have resided on a European-owned plantation for all their worst fears to be confirmed.

To add to the African burden, the governments of Nyasaland and Northern Rhodesia imposed taxes. Protectorates had to support themselves. As early as 1892, an African living in the Shire Highlands found that Johnston's Administration demanded three shillings from him for each of his huts—that is, for each of his wives. By 1894, Johnston raised more than £1,100 a year from this source.[16] In 1901, the British South Africa Company began

---

[13] Land Commission to Acting Commissioner Francis Barrow Pearce, May 6, 1903.

[14] CO 525/49: Pearce to the Secretary of State for the Colonies, June 14, 1913.

[15] S 1/411ii/33: Governor Harold Kittermaster to Philip Cunliffe-Lister, the Secretary of State for the Colonies, December 15, 1934.

[16] FO 2/66: Harry H. Johnston to Lord Rosebery, January 22, 1894 (London).

to collect taxes in northeastern Rhodesia. "The natives," wrote the Administrator hopefully, "consider the tax inevitable."[17]

The pacification of trans-Zambezia attracted increasing numbers of white immigrants and imposed new responsibilities on the respective administrative staffs. The immigrants—most of whom had obtained some experience in South Africa—wanted the services of African labor in order to assist the development of newly alienated lands. They early demanded that their governments should—by any one of a number of means—encourage Africans to forsake their tribal chores for employment on white-owned estates. The administrators themselves sought to obtain labor for a variety of routine tasks; they always needed head porters. Both the Foreign and Colonial Offices frowned on methods of recruitment that approximated impressment. As a result, the governments of Nyasaland and Northern Rhodesia used the tax as an instrument with which to induce Africans to offer their labor to whites in return for artificial rates of pay that were geared entirely to the level of the prevailing tax assessment. The Administrator of Northeastern Rhodesia explained that ". . . the natives are able . . . to pay the three shilling hut tax. It would prove, as . . . in the British Central Africa Protectorate [Nyasaland], a means of getting a certain amount of work out of the natives, and would in this manner greatly assist transport difficulties."[18] Taxation became the main reason behind a new wave of migration that significantly transformed the Central African countryside and effectively destroyed a traditional way of life.

In Northern Rhodesia, the rate of taxation, although it varied according to the wealth of the district in question, increased steadily throughout the interwar period. A leading settler commented: "Poor villagers . . . their tax [has been] put up from five shillings to ten shillings a year as a reward for being loyal. It's the good old policy of exploiting the black man, in this case it's intended to drive him down to the mines in Southern Rhodesia . . . where they're short of labour. . . ."[19] Similarly, measures traditionally used for the collection of taxes were improved. Administrators burned huts of tax defaulters, seized their wives until the tax was paid, and accepted road labor in lieu of taxes.

In 1930, when Lord Passfield (Sidney Webb) briefly became Secretary of State for the Colonies, he decreed that the government of Northern Rhodesia should not impose taxes to the extent that they might disrupt traditional life or compel Africans to offer their labor to the newly opened copper

---

[17] A 2/3/1/4: Robert Codrington to the British South Africa Company (London), annual report for 1902, Lusaka archives.

[18] FO 2/210: Codrington to Administrator (Salisbury), June 15, 1899.

[19] Gore-Browne Papers: Stewart Gore-Browne to Dame Ethel Locke-King, June 15, 1921, privately held.

mines. "Taxation," he wrote, "is not meant to change the life of a people."[20] Nevertheless, it soon appeared perfectly evident that taxation was responsible for decreasing the extent of polygyny; for driving men permanently from the rural areas; for encouraging divorce, adultery, and, in time, prostitution; and for giving rise to all the myriad ills that anthropologists and other critics have lumped under the rubric "detribalization." A government official summarized this argument: "There are causes for unrest: The native is getting nothing out of the white man; we give him no education, nothing and screw ten shillings out of him. The wages are usually six shillings per month . . . and calico you cannot buy."[21]

Like colonial subjects elsewhere in tropical Africa, the peoples of Nyasaland and Northern Rhodesia suffered arbitrary rule by aliens. Their chiefs became servants of the government, and they themselves became subjects seemingly without any important rights. Officials enforced new conservation laws, told Africans where they might and might not farm, and forced them to vacate traditional lands in order to make way for whites. In the towns, the government likewise segregated Africans, restricted their movement, introduced passes, and compelled Africans to recognize the inferiority of their color. Moreover, in African eyes, the positive expressions of colonial interest—the ending of tribal quarrels and the slave trade; the introduction of indirect rule, British justice, British medical care, and British education; and expenditures on railways, roads, telegraph lines, and electric power— seemed essentially negative. On the one hand, Africans believed that they profited little by the white man's way of life; on the other, they believed that the white man had promised them that he would, in time, share his secrets, wealth, and governmental responsibilities with Africans. Instead, whites gave Africans few chances to participate fully in the European way of life. What is more, the white man practiced discrimination widely.

Even the best-dressed Africans could never enter a "white" hotel or restaurant. They addressed Europeans respectfully and doffed their caps to whites of every station. Meanwhile white miners called them "black monkeys." In the rural areas, some white men cohabited with the blacks' wives or had children by their daughters. No redress appeared available. Why, they asked, did Africans need to carry passes in their own country? Why did whites who whipped Africans receive no punishment? They wondered why the governor of Nyasaland prevented a Nyasa living in Glasgow from marrying a white Glaswegian lass.[22] Africans failed to receive suitable answers to these kinds of questions. Instead, their anguish led them to seek political

---

[20] ZA 1/2: Lord Passfield to the Governor of Northern Rhodesia, February 7, 1930, Lusaka archives.

[21] B 1/8/2: Interview with Peter Cookson, Native Commissioner, May 30, 1920, Lusaka archives.

[22] S 2/54/19, Zomba archives.

and religious means of expression. Some even began to prophesy the coming of a new dawn.

INDIGENOUS PROTEST AND THE RISE OF NATIONALISM

Colonial rule, with its many coercive demands and regulations, encouraged a hostile response. In Nyasaland and Northern Rhodesia, Africans contrasted Biblical teachings of equality with the actual performance of the Europeans who had settled in their midst. Not unnaturally, they also queried their own initially rather mute acceptance of the superiority of the white man's approach to modern life. These currents of thought, often influenced by the social or economic circumstances surrounding particular Anglo-African confrontations or by external ideological stimuli, at first stirred gently. In time, however, Africans grafted a wide range of political and religious expression onto the frail stock of tentative protest.

In both protectorates, chiliastic preachers and the leaders of separatist sects early gathered adherents who were presumably attracted by the apocalyptic message of independence. In the early years of this century, a so-called Ethiopian Church flourished in Barotseland. The colonial soil of Nyasaland nurtured Elliot Kenan Kamwana Achirwa, who promised excited fellow Tonga that they would soon see no more of the British government ("We shall build our own ships, make our own powder, and make or import our own guns"), the separatist Charles Domingo ("Instead of 'Give' [Europeans] say 'Take away from' ")[23], and John Chilembwe, the American-educated leader of the Providence Industrial Mission of Chiradzulu.

The government's imposition of an increasingly onerous tax obligation, its stricter administration of African activities, the increase of African pressure on available acreage in the Shire Highlands, and the tendency of white planters to use their indigenous labor as cruelly as possible were factors that all provided an atmosphere receptive to the preachings of Kamwana, Domingo, and Chilembwe. The last publicly complained about the injustices that the government of Nyasaland had heaped on his fellow countrymen. He particularly waxed indignant when Nyasas lost their lives in defense of the white man. His letter to the local *Nyasaland Times* expressed this point of view eloquently:

We understand that we have been invited to shed our innocent blood in this world's war which is now in progress. . . . A number of our people have already shed their blood, while some are crippled for life. . . . Police are marching in various villages persuading well-built natives to join in the war . . . [but]

---

[23] Quoted in George Shepperson and Thomas Price, *Independent African* (Edinburgh, Scot.: Edinburgh University Press, 1958), pp. 156, 163–164.

will there be any good prospects for the natives after the end of the war? Shall we be recognized as anybody in the best interests of civilization and Christianity after the great struggle is ended? . . . we are imposed upon more than any other nationality under the sun. [We] . . . have been loyal since the commencement of this government. . . . And no time have we ever been known to betray any trust, national or otherwise, confided to us. . . . For our part we . . . have reservedly stepped to the firing line in every conflict and played a patriot's part with the spirit of true gallantry. But in time of peace the government failed to help the underdog. In time of peace everything [is] for Europeans only. . . .[24]

Chilembwe and his co-conspirators thereafter plotted rebellion. Then, in early 1915, the rebels killed a few whites, including the managers of the Bruce estate, raided Blantyre, and attacked a Roman Catholic mission station. Admittedly bloody, the rising ended as suddenly as it had begun. The immediately favorable results of the rising were few. Suspected followers of Chilembwe either lost their lives, languished in prison, or spent their remaining days in enforced exile. The government imposed severe restrictions on the activities of the fringe churches and their leaders. When the official commission of inquiry recommended a number of ways of ameliorating the harsh conditions under which Africans lived and labored in the Shire Highlands, the government refused to implement these reforms. Chilembwe, nevertheless, shattered the widespread aura of white complacency. He destroyed the notion that "the natives were happy" under British domination. Unfortunately, however, the government learned this lesson imperfectly, and the rising of 1915 failed to change appreciably the course of colonial rule in Central Africa. The forlorn example of John Chilembwe only later, during a more propitious era, provided the text for a genuine movement of independence.

During the years between the two world wars, Africans in Nyasaland and Northern Rhodesia sought, in every conceivable constitutional way, to better the political, social, and economic order to which they had become subject. Chilembwe's abortive rising signified the end of a defensive era; thereafter, Africans recognized that the colonial governments had come to stay and that the imposed codes of law were not to be removed easily. Using the political concepts and language of their rulers, they claimed a democratic right to participate in the governing process. At first, they wanted no more than the right to have their collective voice heard in matters directly affecting the lives and actions of the indigenous population. To this end, those Africans to whom the white man's ways had become most familiar imitated the settler example by forming associations through which their mutual pleas for reform, and for consideration, could best be expressed.

Among the several widespread manifestations of indigenous protest, the

[24] GOA 2/4/14: Chilembwe to the *Nyasaland Times,* Zomba archives. See also Shepperson and Price, *op. cit.,* pp. 234–235.

establishment of voluntary associations played the most significant role in the development and the eventual emergence of the avowedly nationalist movements of the 1940's. For more than twenty years, the associations sought redress for grievances suffered by Africans. They urged reform on hostile or amused governments. They countered every public move made by the settlers to entrench white privilege at the expense of Africans. They reacted strongly against the settler agitation that favored amalgamation and closer association. They also concerned themselves continually with matters of immediate, even parochial consequence to the otherwise unrepresented people of the protectorates. Perhaps unintentionally, these gentle skirmishes with authority represented an intermediate phase in the history of Central African nationalism during which the indigenous leadership, like its counterpart in West Africa, came gradually to appreciate the essential futility of a strictly constitutional, *ad hoc,* and basically elitist approach to the problems posed for subject peoples by colonial rule.

In both protectorates, the associations responded, if timidly, to the radically charged air that surrounded them. Only in urban Northern Rhodesia did the momentum of protest carry the associations from mere complaint to combination. In 1933, these various urban voluntary societies tried to create a single body to represent the many different peoples of the protectorate. To this end, their leaders, under the chairmanship of I. Clements Katongo Muwamba, a Nyasa Tonga, met publicly at Kafue in order to organize a national association of associations. He advised his participants to think carefully about their peculiar position. "We are here to make a recognition that should cement the existing friendship between the Government, the settlers, and the Africans. Whatever we are going to discuss must be in line with the Government because they are our fathers upon whom we should rely for our progress and welfare."[25] Together they demanded a number of improvements in the status and treatment received by educated Africans. They also asked the governor to persuade the editor of Northern Rhodesia's only newspaper to print their letters. Finally, the assembly of elitist leaders voted overwhelmingly in favor of the immediate amalgamation of all of the various Northern Rhodesian native welfare associations.

The government of Northern Rhodesia naturally moved quickly to eliminate such open subversion. It decided that the activities of the local associations should be limited to matters concerned with the general welfare of "alien and detribalized natives" resident in urban areas. The Chief Secretary instructed his district officials henceforth to prevent members of the associations from dabbling in politics.

In future the activities of welfare associations must be confined to matters strictly pertaining to the township in which they function. . . . African em-

---

[25] Sec/Nat/311: Minutes of the Kafue Meeting, July 10–11, 1933, Lusaka archives.

ployees . . . are debarred from becoming members of any political organization. . . . Native employees must not address public meetings on any but
academic subjects; neither should they write letters to the papers.[26]

For the next ten years, these constraints effectively curbed the associations. African civil servants tried to keep in the good graces of the government; many continued to participate in meetings, but, for the most part, they
confined themselves to the expression of innocuous grievances and to the
furtherance of social and cultural ends. The breezes of change barely blew.
Although several of the associations continued to meet regularly and, despite
the public inactivity of some of their more articulate members, to demand
redress anew for many of their old grievances, they accomplished little, and
again and again forlornly aired matters that had already occasioned an unfavorable official response.

Despite numerous rebuffs, the various African voluntary associations of
Northern Rhodesia and Nyasaland refrained from speaking publicly of self-
government, and, by 1939, they had alluded only in the most tangential
manner to the possibility that Africans might one day be represented in the
respective legislative councils by persons of their own choice. Their leaders
spoke rarely of "freedom" or of the stratagems that might ultimately return
the two protectorates to indigenous control. At the onset of World War II,
they wanted equality of opportunity more than power and status within the
existing society more than its wholesale transformation. Yet, their actions
fanned the breezes of protest. Associational activity also provided training
for future politicians. At the time, Central Africans may also have lacked
the experience or the desire to organize themselves in ways from which
they might have derived greater and more lasting benefit. Nonetheless, their
associations were the logical progenitors of the nationalist-minded congresses.

In early 1943, after President Roosevelt and Prime Minister Churchill
had enunciated the principles of the Atlantic Charter and the Allies had
effectively eliminated the threat of an Axis conquest of Africa, James Frederick Sangala, who had earlier held office in different local associations,
apparently began to seek new organizational ways in which to express the
political thoughts of the day. With the advice of W. H. Timcke, a British
South African businessman residing in Nyasaland, and Dr. H. Kamuza
Banda, then practicing medicine in North Shields, England, Sangala later in
that year summoned at least two meetings of the African leaders of Blantyre and Limbe. As a result of these discussions, on October 1, 1943, Sangala penned a "circular letter to all Africans resident in Nyasaland." It
proposed the organization of an "association" that would seek effectively to
represent their interests. The letter explained that the main reason for creating another association was "because experience has taught that unity is
strength."

---

[26] Sec/Nat/332: circular minute of September 4, 1933, Lusaka archives.

In the past grievances and other vital matters affecting the country and people have been presented to the government and/or other authorities by local organizations who were interested only in their local worries. It is considered that the time is ripe now for the Africans in this country to strive for unity so as to obtain the greater development of the peoples and country of Nyasaland.

In sum, Sangala appealed to "all Africans and leaders of this country to give their support . . . so that our race should have a place among the civilised . . . ." [27]

Sangala and his colleagues envisaged the creation of a new representative body, to be called the Nyasaland African Council, "which should be the mouthpiece of the Africans." They presumed that the proposed council would meet once or twice each year in order to deal with matters affecting "the Protectorate generally." In the reassuring style of the early voluntary societies, these leaders also promised that the council would cooperate with the government, with commercial, planter, and missionary bodies, and with native authorities "in any matters necessary to speed up the progress of Nyasaland."[28] They modeled the structure of their proposed council on that of the local white-led Convention of Associations. Sangala and others expected that the various African interest groups already in existence separately would adhere to the council; it would not, as a matter of principle, enroll individual members. Like the nearly contemporaneous Nigeria National Council (later the National Council of Nigeria and the Cameroons), the Nyasaland Council was designed organizationally as an umbrella under which constituent bodies could find shelter. Sangala specifically reserved a seat on the executive committee of the Council for representatives of each of these existing groups.

In January 1944, Sangala convened and presided over a major session of the *ad hoc* executive committee of what was then called the Nyasaland African Association. (The government, which had been thinking about African political representation, preempted the use of the word "council" for its own undertaking and forced Sangala and his colleagues to use the traditional appellation.) The committee demanded that the government should provide Nyasas with the best possible educational facilities and instruction, offer opportunities for advancement to responsible positions in the civil service and pay salaries commensurate with those "at present enjoyed by Europeans." They wanted the government to build modern houses and to sponsor the kind of recreational experiences that would prevent young Nyasas from spending their free hours in community beer halls. They demanded the right to organize trade unions. They asked that the lands that Europeans had "taken from us" and that still remained undeveloped should be restored.

---

[27] la/1423: circular letter of October 1, 1943, Zomba archives.
[28] *Ibid.*

Then, in a forward-looking departure from the traditional search for economic betterment, the committee forthrightly decided that Africans should henceforth occupy the majority of the seats on all of the bodies that advised the government. They totally rejected the continued representation of "African interests" in the Legislative Council by a nominated missionary. They also condemned missionaries in general for their prejudice and their unwillingness to share power and authority with African clergy and laity.

The committee, like earlier African bodies, stood unequivocally against either the amalgamation or federation of Nyasaland with any of the other British dependencies in Central and East Africa. "We totally refuse to amalgamate," they wrote, "until we have been given at least 99 per cent of the rights we are entitled to enjoy in the administration of our own country."

Sangala and his fellow nationalists simply wanted "whatever is good for Europeans and Asians."

> In conclusion, we beg to state that we have served loyally in any way which His Majesty . . . has asked our boys to serve and we think this is the time that we should ask for justice [so] that our boys and girls may enjoy the freedom of being part and parcel . . . of a British empire. . . . We cannot go on allowing our country becoming a labour centre for the neighbouring territories. We must have justice done. . . . We ask you to give us the right to speak for our people be it in the mission councils or in the bodies that govern our country. . . . We have paid the price and we must be compensated accordingly. . . .
>
> It is not a question of being ungrateful but seventy years of patience is a very long time to wait. . . .[29]

In October 1944, the delegates from seventeen associations held the inaugural meeting of what had come to be known, in the manner of South Africa and India, the Nyasaland African Congress. As president, they elected Levi Mumba, an experienced civil servant who had founded a number of the older associations. Two hundred fifty Africans heard him denounce the continued "exploitation" of Africans by Europeans. Africans desired, he said, all of the attributes of full citizenship and, in a perhaps conscious echo of Roosevelt, "opportunities for all regardless of race, colour, or creed." In words once used by Timcke, he demanded the representation of Africans on the Legislative Council by Africans. And together, he and the many delegates expressed a hope that the Governor would, on their behalf, inform the Secretary of State for the Colonies of their overwhelming opposition to amalgamation.

In a series of policy pronouncements, they condemned the color bar. They deplored the restrictions which reduced Africans to a state of social inferiority and humbly requested the government to permit Africans to enter

---

[29] *Ibid.*, minutes of a meeting of a committee of the Nyasaland African Association, January 21, 1944.

movie theaters, either to distill their own liquor or to buy European-produced spirits, to purchase goods from European-owned stores without being forced to ask for them through a hatch, and to wear shoes and hats in the presence of whites. They also wanted to be paid according to their ability and not exclusively in terms of their color.[30]

The Congress had not yet found a modern political voice. Like the earlier associations, it still felt constrained to seek official blessing for its proposals. For the accomplishment of social and political change, it looked to the government. It eschewed subversion. By late 1945, however, the leaders of Congress had realized that such dependence would bring them little material satisfaction. Therefore, they decided to encourage Dr. Banda to represent them formally at the meetings of the Fifth Pan-African Congress in Manchester and to establish ties with the Fabian Colonial Bureau. At Dr. Banda's suggestion, they also attempted to reorganize the administrative affairs of the Congress and to encourage the quasi-independent branches to relinquish their fragmented control over its finances. Later, however, they rejected Dr. Banda's suggestion that Congress should employ a full-time paid organizing secretary. (Dr. Banda had promised to provide the necessary funds.)

The Congress had clearly not reached the point of political "take off." It still hoped that patient nagging of the government, and the careful drafting of memorials and petitions would ultimately provide them with their rightful share of the political kingdom. They were not yet in a position to appreciate the extent of their struggles; nor could they realize the need for professional efficiency. They lacked vision. But, of even greater importance, they lacked both vigorous personal leadership and the necessary political catalyst.

In Northern Rhodesia, meanwhile, educated Africans had revived the urban and rural welfare associations that had played such an important part in their previous political life. During the years immediately after the 1940 strike, they provided an alternative channel of communication for those who found themselves either frustrated or disillusioned by the limited opportunities for expression available in the government-sponsored urban and provincial councils. For example, the Lusaka African Association, which met regularly after 1943, sought service without reference to color from butchers, banks, the local mill, and the railways. It regarded itself as the legitimate voice of the African community. "I would like this association to make it clear to the authorities," a Lusaka spokesman said, "that it is the mouthpiece of the people of the whole of the Lusaka district and that it does not represent individuals, but the community as a whole."[31]

A number of these associations decided, in May 1946, to create the

---

[30] Minutes printed in a pamphlet entitled *African Congress: First Annual Meeting,* (1944), p. 16.

[31] ACC/65/1/1: J. Y. Mumba, quoted in the minutes of a meeting of the Lusaka African Welfare Association, February 10, 1946, Lusaka archives.

Federation of African Societies of Northern Rhodesia. As its name implies, the Federation, like the Nyasaland Congress, was merely a body with which local societies could affiliate. Together, the representatives of fourteen of these associations subscribed to a constitution that declared that the Federation had been established in order "to speak for and on behalf of Africans . . . and . . . to promote and support any work which is calculated to ensure good feeling between Europeans and Africans. . . ."[32] Two years later, at a time when settlers had begun to agitate for "responsible government" and the specter of a possible tie to Southern Rhodesia had once again cast its evil shadow over their deliberations, the Federation decided to transform itself into a Congress. The founders of the Congress believed that it would provide a more effective platform from which they might attack settler domination and fight the attempt to create a political federation in Central Africa. At this stage, both the Northern Rhodesian and Nyasaland Congresses sought primarily to improve the benevolent exercise of Colonial Office overrule. They did not plot or want its overthrow. Impressed by what they conceived to be the horrors of settler rule, they instead desperately desired to retain their positions as "protected persons" and gradually to obtain the home rule that protection had always implied in their eyes. Only the struggle over "federation" could make them more militant.

The fear of "federation" provided a catalyst sufficient to transform the hesitant original Congresses into militant organizations capable of eventually destroying the governments of settlers. During the years from 1949 to 1953, Africans attempted to persuade the British government not to devolve its traditional responsibilities for African interests to the proposed federal body that would, so they gathered, gradually assume the powers of a unitary state. They understood that the then prevalent racial policies of Southern Rhodesia would, under "federation," poison the comparatively free atmosphere of Northern Rhodesia and Nyasaland. More than anything else, however, they believed that "federation" would mean the end of their long-cherished hopes of someday ruling themselves. Thus, in the two protectorates, and in London, both Congresses first fought energetically against any derogation of imperial trust and, after "federation" had become a reality in 1953, to destroy the federal government itself. Latterly too, the Congresses sought political freedom and national independence for the peoples of both protectorates.

The bitter fight against the imposition of the "federation" failed. But it had involved the interests of all Nyasas and Northern Rhodesians. The masses now joined the educated elite that had always demonstrated a political concern; and, together, under a succession of younger, more determined leaders, they battled to free themselves from all connections with

---

[32] Sec/Nat/353: Minutes of the meeting of the executive committee of the Federation of African Societies, May 18–19, 1946, Lusaka archives.

either the federal or the British government. In Northern Rhodesia, Harry Nkumbula, who had returned from the London School of Economics, became president of that territory's Congress and, with the help of Kenneth Kaunda, he attempted to make of it a useful instrument of change.

The Congress demonstrated its strength on a number of occasions by boycotting beer halls, Asian shops, and European butcheries. Indeed, in 1956, Congress finally breached the color barrier; henceforth Africans could generally enter any butcher shop and expect approximately equal service with whites. Meanwhile, Dunduzu Chisiza, Masauko Chipembere, and Kanyama Chiume had revitalized the Congress movement in Nyasaland. From 1956, both Chiume and Chipembere also sat on the Nyasaland Legislative Council. But neither Congress had, by this time, discovered a method whereby it might persuade the British government to grant the people of the two protectorates their independence. In 1957, Britons and white Rhodesians alike commonly believed that the federal experiment, with its underlying assumptions of "partnership" and "multiracialism," would succeed. They confidently expected the "federation" to remain in existence indefinitely.

In 1958, the return home to Nyasaland of Dr. Banda and Kaunda's decision to denounce Nkumbula introduced new elements into the conflict between white and black in Central Africa. With the assistance of Chisiza, Chipembere, and Chiume, Dr. Banda revitalized the Nyasaland Congress. Gathering new support in rural and urban areas alike, both Congresses determinedly sought the end of "federation" and freedom for their fellow countrymen. While they still hoped to usurp existing institutions constitutionally, their evident grip on the sympathies of large numbers of Africans and their professed militancy posed what the governments of the protectorates could only regard as a severe threat to order. In 1959, after Africans had disturbed the peace in parts of Nyasaland, the respective governors therefore outlawed both Banda's and Kaunda's Congresses. The leading members of both organizations soon found themselves under arrest. Nyasaland and Northern Rhodesia had, at last, crushed those who declared themselves nationalists.

Or so it seemed. In fact, Africans had demonstrated a determination sufficient to resist continued deprivation of what they regarded as their natural rights. The British government recognized that it could not continue to govern Nyasaland and Northern Rhodesia without the consent of the subject peoples. The next developments in the emergence of Malawi and Zambia became, therefore, only questions of time. Both Banda and Kaunda eventually walked from prison to the conference table. The British government introduced new constitutions; white Rhodesians unsuccessfully attempted to keep alive some kind of a settler-dominated federation; Africans began to play an increasing part in the political process; and elections were followed by phases of African political advance, variously labeled "responsible-" and "self-government."

At the onset of their independence, Africans firmly controlled the governments of Malawi and Zambia. Prime Ministers Banda and Kaunda had led their respective peoples to the freedom of which Kadalie had spoken. But, for the two Prime Ministers, new kinds of problems had arisen which threatened to disturb the enjoyment of independence by Malawians and Zambians. For the former, economic development and political control (including the quelling of a rebellion led by Chipembere) took precedence. No easy answers seemed available, although officials confidently expected to use new agricultural and manufacturing techniques to provide higher standards of living for their countrymen. In Zambia, the main problems appeared more political than economic. While Malawians, perhaps because of the Ngoni invasions, characteristically had long ago relegated their tribal loyalties to a secondary limbo, Zambians appeared more conscious of such origins. Kaunda had not inherited a nation; perforce, he had to create one himself before embarking on the economic and social improvements to which his government had committed itself. Personally moderate, he also found himself forced by the general pace of nationalism to try to satisfy some of his more extreme followers, many of whom wanted to claim overnight every part of the political kingdom for which they had fought so bitterly. For the moment, both independence movements, in their governmental guise, had chosen simply to take over the basic elements of the system with which they themselves had competed.

The period of transition opened with few in a position to predict the responses that Malawians and Zambians might give to the problems of their future. No one, in fact, knew whether or not Kaunda and Banda would be able to foster distinct national identities. African they would be, but the particular qualities of that general category remained unspecific.[33]

---

[33] This chapter was presented to a Syracuse University seminar in April 1964.

SELECTED BIBLIOGRAPHY

Conference of the History of the Central African Peoples. Lusaka: 1963.

Duff, Hector Livingston. *Nyasaland under the Foreign Office.* London, Eng.: George Bell and Sons, 1906.

Gray, Richard. *The Two Nations.* London, Eng.: Oxford University Press, 1960.

Jones, Griffith. *Britain and Nyasaland.* London, Eng.: Allen and Unwin, 1964.

Rotberg, Robert I. *The Rise of Nationalism in Central Africa.* Cambridge, Mass.: Harvard University Press, 1965.

Shepperson, George, and Thomas Price. *Independent Africa.* Edinburgh, Scot.: Edinburgh University Press, 1958.

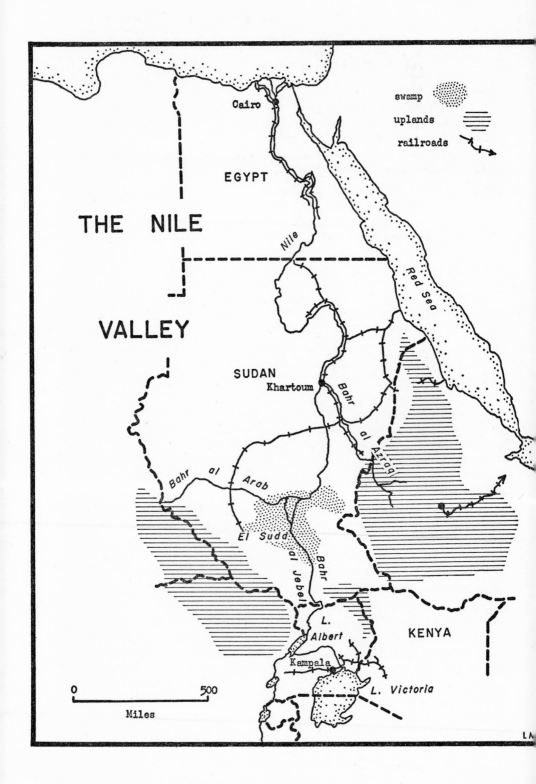

THE NILE

VALLEY

swamp

uplands

railroads

Cairo

EGYPT

Nile

Red Sea

SUDAN

Khartoum

Bahr al Azraq

Bahr al Arab

El Sudd

Bahr al Jebel

L. Albert

KENYA

Kampala

L. Victoria

0   500

Miles

9

The Sudan: Link to the North

Robert O. Collins

NILOTIC MIGRATIONS

Relations between the Sudan and East Africa have historically revolved around the lakes and rivers that combine to form the White Nile.
From earliest times, the Nile has been the traditional highroad along which
Africans, Arabs, and Europeans have moved south into East Africa. Many
customs of Pharaonic Egypt were transmitted up the Nile to eastern and
central Africa, where they are found in modified form today. For example,
the Meroitic iron-working techniques of the kingdoms of Kush probably
reached East Africa by the Nile, and the great migrations of Lwo-speaking
Nilotes came up the Nile Valley into East Africa from the savannah country
of the Southern Sudan. Occasionally the invaders were repulsed by the East
Africans. At times, the intervention of a third party contained the immigrants
north of the great lakes. But the pressure of cultural and population movements up the Nile has never ceased and has left an indelible imprint on those
areas of East Africa reached by influences from the north. In more recent
times, the Arabs followed in the footsteps of the Kushites and the Nilotes.
In the mid-nineteenth century, Arab Moslem Sudanese began to press up the
Nile into East Africa as traders, soldiers, and crusaders. Then during the
half-century of British imperial rule in Africa, these Sudanese encroachments
were momentarily checked, and the floodtide of Arab penetration ebbed back
down the Nile. Now, however, that the *Pax Britannica* has been lifted from
the Nile Basin, the historic tides of cultural encroachment, tribal migration,
immigration, and perhaps even military invasion will again flow into the
heart of Africa from the north. Future relations between the Sudan and East
Africa will certainly be conditioned by the character of the Arab advance
into sub-Saharan Africa and the reaction to this intrusion by the Negroid
people south of the desert.

Although both Cushitic-speaking people from Ethiopia in the east and
Bantu migrants from the west settled in East Africa in the Christian era, the

359

Lwo-speaking Nilotes were probably the first to approach the great lakes regions from the north. The Nilotic cradle land embraced that area of the Southern Sudan along the Bahr al-Jabal, south of Lake No, from which the Lwo-speaking Nilotes were first dispersed, probably in reaction to pressures from other Nilotic peoples living farther east in the basin of Lake Rudolf. One branch of the Lwo, ancestors of the Shilluk and the Anuak, swept north through the Bahr al-Ghazal. Another and larger group moved southward up the Nile and into the territory now known as Uganda, inhabited by Bantu-speaking people. Spread over two or perhaps three centuries, these western Nilotes pushed into East Africa in successive waves, the Lwo vanguard crossing the Victoria Nile sometime at the beginning of the sixteenth century. Once in Uganda, they settled among the Bantu, adopted their speech, and established Bito dynasties. Some of these Bito dynasties survive to this day in positions of authority in Buganda and Bunyoro, while a host of Bito clans still claim a privileged position in spite of the erosion of their rights over land and political authority by European overrule and modern democracy. Throughout the sixteenth century, these Lwo-speaking Nilotes appear to have moved steadily into northern Uganda; but in the seventeenth century, fresh contingents created secondary migrations west of the Bahr al-Jabal where the Nilotes came in contact with Sudanic peoples and east to the country north of Lake Kyoga and beyond. Wherever the Lwo settled, they established themselves as a ruling minority over the Bantu peoples, adopted the Bantu language, and accepted certain Bantu customs. The dramatic impact of the Lwo in northern Uganda appears not so much to have been the result of their military or cultural characteristics, which do not seem to have been decisively superior, but their political and social organization which transformed kinship polities into territorial units under Bito chiefs. The introduction of a leader or chief whose authority was territorial, rather than consanguineous, diminished, if not abolished, the spiral of violence associated with the continual but enervating blood feud of clan relationships. The Lwo invaders from the Sudan introduced into northern Uganda the basic political and social components from which the organization of society evolved until the coming of the Arabs and the Europeans in the nineteenth century.[1]

Pressed from behind by successive waves of Nilotes, the Lwo vanguard in

---

[1] The best summary of the many strands of evidence concerning the Lwo invasions of East Africa is at present: Roland A. Oliver and Gervase Mathew (eds.), *History of East Africa,* Vol. I (New York: Oxford University Press, 1963), 171–180. A detailed account of Lwo migrations is J. P. Crazzolara, *The Lwoo,* Vol. I (Verona, Italy: Missioni africane, 1950), which should be read, however, in conjunction with D. Westerman, *Geschichete Afrikas* (Köln: Greden-Verlag, 1952); Audrey J. Butt, *Nilotes of the Anglo-Egyptian Sudan and Uganda* (London: International African Institute, 1952); and A. W. Southall "Alur Traditional and Its Historical Significance," *Uganda Journal,* XVIII (1954).

northern Uganda soon pushed south and west into the kingdom of Kitara, which included the present territories of southern Bunyoro, Toro, western Buganda, and northern Ankole. Kitara was then ruled by aristocratic Hima pastoralists of probable Cushitic origins who had adopted the language of the Bantu agriculturalists over whom they had established feudal rule. At the time of the Lwo invasions, the political kingdoms of Kitara appear to have been directed by kings of the Chwezi clan of the Hima aristocracy, although other Hima dynasties in the past had traditionally preceded the Chwezi. As in northern Uganda, the Lwo invasion of Kitara in the sixteenth century was the decisive event that set the pattern of social and political organization in the kingdom. Bito dynasties replaced the Chwezi rulers, but clearly absorbed their more advanced culture as well as their Bantu speech. By substituting Bito ruling clans for Chwezi, the Lwo controlled not only the central kingdom of Kitara, now known under its Bito rulers as Bunyoro, but a number of peripheral satellite states as well. In these interlacustrine kingdoms, the Nilotic Lwo were certainly a pastoral minority among the Bantu peasant cultivators and the Hima pastoral aristocracy, but the responsibility for the rise of territorial states seems to belong to the imposition of Nilotic Bito clan control throughout the region. Much farther south in southern Ankole, Rwanda, and northwest Tanganyika where the Nilotic Lwo did not penetrate, the Hima, fleeing before Lwo invaders, moved south and west, introducing into that area a more complex political and social organization than hitherto appears to have existed. The invasion of western Lwo-speaking Nilotes not only created the structure for the evolution of the interlacustrine kingdoms, but triggered the spread of Hima political and social institutions beyond the borders of Uganda to the south.[2]

Farther to the east in Kenya and in northern Tanganyika, a second and older migration of Nilotic peoples from the Sudan had paralleled the southward drive of the Lwo into the region of the great lakes. Known variously as the Eastern Nilotes, the Cushitized Nilotes, or the Nilo-Hamites, these Nilotic-speaking people moved west and south from a dispersal area northwest of Lake Rudolf.[3] Those Eastern Nilotes that migrated west probably caused the dispersal, in turn, of the Lwo-speaking Nilotes to the north and south; and the Lango and Teso who later settled in northeastern Uganda

---

[2] Oliver and Mathew, *op. cit.,* pp. 180–184.

[3] At present, Africanists are divided into American and British schools of nomenclature concerning these Nilotic peoples. On the one hand, Americans tend to prefer Greenberg's phrase "Eastern Nilotes" or Murdoch's adaptation based on Greenberg's linguistic work of "Cushitized Nilotes." British scholars have persisted in their use of "Nilo-Hamites," now employing it almost solely as a linguistic term where previously it had been applied to a particular ethnotype. Greenberg has presented his arguments against the continued use of the term "Nilo-Hamite" in *The Languages of Africa* (Bloomington, Ind.: Indiana University, 1963), pp. 85–95, while Huntingford has championed the British school, defending the linguistic unity of Nilo-Hamitic in "The Nilo-Hamitic Languages," *Southwest Journal of Anthropology,* XII (1956).

appear to have come from the western fringe of the Rudolf basin. The southward movement of Eastern Nilotic peoples from the Sudan was certainly older and of far greater significance for East Africa. Beginning in antiquity, probably before the arrival of the Bantu, the Eastern Nilotes had moved south from Lake Rudolf into Kenya in successive waves, not unlike the Lwo migrations in the west at a later date. When the Nandi, for instance, arrived north of Mt. Elgon in the sixteenth century, other Eastern Nilotic tribes had long preceded them and inhabited large areas to the south. The more famous Masai seem to have been only the last of many groups of Eastern Nilotes who had pressed south from their cradle land in the Sudan at a much earlier date. Here the Eastern Nilotes were exposed to Bantu people moving north and east from central and southern Tanganyika and were reinforced only from time to time by additional groups of Nilotes from the Sudan. Unlike the interaction between the Lwo and the Bantu of the great lakes, contact between the Eastern Nilotes and the Bantu led neither to the formation of states nor to the Bantuization of the Nilotes. Rather, the Bantu appear to have adopted many military and social customs of the Eastern Nilotes, while the Nilotes, at least those long in the region, accepted many Bantu agricultural techniques. But whatever the degree of acculturation between Eastern Nilotes and Bantu, the Nilotic invaders from the Sudan, just as in the interlacustrine kingdoms to the west, decisively influenced the political and social organization of highland Kenya until the coming of the Europeans.[4]

THE ARAB SLAVE RAIDERS

The second group of invaders, the Sudanese slave traders, did not reach the frontier of East Africa until the second half of the nineteenth century. Before that time, the Khartoum merchants had failed to penetrate the swamps of the Nile which blocked the river passage to the Southern Sudan and Uganda. In 1841, however, a Turkish frigate captain, Salim Qapudan, with instructions from Muhammad Ali to seek the source of the White Nile, was able to navigate though the great swamps all the way to Gondokoro, near the present Sudan-Uganda border. Salim never found the source of the White Nile, but he did succeed in opening a river route to Central Africa. European and Arab merchants were quick to follow Salim, seeking to exploit the human and natural resources of the Southern Sudan and East Africa. At first they bartered for ivory with the Nilotic tribes along the Nile banks, but the Nilotes had neither the interest in ivory nor the political and economic organization to meet the commercial demands of the traders. Failing to acquire sufficient ivory from reluctant Nilotes, the traders soon established their own collectors in permanent encampments beyond the rivers. These agents gradually pushed their operations east and west into the interior and

---

4 Oliver and Mathew, *op. cit.,* pp. 199–203.

south up the river to Uganda. But trading posts, agents, and collecting expeditions were expensive, and, to meet increased costs, the traders extended their operations to slaves. Where once the merchants had remained aloof from intertribal quarrels, they now plunged into these internecine struggles, playing one Nilotic tribe against another. While their Nilotic allies acquired looted cattle, the traders obtained ivory and slaves. As with ivory, the greater profits of the slave trade went to the trader who had the energy and resources to seek out new supplies. Within a decade and a half after Salim Qapudan's pioneering voyage, a large and complex network of fortified trading stations laced the southern Sudan and Uganda from which the surrounding countryside was plundered and pillaged.

Here the savannah gave little natural defense against the powerful slavers, nor had the Nilotic inhabitants fashioned such states as the interlacustrine kingdoms to the south. Moreover, increasing numbers of Northern Moslem Sudanese became associated with the trade, either as agents of the traders or traders themselves, and these Sudanese made little effort to hide their contempt for the naked Nilotes whom they despised as barbarous pagans fit only for slavery. As early as the late 1850's, the Acholi region was ravaged by Sudanese agents of the Maltese trader Andrea De Bono, while rival traders were pushing south into Bunyoro. When Gordon and his successors put an end to the riverine slave trade twenty years later, the Sudanese agents and troops of the Egyptian traders Muhammed Ahmad al-'Aqqad and his successor Abu Su'ud had been raiding all along the Victoria Nile and into Bunyoro for over a decade. Both these traders had exploited the rivalries of the interlacustrine kingdoms for their own profit. In 1864, for instance, 'Aqqad had been handsomely rewarded by Kamrasi, King of Bunyoro, with ivory and slaves in return for raids against his rivals; and after Kamrasi's death in 1870, his successor, Kabarega, was even more dependent on the support of 'Aqqad and his men. The power of these Sudanese traders clearly undermined the authority of the Bunyoro kings, but the unholy alliance between these African rulers and the Moslem Sudanese traders laid the foundation for the growth of Islam and the spread of Arabic in Bunyoro which was later to have such fateful consequences during the political and religious struggles throughout Uganda in the 1890's. The Sudanese today may have forgotten the violence of their forebears on the Upper Nile in the third quarter of the nineteenth century, but their raids have not yet been erased from the memory of the Southern Sudanese and the peoples of northern Uganda and Bunyoro.

THE IMPERIALISM OF ISMA'IL

At the same time that Sudanese slave traders were extending their operations up the Nile to the interlacustrine kingdoms, the reports of European explorers, such as Richard F. Burton, John H. Speke, and James A. Grant, who had marched inland from the East African coast, revealed a "fertile and well-watered crescent" stretching from Lake Nyasa to Lake Albert, densely populated with well-organized, territorial, autocratic kingdoms.[5] All the explorers wrote enthusiastically about the great commercial possibilities which these wealthy East African states presented to the outside world. But the route from Zanzibar to the lake country was long and circuitous, passing through country held either by exacting petty chiefs or by the warlike Masai. Both Speke and Grant felt that the kingdom of the great lakes could best be tapped by the Nile route and not from the East African coast.[6] In June 1863, Speke himself outlined to Khedive Isma'il of Egypt a detailed plan to open up East Africa from the north. Educated in Egypt, Vienna, and Paris, Isma'il had absorbed much of the outward drive of the European society as well as inherited Muhammad 'Ali's interest in imperial expansion, and he set about to create a vast Egyptian empire in East Africa. The history of Isma'il's imperialism is well known: he sought to grasp East Africa in a gigantic pincher, one arm of which would strike inland from a base of operations on the coast of Somaliland, while the other arm would sweep eastward from the Upper Nile, gathering the African kingdoms into the fold of the Egyptian imperium. Isma'il's designs were never brought to fruition. His expedition to the East African coast, which seized Barawa in 1875, was quickly withdrawn—frustrated by British power which was determined to keep the Egyptians out of African waters. Isma'il's efforts on the Upper Nile were more rewarding.

In 1869, the Khedive commissioned Sir Samuel Baker to lead an expedition up the White Nile to establish Egyptian hegemony over the equatorial regions of Central Africa. Although the expedition was unable to make its way through the Nile swamps until April 1871, Baker, once he had reached Gondokoro, relentlessly imposed Egyptian authority over the Sudanese traders. He appropriated their trading stations and established an Egyptian government monopoly over the ivory trade so that the Khartoum merchants either withdrew or joined the Egyptian service hoping for better and more profitable days in the future. Baker had less success asserting Egyptian rule over the Africans. On the one hand, he earned the implacable hostility of the Bari by raiding for supplies he could not acquire by any other means, but, on the other, he won the support of the Acholi by curbing the slaving activities of Abu Su'ud and his agents. In April 1872, Baker crossed the Victoria Nile into Bunyoro, hoping to annex that kingdom to Egypt's growing empire in equatorial Africa. He failed. Kabarega had no use for the protection of the Khedive of Egypt and forced Baker back across the Victoria Nile to Fatiko on the Bunyoro frontier. But Kabarega's refusal combined with Baker's tact-

---

[5] Roland Oliver, *The Missionary Factor in East Africa* (New York: Longmans, Green, 1952). p. 29.

[6] Richard Gray, *A History of the Southern Sudan* (New York: Oxford University Press, 1961), Ch. 3.

less actions, if not outright hostility, created a legacy of mutual enmity between African and European which was carried over to the end of the century and was partly responsible for the animosity between Kabarega and the early British authorities who crushed Bunyoro and reduced that once proud kingdom to a petty African administrative district.

Baker soon returned to Europe and fame and fortune. His successor, Charles George Gordon, arrived in Equatoria in 1874. His object was the same as Baker's—to establish Egyptian authority over the interlacustrine kingdoms of the great lakes—but his means were considerably more pacific. He reasserted government control over the stations which, since the departure of Baker, had been used once again as slave centers by Sudanese traders. Gordon also stopped the continual foraging raids against the riverine tribes. But his goal was the lakes not the river, and he sought to convince Bunyoro and Buganda to recognize Egyptian sovereignty. In 1875, despite the opposition of Kabarega, he forcefully established Egyptian stations beyond the Victoria Nile in Bunyoro proper at Foweira and Mruli. This drive into Bunyoro was but part of a more concentrated effort to reach Buganda which had begun two years before when a Bagandan delegation arrived at Gondokoro from Kabaka Mutesa. The real purpose of the mission from Buganda was not to acknowledge Egyptian suzerainty, but to seal an alliance with Egyptian power to crush resurgent Bunyoro. Gordon never appreciated this distinction. He thought the Baganda were ready to acknowledge Egyptian authority and consequently entrusted the negotiations to an eccentric and conceited American, Chaillé-Long. Long failed to persuade Mutesa of the benefits of Egyptian rule. Combining political sagacity with the diplomacy of evasion, Mutesa sent Chaillé-Long back to Equatoria, convinced that Buganda had accepted Egyptian protection, when in reality such a claim appears to be more the invention of Long's imagination than Mutesa's wishes. To capitalize on the mission of Chaillé-Long, Gordon sent a second envoy, Linant de Bellefonds, to Buganda in the following year. Bellefonds knew that Long's claims did not agree with the facts, and, like Long, he was equally unsuccessful in obtaining the Kabaka's recognition of Egyptian sovereignty. In 1876, Gordon tried once again to extend Egyptian authority to Buganda. He sent Nur Agha to negotiate an agreement whereby Egyptian troops could occupy stations on Lake Victoria. In the end, Nur Agha was no more successful than Chaillé-Long or Bellefonds, and, with his resources exhausted, Gordon called off his attempts to incorporate Buganda into the Egyptian empire. At the time, however, Gordon perceived the setback as only temporary, and he left Equatoria convinced that within two years the Egyptian flag would fly on the shores of the Victoria Nyanza. Gordon was wrong. When he returned to Khartoum in 1877, as governor-general of the Sudan, he realized that the resources of Egypt were insufficient to absorb the interlacustrine kingdoms of the great lakes. In 1879, Egypt was bankrupt, and the Khedive abandoned forever his dream of a vast equatorial domain and sailed away on his yacht, the *Mahrusa,* to a gilded exile in a palace on the Bosphorus. Gradually, the Egyptian garrisons in Bunyoro were withdrawn, and, by 1881, all that was left of Egypt's equatorial empire was a riverine rump extending from Lado to Lake Albert under the governorship of that enigmatic German doctor, Emin Pasha. Although this finger of territory pointing into East Africa might have served as a base of operations from which Egypt could press south again at some future time, events in the north soon destroyed such wishful thoughts. In 1881, the Mahdist rebellion erupted in the Northern Sudan, and Egyptian hopes of hegemony in East Africa faded with the dissolution of the Egyptian administration before the militant vigor of Mahdism.

But if Egypt had failed to establish her political dominion over the inter-lacustrine kingdoms, she left behind a religious and cultural legacy that had a profound effect throughout Uganda for another generation. North of the Victoria Nile, Egyptian stations remained as islands of cultural contact between Arab and African, and a half-caste population sprang up through intermarriage and profligate concubinage. The number of camp followers attached to the Egyptian stations became truly astounding. Bastard Arabic became the lingua franca of the Africans within the neighborhood of these stations, and Islam was widely practiced wherever the soldiers were found. These same troops continued for years to play an important role in the clan feuds of the Acholi and of other tribes in what is now the northern province of Uganda. This ethnic intermixture and acculturation by intimate contact was diffused beyond the vicinity of the stations by petty Sudanese traders who roamed the countryside spreading the use of Arabic and the practice of Islam. Although Mutesa refused to allow Sudanese merchants into Buganda, there were many in Bunyoro where they frequently joined the mercenary army of the Omukama, supplied arms and ammunition in return for ivory and slaves, and more generally laid the foundations for a strong Moslem community.

THE MAHDIST INVASIONS

The next Sudanese, Moslem drive to penetrate East Africa from the north was the Mahdist invasions. The Mahdists were the followers of Muhammad Ahmad, al-Mahdi, who rose against Egyptian administration in the early 1880's and established their rule throughout the length and breadth of the country. Although the Mahdists were deeply concerned with fashioning a political kingdom in the Sudan, religion was the driving force of their movement. As the guided one, the Mahdi was to bring equity and justice to earth by returning to the puritan strictures of primitive Islam. In the tradition of the Wahhabi movement in Arabia and of the Sanusiya in Libya, the Mahdists insisted on a more austere, literal interpretation of the Koran than the legal and sophisticated readings of the orthodox Moslems in the northern cities beyond the desert. Like the Wahhabis and the Sanusiya, they were determined to establish the rule of Mahdism throughout the earth by the *jihad,* or holy war. In 1884–1885, a strong Mahdist force under the command of Karam Allah Muhammad Kurqusawi conquered the Bahr al-Ghazal province of the Southern Sudan and moved against the Egyptian troops of Emin Pasha, who still held the stations on the Upper Nile. Only the sudden recall to Umdurman of Karam Allah and his men at the death of the Mahdi in the summer of 1885 saved Emin Pasha forces from being overwhelmed by the Mahdists. Most of the petty Sudanese traders and camp followers joined their kinsmen and retired to the North.

Three years later, the Mahdists returned to the Upper Nile, under the command of Umar Salih, determined to drive out the Egyptian garrisons and spread Islam, by fire and sword if necessary, among the African Negroid population. Seasoned fighters, immune to hardships, and fanatically devoted to the cause of Sudanese Islam, the Mahdists succeeded in driving the Egyptian garrisons south to Wadelai and Lake Albert, where mutiny and divided leadership rendered them impotent. Certainly the Mahdists would have pressed south into the interlacustrine kingdoms had they not been forced to turn west to face the advancing forces of Leopold II, King of Belgium and Sovereign of the Congo Free State. For nearly a decade, the Mahdists and the Congolese struggled for control of the Upper Nile, until 1897, when the Sudanese were decisively defeated at Rajjaf. In the following year, they fled from the Southern Sudan. The intervention of the Congo Free State on the Upper Nile in the 1890's unquestionably prevented Sudanese encroachment into East Africa, where the impact of the Mahdists was consequently slight. In the early years of their campaign, the Congolese drew off the major Moslem influence from Equatoria and Bunyoro and eventually drove them from the Upper Nile before the arrival of the British. Even at the height of their control of the Nile Valley, the Mahdist ascendancy over the Negroid peoples was ephemeral and the fanaticism of their religion repugnant to the Africans. Sir Gerald Portal was convinced that the Mahdists in the Southern Sudan were linked with Moslem activities in Tanganyika, but there is no evidence to support this conclusion. The King of Bunyoro, Kabarega, had hoped to ally with the Mahdists against the advancing European Christians, but nothing came of these overtures. Throughout the Northern and West Nile provinces of Uganda, the Mahdists are today only an unpleasant and bitter memory, rapidly fading with the death of tribal elders.[7]

Although the Mahdists had discredited Islam and the Arabs along the northern border lands of East Africa, the former Egyptian troops left behind by Emin Pasha in 1890 continued to spread Moslem influence in Uganda. These Sudanese troops were the legacy of Isma'il's imperial adventure, a sorry remnant of that most purposeful Egyptian drive into eastern Africa.

---

[7] R. O. Collins, *The Southern Sudan, 1883–1898* (New Haven: Yale University Press, 1962) Chs. 2 and 3.

After the departure of Emin Pasha, these Sudanese troops had remained in the vicinity of Kavalli on Lake Albert until 1891, when they were enlisted into the services of the Imperial British East Africa Company by Captain Frederick Lugard and subsequently posted in a series of stockades in Toro to defend against Bunyoro incursions. They courageously defended these posts until 1893, when they were withdrawn to Buganda. Here they came under the influence of the Moslem party at Kampala, and their susceptibilities to their rebellious co-religionists were only checked by the arrest of the Sudanese leader Salim Bey. Thereafter, the Sudanese continued to serve the Protectorate government loyally until 1898 when they mutinied against their officers. The greater part were hunted down and dispersed into the swamps beyond Lake Kyoga, while a few joined Kabarega in refuge in the Northern Province of Uganda. Speaking Arabic and practicing Islam, the Sudanese strengthened the Moslem party by their presence in Buganda and, until their mutiny, served as a principal agent in the spread of Islam in East Africa by example, inter-marriage, and by their general support for Moslem converts.

In the Southern Sudan, the effects of the Mahdist invasions were more critical than in Uganda. One must regard the Mahdist invasions as extended raids which upset the traditional pattern of tribal life, disrupted the sub-sistence economy, and even depopulated areas where the raids of the North-erners were thorough and unremitting. Many of the tribal leaders were killed or carried off with their tribesmen to captivity. Villages were plundered for ivory and supplies, crops destroyed, and Mahdism forced on the in-habitants. Well armed with Remington repeating rifles and the courage and zeal of their religion, the Mahdists, although small in number, had little difficulty in defeating the Negroid tribesmen. But it was precisely their small numbers which perpetuated the breakdown of tribal society. For though strong enough to defeat the Negroids, they were never sufficiently strong to establish hegemony over them and were compelled to raid again and again, not only to maintain their own position, but also to secure even the most essential supplies. The only lasting result of these continual raids was the ever-increasing depth of the Southerner's hatred for and fear of the Northern Sudanese. The era of the Mahdist in the Southern Sudan must therefore be regarded as the culmination of a long series of misfortunes which had fallen upon that unfortunate land in the latter half of the nineteenth century. Before the coming of the slave traders and the Egyptian administration, the smaller tribes of the Southern Sudan were concerned with survival, while the stronger tended to expand and to assimilate their less powerful neighbors. For example, during the nineteenth century, the Azande had pressed north-ward across the Congo-Nile Divide until halted by the establishment of Egyptian administration in the Bahr al-Ghazal. Small, weak tribes, such as the Bongo, the Kreisch, and the Shatt could not withstand the Azande, who, under their autocratic Avungura chiefs, formed a cohesive fighting machine, efficient in war and stable in peace. It would appear that the Dinka tribes were also expanding at the expense of their weaker neighbors. Less cohesive than the Azande and unwilling to acknowledge a supreme ruler, the Dinka confederation was slowly pushing westward from the swamps of the Nile and, by sheer weight of numbers, driving the weaker tribes before them, frequently into the arms of the Azande.[8]

By the latter half of the nineteenth century, the fluid society of the Southern Sudan had thus been disrupted by the arrival of three successive waves of invaders—the slave traders, the Egyptian Army, and the Mahdists. Each of the three had, in turn, not only dislocated tribal life in the Southern Sudan, but in many cases had caused the breakdown of tribal society. Playing on tribal jealousies and animosities, the slave traders raided and plundered the tribes for slaves who were sent northward to fill the harems and armies of Egypt and the Arab world. The advent of Egyptian administration brought an end to wide-scale slave-raiding, particularly in the Bahr al-Ghazal under Gessi Pasha and in Equatoria under Gordon; but the Egyptian government was never able to persuade the tribes of the Bahr al-Ghazal and Equatoria to accept its administration. Such tribes as the Dinka, or the Nuer, or even the Feroge, or the Njangulgule were as loath to suffer an alien government as slavery. To maintain their rule in the Southern Sudan, the Egyptian government found it necessary to coerce the tribes to accept the administration and to suppress tribal rebellions with punitive expeditions. These repressive measures by the Egyptian Army caused a further breakdown of tribal society. Chiefs were shot, their subjects killed, the cattle seized, and the crops commandeered. Although the tribes of the Southern Sudan were anxious to rid themselves of Egyptian rule, they did not simply wish to exchange the oppressive rule of the Egyptians for that of the Mahdists. Disinterested in Mahdism, the tribes resisted attempts by the new invaders to force Mahdist rule and religion on them. The Mahdists crushed the tribes, smashing what remained of their former traditional way of life and causing in turn a further breakup of tribal society. Although the Mahdists did not remain in the Bahr al-Ghazal, and were confined largely to the riverine area in Equatoria, the fanaticism of their rule and the uncompromising nature of their religion disrupted tribal life in the Southern Sudan as much as, if not more than, did the longer periods of control by the slave traders and the Egyptian government.

ARRIVAL OF THE BRITISH

Mahdist rule in the Southern Sudan was brought to an end by the appearance of yet a fourth wave of invaders, the British. Years of alien oppression had made the tribes suspicious of any new invader, and, although decimated and disintegrated, the tribes accepted Anglo-Egyptian rule with reluctance

---

[8] *Ibid.*, pp. 177–178.

and, in those areas where a semblance of authority and order remained, only after military conquest.

Although the Anglo-Egyptian forces overthrew the Mahdist state at the climactic battle of Karari, in September 1898, the Anglo-Egyptian Condominium Government, created to administer the conquered Sudan, did not begin the pacification and occupation of the southern provinces until considerably later. Not until December 1900 did Sudanese troops, commanded by British officers, embark from Khartoum for the Bahr al-Ghazal where they proceeded to establish a network of posts throughout the province. The following year, riverine stations were erected on the Bahr al-Jabal. The construction of government posts garrisoned by troops and managed by British officials did not mean that the *Pax Britannica* was imposed on the vast reaches of countryside surrounding the isolated stations. Only gradually did British officers win the confidence of the African peoples in the Southern Sudan—sometimes by cajolery, gifts, and peaceful displays of force and, at other times, by offers of protection, threats, and even by playing on the traditional enmities of the tribes. They trekked throughout the countryside visiting chiefs, villages, and tribal gatherings. On occasion, they were accompanied by a large and well-armed escort when respect required force. Frequently a lonely district officer tramping through the bush with a butterfly net and a few porters made a greater impression than legions of well-disciplined troops. With or without arms, however, the purpose was the same —to establish the authority of the Sudan government, hopefully by peace but if necessary by war. The task was enormous, and the men and financial resources few. A generation was to pass before British officers could claim that the unquestioned rule of the Sudan government stretched throughout the length and breadth of the southern provinces.

ADMINISTRATION OF THE SOUTHERN SUDAN

Those tribes residing in the central Bahr al-Ghazal or in Equatoria along the Nile which had experienced the intensive attack from the slave traders, Egyptians, and Mahdists were the first to capitulate to British officers and accept the government's authority. For the most part, they consisted of sedentary cultivators who formed the core of the peoples of the Bahr al-Ghazal and Equatoria and, although badly disintegrated, had been a creative and industrious people in the nineteenth century. On the periphery of these central areas easily accessible from the river ports, British officers faced increasing resistance directly proportional to the distance from the government stations. In the Azande country to the south, the powerful chief Yambio was determined never again to submit to alien rule.[9] In the Dinka swamp

---

[9] Yambio or Mbio had been captured by Egyptian government forces in 1882, where he remained a prisoner for nearly two years. When he re-established his position in his land, he vowed, according to the Zande tradition, never again to be made a prisoner by alien invaders.

country beyond Rumbek, the Agar and the Atwot had fought successfully against slavers, Egyptian administrators, and the Mahdists and regarded the British as just another invader to keep out of their marshland. Further to the north and deeper in the swamps lived the Nuer whose isolation in the heart of such a lonely and inaccessible land had protected them from the encroachments of the nineteenth century and had long sheltered them from British rule in the twentieth. The Nuer did not submit until the early 1930's. South of the Nuer on the upper Pibor in swampland nearly as formidable as that of the Nuer, the Beir defied the government until 1911, when they were finally overwhelmed by a strong punitive expedition. Still farther south on the Uganda frontier, Sudan government control moved eastward very slowly to Lake Rudolf, only establishing its uncontested authority in that region during the 1920's.

This long period of pacification in the Southern Sudan clearly conditioned the form of European imperial rule which emerged and, in turn, shaped the evolution of tribal society. The principal task of the Condominium Government was to establish its authority, and many British officials realized that this could be most easily and inexpensively accomplished by enlisting the cooperation of the traditional tribal chiefs and headmen. General Horatio Herbert Kitchener implied as much when, in 1899, he laid down a general line of policy to be followed by British administrators in the Sudan:

Mudirs and Inspectors should learn to know personally all principal men of the district and show them, by friendly dealings and the interest taken in their individual concerns, that our object is to increase their prosperity. It is to the individual action of British officers, working independently but with a common purpose, on the individual natives whose confidence they have gained that we must look for the moral and industrial regeneration of the Sudan.[10]

What was more natural than to enlist in the task of administration of the district the "principal men" who were the accepted leaders in the community. To enroll the tribal authorities in the task of government was a natural response, arising not from any prearranged plan but simply as a solution to the problem of ruling a vast area of land with insufficient troops and a limited number of British administrative officers. Not only would instructions from the government reach the people through the authorities they had traditionally accepted, but the enforcement could be made along the traditional lines of the customary law of the tribe. Reliance on local institutions precluded the need for a centralized bureaucracy and gave recognition to the tribal leaders without which they would be a threat and a danger to the government. It was practical, logical, and conservative, and, as early as 1910, District Commissioner H. W. Channer Bey wrote from Tambura district in Zandeland: "The policy of the Government here as throughout the country is to support the sultans and chiefs in their dealings with their own subjects

---

[10] *Annual Report on the Administration of the Sudan 1899*, p. 55.

—allowing them to administer according to their tribal customs as far as possible."[11]

In spite of Channer's (and other similar) statements, the actions of British administrators in the Southern Sudan did not conform in practice to this policy. During the first decade of British rule, the administrative officers were actually more concerned with limiting than supporting the power of the tribal chiefs. For instance, in Maridi district, the powers of the great Zande sultan, Mangi, were so restricted that "he could no longer exert effective authority over all his people."[12] Or the case of Chief Oku of Yambio district who, when appointed, had "openly stated that his following was so small that he could not maintain his position if the troops were withdrawn." Within a few months, poor Oku was "continually running away and leaving people in the lurch" —clearly not helping the cause of native administration.[13] Then there was the case of Chief Murad of Kafia Kingi in the western Bahr al-Ghazal who was deposed "owing to his disobedience to government orders and his treacherous conduct toward the Inspector of Raga District."[14] Twenty years later, the district commissioner of this same district commented that "it appears to have been the policy of the D.C. here in the early days to break down any tribal organization that ever existed—with the result that *real* chiefs did not now exist."[15] At the same time, another experienced district commissioner in the eastern district of the Bahr al-Ghazal blamed his predecessors for destroying any sense of tribal unity in the region. The list of deposed Southern Sudanese chiefs could be extended indefinitely, the reasons for such depositions ranging from incompetence to insubordination to personality clashes with British officials. Invariably their successors were men primarily committed to the government and only secondarily to the tribe.

> If we too often interfere the people not only give us little thanks for it, but they cease to look to the Sheikh for their redress or to obey him. They play him and the government off the one against the other and consequently the Sheikh has no effective power, finding himself in an impossible position and is tempted to make a catspaw of the government.[16]

But this contradiction between policy and practice in the administration of the Southern Sudan was not limited to the deposition and the appointment

---

[11] "Report on Tambura District, December 1910," by H. W. Channer Bey, Mongalla, I/5/32, SGA (Sudan Government Archives).

[12] Sudan Intelligence Report No. 69, August 1908, Appendix A, SGA.

[13] A Sutherland Bey to Civil Secretary, December 20, 1905, Palace Papers, III/3/19, SGA.

[14] Sudan Intelligence Report No. 165, April, 1908, SGA.

[15] District Commissioner, Western District, to Governor, Bahr al-Ghazal Province, March 4, 1930, Bahr al-Ghazal, I/1/2, SGA.

[16] "Memorandum on General Administrative Policy, 1924," Civil Secretary, I/9/30, SGA.

of chiefs. The mere presence of a government post frequently made use of traditional authorities in the administration of the surrounding area quite impossible. At the time of the Anglo-Egyptian occupation of Meridi, for instance, many Africans sought the safety and protection of government posts, where by making themselves agreeable and useful to the soldiers, they gained their friendship and protection. Relying on such protection, these settlers were virtually free agents and would invariably flout the authority of the local chief. The British officials soon found themselves on the horns of a dilemma. On the one hand, they did not wish for humane reasons to refuse legitimate protection; yet, on the other, they could not grant asylum without undermining the authority of the local leaders. Those administrators who tried to solve the problem by placing such settlers under the local chiefs were dismayed to find that the chiefs were so intimidated by the newcomers that they failed to enforce their authority over persons living near a government post.[17]

Peace also eroded the influence of the local traditional leaders. The basic aim of the British administration was, of course, the cessation of intertribal warfare and the establishment of a *Pax Britannica* throughout the Southern Sudan. By 1930, the Sudan government was moderately successful in achieving this goal, but, as a consequence, "there is a tendency for tribes to split, as the necessity of one strong leader was no longer apparent to the people."[18] Tribes hitherto united by fear of aggression from a neighbor broke down into parochial kinship groups, confident in the protection that the government had guaranteed, while the chiefs, prohibited by the government from the use of harsh methods, frequently were powerless to keep their followers in line. For example, the Zande chief Mangi gradually lost control of his people, not so much from his own physical infirmities, as from British prohibitions against his "not putting people ruthlessly to death as he did formerly," or the case of the Berri chief Alikori who frankly admitted that "he might have some difficulty in restraining his young bloods."[19]

Thus, after two decades of imperial rule, British officials had failed to resolve the paradox of administration in the Southern Sudan. Although ostensibly claiming to support the traditional authorities and permitting them to rule according to customary practices, more often than not the tribal leaders had to be broken, either to establish uncontested British control or to halt intertribal warfare or both. Yet, ironically, peace tended to undermine the traditional authorities, for the people no longer required leadership as a defense against aggression. As in the more turbulent days of the nineteenth

---

[17] Bahr al-Ghazal Province Report, Meridi and Yambio District, Intelligence, II/26/214, SGA.

[18] Sudan Intelligence Report No. 167, June 1908, Appendix E, "Report on Tagale Merkaz," SGA.

[19] Sudan Intelligence Reports Nos. 146, September 1906, and 169, August 1908, Appendix A, SGA.

century, when the invasions of the slave traders, Egyptian officials, and the Mahdists overwhelmed tribal authorities and broke up ethnic units, the *Pax Britannica* precipitated a similar result by reducing the need for institutions of authority and thereby encouraging the centrifugal forces of clan and kin groups when danger no longer threatened. Between the depredations of the nineteenth-century raiders and the consolidation of authoritarian rule by the British the 1920's there were few chiefs who could be described as the traditional leaders, while the power of those hereditary rulers who had survived had been rendered increasingly ineffective by the demands of the government to conform to Western standards of peace, humanity, and justice. As the British governor of Mongalla province laconically remarked in 1929, "the government support which can be given to the chiefs is not worth their while to have."[20]

By failing to utilize the traditional political organizations of the peoples of the Southern Sudan, administration was concentrated into the hands of the British district commissioner who had to deal directly, not only with executive matters involving the people in his district, but even more so with judicial cases as well. Rather than devoting his time to the larger questions of administration, the British district commissioner found himself besieged with endless civil cases concerned principally with the frailties of women or the ownership of cattle, the adjudication of which would certainly have been handled as well, if not better, by indigenous authority than by a British officer who had, at best, an incomplete knowledge of tribal law and custom acquired by inaccurate experience and incompetent interpretation. Direct administration was, in effect, time consuming, unwieldy, and often quite unjust. Yet the policy of the Sudan government in the southern provinces was regularly reiterated as one of devolution and "decentralized" control. "Administration is to be left, as far as possible, in the hands of the native authorities. . . . Native chiefs are to be encouraged to administer their own tribes in accordance with native customs, in so far as these customs are not entirely repugnant to ideas of justice and humanity."[21] But even the most naïve district commissioner and the most obtuse governor recognized the wide divergence between policy and practice, and, in the 1920's, they set about to close this gap, to support the chiefs, to bolster existing tribal authorities, and to rediscover, if necessary, those customs and traditions which had been lost or fallen into disuse.

I take it that it is now clearly realized that the policy of the Government is to get the administration of affairs which are purely native back onto a tribal basis and that the function of the Government is to supervise, guide, and

20 "Notes on Current Topics in Mongalla Province," by A. W. Skrine, March 1929, Civil Secretary, I/11/36, SGA.

21 Proceedings of the Southern Governors Meeting, March 1922, Civil Secretary, I/9/31, SGA.

mould tribal organization, rather than to destroy such systems of customary law, discipline, and culture as the natives already possess.[22]

British officials in the Southern Sudan first sought to enhance African tribal organization and customs by delegating judicial powers to the chiefs, since both executive and legislative functions of government could hardly be relinquished by the imperial authorities. Drawing their examples from the *lukiki* court of Uganda and imaginatively experimenting with judicial forms most suited to the peoples of their districts, the district commissioners gradually and informally inaugurated courts of African chiefs which considered cases within the tribe with a view to their ultimately acquiring official magisterial powers under the code of criminal procedure.

Although the inauguration of formal chiefs' courts may have enhanced the prestige of the chief, it did not necessarily strengthen his authority. The demands that the administration of justice placed on the chiefs were considerable. No longer was justice merely a matter of dispensing decisions within the context of tribal law from beneath a large tree. Now it involved the keeping of records, fees, and transcripts of cases in the best traditions of the English law courts. Many chiefs had neither the ability nor the competence to contend with court records or financial statements and, consequently, were replaced by individuals who, the district commissioners hoped, could carry on the work more effectively. During this period, the district records contain many revealing statements: "Chief Quoich Kuma has been making efforts at reinstatement, but they are typical and will avail him nothing. . . . Chief Akoavungura has been removed from the list of chiefs' courts for laziness in his work, but has been retained as regent."[23]

Indeed, the principal problem of the administration was to find a sufficient number of able chiefs who could fill the role of servant to the government. V. H. Fergusson, the famous Fergie Bey, district commissioner in the Eastern District, Bahr al-Ghazal, wrote in 1927: "Our most difficult task at the present moment is to find suitable chiefs with sufficient tribal authority to control those under them and at the same time being capable of appreciating the Government's methods to such an extent as to be able to act as teachers of the people."[24]

Fergie Bey had a particularly difficult task in attempting to implement chiefs' courts among the Nuer and the Dinka of the Eastern District. To these tribes, the institutions of a single chiefs' court to decide all cases in which the tribe was involved was indeed a novelty, for neither the Nuer nor

---

[22] "Notes regarding Chiefs Courts and Native Administration in Mongalla Province," December 1, 1924, by A. W. Skrine, Mongalla, I/1/2, SGA.

[23] "Yambio and Rumbek District Intelligence Reports," November 16–December 31, 1929, Civil Secretary, I/3/43, SGA.

[24] "Report by Fergusson Bey on the Eastern District," June 1927, Civil Secretary, I/13/43, SGA.

certain Dinka tribes had ever possessed, as an indigenous institution, a chiefs' court until one was imposed on them by the government. Under these conditions, the attempt to apply the principles of devolution to tribal authorities turned from the sublime to the ridiculous. In March 1927, the governor of the Bahr al-Ghazal admitted failure in attempting to apply chiefs' courts to the Nuer:

> Cattle cases are only heard by the cattle chief, land cases by the land chief, and so on. . . . Unfortunately, when we first started administering this province, this ancient system was not known and it has only recently been realized. In our ignorance we presumed that a chief was a dispenser of justice in every case and was generally paramount in the tribe. Undoubtedly in many instances a kujur or witchdoctor had usurped this paramount right and the old system had fallen into disuse. Through lack of knowledge and inexperience we failed to grasp this point, and jumping over this stage, we appointed chiefs to whom we looked as the responsible head.[25]

The basically alien procedure of the chiefs' courts should not, however, obscure their overwhelming success as judicial institutions. Grafted to African circumstances and nurtured by the district commissioner, the chiefs' courts functioned effectively in many districts even where the indigenous judicial powers of the chiefs had been miniscule. Although regarded as a government institution, chiefs' courts multiplied rapidly throughout the southern provinces, adjudicating a host of civil cases, by tribal custom, mostly of a domestic nature, which before had frustrated the Solomonic wisdom of the district commissioners. Not only did the Africans receive better justice, but they clearly preferred it to that of British officials. The courts at once enhanced the prestige of the chief, even though he was still regarded as a "government man." For the first time in over half a century, the precipitous decline of the chief as a tribal leader was checked; whereas, among those Nilotic peoples who had never recognized a permanent leader, the new institution partially satisfied the needs of a changing society in which the more traditional forms of minimal government were becoming inadequate. The new chief was thus transformed from a symbol of declining authority to a position of predominance, for whether the chief and his court were created without precedent or were simply a revitalized form of an ancient tribal institution, the British acknowledged the participation of the Southern Sudanese chiefs as a part of imperial rule and consequently had to support them. Moreover, as the locus of the court was the chief, the centrifugal tendencies of the more decentralized societies in the Southern Sudan were counteracted. The African was now encouraged to take a part in the regulation of his society, thereby evolving greater interest in affairs that directly and personally affected him. The government appeared less alien, and there was less reason to feel politically restless or hopelessly indifferent.

---

25 Governor, Bahr al-Ghazal to the Civil Secretary, March 21, 1927, Civil Secretary I/10/34, SGA.

British officials were enthusiastic over the introduction of Africans into the administration. Not only did the district commissioners in the southern provinces welcome the relief from petty judicial business, but, in a more positive spirit, hoped to broaden the powers of chiefs' courts to take on administrative as well as judicial functions. Even more than the British administrators in the field, the officials in Khartoum and in Whitehall regarded the chiefs' court as the basis for the continuing evolution of native administration. They were deeply imbued with the principle of entrusting local administration to traditional authorities, commensurate with the dictates of indirect rule, which—among colonial officials—had passed "through three stages, first of a useful administrative device, then that of a political doctrine, and finally of a religious dogma."[26] Like British officials in Nigeria, Tanganyika, and Uganda, those in the Sudan soon revered the principles of indirect rule with mystic awe. Ignoring the fact that the institution of chiefs' courts in the Southern Sudan was in many areas an alien instrument, although in others it had but a tenuous connection with traditional institutions, the Sudan government set out to make the South safe for Africanization.

SEPARATION OF NORTH AND SOUTH

The Sudan is a diverse land inhabited by widely differing peoples, but for centuries a fundamental cleavage has separated the Northern and the Southern Sudanese. Racially, the North claims to be Arab; and the South, Negroid. In religion, the North is Moslem; the South is pagan and Christian. Linguistically, the North speaks Arabic; the South, some eighty different languages. Thus, when judicial responsibilities were devolved on chiefs, and the British administrators sought to rediscover, preserve, and create, if necessary, African customs and traditions, no question was more fundamental or more basic to the future development of African societies in the Southern Sudan than the role of the Arab, Moslem, and Northern Sudanese in the southern provinces. No question of administration, whether it could be one of education, religion, trade, transport, or even health, could possibly be resolved without reference to the advisability of permitting Islamic influences in the pagan, Negroid South. African participation in administration and the revitalization of African customs could hardly occur if such customs were continually eroded by contacts with the Arab-speaking peoples of the Northern Sudan. Thus, a year before the judicial innovations of the chiefs' courts were regularized throughout the southern provinces by the promulgation of the Chiefs' Courts Ordinance of 1931, Sir Harold MacMichael, the Civil Secretary of the Sudan government, issued a secret memorandum restating that: "The Policy of the Government in the Southern Sudan is to build up a series of self-contained racial and tribal units with structure and organization based, to whatever extent the requirements of equity and good

---

[26] Lord Hailey, "Some Problems Dealt with in an African Survey," *International Affairs* (March/April 1939), p. 202.

government permit, upon indigenous customs, traditional usage, and beliefs."[27]

Such a statement of policy was hardly new or secret, but the forceful recommendations to carry out this policy which followed were a startling demonstration of the determination of the Sudan government to preserve the African way of life of the Southern Sudanese. In order to encourage the growth of African customs, whether traditional, rediscovered, or simply created, all Northern Sudanese, Moslem, Arab influences were to be eradicated from the southern provinces. First, all Arabic-speaking administrative staff, including clerical and technical personnel, were to be replaced from local sources, and the language of the government offices was to be henceforth English. Second, Syrian and Greek traders were to be urged to replace Arab merchants in the Southern Sudan. Third, it was emphatically urged that the British staff familiarize themselves with the beliefs, customs, and the language of the tribes they administered. Under no circumstances were they to rely on their knowledge of Arabic and Moslem culture learned in prior service in the North. This new "Southern Policy" put into official practice what many British officers had long felt about the encroachment of the Arabs and Islam into Central Africa. Since the spread of British influence in Africa in the nineteenth century, many Englishmen have deplored the extension of Arab, Islamic influence into Negro Africa. Victorian humanitarians who were also devout Christians could hardly look with equanimity on the spread of Moslem influence up the Nile, when that influence had been so closely associated with the East African and Nilotic slave trade. They would have agreed wholeheartedly with Kitchener's concern about Arab encroachment into the center of the continent, expressed in an 1892 memorandum on Uganda: "Unless the Christian powers hold their own in Africa, the Mohammedan Arabs will, I believe, step in, and in the center of the continent will form a base from which they will be able to drive back all civilizing influences to the coast, and the country will then be given up to slavery and misrule as in the case in the Sudan at present."[28]

Like most basic administrative decisions, Southern Policy was not fully developed in 1910 and was not clearly stated or vigorously and consistently pursued until MacMichael's Memorandum of 1930. Indeed, in 1920, the British governors of the southern provinces voted "that the introduction of Muhammadanism is not undesirable and that active steps to prevent its spread should not be taken, but that no encouragement should be given it."[29] This moderate and indifferent attitude was to exist for nearly a decade thereafter until the inauguration of indirect rule. When the Sudanese forces took

---

[27] Memorandum on Southern Policy, January 25, 1930, by Sir Harold MacMichael, Bahr al-Ghazal, I/1/1, SGA.

[28] Memorandum on Uganda, September 1892, by H. H. Kitchener, Conference Report 185, Cairo Intelligence, III/1/11, SGA.

[29] Minutes of the Southern Governor's Meeting, 1920, Mongalla, I/5/31, SGA.

over the Lado Enclave from the Belgians in June 1910, the question of Northern Sudanese influences in the South was raised by both the Church Missionary Society and the Roman Catholic (Verona Fathers) missionaries who urged that the Sabbath, observed by the Belgians on Sunday, be retained on that day instead of Friday as was practiced generally throughout the Sudan.[30] The British governor of Mongalla Province and the Lado Enclave, R. C. R. Owen, cautioned against retaining Sunday as the day of worship for

> the bigoted Moslems, of which there are always some among both officers, including Imams, and men in every Sudanese Battalion might and I think probably would cause trouble if made to work on Fridays. Unfortunately the army is a great mission agent and all the Sudanese askari make a point of seeing that every recruit does become one and the Imams instruct them from the Koran.[31]

A few months later, Owen suggested that an equatorial battalion be formed for service in the South composed entirely of Southerners, the commands of which would be English and the observances of which would be Christian, and he urged that steps be taken to form "a large Christian population which would eventually link up with Uganda and form a substantial buffer or check to the spread of a faith, such as the Muslim, which may at any time break out into a wave of fanaticism."[32] Sir Reginald Wingate approved Owen's plan for an equatorial corps, and, for the next eight years, local Southern Sudanese recruits were slowly welded by British officers into the Equatorial Battalion which gradually replaced the Northern Sudanese army units. Wingate saw an African counterweight to Arab influence in the Sudan in the Equatorial Battalion. As Director of Military Intelligence in the Egyptian Army and later Governor-General of the Sudan, Wingate knew well the depth of Moslem Sudanese religious emotion which, in the early years of the Condominium, expressed itself in numerous local outbursts against the conquerors. Security in the Sudan depended on Sudanese Moslem troops, whose loyalty to suppress rebellious co-religionists was never certain, and on a thin red line of British regulars to which the Anglicized and Christian Equatorial Battalions could now be added. Moreover, Wingate himself was a devout Christian, and, deeply impressed by Uganda's enthusiastic reception of Christianity, he naturally wished to limit the spread of Islam in the vast adjoining area of the Southern Sudan. On December 7, 1917, the last of the Northern Sudanese troops left Mongalla, and the Equatorial troops remained as the only permanent garrison in the Southern Sudan until their

---

[30] Sir Reginald Wingate to R. C. R. Owen, December 19, 1910, Telegram, Mongalla, I/5/31, SGA.

[31] Owen to Wingate, December 21, 1910, Telegram, Mongalla, I/5/31, SGA.

[32] Memorandum by Owen, March 29, 1911, Mongalla, I/5/31, SGA.

mutiny in August 1955. By January 3, 1918, Sunday was recognized throughout the Southern Sudan as the official day of worship.[33]

But many British administrative officers were not content with simply changing the Sabbath. Wingate himself urged, against the advice of the missionaries, that English, not Arabic, should be taught in the Southern Mission schools. The missionaries argued that a knowledge of Arabic was essential for the future employment of their pupils in government service, but the Governor-General hoped that if the teaching and the use of English was "started very quietly and tentatively—without any fuss and without putting the dots on the *i's* too prominently—the desideratum may become a *fait accompli* almost before anyone has realized that a change has taken place."[34] Owen even went further. He quietly removed "the more fanatical, super-religious" Moslems—soldiers, *gallaba* (merchants), and riffraff alike—hoping that the authorities in Khartoum "will see that they don't return."[35] Although there appears to have been some grumbling by those directly affected by such measures, the population, Moslem and pagan alike, stoically accepted these innovations.

Although the beginnings of Southern Policy are to be found in the creation of the Equatorial Battalion, Wingate's decision, as well as the more inordinate actions of British officers in the South, cannot be regarded as a thoroughgoing policy of excluding Moslem influence from all aspects of Southern society. Arabic and Islam continued to be spread by Northern Sudanese merchants and administrators and, ironically, even by British officials who preferred to speak Arabic rather than learn the local dialect. This contradiction between discouraging, officially at least, Moslem influence and in practice contributing to its spread was quite apparent to British administrators. In 1920, V. R. Woodland, the Governor of Mongalla, wrote in exasperation that "the time has come either to cut off this province from the rest of the Sudan or to institute a more incisive policy as regards its administration."[36] Either sever the Southern Sudan from the Arab North and administer the territory along the lines of Uganda or "allow the development of this country by the Arabs of the Sudan under—of course—the Sudan government."[37] No decision was made at that time. Everyone in the administration talked about the problem. Some, such as Woodland and Sir John Maffey, the Governor-General, urged that the Northern Sudanese be

---

[33] Owen to Private Secretary to Governor-General, January 3, 1918, Mongalla, I/5/31, SGA.

[34] Wingate to R. M. Fielden, Governor, Bahr al-Ghazal, December 27, 1910, Mongalla, I/5/31, SGA.

[35] Owen to C. S. Northcote, Acting Governor, Mongalla, January 10, 1918, Mongalla, I/5/31, SGA.

[36] V. R. Woodland, Governor, Mongalla, to Civil Secretary, Khartoum, August 29, 1920, Mongalla, I/5/31, SGA.

[37] *Ibid.*

permitted a free hand in the Southern Sudan; while others, supported by the ever-growing strength of the Christian missionaries, demanded the complete exclusion of Moslem influences. In 1921, the Southern governors even agreed that in the future English should replace Arabic as the official language.[38] But little more was done than to talk and to propose, and matters drifted for another decade. Administration, as well as development, was hampered and curtailed by this lack of a clearly defined policy. This want of direction certainly contributed to the failure of the administration to govern the tribes short of the constant use of punitive patrols and expeditions.

THE IMPLEMENTATION OF THE SOUTHERN POLICY

In 1930, Sir Harold MacMichael ended the years of vacillation by presenting his Memorandum on Southern Policy, which formulated a program designed to further the development of the Southern Sudan. An able and precise administrator, MacMichael had reshaped British administration in the Northern Sudan and wished to construct a coherent program for the future administration of the South. Like all colonial administrators of his era, MacMichael was deeply influenced by Lugard and the principles of indirect rule which he himself had practiced in Kordofan before World War I.

Practice became policy during the 1920's, and, when seeking principles upon which to govern the Southern Sudan, MacMichael and others sought to apply indirect rule in the South by encouraging tribal units with structure and organization based on indigenous laws and traditional customs. But, in order to encourage indigenous, African customs in the South, all Northern Sudanese, Moslem, Arab influences were to be eradicated, for African traditions, already weakened by a century of chaos, could hardly hope to flourish in the face of the dynamic and expansive culture of the Northern Sudan. First, all Arabic-speaking administrative staff, including clerical and technical personnel, were to be replaced from indigenous sources. Local boys were to be procured from the mission schools and "every encouragement should be given to those in charge of mission schools to co-operate in that policy by sending boys into Government service." Furthermore, Greek and Syrian traders were to be encouraged to trade in the Southern Sudan rather than the Arab merchants, or *gallaba,* whose permits to trade were to be "decreased unobtrusively but progressively . . . only the best type of Gellaba, whose interests are purely commercial and pursued in a legitimate manner should be admitted." Second, the Memorandum strongly stressed that the first duty of the administrator was "*to speak the natural language of the people whom he controls*" and when this was not possible to communicate in English even if the inability to converse freely resulted "in some loss of efficiency." Every effort was to be

---

[38] Memorandum by the Civil Secretary, March 1922, Civil Secretary, I/9/31, SGA.

made to counteract the idea that Arabic was the official and hence the fashionable language, and, although individual administrators might be reluctant to converse with Africans in English rather than Arabic, such "difficulties and dislikes must be subordinated to the main policy." Third, it was emphatically urged that the British staff familiarize themselves with the beliefs, customs, and mental processes of the pagan tribes they administer and under no circumstances rely on their knowledge of Arabic and Moslem ways learned in prior service in the Northern Sudan.[39]

The new policy was greeted with widespread approval by the British administrators in the South, thankful that an ambiguous and anomalous state of affairs had been regularized and that a policy that many felt proper for the development of Negroid Africa was at last being pursued in the Southern Sudan. The British staff in the South set about immediately to carry out the principles of the memorandum with enthusiasm. Indeed, the Governor of the Bahr al-Ghazal himself wrote that "the situation as regards the spread of Northern influences is eminently unsatisfactory (in the Bahr al-Ghazal), and if the declared policy is to be carried out to a successful end, rigorous measures must be adopted without delay."[40] He put forward a host of recommendations ranging from the compilation of Dinka grammars to the removal of Northern clerks, technicians, and traders. So vigorously were his proposals pressed on the government in Khartoum that MacMichael wryly cautioned the governor against solving the problem of Arab influence "on the same lines as Tamburlaine or Genghis Khan would have undoubtedly followed."[41] Throughout the Southern Sudan, Northern Sudanese in the employ of the government were transferred to the North, while Northern Sudanese merchants were encouraged to leave the South and, if recalcitrant, virtually forced to retire. Among the Southerners themselves, the practice of Islam and the speaking of Arabic were discouraged, and those who persisted in wearing Arab clothing or aping Arab ways were publicly berated and chastised.

In most districts of the Southern Sudan few difficulties arose in the implementation of Southern Policy. The Northerners were few, the Arabic language, religion, and culture were not widespread. Only in the Western District of the Bahr al-Ghazal Province was Arab influence long-standing and tradition, and undoubtedly the western Bahr al-Ghazal was the most thoroughly Arabized area in the Southern Sudan. The whole length of its northern boundary adjoined the Arab-speaking areas of Dār Fūr; while such tribes as the Banda, Dongo, and Kreisch had adopted many Arab customs, and such others as the Feroge, the Njangulgule, and the Togoyo even claimed to be of Arab

---

[39] Memorandum on Southern Policy, January 25, 1930, Bahr al-Ghazal, I/1/1, SGA.

[40] R. G. C. Brock, Governor, Bahr al-Ghazal Province, to Sir Harold MacMichael, March 22, 1930, Bahr al-Ghazal, I/1/2, SGA.

[41] MacMichael to Brock, March 26, 1930, Bahr al-Ghazal I/3/17, SGA.

origin. Arabic was the lingua franca of the district, and certainly most of the chiefs were practicing Moslems. Under such conditions, the eradication of Northern Sudanese influence would take more than just the "friendly conversation with the chiefs" envisaged by the authorities in Khartoum.[42] First those Arab emigrants who had settled in the western Bahr al-Ghazal from Dār Fūr and the areas of Wadai, Bornu, and Sokoto farther west were resettled in Dār Fūr.[43] This transfer involved the movement of some 3,000 people, including nearly 700 Mandala, a nomadic tribe that traveled regularly between Dār Fūr and the western Bahr al-Ghazal.[44] During the transfer of these Arab emigrants, the indigenous inhabitants of the Western District who lived in and around the administrative post of Kafia Kingi were grouped together according to tribe and resettled south of the Raga-Kafia Kingi road so that no Southern Sudanese lived more than ten miles north of the Boro River.[45] This created a vast "no-man's land" between the tribes of the Southern Sudan and the Arabs north of the Bahr al-'Arab River in Dār Fūr and acted as a barrier between the two. At the same time, the town and administrative center of Kafia Kingi was abandoned, the shops and headquarters buildings leveled, and "despite precautions the mosque caught fire and was burnt."[46] To prevent any Southerners from again taking up residence, all houses and huts in and around Kafia Kingi were destroyed as well as all villages throughout the "no-man's land" east and west of the town. Raga, the other principal town in the district, was also abandoned; and a new town, smaller in size and containing only limited facilities for Northern Sudanese merchants, was erected nearby on a more satisfactory location.[47]

The chiefs and their followers were specifically advised to give up their Arabic names and abandon Arab mode of dress. Arabic names had been used for so long, however, that the British district commissioner admitted "that it will take constant 'pegging-away-at' before any real noticeable change is effected."[48] The prohibition against Arab dress was more easily enforced by simply instructing local merchants not to supply such dress or to risk the loss of their permits to trade.[49] Occasionally, the British administrators went even further. In 1935, the district commissioner of the Western District apprehended a Greek merchant selling Arab clothing and not only forbade its further sale, but specified that "shirts should be made short, with a collar and opening down the front in the European fashion and NOT an open

---

[42] MacMichael to Brock, May 11, 1930, Bahr al-Ghazal, 1/1/2, SGA.

[43] Acting Civil Secretary to Brock, July 22, 1930, Bahr al-Ghazal, I/1/2, SGA.

[44] "Notes on Meeting at Afifi, 1931," Bahr al-Ghazal, I/3/17, SGA.

[45] Brock to Captain H. F. Kidd, District Commissioner, Western District, June 9, 1930, and Kidd to Brock, August 8, 1930, Bahr al-Ghazal, I/1/2, SGA.

[46] S. R. Simpson, Assistant District Commissioner, Western District, to Brock, April 29, 1931, Bahr al-Ghazal, I/3/17, SGA.

[47] Kidd to Brock, June 10, 1930, Bahr al-Ghazal, I/3/17, SGA.

[48] Kidd to Brock, August 8, 1930, Bahr al-Ghazal, I/1/2, SGA.

[49] *Ibid.*

neck as worn by the Baggara or Darfur."[50] As one British official dryly remarked on hearing of this incident: "The polo-collar, as haberdashers call it, is the key to Southern Policy. The efforts of the administration, however, were not confined solely to social customs, but applied to commerce as well. Northern Sudanese merchants were told to leave the district in 1930, and indeed many were only too glad to accept the government's offer to pay expenses in order to extricate themselves from an unprofitable enterprise. By 1931, only four merchants remained in the western Bahr al-Ghazal out of the twenty-three in business the previous year, and these were either non-Arabs or Northern merchants with close business or family connections in Umdurman which the government did not wish to excite.[51] But even these few Northern Sudanese merchants did not long remain, for, by 1932, only Greek, Syrian, and Jewish traders were to be found in the district.[52]

The execution of Southern Policy in the western Bahr al-Ghazal was generally accepted without widespread complaint. Aside from grumbling about new names and new clothing, the chiefs and their people resigned themselves to the wishes of the government. One exception was Chief Isa Ahmad Fertak, chief of the Feroge. He complained bitterly at first about the use of English and the resettlement of his tribe. Then he wrote to the influential amir of Zalingi, but the letter was intercepted and Isa severely reprimanded.[53] For several years Isa remained silent, and then, in 1936, he wrote again, but this time to the editor of the magazine *Omdurman*, complaining of religious, linguistic, and racial discrimination. The issue was immediately taken up by the Northern Sudanese in Umdurman and Khartoum as a test case against the government's policy in the Southern Sudan. To placate public opinion, an official inquiry was duly instituted by the government which saw to it that the affair was hushed up and quietly forgotten.[54] Isa himself was removed as chief of the Feroge and, "in the public interest and without recourse to legal action," exiled to Yei in the southern reaches of the Equatoria Province.[55]

Although these negative, restrictive aspects of Southern Policy were carried out successfully, the more positive side, that is the growth of the indigenous cultures, progressed very slowly and brought to the fore its latent contradictions. Certainly these contradictions were unavoidable when the govern-

---

[50] D. J. Bethell, District Commissioner, Western District to Emmanouil Lagotaris, January 21, 1935, Bahr al-Ghazal, I/1/2, SGA.

[51] Kidd to Brock, August 8, 1930, Bahr al-Ghazal, I/1/2, and Brock to MacMichael, September 29, 1930, Bahr al-Ghazal, I/3/17, SGA.

[52] Simpson to Brock, July 1, 1931, Bahr al-Ghazal, I/3/17, SGA.

[53] Brock to Simpson, May 13, 1931, and Simpson to Brock, June 2, 1931, Bahr al-Ghazal, I/3/17, SGA.

[54] Civil Secretary to M. W. Parr, Governor of Equatoria, March 3, 1937, and "Memorandum of Case of Isa Ahmad Fertak," by G. S. Symes, Governor-General of the Sudan, Bahr al-Ghazal, I/3/17, SGA.

[55] Bethell to Parr, February 3, 1937, Bahr al-Ghazal, I/3/17, SGA.

ment decided what was indigenous and what was not. Within two years after the announcement of Southern Policy, Captain H. F. Kidd, the district commissioner in the western Bahr al-Ghazal, clearly saw the paradox "in inducing these people (the inhabitants) to re-adopt their own tribal names and customs" when the missions were baptizing the populace with Italian names,[56] or the contradiction between preventing marriages between Moslems and pagans while tacitly encouraging matrimony between Christian converts and pagans. Kidd's successor, D. J. Bethell, expressed himself even more strongly. "The suppression of Mohammedanism is desirable, though whether Roman Catholicism (mostly instilled by Italian peasants) is the best substitute is a matter of opinion."[57] Not only was it many years before the district commissioners qualified in the local vernaculars, but the number of trained Southern Sudanese capable of replacing Northern clerks and administrative staff remained, in spite of the best efforts of the missionaries, discouragingly small. One despondent district commissioner wrote, in 1941, that "perhaps the most disappointing aspect of the working of Southern Policy is the failure to produce in ten years any Southern staff trained for executive work."[58] Even the free English classes held at each district headquarters and the introduction of English words of command in the police did not eliminate the use of Arabic so rapidly as had been anticipated. Indeed, the whole contradiction of Southern Policy was glaringly exposed by the language problem. It was clearly impossible to develop all the languages and dialects of the Southern Sudan, and, at the Rajjaf Language Conference of 1928, certain group languages had been chosen to be imposed on the local tribes in place of their own peculiar dialect or Arabic. When communication in the local vernacular was impossible, of course, English would be employed. By no stretch of the imagination could forcing the Azande language or English on the Kreisch, for instance, be called developing the indigenous customs and traditional usages and beliefs of that tribe. Certainly by massive efforts the British administration in the Southern Sudan might have impressed on the tribes the culture deemed most suitable for them, but the great depression of the thirties, which hit the Sudan very hard, followed by the reduction of staff necessitated by World War II, precluded any such concentrated program.

TO THE NORTH—EMERGENT NATIONALISM

While the indigenous cultures were slowly being nurtured in the Southern Sudan, events in the North began to destroy the air of permanency with which the British officials viewed their governing of the Sudanese. The creation of the Graduate's Congress in Northern Sudan and the rise of a politi-

---

[56] Kidd to Brock, June 17, 1932, Bahr al-Ghazal, I/1/2, SGA.

[57] "Undated Notes on Southern Policy," by Bethell, Bahr al-Ghazal, I/1/2, SGA.

[58] Elliot-Smith to B. V. Marwood, Governor of Equatoria, June 30, 1941, Bahr al-Ghazal, I/1/2, SGA.

cally- and nationally-minded intelligentsia primarily concerned with the future status of the Sudan soon raised the question of the future status of the South. To the Northern Sudanese nationalists, Southern Policy appeared to be, not only a typically Machiavellian device by which the British were to divide and rule, but also seemed to be aimed at severing the South from the North. The strict silence which the government maintained about Southern affairs only further aroused the suspicions of the Northerners, who in their ignorance attributed deep, dark designs where none really existed. For years, Southern Policy was one of "the main topics of (well-informed) conversation at effendi's tea parties in Omdurman," and the reluctance of the government to explain its policies did much to exacerbate relations between the nationalist and the administration.[59] The Sudanese were not alone in their distrust of Southern Policy. To the British administrators in the South, the advancing political consciousness of the North appeared to call for a reaffirmation of Southern Policy and redoubled efforts in order to prepare the Southern Sudanese for their future—a future still to be determined. As the Governor of Equatoria wrote:

> The political future of the Southern Sudan cannot yet be determined, but whatever it may be, we should work to a scheme of self-government which would fit in with an ultimate attachment of the Southern peoples southward or northwards. Northward cannot be excluded if we admit the principle of self-determination, but the policy that is being adopted makes political adhesion to the North improbable from *the Southern point of view*.[60]

As early as 1942, increased efforts in education and in economic and transport development were urged; but little was done during the war years, and development languished in every field. By 1944, however, "it was generally agreed that a policy of more intensive and rapid economic and educational development of the Southern Sudan was desirable and should now be executed."[61] The directors of the departments of Agriculture, Forests, and Education were asked to formulate concrete programs of development, and a complete overhaul of the administration and transport system was begun at once. Southern Policy itself was even reaffirmed and restated by the Governor-General:

> The approved policy is "to act upon the fact that the peoples of the Southern Sudan are distinctly African and Negroid, and that our obvious duty to them is therefore to push ahead as fast as we can with their economic and educational development on African and Negroid lines, and not upon the Middle Eastern and Arab lines of progress which are suitable for the Northern Sudan.

---

[59] "Undated Notes on Southern Policy," by Bethell, Bahr al-Ghazal, I/1/2, SGA.

[60] C. H. L. Skeet, Governor of Equatoria, to King, District Commissioner, Tonj, August 14, 1943, Bahr al-Ghazal, I/1/1, SGA.

[61] Skeet to King, February 19, 1944, Bahr al-Ghazal, I/1/1, SGA.

It is only by economic and educational development that these people can be equipped to stand up for themselves in the future, whether their future lot be eventually cast with the Northern Sudan or with East Africa (or partly with each."[62]

Such plans for advancing the political and economic development of the Southern Sudan were soon subordinated, however, to the political demands of the Northern Sudanese for a greater participation in the government. In 1944, an advisory council was instituted in the Northern Sudan, and, by 1946, the Sudanese were agitating to transform this advisory council into a legislature. Of course, this raised the question of the status of the Southern Sudan. Was the South to be represented in any future legislative council and thereby irrevocably committed to a unified Sudan, or was it to remain outside the council and gradually develop its own political institutions? On April 23, 1946, a special Sudan Administrative Conference was held at the Governor-General's Palace in Khartoum. The conference arranged for two subcommittees composed largely of Northern Sudanese "to deal with the closer association of the Sudanese with the Central Government and Local Government respectively."[63] The Central Government Committee, of course, explored the possibility of bringing the South into a legislative assembly; and, in order to see the problems of the South at first hand, the Committee flew to Juba in June to tour the Southern provinces. Although the Committee could hardly have been expected to grasp fully the problems of the Southern Sudan in a visit of a few days, they returned to Khartoum and, in subsequent reports, urged the fusion of the Northern and the Southern Sudans.[64] The rapid advance of the Northern Sudan toward self-government and the decision to institute a legislative council in the following year, 1947, accelerated Northern Sudanese discussion and criticism of Southern Policy. In order to meet the public canvassing of the Southern Sudan question, the government in Khartoum proposed to settle the future of the South and to crystallize its policy.

Apart from the rapid political development of the Northern Sudan, the failure of East Africa to improve communications or develop trade with the Southern Sudan did not encourage the British officials in Khartoum to seek any political tie with Uganda or Kenya. Indeed, nothing would have been more distasteful to British East Africa than to add the immense liability of the Southern Sudan to a rapidly growing list of difficulties, and it appears that the Uganda authorities were extremely cool toward any pros-

---

[62] Khartoum Secret Despatch No. 89, August 4, 1945, quoted in B. V. Marwood, Governor, Equatoria, to M. B. Stubbs, District Commissioner, Western District, December 23, 1946, Bahr al-Ghazal, I/1/2, SGA.

[63] Marwood to Stubbs, May 25, 1945, Bahr al-Ghazal, I/1/2, SGA.

[64] T. R. H. Owen, Deputy Governor, Equatoria, to Secretary Sudan Administrative Conference, October 6, 1946, Bahr al-Ghazal, I/1/2, SGA.

pect of union with this vast and unproductive land. The Sudan government authorities therefore concluded that "we should not work on the assumption that the Sudan as at present constituted with possibly minor boundary adjustments will remain one" and that the peoples of the Southern Sudan are "inextricably bound for future development to the Middle-Eastern and Arabicized Northern Sudan."[65]

The reaction by the British administrators in the South to the government change of policy was overwhelmingly favorable.[66] Expressions of approval and satisfaction on the part of the British staff, however, soon gave way to consternation and concern. On January 8, 1947, the Sudan Administrative Conference proposed that Southern representatives be sent to Khartoum to participate in the legislative council to be established the following year. When the minutes of the meeting were distributed to British officers in the South, many became greatly disturbed and protested to the central authorities that

> These minutes have given the impression that the future of the South is being discussed by the wrong men in the wrong milieu and that the Government's decision is likely to be thereby directed into wrong channels. The signatories note that no Southern Sudanese were present. . . . They do not believe that any proposal yet made for Southern representation in an Assembly at the capital would amount to such full representation as could guard the interests of two provinces comprising more than a third of the Sudanese people.[67]

The officials urged that the government call an "Administrative Conference for the Southern Sudan" composed of British administrators, Northern Sudanese, and at least ten Southern Sudanese. The conference was to meet in the South and to assume "that the Sudan remains one country," but to determine how best to proceed with the political development of the Southern Sudan in order for the Southerners to take their place as equal partners with the North in the Sudan of the future.[68] On learning of the concern and suspicion of British officers in the South, the Civil Secretary, James Robertson, quickly reassured them that the government had not yet considered the recommendations of the South Administrative Conference concerning the South and had reached no decision in the shape of its future political tie with

---

[65] J. W. Robertson, Civil Secretary, to Marwood, December 16, 1946, Bahr al-Ghazal, I/1/2, SGA.

[66] See Owen to Marwood, January 5, 1947, Bahr al-Ghazal, I/1/2, SGA; E. H. Nightingale, District Commissioner, Rumbek to Owen, January 29, 1947, Bahr al-Ghazal, I/1/2, SGA; J. H. T. Wilson, District Commissioner, Jur River, January 2, 1947, Bahr al-Ghazal I/1/2 SGA; Stubbs, District Commissioner, Western District, to Owen, February 12, 1947, Bahr al-Ghazal, I/1/2, SGA.

[67] Hunter, Ramshaw, Wilson, Mackenzie, Stubbs, Chatterton, Owen, Keen, Ferguson, Eyre, McComas to Civil Secretary March 10, 1947, Bahr al-Ghazal, I/1/2, SGA.

[68] Ibid.

the North. He readily agreed to call a conference to meet in Juba in June and authorized the governors of the southern provinces to select representative Southerners to participate.[69]

The conference opened in Juba on June 12. Composed of six British officials, six Northern Sudanese representatives, and fifteen Southerners, the Conference was presided over by the Civil Secretary who delivered a speech in which he indicated the policy of the government concerning the future of the Southern Sudan.

> It has begun to be clear, I think, that the Southern Sudan, by its history and by the accident of geography, river transport, and so on, must turn more to the North rather than to Uganda or the Congo, and I believe that our policy regarding these areas should now be restated as follows: "The policy of the Sudan Government regarding the Southern Sudan is to act upon the facts that the peoples of the Southern Sudan are distinctly African and Negroid, but that geography and economics combine (so far as can be foreseen at the present) to render them inextricably bound for their future development to the Middle East and the Northern Sudan: and therefore to ensure that they shall through education and economic development be equipped to take their places in the future as socially and economically the equals of their partners of the Northern Sudan in the Sudan of the future."[70]

Although there was no argument about the ultimate future of the Southern Sudan, which had been decided the preceding December, controversy soon arose over the means to implement Southern Sudanese participation in the political development of the Sudan as a whole. The Southern Sudanese, painfully conscious of their political backwardness, were at first reluctant to assume a role in the budding political institutions being created in the North, and it was only after considerable pressure was brought to bear by the Northern Sudanese representatives that the Southerners, during the second day of the conference, agreed to send delegates to Khartoum to take part, for better or for worse, in the Legislative Council.[71] The British representatives at Juba appear to have played the role of honest broker and even regarded the sudden change of mind by the Southerners "as no bad thing."[72] The meeting did reveal to the Civil Secretary and others, however, the Southerner's need for safeguards, and all privately agreed that some measures would have to be devised to protect the Southerners from possible political exploitation by the Northern Sudanese. In August, the Governor-General's Council approved the report of the Sudan Administrative Con-

---

[69] Marwood to Owen, April 30, 1947, Bahr al-Ghazal, I/1/2, SGA.

[70] "Proceedings of the Juba Conference on the Political Development of the Southern Sudan, June 1947," Bahr al-Ghazal, I/1/1, SGA.

[71] *Ibid.*

[72] Letter of Owen, September 23, 1947, Bahr al-Ghazal, I/1/2, SGA.

ference and, in view of the decisions arrived at in Juba, passed the following resolution on the Southern Sudan:

> That the proposal that the Legislative Assembly should be representative of the whole Sudan and that its scope should not be limited to the Northern Sudan be accepted, but that safeguards be introduced into the legislation setting up the new constitution which will ensure the healthy and steady development of the Southern peoples.[73]

This clarification of Southern Policy and the real concern signified by the central authorities to provide adequate safeguards did much to calm the fears of the British staff in the South. In September, the Deputy Governor in the Bahr al-Ghazal, T. R. H. Owen, expressed the feelings of his colleagues when he wrote that "we at least know now that the South's case will not go by default, that the Central Government understand both our needs and wants and that their conscience is very much awake."[74] Unfortunately, Owen spoke too soon. When the Legislative Assembly Ordinance of 1948 was drafted, the Legal Secretary saw no need to include specific safeguards for the Southern Sudan, since all legislation was subject to the reserve powers of the Governor-General who could veto measures that he regarded to be detrimental to the South.[75] The omission of specific references to the Southern Sudan in the Legislative Assembly Ordinance was greeted by a storm of dissent from British officials in the South who demanded that specific protective clauses be written into the legislation.[76] The Civil Secretary, James Robertson, refused to provide such safeguards. He cogently argued that all Northern opinion was firmly against any special treatment of the South and any specific references to the Southern Sudan would only be exploited by Egypt in negotiations with the British over the revision of the Condominium Agreement. There was no need to exacerbate these suspicions unnecessarily when the Governor-General's veto could be used "to prevent anything stupid."[77] Robertson angrily rejected the charge that he was "sacrificing my conscience" to Northern opinion and reiterated his belief that "we shall be long enough in the Sudan to see that they (the Southerners) have a chance to speak, and I have no doubt that they will then be able to make a choice."[78] The British staff in the South reluctantly accepted the decision of the government. No reference to specific safeguards for the South was ever included

---

[73] Robertson to Marwood, August 21, 1947, Bahr al-Ghazal, I/1/2, SGA.

[74] Letter by Owen, September 23, 1947, Bahr al-Ghazal, I/1/2, SGA.

[75] Robertson to Southern Governors, February 10, 1948, Bahr al-Ghazal, I/1/2, SGA.

[76] Owen to Robertson, February 26, 1948, and Marwood to Robertson, March 3, 1948, Bahr al-Ghazal, I/1/2, SGA.

[77] Robertson to Owen, May 25, 1948, Bahr al-Ghazal, I/1/2, SGA.

[78] *Ibid.*

in the Legislative Assembly Ordinance and, on its passage, Southern Policy was no more.

AN ASSESSMENT OF SOUTHERN POLICY

Before 1947, the British had been willing to consider a different future for the Southern Sudan, either some sort of separate status within the empire or even linking the Southern Sudan with Uganda. Events in the Northern Sudan had, of course, made a decision on the future of the South imperative; and since the South could neither support itself, nor did Uganda want to take on the burden of doing so, even the British administrators were convinced that union with the North was the only solution. Indeed, all but one of the British district commissioners in the Southern Sudan agreed that it was morally, politically, and economically best that the two Sudans should be linked together. Once the decision had been made to regard the Sudan, politically speaking, as a unified whole, the possibility or the advisability of retaining Southern Policy was not even considered. The restrictions against travel and trade in the Southern Sudan were revoked, and it was even suggested that Islamic missions be admitted to the South.

If Southern Policy had successfully excluded Northern influence from the southern provinces for a generation, its effects on the Negroid peoples of the South were of even greater importance for the future of the Sudan. Tribal units were certainly preserved and strengthened, and, for the first time since the mid-nineteenth century, tribal society was ordered and secure. The political and social disintegration caused by nearly a century of incomers had been checked, and traditional ways of living and indigenous customs were reinforced, revived, and even re-created. But Southern Policy had never been conceived simply as a return to the past, nor as a negative reversion to the pristine civilization of the noble savage. Its more positive aims, in the best traditions of indirect rule, were to permit guided change of indigenous customs—but guided change without Arab Moslem influence. Yet, as alien rulers, the British themselves could not control without influencing. Although they could eliminate the effects of Arabic and Islam by legislation, they could hardly restrict the impact of their own culture on the Southern Sudanese. This was the essential contradiction of Southern Policy. In trying to restrict Arab or Moslem influence British administration in the Southern Sudan was, in reality, changing the culture of the Southern Sudanese. To return to tribal customs meant to revise them, and revision meant the introduction of a practice alien to the indigenous culture. Forbidden to wear the Arab *jallabia,* the Southerner took up English walking shorts. Prohibited from speaking Arabic, the Southern Sudanese learned English to communicate with tribesmen other than his own. Discouraged from practicing Islam, the tribesman was encouraged to visit the Christian mission station rather than lapse into paganism. Undoubtedly, indigenous customs were stimulated under Southern

Policy, but frequently, instead of African practices, Western customs were substituted to replace Moslem Arab ways. By neither opening to the future nor faithfully reconstructing the past, Southern Policy failed as a guide in the present. In the end, this fundamental paradox proved the bankruptcy of Southern Policy.

To prepare the Southern Sudanese for participation in self-governing Sudan, economic and educational developments were speedily inaugurated after 1947 in a frantic effort to make the Southerners an equal and not inferior partner with the North. The Zande scheme was started, under the direction of the Equatorial Projects Board, to grow cotton and produce cloth in a complex of agricultural and industrial sites in Yambio district on the Congo border. Sawmills were established at Kateri, Gilo, and Loka. All-weather roads were constructed to link the principal southern towns, and permits to trade were now given to anyone who could meet the commercial requirements. The government subvention to mission schools was increased, and a more unified system of education was enforced by the ever-increasing supervision of government inspectors. Indeed, the policies and plans of the Sudan government were impressive, but, as in so many other colonial areas of the world, the British in the Southern Sudan began with too little too late. As one administrator wrote late in 1947: "The ideal safeguard for the South would be a British Administrator for the next fifty years."[79] Five years later, time had run out, for the Sudan became self-governing in 1953. Between 1930 and 1947, Southern Policy had precluded the Southerners any identification with the Sudan as a whole as a necessary restriction to enable the administration to create a viable system of native administration throughout the southern provinces. But the development of native administration provided only a fragile and spotty veneer of Christian-Afro-English culture to withstand, in an emerging Sudan, political, cultural, and economic encroachment from the rapidly developing and dynamic North. Such a veneer was patently insufficient either to resist their encroachments or to deal with them on equal terms.

INDEPENDENCE AND NORTH-SOUTH RELATIONS

The Southern Sudan was ill-prepared for the rapid political transition from colonial rule to participation in a self-governing and independent Sudan. Devoid of political experience, except in the confines of the chiefs' court, and protected by the watchful eye of a parental British official, the Southerners' loyalties were still predominately to clan or tribe rather than to region or nation. Accustomed to a traditional way of life, either cultivating the soil

---

[79] "Note on Situation Regarding the Southern Sudan, December 1947," Bahr al-Ghazal, I/1/2, SGA.

or grazing herds of cattle and sheep, the Southern Sudanese were over-whelmingly illiterate and almost totally unaware of the changing world that was relentlessly closing in on them. When suddenly deluged by "rash and irresponsible promises" of Northern politicians who sought to win their votes and flattered by the visits of important Egyptian officials who frequently made themselves ridiculous by their extravagant politicking, the Southern Sudanese were bewildered, mystified, and not a little suspicious.[80] Suspicion soon deepened into distrust after the elections were over and a Sudanese national government was installed in Khartoum, for the Northern-dominated political parties in the South continued to hurl charges and countercharges at one another with little thought of Southern interests and even less of the aspirations of Southern representatives, many of whose decisions were ap-parently guided more by monetary reward than political principles. Wooed, won, then ignored if not corrupted, there was little cause for the Southern Sudanese to place much faith in the intentions of Northern politicians. This deterioration in relations soon turned into open hostility when the results of the Sudanization commission were announced in October 1954. The committee had been commissioned with the uneviable task of phasing out British officials and promoting Sudanese to fill their positions. Not only did the committee Sudanize positions more rapidly than had been anticipated, but, in the South, only four minor posts were given to Southern Sudanese, while all the principal positions were taken up by Northern civil servants. The reaction was one of bitter disenchantment. This attitude of despair was perhaps best summed up by a Southern merchant in Gogrial: "The results of Sudanization have come with a very disappointing result, i.e., four Assistant District Commissioners and two Mamurs. Well as it appears, it means our fellow Northerners want to colonize us for another hundred years."[81]

In spite of the startling, one-sided Sudanization, the confidence of South-erners might not have been totally lost if the Northern officials sent to posts in the South had acted with either wisdom or prudence. To most Northern officials, service in the Southern Sudan was regarded with distaste, not only as hardship duty, but as exile from the mainstream of a professional career in the Sudan Civil Service. Thus, experienced and effective British officials were replaced by inexperienced and ineffective Sudanese, the unscrupulous bureaucrat, and the party hack, who frequently used his office for personal profit or to promote party interests. "A series of blunders followed (Sudaniza-tion) in the administrative, political, and industrial fields."[82] Administrative duties were neglected, local Southern officials were bullied and badgered, and a Southern member of Parliament was arbitrarily and illegally imprisoned.

---

[80] *Southern Sudan Disturbances, August 1955,* Report of the Commission of En-quiry, p. 20.

[81] Quoted in *Southern Sudan Disturbances, August 1955,* p. 114.

[82] *Ibid.,* p. 21.

The central government in Khartoum did nothing to ease the mounting tension and only exacerbated Southern sensibilities by threatening over radio and press those Southerners who criticized the government. When 300 Southern workers in the Zande scheme were summarily dismissed, in July 1955, the precipitate action was regarded as a "deliberate attempt by the management (which is Northern) to deprive Southerners of a livelihood and bring in Northerners instead."[83] Neither understanding nor sympathy was wasted on the unemployed Southern workers in the scheme, and when they demonstrated against the dismissals, they were shot down by the army and the police. This was the decisive event, for the Southerners regarded the incident "as the beginning of a war; and if there was some confidence left in the administration it then disappeared completely."[84]

On August 18, the Southern soldiers of the Equatorial Corps stationed at Torit mutinied, triggering a general revolt throughout the Equatorial Province. Although the mutiny itself appears to have been precipitated by a series of immediate and local misunderstandings, the fundamental cause of the rebellion belongs to history. Long accustomed to the impeccable justice of paternal British administrators, the Southern Sudanese could hardly adapt themselves to the rough-and-tumble politics of the emerging Sudan. The Northerner was still a symbol of fear and hostility. Although his predatory habits of the nineteenth century had been modified by British rule in the twentieth, the earlier restrictions against intercourse between the two Sudans prevented either the North or the South from understanding the changes undergone during British rule. Even after the abandonment of Southern Policy, the lack of development and the paucity of resources in the South only enhanced the feeling, real or imaginary, that the South would be exploited by Northern politicians and profiteers. Even the rudimentary political consciousness, fostered by British officials in the South since 1947, was regional rather than national, whereas, the scornful attitude of newly arrived Northerners in the South tended to convince the Southern Sudanese that their regional interests were of greater value than the larger association with the Sudan as a whole.

Although only 261 Northern Sudanese and some seventy-five Southerners were killed before Northern Sudanese troops re-established the central government's control in Equatoria, the rebellion electrified the Northern Sudan. Catering to Southern susceptibilities, Northern politicians hastily agreed to consider a federal solution for the Sudan. On the strength of this promise, the Southern representatives in the Parliament at Khartoum consented to a declaration of independence on January 1, 1956. Moreover, in spite of the trials, executions, and deportations of those Southerners who took part in the mutiny, the central government made considerable efforts to regain the

---

[83] *Ibid.*, p. 102.

[84] *Ibid.*, p. 102.

confidence of the Southern Sudanese. The most able Sudanese civil servants were rushed south to replace those whose incompetence had done so much to foment rebellion, and numerous Southern officials were quickly promoted to key posts in the provincial administration. Even party politics, so rough and ready before the mutiny, was at first restricted and then prohibited so that the ubiquitous Sudanese politicians had no excuse to venture up the Nile to stir up political emotions. In fact, the Sudan government deported Egyptian and Northern Sudanese agitators and resuscitated the old Closed District Ordinance which the British had utilized during the days of Southern Policy to exclude anyone they wished to keep out of the Southern Sudan. At the same time, greater efforts were made to correlate educational practice in the North and South. Arabic was introduced in mission schools where classes had previously been conducted in English, and missionaries themselves as well as many foreign teachers, who in the eyes of the Northern Sudanese represented an alien, heretical, and therefore undesirable element in the South, were not permitted to return from leaves of absence. By the summer 1956, all of these measures began to have a tranquilizing effect; and, except for the occasional army mutineer who emerged from the bush to shoot up isolated government posts, the Southern Sudan appeared resigned to its future, in union with the North.

Although these measures did much to check further deterioration of relations between the Northern and Southern Sudan, the South remained passive, not through constant attention, but rather through neglect. During the two years of parliamentary rule in the independent Sudan from 1956 to 1958, the central government at Khartoum was completely preoccupied with national economic and political difficulties. Three years' supply of cotton was still unsold, and the foreign-exchange reserves soon fell perilously low. Political bickering and corruption intensified sectarian differences between the two powerful Moslem sects, the Ansar and the Khatmiyya. The coalition government that ruled the Sudan was, at best, the result of political opportunism, personal interest, and sectarian loyalty all held together by parliamentary manipulation. When the tactics of party management were exhausted, parliamentary institutions were left debased, benefiting only those politicians who reaped the rewards of power and patronage. Unable to rule effectively in the Northern Sudan, the politicians could hardly hope to govern firmly in the South. Thus, during this period, the Southern Sudanese continued their local instruments of government begun under British tutelage, dealing only with Northern administrators when necessary and disappearing off into the bush when pressed by the demands of the administration or when their customs were openly challenged by the latest intruders.

On the night of November 17, 1958, the Army under the command of General Ibrahim 'Abbud took control of the government in a bloodless, predawn *coup d'état*. Parliamentary democracy came to an end in the Sudan. Few mourned its passing. The mass of Sudanese had regarded the maneuvers of the politicians with bitter cynicism. Indeed, the last prime minister, 'Abd Allah Khalil, appears to have urged the military to take over to counter growing Egyptian influence. The large politicians were pensioned off and, in fact, seemed quite willing to hand over the task of governing. Both the two great religious leaders, Sayyid 'Ali al-Mirghani, leader of the Khatmiyya sect, and Sayyid 'Abd ar-Rahman, head of the Ansar, welcomed the army's seizure of power. Sayyid 'Ali could now retire from politics, which he had never liked, and Sayyid 'Abd ar-Rahman died on March 24, 1959, depriving his followers of their active and respected leaders. The change of government did not at once have any immediate impact on the Southern Sudan, for like the parliamentary regime before it, the military dictatorship of General 'Abbud was confronted not only with the economic problems of the previous regime but with dissident groups within the Army itself. During the first year of army rule, factions and personalities within the Army struggled for control of the Supreme Council which governed the country. 'Abbud himself seemed above all this. A fatherly figure whose gentle demeanor and courtly manners impressed foreigners and charmed the Sudanese, he remained passive and quiescent. He preferred to act as head of state, leaving the real power to the younger generals who vied for control of the Council. In March and November 1959, the internecine struggles among the army officers erupted into open attempts to seize control of the government. Both failed, and the ringleaders of the November rising were tried and executed. The executions sobered the Northern Sudanese who hitherto were proud of the bloodless method by which the 'Abbud government had seized and maintained power and seemed to have discouraged further attempts to take over the Sudan. 'Abbud remained firmly, if benevolently, in control of the Sudan.

In spite of these internal struggles, army rule brought rapid improvement in the Sudan's deteriorating economic position. The parliamentary government had always insisted on selling the cotton crop at a fixed price. Thus, when cotton prices slumped on the world market in 1958, Sudan cotton went unsold at its unrealistic, high price. Nearly 250,000 bales remained from the 1958 crop with a second bumper harvest expected in 1959. The 'Abbud government at once abolished the fixed price, and, within six months, had sold all the Sudanese cotton. Although disposed of at lower rates, the ultimate effect of the cotton sale was to give the Sudan a surplus revenue and to rebuild dramatically the nation's foreign reserves. The other great achievement of the military government was the conclusion of a Nile Waters agreement with the United Arab Republic. A Nile Waters treaty was signed on November 8, 1959. The Nile Waters agreement was more far-reaching than the technical treaty implies, for the United Arab Republic not only recognized but appeared to be reconciled to an independent Sudan.

By 1960, the rule of the military regime was unchallenged; the threat of counter-revolution had disappeared, and the Sudan appeared as a model of authoritarian, progressive government. But the problem of the Southern Sudan remained. During the short-lived parliamentary government, the politicians had no coherent policy for the South, except to win the votes of its representatives first by promises and then by threats. Neither was effective, and, when the Equatoria Province erupted into rebellion in 1955, the principal object of the government was to maintain its control and to preserve a united Sudan. Although military force succeeded in suppressing the rebellion, the determination by Northern Sudanese to continue the union of the two disparate regions of the Sudan was rooted in Sudanese nationalism.

Built on the skeleton of British imperial rule, nationalism in the Sudan has been the dominant unifying force in this vast and diverse land. Thus, when the forces of Sudanese nationalism were called on by Sudanese leaders to unify the country, they appealed to ideas and passions primarily associated with Arabization and Islamization. These are strong and effective themes in the Northern Sudan, but they have little relevance in the South. The multiplicity of weak local cultures in the South could hardly withstand the more powerful and vigorous culture of the North. In effect, the paramountcy of indigenous cultures in the Southern provinces and the primary concern for their growth in an African environment died with the abandonment of Southern Policy in 1947. If Sudanese nationalism was to remain a viable ideology for the continuance of a united Sudan, the indigenous customs of the South would inevitably be challenged by the Arabic, Moslem practices of the North. Partly in fear of another rebellion and partly restricted by the moderation imposed on them under a parliamentary system, the politicians failed to press Arabization and Islamization in the South. The army officers of the military government were under no such restraints, and discontent was controlled by military might unhindered by parliamentary majorities. As the Governor of Equatoria put it in a speech in Juba in 1961:

> We thank God that by virtue of the marvellous efforts of the Revolution Government, the country will remain forever united. You should turn a deaf ear to any evil talk which comes from politicians, as you well know what has come of them in the past few years and you certainly don't want "bloodshed again in the South." You are aware that anybody who interferes with public peace and tranquillity will be dealt with severely and at once.[85]

Once the military regime had achieved stability in the North, it was free to complete the feeble attempts of the politicians to obliterate, in the name of unity, the cultural differences between the Northern and the Southern Sudan. Arabization and Islamization were thus increasingly employed by devoted army officers who saw no contradiction in binding the manifold diversities of the Sudan with the cords of Sudanese nationalism. In the North, their policy was overwhelmingly successful where Arab culture and Islam are at least recognized, if not rigid, practices. In the South, however, these Northern traditions have little meaning, and, consequently, they have clashed

---

[85] Speech of Governor 'Ali Baldo delivered in Juba and reprinted in *Morning News* (Khartoum), March 29, 1961.

with Southern cultures, deriving their inspiration from African, Christian, and European sources. Since 1960, the military government of the Sudan had introduced numerous measures designed to strengthen its hold on the South and to facilitate the spread of Arabic and Islam. The Southern Liberal party, which represented the views of the core of Southern intellectuals, was banned along with all other political organizations. All the principal administrative posts, governors, deputy-governors, and district commissioners in the Southern Sudan, were held by Northern officials, while those Southerners occupying more junior positions were transferred to the North where their influence is negligible. The army and police were predominantly staffed by Northern Sudanese. Provincial councils were introduced ostensibly to provide a medium for discussion and debate; but the Southern members were nominated by the governor and the executive councils were completely controlled by Northern administrators and residents.[86]

If a unified Sudan had been achieved by political power, the Northern-dominated administration in the South was to be cemented by education in Arabic and religious instruction in Islam. Ironically, Arabization and Islamization through education and religious instruction will have a greater impact in the long run than the more overt displays of political and military control, and, consequently, the central government at Khartoum made its greatest efforts in these two fields. Since the early days of the Condominium, education in the Southern Sudan had been exclusively in the hands of the Christian missionaries. After World War II, the mission schools, which had received government subsidies since 1927 and had in turn submitted to government inspection, were supplemented by government schools. Soon after independence, the missionary schools were nationalized and integrated into the system of government schools that flourished in the North; while the missions or any Southerner were prohibited from opening a private school in the South, although such privately owned (ahlia—Arab-owned) schools continued to provide a valuable supplement to the government schools in the North. The language and curriculum of the Southern schools rapidly shifted from English to Arabic. Several years were necessary to accomplish this transition from mission to government-operated schools with an Arabic, Islamic orientation; but, in 1961, The Sudan Almanac reported:

A national system of education which is government controlled has been firmly established in the three Southern Provinces since the takeover of mission schools in April 1957. These schools have now been integrated into the system of government schools already in existence forming a unified system which is now being gradually assimilated to its counterpart in the Northern Provinces.[87]

---

[86] Joseph Oduho and William Deng, The Problem of the Southern Sudan (London: Oxford University Press, 1963), pp. 43–44.

[87] The Sudan Almanac (Khartoum: Republic of the Sudan Information Office, 1961), p. 186.

Although a national system of education is a most powerful instrument in welding a united Sudan, the Sudan government lamentably, if not deliberately, failed to expand educational facilities in the Southern Sudan, while rapidly increasing the educational system in the North. At the time of the declaration of independence in 1956, there was one secondary school at Rumbek and another under construction at Juba. By 1964, no additional secondary schools had been established in the Southern Sudan, which comprises nearly a third of the Nation's total population, but a host of new secondary schools were opened in the North.[88] Today the two secondary schools in the South produce less than 100 graduates a year, with the result that few Southerners are equipped to continue their education at the University of Khartoum, where less than 100 Southern students are enrolled in a student body of about 1,800.

Even more far-reaching have been the efforts by the government and Northern Sudanese to propagate Islam. These attempts to proselytize in mid-twentieth century originate from the deepest religious traditions of the past. The emotional appeals of the Sufi orders, which have played such a vital role in Sudanese history, have fused with the apocalyptic mission of Mahdism to continue the spirit of the *jihad* without its more belligerent overtones. Whether in the name of Allah or a unified Sudan, to spread Islam throughout the country is a duty on which all Northern Sudanese can agree, irrespective of political persuasion. To encourage the growth of Islam in the South, the Sudan government has constructed mosques, established institutes of Islamic higher learning (*maahad*), and subsidized Moslem propaganda under the direction of the Department of Religious Affairs. Even before the military *coup d'état,* the parliamentary government of the Sudan had begun to curtail the activities of Christian missionaries in the Southern Sudan. Not only were mission schools nationalized, but the missionaries were forbidden to open new schools on their own resources or even seminaries for the training of Sudanese clergy. Following the seizure of the government by the army, efforts to restrict the missions were intensified. The missionaries were regarded as an undesirable element because they were aliens as much as Christians, and they were soon regarded by Northern Sudanese as the principal instigators for the growing discontent among the Southerners. In 1960, Friday was exchanged for Sunday as the day of rest in the South, reversing a custom begun half a century before. In 1961, all religious gatherings for prayer, except in a church, and catechetical teaching

---

[88] On June 27, 1963, *Al Thawra,* the government newspaper, published the Sudan Secondary Certificate Results. There were some 1,300 graduates from twenty-three secondary schools in the North, including some 130 private candidates. The two secondary schools in the South (Juba Commercial and Rumbeck) graduated only fifty-nine. On June 23, 1963, *Al Thawra* reported the distribution of twelve new secondary schools which were all located in the North. None were allotted to the Southern Sudan.

were forbidden. Missionaries home on leave were not permitted to return, and those who remained found themselves increasingly harassed and restricted. In May 1962, the Supreme Council promulgated "The Missionary Societies Act," whose sweeping limitations left the missions at the whim of the government. Even the most optimistic Christian missionary realized that his activities in the Southern Sudan would soon be terminated. On February 27, 1964, the Ministry of the Interior announced the immediate expulsion of all Christian missionaries. Within a fortnight, the missionaries were gone, leaving behind an immature Sudanese Christian Church, struggling to preserve itself against the growing strength of Islam backed by the power and resources of the Sudan government.

Although the military government in the Sudan steadily imposed its policies throughout the Southern Sudan, it noticeably failed to gild the bitter pill of Arabization and Islamization with economic development. When the British left the Sudan in 1956, there were numerous schemes for developing the Southern Sudan. As with education, however, most of those projects have been postponed or abandoned in favor of economic undertakings in the North. The plans for growing sugar cane at Mongalla and Malakal in conjunction with a sugar refinery constructed in joint partnership between the Sudan government and the Boxall Company have been given up in favor of inferior sugar schemes in the North at Junayd and Khashm al Qirbah. A paper factory planned for Malakal has been forgotten as well as a fish-canning plant, which has been moved north to Jabal al 'Awliya. Plans for a meat-canning factory in the Bahr al-Ghazal remain stillborn. True, a large rice-growing scheme has been inaugurated at Aweil, but Southern participation appears limited to labor. The important strategic railway has been extended from Babanusah in Korodofan to Wau, the capital of the Bahr al-Ghazal, but the line represents an iron tie that binds the South to the North as much as an important link in the Sudan's economic infrastructure.

The reaction on the part of the Southerners to these political and religious pressures and the economic and education neglect was flight and rebellion. Ever since the disturbances in 1955 the Southern Sudanese have fled to Uganda and the Congo, particularly those from the border tribes where kinsmen live on either side of the frontier. The flow of refugees decreased to a trickle during the dying days of parliamentary government in the Sudan. The military seizure of the government did not at first precipitate a fresh flight or outbreak of new disturbances, but after 1960, when the military government began pressing Arabization and Islamization on the South, the trickle again became a flood. Many Southern intellectuals and members of the proscribed Southern Liberal party who had not been associated with the disorders in 1955 fled the country. The refugees established the Sudan African National Union to present the Southern point of view and to work peacefully, if with futility, for the Liberal's old demand for a federated Sudan. The tribesmen were simply herded into refugee camps by the harried and somewhat embarrassed government officials of the Congo and Uganda.

In the Southern Sudan itself, the measures of the central government were greeted by ever-increasing resistance. In October 1962, a widespread strike in Southern schools resulted in anti-government demonstrations, followed by a general flight of students. During the spring and summer of 1963, feelings relaxed and affairs appeared to improve as most of the discontented had fled. Furthermore, the Sudan government had reinforced its army and police units in the Southern provinces. Suddenly, however, on September 18, 1963, rebellion erupted again in eastern Equatoria and in the Upper Nile Province led by the Anya Nya Society, a Southern Sudanese terrorist organization. Bitterly opposed to the policies of the government and disenchanted with the more peaceful attempts by the leaders of the Sudan African National Union to reach a settlement, the Anya Nya declared open hostility toward the Arabs in the South in the belief that only violent resistance would make the government of General 'Abbud seek a solution acceptable to the Southerners.

Although the Sudan government had temporarily suspended the Closed District Ordinance, which had been used to seal off the Southern Sudan, the Ordinance was reimposed at the outbreak of these fresh disturbances. A grass curtain once again obscured events in the South and eclipsed the clash of cultures in that unhappy land. Seeking refuge in the vastness of the bush, the terrorists continued their sporadic attacks on isolated posts of the Sudan Army, while the Southern Sudanese carried on their way of life much as before, wandering off when the pressure of government became too great, returning when the weight of administration relaxed. Without confidence, however, there was little growth or progress in any field. Thus, while economic and educational developments are transforming the North, the South remains a stagnant backwater in a rapidly changing world. Blind to the aspirations of the Southern Sudanese and devoid of imagination in their dealings with them, the generals in Khartoum sought to establish their authority by negative repression which appeared to increase proportionately with Southern resistance. To prevent the flow of refugees to neighboring countries, the Sudan negotiated extradition treaties in the spring of 1964 with Ethiopia and Uganda. But where Ethiopia agreed to return all criminals, Uganda reserved the right not to extradite those convicted of political crimes. These measures had little effect, however, and most of the Southern Sudanese in exile in Ethiopia sought refuge in Kenya after the signing of the treaty. Their flight was but another example of the Sudan government's failure in the South.

Unable to recover internal security in the Southern provinces, the Sudan government announced, in September, that a twenty-five-man Commission of Enquiry, under the leadership of Sayyid Ahmad Muhammad Yassin, would investigate conditions in the Southern Sudan in a desperate attempt to find a solution. The formation of such a commission was itself a confession of the government's failure to acquire control or to restore confidence, and, with every passing month, the magnitude of this failure became increasingly apparent to the Northern Sudanese and even to the world beyond. Although many Northern Sudanese had little sympathy for their Southern countrymen, they were able to use the government's failure there to assail military rule in the North. The Northern Sudanese had at first welcomed General 'Abbud's government and then tacitly accepted it. By 1962, however, numerous urban elements, including the intelligentsia, the trade unions, and the civil servants, as well as the powerful religious brotherhoods, the *turuq*, had become bored and disenchanted with the military regime. In 1958, these groups had applauded the efforts of the patriotic and progressive army officers to clean the Aegean stables of Sudanese parliamentarianism and to solve pressing economic and international problems. But within a few years, after the military government had consolidated its power, the intelligentsia resented its exclusion from the councils of government, the trade unions chafed at the restrictions placed upon their activities, and the civil servants sulked at orders from their military superiors. Even the conservative religious brotherhoods grew restless when they were unable to carry on their former political activities. Moreover, the tribal masses and growing proletariat had become increasingly apathetic toward the government, for even if the parliamentarians were corrupt, they were at least exciting and colorful. Military reviews, parades, and heroic pronouncements were no substitute for the enthusiasm generated by party politics and the passions stirred by political action. The military government never provided an outlet for the political frustrations of the Sudanese, and, in the end, the regime was overwhelmed by boredom and overthrown by the reaction to its lassitude. The means, not the cause, was the Southern Sudan.

Following the establishment of the Commission of Enquiry in September 1964, students at Khartoum University created their own discussion groups to express their dissatisfaction with the government's policies in the South. On October 22, the students held a meeting in defiance of a government prohibition in order to condemn publicly these policies and to denounce the regime. In the ensuing and inevitable clash with the police, one student was killed and several were wounded. The funeral of the martyred student on the following day sparked even larger demonstrations—in Khartoum, Umdurman, and Khartoum North—which were only contained, not suppressed, by troops with tanks and armored cars. Numerous Sudanese were killed and many wounded. With most of its forces committed in the Southern Sudan, the Army was unable to impose its complete control in the three cities; and the disorders soon spread to other towns along the Nile and in the interior. The extent of the disturbances and the failure of the Army to suppress them strengthened the position of those members of the military regime who recognized the government's failure in the South and divided the generals more deeply. Unable to govern without civilian support and unwilling to crush the disturbances with massive repression, General 'Abbud announced the dismissal of the Supreme Council and the Cabinet on October 26 and began consultation with the influential political and religious leaders. Meanwhile, a general strike called by the United National Front, a hastily organized alliance of proscribed political parties, trade unions, and even the Moslem Brotherhood, paralyzed communications and brought the commercial life of the country to a standstill. Under pressure from the strikers and the civilian leaders, 'Abbud capitulated and, on October 29, announced the end of the military government. Although 'Abbud himself was to remain the titular head of state, he too resigned shortly thereafter. A transitional government was appointed to take the place of the military rulers, consisting of sixteen men under the Prime Minister, Al-Khatim al-Khalifa, former Deputy Permanent Secretary of the Ministry of Education. The transitional government was to rule under the provisional constitution of 1956 until parliamentary elections could be held to determine the composition of an elected government. Censorship of the press was removed, and the prohibition against political parties was rescinded. Political prisoners were released.

Although the success of the civilian *coup d'état* was made possible by conditions in the Northern Sudan, it was the failure of the military government in the South that precipitated its downfall. Indeed, the appointment of Al-Khatim al-Khalifa as Prime Minister and the inclusion of two Southerners in the Cabinet was a direct attempt to reverse the repressive policy of the military government and to re-establish good will, if not confidence, throughout the South. But more than gestures are required in the Southern Sudan. Already racism has fanned the flames of the religious intolerance and the political repression of the military regime. On December 7, 1964, Southerners in Khartoum rioted in protest against Northern domination and were attacked in turn by mobs of Northerners seeking retaliation. Over a score of Sudanese were killed, and hundreds injured before the army succeeded in restoring order. These race riots were symptomatic of Southern bitterness, and they exacerbated, as well as hastened, the government's determination to seek a political solution to the problem of the Southern Sudan. The transitional government quickly seized the opportunity of Kenya's republic celebrations held on December 12, to send two representatives to Nairobi to open negotiations with the leaders of the Sudan African National Union. Clearly the transitional government appears willing to concede a liberal political settlement in order to preserve a united Sudan and to restore confidence in the South. Indeed, the Sudan African National Union has consistently asserted that the problem of the South was principally political.[89] Many in the transitional government are of the same opinion, arguing that a political solution will solve the Southern Sudan question. This is misplaced optimism. Unfortunately, the question of the Southern Sudan is not just political, but religious, economic, and, above all, cultural. To succeed, any political agreement must be accompanied by a modification in the intensity

---

[89] *Voice of Southern Sudan,* I, No. 2 (n.d.), p. 3.

with which Arab customs, language, and religion have so recently pressed up the Nile. It must no longer restrict the Southern Sudanese to an inferior economic position. It must provide the means to sublimate the superior attitudes assumed by many Northerners toward their Southern countrymen. It must recognize that Sudanese nationalism must include peoples for whom Arab nationalism has little or no appeal. These hereditary states of main and traditional relationships, not just the immediate political problem, must accommodate themselves to any political settlement. If the more autocratic traditions of the Northern Sudanese are not altered and if Sudanese nationalism is not sufficiently viable to encompass the more disparate societies within the country, the liberalism of the transitional government and its successors cannot hope to achieve an enduring union. Mutual help, respect, and toleration, as much as political agreements, will be required to bind the two nations until that time when the Sudan—in culture, race, and religion, if not in politics—will cease to be a house divided against itself.

BIBLIOGRAPHICAL ESSAY

An interpretive essay is usually the product of wide reading in both published and unpublished sources, combined with critical reflection and a sense of synthesis uncommon in more specialized studies. Such is the case with "The Sudan: Link to the North." The historical literature of the Sudan is large, particularly concerning the Southern Sudan in the nineteenth century, but with few exceptions neither comprehensive nor disquisitional. For the diligent student who seeks to pursue a particular aspect of Sudanese studies, one need only turn to the excellent bibliographies of Richard Leslie Hill, *A Bibliography of the Anglo-Egyptian Sudan from the Earliest Times to 1937* (London: Oxford University Press, 1939), and Abdel Rahmanel Nasri, *A Bibliography of the Sudan 1938–1958* (London: Oxford University Press, 1962). The literature published after 1958 will usually be regularly listed in *Sudan Notes and Records*. If the reader desires only a single, comprehensive history of the Sudan, Peter Malcolm Holt, *A Modern History of the Sudan* (New York: Grove Press, 1961), is an excellent survey, but one in which the Southern Sudan is regarded more as an appendage of dubious historical value to the North than as a link with East Africa. The history of the Southern Sudan in the nineteenth century is well covered by two complementary works: Richard Gray, *A History of the Southern Sudan 1839–1889* (London: Oxford University Press, 1961); and Robert Oakley Collins, *The Southern Sudan, 1883–1898* (New Haven: Yale University Press, 1962). After the establishment of the Anglo-Egyptian Condominium in 1898, the historical literature of the Sudan, both North and South, is reduced to delightful but superficial surveys such as Sir Harold MacMichael, *The Sudan* (London: Ernest Benn, 1954); and John Spenser Ritchie Duncan, *The Sudan, A Record of Achievement* and *The Sudan's Path to Independence* (London: William Blackwood & Sons, 1952 and 1957 respectively); journalistic accounts of questionable taste and accuracy, such as Michael Langley, *No Woman's Country* (London: Jarrold's, 1950), and Anthony Mann, *Where God Laughed* (London: Museum Press, 1954); or to such charming personal memoirs as those of Sir Douglas Newbold (Kenneth David Druitt Henderson), *The Making of the Modern Sudan* (London: Faber and Faber, 1953) and Henry Cecil Jackson, *Sudan Days and Ways* (London: Macmillan & Company, 1953), and *Behind the Modern Sudan* (London: Macmillan & Company, 1954). An even more analytical approach to British administration in the Sudan is only foreshadowed in Mekki Abbas, *The Sudan Question: The Dispute over the Anglo-Egyptian Condominium 1884–1951* (London: Faber and Faber, 1952), and is never fully developed in his general discussion of the Condominium conflict. In fact, there is no single, comprehensive history of British administration in the Sudan that laymen and scholars alike can use to acquire a meaningful understanding of the modern Sudan or attempt to intepret its history. It is certainly doubtful whether one could obtain such knowledge from the works cited above or others like them. The policies, problems, successes, and failures of British rule in the Sudan are still to be found among the official records in the Sudan Government Archives, Khartoum, and from the personal papers and memoirs of former British administrators now living in retirement in England. These are the sources which the author has consulted in order to fashion this essay.

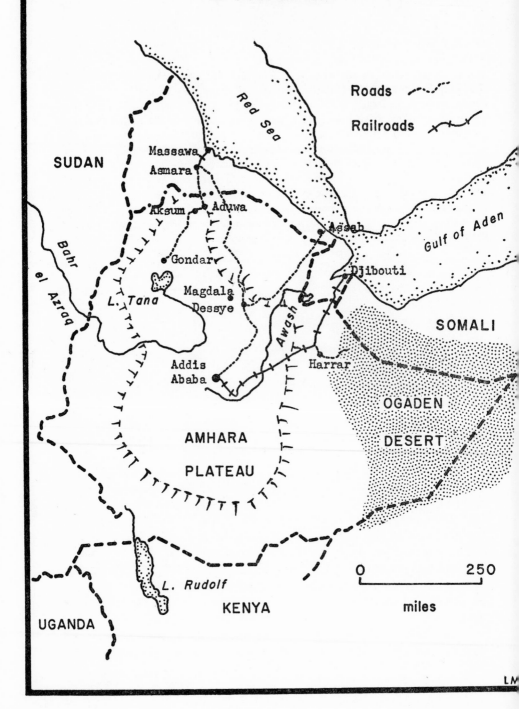

ETHIOPIA

Roads

Railroads

SUDAN

Red Sea

Massawa
Asmara

Aksum   Aduwa

Assab

Gulf of Aden

Gondar

L. Tana

Magdala
Dessye

Djibouti

Awash

SOMALI

Addis
Ababa

Harrar

OGADEN

DESERT

Bahr

el Azraq

AMHARA

PLATEAU

L. Rudolf

KENYA

0   250

miles

UGANDA

LM

10

Ethiopia: A Special Case

Francis A. J. Ianni

OF ALL THE COUNTRIES of East Africa none is better known to the world than Ethiopia, and yet none is less understood; for, in the Horn and in Africa, Ethiopia is unique. Geographically, culturally, and politically, it is all but impossible to find close ties with any of the neighboring countries. In fact, until quite recently, Ethiopia was not a part of Africa, either to Ethiopians, to Africans, or to informed non-Africans. And, even today, there is some question as to where it belongs politically and culturally. Many African leaders maintain, for example, that Haile Selassie has only recently discovered that he is indeed black and that his future rests with the Africans and not with the Arabs. The African commentator is also likely to go on at some length about the political naïveté of the young Ethiopian intellectual and the incongruity of a modern-day African calling himself "King of Kings, The Elect of God, Conquering Lion of the Tribe of Judah, Emperor," and before finishing, one realizes that the lack of knowledge about Ethiopia is as great within Africa as it is elsewhere—and perhaps greater—for the African sees the emerging Africa of today, and Ethiopia is not a part of that blooming.

Other pictures are also commonly painted. The young American Negro intellectual, drawn to Africa by his new awareness of the cultural heritage that he thinks he *should* share with the African, returns, and says over and over again, with a mixture of surprise and irony, "But Ethiopia has been *free* for most of the last 3,000 years. She knew none of the chains of colonialism, and yet she is the most backward nation in all of Africa save one, and that is Liberia." During the recent coup of 1960, the proclamation of freedom by the rebels began, "We have been free for 3,000 years yet we are behind those African sister states who have been free but three years."

These views—along with those of the tourist, the ethnologist, the trade unionist, and white settler—all create the same image, the same conundrum:

407

Ethiopia is a nation which developed its own form of writing (one of the few native to Africa), held suzerainty over diverse lands from Egypt to Yemen, successfully withstood the crushing encirclement by Islam, generated several advanced civilizations, and yet remains relatively unaffected by the African revolution. Why? The following factors are clearly pertinent:

1. The very circumstances that kept Ethiopia free—her physical and cultural self-sufficiency and isolation—have also kept her insulated against the new African dynamism.

2. Though Ethiopia has been spared the convulsions of colonialism, she has also been denied the benefits that came to many other parts of Africa as a result of colonialism. For it demands to be considered that, despite our social and moral condemnation of colonialism, the contact phenomenon—by which I mean the social, the moral, and the economic contacts resulting from colonization—has been the primary factor in preparing other African nations for getting on in today's world. Ethiopia has been left largely to herself, and her resulting uniqueness accounts for her present political posture in East Africa.

Ethiopia provides a prime example of the absence of sustained culture contact, that is contact by conquest or by direct or indirect colonization. From the negative experiences of Ethiopia, some generalizations concerning the social politics of colonization and the sociology of race contact can be drawn. First, however, we must examine Ethiopia's distinct and unique character—in terms of geography, cultural and racial history.

Ethiopia is made typographically distinctive by one important feature: her towering, plateau-topped mountains (*ambas*) surrounded by deserts. These *ambas,* accessible only by a few paths and with sufficient water and grazing on top to support vast armies under siege, have served as almost complete secure, self-sufficient fortresses. Playing a major role in Ethiopian history, they have been strongholds of rebellious tribes, the refuge of *shiftas* (bandits) and, most importantly, centers of resistance to foreign invaders. They still provide excellent sites for enforced contemplation by anyone creating difficulty for the realm. Locked in this mountain fastness, Ethiopia has not only been sealed off from the rest of the world, but the various tribal groupings living within her present boundaries have had little contact even with one another.

RACIAL AND CULTURAL HISTORY

The racial history of Ethiopia also presents, even for East Africa, an intriguingly diverse and distinctive aspect to the country. Even today, very striking racial differences can be observed in moving from one part of the empire to another. These variations reflect the major racial differences that have resulted from the admixture of an indigenous Bushmanoid population in the western portion of the country, Cushitic-speaking Caucasoids farther east, an early (*circa* 3000 B.C.) invasion by Negroid ancestors of the agricultural peoples whom Grottanelli has characterized as pre-Nilotes, and subsequent invasions of Semites from across the Red Sea.[1]

As a result of the pressure from the invasion of pre-Nilotes, the Cushitic Caucasoids broke into three distinct divisions, and the factors of regional geography tended to perpetuate these distinctions. In the southeast of the present empire, cut off from the rest of the plateau by the Great Rift, the Konso cluster of peoples and other diverse groups developed. In the southwest, a second cluster developed which produced the Sidamo peoples made up of the Gibe, Janjero, Kafa, and similar tribes. But the most interesting, at least in terms of the cultural history of the Ethiopians, was the third cluster of plateau Cushites, the Agua peoples. Whereas today only a scattered handful of these people remain in Ethiopia, they once inhabited most of the central and northern reaches of the highlands and were probably among the most dynamic and creative people in all of Africa. Adoptive and inventive agriculturalists, they borrowed from the invading pre-Nilotes and experimented with wild plants, herded cattle, sheep, and goats, domesticated the wild ass, and produced in Ethiopia an important center for distribution of cultivated plants to other parts of Africa.

The descendants of the Agua form the most important tribal groupings in Ethiopia today: the ruling Amhara, a Coptic Christian people in excess of 3 million from whom come the ruling family, almost all responsible government officials, the church hierarchy, and the leaders of the armed forces; the Gurage, a Semitic-speaking group numbering about 400,000, some of whom are Christian, some Moslem, some pagan, but all regarded as virtually a slave caste; the Tigrinya, a predominantly Christian group numbering about 1.25 million over one-third of whom live in Eritrea; the Harari, an Islamic group of 40,000–50,000 who live in and around the city of Harar; the Falasha, an Agua remnant of some 20,000–30,000 people, believed by some to have been converted to Judaism during the Diaspora and today still following this religion; and other scattered remnants of the Agua, such as the Awiya, Kamir, and Kemant.

In addition to these plateau people, who are primarily agriculturalists, three important groups of independent pastoralists make up the bulk of the remaining population of Ethiopia. Two of these groups, the Afar and the Somali, inhabiting the desert region of the Ogaden and the semidesert region of the Danakil Plain, are primarily nomadic pastoralists, although agriculture is practiced by some Somali, and the coast-dwelling members of the Afar group are fishermen. The latter are, with few exceptions, followers of Islam. The Afar—who, along with the kindred Saho, number about 150,000—still retain a measure of independence, and their local rulers (still called "sultans" in a holdover from the Turks) exercise considerable local power. The Somali,

---

[1] Vinigi L. Grottanelli, "I Pre-Niloti," *Annales Lateranensi,* XII (1948), 282–326.

who number about 2.5 million, are even more independent and are currently agitating for secession from Ethiopia and incorporation into a "Greater Somalia" with their Somali brethren in Somalia and northern Kenya. The third group, originally pastoral nomads, consists of the pagan Galla tribes, many of whom invaded the plateau regions and adapted the agriculture and Christianity of the region. Numbering about 3 million, the Galla today cover extensive portions of Ethiopia and generally support the Amhara ruling classes.

It seems clear that, from ancient times, Ethiopia has been inhabited by a variety of peoples with the greater part of the area originally occupied by Hamito-Semitic–speaking Cushites. The origin of the Cushites is still an unresolved question, but the weight of evidence points to Arabia rather than elsewhere in Africa as was once believed. In any event, there is enough evidence of subsequent invasions from Arabia to support the view that in race, culture, and speech the Ethiopian shows close affinity to the Arabian peninsula.

One of the important invasions from Arabia in the early centuries before Christ led to the establishment of the kingdom of Aksum and constitutes one of the great periods in Ethiopian history in legend and in fact. The kingdom of Aksum, resulting from a gradual federation of Arabian immigrants who came to trade rather than conquer, was well known to classical and early Christian writers. Its importance as a trade center on the Red Sea is seen in the frequent mention it received as a trade center in various early historical works, such as the anonymous first century A.D. *Periplus Maris Erythraei;* Pliny's *Natural History,* the historian Procopius' *De Bello Persico;* and *Topographia Christiana,* written in the sixth century A.D. by the Greek monk Cosmos Indicopleustes. But, more important, it was probably through Aksum and the Greco-Roman merchant communities on the Red Sea coast that Christianity was first introduced into Ethiopia and to Ethiopians. Spread among the ruling classes by St. Frumentius, a Syrian traveler shipwrecked on the Red Sea coast in the early part of the fourth century A.D., Christianity formed the strongest link between Ethiopia and the Western world. When subsequent events cut the country off from the rest of the world, Christianity became a dominant element in the distinctive Ethiopian culture.

Up until the middle of the seventh century, Ethiopia retained these ties with the world of Christendom, but with the expulsion of the Akumite forces from southern Arabia by the Persians (probably about 572) and the later rise of a militant Islam, Ethiopia became isolated from the Mediterranean. Eventually, Moslems took over the desert regions surrounding the mountain fastness and converted the indigenous peoples. Forced back to the high interior lands of the *ambas,* the ruling Christian Amharas entered the Ethiopian middle ages. No longer in contact with the outside world, Ethiopia began to develop her own culture and to erect the physical, emotional, and cultural barriers that served to keep out the rest of the world.

Little is really known about Ethiopia during the next four or five centuries. The Zaque dynasty (of Agua origin) flourished during this period and built the splendid monolithic churches of Ethiopia. In 1270, the Zaque dynasty was overthrown by the Solomonoid dynasty, which in popular Ethiopian belief (and in official government tradition) traces its genealogy back to Menelik I, son of Solomon and the Queen of Sheba.

A series of conflicts between Christian Ethiopia and the Moslem world gradually forced the Ethiopians farther back into the mountains. Here, the power of the Coptic church greatly increased, and the religious influence on the governing kings became intense. Little came into Ethiopia, and virtually nothing came from it, except some rather fabulous (in both senses of the word) tales of a great Christian monarch in Ethiopia.

About 1165, a letter said to be written by one "Presbyter Joannes, by the power and virtue of God and of the Lord Jesus Christ, Lord of Lords," the greatest of Christian rulers who controlled a vast land somewhere in Africa, was published in Europe. The letter alleged that seventy-two kings, reigning over as many kingdoms, joined with twelve archbishops in giving "Presbyter Joannes" homage and that he had a vast and miraculous mirror that allowed him to keep an eye on all of these kings and, indeed, over all of his empire. His domains contained the "ants which dug gold" and the "fish that gave the purple"; he went to war, so it was said, preceded by thirteen golden and jeweled crosses each followed by 10,000 knights and 100,000 warriors. In his lands, where there were no thieves, no poor, no lies, and no vices, he was served by seven kings at a time, by sixty dukes and 365 counts and had an untold number of ecclesiastics surrounding him on all sides.

The story of "Prester John," as he came to be known, spread far and wide, particularly since the import of the letter was that he was planning to march to Jerusalem and stamp out the infidel. Although Prester John was never found, this legend and its promise of riches served to develop an interest in Ethiopia on the part of the Europeans, notably the Portuguese. Portuguese interests in the trade routes to India also whetted this concern, and, in the fifteenth and sixteenth centuries, a number of missions were sent by the Portuguese in Ethiopia.

After the Turkish Sultan Selim I conquered Egypt in 1517, the Portuguese concern for the Red Sea route became extreme, and, when a Moslem fire-brand from the Danakil Desert, Mohammed Grañ, set out to place much of Ethiopia under the Star and Crescent, the die was cast for Portuguese intervention. So great was the success of Grañ, who was helped considerably by a force of armed Turks from Yemen, that in 1541 Estevan de Gama, son of Vasco da Gama and then Viceroy of India, dispatched his brother Christovam to aid the seemingly helpless Ethiopian forces under King Claudius. In the course of the war, Christovam de Gama was captured and beheaded, but Mohammed Grañ was himself killed in a later battle. In 1542, the Moslem threat was temporarily halted. In 1551, however, a new Moslem leader, Nur Ibn Mujahid, married the widow of Grañ, promised her revenge, and again proceded to attack the Ethiopians. He defeated and killed Claudius in March 1559; but, with the exhaustion caused to both sides by this long and bitter struggle, both Christian and Moslem soon fell prey to a new threat from the south. The pagan Galla tribes drove the Moslems from Harrar to the sultanate of Aussa in the midst of the Danakil Desert and the Christian Amhara northward to a new capital in Gondar.

During this period, the Holy See and the Portuguese sought to use the advantage of the Ethiopians' military plight and need to bring about some union between the Ethiopian church and Roman Catholicism. Missionaries, principally the Jesuits, were sent into Ethiopia and, for a period, succeeded in working with the Ethiopians. They failed, however, in convincing the Ethiopians that the monophysitic tradition of the Coptic church was in error. Finally, in 1603, the great Spanish Jesuit Pedro Paez converted King Susenyos, who accepted the two natures of Christ and proclaimed his acceptance to Pope Urban and the King of Spain and Portugal. Paez died in 1622, and reaction against the conversion began almost at once. So great was the public outcry that Susenyos abdicated in favor of his son Fasilides, but not before a period of severe repression set in and many of the missionaries fled, were killed, or were sold into slavery.

Once again, the contact with the outside world was ended in a manner that caused the Ethiopians to withdraw even more into themselves. The last link with the Mediterranean was now severed and a two-century-long period of complete isolation and gradual decay followed in the face of Galla pressure against which the Ethiopians could not or would not turn to Europe for aid.

From this depth to which the country had fallen as a result of the constant struggles with Islam and the Galla and the equally constant internecine struggles among the chiefs and nobles emerged one of the great controversial figures in Ethiopian history—the mad Emperor Theodoros II. Of lowly birth and at first little more than a bandit leader, Theodoros, whose real name was Kassa, achieved the throne by a succession of victories over feudal chiefs and had fairly well unified the country by the time of his coronation in 1855. But even then, there were still numerous uprisings by the recalcitrant chiefs, and Theodoros became increasingly repressive and embarked on a series of punitive expeditious massacres, utilizing torture and mutilation in an effort to bring the country under his control.

During the reign of Theodoros, Europe began again to show an interest in Ethiopia; and both France and Britain sent representatives—the French to the chief of the Tigré and the British to the court of Theodoros. At first, the British fared well with Theodoros, but with the arrival of the second British emissary, Charles D. Cameron, difficulties began to develop. As Theodoros became older, he began to have fits of madness, drank heavily and, under the combined weight of his own vices and the continued hostility of the feudal chiefs, began to lose control of himself and of his people. He embarked on yet another wave of terror and destroyed village after village, burning thousands of his subjects alive. He suspected Cameron of intercourse with his Moslem antagonists and of joining in an Egyptian plot to unseat him. To add to his difficulty, an incredibly important little mishap occurred. Theodoros had written a letter to Queen Victoria, but in the vast entanglement for which civil service around the world has become infamous, the letter went unanswered. Theodoros became violent and finally imprisoned Cameron along with other British subjects and European missionaries. In turn, the British sent a punitive expedition complete with modern weapons and elephants under the command of Sir Robert Napier. Napier, with 3,400 men, defeated Theodoros in April 1868, in a battle marked by reckless bravery and defiant charges by the Ethiopians. Surrounded in his stronghold at Magdala, Theodoros shot himself on Easter Monday.

Despite his despotism and madness, Theodoros did more than any previous king to set the stage for unification of Ethiopia, which at that time was little more than a series of hostile and antagonistic kingdoms, each ruled by a *negus* or king who aspired to dominate all of the others. Inevitable chaos and decay followed his defeat, as rival chieftains sought to gain control. It is interesting to speculate what might have happened had not the British been busy elsewhere and had they decided to capitalize on Napier's victory to set up a colony in Ethiopia. Certainly the Ethiopian highlands were every bit as healthy and productive as the highlands of Kenya. But this was not to be, and Napier left after freeing the European prisoners.

Subsequently Ethiopia was once more rescued from internal disorder by the emergence of a great leader from within, Menelik II, the greatest of all Ethiopian rulers and the one individual most responsible for the unification of the Ethiopian Empire. A Shoan *negus,* Menelik proceeded by force of arms and strategic marriages to bring most of what is today Ethiopia under his control. Menelik fought a long succession of battles, particularly with Ras Kassa, chief of the Tigré, who had been crowned Emperor Johannes IV in 1872. Johannes had defeated the Egyptians at Gura in 1876, but was constantly threatened by the forces of the Mahdi from the Sudan and of the Italians who had taken over what is today Eritrea. As the Mahdists and Italians advanced, Johannes was set upon by Menelik who, after being imprisoned by Theodoros, had re-established himself as king in Shoa. With the help of arms supplied by the Italians, Menelik sought to overthrow Johannes and re-establish the Solomonoid (Shoan) dynasty. As he marched to meet Menelik, Johannes was killed by a Mahdist army at Metamma in March 1889. In November 1889, Menelik was crowned *Negus Negusti* (King of Kings).

Having acquired Somalia and Eritrea, Italy was desirous of linking the two by acquiring Ethiopia. Remembering the fiasco of the Ethiopian attempts against Napier and forgetting that this was now a unified Ethiopia and that their own King Umberto had given Menelik a gift of thirty cannon and 38,000 rifles, the Italians attempted a surprise attack at Adoua on March 1,

1896. A disastrous rout of the Italians and the first and last great victory achieved by an African leader against a European power followed. The Italians lost 8,000 of their own troops and four thousand Eritrean *askaris*. Only 600 of the invaders escaped, and almost 2,000 were captured. Menelik agreed to free the Italian prisoners in exchange for Italian recognition of his sovereignty, but, in express disobedience of his orders, a company of Italian soldiers was mutilated. Menelik's pity for the Italians did not extend to the Eritrean troops who fought for the Italians, and he ordered that 406 of them should have their right hands and left feet cut off as a sign of treason. Eritreans still remember this. With the defeat of the Italians, Ethiopia was once again brought to the attention of Europe, and representatives from the great powers poured into the country. Menelik put them to good use, and, for the rest of his long reign, he began to unify and, as much as possible, to modernize Ethiopia.

Menelik died in 1913, having proclaimed as his successor his twelve-year-old grandson Lij Yasu, yet another tragic figure in the history of the Ethiopian throne. Before he could be crowned, World War I had broken out; and, within Ethiopia, the age-old tradition of intrigue was at work. The dowager Empress Zauditu, Menelik's widow, schemed from the very outset to replace Yasu with Menelik's daughter Zauditu. In the wings at this drama were two other contenders—the old Minister of War Fiturari Hapte Giorgis and the young but determined twenty-one-year-old governor of the city of Harrar, Ras Tafari Makonnen, the son of a great general under Menelik, Ras Makonnen.

Finally, Yasu presented these aspirants to his throne with the opportunity they needed. Always a clever but unstable youth, he began to give clear evidence of his preference for Islam and his sympathy for the Central powers and Turkey. He began to associate more and more with Moslems and finally proclaimed himself a follower of Islam and disposed of his Christian wife. The feudal chiefs of Shoa, encouraged by the allied powers, were outraged and joined forces behind the Cross of the Coptic church as the *Abuna* (Archbishop) released them from their oath of fealty to Yasu and proclaimed that all who followed the Moslem Emperor were "cursed by God," and "would incur" the wrath of the Father, Son and Holy Ghost, of the twelve apostles and of all the fathers of the Council of Nicaea, the curse of Arius, and the approbation of Judas." Yasu fled to the Danakil Desert and attempted to raise the Moslem Danakil and Somali tribes. Six years of turmoil followed until Yasu was captured, fettered (as tradition demanded) in chains of gold, and spirited away. What eventually happened to him no one quite knows. The Danakil, who still revere him, say that he was poisoned, some Ethiopians say he was drowned, but all agree that he was disposed of in such a way that "no royal blood was shed!"

As might be expected, a struggle for power then developed among the Empress Zauditu, old Hapte Giorgis, and young Tafari Makonnen. Eventually Hapte died, and Zauditu's favorite, Taitu, was named Empress with Ras

Tafari as heir apparent to the throne. In 1930, the Empress Taitu died, and Ras Tafari became Emperor with the throne name Haile Selassie (Power of the Trinity).

ETHIOPIA TODAY

Haile Selassie I, Elect of God, Conquering Lion of the Tribe of Judah, King of Kings, and 225th in the somewhat-less-than-unbroken line of the Solomonoid dynasty of Ethiopia, came to the throne well prepared. Educated at a French Jesuit mission school in Harrar where his father was governor, he himself became governor of a town in that province at the age of fourteen. A great-nephew of Menelik, Tafari distinguished himself early as an able if ruthless administrator and was so well versed at intrigue that he was exiled to the remote province of Kaffa. When Menelik died, Tafari went back to Harrar, this time as governor of the province.

An accurate assessment of Haile Selassie as ruler, distinct from the country itself, is almost impossible for today, as, always during his rule, he *is* Ethiopia. Although the world tends to think of him as a pathetic little figure in a pith helmet and cape, pleading with the League of Nations for his country, there is the other Haile Selassie, and, in that image, he is one of the most ruthless yet benevolent, suspicious yet intelligent and dedicated rulers in the world.

Soon after Haile Selassie took the throne, trouble erupted between the Italians and Ethiopia. On October 3, 1935, Italian expeditionary forces from Eritrea and Italian Somaliland began penetrations into Ethiopia. In May 1936, the Emperor fled the country, going first to Jerusalem, and eventually to exile in England, where he remained for nearly five years. In Ethiopia, the tough old war lords, such as Ras Kassa, Ras Imru, and Ras Desta, fought, but eventually almost all were overwhelmed.

The results of the five-year occupation of Ethiopia by the Italians are difficult to assess. There is little question of the harsh, repressive measures inflicted on the population by the Fascist conquerors, particularly after the attempt on the life of the Viceroy Marshal Rodolfo Graziani in February 1937. The succession of the Duke of Aosta as viceroy later that year led to somewhat milder methods, but the resistance continued under Ras Imru and Ras Abeba Arregai (Minister of Defense under Haile Selassie until he was executed by the rebels during the *coup d'état* of 1960) and so did the repressions. On the other hand, the Italians did embark on an ambitious program of public works. They built vast networks of roads, tunnels, and bridges, which still remain the only major highway systems in Ethiopia. They introduced and measurably developed medical organization and established elementary, technical, and agricultural schools. They began a conscientious plan of agricultural development and erected factories and electric generating plants. Although they did these things for the benefit and greater glory of

Italy rather than the development of the country, they still remain as a legacy of Ethiopia's brief period of colonialism.

When Haile Selassie returned to Addis Ababa in May 1941, he must have found it quite changed from his departure five years earlier. His experience outside of Ethiopia had given him a perspective, however, which must have also changed him. He set about to redevelop his country. But even though he was the first Ethiopian monarch to view the outside world at close hand, he was still too traditional to want to see the ancient monarchy modified greatly in his lifetime—or he might have been too intelligent and practical to expect to transform his medieval kingdom overnight into a modern nation.

Shortly after his return from exile, he convened the parliament provided for in his Constitution of 1931. In 1955, he issued a new constitution which gave evidence of his determination that, while Ethiopia will show continued progress under his rule, there will be no "deliberate speed." The constitution called for a Senate, which is an advisory body made up of nobles and chieftains, and an equally advisory House of Deputies, which was to be elected by a very small number of "qualified" voters who could pass a rigorous property qualification. Since 1957, the members of the House of Deputies have been elected by "universal suffrage," but since political parties are banned and so few Ethiopians literate, representative government simply does not exist. Ethiopia today continues as a feudal monarchy with the Emperor making every decision—even on matters that would be considered trivial in modern governmental systems.

Regulating this government is an involved and antiquated law system— or rather series of law systems—based on biblical, Roman, and customary law, making legal actions in the courts such long drawn-out affairs and so unpredictable that Ethiopians and foreigners alike are loath to use the courts as a means of recourse. In effect, the Emperor himself is the supreme court, and, although some serious attempts at legal reforms are now under way, it seems unlikely that any great progress will be made in the immediate future.

Ethiopia's economy is still primarily agricultural and pastoral as are almost all of her few exports. The economy has not been kept backward by any lack of natural resources, for the country is rich in fertile land, waterpower, and, to a lesser extent, mineral resources. Ethiopia probably has more arable land than any other country in Africa, and it is rich land. Mussolini boasted that he could feed all of Europe from the Italian farms in Eritrea and Ethiopia, and, more recently, United States Assistant Secretary of State for African Affairs G. Mennen Williams told a meeting of the African Studies Association that State Department experts estimate that the Ethiopian highlands ". . . if properly cultivated, could produce sufficient food (to feed) all of Western Europe."[2] There are vast systems of rivers available for hydro-

---

[2] *Department of State Bulletin*, XLVII (October 29, 1962), p. 692.

electric power and potential source waters for irrigation schemes. Ethiopia, including Eritrea, has sizable proven resources of nickel ore, copper, coal, potash, gold and platinum, and lesser supplies of other minerals. Rather than a lack of natural resources, it would seem that the economy has been hindered by the age-old suspicion of the foreigner—whether providing aid, capital, or advice—and the almost complete lack of trained manpower to exploit these riches.

Since 1950, the Emperor has shown less reluctance to accept foreign aid and has concluded large aid agreements with the United States and the Soviet Union and lesser agreements with such countries as Yugoslavia, Czechoslovakia, Israel, and West Germany. Though Selassie's willingness to accept aid from a variety of sources is not unusual among developing nations in Africa and elsewhere, his reluctance to place complete dependence on any one nation or bloc of nations and his determined attempt to balance foreign influence in Ethiopia are unusual, even in Africa. Whereas American officers advise the Army and Imperial Bodyguard, the officers for both of these forces are trained in a military academy run by the Indians. The Imperial Ethiopian Navy is made up of ships supplied by the United States and seamen and officers trained by the Norwegians; the Imperial Ethiopian Air Force of Ethiopian pilots is trained by the Swedes to fly American planes. In the economy, British firms are alternately favored with American ones, although Italian products are still the most common; the Yugoslavs, the Bulgarians, and the Czechs are all providing factories, and Israel is helping to build roads. Significantly, this ménage of foreign advisors does not stem from any attempt to woo many nations, but rather from the historic fear that too much dependence on one nation may produce undue influence.

Ethiopia's role in Africa is also complicated by her cultural history. Long rejecting any ties with Black Africa, the early history and tradition of the country looked toward the Near East rather than Sub-Saharan Africa. But the Emperor has now seen clearly that the fate and future of Ethiopia resides in Africa, and no one has helped him to see this more clearly than Gamal Abdul Nasser. Nasser's continuous appeals for activism among the Moslems of East Africa beamed into Ethiopia are far more popular in the Danakil and Ogaden and throughout Eritrea than is Radio Addis Ababa. More recently, Nasser's strong pro-Arab support for the nationalistic claims for a "Greater Somalia" seems to have influenced the Emperor to establish closer ties with Israel. Even before these difficulties and before the coup of 1960, however, he tended to align himself with the Union of African States, Malagasy, and the Monrovia bloc against the Casablanca bloc of Nasser, Nkrumah, and Sékou Touré.

The Emperor has placed his greatest reliance on education to help Ethiopia take her place in the world. Early after his return from exile in 1941, he instituted an ambitious ten-year plan to advance elementary, secondary, and post-secondary education and to combat widespread illiteracy. Since

that time, he has continued to pour major portions of the budget into education and to build more schools. In the 1962–1963 school year, school enrollment had increased to the point that 304,138 students were in schools.
In addition to the University of Addis Ababa and the newly formed Haile
Selassie I University, which provide higher education for Ethiopians and
scholarship students from elsewhere in Africa, there are agricultural,
engineering, and public-health colleges. Over 700 Ethiopians have received
university education in the United States and Canada, and others have gone
to England, Western Europe, and to universities in the Soviet bloc. Nevertheless, the literacy rate is almost certainly still under 10 per cent, and the
Emperor's dream of a literate nation is still a long way off.

Modern Ethiopia is a political and economic, but not a cultural or even
religious, unification of a number of different and often dissident tribal groupings. She is held together today largely through the forceful personality of a
benign, beloved, but dictatorial ruler, the Emperor Haile Selassie. The most
dissident, or at least the most vocally dissident, tribal groupings are the
Somali and the various Eritrean political groups, with the Somali actively
seeking merger with their co-religionist and culturally related fellow Somalis
in the Republic of Somalia and Northern Kenya, and with the Eritreans
becoming increasingly activist in their desire to end the federation which
many of them oppose. Other groups, such as the nomadic Afar or Danakil, are
less actively hostile to the realm, but the typical Amhara does not feel any
safety in traveling in their lands.

Despite the attempts of the Emperor to ease Ethiopia from a feudal
monarchy into the twentieth century, the Empire remains socially, economically, and politically one of the most backward—and, in some ways,
the most backward—of African nations. The long-standing policy of isolation from the outside world, aided and abetted by a geographical condition
which allowed for this, deprived Ethiopia and Ethiopians of cultural contact
and knowledge of social and technological advance in the rest of the world.
Late nineteenth-century imperialism suddenly fell on Ethiopia, but, instead
of bringing social contact, it created a fear of contact with foreign nations
which, however justifiable, still accounts in part for Haile Selassie's "too little,
too late" efforts to modernize the nation. Meanwhile, he continues to retain
the most feudal aspects of the monarchy—the power of the church, personal
and church ownership of much of the land, domination of the government by
ruling Amhara, and suspicion, fear, and court intrigue as instruments of
domestic and even of foreign policy.

The abortive *coup d'état* of December 1960 was carried out by a relatively
small group of Western-educated intellectuals and Imperial Bodyguard
officers who had been exposed to Western institutions and were bent on
change. Ostensibly, their chief charge against the Emperor was that he was
holding Ethiopia back from the progress evident elsewhere in Africa. The
coup was unsuccessful, and the Emperor returned in triumph, announced

that his son, Crown Prince Asfa-Wossen Haile Selassie, had participated in the plot only under strong "duress," and promptly forgave him.

What of the future? As with everything else in Ethiopia, the future is dependent on the whim and fate of Haile Selassie. It seems certain that, while he is alive, only a massive revolution could bring reform to the government and do away with the neo-feudal system. But without the guiding genius of the Emperor, only chaos would remain, and the real crisis in Ethiopian affairs will come with his death. More than anything else, the coup indicated that without Haile Selassie, for the present, there can be no collective entity known as Ethiopia.

Ethiopia's 3,000 years of independence—save only for five years of Italian occupation—has combined with isolation to insulate her against the winds of change in Africa. Spared the humiliation of colonialism, Ethiopia has consequently failed to reap the benefits of the culture contact that comes with colonialism. The new values, the new material advances, the feeling of nationhood, education, and leadership, the growing political awareness of the people, the trade-union movement, and all of the social niceties which mark the advance from an underdeveloped to a developing nation must, however grudgingly, be seen as the legacy of colonialism. This does not justify imperialism or even colonialism—nor does it suggest that colonialism is the only means of culture contact for a nation. But for Ethiopia, given her isolation from trade routes, her hostility to the outside world, her insulation as a Christian nation in a sandy sea of Islam, it is suggested that only colonialism would have served to produce in Ethiopia the same level of political, economic, and social sophistication—in the Western sense—that is found elsewhere in Africa. Admittedly, in those colonies such as northern Nigeria, where the British retained the feudal system and used indirect rule, the acculturative experience has also been retarded, but even this example suffers from our tendency to view colonialism as all bad, always bad, and always the same.

THE SOCIAL POLITICS OF COLONIALIZATION

With this general proposition in mind and with reference to the special case of Ethiopia, the relationship between colonialism and culture contact should be examined from the point of view of political anthropology. Perhaps positive generalizations can be drawn from this negative case history. Most certainly, it will add to our understanding of Ethiopia.[3] First, colonies

---

[3] This analysis is heavily indebted to the pioneering work of René Maunier on the sociology of colonies and to Fred Burke and others for political and governmental aspects of race contact in Africa. See René Maunier, *The Sociology of Colonies* (London: Routledge and Kegan Paul, 1949), Vol. I; and Fred G. Burke, *Africa's Quest for Order* (Englewood Cliffs, N.J.: Prentice-Hall, 1964).

should be seen for what they are. A seemingly simple matter, perhaps, but still a complex one, for democratic and humanitarian ideals quite naturally lead one to view colonialism as a dreadful form of social and political domination of a subject racial grouping by another and to ignore its other aspects. But even the word "colony" is often misused.

Basically, for a colony to be worthy of being called a colony, three characteristics should be present; (1) There must be a historical and cultural difference—usually quite marked—between the colonizers and the indigenous population. Thus, the present western movement of our American population cannot be compared with the "colonizing" movements of the 1800's. (2) There must be occupation—that is, there must be an emigration of people from the colonizing country to the colony. (3) There must be government—the colonizing country must rule, directly or indirectly, the colony; there must be some form of active administration of the area by colonizers. Thus, for a colonial situation to exist, there must be relatively permanent face-to-face contact between a dominant and a relatively subordinate population. The so-called Italian or Irish colonies in the United States and the artists' colonies in metropolitan areas are not really colonies at all, but cultural enclaves. Neither, by this definition, would situations where only a few managing directors or garrison troops occupy an area be colonies. Colonialization, in the true sense, requires intensive and relatively permanent emigration from the "mother country" to the colony. The very term "mother country" gives the proper connotation to what develops—a population group leaves one country and attempts to set up an extension of its native land in some other country. Thus, as Plato said in *The Republic,* "Colonies are like children in whom the life of the nation continues." And, in addition to people, of course, goods and ideas—material and nonmaterial culture—emigrate from the mother country to the colony.

It is important also to consider why the people who go to a colony go there, for it is wrong to assume that all colonizers have the same motivation. Many go for political or economic reasons. Others go because they are sent. Some, perhaps few, but still some, go for what they consider, rightly or wrongly, humanitarian reasons: to teach or to preach, to heal or to build. Certainly many go to dominate and to subjugate; but some do go to "dominate for development" through some sense of *noblesse oblige.* And even among those who go for reasons of economic or political domination, there develops in many of them or in their descendants the sense of "the White Man's burden"—not in all and not to the same degree or for the same reason among those who do develop this sense, but it is true that a significant group of colonists in any colonial situation develop a sense of social responsibility for the native population. In many, it is a condescending and paternalistic expression, and in others even this never appears. But from the writer's own experiences and from those related by others who have spent years in Africa, the proponent of apartheid and the exponent of white supremacy are not nearly so common as is sometimes believed. Many of the remaining colonists in East Africa feel a real love for the land and a genuine affection for Africans. Even though their reasons for staying and their rationalizations for their claim to African heritage are less than realistic, they have a genuine interest in improving the lot of the African.[4]

To summarize then, colonization is often an outcome of imperialism but is not the same as imperialism. When a territory is acquired, annexed, or occupied, there is an emigration of people and of goods and ideas from the mother country to the colony. Along with these people, ideas, and things, there usually comes, either from the beginning or in succeeding generations, some feeling of responsibility for the indigenous peoples. With characteristic French sagacity, Maunier has ascribed this "New Imperialism" to the British when he says of their recent colonial experience:

> Creative, constructive rather than destructive, it is much more a means than an end; it finds its justification in right, no doubt, but also in duty and lastly in profit. If you wish to rule, it is because you *ought*, because you *must*—to the benefit of the entire world. To bestow on all men two good gifts, ill-appreciated by inferior peoples: *security* and *prosperity*. To this end the chosen race devotes its efforts. The *"Imperial Task"* laid upon the chosen people is to give civilization to the whole world, civilization in the Anglo-Saxon meaning of the word, that is in its material sense.[5]

So much then for the rulers, their motives, and the milieu which they create. What about the ruled? The effect of colonial status on the ruled should be considered from two points of view. One, political and governmental is the concept of sociation and its processual occurrence in Africa. The other, from culture-contact theory, is the psychological reactions to culture change. The concept of sociation is defined by Fred Burke as a process whereby individuals "shed values, beliefs, and behavior relative to membership in certain groupings; are exposed to new values and beliefs; modify their behavior and human inter-relationships; and act in such a way as to form new groupings which give expression to the new or altered values, beliefs, and behavior."[6] Burke has done an excellent job of charting the process of institutional formation and dissolution in Africa. In summation, he says,

---

[4] Examples are the Italian farmer in Eritrea, who explained, quite vehemently, that he had bought his land and that, after all, the ports of Assab and Massawa and much of Eritrea had been sold to the Italian Rubbatino Navigation Company by a local sultan and the Portuguese colonists from Angola who could not understand the Americans' "holier than thou attitude" toward Portuguese Africa and insisted that, while the Americans had wiped out the Red Indians, the Portuguese live in relative harmony with the Africans.

[5] Maunier, *op. cit.*, Vol. I, p. 33.

[6] Burke, *op. cit.*, p. 2.

The new order, seeking to emerge, draws its sustenance from a legacy of European conquest and from an imposed and alien order as well as from Mother Africa. The rapid disintegration and subsequent integration that characterize the quest severely try human endurance and capacity, shattering status and interest, demanding a revolution in leadership; governments' fortunes and egos are made overnight. Violence, just under the surface, erupts here and there as the limits of human endurance and capacity to reorder are exceeded or are knocked askew by the intervening pressures of an external world, which itself is characterized by a powerful quest for some sort of order. Devoid of generations of sanctity, the new institutions and leaders, as they seek the proper path, are extremely vulnerable. In 1962, hardly an African premier or president could report that his assassination had not been attempted.[7]

As bad as this sounds, at least to those of us who are lovers of peace, stability, and tranquility in the affairs of nations, it has some positive aspects as well. (1) This demand or, if you will, "quest" for political and social meaning for the new nations of Africa reveals that they do, indeed, regard themselves to some degree as nations. Despite the continuing threat of tribalism, one sees at least the beginnings of nationhood emerging from European domination which, more than any other factor, gave a focus—albeit the negative focus of opposition—for a sense of national unity. The fact that the new national units themselves were often alien as well should be set aside for the moment, since only time can tell how long tribalism will continue to be a major block to nationhood in Africa. (2) Colonial domination also led to a need for national—as opposed to tribal—leadership and to the replacement of normative, generational rule by young activists, many of whom received their formal education under colonial regimes and their political indoctrination in overthrowing these regimes. (3) Finally, obviously, the new, emerging institutions of Africa could not have come about without the challenge of European institutions in conflict with African institutions. It is just this sense of conflict which leads to the development of new responses and institutional formations.

And how does the individual African himself react to colonialism? One would suspect that he reacts in much the same way as any individual in an acculturative situation. For, at the risk of repetition, it should be pointed out again that colonialism is more than imperialism; it is a special case of culture contact. The same social laws that govern adaptation, assimilation, acculturative experience, and innovation are operative here. That this is true can be illustrated by a quote from the author's own works on the acculturation of immigrants in the United States:

In some cases, the adjustment of the second generation to this conflict was extreme—the name was changed, all association with the motherland was cut off, and the individual rushed to become an American. In some cases, the

---

[7] *Ibid.*, p. 170.

reaction was equally extreme but in the other direction—the second generation families re-embraced the old cultural pattern, preferred to remain in the ethnic enclave close to the parental home, and insulated themselves against further pressures toward acculturation. The most common reaction, however, was to attempt some compromise adjustment, earnestly to seek integration into the American culture while still retaining intimate contact with the immigrant family and way of life.[8]

These same polar reactions occur in Africa, except that we call them Westernization and Africanization. But they still result from the culture-contact phenomenon. Whereas it is usually the indigenous population which borrows most from the colonists, imitation, fusion, and diffusion of ideas all work both ways, for the European colonist borrows the burnoose, or African art, and other local customs. Even revitalization movements—nativism, Africanization, call them what you will—are impossible without colonialism. Neither pan-Africanism nor Negritude would have any meaning without the history of colonialism.

Although this is not meant as a defense of colonialism, it should be noted how the lack of a macrotemporal experience with the culture contact brought about by colonialism has combined with geographic and cultural isolation to retard the political and social development of Ethiopia—at least if the present definition of progress in Africa is to be accepted.

Without the challenge of domination by a foreign power, political protest movements simply did not develop in Ethiopia. It is significant that only in Eritrea, with its nearly eighty-year history of colonialism under the Italians and now under the Ethiopians, has there developed any political protest movements, and frankly any political awareness. Even the abortive coup of 1960 was indicative of the political naïveté of the Ethiopian. Planned but a short time in advance, apparently with *no* plan beyond the initial takeover, the rebels firmly believed that if they held the capital—in fact, not even the entire capital, but just the palace and the downtown area—they held the nation. The student body at the University belatedly acted like students in other parts of the world and paraded in favor of the rebels, but it did little else and took no active part.

There is no Ethiopian intelligentsia as such—at least not in the sense that one uses this categorization elsewhere. There are intelligent Ethiopians, there are artistic ones as well, but there is no active, fermenting, intellectual elite. The young, educated would-be reformers who return from the United States after their education are quickly absorbed into the government and soon take on the "*Ishi nega*" ("yes, tomorrow") complex which seems to go with civil servitude everywhere. At the University, one is impressed with the political awareness of the non-Ethiopian African scholarship student who

---

[8] F. A. J. Ianni, "The Italo-American," *The Annals,* CCCXXXVIII (November, 1961), 75.

invariably looks at his Ethiopian fellow student with amazement and, while accepting the bounty of the Emperor's scholarship, cannot understand how the Ethiopian can tolerate the monarchy and, even by African standards, backwardness of the country.

Just as there is no literary or commercial or educational elite, in the present African sense, in Ethiopia, neither is there a political elite because the sources of leadership in Ethiopia differ from modern-day Kenya, or Nigeria, or even South Africa. Leadership positions are still tribal, largely restricted to the Amhara, and generational. And more, they exist at the sufferance of the Emperor, and kinship with him is an important factor. Positions in the civil service, no matter how far down the status scale, still require his personal approval. Who is to challenge such a system?

The recent coup gives some indication of the difficulty of organizing a revolution where there is no political elite to challenge an existing government. The leaders of the coup were an amazing collection of individuals. The intellectual leadership came from the young governor of Jigjiga, Germame Neway, who had studied political science at Columbia University. The military leadership came from three highly placed military commanders: Mengistu Neway, the commanding general of the Imperial Bodyguard (and Germame Neway's brother); Tsigae Dibou, the commander of the police force; and Workener Gebreyehou, a bodyguard officer and the head of the secret police and intelligence service.

With the exception of Tsigae Dibou, who seems to have gone along largely because he was a close friend of General Mengistu, each of the leaders was exposed to Western (not Eastern or Soviet) ideas and ideals as a result of being out of the country—Germame, while in school, and the military leaders, while fighting in Korea. The principal reason for the failure of the coup was that there simply was no political protest movement to follow this small group of very amateur revolutionaries who were seemingly not even aware that popular support was necessary. There was no popular uprising— even university students made only feeble (and entirely vocal) gestures at support. There had been (and still is) a political protest movement in Eritrea which could have provided popular support necessary to sustain the coup, but, as one of the leaders of the Eritrean dissidents complained, no one bothered to tell them that the coup was coming. So it failed and with it went the small corps of potential political-military revolutionaries. And, since they took with them the nucleus of the ultra-conservatives, the ministers, secretaries-general, and conservative generals who were executed by the rebels in the last desperate agony of the coup, the political vacuum has become even more pronounced. If any leadership were to arise to challenge the Emperor—a most unlikely possibility—it must surely come from the military following the pattern of the Near East, Southeast Asia, and South America, and now Africa as well.

If, as seems to be the case, youth movements and the trade-union movement are the two principal forms of sociation which cut across regional and tribal boundaries to foster unity, nationalism, and pan-Africanism, the almost complete absence of either movement in Ethiopia again provides the negative example, which underscores the principle. The few such movements found in Ethiopia are only in Eritrea. In Eritrea, youth movements among the Moslems were formed to oppose Italian colonial and Ethiopian federational rule, and the trade-union movement was introduced by the post-World War II British Labour government, which administered Eritrea until it was federated with Ethiopia. Again, colonialism provided the challenge which led to the development of a response.

National unity, or at least a focus for national unity, is emerging in much of Africa, even though, as Burke points out,[9] tribalism persists and is often more intense after independence and the withdrawal of colonial rule. Not so in Ethiopia. Tribalism is becoming more rather than less intense as various tribal groupings—the Somali, the Afar, the Boran—unite themselves to oppose the Amhara. The absence of a European colonizer to serve as the focus for collective efforts that crossed tribal boundaries simply was not operative in Ethiopia, and consequently today there are no associations, no movements, no group which has the national unity of a country called Ethiopia as its purview.

Finally, the factor that Ethiopia has missed most by her lack of colonial status has been the long multi-generational contact with Europeans. As indicated earlier, this might have come without colonialism if Ethiopia had not been so isolated and so hesitant to accept contact with the outside world. Perhaps if there had been a Commodore Perry to help open Ethiopia to the outside world, Ethiopia might today be a Black Japan rather than a Black Tibet. Even the short period of colonization by the Italians and the comparison offered by the longer colonial experience by the Eritreans indicate what Ethiopia might have acquired through colonialism. All of the non-essential idioms of Italian culture are present in Ethiopia today—the pasta, the pizza, Italian music (which competes only with a Japanese influence on Ethiopian music brought back from Korea), Italian work styles, and manufactured goods. Eritrea, however, is another story.

There is little question that the record of Fascism in Eritrea is one of harsh reprisal and totalitarian control of administrative procedures. There is equally little question, however, that the Italians brought administrative order and system where there had been chaos and internecine warfare. They brought to Eritrea advanced farming techniques, a money economy, sanitation, and a higher standard of living than Ethiopia had ever known. They built excellent roads, began irrigation schemes, established railroads (and even an ingenious aerial ropeway), and developed commerce; these continue to be the mainstay of the economy. In fact, the Eritreans have a saying: "When the Italians were here, we had plenty of work but we could not speak.

---

[9] Burke, *op. cit.,* p. 29.

Then the British came and we were allowed to speak but there was no work. Now the Ethiopians are here and we can neither work nor speak."

Despite the legacy of Fascism and the earlier colonial record of the pre-Fascist Italian imperialists in Eritrea, the majority of Italian farmers seem to have gotten on fairly well with the Eritreans. This relationship continues today, and the amount of intermarriage of Italians and Eritreans continues to be high. One of the reasons often advanced for this is that, after all, there is not a great deal of difference between the southern Italian peasant and the Eritrean peasant. If few Eritreans were afforded the opportunity to go beyond elementary school, they were no worse off than most of the population of Calabria or Sicily. These are minimal achievements, but they do suggest what might have been in Ethiopia.

There are, of course, Europeans living in Ethiopia today, but their relationship with the population is slight and, for the most part, they are in contact with the Western-educated Ethiopian. Their positions as advisors to the Air Force, or the Navy, or the Ministry of Pen keep them isolated from the masses of the population and, except for a handful of missionaries, Italian technicians and lorry drivers, Greek and Armenian merchants, and an occasional British or American Desert-Locust-Control-Program expert wandering through the area, most Ethiopians seldom see white men.

It is somewhat less than wise to speculate on what might have been. But if Ethiopia had been colonized by the British at the time of the Napier expedition, by the Italians, or by any other European power, things might be quite different there today. Certainly, the proud record of independence would have been lost and the dignity that goes with freedom would be missing. But the benefits which Ethiopia would have received from culture contact with the Western world would have fitted her for getting on, in a world of Western values, far better than she does today.

SELECTED BIBLIOGRAPHY

ETHIOPIA

Buxton, David R. *Travels in Ethiopia.* New York: M. McBride Company, 1950.

Cerulli, Ernesta. *Peoples of Southwest Ethiopia and Its Borderland.* London: International African Institute, 1956.

Cole, Sonia. *The Prehistory of East Africa.* Harmondsworth, Middlesex: Penguin Books, 1954.

Grottanelli, Vinigi L. "I Pre-Niloti," *Annales Lateranensis,* Vol. 12, pp. 282–326, Città del Vaticano, 1948.

Huntingford, G. W. B. *The Galla of Ethiopia.* London: International African Institute, 1955.

Leslau, Wolf. Falasha Anthology. New Haven: Yale University Press, 1951.

Lewis, I. M. Peoples of the Horn of Africa. London: International African Institute, 1955.

Nesbitt, Lewis M. Desert and Forest: The Exploration of Abyssinian Danakil. London: J. Cape, 1935.

Pankhurst, Estelle S., and K. P. Richard. Ethiopia and Eritrea. Essex: Lalibela House, 1953.

Perham, Margery. The Government of Ethiopia. New York: Oxford University Press, 1948.

Plowden, Walter C. Travels in Abyssinia and the Galla Country. London: Longmans, Green, and Company, 1868.

Trimingham, John S. Islam in Ethiopia. London: Oxford University Press, 1952.

PART III

REGIONAL PROCESSES
AND
PROBLEMS

11

The African Elite

Gordon M. Wilson

INTRODUCTION

The difficulties of conducting research in the formerly British-controlled territories of East Africa are no different from those encountered elsewhere,
only more intense because of the lack of basic bench-mark data and basic
socioeconomic data. Stratified probability sampling in more advanced societies can be designed in many ways. Voters rolls, rate-payers registers, and
the like are usually up to date and easily available to the researcher—such
data do not exist in East Africa. Survey research must be designed, therefore,
on what data are available. There is little constructive value in the criticisms
of the purist that sampling techniques used in Africa do not fit acceptable
Western standards. It is true that they do not, but this writer agrees with
Leonard Doob that, "The scholarly or scientific gains to be derived from
valid results are so staggeringly inviting that the frustrations of the moment
are rendered almost impotent." Doob continues,

> Africa is no research Utopia; any research project must emerge with more
> than the usual burden of imperfections. Let there be no illusions, let aspirations
> not be too high, let expectations be modest. Any survey cannot be altogether
> solid: some sagacious guessing, some intuition is unavoidable; interviewing in
> Africa can be efficiently conducted only when investigators declare a mora-
> torium on hair-splitting and agree on a set of categories to guide the work.[1]
> It is with this thought in mind that this study proceeds.[2]

---

[1] Leonard W. Doob, "Periodic Surveys in sub-Saharan Africa," an informal paper
given to the Committee on Comparative Politics, Social Science Research Council
Conference, May 10–11, 1963, New York City.

[2] This writer has been engaged in a wide range of research surveys in East and
West Africa for fourteen years. My associates in Marco Surveys, Ltd., and I now
think that we have designed a sampling technique that is as effective as is possible when
we are concerned about the whole population as the universe for marketing research,
consumer research, media surveys, and public-opinion polling. The numerous surveys
of this type, conducted almost continuously in East Africa since 1955, have provided

The data in this chapter are presented on a comparative basis to illustrate, by the basic classificatory data, the differences and similarities of the African elite of the three countries—Kenya, Uganda, and Tanganyika. Zanzibar has been included and treated separately in most of the tables, but it must be pointed out that many of those originally interviewed were

---

us with accurate information about the socioeconomic characteristics of the East African rural and urban populations. We are able to use these data to stratify the population of East Africa by income groups, education, tribal composition, sex, occupation, and other factors. We are able, therefore, to work on the basis of quota samples in specific areas.

It was with this knowledge that we decided to publish *Who's Who in East Africa* in 1964 (*Who's Who in East Africa 1963–1964* [Nairobi: Marco Surveys, Ltd., 1964]). The original data for this publication, in part, are the basis for this study. We knew, at the planning stage, that there would be no economic gain in the publication because of the high costs of gathering the biographies by direct personal interview. We were convinced, however, that a publication of this type would provide a universe from which random quota samples could be drawn for periodic surveys for the accumulation of many different kinds of data. Moreover, an analysis of the biographies by standard quantitative methods could also provide an accurate description of the elite of East Africa. The details of the quantitative analysis would also provide the necessary facts for determining sample size and quotas for surveys, which do not require probability sampling. The fact that Africa is no research utopia was realized when the task of gathering the biographies was begun. We estimated that the field-work period required would be three months, and writing, checking proofs, and printing would require another three months. Costs, apart from printing, were estimated at £5,000. Work began in August 1963, and, after the work was completed, we were to experience a revolution, two mutinies, and two cabinet changes. Consequently several revisions were required, even before the first proofs were ready. The final proofs were returned to the printer in April 1964, nine months from the starting date and after an expenditure of more than twice the estimated budget. *Who's Who in East Africa* was published by Marco Surveys, Ltd., in May 1964.

Deciding who was to be interviewed for the publication took several months of careful planning. Staff lists prepared by the four governments; directories of commerce and industry; membership lists of all available professional, cultural and welfare organizations and societies were examined. Finally, the wage structures of the largest companies were checked and compared to the wages paid by the four governments. Every interview was planned, and every respondent was preselected. There were no direct mail interviews, and each respondent signed the completed form as correct after the interview.

The criteria for selection of persons to be interviewed for *Who's Who in East Africa* were three. The first criterion was income. The optimum cut-off point was an income of £1,000 per annum, which is higher than the average European or Asian income and is also higher than the starting government scales for university graduates. The second criterion was the position held by the respondent. In some cases, therefore, the respondent was included—for example, the mayor of a local town—even though he did not qualify by the criterion of income. Women who have been included are elites in their own right and not persons who are simply wives of elites. (There are only sixty women in the total of 1,423 interviews, about 4 per cent, so sex was not used as a basis of tabulating the socioeconomic data.)

The third criterion was the power position of the post occupied—for example, all

dropped when the data from Zanzibar were revised after the revolution. Consequently the category, "elected/appointed representatives," is smaller than was the case before the revolution and subsequent union.

This study refers only to African and not to European or Asian respondents. For the purpose of this survey, an African is defined as anyone who is not designated an Asian or a European. The survey includes, therefore, all the combinations—particularly in Zanzibar and on the coast—of Arabs, Afro-Arabs, Coloreds, and Swahilis.[3]

This study is divided into three parts. The first is an analysis of the elite in East Africa based on the basic classificatory data that were collected in the original research for *Who's Who in East Africa*[4] and two additional studies which, in addition to describing the elite, give insight into their opinions, attitudes, and beliefs. The second is an analysis of urban elite opinions on basic social and economic problems and technical assistance. It is based on a stratified probability sample of those who most closely resemble the elite in the three African capital cities. The third describes a

---

elected or appointed members of central and regional governments qualified, regardless of other factors. African professionals qualified, regardless of other factors. The criterion of income applied in almost all cases for those selected from the civil service, commerce, industry, and agriculture. Trade unionists, politicians, religious leaders, leaders of cooperative unions, and voluntary associations were selected on the basis of the executive or senior position held by the respondent.

Approximately 6 per cent of the Africans listed for interview refused to be interviewed. There were numerous reasons given for refusing, but the chief factor was education. Some respondents were embarrassed by the prospect of publishing facts about their low formal educational accomplishments. Others refused for personal reasons, claiming that they were not important enough to be included. Some Europeans refused because they were planning to leave East Africa, and some Asian and European professionals refused because of their interpretation of their professional association's rules regarding advertising. Inevitably, some of those listed were not available for interview. Five attempts were made in every case of this type before giving up. An estimated 10 per cent of those listed were "not available" for interview, for one reason or another.

The interviews were conducted by permanent senior research assistants. All of these have at least a B.A., or its equivalent, and are either nationals of the country in which the interviews were conducted or had many years' residence there.

Standard codes were used to clarify the data, and cards were punched for 80-column I.C.T. data-processing equipment in Nairobi. These cards are being maintained by adding new respondents and dropping those who die or who leave the country. Changes in position and status are also being recorded regularly for each of the four countries.

[3] This article was written after most of the biographies for *Who's Who in East Africa* were collected; it in no way influenced the process of selection of those who were interviewed.

[4] *Who's Who in East Africa 1963–1964* (Nairobi: Marco Surveys, Ltd., 1964). For a discussion of this publication see footnote 3, *supra*.

survey which is the beginning of a series of basic sociological studies to provide periodic research into changing attitudes and knowledge that will indicate social change in the fields of temporal orientation, science and determinism, loyalties, attitudes toward government, confidence and optimism, tribalism and traditionalism. The sample will be described at the beginning of the second part and third part for each of these surveys, and a few sample tables will be given to illustrate some of the results of this research.

ANALYSIS OF WHO'S WHO IN EAST AFRICA

The Age Factor

The age of the elite of East Africa shows some significant differences among the four countries. Table 11–1 is the percentage distribution by age. If we disregard the "not stated" categories, the average ages are as follows: Kenya, 31–35 years; Uganda, 36–40 years; Tanganyika, 31–35 years; Zanzibar, 41–45 years; East Africa, 36–40 years.

Table 11–1

East African Elite Age Factor by Per Cent

	Kenya	Uganda	Tanganyika	Zanzibar	Total
up to 25 years	5%	1%	1%	2%	3%
26–30 "	18	15	18	8	16
31–35 "	26	15	21	5	17
36–40 "	21	20	20	9	20
41–45 "	12	16	11	17	14
46–50 "	4	8	8	5	6
51–55 "	2	9	2	10	4
56–60 "	1	4	2	8	3
61–65 "	1	3	—	7	2
66 and over	a	1	—	3	1
not stated	10	8	17	26	14
Total	100%	100%	100%	100%	100%
Base	457	409	444	113	1423

a Less than .5 per cent.

Table 11–1 on age of elite shows the average to be higher in Uganda and Zanzibar than in Kenya or Tanganyika. Uganda has 17 per cent over fifty years and Zanzibar 28 per cent; while only 4 per cent are in this age group in Kenya and Tanganyika. Later analysis will reveal that one-third of the Uganda elite are Baganda; thus, the explanation of the older average age may be that Baganda has had a strong traditional, centralized government for many years, and, therefore, positions of power and authority have been open to the Baganda for a much longer period than for other East Africans. The same explanation can apply to the elite of Zanzibar.

The Occupation Factor

Table 11–2

Sample by Percentage Distribution

Occupational Classification	Kenya	Uganda	Tanganyika	Zanzibar	Total
civil servants	27%	42%	51%	46%	40%
elected appointed	41	34	23	10	31
commerce/industry	12	10	9	19	11
trade union politician	13	5	4	6	8
education	6	6	7	9	7
professional	3	1	1	7	2
cooperatives/trade	1	1	3	1	1
religious/welfare	2	4	6	—	4
agriculture	1	2	1	3	1
miscellaneous	2	3	3	2	3
Total[a]	108%	108%	108%	103%	108%
Base	457	409	444	113	1423

[a] In a few cases the same person qualified in more than one classification.

The Zanzibar interviews were redone after the revolution in January, but the interviews were completed before the union of Zanzibar and Tanganyika, therefore the tables refer to facts as they were prior to March 30, 1964.

The process of Africanization can be seen in Table 11–2. There is a smaller percentage of Africans in the civil service in Kenya than in the other two countries, but a higher percentage of elected and appointed representatives due to the regional form of government. Kenya also has a higher percentage of elite who qualify as trade unionists.

There are several ways of describing occupation; civil servants, for example, can be in medical, education, or other services. Table 11–3 gives occupation of the elite by a different set of criteria.

Table 11–3

Specific Occupations	Kenya	Uganda	Tanganyika	Zanzibar	Total
education (administration)	5%	4%	6%	7%	5%
education (teacher)	1	3	1	2	2
medical practicing	4	5	3	5	4
sciences	1	1	1	2	1
law/judicial	1	6	2	8	2
accountancy	2	1	2	—	1
farmer	1	2	1	3	1
entrepreneur	2	2	1	9	2
senior executive	34	36	61	44	45
junior administrator	7	14	14	3	11
legislator (only)	38	20	7	8	21
party/union officials	13	5	4	6	8
editors/arts/authors	1	1	1	5	1
clergy senior	1	3	4	—	2
others (unclassified)	2	5	3	2	3
Total[a]	113%	108%	111%	104%	109%
Base	457	409	444	113	1423

[a] Some individuals have been classified in more than one category as in Table 11–2.

The Education Factor

Table 11–4 on education shows the position by this factor for East Africa as a whole.

The mean educational level for the East African elite is more than secondary, but less than "university non-graduate." The mean for Kenya is Cambridge School Certificate, a point lower than the average. Uganda is a point at or slightly higher than the average; Tanganyika at the point of the average; and Zanzibar also at the point of the average. The first two categories should be taken together because of the dissimilarity in the terminology used between the three countries. When this is done, we find that Kenya has 43 per cent in these categories while the rest have between 31–34 per cent.

In the categories university and above, East Africa rates 25 per cent— with Kenya 25 per cent; Uganda 24 per cent; Tanganyika 19 per cent, and Zanzibar 32 per cent. The high number in the last country is accounted for in Table 11–6, "East African Elite—Where Educated." A higher percentage was educated in the United Kingdom and India/Pakistan (52 per cent) because of the lack of local secondary schools. Another factor is that a well-established social-class structure was part of pre-independence culture.

Table 11–4

East African Elite by Education

Educational Level Reached	Kenya	Uganda	Tanganyika	Zanzibar	Total
	%	%	%	%	%
no formal education	—	—	—	—	—
attended junior secondary	22	13	8	21	15
attended senior secondary	21	18	23	13	20
obtained Camb. Sch. Cert.	12	8	3	10	8
obtained Higher Sch. Cert.	a	a	a	—	a
nonuniversity technical studies	5	7	19	6	10
nonuniversity teaching studies	4	6	7	—	5
university studies non-graduate	10	22	20	17	17
university studies first degree	17	15	16	26	17
post-graduate studies nongraduate	—	1	a	—	a
post-graduate studies master's degree	5	7	2	4	7
post-graduate studies higher degree	2	2	1	2	1
not stated	1	—	1	1	a
Base (all Africans interviewed)	457	409	444	113	1,453

a Less than .5 per cent.

The upper class in Zanzibar and, to some extent, those among the Baganda could afford overseas education whereas those from other countries were dependent on financial help from government and overseas sources.

The higher percentage of elite in Kenya who are found in the lower educational categories finds an explanation in Table 11–5. There was a higher percentage of elected or appointed representatives in Kenya, and this category was not so highly educated as the "civil servant" of "all others" category.

It can be seen that there are more elected/appointed representatives than civil servants or others in the lowest category of education. In the highest educational brackets, we have more civil servants in the elite of all three countries than in the other two classifications. Civil servants in Uganda are more highly qualified than in the other three countries: 59 per cent have university education. In Kenya 56 per cent, Tanganyika 42 per cent, and in Zanzibar 56 per cent have university education. Elected and appointed

Table 11–5

The Education Factor by Occupational Groupings by Percentages

	KENYA			UGANDA			TANGANYIKA			ZANZIBAR		
	Civil Servants	Elected/ Appointed Representatives	All Others	Civil Servants	Elected/ Appointed Representatives	All Others	Civil Servants	Elected/ Appointed Representatives	All Others	Civil Servants	Elected/ Appointed Representatives	All Others
attended junior secondary	11%	28%	24%	9%	12%	18%	3%	11%	12%	6%	(3)	35%
attended senior secondary	15	22	22	11	21	27	21	30	18	10	(1)	19
obtained Cambridge School Certificate	11	15	10	7	10	6	4	1	4	15	—	6
obtained Higher School Certificate	—	—	2	1	1	—	—	—	1	—	—	—
nonuniversity technical studies	3	2	10	9	9	5	21	25	4	11	—	2
nonuniversity teaching studies	2	6	4	3	9	7	7	7	8	—	(4)	—
university degree	12	9	11	24	23	19	19	14	26	19	—	11
post-graduate studies nongraduate	37	7	12	24	8	8	21	11	11	33	(1)	21
post-graduate studies master's degree	—	—	—	3	—	—	—	—	—	—	—	—
post-graduate studies higher degree	7	6	2	8	6	7	2	1	4	4	(1)	6
not stated	2	5	3	1	1	3	1	—	2	2	(1)	—
Total	100%	100%	100%	100%	100%	100%	100%	100%	100%	100%	(11)	100%
Base	123	190	183	173	139	143	223	107	147	52	11	52

representatives generally have less education. In Kenya 22 per cent, Uganda 37 per cent, Tanganyika 26 per cent (Zanzibar could not be tabulated) have university education. Uganda is still the highest among the three countries.

In the "all others" category, Tanganyika leads with the best educated men, 41 per cent, while Kenya has 24 per cent, Uganda 34 per cent and Zanzibar 38 per cent who have university education.

Country Where Education Was Obtained

Table 11–6 gives details about the country in which the respondent was educated in his final year of education. It can be seen that the highest percentage of the elite were educated in local East African schools (58 per

Table 11–6

East African Elite—Where Educated

country of education	Kenya	Uganda	Tanganyika	Zanzibar	Total
educated in East Africa only	67%	54%	57%	42%	58%
educated in Africa— outside East Africa	3	4	4	1	4
educated in the U.S.	8	5	8	2	7
educated in the U.K.	18	38	27	38	28
educated in India/Pakistan	4	3	3	14	4
educated in Australia/New Zealand	a	—	—	—	a
educated in Canada	—	a	—	—	a
educated in Western Continental Europe, i.e., Germany, Norway	1	1	3	2	2
educated in U.S.S.R./China or Eastern European countries	—	—	a	—	a
educated elsewhere outside Africa	1	1	1	—	1
not stated	1	—	a	2	1
Total	103%	106%	103%	104%	105%
Base (all African interviews)	457	409	444	113	1423

a Less than .5 per cent.

cent). The United Kingdom came next (28 per cent), followed by the United States (7 per cent), India/Pakistan and other African countries. There are very significant differences between the East African countries, however, which are worth noting. Zanzibar and Uganda have many more elite who were educated overseas and in the United Kingdom, particularly, than the other countries. Kenya had fewer by 10 per cent than the next lowest, which was Tanganyika.

It would be a waste of effort to detail all of the East Africa schools attended by the East African elite. There were nearly 100. What is significant, however, is to show that out of this total only a few schools account for more than 5 per cent of the elite in each country and, moreover, that this handful accounts for a very significant percentage of the elite.

In Zanzibar, the Government School, Zanzibar, had 37 per cent of the elite as former students, and no other school had even 5 per cent. In Tanganyika, the Tabora Government School accounted for 30 per cent and St. Andrew's, Minaki, for 8 per cent. No other Tanganyika school had more than 9 per cent: St. Mary's, Tabora, and Old Moshi Secondary School each had 5 per cent. Uganda elite went to King's College, Budo. This school educated 33 per cent. St. Mary's College, Kisubi, can count 9 per cent; Nyakasura High School, 6 per cent; and both Namilyango College and Busoga College, Mwiri, 5 per cent. The rest had less than 5 per cent. The Kenya picture is relatively the same: 24 per cent of the elite attended Alliance High School, 9 per cent Maseno High School, and 7 per cent The Holy Ghost College, Mangu. The remainder had less than 5 per cent of the elite as students.

The British emphasis on the "old school tie" type loyalty was instilled into the spirit of each of these schools. The term, *walimu,* teacher, has an honored meaning in East Africa as evidence the fact that Mr. Nyerere prefers the press and radio to address him as such. We can speculate that much of the so-called nepotism that is said to exist is at least partly due to the "old school tie" spirit. All East African schools did, in fact, have a school tie, a uniform, and a crest or coat of arms still worn with pride by many of the alumni.

The Factor of Religion

This survey did not include Zanzibar, and, therefore, we are unable to provide comparative figures for Zanzibar or for East Africa as a whole. One would logically expect to find relatively the same number of elite as the general percentage for the population as a whole in each religious grouping. Table 11–7 is complicated by the category among the elite of "nominal Christian," which did not appear in the first survey. This category has been added because many of the sophisticated Africans were educated in Christian schools so they do not regard themselves as pagan, and yet they do not belong to any formal church. The category "nominal Christian," or simply Christian, is used to describe them. We can generalize that fewer Moslems are among the elite then one would reasonably expect from the above figures, particularly in Tanganyika. Fewer Roman Catholics in Kenya and Uganda

Table 11–7

East African Elite by Religion/to Population Percentage

	Kenya		Uganda		Tanganyika		Zanzibar	Total
	Elite	Others[a]	Elite	Others[a]	Elite	Others[a]	Elite	Elite
Roman Catholic	21%	29%	25%	34%	26%	28%	4%	22%
Protestant	54	45	65	50	22	26	—	43
Moslem	4	16	3	10	16	39	88	14
pagan	—	8	—	6	—	7	—	—
nominal Christian	15	—	2	—	24	—	1	13
other	—	—	—	—	1	—	7	1
not stated	6	2	5	—	11	—	—	7
Total	100%	100%	100%	100%	100%	100%	100%	100%
Base	457	2400	409	2600	440	2000	113	1423

[a] The percentages for "others" is based on the probability sample (7,000) of a survey conducted for Fred G. Burke. See Fred G. Burke, "Some Grass-Roots Attitudes Affecting Political and Social Integration in East Africa," paper delivered to the African Studies Association, San Francisco, October 26, 1963.

are among the elite than one would reasonably expect from the above figures, about the proportions to be expected.

Moslem education in East Africa is less developed than education among the other religions. Protestant missions have been strongest in education since earliest times in East Africa, and this is reflected in Table 11–7. Even in government schools in the old colonial tradition, the Church of England, as the state church, dominated the educational field. In the British system and in England today, religion is taught along with the three *R's*. This will explain the larger number of Protestants in the population as a whole and among the elite of Uganda and Kenya. Zanzibar, of course, is a Moslem country. Most of the 7 per cent "other" in Zanzibar were Bahai. The White Fathers of Tanganyika dominated the field of education in early German times and remained a powerful force throughout the Trusteeship period.

The Factor of Voluntary Associations

The degree to which individuals in African societies join groups of voluntary association is a measure of social change. The comparison between the four countries which is given in Table 11–8 shows significant differences between them. Tribal associations are much stronger in Kenya than elsewhere: 21 per cent as against 2 per cent to 8 per cent in Zanzibar, Tanganyika, and Uganda. This underlines the felt need of the Africans of Kenya for security among their own people in face of the insecurities of the old colonial system and its concomitant privileged European and Asian classes. Nowhere else in East Africa was the position of the settler or trader so strong. Moreover, political parties were banned in Kenya on a national basis until comparatively recently, although district associations were encouraged by the administration.

Kenya elite rates highest in political party membership (35 per cent) as against 17 per cent to 22 per cent and trade-union membership (20 per cent) as against 5 per cent to 12 per cent.

Table 11–8

Membership of Clubs, Associations, Political Parties, etc.

	Kenya	Uganda	Tanganyika	Zanzibar	Total
member of a tribal association	21%	8%	3%	2%	10%
religious society/union	6	16	6	9	9
business society	5	8	6	4	6
professional society	9	15	4	11	9
academic society	12	20	7	15	13
political party	34	21	22	17	25
charitable organization	5	13	12	9	10
social club	23	36	25	42	29
sporting club	6	16	11	9	11
other organizations	11	4	5	15	8
cultural organizations	6	16	11	10	11
trade union	20	5	12	5	12
belong to none	18	17	33	17	22
Total[a]	176%	195%	157%	165%	175%
Base (all African interviews)	457	409	444	113	1423

[a] Many individuals belong to more than one group.

Uganda elite join more groups of voluntary associations than the elite of the other countries. The average Uganda elite has membership in two groups; Kenya, 1.7; Zanzibar; 1.6, and Tanganyika, 1.5. Moreover, the kind of groups that the Uganda elite support are more sophisticated. The Uganda elite rate much higher in the religious (16 per cent) versus 6 per cent to 9 per cent; professional (15 per cent) versus 4 per cent to 11 per cent; academic (20 per cent) versus 7 per cent to 15 per cent; and cultural (16 per cent) versus 6 per cent to 11 per cent. The Uganda elite is only second to the Zanzibar elite (42 per cent) as members of social clubs (36 per cent) but significantly higher than the Kenya elite (23 per cent) and the Tanganyika elite (25 per cent). One in three of the Tanganyika elite

(33 per cent) does not belong to any voluntary association, compared to only 17 per cent or 18 per cent for the elite who do not belong to at least one in the other East African countries. Business societies are represented equally in each of the four countries.

Table 11–8 is one of the most significant of the survey. The Uganda elite, of whom one in three was a Baganda, have had a university at Kampala for many years. It was once the only center for higher education in East Africa. Therefore, culture, in the Western sense, was for many years a factor of influence on the elite of Uganda which was not available in either Kenya or Tanganyika.

The Tribal Factor

The percentage of the elite in each country by tribe, compared to the percentage of the population represented by that tribe, should give an interesting index of the degree to which the tribe has progressed and, indirectly, of the influence of its members. (See Table 11–9.)

Table 11–9

Tanganyika Elite by Tribal Group

Tribe	Per Cent of Population	Per Cent of Elite
Sukuma	19%	3%
Nyamwezi	7	2
Makonde	6	—
Haya	6	7
Chagga	6	12
Goga	6	—
Ha	5	—
Hehe	4	1
Nyakusa	4	3
Luguru	4	—
Sambaa	3	1
Zaramo	3	1
Yao	3	—
Mweru	2	—
others (less than 2%)	13	22
stated Tanganyikan	?	9
Kenya tribes	?	30
Uganda tribes	?	2
Zanzibaree	?	5
Total	100%	100%
Base	5,682,419 (1957)	444

The first significant fact which emerges is that 9 per cent called themselves "Tanganyikans" and would not use the label "tribe." We can only assume that the actual percentage by tribe of this group is about the same as described in Table 11–9 with the obvious inclusion of some who are of mixed parentage. The most significant fact is that there were 30 per cent who belonged to Kenya tribes, 2 per cent Ugandans, and 5 per cent Zanzibarees. No other East African country had as high percentages in these categories. That amounts to 37 per cent who were of tribes other than those of Tanganyikans. We shall attempt later, in Table 11–12, to give a tribal breakdown by the three main occupational categories to determine how these are grouped by that factor. The major tribe, the Sukuma, represents one in five of the Tanganyika population, yet has only one in thirty-three among the elite. There are twice as many Chagga among the elite as their tribal percentage would warrant. Surprisingly, the Haya have more elite than their share, although all the rest have fewer, except the very small "other" tribes who have nearly twice as many.

Table 11–10

Uganda Elite by Tribal Group

Tribe	Per Cent of Population	Per Cent of Elite
Baganda	16.2%	33%
Banyankole	8.1	3
Iteso	8.1	3
Basoga	7.8	4
Bakiga	7.1	1
Lango	5.6	2
Bagisu	5.1	3
Acholi	4.4	3
Lugbara	3.7	1
Batoro	3.2	4
Banyoro	2.9	3
Karamojong	2	—
Alur	1.9	1
Banyole	1.4	—
Kumam	1	1
others (less than 1%)	9.4	6
not stated	—	1
stated Ugandan	—	28
Kenya tribe	—	1
Tanganyika tribe	—	1
Total	100%	100%
Base	6,449,558 (1957)	409

We would expect to find the Baganda overrepresented in the elite (see Table 11–10). They have, like the Chagga, twice as many (33 per cent) as the tribal percentage would warrant (16.2 per cent). An even higher percentage, 28 per cent, claimed to be "Ugandans," a classification not recorded in the official census figures. Only 1 per cent are from Tanganyika and 1 per cent from Kenya. Unlike Tanganyika, the smaller tribes, which each represent less than 1 per cent each of the population, have only half as many elite (6 per cent) as their combined percentage (9.4) would expect. Tanganyika had twice as many. The Batoro was the only other tribe in which the percentage of the elite exceeded that of the tribe, 4 to 3.2.

Table 11–11

Kenya Elite by Tribal Group

Tribe	Per Cent of Population	Per Cent of Elite
Kikuyu	19.5%	23%
Luo	14.4	19
Luhya	12.5	19
Kamba	11.7	6
Meru	6.9	2
Kisii	4.9	3
Embu	3.9	1
Kipsigis	3	2
Nandi	2.2	1
others (less than 3%)	16.1	22
stated Tanganyikan	—	2
Total	100%	100%
Base	5,251,120	457

N O T E : Though the percentages taken are those of the 1948 census, this introduces no serious error, assuming a proportionate rate of increase among the tribes over the past years.

Kenya is unique in that there are several tribal groups that exceed their quota of elite and by almost the same ratio. (See Table 11–11.) The Luhya have a slight margin by ratio over the Luo and Kikuyu. The Kamba, Meru, and Embu, related tribal groups, are all seriously under their expected percentages. Like Tanganyika, but unlike Uganda, the small tribal groups— each of less than 3 per cent of the total population, but representing 16.1 per cent of it—have 22 per cent of the elite. A high percentage of this group of elite are from the numerous coastal tribes (8 per cent), only 2 per cent are Tanganyikans, and the Ugandans did not rate statistically.

Examining the tribal factor by profession in Uganda, the Baganda again

Table 11–12

Tribal Factor by Profession—Uganda

Tribe	Civil Servants	Elected or Appointed Representatives	All Others
Baganda	27%	25%	50%
Acholi	6	2	2
Iteso	4	4	—
Kumam	1	2	—
Lango	2	4	1
Alur	2	1	2
Bagisu	3	2	2
Basoga	3	5	6
Batoro	4	6	3
Bakiga	1	1	1
Banyoro	1	3	6
Banyankole	2	5	3
Bakedi	—	1	—
Badama	1	—	—
Banyoli	—	1	—
Lugbara	1	1	—
Karamajong	—	—	1
others	5	10	3
not stated	—	1	1
stated Ugandan	37	23	15
Kenya tribes	—	—	3
Tanganyika tribes	—	3	1
Total	100%	100%	100%
Base	173	139	143

dominate all of the professional categories (see Table 11–12). Their percentage of "All Others" is 50, which is unexpectedly high. The "stated Ugandan" group are unknowns tribally and constitute over one-third of the "Civil Service" classification, but only 15 per cent of the "All Others." The Kenya elite are all in the "All Others" category, which is very different from the Tanganyika picture. Similarly, none of the Tanganyika elite are in the Civil Service category.

In examining the tribal factor by profession in Tanganyika, the Chagga again dominate the field of elite in the "Civil Service" and "All Others" categories. (See Table 11–13.) Surprisingly, however, the Haya have the highest percentage among the elected/appointed representatives. "Kenya

Table 11–13

Tribal Factor by Profession—Tanganyika

Tribe	Civil Servants	Elected or Appointed Representatives	All Others
Sukuma	4%	4%	2%
Nyamwezi	5	—	2
Makonde	—	—	—
Haya	5	8	9
Chagga	11	5	15
Gogo	—	—	—
Ha	—	—	1
Hehe	1	2	1
Nyakusa	5	5	1
Luguru	—	—	—
Sambao	1	—	1
Zaramo	1	4	1
Yao	—	—	—
Mwera	—	—	—
others	22	24	20
stated Tanganyikan	5	22	7
Kenya tribes	30	24	33
Uganda tribes	3	1	3
Zanzibaree	7	1	4
Total	100%	100%	100%
Base	223	107	147

tribes," as a group of elite, dominate all the three professional groupings. Even the Uganda tribes and Zanzibarees have higher percentages among the elite in the civil service than many of the major tribes of Tanganyika. In Kenya, we find that there are more Kikuyu elite in the civil service than elite of any other tribal group. (See Table 11–14). The Luo elite are more numerous than the Luhya followed by the Wakamba. The latter have more elite in the "Civil Servants" than in the "All Others" category, which is the reverse of any other major tribal group.

URBAN ELITE OPINION

A recent study poses the hypothesis that the role of the city in Africa is that of generator, communicator, innovator, and integrator.[5] We accepted

---

[5] Fred G. Burke, *Africa's Quest for Order* (Englewood Cliffs, N.J.: Prentice-Hall, 1964), Ch. 4.

Table 11–14

Tribal Factor by Profession—Kenya

Tribe	Civil Servants	Elected or Appointed Representatives	All Others
Kikuyu	29%	17%	27%
Embu	—	3	1
Meru	1	4	2
Luo	23	12	26
Taveta	—	—	—
Masai	1	4	1
Nandi	2	1	—
Wakamba	9	6	5
Kipsigis	2	3	1
Luhya	20	13	25
Iteso	1	—	—
Taita	2	2	—
Non-Somali N.F.D.	—	2	—
Kisii	1	5	—
Kalenjin	1	9	—
Coast	4	12	7
stated Kenyan	—	—	—
others	—	2	—
Tanganyika tribe	2	—	3
not stated	2	5	2
Total	100%	100%	100%
Base	123	190	183

this hypothesis and designed a stratified probability sample in each of the capital cities of East Africa to test the attitudes and opinions of the city African on certain questions involving their personal life, international affairs, and social problems. The sample was stratified by age and education. The respondent had to have had some secondary education and had to be at least eighteen years of age. It cannot be said that the attitudes and opinions expressed in answer to the questions are those of the elite, but they do represent the opinions and attitudes of a probability sample of urban Africans, eighteen and over, who have had some secondary education and who live in the capital cities of East Africa. Therefore, the opinions of this group will be closer to those of the elite than a sample based on the population as a whole.

The people to be interviewed were chosen in the following manner. Each city, including peri-urban and dormitory areas, was divided into geographical units using a grid method on a base map. Each square of the grid was numbered, except for those that were in the business area—marshalling yards, ocean, and the like—and 10 per cent of the squares were chosen by using a table of random numbers. The number of units of housing in each was then determined, and the quota was divided proportionately between each. The interval between units was determined and a starting point selected.

The interviewers continued interviewing to the set interval, until the quota was completed. Three callbacks were made, where necessary, for each respondent before declaring that interview void. The household was defined as that group which regularly takes its meals together. The head of the household was interviewed to determine how many in the household of either sex were over eighteen and who had some secondary school education. These were then listed, and the person to be interviewed was selected by a system of random numbers. Only one person was interviewed in each household. If the unit did not have at least one person as defined by education, the interviewer then proceeded to the next household by the fixed interval. Ten per cent of the interviews were checked by field supervisors. The interviews were conducted in English for the most part, but some Swahili was used in Dar es Salaam.

The questionnaires were pretested in each of the capital cities, and the questions modified where necessary. The translation of Swahili was made in the usual way of two separate translators who worked from English to Swahili and vice versa.

The interviews were conducted from April 15–May 5, 1964. The tables have been shortened for printing convenience by grouping items that have less than 5 per cent response into the category, "others." Percentages were rounded to the nearest whole number, or, if the percentage was too small in a subsample, whole numbers were given in parentheses ( ).

Future studies will contain these same basic questions when samples of similar size are employed in the urban centers of East Africa. We hope to provide, in this way, comparative data on changing opinions on the subjects covered. Only a few of the questions have been included in this chapter.

QUESTION 1. *What, in your opinion, is the most important problem facing our country at the present time?*

	Nairobi	Dar es Salaam	Kampala	Total
education	22%	29%	28%	27%
poverty/famine	13	24	18	19
unemployment	41	6	18	18
economic development	6	24	12	14

QUESTION 1. (*Continued*)

	Nairobi	Dar es Salaam	Kampala	Total
high cost of living	10	3	9	8
health	3	6	1	4
border disputes—Inter-African disputes	3	1	5	3
political instability	1	6	3	3
tribalism	2	—	2	1
land apportionment	3	—	—	1
public laziness	1	—	1	1
other problems	2	4	5	4
don't know/not stated/refused to answer	2	2	3	2
Total	109%	105%	105%	105%
Base	389	451	395	1235

QUESTION 2. *All things considered, how satisfied are you with your present standard of living—very satisfied, fairly satisfied, somewhat dissatisfied, or very dissatisfied?*

	Nairobi	Dar es Salaam	Kampala	Total
very satisfied	6%	13%	4%	8%
fairly satisfied	32	50	25	36
somewhat dissatisfied	32	26	37	31
very dissatisfied	29	11	32	24
don't know	1	—	1	1
refused to answer	—	—	1	—
Total	100%	100%	100%	100%
Base (all interviews)	389	451	395	1235

QUESTION 3. *Do you think political matters should be left to the government or should people like yourself take some active part in political affairs?*

	Nairobi	Dar es Salaam	Kampala	Total
left to government	26%	24%	13%	21%
people take an active part	72	72	73	72
other answers	1	1	4	2
don't know	—	2	8	3
refused to answer	1	1	2	2
Total	100%	100%	100%	100%
Base (all interviews)	389	451	395	1235

QUESTION 4. *All things considered, how satisfied are you with the amount of influence people like yourself have on affairs in our country—very satisfied, fairly satisfied, somewhat dissatisfied, or very dissatisfied?*

	Nairobi	Dar es Salaam	Kampala	Total
very satisfied	13%	15%	8%	13%
fairly satisfied	33	49	28	37
somewhat dissatisfied	32	22	26	26
very dissatisfied	18	10	31	19
don't know	4	4	5	4
refused to answer	—	—	2	1
Total	100%	100%	100%	100%
Base (all interviews)	389	451	395	1235

QUESTION 6. *Which one of the following do you think our country needs most at the present time: more schools, more hospitals, more housing, more factories, or more roads?*

	Nairobi	Dar es Salaam	Kampala	Total
more schools	40%	44%	51%	45%
more factories	40	37	28	35
more hospitals	17	10	15	14
more housing	1	6	5	4
more roads	2	3	1	2
don't know	—	—	—	—
Total	100%	100%	100%	100%
Base (all interviews)	389	451	395	1235

QUESTION 7. *Now, which one of these do you think our country needs most: an honest government without corruption, a government that gets things done, fair distribution of wealth, national unity, or individual freedom?*

	Nairobi	Dar es Salaam	Kampala	Total
an honest government without corruption	44%	38%	51%	44%
a government that gets things done	23	18	17	20
national unity	22	20	17	19
individual freedom	6	14	6	9

QUESTION 7. (Continued)

	Nairobi	Dar es Salaam	Kampala	Total
fair distribution of wealth	5	9	8	8
don't know	—	1	—	—
refused to answer	—	—	1	—
Total	100%	100%	100%	100%
Base (all interviews)	389	451	395	1235

QUESTION 8. *Which do you prefer—government ownership or private ownership of major industries?*

	Nairobi	Dar es Salaam	Kampala	Total
government ownership	51%	43%	38%	44%
private ownership	38	38	31	36
mixed (voluntary answer)	10	18	29	19
don't know	1	1	1	1
refused to answer	—	—	1	—
Total	100%	100%	100%	100%
Base	389	451	395	1235

QUESTION 9. *Are there things which African nations have or can do to help the rest of the world?*

QUESTION 9a. *(If "yes") What things do African nations have or can do to help the rest of the world?*

	Nairobi	Dar es Salaam	Kampala	Total
yes	89%	94%	75%	86%
no	5	4	11	6
don't know	6	2	14	8
Total	100%	100%	100%	100%
natural resources	24%	42%	24%	31%
contribute to peace, mediate, take neutral position	27	34	17	27
culture, art, music, literature	17	16	23	19
example of racial harmony	19	24	7	17
African socialism	1	—	—	—
not reported/refused to answer	1	—	4	1
have or can do nothing	11	6	25	14
Total	100%	122%	100%	100%
Base (all interviews)	389	451	395	1235

QUESTION 10.   *Which African governments would you say are the most sympathetic to the hopes and wishes of our country?*

	Nairobi	Dar es Salaam	Kampala	Total
Nigeria	4%	40%	15%	22%
Tanganyika	49	—	2	16
Ghana	11	7	26	14
Kenya	—	10	22	11
Ethiopia	13	2	3	6
Uganda	11	6	—	4
Algeria	—	9	2	3
Guinea	—	8	—	3
Zanzibar	—	2	—	1
Sudan	—	—	1	—
Egypt	—	—	—	—
Mozambique	—	—	—	—
others	—	—	—	—
none	—	—	—	—
don't know	12	16	31	20
Total	100%	100%	100%	100%
Base (all interviews)	389	451	395	1235

QUESTION 12.   *Do you favor or oppose closer ties among African states?*

QUESTION 12a.   *(If "favor") As you know, there are many different ways in which African states can establish closer ties among themselves. Which of the following ways would you favor: an organization for settling disputes between African governments, closer economic relations, political federation, African military organization, cultural exchanges?*

	Nairobi	Dar es Salaam	Kampala	Total
favor	94%	96%	85%	92%
oppose	3	3	9	5
don't know	2	1	4	2
refused to answer/not stated	1	—	2	1
Total	100%	100%	100%	100%
Base (all interviews)	389	451	395	1235
closer economic relations	22%	49%	53%	41%
political federation	26	39	27	31

QUESTION 12a. (*Continued*)

	Nairobi	Dar es Salaam	Kampala	Total
an organization for settling disputes between African governments	34	32	15	28
an African military organization	15	18	11	15
cultural exchanges	3	10	3	6
don't know	—	1	1	—
Total	100%	149%	110%	121%
Base (all those who favor)	366	432	337	1135

QUESTION 14. *Which political leader in Africa do you admire most?* (Weighted 2)

QUESTION 14a. *Which other African political leader do you admire after the one you have already told me?* (Weighted 1)

	WEIGHTED SCORE (*African leaders*)			
	Nairobi	Dar es Salaam	Kampala	Total
Kenyatta	485	293	283	1061
Nyerere	204	486	108	798
Nkrumah	142	197	207	546
Obote	17	11	265	293
Sekou Toure	6	80	2	88
Mboya	77	5	2	84
Tafawa Balewa	17	30	35	82
Haile Selassie	41	23	17	81
Ben Bella	10	52	8	70
Kaunda	5	10	14	29
Azikiwe	2	11	11	24
Banda	1	15	6	22
Karume	—	21	—	21
Nasser	7	5	3	15
Ngala	7	4	2	13
Kabaka	8	—	3	11
Luthuli	1	2	5	8
Nkomo	—	4	—	4
others	104	5	15	124
don't know	33	99	199	331
Total	1167	1353	1185	3705

QUESTION 14b. *What non-African world leader do you most admire?*
(Note: Kennedy was allowable, but if mentioned the
respondent was answered as follows: "As Mr. Kennedy
is dead, could you please name another?")

	Nairobi	Dar es Salaam	Kampala	Total
Lyndon Johnson	24%	30%	8%	21%
Khrushchev	10	19	7	13
Nehru	10	3	2	5
Douglas-Home	4	3	4	4
Macmillan	5	—	2	3
U Thant	1	6	—	3
De Gaulle	2	1	1	1
Churchill	1	2	1	1
Queen Elizabeth	2	—	2	1
others[a]	7	—	—	—
none admired	11	7	7	9
don't know	23	29	66	39
Total	100%	100%	100%	100%
Base (all interviews)	389	451	395	1235
Kennedy mentions	34%	17%	30%	27%
Base (all interviews)	289	451	395	1235

[a] Others include: Sandys, Butler, Fenner Brockway, D. Pritt, Harold Wilson, Tito, MacDonald, Chou En Lai. Each of these recorded a frequency of responses less than .5 per cent in the "total" column.

QUESTION. *Would you tell me what your feelings about the following countries are?*

The countries on the list were India, Soviet Union, Ghana, United States, Algeria, Red China, Israel, United Kingdom, Liberia, and Somalia. The respondent was asked if he had a "very good opinion," "good opinion," "neither good nor bad opinion," "bad opinion," or "very bad opinion." The order of the list of countries was changed with each interview. Answers were weighted when the answers were tabulated by score of +2, +1, 0, −1, −2, respectively. The following table is the result by weighted score totals by country and by the grand total.

Country	Kenya	Tanganyika	Uganda	Total
United States	247	233	187	221
United Kingdom	156	179	219	203
Israel	194	157	188	170
Ghana	183	164	148	166
India	113	148	51	104
Algeria	77	215	0	103

QUESTION. (*Continued*)

Country	Kenya	Tanganyika	Uganda	Total
Liberia	67	132	19	92
Soviet Union	−29	57	−15	4
Red China	−55	27	−39	−15
Somalia	−251	−75	−97	−136

BASIC SCALE FOR PERIODIC RESEARCH

The following is a description of a few of the questions which were used in pretesting a series of eighteen questions in three capital cities of East Africa to establish eight scales to assess opinions and attitudes about temporal orientation, government, confidence and optimism, patriotism, science and determinism, conception of people, politics and political leaders, and tribalism or traditionalism. It is intended that the scales, when adequately tested, revised, and evaluated, can be used for periodic surveys at fixed intervals over the next five years. Such surveys will provide scales that can be used to measure social change and that can be used to compare data from the three capital cities and also to compare the basic data between the elite of the urban areas and probability samples from selected rural areas.

The pretests were carried out in Nairobi, Kampala, and Dar es Salaam. Each was based on a probability sample of 150 people, stratified by age, eighteen and over, and education; the respondent must have had some secondary education. In fact, the samples for the pretests were chosen on the same basis as the survey described in the third part. A probability sample of this type is unavoidably composed mostly of males, young adults who are relatively wealthy, engaged in the more skilled occupations and professions, from the higher social groups, having a better than average education, representing the politically and socially important members of the community, and it closely resembles the elite described in the second part of this chapter. We have selected only a few questions to illustrate the possible value of the results. It is patently evident, however, that though these "one-shot" results are "merely interesting" or suggestive—they will become significant and really helpful when comparative data are obtained over a period of time so that trends, knowledge, and public opinion can be detected and measured by established scales.

The Results Suggest Possible Favorable Areas of:

(A) Knowledge

Scale I.   It does not help much to try to prevent crops from being damaged by insects and diseases: such losses can never really be prevented.

		Kampala	Dar es Salaam	Nairobi	East Africa
agree	%	8	12	12	11
disagree	%	88	85	87	86
uncertain	%	4	3	1	3
Base		153	156	150	459

(B) Public Opinion/Traditionalism

Scale II.   A man should never marry a woman who does not belong to his tribe.

		Kampala	Dar es Salaam	Nairobi	East Africa
agree	%	12	10	17	13
disagree	%	81	83	80	82
uncertain	%	7	7	3	5
Base		153	156	150	459

Not only does Scale I illustrate a sound basic knowledge of modern methods to prevent crops from being damaged, but it also illustrates a similarity of knowledge between the three sample areas which are widely separated geographically. Scale I will be invaluable when comparing the results of our first rural study, the fieldwork of which has been completed and is at the stage of processing.

Scale II also illustrates, but not so conclusively, similarities between the three areas. Nairobi had 17 per cent agree, whereas Dar es Salaam had only 10 per cent, with Kampala somewhere in-between. One could say, therefore, that there is a higher degree of tribalism among the elite of Nairobi than among the elite of Dar es Salaam.

The Results Suggest Possible Unfavorable Areas of:

(A) Knowledge

Scale III.   People have it within their power to bring harm and misfortune to others through magic.

		Kampala	Dar es Salaam	Nairobi	East Africa
agree	%	26	28	30	28
disagree	%	45	46	61	51
uncertain	%	29	26	9	21
Base		153	156	150	459

Scale IV. Science and knowledge are useful, of course, but many important matters can never be positively understood by the human mind.

		Kampala	Dar es Salaam	Nairobi	East Africa
agree	%	80	79	86	83
disagree	%	9	12	13	11
uncertain	%	11	9	1	6
Base		153	156	150	459

(B) Public Opinion

Scale V. A man ought always to obey his traditional chief.

		Kampala	Dar es Salaam	Nairobi	East Africa
agree	%	42	38	45	42
disagree	%	42	46	49	46
uncertain	%	15	16	6	12
Base		153	156	150	459

While Scale III shows a similarity between the three areas, it shows that the respondents of Nairobi are much more sophisticated in regard to magic than in the other sample points and that fewer are uncertain. A significant number in each area, however, believe that magic can be used to bring harm and misfortune to others.

Scale IV also shows a consensus between the three areas, but shows an over all unfavorable knowledge about science and knowledge. The majority, 83 per cent, believe that many important matters can never be positively understood by the human mind. The question can provide a very useful comparison in changing patterns of knowledge regarding science in the future.

Scale V shows an unfavorable public opinion about the role of traditional chiefs and the dichotomy caused by loss of status in recent years by traditional chiefs whose role has been largely taken over by the political appointee of the ruling party. The question will also provide useful comparative data between rural/urban and will be useful in the future to measure changes in attitudes and opinion about traditional chiefs.

The Results Suggest Possible New Problems in the Areas of:

(A) Knowledge

Scale VI. Government and politics are so complicated that the average man cannot really understand what is going on.

		Kampala	Dar es Salaam	Nairobi	East Africa
agree	%	81	65	72	72
disagree	%	16	24	22	21
uncertain	%	3	11	6	7
Base		153	156	150	459

Scale VII. If I had the choice, I would prefer to be given a small sum immediately, rather than be promised a very large sum one year from now.

		Kampala	Dar es Salaam	Nairobi	East Africa
agree	%	62	54	62	60
disagree	%	24	37	30	30
uncertain	%	14	9	8	10
Base		153	156	150	459

(B) Public Opinion

Scale VIII. Fundamentally, the world we live in is a lonesome place.

		Kampala	Dar es Salaam	Nairobi	East Africa
agree	%	37	39	43	40
disagree	%	43	46	49	45
uncertain	%	20	15	8	15
Base		153	156	150	459

Scale VI not only shows an area of new problems for East African elite, but also the wide divergence of response between the three sample points. In Kampala, 81 per cent agree with the statement and only 3 per cent are uncertain; whereas, in Dar es Salaam 65 per cent agree, while 11 per cent are uncertain. The statement will provide a useful measure in the future of the attitude of the elite toward government in each of the three sample points.

Scale VII is a new problem of investment and saving which, as you can see, has brought out differences between the three sample points and will provide in the future a useful measure of changing attitudes toward savings and the postponement of rewards.

Scale VIII shows similar responses in the three sample areas and will provide a useful measure between urban and rural areas, if we accept the hypothesis that those who change in their central beliefs are less secure than those who have not changed. We can expect that the responses from the rural area will show a higher percentage of disagreement if the hypothesis is valid.

The Results When Compared with Data from Comparable Samples Elsewhere Suggest:

(A) Similarities

Scale IX.   A woman's place is in the home.

		Kampala	Dar es Salaam	Nairobi	East Africa
agree	%	45	36	45	42
disagree	%	46	61	51	52
uncertain	%	9	3	4	5
Base		153	156	150	459

(B) Dissimilarities

Scale X.   The traditional ways of the past are the best, and all the changes nowadays only make things get worse; hence, the best way is to work hard and to keep up the old ways and to try and bring them back when they are lost.

		Kampala	Dar es Salaam	Nairobi	East Africa
agree	%	15	33	33	27
disagree	%	68	58	56	61
uncertain	%	17	9	11	12
Base		153	156	150	459

Scale XI.   The present is all too often full of unhappiness; it is only the future that counts.

		Kampala	Dar es Salaam	Nairobi	East Africa
agree	%	29	50	60	46
disagree	%	44	27	32	34
uncertain	%	21	23	8	20
Base		153	156	150	459

There are other examples above of similarities and dissimilarities which perhaps are even better than Scale IX. It does show, however, a close correspondence between Kampala and Nairobi, while Dar es Salaam shows a more tolerant attitude in their response to this statement. Once again, the comparison between urban and rural should show an interesting and significant difference.

Scale XII. The government is doing all it can to develop our country.

		Kampala	Dar es Salaam	Nairobi	East Africa
agree	%	51	86	84	74
disagree	%	21	5	10	12
uncertain	%	28	9	6	14
Base		153	156	150	459

Scale X shows significant statistical differences between the responses from Kampala and those of the other two sample points. This fact is even more interesting when we know that in Uganda the present form of government has been designed to maintain traditional ways of the past; whereas, in the other two areas, the present government has been designed to change, politically at least, traditional ways. The reactions of the Kampala respondents, therefore, are a significant indication of their dissatisfaction with efforts to maintain traditional ways.

Scale XI also illustrates that Kampala has a different reaction than the other two sample points, although there are less significant differences between Dar es Salaam and Nairobi.

Scale XII is a really significant indication of the basic dissatisfaction of the Kampala respondents with the status quo. The dissimilarity was also reflected in Scale X.

In conclusion, the few examples given above illustrate a basic effort to provide techniques that will standardize, by periodic surveys, scales that will measure social change in the broad areas of knowledge and public opinion.

The project is in its early stages, but it is hoped that, after the scales have been standardized for significance, regular studies will be continued to provide basic comparative data. It is also possible, by use of these scales, to test many hypotheses about social change, particularly in the fields of security, attitudes toward modern education and science, as well as to give a basic indicator of public reaction to the performance of the new governments.

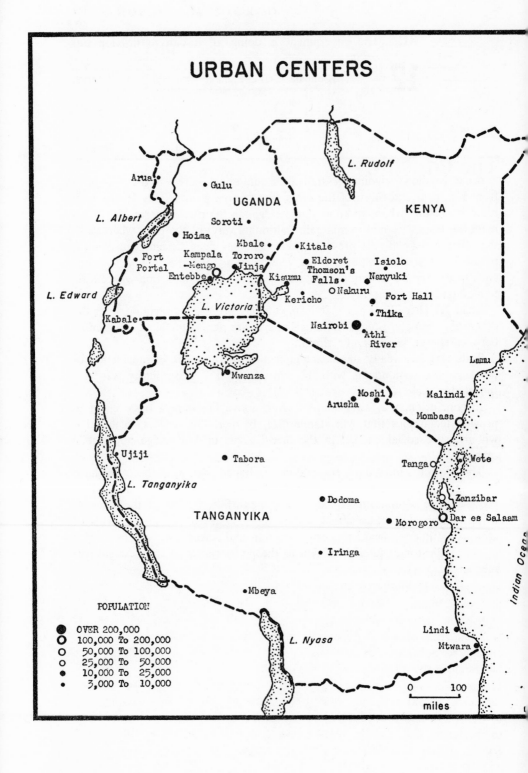

URBAN CENTERS

L. Rudolf

Arua •

• Gulu

UGANDA

KENYA

L. Albert

Soroti •

• Hoima

Mbale • • Kitale

Fort
Portal •

Kampala Tororo
—Mengo • Jinja

• Eldoret
Thomson's
Falls

Isiolo
•

• Nanyuki

Entebbe

Kisumu

L. Edward

○ Nakuru

Fort Hall

Kabale •

L. Victoria

Kericho •

• Thika

Nairobi ● Athi
River

• Mwanza

Lamu

Moshi •

Malindi •

Arusha •

Mombasa ○

• Ujiji

• Tabora

Tanga ○ • Wete

L. Tanganyika

• Dodoma

Zanzibar

TANGANYIKA

Morogoro • Dar es Salaam

• Iringa

Indian Ocean

POPULATION

● OVER 200,000
○ 100,000 To 200,000
○ 50,000 To 100,000
○ 25,000 To 50,000
• 10,000 To 25,000
• 3,000 To 10,000

• Mbeya

L. Nyasa

Lindi •

Mtwara •

0   100

miles

12

The Growth
of Urban Society

A. W. Southall

THE CAPITAL CITIES AND OTHERS

Nairobi, Dar es Salaam, and Kampala, the three metropolitan cities of formerly British East Africa, represent different combinations of the major historical themes of the past century. Nairobi, the most accidental of the three, was a construction camp on the Uganda Railway which was being built up from the coast at Mombasa in 1899. It marked a pause after the successful crossing of the high and open grassy plains of Masailand before pushing on through the forested southern edge of Kikuyu country and on over the Great Rift Valley toward Uganda. The Kikuyu were a vital source of foodstuffs between the empty grasslands to both east and west. There were no indigenous centers of population concentration or political organization to act as a counterattraction.

Dar es Salaam was a fine harbor on the midpoint of the long coast line of the new German East Africa and the natural place to choose as headquarters in the absence of any counterbalancing focus of interest in the interior. Had the scales been differently weighted, the more centrally placed Tabora might have been such a focus, fostering the growth of a capital in association with the large Nyamwezi kingdom of Unyanyembe. It had been the main interior caravan base since the early nineteenth century, but neither the natural resources of the region, nor the political organization and influence of the Nyamwezi, nor the attractions of its climate were enough to outweigh the convenience of a coastal capital. Dar es Salaam has retained the disadvantage of being rather isolated from any other major centers of development in Tanganyika. The previous Arab and Swahili settlement at Dar es Salaam had been of little importance. Kilwa, 150 miles to the south, and even the tiny village of Tongoni near Tanga, 150 miles to the north, had a much greater history as trading posts. But Arab and Swahili traders with their mercantile interests and their partly literate urban

463

culture were easily attracted to any new center, so that their Swahili coast culture dominated the life of Dar es Salaam and was, to some extent, spread by the Germans to most of the interior stations that it had not already reached before in the caravan age of the slave and ivory trade.

Although Kampala was founded on a hill where no previous settlement of any importance had been, it was sited there because of its immediate proximity to the capital of the king of Buganda, on Mengo Hill a mile away. As a consequence, urban development has retained a dual character ever since.

To this trilogy should be added Zanzibar City, with a population of 57,923 in 1958, capital of the sultans of Zanzibar since their move from Oman in 1840 until their deposition and flight in the 1964 revolution. At first, a city of Arab and Afro-Arab traders and plantation owners, with a few Indian merchants and a mass of African slaves, it acquired contradictory characteristics after the abolition of slavery and the imposition of the British protectorate. Indirect rule maintained the general rank and political status of the sultan and the Arabs, but the greatly expanded general commerce that followed after the trade in ivory and slaves under the *Pax Britannica* was largely captured by Indians. The African population, swelled by considerable immigration from Tanganyika, became one of free servants, employees, and petty traders. A new town grew up to accommodate them, similar to the African quarters of most coastal towns, with its square, mud-walled, palm-thatched houses, called *ngambo* (across) because it is across a creek from the old "Stone Town" which represents the nineteenth-century Arab city, with the sultan's palace and fort, the narrow, winding streets between lofty, massive houses, airy rooms above, and dark slave quarters below.

Besides these capital cities, there are few towns of any importance. The town on Mombasa Island is as old as any in East Africa, and its harbor is noted in the earliest records. For most of its history, it formed an independent Arab trading city-state, with long interludes of Portuguese domination from the sixteenth to the eighteenth century, and eventually falling under the general suzerainty of the Zanzibar sultans in the nineteenth. However, suzerainty was never effective, and the dominant Mazrui family remained an almost independent force in Mombasa and in other neighboring settlements on the coast. In 1895–1896, the Mazrui revolted all along the Kenya coast against the growing encroachments of British power. They were defeated, and Mombasa came effectively under direct British rule, despite continued legal recognition of the sultan of Zanzibar. Until superseded by Nairobi a few years after 1900, it was the first colonial capital of what is now Kenya. Mombasa remains East Africa's largest port and—because of its ethnic, religious, geographic, climatic, and economic distinctiveness and isolation from the rest of Kenya—retains something of the status of a capital. It has by far the largest Arab, Swahili, and Moslem population in the country and dominates the narrow, fertile coastal strip with its fish and its crops of coconut, cashew, and citrus, which are not found up country from which it was effectively segregated by the Taru Desert until the advent of the railway. In addition, the political status of Mombasa and the coast as a protectorate, legally owned by the sultan of Zanzibar and not a colony like the rest of Kenya, remained a paramount anomaly up to the time of Kenya's independence.

Nakuru has, perhaps, been the most solidly European town in East Africa, lying 100 miles northwest of Nairobi in the middle of the Great Rift Valley and the large farms of the former White Highlands. It is a farmers' capital, despite their numerical minority, dominated less by Asian commerce than most other areas, with nearly all its African population employed until recently in subordinate positions. Before 1900, the whole area was only occasionally occupied by nomadic Masai, who do not take to urban employment, so that its present African population is entirely derived from elsewhere, the vast majority being Kikuyu.

Tanga is another natural harbor which, though of little importance before the German conquest of Tanganyika, has become the third largest port on the coast after Mombasa and Dar es Salaam, serving the main sisal-growing area, which produces Tanganyika's most valuable export crop.

Tabora is the oldest inland town of consequence and has the most African flavor, a result of its Islamic Arab and Swahili background, which provides the gentlest induction of Africans into town life. Unlike Christianity, Islam seems to be untainted by the West to the African nationalist. The intermarriage and interbreeding of Arabs and Africans on the coast for over a thousand years, coupled with the full status accorded to offspring irrespective of color, makes Islam appear capable of providing a channel to self-respecting civilization and equality without subordination to the West, although its lack of wealth and educational resources are a very serious disadvantage. Four hundred miles from the coast, in the middle of Nyamweziland, with the headquarters of the chief of Unyanyembe just on its outskirts, Tabora is something of a regional metropolis.

Jinja is Uganda's second town, strategically situated on the Nile where the dam foretold by Sir Winston Churchill in 1908[1] was finally opened in 1954. It is the distribution center of a prosperous and populous countryside, the greatest cotton-growing area in Uganda. Its core consists almost entirely of the small shops of Indian merchants, though various industrial enterprises, such as a textile factory, brewery, and copper smelter, have been established on the basis of the electric power supplied by the dam.

RACIAL PROPORTIONS

Table 12–1 shows that there are some significant differences in the proportional numerical contribution of the main races to the population of the

---

[1] Winston S. Churchill, *My African Journey* (London: Hodder and Stoughton, 1908).

Table 12–1

Proportional Numbers of Main Ethnic Groups in Main Towns

	African	Arab	Asian	European	Non-African
Kampala	51.5%	0.09 %	41.1%	6.8 %	48. %
Kampala-Mengo	71.6	0.10	24.5	3.3	28.
Mengo (Kibuga)	87.3	0.11	11.5	0.6	12.2
Nairobi	58.6	0.37	32.4	8.05	41.4
Nakuru	79.1	0.47	16.2	3.7	20.5
Mombasa	62.3	9.9	24.3	2.95	37.7
Kisumu	60.	1.6	35.5	2.5	39.6
Lamu	31.1	64.6	4.0	0.22	68.8
Dar es Salaam	72.5	2.0	21.3	3.5	27.5
Tanga	73.5	3.7	19.5	2.0	26.5
Tabora	78.2	2.0	15.9	2.2	21.8
Mwanza	76.7	1.2	19.9	1.8	23.3
Dodoma	77.3	2.0	16.9	2.6	22.7
Lindi	81.1	0.3	17.5	1.0	18.9
Moshi	68.5	0.5	26.6	3.2	31.5
Arusha	51.4	0.7	34.8	8.7	48.6
Morogoro	85.8	1.5	10.5	1.9	14.2
Mtwara	91.9%	.003%	5.7%	2.0 %	8.1%

SOURCES: East African High Commission, East African Statistical Department, *General African Census, August 1957,* "Tribal Analysis: Tanganyika Population Census 1957" (Nairobi: 1958); East African High Commission, East African Statistical Department, *Uganda General African Census 1959* (Nairobi: 1960); Kenya Ministry of Finance and Economic Planning, *Kenya Population Census 1962* (Nairobi: 1964).

main towns. Separate figures are shown for Kampala-Mengo, Kampala, and Mengo to illustrate this. Visitors have often remarked that Kampala gives the impressions of being an Asian town. The figures show that Kampala, when taken alone, is indeed the most Asian (41.1 per cent) of all the main towns.[2] Complementarily, Mengo (the Kibuga[3]) is by far the most African of all the main towns. In other words, there is a polarization of racial groups in Kampala-Mengo. This looks like a kind of segregation, but is very different from what is usually understood by the word. The concentration of non-Africans in Kampala and of Africans in Mengo reflects the tacit agree-

---

[2] Asian here somewhat arbitrarily includes only Indians, Pakistanis, and Goans. The number of Indians is six or more times as great as the numbers of Pakistanis and Goans put together.

[3] See A. W. Southall and P. C. W. Gutkind, *Townsmen in the Making* (Kampala: East African Studies, No. 9, E.A.I.S.R., 1957), pp. 1–18.

ment between the British and the Ganda that their capital (Kibuga) of Mengo should be left for them to run in as autonomous a manner as possible. The very choice of the official capital of the Uganda Protectorate at Entebbe, over twenty miles away, represented the same desire to keep the two political presences distinct, disentangled, so that neither would foul the other. But the economic importance of Kampala always gave it a claim to be unofficially regarded as the capital. The government vacillated constantly for half a century over whether to transfer the capital (in the shape of the ministries and departments of the central government) to Kampala. In fact, over the last decade, this has been largely done in a piecemeal fashion, so that Kampala is now the capital of Uganda in almost everything except the legal name.

Nairobi is the most European of the East African cities, as would be expected, although Europeans form only 8 per cent of its population. In fact, Nakuru is more dominantly European than Nairobi. Its Asian population is relatively the smallest of any big town (except the exceptional Mengo), and its European population is the largest next to that of Nairobi; while its Africans, though so numerous, have no traditional roots in the area, are low in the scale of income, skill, and status and had very little influence until recently.

The figures for the Arabs are given separately from those of the Asians as a matter of historical interest, showing how tiny their numbers are despite their past importance. Only in Lamu are they really dominant, even numerically, and Lamu is a small town of only 5,828 people. There are several larger towns in Kenya which have not been included in Table 12–1. Arusha, like Nairobi, is almost half Asian and European.

NUMERICAL RANK ORDER

We may now explore some further demographic characteristics of East Africa's main towns and their social implications. Despite their different local origins, such as Arab port, railway supply dump, or tribal capital, in their present form as modern cities, they have all faced the same problem of growing from virtually nothing into large cities in little over half a century. Their multiracial, polyethnic composition has caused similar problems everywhere, although there have been different approaches to them. Just as in the early days, the European colonial rulers were concerned to protect their health against very high death rates from tropical diseases, so recently the most pressing problem has been the health and housing of the poorest African and Asian town-dwellers, with the attendant issues of national and municipal capital investment, land tenure, and wage rates.

Some demographers have argued that in any developed and properly defined urban region, the size of cities is proportional to this numerical rank order.[4] That is, the second largest city is about half the numerical size of the first; and the tenth largest, a tenth the numerical size of the first; and so on. Others have also drawn attention to the increasing dominance of very large cities in the underdeveloped parts of the world, where post-industrial urban growth is new, yet exceptionally rapid. Although most parts of Africa and East Africa, in particular, are obviously at a fairly early stage of this process, it would appear to be occurring there, as far as inadequate statistics will show. (See Table 12–2.)

At present, it is quite impossible to state with precision the proportional numerical size of urban areas in East Africa because there is no consistent definition of such areas. In other words, it is easy to find areas that by common-sense criteria seem urban, but are not officially included in an urban area; whereas, on the other hand, it may be that seemingly rural areas are urban. However, after allowing for some variability in the definition of urban areas of the figures in Table 12–2, it is quite obvious that East African towns do not conform to the numerical size order-ranking hypothesis at all. This hypothesis requires some conception of a social and spatial system of cities with definable limits, but it is arguable that, in the East African region, several urban systems have left their mark, in the context of various political and economic situations, so that no unequivocal spatial system of cities could be viably defined on the basis of synchronic factors alone.

This problem points strikingly to the ambiguity of status between East African cities and countries. Is Nairobi the first city numerically in an East African urban system or only in a Kenyan urban system; and, correspondingly, are Mombasa, Dar es Salaam, or Kampala-Mengo first cities in separate spatial systems, or partially separate subsystems, or second, third, and fourth cities in a single system? The correct answers can only be for certain purposes yes and for certain purposes no, so that it is difficult to see how any unilinear rank ordering of East African cities, either in one or several spatial systems, can possibly be sociologically meaningful or valid. In the thirteenth century, Kilwa was probably the most important city of the East Coast; throughout most of the nineteenth century, Zanzibar was; and Mombasa may have been in the sixteenth century and regained this position briefly under very different circumstances at the end of the nineteenth. Obviously there was nothing like a spatial urban system in the hinterland until well into the twentieth century, and only a rather tenuous system or plurality of systems could be demonstrated today.

As to the numerical dominance of the capital cities as central cities, it is very marked and seems to be becoming increasingly so. The capital cities have already far outstripped all other urban centers, and Nairobi has far outstripped them all. Mombasa remains somewhat anomalous, having enjoyed something of the status of a coastal capital.

---

[4] See, for example, R. Vining, "A Description of Certain Spatial Aspects of an Economic System," *Economic Development and Cultural Change,* III (January 1955).

Table 12–2

The Numerical Ranking of Towns in East Africa

Kenya (1962)		Tanganyika (1957)		Uganda (1959)	
1. Nairobi	266,794	1. Dar es		(Kampala	46,731)
2. Mombasa	179,575	Salaam	128,742	(Mengo	60,374)
3. Nakuru	38,181	2. Tanga	38,053	1. Kampala-	
4. Kisumu	23,526	3. Mwanza	19,877	Mengo	107,105
5. Eldoret	19,605	4. Tabora	15,361	2. Jinja	19,828
6. Thika	13,952	5. Morogoro	14,507	3. Entebbe	10,941
7. Nanyuki	10,448	6. Moshi	13,726	4. Kabale	10,186
8. Nyeri	7,857	7. Dodoma	13,435	5. Mbale	8,433
9. Kericho	7,692	8. Mtwara	10,459	6. Lugazi	7,744
10. Kitale	7,000	9. Lindi	10,315	7. Fort Portal	7,647
11. Gilgil	6,452	10. Arusha	10,038	8. Tororo	4,818
12. Lamu	5,828	11. Ujiji[a]	10,000	9. Soroti	4,618
13. Malindi	5,818	12. Iringa	9,587	10. Gulu	4,043
14. Athi River	5,510	13. Mbeya	6,932	11. Arua	3,991
15. Isiolo	5,445				
16. Fort Hall	5,389				
17. Thomson's					
Falls	5,316				
18. Embu	5,213				

Zanzibar (1958)

Zanzibar Town	57,923
Wete (Pemba)	7,507

SOURCES: East Africa High Commission, East African Statistical Department, *General African Census, August 1957*, "Tribal Analysis: Tanganyika Population Census 1957" (Nairobi: 1958); East Africa High Commission, East African Statistical Department, *Uganda General African Census 1959* (Nairobi: 1960); Kenya Ministry of Finance and Economic Planning, *Kenya Population Census 1962* (Nairobi: 1964).

[a] Not included in the official census list of towns because of its different legal status.

NAIROBI

In 1962, the population of Nairobi was 266,794; whereas, in 1902, it was about 9,000. The railway only reached the bare and empty Nairobi plain in 1899, some ten years after the founding of both Dar es Salaam and Kampala as central colonial cities. Sir Edward Grigg, former governor of Kenya, said that the country was not conquered by force of arms but by a railway. "The railway is the beginning of all history in Kenya. Without it there would be no history of Kenya."[5] The Uganda Railway was built, without any thought for the Kenya Highlands, as the easiest route to Uganda to secure the Congo Basin, the Sudan, Egypt, and the Nile.

The site of Nairobi was chosen because it was convenient for the railway, as a headquarters and as a base for the further construction towards the lake [Victoria]. For these purposes the site may have been well chosen, but it was not an ideal site for a town which was later to become the capital of Kenya Colony. [Major Patterson, the lion killer of Tsavo, was in charge of the first layout.] There was an immense amount of work to be done in converting an absolutely bare plain, 327 miles from the nearest place where even a nail could be purchased, into a busy railway centre . . . Wonderfully soon, however, the nucleus of the present town began to take shape, and a thriving bazaar sprang into existence with a mushroom-like growth. In this, however, a case or two of plague broke out before very long, so I gave the natives and Indians who inhabited it an hour's notice to clear out, and on my own responsibility promptly burned the whole place to the ground.[6]

But, in 1901, the commissioner (governor), Sir Charles Eliot, had reported favorably on white settlement, and, by 1903, there were 100 European settlers in Nairobi. By 1906, the town was growing rapidly, with more and more white settlers, expansion of the Asian bazaar, and a corresponding influx of their African employees. Nairobi is an example of the triumph of culture and technology over ecology and indeed the creation of a new ecology.

The choice of Nairobi as the capital of Kenya was geographically sound. Government came here for the same reasons as those which attracted the traders and later the manufacturers—it has better communications by rail and road than any other place in Kenya, and it is not too far from any part of the well-populated areas of the country—the Highlands, Nyanza, and the Coast . . . Shortage of water and power; the unhealthy nature of the ill-drained black cotton soil and its unsuitability for the foundations of buildings; shortage of houses; traffic congestion and other difficulties of transport . . . are all being overcome because the forces favouring the growth of the city are so powerful.[7]

But, in fact, Nairobi is the center of communications and of urban growth because it is the capital and not vice versa. Furthermore, it has often been an example of the triumph of sheer marginal utility over apparently discouraging political circumstances.

A somewhat paradoxical feature of Nairobi's recent development is the

---

[5] M. F. Hill, *Permanent Way* (Nairobi: East African Railways and Harbours, 1950), pp. 199, 244.

[6] *Ibid.*

[7] R. W. Walmsley, *Nairobi—The Geography of a New City* (Nairobi: Eagle Press, 1957), pp. 8, 12.

extreme speed with which Nairobi grew and with which its central business district was almost completely transformed during and immediately after the Mau Mau Emergency, in many ways one of the darkest episodes in the history of Kenya. However, the vast operations within the military, police, penal, and general administrative sphere and the high amount of construction and reconstruction required meant colossal spending on an unprecedented scale. Much of this spending was inevitably siphoned through Nairobi in the form of increased consumption and ultimately came to be reflected in the pulling down of old buildings, many of which had survived with their one or two stories and their corrugated iron roofs from before World War I. These buildings were replaced by multistory blocks of shops, hotels, and offices of a highly contemporary style.[8] (See Table 12–3.)

Table 12–3

Visible Balance of External Trade

	Kenya	Tanganyika	Uganda
1951	—	+12,225	+25,305
1952	−29,595	+9,918	+23,409
1953	−28,780	+7,183	+7,948
1954	−37,560	+5,813	+15,830
1955	−43,506	−6,118	+8,330
1956	−36,789	+10,422	+13,402
1957	−40,754	+1,771	+17,963
1958	—	+10,260	—
1959	—	+12,762	—

N O T E : These figures are in thousand £'s.

Underpinning this process was the appearance of large numbers of new foreign firms in East Africa, most of which set up their regional head offices in Nairobi. With the coming of independence to Tanganyika in 1961 and Uganda in 1962 (Kenya following in 1963), many firms had to make the formal gesture of establishing independent representation in Dar es Salaam and Kampala, but the economic and institutional dominance of Nairobi continues to make an important contribution to Kenya's peculiarly poised balance of payments (see Table 12–3). Mombasa remains the only effective

[8] The Kenya government spent over 56 million £'s sterling on the Emergency from 1952 till 1959, and all of this must be regarded as abnormal extra spending. The British government made loans totaling 29.5 million £'s to Kenya, specifically for Emergency expenditure and another 5 million £'s for the Swynnerton Plan of agricultural development which arose directly out of the impetus of the Emergency. Nor is it possible to state the further spending by the British forces in Kenya and in other concealed ways not included in this reckoning.

port of entry for goods to or from overseas both for Kenya and Uganda, so that most of the latter's imports and exports pass through Nairobi. Meanwhile, Nairobi also retains its position as big-game hunting and filming "capital of the world." This is the core of an increasingly flourishing international tourist industry. Finally, since World War II, Nairobi has been the headquarters of the East African High Commission, which became the East African Common Services Organization when the East African countries achieved independence. This not only reinforces the emphasis on Nairobi as metropolis and implicit East African capital city, but carries with it important contributions in finance and employment through the presence of the headquarters of the East African Railways and Harbours, East African Posts and Telecommunications Administration, and a number of other major services common to all the East African countries, including most of the research institutes for the applied sciences.

No matter how much political, economic, or cultural interests may wish to resist the snowball effect of concentration in Nairobi, they find it inconvenient and costly to do so. Inevitably, Nairobi is at first sight the obvious capital city for any East African federation. The relative geographical positions both in their own countries, as well as in East Africa as a whole, of Nairobi, Dar es Salaam, and Kampala, drives the same point home and encourages the development of a system of communications by both land and air, national and international, which further entrenches it. Since the success of an East African federation must depend in large part on the satisfaction and sense of equality of its component states, any tendency of Kenya and Nairobi to dominate could be disastrous. But it must be admitted that the fundamental objection to Nairobi as East Africa's capital is precisely its dominance. Hence, we have the canvasing of neutral compromises, such as Arusha in northern Tanganyika, which is attractive, salubrious, and well placed as the geographical center of East Africa, but would be vastly expensive to establish as a new capital along the lines of Brasilia, Canberra, or Washington.

We must now look more closely at the composition of Nairobi's population. Although the European population seems large at 21,477, it is only 8 per cent of the total; while Africans form 59 per cent, and Asians 33 per cent. The Arabs themselves, despite their importance in the history of East Africa, form only 0.4 per cent (see Table 12–1). The proportion of the different racial and tribal or ethnic groups and the proportion of women to men and of children to adults are important indicators of what is going on in these cities. Within the African 59 per cent of Nairobi's population there are many subdivisions. Since the traditional tribal peoples have long lost their political autonomy and are now incorporated in the new Kenya state, I shall refer to these subdivisions as ethnic groups, recognizing that many of them still retain important linguistic and cultural differences, together with a strong sense of their distinct identity.

The largest of these ethnic subdivisions in Nairobi's African population are those of the Kikuyu, Luyia, Luo, and Kamba, also corresponding to the largest traditional ethnic groups in Kenya as a whole. Since the colonial administration held the Kikuyu people principally responsible for the Mau Mau Emergency and, to a much lesser extent, the Kamba, the Mau Mau period in Nairobi was the occasion of a violent swing of population in which the Kikuyu and Kamba were rounded up and screened by the security forces, large numbers of them being deported from Nairobi, while their places in the residential and employment structure of the city were taken by members of other Kenyan ethnic groups, but particularly by the Luo and Luyia.[9] After the Emergency was over, the pendulum gradually swung back to the earlier predominance of Kikuyu. The relative numbers of Luo and Luyia fell, although the absolute numbers of all groups had risen greatly since the beginning of the Emergency.

However much suffering and privation may have been caused to many thousands of individuals and families in the course of this major and partly compulsory movement of population to and fro, it is doubtful whether either the structure or the pattern of development of urban Nairobi was greatly affected by it, except insofar as there was a very general determination to ameliorate housing and general social conditions in Nairobi after the Emergency. Indeed, one of the fascinating if intangible aspects of this period, from the point of view of a study of ends and means, is that the open and violent confrontation of racial, ethnic, and political groups in the Emergency does not seem to have led, as might have been expected, to even greater bitterness, antagonism, and polarization—although, undoubtedly, it rendered the whole basis of law, order, and social control in Kenya unfortunately fragile—but, rather, eventually to a more mature heart-searching on all sides, out of which arose a widespread determination to transcend hostilities and hatreds in discovering the requisite foundations for building a new society. This is nowhere more strikingly symbolized than in the transition, for which Nairobi was the setting, from the characterization of Jomo Kenyatta as "leader to darkness and death" by one governor of Kenya to the successful and mutually respectful association of his successor with Kenyatta as Prime Minister.

In the case of all these major ethnic groups of the Kikuyu, Luyia, Luo, and Kamba in Nairobi, males are nearly twice as numerous as females. This

---

[9] From 1952 to 1957, some 419,000 arrests were made in Kenya in connection with the Emergency, a substantial proportion being in and around Nairobi. In Nairobi City, the percentage of Kikuyu, Embu, and Meru in the total labor force fell from 47 to 22 between 1953 and 1956, while that of the Nyanza province peoples (Luo, Luyia, and Kisii) rose from 27 to 38, and that of the Kamba from 18 to 28. While the figures for male residence are not precisely comparable to these, they are very highly correlated—so the swing back can be seen from the fact that, at the 1962 census, Kikuyu, Embu, Meru males formed 44 per cent; Luo, Luyia, and Kisii 33 per cent; and Kamba 17 per cent of the male African population of Nairobi City.

is a general characteristic of East African cities and indeed of the newer, rapidly growing cities all over Africa. Where the figures are available and children and adults are adequately distinguished, this disparity is shown to be clearly due, as might be expected, to the preponderance of adult men over adult women in town, the proportions of boys and girls in the category of children being approximately equal. However banal this fact may have become to Africanists, it is worth noting that it is in direct contradiction to the general statement, often found in works of urban sociology, that cities are characterized by a predominance of women over men. This conflict is probably due to the extent to which African cities recruit their populations on the basis of the system known as migrant labor and the extent to which Africans do or do not look on urban communities as truly their own.

Insofar as African urban populations depend on migrant labor for their recruitment, large numbers of men come to live and work in town, leaving their wives and children in rural areas. This indicates an unwillingness to switch either their economic or social dependence irrevocably from rural to urban society. Despite the high cost in many ways, both to society and the individual and family, of this splitting of the domestic unit between town and country, the average African family, in general, and its responsible head, in particular, is able to ensure itself certain economic and social gains that would still be difficult to attain in any other way. At the level of unskilled labor, which absorbs the vast majority of employed Africans, the family gains an advantage by securing an urban wage, while, at the same time, supporting its wives and children rurally through maintenance of the largely traditional subsistence economy—even if, through lack of its traditional manpower, it is sometimes at a slightly impoverished level. By the same combination, that social security—which neither state, city, nor employer provides for the unskilled worker—can be ensured by retaining the ever-present possibility of return to the rural family in case of unemployment, illness, or any other misfortune, and finally old age. In addition, this situation is caused by and perpetuates the remaining exclusiveness of the rural communities with their background of former tribal solidarity and their fairly profound linguistic and cultural differences, which still make most Africans (and, of course, this always means the least educated and least skilled) feel that they do not fully or safely belong anywhere else. This certainly constitutes a vicious circle in which both urban and rural economies are retarded. But escape from the circle is difficult, and, meanwhile, it appears that no conceivable level of urban unskilled wages can hope to compensate for the advantages of remaining a member of two almost separate economies and social systems at the same time.

From the above argument, it may be inferred that the mass of the Kikuyu, Luyia, Luo, and Kamba in Nairobi do not regard it as their city to the extent of feeling able to commit themselves and their families to it and that, correspondingly, their interests, goals, and identifications are but partially urban. Exceptions to this general statement will be noted, but it needs to be stressed all along that it is not an exception to recognize the importance of social stratification in East African cities. Nonetheless, the small but important minority whose status, education and income are higher has a much deeper commitment to urban life (although it is rarely cut off from its rural roots) and increasingly occupies a different position in the urban structure. African businessmen or officers in large firms, teachers and professional men, civil servants and politicians also usually retain close links with rural kinfolk in their traditional areas of origin; they may well buy land there and put up improved houses; it is profitable for them, directly or indirectly through relatives or employees, to invest in improved cash-crop farming and in small-scale rural business, such as shops, bars, gas stations, or transport. Yet, despite this potential rural involvement, the prospect of any permanent or even long-term return to rural residence and full participation in rural society is much more remote for them. Furthermore, their daily energies and their goals and interests are much more fully incorporated in urban society. Precise figures cannot be given, but we know from personal experience that there are now many African families of the top elite in Nairobi with their nuclear membership of husband, wife, and children firmly established in long-term urban residence. Since this elite category is nonetheless a small numerical minority, official figures nearly always express the quantitative characteristics of the masses. Not only is the ratio of African women to men in Nairobi abnormally low (40 per cent), but so also is that of children to adults. This is particularly striking in view of the preponderance of children (exceeding the number of adults) in the population of the country at large, which is common in underdeveloped parts of the world with very high birth and death rates and may even be intensified in the early stages of improved health conditions, permitting rapid population growth. Thus, we find that in Nairobi the number of girls is only 79 per cent of the number of women and the number of boys only 34 per cent of the number of men. But among the elite, we should expect to find greater numerical equality between the sexes and a preponderance of children, since large families are common.

It must further be noted that the relative distance or proximity of these peoples to Nairobi does not seem to have been a major influence as far as these figures go. Strictly speaking, the site of Nairobi was in Masailand, Nairobi meaning "cold" in Masai, probably with reference to the Nairobi River. However, it is on the very edge of Kikuyuland, and they, if any people (since the special position of the Masai precludes them), might be expected to go furthest in claiming Nairobi as their city in a proprietary sense. This would be all the more to be expected in view of the extreme land hunger in the very dense Kikuyu areas of Kiambu on the outskirts of Nairobi. But until very recently, Nairobi has appeared to most Kikuyu as a hostile expression of colonialism rather than as a city. Doubtless, this reflects the alienation of much land in and around Nairobi to exclusively European use and ownership during the first half of the twentieth century, as well as the continued restriction of most Kikuyu land rights to the traditional channeling of small, highly localized lineages, which made it psychologically impossible for the average Kikuyu to get security or satisfaction from land which might be available elsewhere. This is in high contrast to the flexible system of land tenure around Kampala-Mengo. Although the Luyia and Luo are, for the most part, 250 to 300 miles farther from Nairobi than the Kikuyu, this does not appear to have affected the ratio of females to males through causing any fewer Luyia and Luo men to take their wives to town than in the case of the Kikuyu on the doorstep of Nairobi. (See Table 12–4.)

Table 12–4

Nairobi

RACE	TOTAL	MALE			FEMALE		
		Total	Adults	Children	Total	Adults	Children
African	156,246	101,842	75,947	25,895	54,404	30,378	24,026
Asian	86,453	45,460	25,236	20,224	40,993	21,884	19,109
European	21,477	11,103	7,857	3,246	10,374	7,402	2,972
Arab	982	537	327	210	445	196	249
other	1,636	786	439	347	850	528	322
Total non-African	110,548	57,886	33,859	24,027	52,662	30,010	22,652
Total all races	266,794	159,728	109,806	49,922	107,066	60,388	46,678

SOURCE: Kenya Ministry of Finance and Economic Planning, *Kenya Population Census 1962* (Nairobi: 1964).

There are certain conditions in which some of these processes operate differently, and a contrasting pattern results. In Nairobi, this may be exemplified by the Ugandan population, in which the number of females is 76 per cent of the number of males, thus nearing equality; whereas Kikuyu, Kamba, Luyia, and Luo females are only 55 per cent, 41.5 per cent, 53 per cent, and 59 per cent of males respectively. It can confidently be suggested that this is due to the following causes: the figures refer mainly to adults and relatively few children are included; while classified as "Uganda," the majority are "Ganda";[10] the Ganda are the most highly educated of the large ethnic groups of East Africa, both in terms of the number of generations that have experienced school education and the average level reached; there are correspondingly more educated Ganda women than there are in any

---

10 The Ganda people supplied the name for the whole country of Uganda, although they form only one-quarter of its population and occupy one of its four regions which is distinguished as Buganda.

other indigenous East African ethnic group; this, combined with other factors, has led to a considerable emancipation of Ganda women from the control of parents, husbands, brothers, and men generally; this has undoubtedly led to greater equality between the sexes and to the emergence of women leaders and women professionals; it has also inevitably led to the escape from male authority of even larger numbers of Ganda women of lower levels of education and family status; it is the towns which offer the greatest possibilities of employment and maintenance of some kind of economic and social independence to such women; some find wage employment; and others, as an alternative or in combination with this, form temporary unions with men whose wives are in the country, or in more extreme cases become commercial prostitutes.[11] It is this background of factors which most probably accounts for the fact that the number of females is more nearly equal to that of males in the case of the Ugandans than in that of any other indigenous ethnic group in Nairobi, and that, in certain senses, these Ugandan women have been able to become more committed to urban life than most other women. Of course, the figures fail to reveal how many women in the larger groups, such as the Kikuyu, Luyia, Luo, and Kamba, are leading similarly emancipated lives; but their numbers are certain to be fairly considerable in the case of the Kikuyu, to whom the city is nearest, although not large enough to affect the over-all ratio of Kikuyu women to men as they do in the case of the Ugandans. The special characteristics of the Ugandans, and especially the Ganda, will be further revealed when consideration is given to the cities of Kampala and Mombasa. It is to be noted that in this case relative numerical parity of the sexes is by no means an indicator of stable marriage and family life.

KAMPALA

By the nineteenth century, the capital of the Ganda people was the headquarters of an increasingly centralized political state,[12] but the capital still moved about from place to place as did those of early English kings. It happened to be on Mengo Hill, in 1890, at the time when Lord Lugard established the first stable and lasting political relationship between the outside world and the rulers of the Ganda people.[13] Though his position was most delicate and insecure, Lugard set the tone of future relationships by refusing to accept the site suggested to him by the Ganda king for his camp

---

[11] G. M. Wilson found that in a sample of prostitutes in Mombasa in 1956, 49 per cent of the African prostitutes were women from Uganda, 43 per cent being Ganda and the others mainly Nyoro, Toro, and Soga. Another 13 per cent were Haya, another interlacustrine Bantu group from the neighboring part of Tanganyika.

[12] See Lloyd A. Fallers (ed.), *The King's Men* (New York: Oxford University Press, 1964). Southall and Gutkind, *op. cit.*

[13] *Ibid.*

and establishing himself on the neighboring hill of Kampala, after which the metropolis of Uganda has been called ever since. However, the duality and ambivalence persisted between the continuity of the Ganda capital, on the one hand, and, on the other, Lugard's new town, of the British administration, the Asian merchants, and, ultimately from 1962 on, the new African national government of Uganda.[14]

The gradually increasing autonomy of Kampala as a self-governing urban entity was marked by its recognition as a township in 1906, a municipality in 1949, and a city in 1962, when Uganda also became an independent state. Similarly, but more slowly, the older Ganda capital of Mengo was officially recognized as a township in 1931 and was made a municipality in 1962. Although Kampala (city) and Mengo (municipality) remain institutionally separate and are likely to remain so for some considerable time to come, they form a concentrated and continuous urban agglomeration which must inevitably be referred to as Kampala-Mengo.

These historical factors are stressed, not only for their intrinsic interest, but because they are essential to an understanding of the contemporary significance of the urban metropolitan area of Kampala-Mengo. The same continuity and cumulative development of traditional and modern urban influences could have occurred, had the coincidence of political and economic factors been favorable, in the case of other headquarters of East African kings or chiefs, such as those of the other interlacustrine monarchs in Bunyoro, Toro, Ankole, Bukoba, Rwanda, or Burundi, or conceivably those of the Chagga, Sukuma, Nyamwezi, or Hehe in Tanganyika. But the required combination and coincidence of factors occurred fully only in the case of Kampala-Mengo, making it somewhat unique in East Africa, but calling for comparison with other varying African instances of the combination of traditional and modern population concentration, such as Addis Ababa, Benin, Ibadan, Ife, Kano, or Kumasi. Bureaucratic myopia has always prevented recognition of the significance of Kampala-Mengo. This has appeared nowhere more fantastically than in the census association of Kampala with the counting of the non-African population and of Mengo with that of the African population, thus effectively misrepresenting them both and concealing their intense relationship.

The European population of Kampala grew slowly; but, like many other African cities, it illustrates the surprising fact that European populations grew particularly fast during the period of Africanization in which independence was approaching and even after it was achieved. The number of Europeans in Kampala was estimated at only 359 in 1926, 505 in 1931, 1,297 in 1948, and 3,179 in 1959. In the same years, the Asian population was estimated at (800 already in 1914) 1,700 in 1926, 3,106 in 1931,

---

[14] *Ibid.*

10,824 in 1948, and 19,268 in 1959. Africans numbered 11,905 in Kampala by 1948 and 24,052 in 1959.

The adjacent area of what is now the municipality of Mengo, although it contained a growing urban nucleus next to the boundary of Kampala, in fact, contained large areas which, though quite densely populated, were comparatively rural until recent years. Thus, its African population—already 32,441 in the admittedly unreliable census of 1911—had only risen to 34,337 in 1948 and reached 52,685 in 1959. The total population of Kampala-Mengo rose from just under 60,000 in 1948 to 107,105 in 1959. Yet the anomalies and obscurities of the local figures are reflected in the fact that the *United Nations Demographic Yearbook* recognizes no urban area of a population of 100,000 in Uganda and refers only to the titular capital of Entebbe with its population of 10,941 (1959).

The average level of rural prosperity has, from the first decade of this century, been far higher among the African population of Uganda than that of either Kenya or Tanganyika. This has been associated with the rather limited growth of something like an urban proletariat or working class. At the same time, this rural prosperity has not been able to expand much during the last five years in which the export prices of relevant primary products, such as cotton and coffee, fell below their postwar-boom level, and, correspondingly, the employed urban labor force has not expanded during this period.

The distinctive history of Kampala-Mengo and the different urban structure that resulted from it are objectively illustrated in such demographic figures as are available, as well as in the different significance which the town has, at least for the local Ganda people in whose country it is situated. Of all the African ethnic groups represented in Kampala-Mengo, the Ganda is the only one in which females outnumber males. Ganda constitute one-third of the total Kampala-Mengo population and three-fifths of the African population. The percentage relation of Ganda females to males is 102 per cent. The next highest percentage of females to males among the African ethnic groups in Kampala-Mengo is that of the Soga (76), followed by the Nyoro (64). Far behind come the Acholi (53.5) and the Jonam (50).[15] In all other cases, females are less than half as numerous as males. (See Table 12–5.)

It is suggested that the numerical equality of urban Ganda females and males reflects the following factors: the continuous tradition of concentrated, almost urban residence of Ganda families dating back to the pre-colonial capital of the Ganda kings and the expansion of Mengo from this nucleus during the colonial period; the relative emancipation of Ganda

---

[15] Haya women outnumbered men in Mengo-Kisenyi (Southall and Gutkind, *op. cit.*) where indeed there was a high concentration of prostitutes, but they did not do so in Kampala-Mengo as a whole.

Table 12-5

Kampala, Mengo (Kibuga), and Kampala-Mengo Combined. Ethnic Groups in the African Population and Ratio of Females to Males (1959)[a]

ETHNIC GROUP	Total Population			Per cent Total		Kampala			Mengo			Kampala-Mengo		
	Kampala	Mengo	Both	African	All Races	Men	Women	Per cent Women	Men	Women	Per cent Women	Men	Women	Per cent Women
Acholi	1,499	581	2,080	2.7	1.9	1,005	494	49.2	350	231	66.0	1,355	725	53.5
Alur	304	158	462	0.6	0.4	216	88	40.7	109	49	45.0	325	137	42.2
Ganda	4,518	32,946	37,464	48.8	35.0	2,226	2,292	102.9	16,331	16,615	101.8	18,557	18,908	101.9
Kiga	810	1,172	1,982	2.6	1.9	673	137	20.4	979	193	19.7	1,652	330	20.0
Ankole	821	1,671	2,492	3.2	2.3	619	202	32.6	1,384	287	20.7	2,003	489	24.4
Nyoro	619	1,301	1,920	2.5	1.8	380	239	62.9	789	512	64.9	1,169	751	64.2
Soga	475	534	1,009	1.3	0.9	264	211	79.9	308	226	73.4	572	437	76.4
Toro	2,346	3,486	5,832	7.6	5.4	1,668	678	40.6	2,433	1,053	43.3	4,101	1,731	42.2
Teso	782	539	1,321	1.7	1.2	497	285	57.3	395	144	36.5	892	429	48.1
Luo	3,450	2,094	5,544	7.2	5.2	2,359	1,091	46.2	1,448	646	44.6	3,807	1,737	45.6
Jonam	309	48	357	0.5	0.3	203	106	52.2	35	13	37.1	238	119	50.0
Ruanda	867	1,962	2,829	3.7	2.6	624	243	38.9	1,420	542	38.2	2,044	785	38.4
"Kenya"	1,481	1,337	2,818	3.7	2.6	1,059	422	39.8	927	410	44.2	1,986	832	41.9
Lango	478	184	662	0.9	0.6	319	159	49.8	139	45	32.4	458	204	44.5
Lugbara	566	348	914	1.2	0.9	388	178	45.9	266	82	30.8	654	260	39.8
Madi	463	173	636	0.8	0.6	299	164	54.8	128	45	35.5	427	209	48.9
Samia	628	442	1,070	1.4	1.0	415	213	51.3	311	131	42.1	726	344	47.4
Total African	52,673	24,056	76,729	100.0	71.6	15,753	8,303	52.7	30,323	22,350	73,7	46,076	30,653	66.5

Total population, Kampala-Mengo (all races): 107,105
Total Uganda population: 6,636,616

SOURCE: East African High Commission, East African Statistical Department, *Uganda General African Census 1959* (Nairobi: 1960).

[a] The columns headed Per cent Women show the proportion which the number of women bears to the number of men, that is, if there were equal numbers of women and men, women would be 100 per cent, if women were only half as numerous as men, women would be 50 per cent, and so on.

women from familial and domestic authority, itself a product of interaction between the Ganda family and marriage system itself; and the rising level of education and income facilitated by the relatively favorable relationship between the Ganda people, their rulers, and the British missionaries and administrators.

The leading Ganda chiefs were traditionally obliged to spend much of their time in residence in the capital at the king's court. There has been a continuous transition from this to the contemporary residence of elite Ganda families in Mengo, reinforced in recent years by increasing numbers of Ganda civil servants and professional men living with their families in Kampala. Some of these influences have been similarly, but less strongly, operative among the interlacustrine Bantu neighbors of the Ganda, such as the Soga and Nyoro.

However, the exceptional advantages of freehold or securely rented land in Buganda have favored the development of a suburban middle-class ethos among the Ganda working in Kampala-Mengo. White-collar workers aim at acquiring a plot and house outside the city but within motoring (formerly cycling) distance of their daily work. By this means, they relieve the middle-class housing problem in the city; carry urban influences into the country; and blend tribal, traditional, rural, and modern urban features in their own lives. They also gain greatly by being able to grow much of their own foodstuffs and often crops for sale also, hiring labor for the purpose and, thus, further intensifying the influence of the urban cash economy in the surrounding countryside.

Although it is not difficult for them to qualify, very few Africans other than Ganda have taken advantage of these possibilities, except for a few prominent and wealthy figures from other tribes. Consequently, the incipient non-Ganda middle class is particularly conspicuous in the housing estates that were developed for Africans during the 1950's on the eastern side of Kampala. Here, they form an increasingly important third element to the older duality of Kampala-Mengo.[16]

DAR ES SALAAM

Sultan Seyid Majid of Zanzibar founded the settlement of Dar es Salaam in 1865, with an Arab garrison and slaves to clear the bush and plant coconuts. The leading men of several Zaramo fenced villages of the area received presents of cloth and money from the sultan and welcomed the new settlement. There were also a few small settlements of Shirazi fishermen in the vicinity. But the sultan died in 1870, and there were said to be only three houses left of the old Dar es Salaam by 1873. Then, the Germans chose it as the capital of German East Africa in place of their previous headquarters

---

[16] See Southall and Gutkind, *op. cit.*, pp. 46–50.

at Bagamoyo, and, by 1886, its population was estimated at 5,000, reaching 18,000 by 1900 (twice the size of Nairobi at that time), and then growing little until after World War I. Only 20,000 in 1921, it nearly doubled to 37,000 in 1943, 72,000 in 1951, 92,330 at the 1957 census, and 128,742 in the 1960 estimate.

The Zaramo and Shirazi were unable to make any special claims on the city that grew up in their midst, as the Ganda did in Kampala-Mengo, because of their lack of political integration. But the Zaramo have remained the most numerous ethnic group in Dar es Salaam, forming over one-third of the African population in 1957. The leading elder of the Zaramo also remained, perhaps, the most strongly established of the ethnic leaders, though such tribal elders have now lost most of their influence in Dar es Salaam.

As a German colonial capital for thirty years and a British one for forty, Dar es Salaam was a largely Western, non-African creation like other East African cities, but its original founding from Zanzibar and its subsequent supersession of Bagamoyo as the chief base for the penetration of the hinterland classes it, in certain respects, with the old Arab-Swahili settlements of the coast and gives it a special quality as the chief disseminator of urban culture in Tanganyika. Although no categorical definition of Swahili culture can be wholly satisfactory, its cardinal attributes are the Swahili language, the religion of Islam, Islamic law, and urban living. By way of this cultural milieu, it has been possible for Africans of any tribe to be inducted and incorporated into town life with a certain coherence. This is equally true of other coastal towns, such as Tanga and Mombasa, but the effect was less pervasive in the latter case because of its geographical, ethnic, and political isolation from the hinterland. The latter is also true of Tabora, the inland metropolis of the old caravan route. The Germans strengthened and generalized the older influence of the Arab and Swahili slave caravans in establishing Swahili as the accepted national language of Tanganyika and giving all administrative centers and towns an important Swahili element. In light of this, it is somewhat surprising to find that, at the 1957 census, there were only 1,000 Swahili and 400 Shirazis in Dar es Salaam. This underlines the fact that the Swahili language, culture, and way of life, pervasive and important though it is in Tanganyika, is a secondary culture, knitting together diverse peoples through their adoption of it; but it is the sole or primary culture of only a very few. It is consistent with the argument that Swahili culture both represents and facilitates an urban way of life that we find the two sexes much more equally balanced numerically in Dar es Salaam than in Nairobi, Kampala, and most other towns of the interior. In the African population as a whole, females are 73.4 per cent of the male numbers in Dar es Salaam. The highest relative percentage of females to males is found in the case of the Haya (245), Manyema (115), Zaramo (88), Shirazi (86), Doe (83) and Ndengereko (80). (See Table 12–6.)

Table 12–6

Dar es Salaam (1957)

ALL RACES	
African	93,363
Arab	2,545
European	4,479
Indian	27,441
Somali	11
others	903
Total	128,742

AFRICAN ETHNIC GROUPS			
Tribe	Male	Female	Total
Zaramo	18,085	15,875	33,960
Rufiji	3,693	2,694	6,387
Luguru	3,615	1,978	5,593
Nyamwezi	2,341	1,713	4,054
Ndengereko	1,933	1,546	3,479
Ngindo	1,762	1,352	3,114
Yao	1,707	1,189	2,896
Nyasa	1,530	1,022	2,552
Ngoni	1,393	964	2,357
Pogoro	1,567	784	2,351
Makonde	1,388	743	2,131
Mwera	1,314	577	1,891
Manyema	777	893	1,670
Matumbi	905	711	1,616
Hehe	741	433	1,174
Haya	325	798	1,123
Swahili	600	423	1,023
Zigua	590	431	1,021
Makua	546	248	794
Sukuma	488	299	787
Nyakusa	460	261	721
Bondei	388	270	658
not stated	495	152	647
Gogo	458	127	585
Luo	394	188	582
Kutu	321	225	546
Kwere	305	196	501
Digo	292	198	490

Table 12–6 (*Continued*)

Tribe	Male	Female	Total
Rangi	358	90	448
non-Africans	240	183	423
Chagga	299	102	401
Shirazi	211	181	392
Mbunga	220	152	372
Doe	178	147	325
Mawia	193	121	314
Fipa	186	123	309
Wemba or Bemba	150	102	252
Sambaa	178	72	250
Kuria	154	91	245
Sagara	143	96	239
Kinga	184	49	233
Bena	157	70	227
Pare	149	68	217
Turu	120	84	204
other immigrants	94	110	204
Kenya	133	62	195
Iramba	113	80	193
Nyika	93	73	166
Northern Rhodesia	100	58	158
Ganda	88	63	151
others	85	58	143
Zanzibar and Pemba	83	45	128
Segeju	63	50	113
all others	1,462	896	2,358
Total	53,847	39,516	93,363

SOURCE: East African High Commission, East African Statistical Department, *General African Census, August 1957,* "Tribal Analysis: Tanganyika Population Census" (Nairobi: 1958).

As the local people, the Zaramo have obviously taken extensively to town life, although they have not been able to dominate it socially or politically. The same is likely to be true of their immediate neighbors, the Ndengereko, who are very similar. The extraordinarily high figure for the Haya reflects the fact that for various historical reasons Haya women are attracted from the distant western shores of Lake Victoria to practice prostitution in Dar es Salaam and, indeed, also in Kampala, Nairobi, and Mombasa, whereas only small numbers of Haya men migrate because of their involvement with a relatively prosperous coffee-growing economy at home. The Manyema are an essentially urban group, made up of descendants of slaves and mutineers from the Congo, without attachment to any rural part of Tanganyika. The small Doe group belongs to the vicinity of Bagamoyo and probably acquired a fairly long-term acquaintance with small-scale urban living in that town.

HOUSING AND SEGREGATION

Although the European colonial ruling class established the East African towns in their present form and the heterogeneous Asian population moved rapidly into them for purposes of trade, commerce, and lower civil service employment, the urban participation of Africans was little considered at first, except on the coast where small mixed urban populations of Africans already existed, though most of them were probably of slave status.

In the colonial situation, the towns were an administrative necessity and inevitable communications centers. Africans were immediately involved as headmen, laborers, servants, police, and soldiers. But in all these capacities, they were even domestically, as well as economically, dependent on the plans made for them by non-African employers and rulers. Their needs were recognized early in Dar es Salaam, where the Germans efficiently laid out the town in plots where Africans could erect their own simple house structures of coral blocks, mud and wattle, and coconut-palm-leaf thatch, as they are still doing there to this day. Undoubtedly, this made for a more balanced urban development in Dar es Salaam from certain points of view, if we neglect, for the moment, the complicated question of what effect this urban involvement had on the Africans concerned. The Zaramo, who form the largest African ethnic group in Dar es Salaam, are characterized by considerable family and marital instability. Nor can they be said to have made a well-recognized contribution to the development of Tanganyika. How far their present characteristics are due to their traditional culture, or its reaction to Islamic religion, Islamic law, and urban life, cannot be certainly stated.

Something of the same development of African built and owned housing occurred in Tanga and, to a lesser extent, in Mombasa where less adequate provision was made for it, and land on Mombasa Island was severely limited. There was a similar self-built estate in Nairobi, but of very limited extent, so that rather than setting a standard in housing and family life, it became notorious for high rents, overcrowding, bad sanitation, prostitution, violence, and crime. Africans in Nairobi were forced to depend mainly on the always inadequate housing which various local authorities were prepared to provide.

It is important at this point to note the inevitable quantitative inadequacy of officially provided housing in these circumstances. For Africans at this stage of economic development, adequate housing could not conceivably have been provided unless the efforts of Africans were themselves harnessed to the constructive effort, as was generally the case in Tanganyika, but not in Kenya. In Uganda, the situation was slightly different. Very little housing was officially provided, except for civil servants, until some years after World

War II when the government woke up to the magnitude of the problem with something of a shock. Nor, however, were Africans specifically prevented from providing their own accommodation, since this was often possible on African-controlled land quite near the towns; whereas, in Kenya, the rigid non-African control of land use, both in and around many towns, precluded this.

No African country, whether colonial or independent, liberal or oppressive, can afford to build enough housing for its urban population, with the possible exception of the few very rich mining centers, such as the Rhodesian and Katanga copperbelt, the Williamson diamonds town at Mwadui in Tanganyika. Indeed, it is often paradoxically the least liberal countries that have the most to show in urban housing development, as a conscious effort to support their emphasis on economic rather than political development.[17]

At the beginning of the century, the European, Asian, and African racial blocks—highly divided by faction and heterogeneity, though they were also divided internally—had hardly anything in common. Food, dress, language, religion, and family structure divided them fundamentally. It would have taken more than starry-eyed idealism to get them all to live together in an unsegregated fashion. *De facto* segregation was inevitable at this stage, undoubtedly taken for granted and desired by all. It was only the quality of facilities that was in dispute.

The Europeans usually took the hills and slopes as more salubrious and attractive. Selfish though this may have been, it was also obviously inevitable. Europeans were still dying like flies from blackwater fever and other tropical diseases (even Nairobi was highly malarial). If they were to survive at all, they had to take the best there was. Indeed, for this reason, the government medical service was given almost a stranglehold over urban planning, which it retained until the last few years. A striking corollary of this arrangement was that, except in Tanganyika, any structure of the simple kind that Africans could hope to build with their slender economic resources was legally prohibited in all towns. There was understandable panic about possible outbreaks of plague. When plague actually occurred in the early days of the Asian bazaar in Nairobi, the European administrators burned it down several times. Perhaps credit must be given to this efficiency for the increasing rarity of plague in towns, but the threat of it was still invoked half a century later in support of the rigid housing rules.

As economic differentiation of the African population proceeded after World War II, these restrictive housing rules became less completely cramping, as more and more better paid employees could afford accommodation of the officially provided type. Besides, the rules themselves were being relaxed in most places by this time. But it still remains true that housing for the unskilled workers who remain the majority is totally inadequate in

---

[17] Estimates (never very reliable and usually conservative) gave Nairobi requiring accommodations for 26,000 people in 1947, 20,000 in 1953. Mombasa needed housing for 27,000. (East Africa Royal Commission, *Report 1953–1955*, Cmnd. 9475, p. 211.)

Kenya and Uganda. For them, urban family life is hardly possible, even if desired. The main alternatives are to sponge on better-off relatives, to live in bachelor accommodation such as bed spaces, whereby legally perhaps four or illegally twice as many men live in the same small room, or else to go outside the city limits where temporary grass huts can be built and occupied with impunity. In many ways, the latter alternative seems to them the most desirable.

The segregation issue itself was settled gradually. Since, as already remarked, the towns inevitably start with a *de facto* segregation, this set the pattern for some time to come, and it was only with the building boom of the 1950's that towns were sufficiently expanded to eclipse the original pattern. Medical and planning authorities in Kampala during World War I intended to impose a rigid regime of racially segregated areas with wide unoccupied sanitary zones between each. However, the secretary of state for the colonies in London ruled against this after the war, and, from that time, segregation in Uganda had no legal basis, though a few tied-plot covenants may have remained. Nonetheless, it is doubtful whether as many as half a dozen middle- or upper-class Africans lived in private housing in Kampala by the mid 1950's. Most superior housing was still provided by the government or commercial firms for their senior European and, to some extent, Asian staff. Both Europeans and Asians were beginning to invest in housing in the town, partly because, in any case, it was difficult legally for them to get sites on African land outside. Correspondingly, it would have been foolish, however desirable from the point of view of social policy, for a wealthy African to build in Kampala, when both sites and building costs were so much lower outside in Mengo and the surrounding countryside where their relatives, friends, and familiar way of life were all to be found. The poorer Africans in town were either in domestic quarters attached to non-African housing; in special estates, such as those of the railways or the police; or in spatially, though not necessarily legally, segregated African housing estates.[18] In all the towns of East Africa, it was only on the eve of independence, by the late 1950's, that both governments and commercial firms were beginning to acquire appreciable numbers of senior African staff and to house them freely in what had previously been, if only by default, European and Asian urban housing.

URBAN STRATIFICATION

We have seen how far the towns of East Africa have been a European and Asian rather than an African enterprise, despite the steps toward urban life that had already been taken in the ancient Afro-Arab settlements of the

---

[18] It was a final absurdity of the system which had accumulated that Asians could not be accommodated in the Kampala Housing Estates because they were partly built with African Development funds derived from the levy on African-grown cotton and coffee and therefore were required to be spent exclusively on welfare of Africans.

coast and in the capitals of the kings of Buganda and some other lesser inland potentates. This is inevitably a sore point with the rulers and leaders of new African nations, who are bound to seek desperately for means of making their towns seem and feel more African. The fact that Africans did not—and most still do not—wish to live permanently in towns has meant that their temporary presence there was not taken very seriously, and arrangements made for them often had a makeshift quality until recently.

The towns have already been transformed by the corollaries of independence, the transfer of large numbers of senior posts—both in government and business—to Africans, bringing a sizable African elite into urban residence for the first time. Meanwhile, higher education has been proceeding apace and swelling the ranks of urban professional personnel. Despite the handover of power, the number of Europeans has not fallen. There are even more foreigners now, with diplomatic missions and technical aid, as well as the remaining teachers, missionaries, and businessmen, than there were before; but many of them are even more short-term residents of these African towns than the previous administrators were. So there is an important but unstable plural element in the urban community. The African elite, with its great internal ethnic diversity, must now form the focus for the activities of most of the non-African population, as well as tie together—through their urban and national participation—the diverse threads which run out into the multiplicity of languages and cultures and local ways of which the new nation is composed. Many of the crucial events in the establishment and development of the new East African nations necessarily take place in their capital cities and are part of their urban life.

The status of an African in the urban community depends on much the same factors that it would anywhere else, but with a somewhat different emphasis. It depends mainly on the length of time he stays in town, his education, and occupational status. Inherited wealth is not yet very important, except among the Baganda and small numbers of notable families elsewhere. But birth in an educated family is of great importance, because of the enormously greater chance it gives of another good education, which is more a key to status here than in most communities, because of the flexibility of the urban structure in this formative stage. Kinship undoubtedly tempers status differences and inhibits the hardening of class lines. Whether through polygamy or repetitive monogamy, kin networks remain extensive, so that many people of very different status, wealth, power, and sophistication, nonetheless, retain a profound sense of mutual belonging and obligation. Although kin groups, as such, do not survive in town, great efforts are made to restrict kin obligations by those sufficiently well placed to suffer heavily from a superfluity of begging relatives.

All people in town move in an urban structure, not a tribal structure. But tribal bonds are invoked, according to position. The unskilled move in work situations where tribal values cannot prevail; although jobs may be obtained and passed from kinsman to kinsman, and small enclaves of tribal monopoly become established. But outside work, they depend greatly on such elements of tribal culture and tribally based relationships that they can cling to in town, for they have little else. This may be somewhat less important in Dar es Salaam and Tanganyika generally, where Swahili urban culture provides more of an acceptable common medium than exists elsewhere. It is also true that a number of the most numerous peoples in Dar es Salaam are in any case much less distinct in language and culture than is the case either in Nairobi or Kampala-Mengo, with their greater ethnic gulfs between Bantu, Nilotic, Nilo-Hamitic, Sudanic, and others.

In all big towns, tribal associations are formed, though it is only a minority who are really active in them at any one time. They are an important mechanism of social security and even provide channels for the gradual transcendence of tribal separatism. Whereas the unsophisticated form intimate, though often ephemeral groups of close tribal relatives, the more ambitious organize more formal bodies purporting to influence and speak for whole tribes. Even more successful social climbers have to divest themselves tactfully of direct tribal involvements as they move into the interethnic social world of the elite. But very few, even of the elite, can dispense with tribal ties, for they are an indispensable source of clientage and support. A leader who fails in this field will rarely succeed in any other. But such tribal support, though essential, must be manipulated with discretion and somewhat behind the scenes, since national and international contexts must be phrased in a totally different idiom.[19]

URBAN ADMINISTRATION

The colonial urban administration was simply an aspect of general administration. The smaller urban settlements were dealt with directly by district commissioners as a minor but troublesome part of their duties for many years. The developments of the last few decades, and more particularly during the 1960's, have been to give the larger towns administrative boards, nominated at first, but increasingly elected in recent years. Their membership was largely European at first, but since World War II has become increasingly Asian and African, culminating in recently achieved African majorities, while retaining a number of full-time expatriate professional staff. Nairobi became a municipality in 1919,[20] Dar es Salaam and Kampala

---

[19] For more detail on this question, see D. J. Parkin, "Urban Voluntary Associations as Institutions of Adaptation," *Man*, Vol. I, No. 1 (March 1966); and A. W. Southall, "The Concept of Elites and Their Formation in Uganda," in P. C. Lloyd (ed.), *The New Elites in Tropical Africa* (New York: Oxford University Press, 1966).

[20] Mary Parker, *Political and Social Aspects in the Development of Municipal Government in Kenya, with Special Reference to Nairobi* (London: Colonial Office, 1950).

in 1949. Now there are over a dozen municipalities in East Africa, consisting of the largest towns, with the most promising revenue opportunities, which can be handed over to the responsibility of elected mayors and councils, though the central government still has to provide up to half the finance and inevitably retains ultimate control over certain policy decisions. This process has also been accompanied by increasing unification of responsibility, bringing African housing areas, formerly often under other authorities, directly into the orbit of city councils. This was particularly vital in view of the fact that such areas are now likely to supply a substantial proportion of city councillors.

The concentration of Asians, Europeans, and non-Africans generally in the towns, and Europeans now mainly in the larger towns, coupled with the ethnic spatial differentiation which persists from early segregation, gives non-Africans much greater representation in urban authorities than in national parliaments. This may continue for some time, but depends partly on the reaction of non-Africans to the new citizenship laws, which is itself not yet clear. Most probably there will be comparatively few European citizens, but a substantial number of Asians, despite the undoubtedly large flow of the latter back to India. Citizenship problems obtrude even on the Africans, for the large numbers of Kenyans in Kampala, including many highly paid professionals, do not have the rights of citizens and feel very insecure.

The highly bureaucratic, civil-servant type of urban administration during the colonial period was relatively immune to the pressures of undue influence and graft. A certain *esprit de corps* among the close-knit small groups of Europeans tempered such influences or simply removed them to a different context. If the old-boy network, based on former school ties, works well enough on a personal basis, corruption as such is unnecessary. Until recently, Africans were not in an economic position to exert corrupt pressure. It was the Asians who were almost forced into such methods. Their anxious situation as neither rulers nor indigenous inhabitants, the undoubted prejudice displayed toward them by many Europeans and Africans alike, their restriction to the towns, and the narrow outlets permitted to their wealth and initiative when successful left them few alternative methods and subjected them to almost irresistible temptations. A permit for a shop, a license for a bus route, a blind eye to some tax offense—all these and many other such familiar contexts could lead to the dispatch of welcome gifts, such as a case of whiskey to the crucial official whose favorable word or silence was required. It is doubtful whether it worked very often. But the growth of the urban economy and democratization of its government will lead to the same problems as anywhere else in the world. Whether the new East African city councillors set out to profit from their positions or not, they are faced with a problem new to East Africa—how to represent popular interest and how to mould powerful economic pressures into some conformity with them. Kampala City Council's refusal, early in 1964, to accept the low tender for construction of a new gasoline station and insistence on accepting a high tender, proffered on behalf of one of its own members, was a sign of things to come.

CONCLUSION

Apart from the three capitals and the three or four other important towns, all the rest are very small. Moreover, the dominance of the capital cities is increasing. Sociologically, they are becoming more like true cities. Their elites largely coincide with the national elites, and now these belong irrevocably to the country, not to some motherland overseas, thus redeeming the foreign intrusion of the modern city into rural Africa. The dramatic events of nationhood are played out in these cities, which are the planning centers of the nation as well as the models for all other towns in it.

There remains an ambiguity and ambivalence about the nascent culture of these cities, which is again a sign that they are playing something of the historic cultural role of cities. For the ambiguity and ambivalence of new African nationhood is most agonizing in them. All the crucial unanswered questions affect them deeply: the type of national economy which is to emerge; the longer-term political goals; the roots of nationhood in the multiplicity of subcultures and mutually unintelligible languages out of which a national and urban culture must be forged; how such culture will stand in relation to the future of the subcultures, on the one hand, and, on the other, the strong currents of pan-Africanism and the powerful penetration of world culture and technology from both East and West. The fine efforts of the national theaters, though led by expatriates, have created African national forms of drama, music, and dance. The changing of street names from colonial to national heroes, from Delamere to Kimathi, Lugard to Lumumba; the crowds at the football matches; the lack of African films and low attendance; the sundowners and the nightclubs are all indicators of the contemporary cultural situation—of the efforts being made and of the inherent difficulties of urban decolonization.

The integrating forms of a new African urban culture can only be worked out by the elite; for however much they too depend ultimately on local and tribal support, they have more chance to see above the welter of these factions. The urban middle class is still small, flexible, mobile, and unstable—not yet clearly or acceptably differentiated from strata above and below. But this process is proceeding apace, and it is certain that class differentiation is increasing, however contrary to national and pan-African philosophy this may be. The mass of unskilled workers are the most temporary and the least involved. Apart from the work situation, which is effectively beyond their control (for those influential in labor unions are of much higher, almost elite status), the masses will inevitably continue to live much of their urban life in the solace of ethnically based networks and subcultural pockets.

The urban culture which is emerging is not only heterogeneous but pluralistic. It has many parts and no single focus, nor is any body of influential persons clear as to what such focus should be. It reflects its multitribal background and the fact that the very necessary transcendence of this leaves the emergent African in something of a vacuum, feeling either saddled with a second-hand version of some European culture or with a vague pan-Africanism which gives no more sense of intrinsic belonging to his own nation than to any other in the continent. It reflects the colonial past in the number of foreigners at the higher economic and social levels of the urban community, however much the older ingredients of British, German, Greek, Italian, or Indian have been flavored with new elements from these nations and the addition of Americans, Israelis, Russians, and Chinese. The most crucial cultural requirement is probably the further coalescence of the urban elite, with a way of life which is its own, whatever it may be. The process has begun and will undoubtedly continue; but even in these days of rapid social change, it is very doubtful whether much can be done to speed it up before at least another generation is reared into this new world.

SELECTED BIBLIOGRAPHY

Abrahams, R. G. "Kahama Township, Western Province, Tanganyika," in A. W. Southall (ed.), *Social Change in Modern Africa*. New York: Oxford University Press, 1961.

Blij, Harm de. *Dar es Salaam*. Evanston, Ill.: Northwestern University Press, 1964.

Churchill, Winston S. *My African Journey*. London: Hodder and Stoughton, 1908.

Fallers, Lloyd A. (ed.). *The King's Men*. New York: Oxford University Press, 1964.

Great Britain, *East African Royal Commission 1953–1955 Report, Part IV, Conditions for Urban Development*, Cmnd. 9475, London: H.M.S.O., 1955.

Gutkind, P. C. W. *The Royal Capital of Buganda*. The Hague: Mouton and Company, 1963.

———. "Some Problems of African Urban Family Life: An Example from Kampala," *Zaire*, XV (1961).

Hill, M. F. *Permanent Way, East African Railways and Harbours*. Nairobi: East African Railways and Harbours, 1950.

Kendall, H. *Town Planning in Uganda*. London: Crown Agents, 1955.

Larimore, A. E. *The Alien Town, Patterns of Settlement in Busoga, Uganda: An Essay in Cultural Geography*. Department of Geography Research Paper No. 55., Chicago: University of Chicago, 1958.

Leslie, J. A. K. *A Survey of Dar es Salaam*. London: Oxford University Press, 1963.

Molohan, M. J. B. *Detribalization*. Dar es Salaam: The Government Printer, 1957.

Munger, E. S. *Relational Patterns of Kampala, Uganda*. Department of Geography Research Paper No. 21, Chicago: University of Chicago, 1951.

Parker, Mary. *Political and Social Aspects in the Development of Municipal Government in Kenya, with special reference to Nairobi*. London: H.M.S.O., 1950.

Parkin, D. J. "Urban Voluntary Associations as Institutions of Adaptation," *Man*, Vol. I, No. 1 (March 1966).

Smart, J. *Nairobi, a Jubilee History*. Nairobi: East African Standard, 1950.

Sofer, C., and R. Sofer, *Jinja Transformed*. London: East African Standard, 1955.

Southall, A. W. "Determinants of the Social Structure of African Urban Populations," in *Social Implications of Industrialization and Urbanization in Africa South of the Sahara*. For UNESCO by International African Institute, 1956.

———. "Kinship, Friendship and the Network of Relations in Kisenyi, Kampala," in A. W. Southall (ed.), *Social Change in Modern Africa*. New York: Oxford University Press, 1961.

———. "Population Movements in East Africa," in K. M. Barbour, and R. M. Prothero (eds.), *Essays on African Population*. London: Routledge and Kegan Paul, 1961.

———. "Race and Class in an African Town," *Sociological Journal* (Makerere), I (1963).

———. "The Concept of Elites and Their Formation in Uganda," in P. C. Lloyd (ed.), *The New Elites in Tropical Africa*. New York: Oxford University Press, 1966.

———, and P. C. W. Gutkind. *Townsmen in the Making*. Kampala: East African Studies, No. 9, E.A.I.S.R., 1957.

Vining, R. "A Description of Certain Spatial Aspects of an Economic System," *Economic Development and Cultural Change*, III (January 1955).

Walmsley, R. W. *Nairobi: The Geography of a New City*. Nairobi: The Eagle Press, 1957.

White, Thornton. *Nairobi: Master Plan for a Colonial Capital*. London: H.M.S.O., 1948.

Wilson, G. M. "Mombasa, a Modern Colonial Municipality," in A. W. Southall (ed.), *Social Change in Modern Africa*. New York: Oxford University Press, 1961.

———. *Mombasa Survey*. Unpublished manuscript.

13

Education

Carol Fisher

INTRODUCTION

Western-oriented education was begun in East Africa in the late 1890's and early 1900's with the coming of the Christian missionaries. Mission schools were opened as early as 1860 in Malawi and 1877 in Uganda. Though spread thinly, the missionaries, in cooperation with colonial administration, slowly began to develop a systematic program of education for Africans. By the end of World War II, awakening nationalism and interest in East Africa developed pressures for an increase in the quantity and quality of education. Table 13–1 shows the growth of pupil enrollment over the last twenty years.

Though the educational emphasis was often on simple literacy and on the development of basic technological skills, the African student absorbed much more than this from the beginning. The humanities, history, government, and social sciences became a part of the intellectual heritage of the schools. Expectations of higher standards of living and of justice and equality in government developed as the students applied these concepts to the facts of their own lives. As they experienced the frustration of non-fulfillment of these new expectations, the generative spirit of nationalism grew and flourished. The schools then, especially the secondary schools from which only a few found opportunity for higher education, fostered the leaders in East African nationalism.

This process, ably described by Helen Kitchen in *The Educated African,*[1] is a phenomenon of prime importance in the twentieth-century history of East Africa, but today it is just that—a phenomenon of the past. East African nationalism has achieved its initial goal. Independence has been won. The expectations of justice and equality, of freedom and a better life, must now become institutionalized within the fabric of newly independent political states. The next commanding task of the leadership is to institutionalize the revolutionary spirit—to give form, meaning, and stability to

---

[1] Helen A. Kitchen (ed.), *The Educated African* (New York: Frederick A. Praeger, 1962).

Table 13-1

African Enrollment—Uganda and Tanganyika, 1955–1960

	1955	1960
Uganda[a]		
primary	246,081	345,834
junior secondary	6,799	18,122
senior secondary	2,946	3,815
teacher-training	3,310	3,182
technical-vocational	3,239	4,348
Total	262,375	375,301
Tanganyika[b]		
primary and		
middle school	340,574	431,056
secondary	1,893	4,645
teacher-training	2,442	1,441
technical-vocational	929	2,075
Total	345,838	439,217

[a] *Uganda Government Statistical Abstract 1962* (Entebbe: Government Printer, 1962). Aided Schools Only.

[b] *Tanganyika Government Statistical Abstract 1962* (Dar es Salaam: Government Printer, 1962).

national independence.[2] A great part of this task rests squarely on the educational system and on those responsible for its direction and administration.

The pattern of education throughout East Africa is an inheritance from the colonial administration and is an adaptation of the British educational system that requires a number of set selection examinations. In general, the system included a lower primary, Standards I–IV, followed by a selection examination for admission to the upper primary or middle school, Standards V–VIII. An examination set by the mother country was administered after Standard VIII to determine admission to four-year secondary schools. After two years of secondary, Forms I and II, another examination, the Junior Certificate, was required for continuation. After Form IV, students took an external examination, the Cambridge Overseas School Certificate examination, prerequisite for admission to institutions of higher learning. The four years of secondary curriculum was largely determined by the requirements of the Cambridge examinations. A few schools offered an additional two years of secondary, Forms V and VI, leading to the Higher School Certificate, receipt of which qualified for admission to British universities and to Makerere. The latter is now a branch of the University of East Africa in

[2] Fred G. Burke, *Africa's Quest for Order* (Englewood Cliffs, N.J.: Prentice-Hall, 1964), p. 8.

Kampala, Uganda. In addition, each country also developed specialized vocational and teacher-training institutions. Malawi introduced a junior secondary of two years after Standard VIII leading to the Junior Certificate to prepare pupils for vocational and teacher training. This 4 4 4 system was designed to offer a four-year minimum program for all children initially and eventually, as expanded facilities developed, eight years of schooling for all. At each of the separation stages, enrollment dropped off sharply. (See Tables 13–2 and 13–3.)

Table 13–2

African Enrollment—Kenya, 1960

secondary	Form IV	975
	Form III	1,177
	Form II	1,545
	Form I	1,712
intermediate	VIII	17,153
	VII	23,230
	VI	29,606
	V	37,745
primary	IV	147,555
	III	145,782
	II	153,138
	I	171,656

SOURCE: Great Britain, Colonial Office, *Report on the Colony and Protectorate of Kenya, 1961* (London: H.M.S.O., 1961).

Table 13–3

African Enrollment—Malawi, 1960

secondary	Form IV	104
	III	104
junior secondary	II	544
	I	726
senior primary	VI	6,092
	V	7,515
	IV	9,802
junior primary	III	25,764
	II	29,610
	I	41,705
	B	62,981
	A	101,694

SOURCE: *The Phillips Report, Committee of Inquiry into African Education* (Zomba, Nyasaland: The Government Printer, 1962).

Recently introduced changes include an integrated system in Tanganyika with an eight-year primary and a four-year secondary program, though the new five-year development plan includes provisions for developing a seven-year primary program;[3] Kenya retains the three four-year system of primary, intermediate, and secondary. Uganda's program contains a primary course of six years, two years of junior secondary, and a four-year secondary school. Here, too, it has been recommended that the primary course absorb the junior secondary and extend for a total of seven years.[4] Malawi has recently shortened the primary course to six years and lengthened the secondary to five years.

The educational system inherited from colonial days not only nurtured the technological and governmental expectations that led eventually to independence, but it also fostered the disassociative processes characteristic of rapid acculturation and introduced a new series of disparities in areas already handicapped in achieving national unification by disparate peoples and cultures.

It is the purpose of this chapter to examine the nature of the disparities fostered by Western-oriented educational systems and contemporary East African policy in this regard.

DIFFERENTIATION IN EDUCATIONAL OPPORTUNITIES

One of the earliest differentiations made in the administration of schools in East Africa was the decision to segregate schools primarily on a racial basis and secondarily on religious grounds. It was reasoned that educational, cultural, religious, and racial differences necessitated separate and often separately administered schools. Different emphases, techniques, and curriculums would permit the educational system flexibility in meeting the needs of different groups. Missionary officials argued that their facilities were often overextended simply in administering to those of their persuasion—therefore, necessitating selection on the basis of religion. Moslem education concentrates almost exclusively on religious instruction with little room for a formal educational curriculum. In the early days of the establishment of the missions, the need for home support brought on competition between missions, both for converts and pupils, and, consequently, the burden of teaching became conversion. Table 13–4 shows the differentials in population and enrollment in segregated schools just prior to independence.

Apart from the psychological significance of racial and religious perception engendered by educational segregation, it soon became apparent that the schools differed in quality and quantity of education provided. Africans

---

[3] *Tanganyika's Five-Year Plan for Economic and Social Development, July 1, 1964–June 30, 1969* (Dar es Salaam: Government Publication, April 1964).

[4] *Report of the Uganda Education Commission, 1963* (Entebbe: The Government Printer, 1963).

Table 13–4

Population Estimates and School Enrollment—1961

	AFRICAN		EUROPEAN[a]		OTHER[b]	
	Population	Total Students	Population	Total Students	Population	Total Students
Kenya[c]	6,988,000	824,180 secondary 6,422	66,000	11,282 secondary 3,069	223,000	52,420 secondary 8,814
Uganda[d]	6,751,000	403,757 4,108	11,600	1,224 —	82,000	21,953 2,591
Tanganyika[e]	9,119,000	515,375 6,031	22,300	2,606 669	119,500	27,853 9,931
Malawi[f]	2,931,100	289,812 1,713	8,800	1,605 395	12,300	3,931 482

a Does not include students in schools outside the country.

b Includes Indo-Pakistani, Arab, Colored, and others.

c *Colonial Office Report on the Colony and Protectorate of Kenya* (London: H.M.S.O., 1963).

d *Uganda Government Statistical Abstract 1962* (Entebbe: Government Printer, 1962).

e *Tanganyika Government Statistical Abstract 1962* (Dar es Salaam: Government Printer, 1962).

f *Ministry of Education Yearly Report 1962* (Zomba: Government Printer, 1962), and *Statesmen's Yearbook 1963:* London: Macmillan & Company, 1963.

became conscious of a rank order of quality in schools. European schools were better equipped and staffed, and, though the pupils were charged a much higher tuition, it nevertheless appeared that more administrative time and money was devoted to European schools. The African held much the same view of the Asian schools. Though perhaps not so good as European schools, they appeared far superior to African schools. Thus the educational system fostered, not only a consciousness of racial and religious differences, but engendered a rank ordering in terms of associated superiority and inferiority.

In Uganda, as in the other areas, primary education had been segregated racially and religiously. Secondary education was in a different position, however, since European secondary students were sent abroad to Kenya's European schools. Nevertheless, in response to political pressure, in 1957, the Uganda government adopted a policy of ultimate integration of schools. In fact, the first integrated primary school in Uganda was opened in Entebbe in 1957. Intended for children of African members of government, the standards and fees were the same as in European primary schools, and English was the medium of instruction. Successful experiences led to qualified African and Asian children being admitted to European schools throughout the country.[5] Today the government policy is one of total integration—acceptance of students based solely on academic qualifications.

In Tanganyika and Kenya, a separate administration was maintained for Africans, Europeans, Asians, and "other non natives." Since the 1950's, there have been pressures in both countries toward integrated education. As early as 1950, a multiracial government school opened in Nairobi. Though a full primary school, plans today include expansion into a secondary school as well. In 1958, Tanganyika formed a committee to study integration. In the report published in 1960, the committee recommended a system for integration of the schools to be initiated in 1962.[6] A government White Paper incorporating the substance of the committee report was approved in Legislative Council, and the plan is now being implemented.

During Federation in the Rhodesias and Nyasaland, separate schools for Europeans, Asians, and Colored were maintained by the federal government. African education was the responsibility of the territory. With self-government and the dissolution of the Federation, Malawi (formerly Nyasaland) paradoxically, because the pressure for education is so great and the available schools so few, has made a decision to maintain temporarily separate European schools. Here too, however, there is great pressure for integrated schools.

A governmental decision to integrate schools—to determine admission solely on academic qualifications—relieves the political pressures but is fraught with problems of implementation and secondary decisions. What standard of academic qualification is to be adopted? What kind of tuition and fees when, typically, African schools are supported by government and European schools by tuition? What distribution of grants-in-aid to mission schools? How can the needs of the different interest groups be accommodated? What kinds of accommodations need to be made for the varying dietary, cultural, and religious backgrounds? In areas where there are too few schools, what will be the priorities for admission to primary schools? What is to be the language of instruction in integrated primary schools? These and a host of other secondary decisions are now slowly being worked out. Such plans for integration, however, are directed at racial segregation. Differentiations on religious grounds are more subtle.

Early missionaries in East Africa had nearly autonomous control over their schools and school policies for some years. Not until 1911 did Kenya have an education department. Tanganyika had its first Director of Education in 1911. Uganda established a Department of Education in 1925.[7] Even then, the missions maintained autonomy in instruction and administration.

---

[5] Wendell P. Jones, "An Overview of East African Education," *Phi Delta Kappa,* XLI (1960), p. 185.

[6] *Tanganyika—Report of the Committee on the Integration of Education 1959* (Dar es Salaam: Government Printer, 1960).

[7] G. W. Kingsworth and Zoe Marsh, *Introduction to the History of East Africa* (Cambridge: Cambridge University Press, 1963), p. 88.

The governments were responsible for setting standards, supervisory service, and providing financial subsidies. As the governments began to build schools, a three-fold system grew up—government schools administered and financed directly through government; grant-aided schools, generally mission schools subsidized by government funds; and private or nonaided schools, generally mission or African church schools independent of government subsidy. Today this division still exists, but nationalist fervor brought with it pressures for more central control and supervision for common curriculums and standards. In all cases, however, the governments have recognized the contributions that mission-supported schools are making in the education of African youth. Table 13–7 shows the number of African pupils in government schools, aided schools, and unaided schools in Kenya in 1960 and 1961. Most of the schools in the latter two categories are mission-operated or supported. (See Table 13–5.)

Table 13–5

African Enrollment in Kenya Schools by Category

	1960	1961	1962
primary			
government schools	841	998	1,663
aided schools	578,507	635,518	616,160
unaided schools	39,820	25,339	19,347
intermediate			
government schools	1,112	688	797
aided schools	104,298	152,136	245,001
unaided schools	2,314	3,079	1,837
secondary			
government schools	36	—	2
aided schools	4,770	6,224	8,119
unaided schools	603	198	934

SOURCE: 1960 and 1961 figures are from *Colonial Office Report on the Colony and Protectorate of Kenya* (London: H.M.S.O., 1963). 1962 figures are from *Kenya Government Statistical Abstract 1963* (Nairobi: Government Printer, 1963).

In the 1950's, East African governments began to charge local authorities with responsibilities for area education, generally primary education. With this development, the missions have a threefold administrative system: central government, the mission board, and the local authorities. The central ministries of education in each country are developing increased supervisory and administrative controls over mission schools. In Malawi, for example, placement of students in secondary mission schools is now formally on the basis of the Standard VII selection examination, and placement in the available schools is done by the central ministry. A count of students by religion in a Catholic secondary boarding school in 1963 shows thirty Catholics and one non-Catholic in Form III and twenty-six Catholics and twenty non-Catholics in Form I.

A recent education ordinance in Malawi establishes a new board of governors for a secondary Catholic school.[8] The board consists of ten members: four representatives of the Ministry appointed by the Minister; three representatives of the "proprietor" appointed by the proprietor; and three representatives of the community served by the school, two appointed by the Minister and one by the proprietor with the approval of the Minister. The board is responsible for general management, curriculum, and finance, though the property remains vested in the proprietor. Such central policies will be inclined to reduce the disparities that have grown out of selective religious identifications.

A third disparity heightened by East African education has been family and kin isolation. For the most part, missions tended to develop boarding schools. Especially from upper primary on, they were a means to ensure regular daily attendance, to provide systematic religious instruction and to accommodate students from distant areas. Until recently, filling the secondary schools and teacher-training institutions depended on recruitment over wide geographic areas and required boarding facilities. Still, today institutions of special character either teacher-training, vocational, or secondary, with special emphasis on science or the arts, as in Malawi, continue to draw from wide areas. Thus, a student who continues through Form IV might as well be away from home, except for an occasional holiday, for eight or ten years—or as much as fifteen or sixteen years if he goes on for higher education. His schoolmates during these years probably include few from his own area.

Combined with the isolation imposed by distance are the factors of developing cultural differences and new age-group associations among schoolmates. Reinforcement of traditional social values arising from family and kin solidarity is disrupted in the new circumstances, and such group solidarity as arises is based on developing values and school associations. In the earlier times of intense nationalism and today, as these nations attempt to build a national solidarity, this disassociative tendency is viewed as a not altogether unwelcome one. As the ties to isolate family and kin units weaken, the likelihood grows that the energies and loyalties of this group can be turned to the national unit. Nevertheless, if the distance—social and geographic—grows too great, this generation cannot act as the agents of cohesion between local and national purposes and loyalties. Though they have been initiated to meet a number of needs, several developments are relevant to this problem: local government has been strengthened in its responsibility for and contact with education in the local areas. Formal and informal contact between school personnel and parents of school children

---

[8] Government Notice No. 241, *The Education Ordinance* (Zomba: Government Printer).

has been increased. Where possible, graduates of sufficient education are given party and government positions in their areas of origin. A number of day schools are being constructed in population centers.

Each of these action programs, however, develop additional problems that must be met by administrative action. For example, since day schools are a new innovation, they may be viewed as less adequate than established institutions. Home-study conditions and supplies are often not adequate in these new schools. With reference to personnel placement, in Tanganyika and Malawi especially, trained personnel are in such short supply that national programs tend to use up those available. Local control of educational activities has been urged for some years. In a special study report to the United Nations in 1954, local control by the indigenous people was recommended as the only effective way to ensure the success of a rural school system, but by 1960 another special study again criticized all but Uganda for inadequate local participation.[9] Both reports, however, emphasized that the governments must provide adequate safeguards against inefficiency, injustice, or financial suicide.

Closely related to family and kin isolation is the rural-urban disparity initiated by the processes of colonial settlement and economic development but fostered also by education. As the governments began to respond to pressures for more education, they often located government schools in urban centers where the pressure was greatest. Though the students for these schools came from large areas of the country, it nevertheless prompted an image of governments favoring urban centers. More significant, graduates and those with vocational training gravitated to the urban centers for employment, further removing rural areas from the mainstream of economic and educational development. With independence, increased attention is being given to drawing the rural areas into full participation in the new national life. The effective networks of grass-roots politics have brought about an enormous increase in rural awareness. The educational policies mentioned above that are being implemented to ease the family and kin isolation relate also to this problem. The role of education, however, in the rural-urban dichotomy is paradoxical. Though rural education is increased, population centers will continue to have the higher enrollments and favorable employment for graduates. Education seems designed to foster the rural-urban dichotomy. However, imaginative educational development can do much to alleviate a disparity for which education is, to some extent, universally responsible.

A fifth disparity fostered by educational development in East Africa is the differential in the education of boys and girls. Table 13–6 shows this differential in Malawi in 1955 and 1960. Education for women and girls did

---

9 *U.N. Special Study on Educational Conditions in Non-Self-Governing Territories* (New York: U.N. Publications, 1954); and *United National Special Study on Educational Conditions in Non-Self-Governing Territories* (New York: U.N. Publications, 1960).

Table 13–6

Number of Girls in Schools in Malawi, 1955–1960

	Primary		Secondary		Teacher-Training		Vocational	
	1955	1960	1955	1960	1955	1960	1955	1960
government schools	119	1,337	—	32	—	—	—	—
aided schools	33,117	51,077	35	170	141	235	—	61
unaided schools	54,526	50,005	6	56	5	11	18	207
	87,762	102,419	41	258	146	246	18	268

SOURCE: *The Phillips Report, Committee of Inquiry into African Education* (Zomba, Nyasaland: Government Printer, 1962).

not receive the support and encouragement given to education for men and boys until recently. In Kenya in 1961, 1,391 pupils took the Cambridge Overseas School Certificate, of whom only 182 were girls.[10] In Tanganyika's secondary schools in 1961 there were 5,458 boys and 850 girls.[11] Though, in recent years, the situation is improving, still, in 1962, there were about seven times as many boys as girls in secondary schools in Malawi and about twice as many in all schools in Tanganyika. In all of East Africa, there are only a few women with university education. (See Table 13–7.)

Table 13–7

African Enrollment, Girls and Boys, 1955–1961

	1955		1961	
Uganda[a]	190,115	65,711	275,289	128,468
Tanganyika[b]	264,179	99,659	388,924	176,451

[a] Uganda 1955 figures from *Uganda Government Statistical Abstract, 1957* (Entebbe: Government Printer, 1957). Aided only. 1961 figures from *Uganda Government Statistical Abstract 1962* (Entebbe: Government Printer, 1962).

[b] *Tanganyika Government Statistical Abstract 1962* (Dar es Salaam: Government Printer, 1962).

A number of factors have militated against education for girls. Limited resources of parents and their belief that education for girls would yield no financial return led to a preference for investing what money they had in the education of their sons. Traditionally sons had greater freedom to seek out their fortunes away from the nuclear home—thousands in Malawi journeyed to the mines in Central and Southern Africa for work. Women, however,

[10] *Colonial Office Report on the Colony and Protectorate of Kenya* (London: H.M.S.O., 1963).

[11] *Colonial Office Report on the Colony and Protectorate of Tanganyika* (London: H.M.S.O., 1963).

remained at home. Thus, boarding schools fit more easily into the pattern of life for boys, but seriously disrupted the traditional values for girls. Many felt that a curriculum emphasizing literacy inculcated values and behavior in girls contrary to the traditional needs of rural life. In addition, parents often preferred early marriage for girls. Higher education delayed marriage. In some cases, parents disliked their daughters' being taught by men. Today adequately qualified women teachers are still in great shortage.

In the face of parental reluctance to send girls to school, the shortage of schools and teachers brought administrative decisions to concentrate on the education of boys. In recent years, however, the governments have recognized the seriousness of the educational gap that has developed. In 1962, the *Phillips Report* on education in Nyasaland emphasized the seriousness of this gap pointing up the importance of women for health and nutrition in the home, for rural improvement in areas where men are away for long pediods, for early socialization of children, and, with independence, for responsible political expression.[12]

A number of programs have been initiated to narrow the gap. Simply increasing the number of schools itself offers greater opportunity for girls. Emphasis on acceptance of qualified students, regardless of sex, has helped where there are coeducational schools. In some areas, schools formerly for boys have become coeducational. Curriculum adjustments for girls include domestic science, home care, garden care, and the care of children. There is an increase in teacher training available for girls. As early as 1954, Kenya government plans called for at least two women teachers in each primary school. Conversely, by 1957 in Tanganyika, some rural schools opened only for three or four years were closed for lack of enrollment, partly because of a department ruling that one-third of the school population must be girls.[13] The 1963 report of the Uganda Education Commission notes considerable progress in recent years, but re-emphasizes the problem of traditional attitudes toward the status of women. They make a number of recommendations, including an increase in the number of girls' high schools, curriculum modifications, financial assistance to parents, and appointment of a senior woman's officer in the Ministry of Education.[14] Community-development programs are emphasizing the role of women, and a number of special community training programs are for women. The women's arms of the national parties are sponsoring women's education programs and emphasizing the importance of education for girls.

There has often been an educational gap between husbands and wives,

---

[12] *The Phillips Report, Committee of Inquiry into African Education* (Zomba: The Government Printer, 1962).

[13] J. C. Stewart, "Problems in Southern Tanganyika," *Overseas Education,* XXVIII (1957), pp. 157–162.

[14] *Report of the Uganda Education Commission, 1963* (Entebbe: The Government Printer, 1963).

and, as the men in responsible positions are increasingly taking travel-and-study grants abroad, this gap increases. Seldom in the past have wives accompanied their husbands on such trips. Programs have been initiated for in-country training, generally in domestic science, for wives whose husbands are away. With the limited funds available, it is difficult to finance whole families abroad, but today each government favors such a policy whenever possible. In addition, Agency for International Development, Africa-America programs, and special foundation programs have sponsored travel-and-training grants just for East African women. In Kenya and Tanganyika, the women's seminar programs have organized women's groups to work together to foster increased opportunities for women. The gap is great, however, and again limited funds and the lack of trained personnel militate against a quick or easy solution.

Differences in language have always been responsible for disparities between people in East Africa. In Tanganyika alone, 120 languages are spoken. Early mission schools are generally taught in the vernacular of the area in the early grades, introducing the language of the mother country in the later grades. Today in Tanganyika, Swahili is used in the early grades; English in the higher grades. In Malawi, three languages are found in the lower grades. English is the medium of instruction throughout secondary school. Though the problem of language disparities permeates all areas of national development, its special relevance here has been the extent to which knowledge of the language of the mother country—English literacy—was a tool of educational and vocational advancement—the extent to which English became the difference between the "haves" and "have-nots." Each of the disparities that we have described above has been furthered by the language of education. Differentials between men and women, between the school boy and his family, between rural and urban areas, have been intensified by the mark of education—English literacy. The problem of racial consciousness and status inferiority was heightened by a recognition that vocational and educational advancement came through a rejection of the language of the ancestors.

With independence has come pressure for an indigenous lingua franca—an African language for an African nation. In Tanganyika, Swahili has been adopted as the national lingua franca. In Malawi, Chinyanja has been proposed as the language of the Legislative Council. Yet admission to schools of higher learning, external examinations, and participation in overseas training programs require a full command of English. Most of the textbooks and learning aids from Standards VII on are in English, and the task of re-equipping the schools, let alone retooling an indigenous language to include modern concepts in the social and physical sciences, at present demands too much of the limited financial and personnel resources available. English remains the language of instruction at the University of East Africa; and, in Malawi, a new curriculum introduces English in Standard I.

A more subtle, but nevertheless significant, effect of education is related to the expectations that parents and students hold about the results of education—from a promise of heaven to better jobs expectations. But, on the whole, the desire for education has mounted to monumental proportions in recent years. Throughout East Africa, there is a belief in schooling as an almost magical way to achieve money, prestige, status, power, health, a better life. Some expected too much and were bitter in their disappointment. Some expected the disassociations and value changes, the developing distance between the student and his family. Others did not, and the distance was thus intensified. But, generally, the positive expectations worked to heighten the disparities we have already discussed. As the numbers of young people wanting education rose beyond the capacity to place them in schools, money, background, influence, religion, location, and language facility became bases for selection and, in turn, focused attention on the educational importance of these differences. In some areas, precolonial disparities were reinforced by this effect. For example, by accident of location, some early mission schools favored the education of the ethnic group in their area, thus starting some tribes on the move to better education and jobs earlier than others—a head start still to be seen in the Northern Province of Malawi and in Uganda.

The system of examinations utilized in East African schools was a partial answer to this increased pressure on the school facilities. It was a natural answer, based on the British educational system. Higher education was geared to the British system, and admission depended on success in the externally set Cambridge examinations. Tables 13–2 and 13–3 show the sharp break-off points and pyramidal effect of this system. Examinations alone, of course, are not totally responsible for the severe dropouts or "wastage," but are in part a symptom of lack of facilities at the higher levels. In 1962, approximately 10,000 students in Malawi took the School Leaving Examination in Standard VIII. According to officers in the Ministry of Education, approximately one-half of these met passing standards, yet there were places in Form I for less than 1,000 new students. Each January, as the new school year began, the secondary school grounds were full of youngsters with school leaving passes but no school assignment, hopeful that somehow room could be found for them. This shortage has increased the importance placed on examination scores and not just passes, and the curriculum came to be tailored to the examinations. The higher the examination passed, the more status and prestige associated with it. Since most teacher-training institutions did not offer a curriculum leading toward one of the upper examinations, students in teacher training or vocational training felt they had less prestige and less chance to achieve prestige. Often, the students enrolled in these institutions were those who, though passing, had not scored high enough in the examinations to win a place in secondary schools. The headmaster of a teacher-training school in Malawi argued that a curriculum tailored to pass the Junior Certificate examination left little time for its primary job—that of teacher training. Yet, if the Junior Certificate were not included, the better students either did not come or spent their time studying on their own to sit for the examination. An astonishing number of people in teaching, clerical jobs, and the junior civil service are studying independently, preparing to sit for an examination, or are enrolled in correspondence courses in preparation for one of these examinations.

In areas where there are inadequate places in secondary schools for those qualified, a system of independent study for external examinations offers hope to those who do not get into regular schools. But to the extent that examination scores alone have become the measure of education, to the extent that each hour of each school day must be designed toward passing a section of an examination, to the extent that the level of examination passed measures the worth of the man, to that extent, the educational system has failed to meet the urgent needs of nation-building. The broader phenomenon of which each of these disparities are only a part is the social, cultural, economic, and valuational distance that develops between the educational "haves" and "have-nots"—phenomena related to education throughout the world, but especially acute in areas where "the nation" is a new and untried concept—where the "haves" are so few and the "have-nots" so many.

In 1953, Margaret Read made an eloquent and prophetic plea to the schools in Africa to use education creatively and imaginatively to bridge the gap between villages and the changing national directions.[15] In 1960, Edward Shils had this to say:

> The closing of this gap between the modernizing elite and the mass of the population is of prime importance. You close the gap through educating the masses. There is nothing quite comparable in Western countries like the wide divergence in the styles of life and the associated outlook of Africans with a Western education and those without it. . . . Where education is highly valued, on traditional religious grounds, on practical vocational grounds and because of the "mystique" of modernity, those who do not have it tend to feel themselves inferior to those who do and to feel cut-off from them.[16]

Both the amount and content of education are significant if the cultural gap is to be bridged. Most of the policies outlined here have been in response to the need for more education for the African, but this broader problem poses the question of content revision as well. The burden of the conversation today turns on "Africanization" of the curriculum.

In the judgment of many commentators on East African education, this social and cultural distance has been, in large measure, because the educational system has been too much a product of the Western mind and not enough of a reflection of the African mind. Examinations, set and administered in England, as we have seen, tended to cast the curriculum into

[15] Margaret Read, *Africans and Their Schools* (London: Longmans, Green and Company, 1953).

[16] Edward Shils, "Political Development in the New States," *Comparative Studies in Society and History*, II (1960).

rigid Western forms. In mission schools, the religious significance of old tribal customs was seen as interfering with the teachings of the new religions and often forbidden. Even though British educational policy formally took the position that education in East Africa ought to be adaptable to traditions and customs of Africans, informally, the pattern seldom took on such adaptations. "In Tropical Africa the educational needs are so obvious and compelling that extraordinary humility and perception is needed not to presume that the good in the indigenous system is so small that little harm can be done, and much time saved, if it were all done away with."[17] Reginald J. Mason goes on to say that, in their determination to eradicate ignorance and superstition, Western educators failed to utilize the indigenous systems.

The "mystique" of education, the belief in a magical quality in education, and the eagerness with which it is sought combine with the total Western character of education to intensify the inevitable distance between those with and those without education. Further, it tends to denegrate the worth of things "African" for those in, as well as out of, schools. Nationalism has brought with it the desire and the need to re-establish the worth and dignity of the African heritage. To this end, each country has undertaken extensive curriculum studies. One obvious approach is the present increase in African teachers—not only at the primary level, but in secondary schools, in teacher-training institutions, and on the staff of the University of East Africa. Inevitably, the curriculum from primary school on will tend to reflect more of the African milieu under the influence of an African teacher. But revision of the curriculum itself is a veritable Gordian's knot. To be done effectively, it must be consistent with and reflect national needs in all sections of politics and the economy. Further, curriculum revision quickly comes up against the requirements of the examination system. Students themselves are likely to be the first to object to a curriculum change that departs from the standard syllabus for the Cambridge examinations. Many of the officials responsible for the direction and content of education are themselves a product of this system, justifiably proud of its results and uneasy with deviations, though the 1961 Education Conference in Addis Ababa set curriculum revisions as the second order of priority in the development of African education.[18]

Africanization of the curriculum leads inevitably to the question of which traditions and values are to be introduced since there are wide cultural differences between peoples of East Africa. For example, in Malawi recently, a debate at a secondary school in English on whether *lobola* (the custom whereby a husband-to-be offers his prospective father-in-law a certain quantity of goods for his bride) ought to be abandoned ended with a near-tie among the students. Curiously, those who had practiced *lobola*

---

[17] Reginald James Mason, *British Education in Africa* (London: Oxford University Press, 1959).

[18] *Final Report, Conference of African States on the Development of Education in Africa, Addis Ababa (May 15–25, 1961)* (New York: U.N.).

traditionally tended to view it with disfavor and those whose cultural heritage did not include *lobola* tended to favor it. If the desire is to combine African and Western traditions, to what extent could a reaffirmation of African heritage be convincing in a secondary school classroom when the language of reaffirmation is itself non-African?

In 1955, Margaret Read listed three areas of African traditional education that, in her judgment, had been abandoned in the Westernized school systems. First, training for physical development and social recognition which included sex education; second, training in citizenship related to their particular ethnic group; and third, the activities that illuminated directly the deep emotional content of African life—i.e., music, folklore, art, and tribal dress.[19] Today these patterns are reappearing in East African schools; slowly and experimentally, they are working their way from extracurricular interests into the classroom itself.

These areas, however meaningful they are to traditional African life, are perhaps not really what is meant when an African speaks of Africanizing education. More to the heart of the matter is an elusive quality of African heart and mind that is illuminated in Professor Diamond's definition of "the primitive."[20] Among the attributes of the primitive identified by Diamond and directly relevant to Africanization are such qualities as these: "The ritual expression of the primary needs of the person in nature and society," "the responsibility of the individual to self and society," "the apprehension of consciousness throughout society and nature," "the emphasis on concrete particulars and contexts," "the full and manifold participation of individuals in nature and society," "the expression of society in the person and the person in society." Diamond goes on to say ". . . what primitives possess— the immediate and ramifying sense of the person, . . . we have largely lost. If we have the means, the tools, the forms, the rational imagination to transform the face of the earth and the contemporary human condition, primitive society at its most positive, exemplifies an essential humanity. That is what civilization must selectively incorporate."[21] This is what Africanization must mean: a creative integration of qualities such as these with the essentially Westernized educational system, rather than a mere re-establishment of specific cultural forms. If these attributes can be meaningfully integrated into the educational patterns of East Africa, the creative system thus delineated will fulfill its responsibility to the search for a meaningful national dignity.

---

[19] Margaret Read, "Education in Africa: Its Patterns and Role in Social Change," *The Annals of the American Academy of Political and Social Science,* CCLXXXXVIII (1955), pp. 170–179.

[20] Stanley Diamond, "The Search for the Primitive," in Iago Galdspon (ed.), *Man's Image in Medicine and Anthropology* (New York: International Universities Press, 1959), pp. 110–111.

[21] *Ibid.*

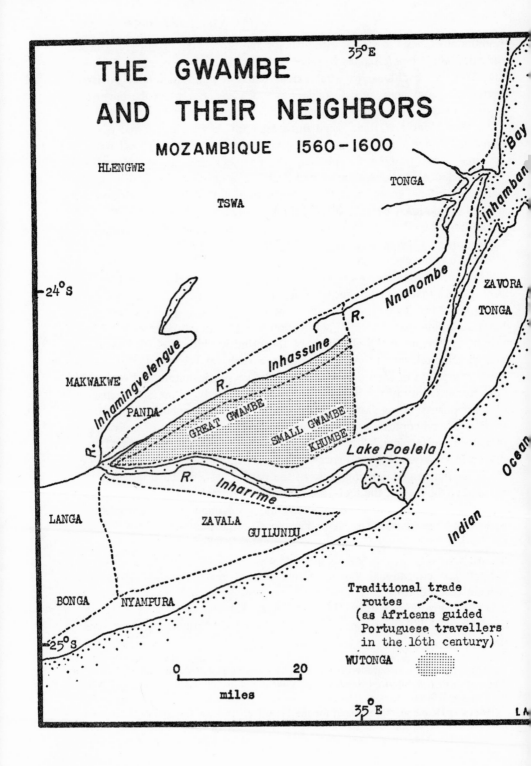

THE GWAMBE
AND THEIR NEIGHBORS
MOZAMBIQUE   1560-1600

35°E

HLENGWE

TONGA

Inhambane Bay

TSWA

24°S

R. Nnanombe

ZAVORA

TONGA

R. Inhamingvelengue

R. Inhassune

MAKWAKWE

PANDA

GREAT GWAMBE

SMALL GWAMBE

KHUMBE

Lake Poelela

R.

Indian Ocean

R. Inharrme

LANGA

ZAVALA

GUILUNDU

BONGA   NYAMPURA

Traditional trade
routes
(as Africans guided
Portuguese travellers
in the 16th century)

25°S

WUTONGA

0   20

miles

35°E

L A

14

Native and
Missionary Religions

Charles Edward Fuller

INTRODUCTION

Fr. Gonçalo da Silveira, a Jesuit missionary and the first to record ethnological observations of the Gwambe, a southeast African Bantu society, in 1560 and 1561 wrote firsthand of these people among whom he lived almost two years.[1] His letters, in addition to preserving useful descriptions, illustrate problems of field investigation and the difficulties of escaping a cultural bias. This priest, fully identified with Roman Catholicism, well educated in the contemporary Christian view of the beliefs and practices of Islam, found the Gwambe and other Bantu lacking in the familiar aspects of religion and wrote:

---

[1] In the map, the area of first pioneer missionary activity in East Africa is shown as Wutonga, the land occupied by the Gwambe, who had migrated there from the mountainous interior of East Africa prior to the sixteenth century. All the tribes or culture units marked in capital letters then occupied, and now occupy, approximately the same areas.

The missionary activities of Father Gonçalo da Silveira and his companion among the Gwambe took place in Wutonga. Traveling from the town of Inhamnae, on the Inhambane Bay (existent in the fifteenth century under these same names), the priests followed the River Matamba route to the Gwambe. Later they traveled down the Nyanombe and traded with the people of this fertile area. The entire "court" of the Gwambe was converted to Christianity and remained nominally true to certain Christian beliefs and customs several decades after the departure of the priests. The Jesuits also evangelized near Inhambane during their travels.

Father Gonçalo da Silveira was martyred among the "Monomotapa" people northwest of Hlengwe, where he traveled to convert the "emperor" of Monomotapa, the head of one of the Shona groups then bearing the name still extant among the Shona as a major division, the Karanga. His records lead us to believe that the Gwambe had migrated from Karanga territory to escape the imposition of the military rule there.

This area is unique in East Africa as being the first to have a fully documented record of the pioneer missionary effort of Christian organizations on this coast.

"They seem to have no religion." A few lines later, he spoke of their worshipping a god whom they called Umbe and accurately described many of their beliefs and rites.[2]

In spite of a claim to objectivity, the ethnologist is one whose religiousness, anti-religiousness, or other attitude runs at some depth, conditioning his evaluation of religious beliefs and practices. A tinge of ethnocentricity, on one hand, or a romantic attachment and identification with "his people," on the other, makes a difference in his manner of seeing, reporting, and interpreting facts. Personality features which enable one to participate in and to understand an alien culture and require another to remain aloof, even beyond the pale of understanding, prescribe the limits of an anthropologist's characterization of the religion he observes. Every informant, too, is one in whom liabilities combine with assets, and one can never be sure when the African or other indigenous assistant is clearly thinking and reporting in the precise categories of culture which the questioning ethnologist is seeking to sound. Complications in communication, with or without an interpreter, are so apparent that most of us would agree in principle, at least, with Bronislaw Malinowski's insistence on prolonged residence in the society to be studied. These and many other peculiar conditions will confront the investigator of culture, determining the kinds of phenomena he will see or miss as he describes its religion.

The problems of field investigation are complicated by the long-recognized problem of definition which cannot be reviewed here. The greatest of all difficulties is the common tendency to define religion in terms of one of its aspects or with special deference to one's own particular religious inclinations. For the purpose of this account of East African religions, and basically applicable to the study of religion anywhere, religion is conceived in the following manner. Religion is a form of human behavior, an aspect of culture. It is the way in which members of a society perceive, think, will, act, and feel in relation to some superhuman powers by which they believe they are helped to fulfill one, another, or all human needs which individual and group effort, unaided, is inadequate to supply. Religion is not limited to some particular form of behavior, not to any specific function or need. In form, in function, or in both, religion may be almost indistinguishable from some other aspect of culture dealing with a similar human need. The difference is in meaning, for, in religion, behavior directed to various ends is related to some power not ordinarily conceived as pertaining to normal humans without some special endowment. This need not be conceived in some conventional notion of deity, but does carry an air of sacredness.

In approaching religion in this way, the student will not seek some pre-

---

2 A letter from Gonçalo da Silveira, August 9, 1560, from Gwambe to Goa, Reported in George McCall Theal, *Records of South Eastern Africa,* Vol. II (Capetown: Cape Colony Government, 1898), p. 81.

conceived pattern of rites and beliefs, nor will he confine his attention to some so-called spiritual function. Instead, he will be alert to observe any form of behavior with the function of meeting any human need. The distinctive feature for which he will search is the relation of the behavior to some power beyond normal human capacities, a power either helping or hindering in the satisfaction of the needs. No stereotyped concept of deity can be visualized as the goal of investigation, but only the result of empirical search and observation among the people being studied.

This definition and the conceptualization of research which is its corollary underlie this enquiry into East African religions. In contrast, we are forced by convention to think of Christianity and Islam in the institutional terms by which they have become familiar, and it is obvious that easy comparisons between the empirically observed, on one hand, and the conventionally described, on the other, could be misleading. For example, the elements of magic, spiritism, and divination persisting in Christianity, noted by trained, objective observers, are more easily overlooked because of our conventional conception of Christianity than are the same elements in an indigenous Bantu religion.

In this study of East African religions, the initial approach will be to examine the earliest records available, representing religious behavior found when the pioneer Europeans made their first contacts with Africans. Then, with some sense of historical perspective, the effort will be made to note the course of relationship of Christian missions, Moslem penetration, and indigenous Bantu religion.

HISTORY OF RELIGION IN EAST AFRICA

Occasional records of antiquity and persistent legends reaching Europe in the Middle Ages assure us that there were contacts between Africa and the outside world. In view of both archaeological findings and some literary reports in various places, it cannot be seriously questioned that travelers from Egypt and other parts of the Near East, and even traders from India, China, and other sections of Asia, had been in contact with African cultures long before the time of Vasco da Gama.

Egyptian records from the time of Sankh-ka-Ra, about 2500 B.C., speak of the Punt, a term that Clement M. Doke believes to be a transliteration of Bantu, a common Bantu expression denoting their own habitation,[3] although he recognizes the suggestion of Carl Meinhof and E. Zylharz that there is some argument for relating Punt to Swahili locative form, *pwani*. Later writings from Arabic sources include tenth-century works. Hamadani, in 902 A.D., speaks of the Zang, considered to be the Bantu, worshiping a god known as Lmklwglw, a term that Masuci, about 956 A.D., records as

[3] C. M. Doke, "The Earliest Records of Bantu," *African Studies*, XIX (1960), 26.

Mlknglw, interpreting this to mean "the great Lord."[4] Many variations of spoken Arabic are found, but all are reasonably seen to bear close resemblance, at least, to the name for God as the "great great," or in one Thonga variant, "the great pig." Nkulunkulu, Mukulugulu, Nkulunkhumba, and other variations persist on the east coast of Africa as the title of the high God.

Bulaq (c.a. 1283) also reports the name, Nkulunkulu, and his *Geographical Dictionary* mentions Langujah, an island in the land of the people of Zing, which would identify the location of the Bantu concerned as the region of Zanzibar (known currently to the Nyamwezi as Lunguja and to the Swahili-speaking peoples as Unguja.[5] The fact that the concept of the "great great" (Nkulunkulu) was current in the mainland across from Zanzibar in this early period, as an area where variants of the name Mulungu are now used to designate God, while the followers of Nkulunkumba are to be found farther south, indicates something of the migration of people between the tenth century and the present.

Sixteenth-century Portuguese writings give us several morsels of information that assist in reconstructing something of the religious history of the Bantu. In his *Da Asia,* written in 1552, De Barros reports, without giving his sources, that in c. 740 A.D. a town of Magadaxo was ruled by Moors, who likewise ruled the region thereabout. He adds:

> . . . but as the first tribe who came there, called Emozaydy (those of Zaide), held different opinions from the Arabs with regard to their creed, they would not submit to them, and retreated to the interior, where they joined the Kaffirs, intermarrying with them and adopting their customs, so that in every way they became mestizos. These are the people whom the Moors of the seacoast call Bacuys, a common name, as in this country we call the country people Alarves (Portuguese equivalent to rubes).[6]

Religious intolerance is implied here, whether documented or not by De Barros. Likewise, the reason for migration into the interior by a group of early immigrants, whose first stand was in Swahili territory before the coming of the Moslems, appears to be religious. The name Emozaydy, as in Bacuys, is certainly Bantu, but De Barros suggests that they become mestizos or mulattos as a result of displacement by the Moslem conquerors of the land.

Little documentation is found for the actual distribution of any but Moslem intrusions into East and Southeast Africa prior to the sixteenth

---

[4] *Ibid.,* pp. 26, 27.

[5] *Ibid.*

[6] De Barros, *Da Asia,* First Decade, translated from the Portuguese in George McCall Theal, *Records of South Eastern Africa* (Capetown: Cape Colony Government, 1898–1902), Vol. VI.

century. Legends and speculations suggest Jewish influence moving down as far as the Limpopo River. The legendary Prester John, for whom many expeditions were sent out by European monarchs in order to make treaties with his reportedly wealthy and Christian empire, has never been satisfactorily identified or written out of African history. Areas of Coptic influence may have been confined within the northern coastal regions. However, when Vasco da Gama, at the turn of the fifteenth century, employed Moslem pilots to guide him from East Africa to India, his first employees rioted when they discovered among them one who practiced Christian rites. Insufficient records prevent more than speculation as to where the Christian African was led to this faith.

On the whole, the Moslems on the east coast of Africa, from Kenya to the mouth of the Zambezi (and perhaps the Limpopo), met the first Portuguese with hospitality and friendliness. It was only after Portuguese nationalism and religious fanaticism joined personal tendencies to violence that hostility was engendered along the coast and the followers of Islam resisted the Europeans. General J. J. T. Botelho, official historian for the Portuguese government, recounts that, in 1500, the Portuguese sent an expedition under Pedro Alvarez Cabral and Bartholomew Dias, accompanied by Father (later Bishop) Henrique, six Franciscans, ten chaplains, and military forces, to conquer the East Coast. He records: "The regiment of Cabral had this norm of procedure: to convert the idolatrous Moors to Catholicism, and if spiritual arms should not succeed, to utilize the material power of the sword."[7]

At the outset of Portuguese exploration, missionary activities were confined to the immediate vicinity of the factories or trading centers, which were established in agreement with indigenous authorities. Some of the employees of the Portuguese became Christians. One of these, a worker at Sofala, was attached to the captain at the fort and became an intimate friend of the Jesuit priests, whom he begged to visit the home of his father, the chief of the Gwambe. Baptized by Fr. Gonçalo da Silveira, the young Gwambe succeeded, a year later, in his appeals to the priests, who visited Wutonga, the land of the Gwambe, and there established a Christian base of operations which operated from 1560 through 1561. From these Jesuit priests and a lay assistant came the earliest description of an East African culture.

Fr. Gonçalo da Silveira and Fr. Andre Fernandes, accustomed to their own cultural distinctions, searched in vain for justice in terms of European courts and prisons and for religion as a formalized system of creeds, ritual, and divinely sanctioned morality. They looked for, and found, traditions of a "venerable Moslem" who once had lived among the Tonga, leading them

---

[7] J. J. T. Bothelo, *História Militar e Política dos Portugueses em Moçambique da Descoberta a 1833* (Lisboã: Centro Tipografico Colonial, 1934), p. 51.

to follow Moslem rites and beliefs, including circumcision.[8] They explained the absence of circumcision and of "idolatrous" practices among the Gwambe as a result of their isolation from Mohammedan influence. Although Fr. Silveira had suggested a lack of religion among the Gwambe, he described their worship of a deity known as Umbe, described as the god of fate. Fr. Fernandes spoke of the people worshiping the Mozimo, first mentioned as one god, but later explained as follows:

> They honor one whom they call Mozimo, and by the attributes which they give him, he seems to be like that which the Moors and heathen call Nacibo, which is much like fate or fortune, and so they say that it is the good luck of their ancestors and that it favors them in their things, so that they should be well loved, and that they should succeed well in their transactions. And they say that this Mozimo comes at night, while they are sleeping, and asks them for food, and they give them to eat and drink, as by throwing it to them at the foot of a tall and green tree. And they say that the Mozimos of some kill the family of others when they require them to do so, and near where I was staying a Kaffir threatened a sheik with his Mozimo if he did not do a certain thing he would kill him, with the effect that he died as the Kaffir said.[9]

The name Umbe, which may have been derived from the Central African name for God, Njambe, the local name for a potter, Muumbi, or the name for the "great great" (Pig), Nkulunkhumba, is not difficult to place in the Southeast African theology. Nor is the word Mozimo, with its various spellings as recorded in this early letter and its various meanings in contemporary Shona belief in the interior land from which the Gwambe traditionally are supposed to have migrated. In different forms, the root is used to designate the spirit that Shona people as a whole venerate, a spirit of a specific ancestor to some sin, and occasionally a spirit of some migrant in the land, now unfriendly because of the nature of his death or the manner in which his body was treated by the inhabitants of the land. Modern Shona people still relate the action of the spirits to fate, as do most people in the region.

Letters from the Jesuit missionaries to their colleagues in Goa revealed other concepts of the Gwambe people which we know to be common to most Bantu, revealing little change since the mid-sixteenth century. All sickness and misfortune was believed to be the result of the action of some mysterious force, known or unknown, to the person carrying it. A woman who had illicit relations with another man could carry an evil force to members of her outraged husband's family, to her partner in infidelity, or to herself. Should this force bring misfortune to her husband or his family, this fact could be revealed through divination, and the one responsible

---

[8] Theal, *op. cit.*, II, 94.

[9] Henri Philippe Junod, *Os Indígenas de Moçambique no Seculo XVI e Comeco da XVII* (Lourenço Marques: Imprensa Nacional, 1939), p. 18.

could be forced to bring compensation to the injured family or die. One intangible force or type of force was related to the criminal in adultery, theft, murder, or other evil; while another tangible force could be invoked by the diviner as the agency of judgment and redress. These facts are evident in the following descriptions made by the priests of the sixteenth century:

> One sorcerer (diviner, or nanga) whom this king consulted about the death of a son and a daughter told him that the son was killed because some men put their feet on his footprints; and as to the daughter, that my neighbor woman killed her, because, seeing her outside perspiring, she wiped off her perspiration and carried it into the house along with the dirt which was on her own face, and thus she died; and they killed the poor neighbor. When I reproved the king for this thing he told me that that was their law to do what the sorcerer ordered, so that he himself would not remain (guilty of) homicide in the death of his children . . .
>
> About the nephew of the king, they said that his daughter, a nursing infant, had died because one of her uncles had worn the cloth in which she had urinated. Another, because his wife borrowed a pan from another, which when she sent it to her, carried death in itself, and killed the son of the one who had lent it. They made him give her another (son). About another, whose wife had left him, they said that just for this he had died, and he whom she later married was sentenced to pay, as he in fact did, a youth, as they did not wish this to be a girl, because she might give birth, and give to the child the name of this death. Commonly these pagans do not accept males because they are costly, and females work, however, they call these demands among themselves *milandos*.[10]

Whether the priests from Portugal had accurate information is no more clear than in the case of modern anthropologists who are sometimes unconsciously deceived by informants failing to communicate accurately. Fr. Gonçalo da Silveira believed that where the natural cause of a difficulty was obvious, no social action was taken, as, for example, when a drunken man killed another with whom he had been quarreling.[11] Fr. Fernandes wrote: "It is of such a nature that things of this kind, misfortune attributed to magic or to mystical powers, are punished with great rigor, but thefts and murders are not punished in any manner."[12] Elsewhere he commented, "All the deaths and sicknesses are said by some to be caused by others, and because of this they employ divination."[13]

The belief in unseen forces which carry misfortune from one to another through the spoken word, contact with some object belonging to the person, or by some other mystic process caused people to take every precaution,

---

[10] *Ibid.*, pp. 16–17.

[11] *Ibid.*, p. 8.

[12] *Ibid.*, p. 17.

[13] *Ibid.*, p. 15.

especially when a member of their family died, making them especially dangerous to others. It was reported: "No one knows when someone dies, nor confesses where he is buried, outside of the persons who are father or son, brother or sister, or the nearest relatives. One of the most important reasons this is so secret is in order not to be thrown into conversations with others so as to be people who are the carriers of death."[14] Except where the cause was clearly known, all cases of sickness and death were taken to the diviners, whom the missionary called *songos,* known today as *tinanga.* These, he explained, were not "witches," that is, *feticeiros,* but were the ones who indicated the guilty party by means of lots. Description of the diviner could be retold in many Bantu societies in the twentieth century as appropriately as in the sixteenth, for the pioneer priest reports:

> In order to know the sicknesses they cast lots, which are cowries fastened by the edges, and full of wax of black wasps, and have luck and misfortune, as in dice. These they throw, using many, which is most difficult, or few, some of which are officials (that is, they represent the chief, the diviner, and other social authorities and members of their social system).
>
> When one is sick, he orders the lot to be cast after paying or promising to pay to know of what he is sick, and the lot comes out asking why he ate from an old pan, slept on an old mat, or touched something of some dead person.
>
> The cause known, the sick says that he would know what is (needed) to be healthy, and at his will takes (a specimen of) a tree or herb, and if the lot falls that this is not good, he takes another until the lot confirms it.
>
> Then he goes to search the herb or leaves and stamps them, and with that juice and with water mixed, wets the part which is sick, or the entire body, and the things in the house which the lot said were the cause of the infirmity.[15]

Some diviners would kill roosters or rats in order to divine from the content and condition of the entrails. Bottle gourds were utilized in some way for the same purpose, and there were diviners, according to the observers, who "studied the water."[16] A "smelling out" process, well known to modern Bantu, was said to be the most important method of divination, as it is in the practice of *kunyamasoro* in many East African cultures. The priests wrote:

> The most famous divine by tracking, as bloodhounds, going about searching and smelling a whisk of long bristles which I believe are those of the wild ass which are numerous in this country. At times they put it on the ground, that is, the whisk of hairs, and turn them to the nose, and thus divine the house

---

[14] *Ibid.*

[15] *Ibid.,* pp. 15ff.

[16] *Ibid.,* p. 18. This may be similar to contemporary Bantu practices in Mozambique, where the diviner, under possession, is believed to go under a lake, river, or sea, spending months to search out a crime or evil.

where the charms are, and why the dead was killed, the manner in which he was killed, and all are very great lies and totally impossible, and I will tell some of the silliness of these in my own time.[17]

When the diviner had discovered the cause of the evil, he would divine further, as has been indicated, to discover the proper treatment. In addition to herbal cures, there were amulets (*mexinha,* as the Jesuits named them), tied about the neck. Sometimes the patient had to compensate injured persons or spirits if the divination showed him to be in guilt. Often it was required that the patient and his family abandon the house in which they lived, because it was judged to be contaminated by evil.[18] In any case, the person judged by divination as guilty of a mysterious contagion, should he have sufficient courage might deny guilt and demand that his accuser (diviner or layman) submit with him to a trial by ordeal. Implicit in the ordeal was the idea that fate would declare the truth. The Jesuit missionary reports that the two contestants would

take the *motro* (a name still used today), which is a poison which an official of that thing has, and then the place where they say the ordeal is to be given is set apart. The official is promptly paid fees by both, or at least by the one who is making false accusation, and after giving them proper things to drink to prepare them, he gives them a poison which he brings on his thumb nail, which is very long, and takes a bowl of water which he has commanded to be brought, and gives them to drink, to the one whom he does not wish to kill, pure water, and to the other he lowers his thumb and touches the water and so kills him, and his generation remains infamous forever.[19]

The people believed that the *songo* performing the ordeal did not do his own will, but that of fate in preparing the contestants in the ordeal. The aim of these practices, as in the case of feeding the Mozimo with libations, consulting the diviners, working cures and rites, was always to restore social equanimity when disturbed by some evil. If the spirits of one family molested the members of another family, the human instrument of that offense had to be punished, and his family was required to make restitution for the resulting damage, so that a harmonious society, which required the satisfaction of the dead as well as of the living, could be made to function effectively.

The reports of Fathers Gonçalo da Silveira and Andre Fernandes—although revealing, combined with ethnocentric judgment, of customs foreign to their Portuguese and Roman Catholic enculturation—provide us with an excellent view of the approximate base line of Southeast African Bantu religion when the Europeans first entered into contact with them in the sixteenth century.

---

[17] *Ibid.,* p. 16.

[18] Theal, *op. cit.,* II, 89–93.

[19] Junod, *op. cit.,* p. 17.

Two separate developments are sequel to this missionary interlude among the Gwambe: the first relating to the results of the mission itself and the second referring to the martyrdom of Fr. Gonçalo da Silveira. Fr. Andre Fernandes remained with the Gwambe a few months after his superior returned to the north to seek the conversion of the head of the Monomotapa "Empire." Then the Gwambe mission was abandoned, leaving a St. Mary's Church in the keeping of African converts. When these people became known late in the nineteenth century, no evident remnant of the Christian faith and practice was recognized. One almost insignificant detail catches the attention of the observer, but this is best noted after reading another record in the late sixteenth century.

Under the two priests, it is reported that the entire court of Chief Gwambe and his several neighbors were converted and baptized. Almost twenty-eight years after the priests left Gwambe, a party of survivors from the wreck of the "São Thomé" wandered up from the vicinity of Durban through Zulu, Swazi, and Thonga territories and found welcome refuge among the Gwambe. These people welcomed them with a warm hospitality which revived their spirits after continuous difficulties en route; and details of the Gwambe conversion to Christianity were recounted. The guests were told that all who had been baptized among them had been given new Christian names, of which some were mentioned. But all were given the Christian surname *Sà* (Saint).[20] Gwambe men and men sharing the basic Gwambe culture commonly call to each other using a greeting which they believe to be the mere equivalent of "Hello Fellow!" The words they use are *"He Sà!"*[21]

The other sequel to the missionary service of these Jesuit priests was the martyrdom of Fr. Gonçalo da Silveira and the subsequent intensification of hostilities between East African Bantu peoples and their Portuguese guests. Fr. Gonçalo traveled several hundred miles north and west to visit the reported emperor of the famed Monomotapa monarchy. Details of the tragic expedition vary and add little to the understanding of the major concern. The Jesuit appears to have made initial contacts which were promising. Then a Moslem member of the court of Monomotapa, said to be resentful and fearful of the Christian mission, brought influences to bear on the king which led to the murder of the Jesuit priest, whose ashes were thrown into the river. Conflicting news reached the Portuguese: first that the mission had been successful and then that, on March 15, 1561, Gonçalo had been ambushed and murdered. A miracle myth rose, claiming that the remains of the priest had floated upstream to bear witness against his murderers. Word spread to Portugal and Rome. Soon an expedition was financed and sent out, presumably led by Captain Francisco Barreto for the purpose of opening the

---

20 Theal, *op. cit.*, II, 182f., 218f.; Junod, *op. cit.*, pp. 43ff., 54ff.

21 The Gwambe and Tswa (Mukhamba) people who use this term deny the knowledge of its meaning, recognizing no relationship between the term and the word in Portuguese, *São*. Its localization among the Gwambe is, however, significant.

country for trade in gold, but soon degenerating into a punitive campaign of vengeance under the stimulation of Fr. Francisco Monclaros, one of the two Jesuit priests sent by the queen of Portugal to convert the head of the Monomotapa Empire.

Fr. Francisco Monclaros was the official chronicler of the forces, and he recorded his own, in contrast with the official, motives of the expedition. J. J. T. Botelho, a Portuguese official historian, drawing from the accounts of Monclaros, unequivocally blames the priest for the costly, useless campaign. "Monclaros," Captain Botelho reports, was "blind with sectarian ardor, demanding vengeance." When the commander Barreto would have used either caution or mercy, Fr. Monclaros demanded unyielding, violent movement against the Bantu and challenged the authority and integrity of the commander. Death by battle, disease, poisoning of the water, and other disasters decimated the forces, but Monclaros demanded that they go on. Barreto himself died, according to another chronicler, Diago do Couto, in the midst of serious conflict with Fr. Monclaros, a situation which the priest does not mention in his own chronicles. Because of the expedition, African and Moslem resentments deepened for the Portuguese, who had carried religious war into areas which had had nothing to do with the event for which the party of revenge had come.[22]

Repeated campaigns intensified the bitterness. A treaty between the Portuguese and Chief Manura of Zimbabwa, May 24, 1692, deferring to superior European arms, makes clear the way in which religion, commerce, and political power intermingled. The chief was forced to agree (1) to respect the Portuguese captain, (2) to permit the free activity of Roman Catholic priests and brothers and the construction of churches at their discrimination, (3) to permit free commerce, (4) to consider as sacred the persons of all Catholic priests and religious functionaries, (5) to expel the Moslems, (6) to open the gold mines to the Portuguese, (7) to excuse white people from the necessity of performing the formalities and honors which Bantu custom demanded of those who would confer with their kinds, and (8) to exchange gifts annually with the Portuguese government at the capital of Mozambique.[23] Little wonder the Moslems and Bantu never learned to distinguish between Church, commerciant, and state.

This somewhat extended account of the initial contact of Christianity and the Bantu of East Africa and Islam in the same area serves to underscore the fact that the Bantu religious outlook provided no barricade against the entry of Christian and Moslem teachings. No evidence is forthcoming to suggest that Bantu religionists tried to convert either of the two major alien groups entering their lands. Africans, confronted by Christians and Moslems, tended to receive what they wanted to take from the invaders' faith and practice,

---

[22] Botelho, *op. cit.*, I, 167–201.

[23] *Ibid.*, p. 291.

rejecting what they would. Moslem influence, however strong it may have been to the north of Beira, never successfully penetrated south of Beira, where Islam's only religious inroads were in the families that they acquired through marriage with African women. As will be seen, Roman Catholic influence remained negligible throughout at least three centuries. Unlike the missionary history in the west, East Africa, from the sixteenth through the nineteenth century, had little missionary activity. With few exceptions, Roman Catholic establishments in Portuguese-held territories on the east coast were preoccupied with commerce by which they had to support themselves; the slave trade, over which they gained a virtual controlling interest; and chaplaincy to the Portuguese authorities and merchants.

In 1667, Manuel Barreto, a Portuguese Jesuit, reported six churches of his own order and nine of the Dominicans in the Zambezi Valley, where the Portuguese were concentrating on trade with the interior. He confessed that there was much simony among the priests and degeneration among the Portuguese settlers, many of whom were ex-criminals serving time in Africa rather than in prison. Barreto expressed hope for better conditions, which did not come. The Patriarch of Lisbon blamed the failure of the missions on the presence of Indian clergy from the seminary in Goa, the depth of whose Christian faith and character he doubted. The darkness of their skin and the less significant cultural distance between the Goanese priests and the Africans did not seem to make them more successful missionaries than their colleagues from Portugal. Botelho writes: "the apostolic work of the Dominicans did not perdure except in the villages off the coast, and in those of the Zambezi Valley where the task of conversion of the pagans was strongly aided by living together with the Europeans."[24] Portuguese captains accused the priests of indulging in many affairs, bringing them and the Church into disrepute. Although Botelho found little to commend in any but the very earliest missionaries, he bemoaned the fact that earlier conscientious missionaries were replaced later by "successors . . . not always conforming to the norms the others had followed." To the contrary, he added, "they deviated by interfering in the administration of public affairs and by dedicating themselves to the interest of slave commerce."[25] He quoted François Pyard, another Portuguese historian, as saying that "all the priests were . . . rich, and each individually gained what he could for himself."[26]

From 1572 to 1918 at Chemba, where the Bantu were under political as well as spiritual supervision of the Jesuits from 1645, until their expulsion by the Marquis of Pombal in 1759, scarcely a decade passed without a violent revolution. Only a decisive military defeat subjugated these people. Religious efforts do not appear to have had any influence on them.

---

[24] *Ibid.*, p. 172.

[25] *Ibid.*, pp. 172f.

[26] *Ibid.*, p. 173.

Portuguese historical records abound in accounts of treachery, debauchery, and intrigue among the missionaries, who lost what respect they had among their countrymen and established their own reputation among the Africans as being avid merchants, slavers, and rulers, guided by greed and lust. In 1783, Pedro de Albuquerque reported to the Secretary of State, Martinho de Melo e Castro, that the missionary "convents are collections of libertine and perverse friars, merchants, and administrators of captive negroes and slave negresses and maids within the same cells."[27] One priest, who had been expelled in 1761, returned to the coast as the captain of a slave ship. In 1805, Fr. Francisco de S. João Batista actually excommunicated the governor, José Filipe de Carvalho, for trying to curb the violent behavior of the priests.[28] The innocent priest shared the reputation of the guilty. A few Jesuit priests maintained a strong reputation for opposing these evils, but their opposition was ineffective. Groves tells of Fr. Barroso, who "saw in the condonation of the slave traffic a major cause of ultimate failure of the work of Catholic missionary work in East Africa."[29] Official action by the Vatican had little effect. Although in 1622 Pope Gregory XV had established the Congregation of Propaganda for the sake of unifying missionary work with proposed reforms, much of this effort faded into insignificance even before the disappearance of the Jesuits from the scene.

Protestant missionary activity in East Africa was delayed longer than in other parts of the continent. In 1824, Captain Owen, a British officer fighting the slave traffic in the Indian Ocean, lifted the British flag over Mombasa, and Protestantism had its first encouragement to look toward East Africa. The influence of David Livingstone, missionary, explorer, and enemy of European and African slave systems, began a movement to introduce "advantages" from the culture of Europe along with the Christian religion into Central Africa. East Africa began to hear of his movements. Johann L. Krapf, sent to Ethiopia in 1837, turned eastward and, in 1844, started the first mission in Kenya. Livingstone and Krapf, scientists as well as religionists, inspired others sharing their dual interests to enter Africa. A succession of men—geologists, geographers, biologists, botanists, and later pioneer anthropologists—moved into East Africa, combining interest in a particular science with a concern for the religious conversion of the Africans to Christianity. At Cambridge University, on December 3, 1857, Livingstone fired the imagination of an unrecorded number of people who heard him or read his address and volunteered to go to redeem Africa from the slave traffic and from "superstition."

---

[27] *Ibid.*, p. 417.

[28] *Ibid.*, p. 419.

[29] C. P. Groves, *The Planting of Christianity in Africa* (London: Lutterworth, 1948), pp. 127f., 146.

The entry of Britain into East Africa, the advent of German influence in Tanganyika, the efforts of France in Uganda, and movements northward by Europeans from South Africa led to widening interest on the part of many missionary-sending agencies. With Protestantism came an emphasis on the Bible, denominational and national rivalries, a greater tendency toward individualism, and the specific cultural proclivities of the societies from which the missionaries came.

Earliest pioneers were Scotch Presbyterians, awakened by Livingstone and stirred to action by Dr. James Stewart of Lovdale, who from 1861 through 1875 worked to secure a missionary expedition to Nyasaland. This project united dissident sections of Presbyterianism, which came to cooperate in Livingstonia, at Blantyre. Here missionaries placed Britain at a strategic point, preventing the Portuguese from usurping the only entry to Lake Nyasa. The subsequent establishment by a wealthy Scot of the Livingstonia Central African Trading Company to supply the two missions and to compete with the Arab overland traders laid valid foundation for the claim that missions had commercial ties. When the management of the company, jointly with the Scottish missionaries, tried to prevent the Universities Mission (founded by Fr. Tozer on the Lake in 1873) from spreading Episcopalianism among the Bantu, the rivalry of missions became apparent.[30]

The London Missionary Society (mostly Congregational in character) and the Church Missionary Society (Church of England) both had work in East Africa, the former starting in Nyasaland and Tanganyika, moving to Rhodesia in 1893, and the latter in Uganda, where it set up its work, using Lutheran workers to man its stations.

Roman Catholic missionary activity in East Africa revived largely under the influence of Cardinal Lavigerie, founder of the Société de Notre Dâme d'Afrique, known as the White Fathers. Following the papal sanction by Pius IX in 1868, the Cardinal succeeded in setting up self-supporting orphanages in France and Algiers and began to develop the same idea in East Africa. Here, he worked both with children and with the unattached Africans recently freed from slavery. In compounds of this mission, Africans were helped to set up some form of industry to provide both subsistence and profit.

In appealing to the Pope for sanction of his mission in Africa, Fr. Lavigerie frankly stated the need to correspond to and to rival the existent Protestant establishments and to undertake humanitarian as well as civilizing functions alongside the religious propaganda.[31] Catholic and Protestant missions were now similarly motivated. By 1878, the Roman Catholic mis-

---

[30] Roland Oliver, *The Missionary Factor in East Africa* (London: Longmans, 1952), p. 38.

[31] Oliver, *op. cit.,* pp. 44ff.

sionaries, recruited from lay and clergy, were in the area around Lake Victoria and Lake Tanganyika. This move came in spite of appeals by the Church Missionary Society in Buganda that the Roman Catholic mission not be set up in direct competition with the Church of England Mission there. Bitter rivalries which were to involve Britain, France, and the African tribes, setting one faction against the other in the leading chieftainships, arose from this opposition of Catholic and Protestant missions in Buganda.

To the south, in areas not far from the initial work of the Jesuits among the Gwambe, new Protestant bodies gained a start. Swiss Reformed missionaries moved in among the western Gwambe in northern Transvaal and also sent mission expeditions to Lourenço Marques and northward. American board missionaries of the Congregational Church moved from Natal into the region around Inhambane. During the fifteen years prior to the turn of the twentieth century, various religious bodies, including the Methodist Episcopalians, Free Methodists, British Methodists, the Church of England, and a pentecostal sect known as the Firebrands, moved into the southern half of Mozambique. At times, groups as different as those just listed entrusted a mission station to the care of a common missionary delegated to care for the interests of them all. At other times, leaders of one mission refused to recognize either the validity of the orders or the integrity of profession of the members of another mission. With the influx of Protestant missions into Portuguese East Africa, the Roman Catholic Church was stimulated to start missions in this land neglected by them for the better part of three centuries. Late in starting, the Roman Catholic missionaries in Mozambique, depending on government support and encouragement, identified themselves closely with the government. Protestant missions, on the other hand, were constantly reminded that they were foreign, and the Africans were frequently shown the danger of associating with English, Swiss, and American missionaries. Where pressures were effective, this worked hardship on Protestants, though it also suggested to Africans resenting Portuguese tyranny that their friends were Protestants and their enemies were Catholic. The most important result of Catholic-Protestant rivalry in the Portuguese colony was the Portuguese effort to eliminate Protestant educational institutions and systems which, for the first four decades of this century, constituted practically the only significant educational program of this country. Medical missions, including well-developed hospitals of the Swiss Mission and of the American Methodists, also brought embarrassment as they preceded both government and Roman Catholic medical services in this Portuguese colony. Thus, in the earliest of the East African territories, Portuguese East Africa, the dawn of modern missions was the beginning of violent tensions which were to stir both nationalistic and religious rivalries throughout this century.

A detailed history of missions in the eastern part of Africa would take more space than could be allowed for our purposes here. As unsatisfactory as generalizations always are, they become necessary. Twentieth-century missions in East Africa must be treated mercilessly in a generalized presentation. In the early part of the twentieth century, missionaries of all denominations confronted Africans whom they described as primitive, savage, superstitious, disease-ridden, victims of famine, illiterate, and pagan. The impetus of humanitarianism, linked with antislavery sentiments, was carried over from the nineteenth-century pioneer missionaries. However bigoted and fanatical the presumed religious outlook of some missionaries of the early twentieth century, most of them were preoccupied with down-to-earth, practical needs of the Africans—interpreted, of course, in terms of their respective cultural experiences. To most of these missionaries, there were basic essentials any culture must have: Christianity, the three R's, stable industry (including agriculture, carpentry, and building as the most important), sanitation, and both preventative and curative medicine. Varying with the country and social class of the missionaries, most workers also believed that some reform in social organization was essential.

Many pioneer missionaries, especially those who were able to survive the rigors of climate before disease could be controlled effectively, could be described as Sir Harry Johnson characterized Dr. Laws of Livingstonia Mission:

> This man, with his fifteen years of whole-hearted devotion to Nyasaland, and his energy of doing good which has made him learn to make bricks himself in order that he may teach others, which has led him to become a practical carpenter, joiner, printer, photographer, farmer, boat builder, engineer, and druggist, so that he might induct his once savage people into all these arts and trades, which has made him study medicine and surgery to heal the bodies, and sufficient theology to instruct the minds of these Africans, about whom he never speaks with silly sentiment and gush, but whose faults, failings and capabilities he appraises with calm common sense—Dr. Laws with these qualities of truly Christian self-devotion should justly be regarded as the greatest man who has yet appeared in Nyasaland.[32]

Most early missions, though they set up preaching places, began to gather people into classes of instruction including all that they believed essential to the education of the people whom they could bring together. Since Protestant missions were universally convinced that the African must be able to read the Bible, primary stress was placed on education, and along with teaching came the printing press. In British territories, this dual venture met with little difficulty for missionaries had the support of government and commercial agents in the belief that literacy, both in the indigenous African languages and in English, was essential. Education and printing would increase the

---

[32] Oliver, *op. cit.,* pp. 62f.

usefulness of the Africans and would at the same time make them ready for increased rights and responsibilities. In Portuguese East Africa, the reaction was different. Official opinion vacillated. Education was desirable, but it had dangers. Toleration of missionary educational programs varied, favorable under liberal political leadership, hostile under reactionary and nationalistic control. As the nationalistic movement in Portugal increased, the opposition hardened against the teaching of African languages. Prohibition of any but the Portuguese language in public institutions was so radical in 1939 that some administrators prohibited the use of African languages in churches and schools. African reaction against this was so deliberate and effective that measures were immediately taken to soften the legislation by interpretations which administrators could use with some freedom.

The mission-related African soon became known, in most places, as an educated African—a relative term, referring to grade-school levels of education. Colonials, particularly farmers and industrialists hiring Africans, tended to dislike Christian Africans because they were proud of their education, looked for "white-collar jobs," and tended to think of their rights to an extent not common among the illiterate workmen.

In the majority of missionary programs, education branched out to involve agriculture, industrial training, domestic science, and some elements of health and sanitation. Under the American Methodist Mission, George A. Roberts pioneered agricultural classes, demonstration plots, and extension work among the Africans in Southern Rhodesia before 1910. Dr. Alvord, a Congregationalist agricultural missionary some years later, so impressed the Rhodesian government of the need for agricultural leadership that they persuaded him to become their first Minister of Agriculture, in spite of his being an American citizen. Pliny Keys, a Kansas agriculturalist, pioneered in his field in Mozambique from about 1909, and later became a self-trained builder, electrical engineer, and educator, even taking theological studies to add preaching to his accomplishments. Convinced that Africans needed to conquer the problems of soil and climate, these men helped them to do just that and also taught them the necessary crafts to build modern houses and furnishings to make their lives more comfortable according to the ways the missionaries had learned at home.

In this same early period, just after the turn of the twentieth century, medical men, inspired by the Student Volunteer Movement and the calls of their churches, moved into Africa and began to confront the medical problems of the eastern part of the continent. Malaria claimed the lives of many Africans and colonists alike in the early years. Blackwater fever, typhoid, dysentery, sleeping sickness, smallpox, and numerous tropical diseases claimed many. The induction of Africans into mining operations brought to light the problems of tuberculosis against which people of this continent had no resistance. The high mortality rate of infants and of young mothers was highly publicized. Methods of the diviners, indigenous physicians, and midwives were seen with all their dangers to the health of their patients. Missionaries built hospitals, out-patient centers, and nursing stations—many of them long before the governments of the respective colonies had undertaken any health measures. Again, the difference between British and Portuguese policies was clear. The former, recognizing responsible medical services of the missions, encouraged their development and cooperated with missionary medical programs, while the government built its own program to supplement the other. Slow to start a medical program of their own and struggling with national doctors and nurses who were not readily accepted by the Africans, the Portuguese discouraged, hindered, and in some cases actually prevented medical services by some of the most qualified missionaries, again inciting tensions among the African population who had come to depend on missionary medical assistance.

THE AFRICAN RESPONSE

Viewing education, industrial training, and medical services of the missions from another point of view, that of the African response, this century shows a constant change. In the early part of the century, concerted opposition of traditional political and religious authority combined with fear and suspicion to prevent people from enthusiastically accepting the offered services. Girls, especially, were prevented from going to school. Indigenous practitioners discouraged people from taking medical services of the missions. The customary agricultural practices were so thoroughly in control that the missionary agriculturists despaired of training people to adopt improved methods which would produce greater crops. Altogether, the tenacity of culture and the strangeness of the missionaries' offerings combined to make the progress much less than they desired.

From the mid-thirties, change began to be so rapid, however, that neither the missionary nor the African could keep up with the needs of the program. The African became education-conscious, and, instead of the Chinese "rice Christian," Africa began to produce the "book Christian"—children and youth clamoring for an education and parents with or without learning seeking to have schools for their children. In the past decade, this has developed into a contagion of demands for overseas scholarships in American and European universities. Even in Portuguese East Africa, with an official discouragement of African education, the missionaries have managed to educate young people beyond the limits imposed by the officials; and many students have escaped the borders of their country to attend higher schools of learning in Rhodesia, South Africa, and elsewhere, finally managing to get into colleges and universities in the United States and Britain. Opposition to medical services collapsed quietly in some places and suddenly in others, and hospitals and other medical centers of the missions have developed rapidly in the past thirty years. Indigenous practitioners have themselves been treated by modern medicine. In turn, many herbalists and other indigenous practitioners have re-evaluated their own arts, sometimes trading information with one another, adding insights learned from doctors and nurses, and otherwise increasing, if not improving, their skills. The present generation of Africans in East Africa has imbibed freely of missionary education, industrial training, and health practices as no other generation ever did. Along with these offerings of the missions, most Africans have been involved to some extent in the religious practices of the missions. Many of the educated youth and adults of East Africa know little firsthand of their ancestors' religious practices. Few contemporary Africans with a high school or college education have had any experience which would allow them to understand or believe the descriptions that were made of their grandparents when missionaries first entered East Africa less than a century ago.

Apart from any religious opposition of Christianity to aspects of indigenous African religion which appeared impossible to reconcile with the Christion faith, many African customs fell in the onslaught of education in science, economics, sociology, and other secular studies which missions provided. Rarely can one find an African with education who knows the culture that his forebears once practiced, save in barest outline. The present generation has awakened to find that by means of education, which the mission symbolizes, traditional ways have passed into disuse, except among a few relatively "untouched" groups of people. The loss relates somehow to all that the missions have been doing. The mission comes to mean an authority that has been responsible for the destruction or disappearance of a cultural heritage which the present generation does not know, but now, with a mysterious nostalgia, begins to wish for.

Not only is there a Bible or its easily accepted substitute, books of modern knowledge, in the place of the divining bones; but there are also many replacements for which the missions are at least symbolically responsible. Music from Europe and America is sung by most people except the uneducated followers of traditional religion and the emotionally alive laymen's evangelistic movements in the missionary churches. The educated elite find themselves out of place with either. By the demand of African students in contact with younger missionaries from overseas, dancing follows ballroom and dance-hall patterns rather than the characteristic pantomime which East Africans have always known and in which they excel. Modern medicine has captured every area in which it has been able to provide adequate personnel and hospital facilities. Although the traditional diviner, herbalist, and charm dispenser revive spasmodically, few educated Bantu consult them, except for the ailments that modern science finds incurable or that are elusive to the diagnostician.[33] The piano, organ, banjo, and other musical instruments from overseas are all too obviously popular, to the detriment of fine African instruments which younger generations do not learn to play. The hereditary chieftain claims little respect from the young and has little authority in comparison with the uniformed representatives of the government.

The exotic diviners, possession mediums, and other representatives of a former set of beliefs in regard to religion and magic, medicine, and jurisprudence are to be found here and there, but they are the object of jest and ridicule of students, whose teachers are accorded highest honor. Indigenous languages, although preserved in writing by the work of missionaries and associated linguists and although bearing in print the lore of African past and the thoughts of the African present, are somehow relegated to an inferior position by the Africans themselves, who covet the magic keys which the languages of Europe appear to possess. All these and many more features of change in the African scene present an ambivalence to the educated Bantu, for they have chosen the changes, or accepted them from their parents, and yet are reluctant to see the over-all result: a displacement of vast sections of African culture. Missionary religion must take the responsibility for the change, even as missionaries are asked to provide opportunities for education, health, and other features of the outside world that they have represented along with the central content of their faith.

Within the religious organization of the missions, too, a social development has unconsciously or consciously unfolded throughout the history of Christian missions. Self-government, varying from church to church and country to country, characterized the out-stations of Christian missions and came increasingly to represent the work of the churches. As early as the first decade of the twentieth century, some missions were appointing African superintendents. Mott Sikobele, for example, was then in charge of areas in Mozambique and Rhodesia, working alongside Methodist missionaries until certain differences of opinion and the opportunity to be bishop in an independent church led to his separation.

Positions of high authority and titles of distinction did not move to the African as fast as might be hoped, but training in leadership, experience in self-rule, practice in the use of initiative and ingenuity were a part of normal church life. In Portuguese East Africa, subject to the projection of hierarchical dictatorship from the continent, the African people have known little autonomy in their past century of submission to direct rule by Portuguese administrators. Nevertheless, most Protestant villages, each set up as a community of believers around an African pastor and church, governed themselves—insofar as they did not run into conflict with civil authorities.

---

[33] The same clientele that seeks cure by "quacks" in our society are to be found in Africa, among the elite as well as among the uneducated masses.

Most Protestant bodies in East African territories had their own representatives to sectional and national convocations of their denominations, and progressively increased the proportion of their voting membership to the point of far outnumbering their missionary colleagues.[34]

Outside of Portuguese territories, where a petition or resolution censuring the government would not be tolerated, religious bodies and societies within them frequently reviewed the policies and practices of the colonial government, pointing out abuses, suggesting reforms, and calling for greater African participation in public affairs. Delegations of African churchmen were frequently met in the offices of business executives, calling on them to improve conditions of their workers. Groups of teachers called for educational changes. Christian women's organizations spoke out on the status of women. A Christian laymen's movement in Southern Rhodesia became the nucleus of an outspoken political African Congress which stirred demands for franchise and political progress for the Africans. A generation of *bafundisa,* teachers and preachers, trained in the churches, formed the bulk of self-assured speakers who have been calling for a new Africa in the past decades. In the interchange of ideas in both denominational and interdenominational, national and international, gatherings of mission-related personnel, religious leaders have become conscious of pan-Africanism and have dared dream of the rights of Africans to speak out, against the background of world opinion.

Facing the changing conditions in East Africa from many points of view, contemporary Christian missions are uncertain of the future. Older missionaries—mindful of the intimate relationships of the past and disturbed by the suspicion and distrust of the present—are slowly being replaced by a new generation of workers. Many newcomers are persuaded by misinformation or partial information and think of the past as one characterized by segregation, paternalism, and sheer ethnocentricity. They see their task as turning over to the African what former missionaries have allegedly withheld. Sensitive to the injustices suffered by Africans throughout the colonial control of their lands, some missionaries have allied themselves with African political movements and their most extreme demands. Others, alarmed by the violence of some movements, fearful of leftist relationships, and concerned about providing self-rule and universal franchise to people "not yet ready" for these responsibilities, take moderate or even reactionary positions in relation to the African aspirations. Mission boards represent this same interplay of contrasting opinions and may be subject to the same opposition of liberal and conservative positions that are threatening the secular political scene. It is doubtful if any except the more authoritarian churches, on one hand, or the most uniformly indigenous churches, on the other, have a

---

[34] This freedom of expression has been the occasion of Portuguese opposition to a system inimicable with their own.

clear-cut view of the Christian mission in this disturbing and disturbed generation in Africa.

As to the Africans, positions vary also. In the Chaminuka cult, Muchatera, the Shona national medium and African leader, voices the opinion of the traditional spirit, Chaminuka, calling for moderation, cooperation between Africans and Europeans, and cessation of demonstrations. Vast sections of ordinary Christians speak in the same way. More vocal Christian leaders, like the political spokesmen, are more radical in their demands for African rule. Many of the elite call for the removal of missionaries as well as other white people. Themselves unaware of the beliefs and practices of their ancestors, some cry out emotionally for a return to the ways of the past, uncontaminated by foreign Christian influence. Conferences of African Christians continue to ask the mission boards to send new missionaries, often appending the request with the suggestion that the missionaries learn their language, come to know them better, and work more intimately with them.

In face of the confusion in Africa and in the countries sending missionaries to minister to African needs, any clear, uniform characterization of either native or missionary religion in East Africa must be, at best, an oversimplification and, at the worst, misrepresentation.

THE OUTLOOK

Prediction under the circumstances is impossible. The future of Christianity in any part of Africa must be judged in terms of its history and the cultural situation that it meets today. As to the future of religion in East Africa, a few basic observations may be made. These will be cast in terms of the characterization of religion with which this discussion began.

African religion embraces human behavior at every level. Bantu people have customarily allowed their religious outlook to color their entire gamut of behavior—what they see, think, judge, will, and do. Their emotional life has been fraught with religious undertones. No human need has been omitted from the functions to which their religion has been applied—land use, nutrition, healing, learning, social organization, ethics, art. Every known want has been sought in religion. Religious explanation has been applied to the total human outlook. The materialistic, secular African can only be the creation of an outsider, the product of foreign universities. To expect a few acculturated representatives of anti-religious sentiments to convert the Bantu to a nonreligious way of life would be to look for a miracle greater than their Christianization, for it would be the most violent attack on an essential characteristic of Bantu culture.

The late Melville J. Herskovits frequently spoke of the resilience of the Africans. Their tolerance of deviance is another well-known characterization. This past century has shown their capacity to absorb new features into their culture, and it currently demonstrates their capacity to rise to demand a recognition of their own rights as a people and of the dignity and worth of their culture. These characteristics, together with their religious orientation, would suggest that certain developments must take place in the future. Some form of syncretism appears inevitable. Given a large amount of independence from the directive force of mission authority, the wide distribution of Christian belief and practice would suggest that spontaneous amalgamations of Bantu and Christian elements will take place. Persistent contact of Christian Africans with a world community of the faith will tend to keep the transformation of African Christianity within bounds in which the new meanings can be shared in this wider context. Should missionary authority seek to direct the syncretic moves, American-made "African music" and British-designed "African church architecture" and such hybrids may impede the development of indigenous re-interpretations. If strong opposition is laid to the Africanization of Christianity, centers of rebellion are likely to erupt. One certainty appears: neither Christianity nor traditional Bantu religion will remain the same. Both will be modified, and both will be the richer for the cultural interchange.

SELECTED BIBLIOGRAPHY

Bascom, William R. "African Culture and the Missionary," *Civilisations* (Institut International des Civilisations Différentes), III, No. 4 (1953), 491–504.

Bascom, William R., and Melville J. Herskovits (eds.). *Continuity and Change in African Cultures.* Chicago: University of Chicago Press, 1962.

Botelho, General J. T. T. *História Militar et Política dos Portugueses em Moçambique da Descoberta a 1883.* Lisboã: Centro Tipographico Colonial, 1934.

Davis, Jackson, Thomas M. Campbell, and Margaret Wrong. *Africa Advancing.* New York: The Friendship Press, 1945.

Dodge, Bishop Ralph E. *The Unpopular Missionary.* Westwood, New Jersey: Fleming H. Revell Co., 1964.

Doke, C. M. "The Earliest Records of Bantu," *African Studies,* XIX (1960), 26ff.

Gann, Lewis H., and Peter Duignan. *White Settlers in Tropical Africa.* Baltimore: Penguin Books, 1962.

Gonçalves, José Julio. *Protestantismo em Africa.* 2 vols; Lisboã: Estudos de Ciencias Politicas e Sociais, 1960.

Groves, Charles P. *The Planting of Christianity in Africa.* London: Lutterworth, 1948.

Haines, C. Grove (ed.). *Africa Today.* Baltimore: The Johns Hopkins Press, 1955.

Hatch, John. *Africa Today and Tomorrow*. New York: Frederick A. Praeger, 1962.

Herskovits, Melville J. *The Human Factor in Changing Africa*. New York: Alfred A. Knopf, 1962.

Hewson, L. A. "The Historical Background," in *The Christian Citizen in a Multiracial Society*, Rosettenville Conference Report, Johannesburg: 1945.

Junod, Henri Philippe. *Os Indígenas de Moçambique no Seculo XVI e Comeco do XVII*. Lourenço Marques: Imprensa Nacional, 1939.

Morris, Collin. *The End of the Missionary?* London: The Methodist Missionary Society, 1962.

North American Assembly on African Affairs. *Africa Is Here*. New York: Africa Committee of the Division of Foreign Missions, National Council of Churches of Christ in the U.S.A., 1952.

Oliver, Roland. *The Missionary Factor in East Africa*. New York: Longmans, 1952.

Oliver, Roland, and J. D. Fage. *A Short History of Africa*. Harmondsworth, Middlesex: Penguin Books, 1962.

Ottenburg, Simon and Phoebe. *Cultures and Societies of Africa*. New York: Random House, 1960.

Paddleford, Norman J., and Rupert Emerson (eds.). *Africa and World Order*. New York: Frederick A. Praeger, 1963.

Quigg, Phillip W. (ed.). *Africa*. New York: Frederick A. Praeger, 1964.

Ross, Emory and Myrta. *Africa Disturbed*. New York: Friendship Press, 1959.

Spire, Herbert J. *Politics in Africa*. Englewood Cliffs, New Jersey: Prentice-Hall, 1962.

Sundkler, Bengt G. M. *Bantu Prophets in South Africa*. London: Lutterworth, 1948.

Theal, George McCall. *Records of South Eastern Africa*. 10 vols., esp. vols. II and VI; Capetown: Cape Colony Government, 1898–1902. N.B. This rare, little-known collection of translations of primary sources from Portuguese, French, Dutch, German, and other records of ships, explorers, merchants, and administrators contains rich sources of ethnographical and historical data of great worth to the ethnohistorical study of Southeast Africa.

Wilson, Godfrey and Monica. *The Analysis of Social Change*. Cambridge: Cambridge University Press, 1945.

A NOTE REGARDING PERIODICALS

In addition to the widely known journals dealing with African Studies, World Missionary Movements, and relevant professional interests, much first-hand information about the attitudes, interests, methods, and successes of missionaries has been found interspersed among missionary propaganda in the magazines published by various churches and missionary societies working in East Africa. Among these is the *Africa Christian Advocate,* published quarterly since 1906 in

Johannesburg, South Africa, by the Central Mission Press. The journal *Practical Anthropology,* published in Tarrytown, New York, presents articles which reflect both a missionary motivation and an anthropological orientation, revealing changing attitudes as this religious vocation and the discipline of anthropology become conversant.

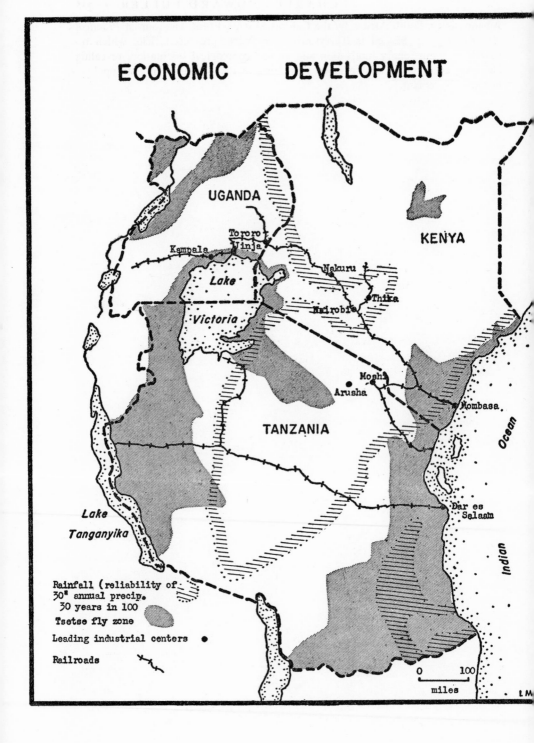

ECONOMIC   DEVELOPMENT

UGANDA

KENYA

Tororo
Jinja
Kampala
Nakuru
Lake
Thika
Nairobi

Victoria

Moshi
Arusha

Mombasa

TANZANIA

Ocean

Lake
Tanganyika

Dar es
Salaam

Indian

Rainfall (reliability of
30" annual precip.
30 years in 100
Tsetse fly zone
Leading industrial centers •
Railroads

0   100
miles

L M

15

Resources and Problems of Economic Development

K. G. V. Krishna

THE FORMERLY BRITISH EAST AFRICAN AREAS of
tropical Africa were largely isolated from the outside world until recent
times. For all practical purposes, the impact of the economic forces of the
modern world was not felt in this region until the beginning of the twentieth
century. At the time of its initial penetration by European powers, the dominant features of economic activity were subsistence agriculture based on
shifting cultivation, primitive pastoral production, food-gathering, and hunting. The nature and the limited range of economic activities suggest that it
was essentially a static society, constrained by serious limitations of an institutional and environmental nature. The pre-colonial economy of East Africa
was, by all available evidence, extraordinarily backward. The African eked
out a miserable living by exerting himself to the utmost in a harsh environment. At its best, the environment provided man with a marginal or perhaps
a submarginal existence; at its worst, it exposed him to the nagging uncertainty of hunger, disease, and fear. As is observed in the *Report of the East
Africa Royal Commission,* "a balance between man and his physical environment, enabling the survival of the former and preventing serious deterioration
of the latter, was maintained by a series of epidemics affecting both man and
animals, by periodic famine and by intertribal raids and wars."[1]

It is not the purpose of this chapter to trace the evolution of East African
economics from the pre-colonial period to the present, except to focus attention on some current assets and liabilities which are attributable to colonial

---

[1] Great Britain, Colonial Office, *East Africa Royal Commission 1953–1955, Report,*
Cmnd. 9475 (London: H.M.S.O., 1955).

537

policy. The important fact about colonial policy is that it laid the foundation of a national economy, just as—in the political field—it created a nation from dissident, warring tribal groups. It exposed the African people, for the first time, to new influences, ideas, and techniques and, thereby, opened up new vistas for African endeavor. It demonstrated the possibility of mastering, at least to a limited degree, a harsh environment and created expectations for a better living standard. It set up the elements of a transportation system, thereby providing the requisite mobility of economic factors. To the African, much of this was a new experience. But, whereas colonial policy was instrumental in releasing these new forces, it did not carry them to their logical fruition and thereby contributed to an immense amount of frustration. Furthermore, colonial policy had the effect of setting in motion a chain of events which gradually contributed to the disintegration of tribal societies without support in the emergence of suitable alternatives.

On the one hand, colonial policy adopted measures aimed at building the base of a market-oriented economy; on the other, it hampered a market economy by ensuring the perpetuation of tribal privileges and differences. The colonial power also underestimated the extent to which the new stimuli would evoke a prompt response from the African people. Both in Kenya and Tanganyika (in the German period), African participation in cash-crop production was deliberately delayed at the same time that the European endeavor was rapidly building the basis of a market-oriented economy. A partial, though not convincing, explanation of this contradictory policy was that it was deemed necessary to insulate poor and inexperienced Africans from the uncertainty surrounding complex transactions with the outside world. The result was that, whereas the African desire for participation in new kinds of activities had been stimulated, its fulfillment was denied both by white-settler intransigence and a queer kind of official paternalism. Thus, the process of breaking away from the stultifying atmosphere of tribal society was paradoxically interrupted.

Colonial policy in East Africa aimed, on the one hand, at maintaining stability and, on the other, at creating conditions for change. The means employed to accomplish these contradictory ends involved the elimination of intertribal conflict, the gradual eradication of both human and animal disease, and the demonstration of the advantages of soil conservation and good husbandry. These measures were basically sound, but the tragedy of colonial policy was that it failed to take cognizance of the responses that the new forces would stimulate. The elimination of intertribal conflict and the progressive eradication of disease brought substantial increases in population in their wake.[2] The growth in absolute numbers assumed such a substantial dimension that traditional methods of land use proved hopelessly inadequate to the growing population.

---

[2] For example, crude estimates of Kenya's African population around the turn of the century put it at about 1.5 million. By 1948, it had increased to 5.2 million.

In the meantime, the Native Laws Trust Ordinance had been enacted in Kenya with the effect of virtually determining, once and for all, the amount of land allocated to each tribal group. This "once-and-for-all" allocation stemmed from the need to assign vast areas for the exclusive ownership and use of the European settler farmers.[3] In retrospect, it may be observed that it was not so much the alienation of valuable tracts of land, but rather the freezing of land ownership on the basis of the then prevalent tribal claims that proved prejudicial to African interests. Insofar as marked discrepancies existed between the man-land ratios in the various tribal areas, the finality of the new allocation hit the more numerous and fast-multiplying peoples hardest.[4] In Uganda as early as 1900, the Uganda Agreement provided for the holding in freehold of those estates in possession of various chiefs and private landowners. These estates termed "*mailo* land" account for about half the area of Buganda. There have been rumblings in Buganda over the issue of *mailo* lands ever since, and, as land shortage becomes more acute, a fundamental alteration in this rigid system seems inevitable.

It is obvious that a fundamental lack of coordination existed in colonial policy between the two distinct but inextricably related aspects, namely, the need to eliminate constant strife over the conflicting claims of tribes and to ensure the availability of land according to changing needs. Where European settlement was actively encouraged (as in Kenya and, to a lesser extent, in Tanganyika), for all practical purposes, the settlers became a "tribe." The practice of delimiting tribal areas proceeded partly from the necessity to delineate and retrace suitable areas for the European farmers; whereas in Buganda, the agreement on *mailo* lands was a concession to influential feudal interests with which the colonial power was not prepared to clash. There is no doubt that this policy contained a serious weakness; it was largely responsible for restraining the free mobility of the factors of production and thereby jeopardized the realization of optimum productive capacity.

The Mau Mau outbreak in Kenya in the early 1950's was in no small measure a reflection of the extent to which land hunger had developed in one area, and it is not surprising that the bulk of the recruits for the movement were drawn from those areas where the most severe distortion in man-land ratios had taken place. Whereas force was readily employed, first, to alienate land and, subsequently, to crush a rebellion largely traceable to land

---

[3] Prior to independence, out of Kenya's total arable land amounting to 10.6 million acres (based on thirty inches or more rainfall per annum with a probability of failure of not more than fifteen years in one hundred), area available for cultivation in the European acres was 2.6 million acres, in comparison with 7.9 million acres in African acres. See B. R. Davidson and R. J. Yates, "Relation Between Population and Potential Arable Land in the African Reserves and the European Highlands," *East African Economic Review,* VI (December 1959).

[4] For example, in some districts inhabited by the Kikuyu people, the density of the population has already reached 1,500 per square mile.

hunger, the government seemed extremely reluctant to redraw tribal frontiers on the basis of actual and anticipated needs.

In any assessment of the natural and human resources of East Africa, it is perhaps appropriate to proceed with data that throw light on the equation between man and land.[5] A combined area of 680,000 square miles (of which 42,000 square miles is water) and a combined population of 26.2 million reveal a density of some forty-one persons per square mile in 1963. (See Table 15–1.) This may convey the superficial impression that East

Table 15–1

Areas and Population Density

Territory	Land Area (Square Miles in Thousands)	Water and Swamp (Square Miles in Thousands)	Total Area (Square Miles in Thousands)	Population Density[a]
Kenya	220	5	225	40.2
Tanganyika	341	21	362	28.7
Uganda	76	16	92	94.6
Zanzibar	1	—	1	319.4
Total East Africa	638	42	680	41.0

SOURCE: East African Common Services Organization, East African Statistical Department, *Quarterly Economic and Statistical Review* (Nairobi).

[a] Persons per square mile of land area in 1963.

Africa does not have a population problem and that there would be no difficulty in absorbing increases in population on the basis of the present growth rates. Although the density of population in East Africa is not high by over-all African standards, it is important to note that land hunger has already developed in important areas of each of the three territories.

In any sensible assessment of man-land ratios, it is axiomatic that only such land be taken into account that will lend itself to profitable exploitation. The criteria that are usually employed in determining this are location, rainfall, soil fertility, water supply, and tsetse-fly infestation. Since deficiencies concerning any of these factors may result in an area being virtually ruled out for purposes of occupation and development, it would be useful to examine land availability through a combined reference to all six factors. (See Table 15–2.) This approach reveals the following. In Kenya, of a total area of 225,000 square miles, about 40,000 square miles is in uninhabitable desert, and another 110,000 square miles is not used at all at present or is only sparsely populated by nomadic tribes. The remaining third constitutes the agriculturally productive part of the country and supports over 90 per

[5] See Appendix A for population statistics.

Areas by Province in Square Miles (at Dec. 31, 1959)

KENYA

Province	Land	Water[a] and Swamp	Total
Rift Valley	17,007	131	17,138
Central	11,091	3	11,094
Nairobi Extra-Provincial District	187	—	187
Nyanza	9,607	1,457	11,064
Coast	25,714	216	25,930
Southern	32,727	55	32,782
Northern Frontier	123,456	3,309	126,765
Total	219,789	5,171	224,960

UGANDA

Province	Land	Water[a] and Swamp	Total
Buganda	16,138	8,958+	25,096
Eastern	10,971	4,395+	15,366
Western	17,297	2,189	19,486
Northern	31,729	848	32,577
Total	76,135	16,390	92,525

TANGANYIKA

Province	Land	Water[a] and Swamp	Total
Central	35,200	—	35,200
Dar es Salaam	50	—	50
Eastern	41,400	—	41,400
Lake	27,600	9,400	37,000
West Lake	11,150	4,200	15,350
Northern	33,100	800	33,900
Southern	55,600	—	55,600
Southern Highlands	44,800	600	45,400
Tanga	14,000	—	14,000
Western	78,250	5,650	83,900
Total	341,150	20,650	361,800

ZANZIBAR

Province	Land	Water and Swamp	Total
Zanzibar Island	640	—	640
Pemba Island	380	—	380
Total	1,020	—	1,020

SOURCE: East African Common Services Organization, East African Statistical Department, *Quarterly Economic and Statistical Review* (Nairobi).

[a] Includes territorial waters of Lake Victoria.

cent of the population. Further increases in population have to be absorbed within the confines of this area.[6]

In Tanganyika, estimates made a few years ago reveal serious short-comings in regard to water supplies and the consequent crowding of population in seventeen areas with a reasonably satisfactory water supply. According to studies, the 10 per cent of the country described as "well watered" accommodated 63 per cent of the population.[7] A further 8 per cent of the land area was classified as "fairly well watered" and provided for a further 18 per cent of the population. Another 20 per cent was designated as "poorly watered" and was occupied by pastoral people making up 18 per cent of the population. The remaining two-thirds of the land area is "virtually waterless" and consequently almost uninhabited. Thus, 99 per cent of the people of Tanganyika are concentrated in about a third of the total land area.

Uganda is more fortunate than Kenya or Tanganyika. About a third of the country has an adequate water supply, though a second third is classified as "areas of difficulty." The balance of the land area has negligible water supplies and is incapable of supporting a significant population. In sum, the position of Kenya gives cause for most concern, whereas, both Uganda and Tanganyika possess a margin of cultivable land. But the position is changing from year to year, owing to uneconomic customary usage and population increases.

East Africa's agricultural potentialities may also be assessed with reference to rainfall. (See Table 15–3.) A thirty-inch rainfall per annum under East African soil conditions is regarded in most areas as the absolute minimum. Of equal importance is the rainfall-reliability factor. Agriculture is generally considered both uneconomic and hazardous in areas where there is danger of failure of rains once every three years. In Kenya, only 13 per cent of the country receives a rainfall of thirty inches per annum with any degree of regularity. In Tanganyika, just under a third of the total area may be regarded as satisfactory from the point of view of rainfall adequacy and reliability. In Uganda, the position concerning both these factors is satisfactory over most of the country, with the exception of the extreme northeast. Thus, only about a fourth of East Africa is adequately and regularly served by rainfall, and agricultural pursuits are essentially limited to this area. Barring the near waterless tracts in the three territories, much of the presently uncultivated area lends itself only to pastoral development.

A further complicating factor in assessing land resources is the presence of the tsetse fly. It is estimated that just over 60 per cent of the area of

---

6 See Appendix B.

7 See International Bank for Reconstruction and Development, *The Economic Development of Tanganyika,* Report of an International Bank for Reconstruction and Development Mission (Baltimore: Johns Hopkins University Press, 1961).

Table 15–3

Rainfall by Major Area and Selected Station

Area/Station	Number of Years	Maxi- mum[a]	Mean[a]	Mini- mum[a]	Standard[a] Deviation	RAINFALL BY INCHES 1957	1958	1959	1960	1961	1962
KENYA											
North—Wajir	34	20.2	9.8	2.9	4.4	20.1	9.9	3.6	13.5	33.6	15.6
North Highlands—Eldoret	49	71.9	38.3	18.2	11.0	38.0	45.4	36.3	41.3	51.4	49.0
South Highlands—Nairobi	55	61.8	34.6	17.2	7.9	34.5	34.9	34.8	34.7	46.0	39.1
—Nyeri	55	52.0	36.3	18.1	11.5	36.2	36.3	36.2	36.1	63.9	32.2
Rift—Naivasha	49	40.8	24.0	15.2	5.9	36.1	23.7	23.7	23.7	37.1	27.7
Coast—Mombasa	69	74.3	47.4	27.9	11.9	47.2	47.1	47.2	47.1	52.6	29.9
TANGANYIKA											
West—Kigoma	36	47.8	36.8	25.9	5.6	39.8	30.4	43.5	37.7	42.3	53.6
Central—Tabora	46	51.3	34.1	15.4	7.4	35.4	28.8	31.3	36.5	54.7	49.5
South Lake Victoria—Mwanza	37	58.5	41.2	28.4	8.0	43.8	37.0	31.7	33.8	66.9	46.9
South Highlands—Iringa	45	43.3	28.0	15.8	6.1	34.8	31.7	—	19.0	24.7	30.7
Coast—Dar es Salaam	57	59.0	41.6	17.2	9.4	57.6	32.4	35.5	40.5	60.3	35.9
North Province—Arusha	37	71.3	48.6	26.3	10.9	52.0	28.4	27.9	33.2	36.1	32.0
UGANDA											
Central—Lira	33	70.6	56.0	40.4	7.2	47.9	58.5	59.4	59.8	66.9	56.6
West—Fort Portal	55	83.4	58.2	42.0	7.9	57.4	52.3	61.6	55.1	77.0	63.8
North Lake Victoria—Entebbe	62	89.0	59.3	39.3	9.7	64.9	65.9	56.5	61.8	72.3	64.5

SOURCE : East African Common Services Organization, East African Statistical Department, *Quarterly Economic and Statistical Review* (Nairobi).

[a] Based on data up to 1960.

Tanganyika, 32 per cent of the area of Uganda, and 10 per cent of the area of Kenya are fly-infested. Though a partial or even total eradication of the fly is now technically possible, it remains a most expensive operation. Where areas are cleared of the fly, there must be prompt settlement and planned systems of land use or the land will revert to bush. Experience has also revealed the difficulty of inducing settlers to move into newly cleared areas either because of tribal prejudices or a reluctance to make a permanent home in an unfamiliar environment.[8]

Another factor which has an important bearing on the issue of the man–land ratio is the possibility of developing irrigation schemes to augment the supply of cultivable land and to enhance the productivity of land currently under use. To date, irrigation has not played a significant role in agriculture in East Africa. Large-scale irrigation schemes require substantial outlays of capital and can only be defended in terms of the returns that they are capable of bringing. Where there is doubt about the return or investment, there exists a possibility that a government will dangerously strain its meager revenues. Also of considerable significance is the fact that comprehensive hydrological surveys have not been completed, and therefore there is as yet only an incomplete appraisal of water resources. In Tanganyika, hydrological surveys are being carried out in the Rufiji, Ruvu, and Pangani River basins. In Kenya, arrangements have been made to carry out a pre-investment survey of the lower Tana River basin. Tentative estimates indicate that the irrigation potential may be of the order of 1 million acres, though the development of irrigation will have to be coordinated with flood-control projects. In Uganda, where the water situation is more favorable, the development of irrigation does not have the same priority, at least, for the time being.

A doubt has sometimes been expressed concerning the advisability of substantial investment in irrigation schemes when the bulk of the African farmers have little or no experience in irrigated farming. However, the farmers have already demonstrated their capacity to switch from dry to irrigated farming without prolonged preparation. The most notable example of this is an irrigation scheme at Mwea-Tebere in Kenya where initially some 400 African families were settled as part of the over-all resettlement scheme.[9] Apart from the novelty of exposure to a new kind of farming, the principal crop chosen for cultivation, rice, was also new. The success of this scheme,

---

[8] I am indebted to my colleague, Mr. James Brain, for the information that an important factor militating against internal population movements is that many Africans are reluctant to leave the site of their ancestral graves.

[9] The scheme has been such a notable success that, at the moment, a further 1,000 families have been settled on 5,500 acres of land. Also, plans have been drawn up for eventually settling a total of 3,000 families by extending the area of cultivation to 14,000 acres.

from its very inception, would seem to demonstrate a capacity for adaptation to new methods of farming.

The ecological phenomenon outlined above is particularly relevant when one takes into account the rate of population increase. This is not to suggest that the present population has already reached a size where it cannot be supported by available resources, though severe local pressures have already appeared in some areas. Rather, it is to indicate that the East African environment demands a carefully thought-out population policy. Considerable energy must be expended to extend the area and fertility of cultivation, by eradicating the fly, by irrigation schemes where surveys have revealed the potentiality of fruitful action, by improved land usage, by inducing settlement in areas suitable for farming, and finally by improving communications requisite to development on the extensive side. In the absence of a well-coordinated policy, the land resources of East Africa will continue to depreciate.

The importance of agriculture in the East African economy is likely to continue to predominate in the foreseeable future. Africa's economic development has been characterized either by an availability of minerals in commercially feasible quantities or by the possibilities of developing cash crops for export—both largely the result of alien initiative, capital, and expertise. The absence of significant mineral finds, with the exception of diamonds in Tanganyika and some copper in Uganda, has tended to orient the economy in the direction of commercial agriculture. In Kenya and Tanganyika, a number of cash crops were introduced by European settlers, and these, combined with livestock development, evolved as the basis of the respective economies. In Uganda, following an abortive attempt by aliens to develop a plantation economy, the production of cash crops proceeded within the framework of a subsistence economy. However, despite a long period of production for the market, this activity still remains of secondary importance to the individual peasant.

In recent years, a few substantial African farming enterprises have appeared, though it is too soon to conclude that it constitutes a definite trend. In Kenya, owing to the presence of a significant number of European farmers, a dual economy emerged with the alien population oriented to the market production sector and the African peasant producing mostly for his own needs. However, important developments have taken place in the field of African production for the market. From almost insignificant beginnings, the value of gross farm revenue from marketed production increased to £10.7 million in 1962. In Tanganyika, some of the more enterprising peoples, such as the Wachagga on the slopes of Kilimanjaro, the Wasukuma on the eastern shores of Lake Victoria, and the Bahaya in the West Lake area, have a relatively long history of producing for the market. (See Tables 15–4, 15–5, and 15–6.)

Table 15–4

Uganda: Gross Domestic Product at Factor Cost by Industry

	1960	1961	1962	1963 Estimate	1964 Forecast
A MONETARY ECONOMY					
agriculture[a]	53.4	52.9	47.6	63.1	77.2
forestry, fishing, hunting	2.3	2.0	2.4	2.4	2.4
mining and quarrying	2.2	2.3	2.6	2.8	2.8
manufacturing	6.0	6.3	6.2	6.9	7.3
electricity	1.9	2.2	2.5	2.8	3.0
construction	3.9	3.6	3.9	3.5	3.6
commerce	14.4	14.5	14.5	18.3	19.9
transport and communication	6.2	5.9	5.8	5.9	6.0
government	6.5	6.6	7.3	7.1	7.1
miscellaneous	10.5	11.5	11.5	12.2	12.8
rents	3.4	3.4	3.6	3.8	3.9
total monetary economy	110.8	111.2	107.9	128.7	145.9
B NONMONETARY ECONOMY					
agriculture	36.4	39.9	42.6	40.8	41.7
forestry and fishing	5.0	5.4	6.1	6.6	6.8
total nonmonetary economy	41.3	45.2	48.7	47.3	48.5
Grand Total (A + B)	152.1	156.4	156.7	176.1	194.4

SOURCE: Uganda Government, Ministry of Finance, *Background to the Budget 1964–1965* (Entebbe: Government Printer).

NOTE: The figures are given in million £'s.

[a] Including cotton ginning, coffee curing, and sugar manufacture.

Table 15–5

Kenya: Gross Domestic Product at Factor Cost by Industrial Origin—1959–1963

Industry	1959	1960	1961	1962	1963[a]
RECORDED MONETARY ECONOMY					
agriculture (including incidental services)	25.32	29.44	28.33	28.46	33.15
livestock	8.57	9.22	8.97	9.62	9.42
forestry	0.79	0.81	0.90	0.97	0.78
fishing and hunting	0.89	0.53	0.52	0.81	0.88
Total	35.58	40.00	38.72	39.86	44.23

OUTSIDE RECORDED MONETARY
ECONOMY

agriculture	38.47	36.10	34.21	46.43	47.87
livestock	11.66	10.99	10.44	11.86	12.83
forestry	2.70	2.94	3.08	4.74	5.78
fishing and hunting	0.20	0.16	0.16	0.19	0.20
Total	53.03	50.19	47.89	63.22	66.68

TOTAL PRODUCT

agriculture	63.79	65.54	62.64	74.89	81.02
livestock	20.23	20.21	19.41	21.48	22.25
forestry	3.50	3.75	3.98	5.71	6.56
fishing and hunting	1.04	0.69	0.68	1.00	1.08
Total	88.61	90.19	86.61	103.08	110.91

RECORDED MONETARY ECONOMY

mining and quarrying	1.12	1.09	0.85	0.83	0.89
manufacturing	20.23	21.62	22.73	23.04	24.38
construction	7.94	7.86	7.80	6.76	4.90
electricity, storage, and					
communications	19.03	20.34	21.15	22.26	24.78
wholesale and retail trade	27.68	28.96	29.56	30.06	31.92
banking, insurance, and real estate	3.46	3.54	3.88	4.01	4.17
rents (including ownership of					
dwelling houses)	8.05	8.70	8.14	8.43	9.36
government services:					
civil departments	16.87	18.33	21.63	22.02	23.44
local authorities	3.15	3.35	3.49	4.11	4.02
defense	1.43	1.37	1.75	1.83	2.01
overseas government (local					
employees)	0.10	0.12	0.14	0.16	0.18
total (government services)	21.53	23.17	27.00	28.12	29.65
services	14.58	15.50	14.14	14.21	15.41
government officers'					
salaries revision	—	1.75	—	—	—
Total	214.79	225.51	224.70	244.09	259.96
recorded monetary economy	161.76	175.32	176.81	180.87	193.28
imputed product outside the					
recorded monetary economy	53.03	50.19	47.89	63.22	66.68

SOURCE: Government of Kenya, Economics and Statistics Division, *Economic Survey, 1964,* Nairobi.

NOTE: The figures are given in million £'s.

a Provisional.

Table 15–6

Tanganyika: Gross Domestic Product at Factor Cost

Industry	1960[a]	1961[a]	1962[a]	1963[a]	Percentage Change 1962–1963
agriculture	112,809	114,087	125,096	139,082	+12.5
mining and quarrying	5,194	5,476	5,128	4,414	−13.9
manufacturing	5,469	6,958	7,853	8,442	+ 7.5
construction	4,565	5,840	6,213	6,640	+ 6.9
electricity and water	1,231	1,360	1,485	1,558	+ 4.9
commerce	20,931	22,062	25,221	27,599	+ 9.4
rent	8,026	8,377	8,782	9,214	+ 4.9
transport	8,734	8,585	9,539	9,781	+ 2.5
services	18,094	20,759	22,924	24,566	+ 7.2
Total	185,053	193,504	212,241	231,296	+ 9.0
Index (1960 = 100.0)	100.0	104.6	114.7	125.0	

SOURCE: Tanganyika, East African Statistical Department, *Budget Survey, 1964–1965* (Dar es Salaam: Government Printer).

[a] The figures given are in thousand £'s.

In Uganda, two-thirds of the gross domestic product is derived from farming, while 90 per cent of all export incomes are derived from agriculture and allied occupations. In Tanganyika, monetary and subsistence activities in the agricultural sector account for about 75 per cent of the gross domestic product, and 80 per cent of export earnings are derived from the sales of agricultural and livestock products. Also, in Tanganyika, African peasant producers account for some 55 per cent of the crops exported and 65 per cent of the value of all marketed crops. In Kenya, about 42 per cent of gross domestic product in 1962 was accounted for by agriculture, livestock, forestry, fishing, and hunting, of which 16.26 per cent was in the recorded monetary economy and 26 per cent outside the recorded monetary economy. Over 80 per cent of the value of all exports was accounted for by agricultural and allied items.

A closer examination of the position of Kenya, however, reveals that the bulk of the export income to date is attributable to production from the European farming areas. In 1962, European agricultural production amounted to £36 million out of the total marketed cash-crop value of just over £42 million. It is also significant that the £36 million from the European farming areas was derived from 1.2 million acres, whereas, the £10.7 million from the African areas was derived from some 18 million acres of African-owned areas.

LIVESTOCK

The position of livestock in East Africa, like the rest of Africa, presents an anomaly. On the one hand, the number of cattle, sheep, and particularly goats is higher for the continent as a whole than for the rest of the world. Available statistics also reveal, however, that the contribution of livestock to the domestic product is very low. Livestock statistics unfortunately are merely rough approximations, except for the European farming sector of Kenya where reliable data are available. In Kenya, an African agricultural sample census in 1960–1961 showed that in Kiambu, Nyeri, Fort Hall, and Embu districts of the Central Province, there were 350,200 head of cattle, 195,600 sheep, 117,600 goats, 10,900 pigs and 380,600 poultry.[10] In the Elgon Nyanza, North Nyanza, Central Nyanza, South Nyanza, and Kericho districts of the Nyanza Province, there were 986,900 head of cattle (excluding Central Nyanza), 888,700 sheep, 759,600 goats, 5,600 pigs and 2,793,-200 poultry. Estimates for the rest of the country are not available, thus leaving a serious gap, particularly in the Masai areas where there are enormous herds of cattle. For the country as a whole, the figures for various categories of livestock must run into several hundred thousands. And yet, if one looks at the gross farm revenue of the African areas, the figure is depressingly low. The combined total for sales of livestock and dairy products originating in the African sector amounted to £2.3 million in 1961 and £2.7 million in 1962. In contrast, corresponding farm revenue in the Scheduled (European) areas—where the numbers relating the cattle, sheep, goats and poultry are much smaller—was £9.3 million and £10.6 million in 1962.[11]

The figures are not strictly comparable in view of the fact that a large proportion of livestock products in the African areas is subject to consumption of the source; but it does provide some measure of the potentialities. Among African rural communities, livestock are generally kept as a store of value and as a symbol of prestige, rather than to augment cash income or to remedy protein deficiencies through increased human consumption. Thus the overriding consideration has been the absolute number of cattle rather than their condition or market value.

It is paradoxical that the continent that has the highest livestock resources is also a net importer of meat and dairy products.[12] Both Tanganyika and Uganda are net importers of meat and dairy products; the deficiencies, in this case, being made good through imports from Kenya. Carefully planned de-

---

[10] *Kenya African Agricultural Sample Census, 1960–1961*, Part I.

[11] Provisional estimates for the value of marketed livestock and dairy products in the European and African areas are £10 million and £2.8 million respectively, in 1963.

[12] United Nations, *Economic Survey of Africa since 1950* (New York: United Nations, 1959).

velopment of livestock resources offers possibly the best means of achieving a measure of "diversification" within the over-all agricultural sector. At present, however, livestock resources not only fail to make a contribution to the economy commensurate with their numbers, but, in some areas, over-stocking and consequent erosion of the soil poses a serious problem to development.

MINING

Mention was made earlier of the importance of mining in African countries. However, East Africa is not generally well endowed with minerals, and even the exploitation of some of the existing mineral deposits is hampered by the absence of a suitable infrastructure. Unfortunately, supplies of some of the minerals that have been making a modest contribution to the economies of the territories have already reached or are feared to be reaching exhaustion. This applies, for example, to the lead mine at Mpanda in Tanganyika which has been closed, and to the copper mine at Kilembe in Uganda where the future of ore reserves is regarded with uncertainty. In Kenya, the value of mineral production has actually gone down in the past few years. The value of gold production in 1940 was £500,000, but, in 1961–1962, it was only £100,000. One of the two big gold mines was exhausted in 1952, and the other ceased operations in 1957. A promising start was made in copper mining in 1953, but in recent years the results have been so disappointing that the Colonial Development Corporation has since written off the £3 million investment. (See Tables 15–7 and 15–8.)

Deposits of various other minerals exist in all three territories, but together add up to very little in terms of their current commercial feasibility. Exploration for oil is proceeding systematically, but so far there have been no positive results. In contrast to this gloomy picture, production of diamonds in Tanganyika has registered a continuous increase until 1961, when the value reached £5.78 million. For 1962 and 1963, however, the value declined to £5.40 and £5.02 million respectively. In 1963, the over-all value of mineral sales in Tanganyika was the lowest since 1959 and was 9 per cent below its 1961 peak.[13] The increased production of mica and tin concentrates in 1963 has to be weighed against the fall in the value of gold production and the permanent closure of the tin mine in Mpanda.

In Uganda, mineral development may be summed up in one word—copper. The importance of copper overshadows that of all other minerals put together. In 1960, for example, copper accounted for £3.4 million of a total mineral export of £3.6 million. In 1963, copper and alloys (unwrought) accounted for an export value of £3.97 million. Tin, the only other mineral of any consequence, accounted for an export value of but £150,000 in 1963. Though deposits of other minerals exist in Uganda, the immediate future of the mining industry depends largely on the fate of the

---

[13] Tanganyika—*Budget Survey, 1964–1965.*

Table 15-7

Kenya—Mineral Production, 1959–1962

Mineral	Unit of Quantity	1959		1960		1961		1962	
		Quantity	Value[b]	Quantity	Value[b]	Quantity	Value[b]	Quantity	Value[b]
cement copper	long tons	1,982	458,391	1,756	412,660	2,524	583,043	2,190	505,000
diatomite	long tons	3,608	57,209	3,385	51,674	3,158	47,584	2,863	41,080
gold	fine oz. troy	9,145	114,290	8,645	108,143	12,299	153,964	9,313[a]	116,176[a]
lime and limestone	long tons	16,733	105,906	24,893	147,483	19,771	106,092	17,995	109,578
salt	long tons	19,242	146,398	21,916	166,772	22,550	182,889	18,568	150,497
soda ash and soda	long tons	153,261	1,757,626	126,981	1,427,422	144,689	1,601,651	124,998	1,374,566
others	—	—	162,894	—	150,236	—	73,869	—	138,176
Total	—	—	2,802,714	—	2,464,390	—	2,749,092	—	2,435,073

SOURCE: Kenya, Ministry of Finance and Economic Planning, Statistics Division, *Statistical Abstract, 1963* (Nairobi: Government Printer).

[a] Provisional.

[b] £'s.

Table 15–8

Tanganyika—Mineral Production, 1959–1962

Mineral	Unit of Quantity	1959		1960		1961		1962	
		Quantity	Value[b]	Quantity	Value[b]	Quantity	Value[a]	Quantity	Value[a]
diamonds	carats	555[b]	4,548	537[b]	4,622	685[b]	5,780	647[b]	5,402
gold	troy oz.	96[b]	1,197	107[b]	1,344	102[b]	1,273	102[b]	1,275
lead	tons	5,715	402	6,087	420	345	22	—	—
building materials	cu. ft.	14,000[b]	209	16,000[b]	255	16,000[b]	293	14,000[b]	195
salt	tons	37,000	251	34,000	274	33,000	271	30,000	282
copper	tons	1,068	258	1,254	293	99	23	—	—
silver	troy oz.	536[b]	177	595[b]	197	64[b]	21	24[b]	9
others		—	155	—	225	—	229	—	326
Total	—	—	7,197	—	7,630	—	7,982	—	7,489

SOURCES: Tanganyika Statistics Division, *Statistical Abstract, 1962* (Dar es Salaam: Government Printer), Tanganyika, the Treasury, *Budget Survey—1964–1965* (Dar es Salaam: Government Printer).

NOTE: The provisional estimate of the value of mineral production in 1963 is £7.2 million.

[a] The figures are given in thousand £'s.

[b] Times 1,000.

Kilembe copper mine, jointly owned by Venture of Canada, the Commonwealth Development Corporation, and the Uganda Development Corporation. This enterprise represents very substantial investment, not only in mining equipment, but in the copper smelter at Jinja and in a large electric power station at the mine. Furthermore, the Uganda government has invested substantially in providing a rail link to the mining area. Despite the fact that production increased steadily in the early years, there is now some uncertainty about the future of mining operations in view of the rapidly decreasing ore reserves. Proved ore deposits could ensure production until 1970 or, if efforts are concentrated only on the best ore, until 1967. The effect on Uganda's economy would be serious and would represent a loss of export earnings of some £3–4 million annually, as well as a drop in wage earnings of some £3 million. A labor force of some 3,000 people who represent various degrees of skills would become obsolete.

The purpose of this cursory survey is to indicate that, on the basis of present knowledge, East Africa's mining sector does not promise to be a prime mover in economic development. Vast areas of East Africa have not yet been subjected to geological or geophysical coverage, and, therefore, there exists the possibility of discovering vast mineral deposits. Further, improvements in transport and communications and the availability of cheap power might improve the commercial feasibility of some enterprises that are currently unattractive. A relevant example concerns the availability of large quantities of good quality noncooking coal in southern Tanganyika in the basin of the Ruhuhu River. But the area is about 500 miles from the coast by existing means of transportation and is inadequately served by transport facilities. Therefore, the possibility of developing a significant mining sector must await large-scale investment in intensified geological mapping and infrastructure development. The size of the initial investment required is so large that it could be pursued, if at all, only by a radical diversion of resources from other sectors of development and, in particular, from agriculture. In view of the present sources and demands on investment capital, it is unlikely that the development of a large mining sector will have a high priority in the foreseeable future.

MANUFACTURING

Manufacturing in the East African countries shows important differences. Both in Uganda and Tanganyika, there has been a relative increase in the size and range of manufacturing activity in recent years. But as a percentage of the value of economic activity, manufacturing still presents only a small figure—about 4 per cent of the domestic product in Uganda and Tanganyika. In Kenya, although manufacturing accounts for nearly 10 per cent of the gross domestic product, there has not been an increase in the share of the

Table 15–9

Kenya—Reported Employment, 1957–1962

	1957	1958	1959	1960	1961	1962	1963
AGRICULTURE AND FORESTRY							
Europeans	1.8	1.8	1.7	1.9	1.6	1.4	1.3
Asians	0.5	0.5	0.6	0.8	0.6	0.6	0.7
Africans	251.1	247.2	249.4	269.1	249.8	243.5	217.6
PRIVATE INDUSTRY AND COMMERCE							
Europeans	11.4	11.6	12.0	12.3	11.7	10.6	10.2
Asians	25.8	24.8	25.1	25.6	25.0	23.5	24.2
Africans	156.8	149.6	148.0	151.1	134.1	133.2	123.6
PUBLIC SERVICE							
Europeans	9.2	9.2	9.0	8.9	8.9	7.8	6.1
Asians	10.9	10.6	11.1	11.8	12.2	12.0	11.6
Africans	146.9	137.9	140.1	140.7	145.9	148.7	139.4
ALL EMPLOYEES							
Europeans	22.4	22.6	22.7	23.0	22.2	19.8	17.7
Asians	37.2	35.9	36.8	38.3	37.8	36.1	36.7
Africans	554.8	534.7	537.4	560.9	529.8	525.4	480.7
Total	614.4	593.2	596.9	622.2	589.8	581.3	535.1

SOURCES: Government of Kenya, Economics and Statistics Division, *Economic Survey, 1964* (Nairobi: Government Printer); and East African Common Services Organization, East African Statistical Department, *Kenya Statistical Abstract, 1963* (Nairobi: Government Printer).

NOTE: These figures are given in thousands.

manufacturing sector over the past seven years—the respective percentages being 9.66 in 1955 and 9.47 in 1962.[14]

In Tanganyika, the manufacturing sector accounted for 3.45 per cent of the domestic product in 1957; its value being £5.7 million. In 1963, manufacturing, with a value of £8.4 million, still accounted for less than 4 per cent of the value of the domestic product. Though there has been a relative increase in manufacturing activity, its share of the domestic product has remained constant over the past seven to eight years.

In terms of employment, the manufacturing sector accounts for only a small proportion of those in paid employment and, recently, there actually

14 The contribution of the manufacturing sector of Kenya has increased in value from £17.44 million in 1955 to £24.38 million in 1963. This shows an increase of 29 per cent over the eight-year period. However, most of this increase was accomplished prior to 1960. Since 1960, the increase is only of the order of some 11 per cent and, thereby, shows the interruption of an encouraging trend.

Table 15–10

Uganda—Reported Employment and Earnings

Year/Race	Private Industry		Public Services		Total	
	Number Employed[a]	Total Earnings[b]	Number Employed[a]	Total Earnings[b]	Number Employed[a]	Total Earnings[b]
1962						
African	126.1	9.4	90.6	9.2	216.8	18.6
Asian	8.1	4.5	1.8	1.3	9.9	5.8
European	2.3	3.3	1.8	3.0	4.1	6.3
Total	136.5	17.2	94.2	13.5	230.8	30.7
1963						
African	122.9	10.6	85.4	9.5	208.4	20.1
Asian	7.9	4.4	1.7	1.2	9.7	5.7
European	2.3	3.3	1.4	2.4	3.6	5.7
Total	133.1	18.3	88.5	13.1	221.7	31.5

SOURCE: Uganda Government, Ministry of Finance, *Background to the Budget, 1964–1965* (Entebbe).

[a] Times 1,000.

[b] These figures are given in million £'s.

Table 15–11

Tanganyika—Employment and Annual Wage Bill

Year	Number of Employees	Annual Wage Bill[a,b]
1962	397,028	42,176
1963	340,490	46,171

SOURCE: Tanganyika, East African Statistical Department, *Budget Survey, 1964–1965* (Dar es Salaam: Government Printer).

NOTES: 1)The fall in employment in 1963 was widespread in every region except Dar es Salaam, but was particularly severe in the Tanga and Morogoro regions, implying further labor economies on agricultural estates. 2) The annual wage bill rose by more than 9 per cent (despite the fall in employment), reflecting another large rise (35 per cent) in the average cash earnings of African employees.

[a] Includes the cash value of free rations.

[b] These figures are in thousand £'s.

has occurred a slight decrease in manufacturing employment. (See Tables 15–9, 15–10, and 15–11.) Ugandan employment in manufacturing and repairs was 29,700 in 1959, 31,200 in 1960, and 25,500 in 1961. In

Kenya, there was a decrease in African employment in the manufacturing sector from 44,200 in 1959 to 35,600 in 1961. The figure for 1962 was 38,700, but it is necessary to view it in relation to the steady addition to the labor force in the country. In Tanganyika, there has also been a sharp drop in numbers employed in the manufacturing sector. The number of Africans in employment in this sector in 1961 was 21,906, but there has been a decrease since then. As a consequence, the East African countries share a very serious unemployment problem. For the whole of East Africa, employment in the manufacturing and repair sector has decreased from 95,500 in 1959 to 81,500 in 1961. And since 1961, the situation has continued to deteriorate. There is no doubt that, during this particular period, investment was adversely affected by political uncertainty. In the case of Kenya, the problem presented itself as late as 1963 and independence. To a lesser extent, the decrease in employment is also attributable to the minimum-wage regulations now in force in three countries. Employment in the manufacturing sector accounts for only 7 per cent of the Africans in paid employment in Kenya, 5 per cent in Tanganyika, and 10 per cent in Uganda. As already stated, figures relating to registered employment in East Africa could be misleading because of the preponderance of the subsistence factor. If, however, employment in manufacturing is viewed as a percentage of the total labor force of the area, the figure would work out at only a fraction of 1 per cent. Generally speaking, the few large-scale industries adopting advanced techniques have a high ratio of capital to labor and, therefore, the prospects of diverting into manufacturing vast numbers of people surplus to agriculture do not appear to be very bright—at least in the immediate future.

Two additional factors need to be considered in relation to manufacturing activity in East Africa. The first of these is that, hithertofore, the initiative, capital, and know-how have been provided almost entirely by non-Africans. It is unlikely that independent African governments will allow this situation to continue indefinitely. All have called for increased participation by local people and have strongly urged development of joint ventures. To date, this principle has only been applied superficially, with a few Africans appointed to positions on the boards of directors. The expansion of the manufacturing sector may well be conditioned by the policies of the East African governments concerning participation by Africans. Secondly, the departure of large numbers of Europeans and Asians constituting the higher-income groups will necessitate a reassessment of the feasibility of developing import to substitute for local industries. Finally, trade with the Communist Bloc countries may actually intensify competition in the East African market and expose both existing and potential local enterprises to still more vigorous competition. For even though trade with the Communist countries may have a salutory effect on agricultural exports, the necessity of conferring reciprocal benefits on these countries would undoubtedly have implications for the manufacturing sector of East Africa.

FORESTS, FISHERIES, AND TOURISM

A survey of the resources of East Africa would be incomplete without a reference to three relatively undeveloped, though potentially highly rewarding, fields of activity, namely—forests, fisheries, and tourism. Uganda has made a promising start in fishery and has already built an export trade of £500,000 a year. The waters of lakes Victoria, Kyoga, Albert, Edward, and George contain vast quantities of fish. Of these, the Uganda waters of Lake Victoria provide about 35 per cent of the annual East African catch. In Tanganyika, the bulk of the fish catch comes from lakes Victoria and Tanganyika. In Kenya, fishing is confined to the coast and Lake Victoria.

It is to be noted that many Kenya and some Uganda and Tanganyika peoples do not eat fish. Nonetheless, fishing is a field that has immense potentialities, both as an export item and as a factor in reducing the dietary deficiencies of the people. Potential markets exist in the Congo, Northern Rhodesia, and in Asia. In the meantime, the waters of the Indian Ocean on the coast of East Africa are vigorously exploited by the fishing trawlers of other nations.

Both Tanganyika and Kenya are fairly well endowed with forests. In Tanganyika, 43,000 square miles or 13 per cent of the territory has been categorized as a forest reserve. The value of forest produce amounts to between £5 million and £6 million per annum. There is a fairly wide range of timber available, besides other forest products, such as honey and beeswax. The government has followed a careful policy of forest conservation and planting to ensure that the requirements of future generations are adequately met. In Kenya, forests are regarded as an extremely important national asset. The value of forest products, both in the monetary and subsistence sectors, amounted to £5.8 million in 1962 and £6.5 million in 1963 (as against 2.7 million in 1955). Forests provide a variety of benefits—such as the regulation and regularization of run-off, which is of vital importance to the lower settled areas, the supply of products both for domestic consumption and export, and as a means of converting wild life. In Uganda, forests are not of major importance to the economy, and the area which is likely to be productive of sawed timber is just about 2,000 miles. Projected estimates related to consumption of timber in the period 1980–2000 reveal serious deficiencies, and an intensified program of afforestation is contemplated.

The present contribution of forestry to the money economy is very small, its share of the recorded monetary economy being less than one-half per cent and, even with the inclusion of the subsistence sector, just under 2.5 per cent. In a United Nations survey of Africa, it is observed that "about 65 per cent of the forest areas in Africa are classified as inaccessible, while in many of the more accessible areas, when overexploitation has occurred, output has had to be restricted to avoid disappearance of the more valuable species."[15] Furthermore, African forests consist of hardwood species with little or no known commercial value. Finally, lack of adequate logging, transport, and other basic facilities, plus a scarcity of skilled labor limit production.

In parts of Kenya, the development of forests may be threatened either by the need to clear them to make room for cultivation or by keeping excessive numbers of stock in the lowland areas surrounding them.[16] Although more pressing human needs must be accommodated, there is no doubt that unplanned clearing will have adverse effects in the long run. Moreover, the clearing of forests for agriculture is not contributing to the establishment of forest-product industries as is evidenced by the low-level output of processed wood products—plywood, pulp, paperboard, and fiberboard. It is only recently that Kenya has finalized arrangements for setting up the first paper and pulp factory in East Africa.

Of all the resources in East Africa, the game parks, the perenially snow-capped mountains, and the rich cultures of her varied peoples hold almost unlimited potentialities. The development of game parks confers a twofold benefit. On the one hand, it helps in the preservation of the flora and fauna which could otherwise become the subject of reckless destruction, and, through its preservation, it facilitates the study of tropical animal ecology and research. And second, it makes available unparalleled attractions to thousands of tourists and, in turn, brings immense benefits to the economy.

The total area set aside for game parks in East Africa is considerable. In Uganda, it totals 5,501 square miles, in Kenya 8,532 square miles, and in Tanganyika 5,954 square miles.[17] Game sanctuaries were initially established on the initiative of the colonial administration. However, an interesting development in recent years has been the transfer of responsibility for the administration of some game parks from the central governments to African district councils. (See Table 15–12.)

The promotion of tourism is in the hands of the East African Tourist Travel Association. But of the three territories, Kenya derives the bulk of the revenue from tourism. Dissatisfaction with an inadequate share of the proceeds from tourist travel led Uganda to decide to withdraw from this body.

In Tanganyika, the famous Serengeti National Park and Ngorongoro Crater together contain possibly the largest collection of wild life in the

---

[15] United Nations, *op. cit.*

[16] It is significant to note that, "as a general principle no forest clearing is allowed on slopes of more than thirty degrees, even if replanting is to follow within two or three years. Not even light-selection fellings are allowed normally on slopes exceeding forty degrees slope." See: B. J. Honore, "Forestry in Kenya," in J. B. Russell (ed.), *The Natural Resources of East Africa* (Nairobi: D. A. Hawkins, Ltd., 1962).

[17] The East African Statistical Department, *Economic and Statistical Review.*

Table 15–12

National Parks and Game Reserves

Territory	Square Miles	Of Which	Square Miles
Kenya	8,516	Tsavo	8,069
Tanganyika	5,954	Serengeti	5,600
Uganda	5,919	Murchison Falls	1,100
Zanzibar	—		
Total			
East Africa	20,389		

SOURCE: East African Common Services Organization, East African Statistical Department, *Quarterly Economic and Statistical Review* (Nairobi).

entire world. The East African governments are fully aware of the immense potentialities of tourism in helping to earn foreign exchange, of the importance of a revival of crafts which may be languishing for want of support, and even in keeping alive certain aspects of traditional culture such as tribal dancing and folk music. Wild game can also serve as a supplementary source of meat, and hippo-cropping has been developed in Uganda in recent years.

PROBLEMS OF TRANSITION

In this section, an attempt is made to examine selected problems facing the East African countries as they seek to ensure steady and orderly economic development. In the pre-independence period, East Africa's leaders resisted the temptation of promising the masses a millennium immediately on the attainment of statehood. President Nyerere's slogan *Uhuru na Kazi* (Freedom and Work) and Prime Minister Kenyatta's catchword *Harambee* (Let us pull together) dramatize the necessity for hard work and indicate that no relaxation of effort is possible. The East African territories were better prepared for independence than their counterparts elsewhere in the colonial world. All inherited stable, well-established administrative machineries, and political transition was orderly. But political independence only marks the beginning of a long, drawn-out process of building a prosperous society on the basis of a growing diffusion of opportunities. It is here that the problems lie. For East Africa, though eager to enter the race for development, is largely without the means to do so.

By far the most important problem facing the East African countries is the transformation of a traditional subsistence economy into a modern, market-oriented economy. The fact that enclaves of highly developed agriculture do exist in East Africa has not been particularly helpful. In Kenya,

European agriculture developed as an island unto itself; and its influence on African farming, if not detrimental, was at best minimal.[18] The European settler community was long averse to the African farmer's entry into the field of cash-crop production and, even when the tide could no longer be stemmed, did little to assist the transition.[19]

The first Lancaster House Conference (1960) contributed to a sense of uncertainty about the future and resulted in an impairment of the performance of the European farming sector. Not only was capital investment interrupted, but existing equipment was allowed to run down. In a few cases, farms were abandoned as the owners hurriedly decided to leave. Livestock resources also were depleted as systematic breeding was interrupted and deliveries for slaughter increased. The demoralization of the European-owned farms added to the already serious problem of unemployment. Perhaps the full impact of this interruption of large-scale agriculture has even not been fully felt yet, but there is evidence to justify the view that the situation has been resolved and that conditions are improving. Uganda and Tanganyika did not have any sizable enclaves of non-African farming, and, hence, the impact of independence on the agricultural sector was less harsh.

The problem of economic development in East Africa can be divided into two broad categories: the immediate and transitional problems and those of a long-range nature. Among the former, the most important is the problem of consolidating the inheritance of the colonial period, which involves making the best of a legacy that is only partly an asset. There exists the need to unshackle the economy from the constraints that the colonial emphasis on stability imposed. In contrast to the broad aims of colonial policy, the requirements of the future are sharply outlined. Until World War II, colonial policy in East Africa was geared toward keeping the peace and maintaining Britain's sphere of influence. Little was done to

---

18 The author is aware of the extremely contentious nature of this statement. Whereas the absence in the past of any significant visible impact of the highly developed European farming areas on African farming activity cannot be denied, it may be argued that the former represents an excellent store of knowledge and experience of local farming conditions, and that this is bound to have a salutory influence on the productivity of African farming in the years to come. Knowledge of soils, the development of hybrid crops, the selective breeding of cattle, etc. would undoubtedly have a profound significance for African agricultural activity. An important development of which there is already some evidence concerns the rearing of high-grade milk cattle in some of the African areas of Kenya. This is in marked contrast to the situation in Uganda and Tanganyika, where the quality of African-owned cattle continues to be very poor. For an extremely interesting discussion of the pros and cons of this question, see Eric Clayton, "A Note on the Alien Enclave and Development" and T. C. I. Ryan, "A Rejoinder to Dr. Clayton's Note on the Alien Enclave and Development," in *East African Economic Review*, X (June 1963).

19 Some highly commendable work has been done by the Kenya Ministry of Agriculture, under the Swynnerton Plan for the promotion of cash farming in the African areas. A brief reference to the Plan occurs elsewhere in this article.

develop the East African countries into independent economic units. Development activity was considerable, but was concentrated in those areas where there was a definite and immediate prospect of return. No special funds were established to further development, and capital investment was limited to a level which current government revenues or borrowing made possible.[20] Public investment was directed largely to those fields that would open up new productive capacity and thereby increase export revenues. Infrastructure investment and, in particular, investment in education was severely limited. On the one hand, the government demonstrated a reluctance to interfere with traditional rights and customs, except for purposes of maintaining peace and effective administration, but, on the other hand, pressure was applied to force people into the market economy whenever revenue requirements or the demand for agricultural labor necessitated such action. The European settlers exercised an influence in political and economic matters quite out of proportion to their numbers.

The end of World War II heralded a departure in colonial economic policy, reflecting the radically altered political realities of the postwar world. A realization that independence was not only inevitable, but on the not too distant horizon, initiated a manifest desire to develop the colonies into viable entities as quickly as possible. Financial assistance was stepped up and began to assume, for the first time, realistic proportions. Attempts at overall integrated development gradually began to replace a previous policy of developing only those activities that were geared to the promotion of exports. There was less reluctance to apply pressure where this was deemed to be in the common interest of the people. In the meantime, pressure for independence grew rapidly, and independence was granted to the three East African countries within an interval of some two years. At this point, responsibility for completing the development task, so recently initiated, fell to the African governments.

Thus, the immediate challenge facing the East African governments is to ensure that programs of development initiated in the closing phases of colonial rule be carried to a conclusion. Although this is a very important first step, it is also simultaneously necessary to formulate well-conceived policies of an intermediate and long-term nature. The transformation from a predominantly subsistence to a market-oriented economy must naturally have the highest priority both in its short- and long-term aspects. The traditional African society and the mode of life therein was geared essentially to the survival of the group rather than to the exercise of individual initiative. It involved a combination of privileges and a corresponding set of obligations. Thus, opportunities for breaking away from the stultifying at-

---

[20] W. E. Moran, Jr., "Tropical Africa and the World Economy," in E. A. G. Robinson (ed.), *Economic Development for Africa South of the Sahara* (London: Macmillan & Company, 1964).

mosphere of the tribe were rare indeed, while an aggressive pursuit of individual welfare was frowned on and frequently punished.

However, the process of tribal disintegration had already begun. It is encouraging that, in all three countries, African people have clearly demonstrated both a willingness and an ability to move away from the irksome confines of a traditional society. The desire for change has not been shared equally by all tribal groups, and this makes the task of the African governments more complex than it might otherwise be. National resources will have to be devoted, not to serve the needs of a single group, but of the country as a whole. Thus, groups with more land than they can profitably use may have to be compelled to share it with others who are facing an acute shortage. This will probably require the introduction of concepts of land ownership, use, and tenure substantially at variance with those currently in force. But there is little doubt that this has to be done. Again, where traditional practices, such as overstocking, are wasteful of resources and inimical to progress, a measure of compulsion may have to be employed to secure adherence to more progressive and practical ideas.[21]

In the predominantly agricultural societies of East Africa, the most important determinant of progress is the sound use of land. Land-use regulations have to be enforced, even if this means undermining traditional rights and privileges. This is no simple task, and the East African governments have no choice but to cajole and, if necessary, to coerce. If they do not face up to the challenge and instead adopt a policy of least resistance, economic transformation, which they so earnestly seek, will not only be delayed but will be rendered increasingly difficult. Independent governments may have to be more ruthless than their colonial predecessors in eliminating barriers to development.

The next immediate problem that the East African territories face is the task of manning the administrative machinery and the various professional and technical services, without which economic development is impossible.

---

21 In a speech on the occasion of issuing title deeds to Masai landowners, the Kenya Minister for Lands and Settlement warned tribesmen that they must change their mode of life to fit in with the new Kenya and develop fully the vast lands occupied by the tribe. The Minister also noted that the number of plots that have been enclosed and registered in the whole of the land united was only sixty-eight as compared with thousands of plots and tens of thousands of acres covered in other areas of Kenya. He pointed out that poverty and backwardness for the Masai meant that Kenya could not progress, and the benefits of the *uhuru* would be dissipated. He stated, "I say this because the Masai people occupy a huge area of land, which almost stretched from the shores of Lake Victoria to within a hundred miles of the ocean and from the Tanganyika border to the outskirts of Nairobi." It contains every variation of climate, and it was true that whatever could be produced in Kenya could not be produced in Masailand. But crops grown in other parts of Kenya were not grown by the Masai, because it was not their custom. If the Masai wanted to develop their land, they must change their customs. *East African Standard,* September 22, 1964.

There is an urgent need to build a pool of African skills. Large numbers of expatriates still continue to perform those tasks that require long experience or high professional skill. It is obvious that a continuation of this situation is inconsistent with the natural and legitimate aspirations of the African people. In all three countries, a policy of Africanization is being vigorously implemented, but, in practice, it is extremely difficult to determine the pace at which Africanization can be carried out without seriously impairing the standards of performance. Moreover, the reach of government has now extended into most aspects of economic life, and, in the years to come, governments will need to equip themselves for even more varied responsibilities. The new governments are faced, not only with the need for the formulation of sound policies, but with their effective implementation as well. Thus, the demands on East Africa's human resources will necessitate important qualitative changes. It is true that the East African countries are now able to draw on a variety of sources for the provision of high-level manpower, but this in itself does not solve the problem and, under certain circumstances, may prove wholly ineffective. For example, a program to eliminate tropical disease or pest control can be handled most effectively by professionals possessing cumulative experience in the field, rather than by an itinerant "expert." The most fruitful plan is, of course, to train Africans. Thus, there is a need for bold and imaginative programs of education and training, but this is an area where governments can at best hasten slowly.

Agriculture and livestock are the dominant sectors in the East African economies. These activities not only account for a very large proportion of the domestic product but are the major sources of cash incomes, export earnings, and employment. But, the dominance of these sectors has often been regarded as a sign of weakness. Hence, it is sometimes suggested that the East African governments must take steps to diversify their economies. This view also derives support from the fact that, since the late fifties, there has been a downward trend in the world-market prices for primary commodities. (See Tables 15–13, 15–14, and 15–15.) The East African countries have only been able to maintain their export earnings through substantial increases in the quantum of exports. A situation in which a fall in the unit export price has to be made good by a steady increase in the quantum would obviously undermine the formulation of any production programs, and thereby would complicate the task of orderly economic development. There is no doubt that one of the basic objectives of developmental policy is to achieve a more balanced distribution in the contribution of the various sectors to the domestic product. The extent to which this objective can be pursued, however, is a function of resource availability. Attempts to push diversification, unrelated to human and material endowments, would be very expensive in terms of scarce resources, time, and effort.

Given a broad desire for change, there will also be undercurrents in the

Table 15-13

Kenya—Value of External Trade

	1959	1960	1961	1962	1963
net imports from countries outside East Africa	61.5	70.1	68.9	69.5	73.7
domestic exports to countries outside East Africa	33.3	35.2	35.3	37.9	43.8[a]
re-exports[b]	5.1	5.0	6.4	7.2	7.1[a]
total value of external trade	99.9	110.3	110.6	114.6	124.6
balance of external trade	−23.1	−29.9	−27.2	−24.3	−22.7

SOURCE: Government of Kenya, Economics and Statistics Division, *Economic Survey, 1964* (Nairobi).

NOTE: These figures are given in million £'s.

[a] Provisional.

[b] Excluding re-exports to Uganda and Tanganyika.

economy which could, by their cumulative impact, inevitably produce changes in the long run. The main deficiencies in the agricultural situation in East Africa are that a large proportion of the activities still takes place outside the monetary economy and that the area of activity that is oriented to the market is narrowly based. In this respect, the position of Uganda is the weakest, since cotton and coffee account for over 80 per cent of the export earnings of that country. In Tanganyika, sisal, coffee, and cotton accounted

Table 15-14

Uganda—Value of External Trade

	1961	1962	1963
net imports from countries outside East Africa	26.5	26.2	30.9
domestic exports to countries outside East Africa	39.2	37.6	51.5
re-exports[a]	2.1	3.3	3.0
total value of external trade	67.8	67.1	85.4
balance of external trade	+14.8	+14.7	+23.4

SOURCE: Uganda Government, Ministry of Finance, *Background to the Budget, 1964–1965* (Entebbe).

NOTE: These figures are given in million £'s.

[a] Excluding Kenya and Tanganyika.

Table 15–15

Tanganyika—Total Value of External Trade

	1959	1960	1961	1962	1963
net imports from countries outside East Africa	34,456	37,817	39,686	39,817	40,418
domestic exports to countries outside East Africa	45,287	54,823	48,667	51,241	63,555
re-exports[a]	1,931	1,747	1,951	2,177	1,408
total value of external trade	81,674	94,387	90,305	93,235	105,381
balance of external trade	+12,762	+18,753	+10,932	+13,601	+24,545

SOURCE: Tanganyika, East African Statistical Department, *Budget Survey, 1964–1965* (Dar es Salaam: Government Printer).

NOTE: These figures are given in thousand £'s.

a Excluding Kenya and Uganda.

for 63 per cent of the value of domestic exports in 1963, and, indeed, since 1961, most of the increase in the value of exports has been achieved through increases in the export value of these items. In Kenya, coffee, tea, and sisal accounted for 56 per cent of the value of total exports in 1963. Here, again, the bulk of the increases in export values has been achieved in sisal and tea.

This kind of concentration in a few select items raises serious problems for the East African countries. Therefore, efforts will have to be made in two directions. One is to increase the range of agricultural commodities produced to reduce the excessive dependence on the items that are currently most significant. This would obviously depend on the speed and the intensity of effort in introducing crop specialities. Second, there is also the need to effect improvements in techniques with a view to reducing costs of production and improving quality to enable producers to absorb price reductions without undue strain. At the same time, programs must be developed for enhancing the nonagricultural sectors and, in particular, manufacturing. Relief from this source will only accrue in the long run; but it is most important that a beginning be made with the least possible delay.

The role of the manufacturing sector in East Africa needs careful assessment. In common with most developing nations, the East African governments are anxious to push ahead with a policy of accelerated industrialization. Apart from the anxiety caused by the recent downward trend in export prices,[22] the case for industrialization is built around the need to widen employment opportunities for a steadily growing labor force. In the East African context, two considerations are particularly significant. A first consideration is the existence of a common market. Industrialization pro-

---

[22] Sisal and tea are exceptions.

grams formulated from a parochial territorial viewpoint could easily result in a situation wherein all the East African countries are pursuing similar or identical industrial efforts. Even on the assumption that the East African market could support the existence of a number of new industrial ventures, it is unlikely that its absorptive capacity could grow at a rate at which it could handle the output of similar ventures in three separate nations. Indeed, uncoordinated development might create new problems without solving existing ones. As yet, there is little indication that the three countries are aiming at the necessary coordination of development policy. One consequence of uncoordinated development is the saturation of the East African market with products that are the easiest to manufacture. Though it is true that the absorptive capacity of the market will probably be based on income levels and patterns of consumption (both of which may change for the better), there is no doubt that considerable frustration may result from the unilateral formulation of industrial programs.

A second important consideration is the necessity to ensure that adequate resources are devoted to continuing the process of agricultural transformation, in which an extremely satisfactory beginning has been made. If, in their desire to achieve accelerated progress in the industrial field, the East African governments were to switch their meager resources to nonagricultural sectors, an unfortunate interruption of what is perhaps the most encouraging trend in the economy, namely, the progress of the African farmer in the field of cash-crop production, might ensue.

In any program of industrialization, the East African countries may have to look inward rather than outward so far as the absorption of the products is concerned. From this point of view, the problem of East Africa is, not to launch an export drive for its manufactured goods, but rather to relate industrialization to the growing potentialities of the internal markets. It is significant that the World Bank missions to all the East African countries emphasized the need to raise the level of earnings in the agricultural sector as a precondition for the establishment of a sizable manufacturing sector. Though there is no doubt that this is an ideal sequence, it ignores considerations of economic nationalism which has played such an important part in developing nations. Nevertheless, it is important that a program of industrialization should be preceded by a scientific assessment of market potentialities, i.e., through feasibility studies. Unplanned industrialization, under cover of tariff protection, may result in a number of high-cost ventures that would impose prolonged hardship on the domestic consumer. (See Table 15–16.)

One other factor may have relevance for East Africa in its program of industrialization. This is the possibility of an enlarged market coming into existence as a consequence of an association between East Africa and the neighboring territories. On the assumption that a greater union of East and

Table 15–16

Value of Inter-Territorial Trade, 1959–1963

	Kenya		Tanganyika		Uganda	
Year	to Tanganyika	to Uganda	to Kenya	to Uganda	to Kenya	to Tanganyika
1959	6,513	5,784	1,848	726	3,640	1,587
1960	7,608	6,163	1,875	450	5,120	1,574
1961	8,901	7,047	1,844	390	5,152	1,704
1962	10,017	7,303	1,954	437	5,386	1,669
1963	10,365	9,425	2,915	508	6,248	1,993

SOURCE: East African Common Services Organization, East African Statistical Department, *Quarterly Economic and Statistical Review* (Nairobi: 1964).

NOTES: 1) The value of inter-territorial transfers excluded excise duty on excisable commodities (i.e., sugar, beer, tobacco, cigarettes, and matches) and customs duty charged on imported raw materials used in local manufactures. Such adjustments have been made annually by the East African Customs and Excise Department since 1959. 2) These figures are given in thousand £'s.

Central African states becomes a reality, it may be possible to re-examine the scope and the range of industrial activity.[23] In this event, East Africa, which is industrially comparatively more advanced, may be able to derive considerable advantage. It must, however, be noted that this would also involve corresponding sacrifices, in view of the fact that the prospective members of a greater union would cast their lot in a greater federal union not merely to improve the viability of East African enterprises.

Any assessment of the balance between the industrial and agricultural sectors must take account of the fact that there are still a number of vital areas in agriculture that need to be strengthened. For example, the present production of food in East Africa is barely adequate to meet the needs of a rapidly growing population. If a responsible calorific intake for the masses is to be achieved, there is an urgent need to increase food production. The precarious nature of the food supply in East Africa was revealed during the drought of 1961 and the subsequent flood in 1962. The deficiencies in communications worsened the problem, and massive famine was averted in many areas by resort to air-dropping of food. When supplies ran alarmingly low, it was necessary to supplement them with food grants from the United States. In view of this, the need to ensure a growing supply of food should be regarded as a matter of the highest priority.

The problems of agricultural transformation in East Africa are so

[23] See B. F. Massell, "Industrialization and Economic Union in Greater East Africa," *The East African Economic Review*, IX (December 1962), 108–123.

numerous and varied that they will probably consume the greater part of governmental energy and resources in the foreseeable future. There is the need to link vast numbers of rural people to the market economy; for this is the only means of diffusing the effects of economic development over a wide area. A significant shortcoming of the colonial period was that the limited economic development that did take place had very little impact on the bulk of the population and succeeded only in creating a dual economy. It is to be hoped that African governments will not be satisfied with the mere replacement of the old dual economy by something akin to it in form and substance. The most promising opportunities for bringing about a diffusion of the benefits of development lie in the agricultural sphere. The reinforcing of the agricultural sector, therefore, would be the most effective first step in building the economy on a firm foundation.[24]

An extremely critical factor in the spread of the market economy is the improvement of communications. In the pre-independence period, the development of the transportation system (both roads and railways) was geared essentially to the need for maintaining a growing volume of exports. Vast areas, therefore, were either inadequately served or not served at all. Hence, the conditions conducive to national economic integration were missing. Recent development projects demonstrate the dramatic impact that a connecting road or a rail link can have on regional development. Of the three East African territories, Uganda has the best road system and Tanganyika has the worst; whereas, Kenya occupies an intermediate position. As population pressure begins to manifest itself, the need to open up new areas for settlement will become critical. Before embarking on new settlement schemes, a substantial investment will be required to extend and improve the transportation network. The extension of the transportation grid will continue to claim a heavy portion of the limited capital resources available to East Africa.

Possibly the most critical factor affecting economic development in East Africa is the availability of capital. The supply from internal sources is

---

[24] For a detailed scheme for raising the productivity of the African agricultural areas see, "A Plan to Intensify the Development of African Agriculture in Kenya," compiled by R. J. M. Swynnerton, Colony and Protectorate of Kenya, Nairobi, 1954. The Swynnerton Plan has, since that time, been the basis of Kenya's government policy in relation to the African agricultural areas. It is generally recognized that the Plan has initiated a virtual "agrarian revolution" in Kenya.

Specific measures for raising agricultural productivity in the African areas are an increased emphasis on land consolidation, the improvement of farming practices, the extension of irrigated farming where feasible, improvement of cattle rearing in low rainfall areas, the provision of credit, the spread of agricultural education, the modification of the inheritance system, and, in particular, the extension services. Many of these measures have already been put into effect, but the attainment of independence has opened up the possibility of much more positive and concerted action.

seriously limited. The combined value of the GNP of East Africa amounted to £590 million in 1962 (Kenya, £243; Uganda, £155; and Tanganyika, £192). On the basis of an estimated population of 25.5 million, the per capita income was approximately £23 per annum. The variations in per capita income are substantial—ranging from Kenya's £28.3, Tanganyika's £20.0, and Uganda's £22.1 per annum. Thus, the possibility of mobilizing considerable domestic savings for investment would appear rather limited. Furthermore, the per capita income figures conceal an important disparity in the average income levels of the three racial groups in East Africa, generally, and in Kenya, particularly. In 1963, the average wage level of Africans in reported employment was £94, of Asians £560, and of Europeans £1,452.[25] On the basis of the average income figures, it would appear that the bulk of domestic savings accrue from the Europeans who constitute a minute segment of the population. Unfortunately, however, the investment requirements of the post-independence years are substantially higher than those of the pre-independence period. Even during the pre-independence period, when the size of development budgets was modest, the greatest part of the required finance was derived in the form of foreign assistance. The three East African countries have recently formulated extensive development places requiring an extraordinary increase in the supply of capital.

The supply of capital must be considered in relation to the balance between public and private contributions. As in most developing nations, the size of private-sector investment in East Africa depends on the nature and extent of supporting public-sector programs. For example, such infrastructure investment as roads, railways, and power supplies have a decisive influence on the scope and direction of private investment. Given their limited resources, the East African governments are unable to finance simultaneously infrastructure- and industrial-capital investment. Barring the Uganda Development Corporation, which had developed a number of manufacturing establishments, government initiative in industry has been slight. Even in Uganda, the Corporation does not wholly "own" the enterprises, but contributes to share capital in varied degrees. Though both Tanganyika and Kenya have established Industrial Development Corporations, they cannot yet be regarded as having a decisive influence on the evolving pattern of manufacturing activity.

The attainment of independence imposes additional obligations. For it is at this critical period that the governments are obliged to undertake substantial investment in social services, which, in the past, were relatively neglected. (See Tables 15–17, 15–18, and 15–19.)

---

[25] In Uganda, the figures of average African wages in 1962 and 1963 were £85.8 and £96.6 respectively, of Asian wages £593 and £597, and of European wages £1834 and £1875 respectively. (Uganda Government, Ministry of Finance, *Background to the Budget, 1964–1965*, [Entebbe: Government Printer]).

Table 15–17

Kenya—Gross Capital Formation, 1958–1963

	1958	1959	1960	1961	1962	1963[a]
PUBLIC SECTOR						
Kenya government	6.4	6.6	8.1	7.2	6.9	5.3
E.A.C.S.O. (including						
trading services)	4.1	3.4	2.2	2.2	2.2	1.8
local authorities	2.8	3.5	3.0	3.2	3.2	2.2
military	—	0.2	1.1	1.8	0.5	0.2
Total	13.3	13.7	14.4	14.5	12.8	9.5
PRIVATE SECTOR						
agriculture	5.7	5.7	5.4	4.6	3.6	3.6
other	21.0	21.0	21.6	12.9	16.9	15.9
Total	26.7	26.7	27.0	17.4	20.5	19.5
PUBLIC AND PRIVATE						
Total	40.0	40.3	41.4	31.9	33.3	29.0

SOURCE: Government of Kenya, Economics and Statistics Division, *Economic Survey, 1964* (Nairobi).

NOTE: These figures are given in million £'s.

[a] Provisional.

Table 15–18

Uganda—Gross Capital Formation, 1954–1963

Year	Public Sector[b]	Private Sector[b]	Total[b]	Per Cent of the Monetary Economy (at market prices)
1954	8.3	10.2	18.6	18.9
1955	9.7	13.5	23.2	21.3
1956	8.4	13.3	21.8	19.9
1957	8.9	11.5	20.4	17.5
1958	8.6	11.0	19.6	17.1
1959	8.3	8.8	17.1	14.6
1960[a]	8.2	10.8	19.0	15.8
1961[a]	6.9	10.4	17.3	14.2
1962[a]	6.3	10.2	16.5	13.8
1963	6.4	13.0	19.4	13.6
(estimate)				

Uganda—Gross Capital Formation in the Public Sector, 1959–1963

Type of Authority	1959[b]	1960[a,b]	1961[a,b]	1962[a,b]	1963[b,c]
Uganda government	5.3	5.0	4.8	4.4	4.8
local authorities	1.9	1.4	1.0	0.8	0.5
E.A.C.S.O.[d]	1.1	1.8	1.1	1.2	1.1
Total	8.3	8.2	6.9	6.3	6.4

Uganda—Gross Capital Formation in the Private Sector, 1953–1963

Type of Asset	1950[b]	1960[a,b]	1961[a,b]	1962[a,b]	1963[b,c]
buildings and works	2.5	2.6	2.6	2.8	3.2
plant, machinery, and equipment	5.2	6.5	7.0	6.1	7.8
vehicles	1.1	1.7	0.8	1.3	2.0
Total	8.8	10.8	10.4	10.2	13.0

SOURCE: Uganda Government, Ministry of Finance, *Background to the Budget, 1964–1965* (Entebbe: Government Printing Office).

[a] Revised.

[b] These figures are given in million £'s.

[c] Estimate.

[d] Includes E. A. R. & H. and E. A. P. & T.

Table 15–19

Tanganyika—Total Gross Capital Formation by Sector

Sector	1960	1961	1962	1963
PRIVATE				
building and construction	7,022	7,433	7,443	8,325
machinery and equipment	8,335	8,027	7,409	8,371
Total private	15,357	15,460	14,852	16,696
PUBLIC				
building and construction	6,725	9,695	8,015	7,883
machinery and equipment	1,099	1,366	1,534	562
Total public	7,824	11,061	9,549	8,445
Grand Total	23,181	26,521	24,401	25,141

SOURCE: Tanganyika, East African Statistical Department, *Budget Survey, 1964–1965* (Dar es Salaam: Government Printer).

NOTE: These figures are given in thousand £'s.

East Africa's economic development depends, therefore, on a constant and massive import of external capital. A review of the role of external finance in gross capital formation in East Africa reveals that there has been a steady increase in the proportion of external finance. In Kenya, since 1960, a steady decline in gross capital formation has been accompanied by an increase in the proportion of external grants and loans. In Uganda, gross capital formation has varied from year to year since 1960, but the 1963 figure is no higher than that of 1960. The amount of external assistance constitutes a lesser proportion than in 1960, and, as in Kenya and Uganda, external assistance in the form of loans and grant aid has shown a marked increase. (See Tables 15–20 and 15–21.)

Table 15–20

Kenya—Grants and Loans Received into Development Account, 1958/1959 to 1963/1964

	1958/ 1959	1959/ 1960	1960/ 1961	1961/ 1962	1962/ 1963	1963/ 1964 Estimates
GRANTS FROM ABROAD						
Colonial Development and Welfare	1.07	0.84	1.57	2.27	3.74	4.28
Agency of International Development and other	0.12	0.22	0.05	0.14	0.22	0.13
LOANS						
United Kingdom Exchequer	—	3.00	5.33	4.45	5.39	6.16
International Bank for Reconstruction and Development	—	—	0.39	0.69	0.64	1.44
others raised abroad	0.57	0.37	0.40	0.16	0.03	0.04
local market issues	3.67	1.75	0.30	0.29	0.05	—
other East African loans	—	0.42	0.10	0.07	—	—
West German loan	—	—	—	—	0.68	0.71
Total grants and loans	5.43	6.58	8.14	9.07	10.75	12.76

SOURCE: Government of Kenya, Economics and Statistics Division, *Economic Survey, 1964* (Nairobi).
NOTE: These figures are given in million £'s.

An interesting trend in the provision of external assistance in recent years has been the diffusion of sources from which capital is obtained. Though assistance from the United Kingdom continues to account for a large proportion of the total, other sources, such as the International Bank

Table 15–21

Uganda—External Financial Assistance

Source of Aid	1961/ 1962	1962/ 1963	1963/ 1964	1964/ 1965	Total
To CENTRAL GOVERNMENT					
British sources	3.60	1.37	2.57	0.81	8.36
Agency of International Development	—	0.07	0.51	1.06	1.64
Federal German Republic	—	—	—	1.40	1.40
international sources	—	0.01	0.14	0.04	0.20
Total	3.60	1.46	3.23	3.32	11.62
To OTHER PUBLIC SECTOR					
British sources	2.40	0.10	—	—	2.50
Agency of International Development	a	a	a	a	0.71
Federal German Republic	—	—	—	0.50	0.50
international sources	1.52	0.77	—	0.08	2.99
Total	3.90	0.87	0.62	0.58	6.71
Total external financial assistance	7.52	2.33	3.86	3.90	18.33

SOURCE: Uganda Government, Ministry of Finance, *Background to the Budget, 1964–1965* (Entebbe: Government Printer).

NOTE: These figures are given in million £'s.

a Details not available.

for Reconstruction and Development, United States, and West Germany, now constitute major sources of capital supply. Still more recently, the Communist countries have begun to supply capital to the East African nations. One important source of assistance (Colonial Development and Welfare funds) disappeared on the attainment of independence. However, the United Kingdom government has agreed that commitments made in advance of independence will be honored. A similar provision also applies to investment commitments made by the Colonial Development Corporation (restyled the Commonwealth Development Corporation).

Also of importance is the fact that, until recently, a substantial proportion of external loans was obtained on an "across the board" basis, with a view toward supplementing the development funds of the recipient country. Discretion in employing the loans remained entirely with the beneficiary nation. Now, however, there appears to be a definite trend toward loans on a "project" basis, with the implication that only approved projects will be financially supported. The finance ministers of the East African territories maintain that this not only limits their independence but also their flexibility and delays the implementation of development plans.

A further complication facing the East African countries is that most loans (apart from Exchequer loans) are "tied," in the sense that they can be used only for buying equipment or obtaining personnel from the lending country. This is a particularly irksome restriction, for not only does it limit the freedom of the recipient country, but it also imposes an obligation to duplicate spares for the foreign equipment so purchased. For example, if the East African Airways Corporation receives a French government loan restricted to the purchase of French aircraft, it is necessary to augment the Corporation's service and spares facilities. In view of the current shortage of skills, the advantages of "tied loans" are often outweighed by the disadvantages.

A further problem in external assistance is proved by the fact that loans are often limited to the value of imported equipment. If the equipment component of a £1 million project is only £250,000, the recipient country is faced with the burden of finding a balance of $750,000. This problem is particularly evident in Tanganyika, where the foreign exchange component of a number of critical projects was less than 25 per cent of the total. What the East African governments badly need is funds flexible across the board rather than segmented inflexible assistance.

Finally, many development projects financed through loans pose problematically high recurrent costs. Some capital projects studied have revealed recurrent costs of as much as 30–40 per cent of the initial capital cost. Thus, in some cases, even when the whole of the initial capital cost is provided by a foreign country, the problems to the recipient nation are considerable. But the recipient nation has little choice in the matter of obtaining foreign assistance and, given the paucity of domestic resources, must attract foreign capital if development is to proceed. Foreign private investment is an important supplementary source of capital, and the East African governments have provided various incentives to attract foreign commercial and industrial finance. This task is frequently complicated by an anxiety to preserve their economic independence and by real and fancied fears that their economic destiny will be decided by alien powers. Also, foreign private capital may demand specific concessions and guarantees which may run counter to economic nationalism or to long-term requirements. The task of developing a workable and acceptable compromise between the need to secure steady infusions of private capital and the imperative of preserving the new nation's economic independence is difficult indeed.

Of necessity, solutions to the economic problems facing East Africa will evolve as part of a long-term effort. Independence and its inevitable attendant expectations place a frightening obligation on the East African governments to deliver the economic advantages which freedom is believed to promise. Governments, if they are to stay in power, have no alternative but to offer some tangible evidence of improved material well-being for the masses. Whereas this requirement will undoubtedly result in a diffusion and dissipation of effort and delay significant progress in a particular economic field, such diffusion will contribute, in some measure, toward reinforcing the economic foundation of the three countries. For example, the necessity to make large-scale investment in the area of social infrastructure will cause a shift of real resources from direct productive activity; but, in the long run, such investment is bound to have important qualitative and quantitative influences on the performance of the entire economy. A decision on investment priorities is always difficult to make, but this is particularly the case when a desperate need for simultaneous development in a number of sectors exists.

An important factor influencing the course of economic progress in East Africa is the degree of realism underlying the direction of economic activity. Despite the attraction of the manufacturing sector, for example, it is imperative that initial efforts be concentrated in the strengthening of the agricultural and livestock sectors. Industrial and agricultural development must not be viewed as alternatives, but as interrelated phases of economic development.

APPENDIX A

East Africa—Estimated Population by Race and Territory[d]

Mid year	KENYA African	Non-African	Total	TANGANYIKA African	Non-African	Total	UGANDA African	Non-African	Total	ZANZIBAR African[a]	Non-African[b]	Total	EAST AFRICA African	Non-African	Total
1948	5,240	159	5,399	7,389	72	7,461	4,900	42	4,942	248.7	16.6	265.3	17,777	289	18,067
1956	6,972	237	7,209	8,489	116	8,605	5,970	76	6,046	274.1	18.7	292.3	21,705	447	22,152
1957	7,181	251	7,432	8,637	122	8,759	6,119	80	6,199	277.5	18.9	296.5	22,214	472	22,686
1958	7,396	256	7,652	8,788	128	8,916	6,272	84	6,356	280.9	19.2	300.1	22,737	487	23,224
1959	7,618	262	7,880	8,942	134	9,076	6,425	88	6,513	284.3	19.6	303.9	23,269	503	23,773
1960	7,847	268	8,115	9,099	138	9,237	6,586	91	6,677	287.8	19.8	307.7	23,819	517	24,336
1961	8,082	270	8,352	9,281	140	9,421	6,751	94	6,845	291.4	20.1	311.5	24,405	524	24,929
1962	8,325	270	8,595	9,467	140	9,607	6,920	96	7,016	295.0	20.5	315.5	25,007	526	25,533
1963	8,575[c]	272	8,847	9,656	142	9,798	7,093	97	7,190	298.7	20.7	319.4	25,622	531	26,153

SOURCE: Kenya, Ministry of Finance and Economic Planning, Statistics Division, *Kenya Statistical Abstract, 1963*. East African Common Services Organization, East African Statistical Department, *Quarterly Economic and Statistical Review*, (June 1964), Nairobi.

NOTES: 1) The population estimates are made as follows: for Kenya, the growth rate for the African population is assumed to be 3 per cent per annum during the period 1952–1962, though corrections have been made in respect of figures since 1956 (on the basis of corrected figures, the mid-1964 estimate of Kenya's population is 9.1 million); for Tanganyika, the assumed growth rate is 2 per cent per annum since 1960; for Uganda, the assumed rate is 2.5 per cent per annum. 2) The latest censuses were held as follows: Kenya, August 1962; Tanganyika, August 1957; Uganda, August 1959; Zanzibar, March 1958.

[a] Arabs, mainland Africans, and Comorians.

[b] Excluding Arabs, but including Asians, Europeans, Somali, and others.

[c] Not corrected for the now assumed growth rate of 3 per cent per annum.

[d] Figures are given in thousands.

APPENDIX B
Kenya—Land Classification

The total area of Kenya consists of 224,960 square miles which are distributed as follows:

land not available for agriculture or grazing, including water, 5,171 square miles; national parks, 8,516 square miles	15,621 square miles
forest areas	5,952 square miles
scheduled areas[a]	12,173 square miles
nonscheduled areas[a]	191,214 square miles

The land areas of the nonscheduled area (85 per cent of the whole) consists of varying qualities and potentials which have been assessed into broad categories for planning purposes by the Department of Agriculture, namely:

A. High potential with adequate rainfall (35 inches and above)
   (1) very high potential land, with adequate rainfall, good deep soils and moderate temperatures (Kikuyu—star grass zones)
   (2) high potential land as above, but too cold to grow two crops per year
   (3) Land with adequate rainfall and deep soil, but with a soil-fertility problem or poor drainage
   (4) Land with adequate rainfall, but with shallow soil unsuited to arable agriculture.

B. Medium potential (20 inch to 25 inch rainfall)
   (1) with good deep soil suited to agriculture
   (2) with soil-fertility problem or with poor drainage
   (3) with shallow soil unsuited to arable agriculture, but suited to grazing.

C. Low potential (20 inch to 25 inch rainfall)
   suited only to ranching except under irrigation.

D. Nomadic pastoral (less than 20 inch rainfall)
   suitable only to poor-quality ranching or wild-life exploitations (latter probably best).

The distribution of these classes of land within each province is set out in Table 15–22.

Table 15–22

Analysis of Land-Use Categories in Nonscheduled Areas by Province[a]

Square Miles

	A1	A2	A3	A4	B1	B2	B3	C	D	Total
Central	1,784	—	234	104	1,058	156	194	2,782	—	6,312
Nyanza	4,192	—	399	1,297	809	755	636	—	—	8,088
Southern	435	—	—	—	1,108	1,177	1,190	4,179	3,861	11,950
Masai[b]	1,535	1,023	485	987	520	—	—	3,618	6,548	14,716
Rift	1,277	345	291	224	1,343	455	1,195	1,491	754	7,375
Coast	445	—	474	643	425	601	679	2,640	14,994	20,901
Northern	—	—	—	—	15	—	—	130	121,727	121,872
	9,668	1,368	1,883	3,255	5,278	3,144	3,894	14,840	147,884	191,214

SOURCE: East African Common Services Organization, Statistical Department, *Kenya African Agricultural Sample Census, 1960/61* (Nairobi: Government Printer).

[a] Originally, the scheduled and nonscheduled areas meant land that was under the exclusive ownership of non-Africans and Africans respectively. The ownership of land on an exclusively racial basis has now ended.

[b] Masai is in fact Kajiado and Narok districts of Southern Province, but it is convenient for this purpose to treat this area separately from the rest of Southern Province— Machakos and Kitui districts.

SELECTED BIBLIOGRAPHY

BOOKS

Elkan, Walter. *Migrants and Proletarians.* London: Oxford University Press, 1960.

Elkan, Walter. *The Economic Development of Uganda.* London: Oxford University Press, 1961.

Fearn, Hugh. *An African Economy.* London: Oxford University Press, 1961.

International Bank for Reconstruction and Development. *The Economic Development of Kenya,* "Report of a Mission Organized by the International Bank for Reconstruction and Development at the Request of the Government of Kenya and the United Kingdom." Baltimore: Johns Hopkins Press, 1963.

International Bank for Reconstruction and Development. Economic Survey Mission. *The Economic Development of Tanganyika.* Baltimore: Johns Hopkins Press, 1961.

International Bank for Reconstruction and Development. *The Economic Development of Uganda,* "Report of a Mission Organized by the International Bank for Reconstruction and Development at the Request of the Government of Uganda." Baltimore: Johns Hopkins Press, 1962.

Robinson, E. A. G. (ed). *Economic Development for Africa South of the Sahara.* London: Macmillan & Company, 1964.

Russell, B. W. (ed.). *The Natural Resources of East Africa.* Nairobi: D. A. Hawkins, Ltd., 1962.

ARTICLES

Belshaw, D. G. R. "Public Investment in Agriculture and the Economic Development of Uganda," *East African Economic Review,* IX (December 1962), 69–95.

Clayton, E. S. "Policies Affecting African Agriculture in Kenya," *East African Economic Review,* VI (January 1959).

Clayton, E. S. "A Note on the Alien Enclave and Development," *East African Economic Review,* X (June 1963), 35–41.

Etherington, D. M. "Land Settlement in Kenya; Policy and Practice," *East African Economic Review,* X (June 1963), 22–35.

Krishna, K. G. V. "Planning and Economic Development," *East African Economic Review,* IX (June 1962), 48–63.

Livingston, I. "The Economic Development of Tanganyika: The World Bank View," *East African Economic Review,* VIII (June 1961), 1–14.

Massell, B. F. "Industrialization and Economic Union in Greater East Africa," *East African Economic Review,* IX (December 1962), 108–123.

Ryan, T. C. I. "A Rejoinder to Dr. Clayton's Note on the Alien Enclave and Development," *East African Economic Review,* X (June 1963), 41–47.

PUBLIC DOCUMENTS

Great Britain, Colonial Office. *East Africa Royal Commission 1953–1955, Report.* May 16, 1955, Cmnd. 9475, London: H.M.S.O., 1955.

Mitchell, Phillip E. *The Agrarian Problem in Kenya,* Nairobi: Government Printer, 1947.

United Nations, Department of Economic and Social Affairs, *Economic Survey of Africa since 1950.* New York: United Nations, 1959.

16

Federation: An Unfinished Portrait

Anthony H. Rweyemamu
Brack E. S. Brown

IT IS NOW MORE THAN a decade since the continent of Africa has captured and held the spotlight of international attention. One region of this vast continent which holds particular attention is what was formerly known as British East Africa, comprising the now sovereign states of Kenya, Uganda, and the United Republic of Tanzania (formerly Tanganyika and Zanzibar).

Transition in East Africa, from colonial dependency to independence and then to the broader tasks of nation-building, has been particularly complex and interesting due to a unique combination of centralizing and separatist forces. Because of colonial and, more recently, African initiatives to expand the framework of the inherited state systems, East Africa has received special notice from those concerned with problems of African economic development, social mobilization, and federalism. In the past several years, a profusion of articles, books, reports, and conferences have been presented to illuminate the issues involved in constructively controlling the future of the 25 million peoples of East Africa. This essay proposes to elaborate and up-date the discussion and analysis of the special issue of East African federation as it has evolved to the present time. Our main concern will be to analyze the relevant issues and events for a federation of East Africa as they appeared by late 1964. We shall also assess the future prospects of East Africa with regard to federation.

HISTORICAL BACKGROUND

The earliest concrete proposal for an East African Federation was prepared by Sir Harry Johnston, special Commissioner to the Uganda Protectorate in 1899.[1] Johnston visualized joining Uganda and Kenya, both

---

[1] Kenneth Ingham, *A History of East Africa* (London: Longmans, Green, and Company, 1962), p. 207.

being under British protection at the time. Also at the turn of the century, the great visionary settler, Lord Delamere, and the intrepid empire-builder, Cecil Rhodes, dreamed their separate dreams of a unified white-settler Dominion of Eastern Africa. From 1905, conferences of white settlers met at frequent intervals to discuss such a linkage. But it was not until Germany's defeat in World War I and the entry of Tanganyika into the British sphere that schemes for federation became a continuing pre-occupation of the colonial administration. A long procession of East African governors, colonial secretaries, and special commissioners were associated with schemes to bring about a closer political union of the territories. These included Edward Grigg, Charles Eliot, Phillip Mitchell, Gerald Portal, Lord Rosebery, Winston Churchill, L. S. Amery, Samuel Wilson, and others. Then, as now, the small but powerful voice of the Buganda government convincingly protested the possibility of becoming a horse in Kenya's stable, although in those early days it was the fear of white-settler domination that agitated the Baganda. Powerful resistance to the federal-minded planners also came from the famous Tanganyika governor, Sir Donald Cameron. He successfully maintained that the idea of federation was not consistent with the League of Nations mandate provisions for the administration of Tanganyika nor with its guarantees of "native rights."[2]

Between 1924 and 1945, a number of investigations were carried out on the federation question. The earliest of these, the Ormsby-Gore Commission, concluded that federation was not a wise step due to the inadequacies of communications, the extra expenses, political difficulties of large-scale government, and the unwillingness of the various governments to depart from their separate territorial development schemes.[3] Subsequent reports such as the Hilton Young Commission Report of 1929 and the Joint Select Committee Report of 1931 reached similar conclusions. Interesting enough, these conclusions bear striking resemblance to arguments that have been made against federation in post-independent East Africa. In every case, the earlier recommendations stressed the necessity to encourage economic cooperation between the various governments—a position that is again not unlike present-day recommendations.

Despite the reiteration in these reports that the time was not yet ripe for political federation, a number of related measures were implemented by the colonial regime. Such policies steadily strengthened the base on which a federation might one day be built. A persistent aim of those favoring federation was to establish a high commission with responsibility for coordinating the entire economic development of the area. The first practical step in this direction, inspired by the Ormsby-Gore Report, was the acceptance, in 1926,

---

[2] Sir Donald Cameron, *My Tanganyika Service and Some Nigeria* (London: Allen and Unwin, 1939), *passim*.

[3] Great Britain, *Report of the East African Commission*, Cmnd., 2387 (London: H.M.S.O., 1925), p. 7.

of a periodic conference of the governors of the three territories. L. S. Amery, the Colonial Secretary, intended to use this machinery as an instrument to create a full federation. However, he was frustrated at the outset by resistance from traditionalist elements in Uganda and by the Governor of Tanganyika. Nevertheless, the governors' conferences and a variety of other piecemeal measures that were introduced over the years did achieve a substantial degree of interterritorial cooperation and especially in such fields as trade, customs, posts and telecommunications, and other public services.

In 1944, the Colonial Secretary, Oliver Stanley, appointed Sir Phillip Mitchell Governor of Kenya, with specific instructions to devise some form of East African authority capable of dealing with common problems of East Africa.[4] Sir Phillip's efforts resulted in the creation of the East African High Commission in 1948. The stated purpose of the new body was "to improve and build up the limited common services already existing."[5] All decisions of the High Commission, however, were subject to the discretion and approval of each of the three governments concerned. The unabating fears that the Commission was the thin edge of the wedge of federation forced the organization to walk a straight apolitical line in the interests of its survival.

By the mid-1950's, there were a number of encouraging signs that the shadow of colonialism might be lifted from East Africa within the foreseeable future. The decolonization of Asia, North Africa, and Ghana, coupled with a more vigorous demand for self-determination on the part of pan-Africanists, constituted the new wind of change that was inevitably felt in East Africa. In Kenya, positive steps were being taken to liberalize the government in the wake of insights gained through the emergency. Tanganyika had established a dynamic new African political party (TANU), whose leaders demonstrated extraordinary organizational ability and unrelenting demands for independence. In Uganda, there was a rising spirit of self-assertion illustrated by the fierce reaction in the country to a colonial secretary's ill-timed suggestion, in 1953, of eventual federation.[6] These events led to a more vigorous and more coordinated campaign by the nationalists for self-determination and self-rule.

THE PAFMECA ERA, 1958–1963

In 1958, East African opposition to British colonialism and separate plans for liberation found common expression in the establishment of the Pan-African Freedom Movement of East and Central Africa (PAFMECA). This organization had several distinct antecedents including the Makerere College

---

[4] *Kenya Weekly News,* October 23, 1964, p. 11.

[5] Great Britain, Colonial Office, *Inter-territorial Organization in East Africa,* Colonial No. 191, (London: H.M.S.O., December 1945).

[6] B. T. G. Chidzero, *Tanganyika and International Trusteeship* (New York: Oxford University Press, 1961), p. 101.

Political Society, founded in 1953 by a number of students who have since become important figures in the East and Central African governments. In its journal, the Society published a draft constitution for an East and Central African Federation.[7] In 1954, Kenneth Kaunda called a meeting of East and Central African nationalists to discuss regional problems. At the first meeting of independent states in Accra, March 1958, Julius Nyerere, Joseph Murumbi, and Sheikh Ali Muhsin discussed the question of regional association with George Padmore and Kwame Nkrumah.[8] Before the December 1958 All African Peoples Conference in Accra, Tom Mboya was visited by Nyerere in Nairobi. They decided that it would be an opportune time to bring together the nationalist movements of East and Central Africa.[9]

On September 17, 1958, PAFMECA was established to "coordinate regional activities towards the achievement of independence for territories in East and Central Africa," but, at both this and its second meeting, PAFMECA affirmed that an East African Federation prior to independence was irrelevant.[10] Federation was still seen as an imperialist plan to maintain control over the still dependent countries.

Subsequent meetings of PAFMECA were held in Zanzibar (April 4, 1959) and in Moshi (December 8–12, 1959), and a number of PAFMECA-sponsored committees were sent to the individual territories to survey political situations. Julius Nyerere was meanwhile canvassing the feeling on federation. At the Second Conference of Independent African states held in Addis Ababa (June 14–24), he announced that a dignified African personality required political unification in East Africa and that Tanganyika would be willing to delay her independence to achieve this end.[11] At the fourth General Meeting of PAFMECA on October 24, 1960, at Mbale in Eastern Uganda, President Nyerere presented his famous "Freedom and Unity" speech in which he rejected any uninvited participation by an imperialist power, insisting that a decision on federation "must be willed, designed and put into effect by the peoples of East Africa themselves."[12] Even though the original focus of PAFMECA was on liberation movements, it added federation to its goals by formally endorsing Nyerere's proposal. At another meeting in Nairobi in January, PAFMECA delegates affirmed, in their final resolution, that:

---

[7] Richard Cox, *Pan-Africanism in Practise* (London: Oxford University Press, 1964), p. 5.

[8] *Ibid.*

[9] Tom Mboya, *Freedom and After* (Boston: Little, Brown and Co., 1963), p. 206.

[10] "Political and Regional Groupings in Africa," *International Organization,* XVI (Spring 1962), 446.

[11] Cox, *op. cit.,* p. 36.

[12] *Memorandum on Federation and Self-Government,* address to the PAFMECA Conference, October 24, 1960, Mbale, Uganda.

> A federation was politically and economically essential, that it could only be brought about by elected and African controlled governments and that . . . such governments should confer and work out the details of the federation and that no reactionary and imperialist elements should interfere with the designing of the federation . . .[13]

Nyerere's sense of timing on federation involved a strong belief that federation should come about when each of the territories reached the stage of self-government. If it occurred before self-government, it could not be a true expression of the will of the African majority. If it came after independence, the countries might refuse to give up the attributes of sovereignty, especially their international representation on such bodies as the United Nations.[14] To this end, Nyerere pressured the British government to accelerate the granting of internal self-government to both Uganda and Kenya. A few months later, the press reported that the governors of the three territories had discussed with the Colonial Secretary how they could help African leaders achieve federation[15] Macleod, the Colonial Secretary, was asked in the House of Commons "whether the timing of the grants of independence in East Africa were being considered so as to assist in the establishment of a federation."[16]

The answer to this and other unanswered questions about the British approach to federation is contained in the report of the *Proceedings of the East African Conference, 1961*. The major theme at this conference, attended by the Colonial Secretary with his major advisors, the three East African governors and the Resident at Zanzibar, was federation. It was agreed that the major objective of British policy in East Africa was to be a federation with separate independence for individual territories as a stop gap if they could not obtain federation.[17] The delegates discussed a political timetable which envisaged an independent federation in 1964. They agreed that everything possible should be done to support Nyerere's desire for bringing all territories to self-governing status at the same time, but cautioned that Britain must appear to take no overt initiative in the matter. One of the deputy secretaries, in a discussion of the impending release of the Raisman Report on the East African Common Market, raised the point as to whether the government should give it open support, since, he said, "this was after all a small step along the road to federation and any support might run counter to our policy of letting local opinion initiate support for federation."[18]

---

[13] A. J. Hughes, *East Africa: The Search for Unity* (Baltimore: Penguin Books, 1963), pp. 227–236; and *Africa Report*, I (February 1961), 11.

[14] *The Times,* November 5, 1960, p. 6.

[15] *Uganda Argus* (Kampala), January 14, 1961, p. 1.

[16] *East Africa and Rhodesia,* January 5, 1961, p. 521.

[17] *Proceedings of East African Conference 1961,* African No. 1203, Colonial Office, January 4–10, 1961, p. 135.

[18] *Ibid.,* p. 42.

Why then did the British government not grant internal self-government to the territories at the same time, despite the clear awareness of Nyerere's demand that it was a prerequisite to federation?[19] In the conclusions of the East African Conference, it was stated that "The establishment of an East African federation should be the aim of policy, but this must not prejudice the possibility of establishing stable government, and particularly in Kenya, of solving special problems."[20]

The various ways in which the report reiterated this point suggest that it was Britain's judgment that Kenya and Uganda's prospects of stability did not satisfy British requirements and therefore compelled the government to stagger the timing of self-government in all three territories. Accordingly, Tanganyika was granted self-government in March 1961, and independence on December 9, 1961; Uganda attained self-government in March 1962, and independence on October 9, 1962; Kenya's dates were March 1963 and December 12, 1963; Zanzibar's were July 1963 and December 10, 1963. There is no question that the British government knew that this timing was bad with respect to the prospects of federation, since they had explicitly agreed with Nyerere's assessment of the political situation, though obviously not with the remedies. Had the British acceded to Nyerere's wish, for simultaneous independence, they, like Pilate, might have been able to wash their hands and say they had done all they could to help.

Given the recognition by all parties that the High Commission and Common Market would be difficult to hold together as the three territories advanced along separate schedules to independence, it was agreed, in 1961, to continue and even to broaden the activities of the High Commission. Consequently, the organization was modified to be compatible with Tanganyika's new sovereignty, and it restyled the East African Common Services Organization (EACSO). Promises were also made to preserve and defend the East African Common Market, the common tariff and customs arrangements, and the East African Currency Board, in line with the recommendations of the Raisman Report.[21] Tanganyika's willingness to adjust to these ties after its independence, in light of disappointments over the staggered timing of independence, was highly praised by the distinguished Secretary-General of EACSO, A. L. Adu.[22] Indeed, the combination of PAFMECA and the new representative Central Legislative Assembly of EACSO was viewed as "excellent forums for informal discussions of federation and for the launching of trial balloons."[23]

---

[19] *Memorandum of Federation and Self-Government.*

[20] *Proceedings of East African Conference 1961*, p. 139. See also pp. 47, 53, and 84.

[21] See Great Britain, Colonial Office, *The Report of the Economic and Fiscal Commission*, Cmnd. 1279 (London: H.M.S.O., 1961).

[22] "Adu Praises Nyerere's Act of Faith," *Tanganyika Standard,* July 26, 1963, p. 5.

[23] Aaron Segal and Carl Rosberg, "An East African Federation," *International Conciliation Series* No. 453 (May 1963), p. 63.

PAFMECA continued to grow in influence with both Somalia and Ethiopia, seeking invitations to join in talks on federation and to participate in EACSO. At the February 1962 annual PAFMECA conference, the two countries committed themselves to federation, and several Southern African countries joined the movement to participate in its liberation activities.[24] A resolution was passed at this meeting urging relentless efforts on behalf of federation, but during 1962, constitutional crises in Kenya and difficulties in the Congo and Central Africa diverted attention from the goal of federation. East African newspapers and magazines, however, vigorously supported and promoted the idea of federation during this period. Yet there was considerable evidence that powerful elements in Uganda resented the efforts of other territories to push her into a political federation, even though the movement was now wholly African-sponsored.[25] A week before Uganda's independence, the three East African countries demonstrated their continued desire for association when they agreed to negotiate as one bloc in discussing the offer of associate status in the European Common Market.[26] At about the same time, a group in EACSO was preparing an elaborate plan for further economic unification of East Africa.[27]

Additional dynamism for federation was generated at the history-making summit conference of Independent African States held in Addis Ababa, May 22–23, 1963. A charter of African unity was agreed on by the thirty leaders as a guide for a new Organization of African Unity (OAU). One of the first duties of OAU was to establish an African Liberation Committee of Nine to guide liberation movements throughout the continent. In one stroke, half of PAFMECA's *raison d'être* was transferred to the new organization, although headquarters for the Committee of Nine was to be in Dar es Salaam. When the heads of the East African states arrived back in Nairobi, they met for two hours to draft their famous June 5 Declaration of Federation, which committed the three governments to press for federation in 1963. Thus, within a month, PAFMECA's two goals—liberation and unity—were transferred to the new OAU, in the first instance, and to the constituent East African governments, in the second. PAFMECA was never formally dissolved, though Richard Cox writes that Kaunda sounded out opinion for a final formal meeting in October 1963, but was not successful.[28] Tom Mboya wrote the epitaph of PAFMECA in anticipation of its death: "It has served a most significant purpose in East and Central Africa. It has helped to coordinate nationalist efforts and strategy in the struggle for *uhuru* as well as the

---

24 Cox, *op. cit.* (The name PAFMECA was changed at this time to PAFMECSA to account for the addition of Southern Africa.)

25 *Reporter* (Nairobi), January 12, 1963, p. 1.

26 Mboya, *op. cit.,* p. 188.

27 Private interview with A. L. Adu, Nairobi, September 25, 1964.

28 Cox, *op. cit.,* p. 70.

struggle against the Central African Federation. It has also helped to keep alive and promote the idea of East African Federation."[29]

THE AFTERMATH OF THE JUNE DECLARATION

The main principles of the Declaration of June 5, 1963, included setting up a six-man ministerial working party which was charged with drafting a constitution for a federation. In its original conception, the working party comprised Tom Mboya, Minister for Justice and Constitutional Affairs, and Joseph Murumbi, Minister of State in the Prime Minister's Office (Kenya); Oscar Kambona, Minister for External Affairs and Defense, and A. H. Jamal, Minister for Communications Power and Works (Tanganyika); Godfrey Binaisa, Attorney General (Uganda), and John Kakonge, Secretary-General of Uganda's ruling Peoples Congress party. The working party was asked to report back before the third week of August when a full-scale conference of representatives and leaders of the governments concerned was scheduled to consider the forthcoming proposals.[30]

The first meeting of the working party was held in Dar es Salaam on June 9 and 10. After the meeting, the delegates were very optimistic and issued statements to the press claiming agreement on every issue that was raised. The working party then instructed the attorney generals of the respective countries to draft the actual terms of the constitutional instrument for the proposed federal government. The document was to be ready in time for the next meeting of the working party, which was slated for June 29. Secondly, the working party asked the United Nations, through its Dar es Salaam representative, George Ivan Smith, to provide three experts to help with the delineation of the financial arrangements that federation would require, the reorganization of the civil service, and also to study and advise on the implications of federation for the East African Common Service Organization. It was hoped that the U.N. report would also be ready by June 29. Meanwhile, Kambona was quickly dispatched to Nyasaland and Northern Rhodesia to bring Dr. Banda and Kaunda "into the picture."[31]

The public response to the East African governments' intention to federate was spontaneous and enthusiastic both within East Africa and elsewhere. Trade unions, chambers of commerce, farmers' unions, etc. declared their support for a federation and laid plans for the amalgamation of their unions and associations on an East African basis.[32] Outside East Africa, support came from Nigeria, India, the United States, Chile, Iraq, and the United

---

[29] Mboya, *op. cit.,* p. 214.

[30] *Tanganyika Standard,* June 6, 1963, p. 1.

[31] *Tanganyika Standard,* June 14, 1963, p. 1.

[32] *Reporter* (Nairobi), June 22, 1963, p. 64; *East African Standard,* September 3, 1963, p. 5.

Kingdom. The Nigerian Foreign Minister expressed a desire and hope for close cooperation between Nigeria and an East African federation.[33] In September, the British government appointed Sir Geoffrey de Freitas, then serving as British High Commissioner to Ghana, as the first head of the British Mission to an independent Kenya. It was hoped that Sir Geoffrey would subsequently fill the role of British High Commissioner to the proposed East African federation.[34]

With this enthusiastic world-wide support, the working party met in Kampala on June 29 for its third meeting. Prior to the meeting, the heads of governments also assembled in Kampala to meet and talk to Uganda's traditional rulers who were still in doubt about their future role within an East African federation. Conceivably, the traditional rulers were assured that the federation would not usurp their long-established authorities. The heads of government also wanted to make themselves available for consultation by the working party, in case the need to do so should arise.[35]

As events transpired, the Kampala meeting was marked by the absence of a communiqué. It was obvious that the members of the working party had discussed the actual constitutional instruments of a federation and that they had encountered fundamental disagreements. It is reported that the Uganda government changed its views on previous agreements that had been reached by the representatives of the three governments on the proposed federation. This change of attitude on the part of Uganda was further reflected by a change of one of its representatives on the working party. Previously Uganda was represented by Godfrey Binaisa and John Kakonge, and it was these two delegates who had taken part in the deliberations of the working party. It was also Binaisa who, in his capacity as Uganda Attorney General, had participated in drafting the federal constitution that Uganda now opposed. At the Kampala meeting, Binaisa was replaced by Adoko Nekyon, Minister for Information, who subsequently became the chief spokesman of the Uganda delegation, with Binaisa attending only as an advisor. In this and subsequent meetings of the working party, Nekyon (reflecting a sudden shift in Obote's attitude to federation) reversed the stand that had been taken by his predecessor.[36]

Despite basic disagreements raised by the Uganda delegation, the working party decided to meet again after consultation with their respective govern-

---

[33] *Tanganyika Standard*, July 6, 1963.

[34] *Reporter* (Nairobi), September 14, 1963, p. 11.

[35] The heads of state met with all the traditional rulers except the Kabaka of Buganda. The latter could not find time for the meeting. See *Uganda Argus*, July 2, 1963, p. 1.

[36] These and other deliberations of the working party were subsequently revealed by Tanzania's Minister for External Affairs, Oscar Kambona, in a speech to the National Assembly on June 23, 1964. See Parliamentary Debates (Hansard), *National Assembly Official Report*, 13th Meeting, June 16–July 3, Col. 342–350. 1964.

ments. In the third meeting in Dar es Salaam on August 10 and 11, the working party included not only the attorney generals and other representatives, but a delegation from Zanzibar as well. The Zanzibar contingent consisted of the Minister for Home and Legal Affairs, Sheikh Ali Muhsin; the Minister for Health, Sheikh Ahmed Bualawy; and the Attorney General, J. F. Rumboldo. The East African Common Services Organization was represented by its Secretary General, A. L. Adu and D. C. Lutta.

It was only after the third meeting that the differences that had beset the working party were publicly aired. On his return to Kampala, Nekyon told reporters that there were a number of issues that were still outstanding and that would have to be settled before taking the next step toward a federation. He listed (1) matters affecting the civil service, (2) siting of the federal capital, (3) whether to have a single or a bicameral legislature, (4) if there are to be two chambers, what powers would be allocated to each, (5) disagreements concerning citizenship, and (6) division of powers and responsibilities between federal and state governments.[37] Nekyon added that, as a small state, Uganda needed certain guarantees for her future within a larger unit. "I want to see that Uganda knows exactly where she is going. I am not prepared just to throw my nation to darkness, so I must know exactly where we are going and to whom we are surrendering our powers."[38]

Early in September, Julius Nyerere said in Stockholm, while touring Sweden, that "there were justifiable doubts about the setting up of an East African federation this year."[39] He indicated that there would be a meeting soon of East African leaders to determine whether "we were overambitious or not."[40] The meeting in question took place in Nairobi on September 20, 1963. As it turned out, the meeting did, in fact, determine that the heads of state were "overambitious." Prime Minister Obote could not find time to attend the summit, while Kenyatta and Nyerere waited with their delegates for Dr. Obote in Nairobi for the meeting. At the last moment, Obote sent his Minister for Communications instead. This incident marked a final blow to the hopes for federation that Prime Minister Obote himself helped raised on June 5, 1963. The door to federation was thus closed, at least for 1963.[41] Referring to this blow, President Nyerere said, on December 9, 1963, the anniversary of Tanganyika's independence, that the failure of federation was his biggest disappointment of the year.[42]

Uganda, smaller in size and population than either Kenya or the United Republic of Tanzania, has reservations regarding complete merger with her

---

[37] *Reporter* (Nairobi), August 24, 1963, pp. 10–12.

[38] *Loc. cit.*

[39] *Tanganyika Standard,* September 14, 1963, p. 1.

[40] *Loc. cit.*

[41] *Tanganyika Standard,* September 21, 1964, p. 1.

[42] Cox, *op. cit.,* p. 75.

two neighbors, and there is some doubt as to whether Uganda was ever really serious. While speaking on an opposition member's motion in the National Assembly, seeking information on the status of negotiations on the proposed federation, Nekyon, now Minister for Planning and Community Development, listed a number of points on which the Uganda government could not compromise. They are the following. (1) The capital must be in Uganda to avoid its becoming forgotten by larger member-states. (2) Uganda must be able to remain its seat at the United Nations, and its sovereignty must also be retained. (3) Member-states of a federation must retain their independent powers to raise money abroad. (4) Agriculture (including marketing boards) must remain a responsibility for each member-state. (5) Higher education, trade unions, lands, and mineral resources must be controlled by the individual states. (6) Interterritorial movement of people must be controlled to protect Uganda against being swamped by Kenya's urban unemployed. (7) Representation in the projected federal House of Representatives may be based on apportionment, but Uganda contends that each member-state must have equal representation in the Senate.[43]

Assuming that the above demands were granted, one fails to see what form of federation Uganda desired, for such arrangements could hardly even qualify as a confederacy. In rationalizing her stand regarding retention of sovereignty, the Uganda government advanced two arguments. First, because Uganda herself is federal, the government would need to retain certain autonomy over and above that enjoyed by her constituent provinces. If this were not the case, Uganda would disappear as a state, leaving her constituent provinces and kingdoms as constituencies in a larger federation. A second argument advanced by Uganda government in favor of retaining complete autonomy concerned Uganda's attitude toward pan-Africanism. During the meeting of the working party, which took place in Kampala on May 30, 1964, the Uganda delegate, Nekyon, was reported to have put the following question before the members: "What powers Uganda would surrender to the Continental Government of Africa, if and when established, if Uganda now surrenders foreign affairs to the Federal Government in East Africa?"[44] Ironically, Uganda comes close to Nkrumah's stand with reference to the dialectic regarding approaches to a future continental African government.

President Kwame Nkrumah of Ghana objects to the concept of regional associations as contrary to the ultimate objectives of pan-Africanism. Both in his writings and at conferences of African heads of state and government, Dr. Nkrumah has persistently objected to what he calls "The new and dangerous doctrine of the 'step by step' course."[45] Nkrumah's dialectic

---

[43] *Africa Report,* August 1964, p. 25. See also Kambona's statement to the National Assembly.

[44] *Loc. cit.*

[45] See Nkrumah's speech to the Assembly of African Heads of State and Government, Cairo, United Arab Republic, July 17–21, 1964.

scheme calls for the creation of a Union Government of Africa, now claiming that "to say that the Union Government of Africa is premature is to sacrifice Africa on the altar of neo-colonialism." Dr. Nkrumah has urged all states agreeing with him to immediately designate representatives to a constitutional convention to draft a constitution for the Federal Union Government of Africa. According to the plan, the heads of states and government should meet within six months and "proclaim to the world the Federal Union Government of Africa."[46] According to Nkrumah, the Union Government should consist of an Assembly of Heads of States and Government headed by a President elected from among the heads of states and government of "Independent African States." The Executive of the Union Government would consist of a Cabinet or Council of Ministers with a Chancellor or Prime Minister at its head, and a Federal House consisting of two Chambers —a Senate and a House of Representatives.[47]

In his drive to secure support for his approach to a Union Government of Africa, Dr. Nkrumah has urged his fellow African leaders contemplating the establishment of regional transnational associations to cease from taking that "dangerous" course. Kenya's Mwai Kibaki wrote early in 1963: "The debate seems to be between those who think that the independent African states should aim at forming a 'political union' . . . directly; and those who think the best approach lies in 'functional cooperation' and the promotion of 'regional associations' which would then work out the political unification of all Africa. To us . . . the regional approach is the most practical."[48] There is evidence that, in the case of East Africa, Dr. Nkrumah did try and may still be trying to influence those in authority and positions of influence to frustrate attempts to establish an East African federation. Toward the close of 1963, Ghana's activities in this direction were very intensive, demonstrated by the increased staff of the Ghanaian High Commission—particularly in Kampala. It is reported that on June 26, 1963, the Ghana High Commission in London arranged for a cocktail party to which a number of government officials were invited. On entering the house of the High Commission, Tom Mboya was handed a paper by an official in the High Commission outlining Ghana's objections to an East African federation.[49] It is interesting to note that D. Basumtwi-Sam, who was Ghanaian High Commissioner to Uganda at the time of Uganda's about-face on federation, was subsequently appointed head of the Ghanaian delegation to Nairobi. It was at about this time that the Kenya government also began to evidence a reluctance to forge ahead and federate with the United Republic of Tanzania.[50]

---

[46] Kwame Nkrumah, "Why Africa Must Unite," *Africa and the World* (October 1964), pp. 11–16.

[47] *Loc. cit.*

[48] *Spearhead*, II (April 1963), 14.

[49] Cox, *op. cit.*, p. 77.

[50] For the United Republic's offer to federate with Kenya alone, see Kambona's speech to the National Assembly, *op. cit.*

What is not completely clear is whether or not Dr. Obote in fact agrees with Dr. Nkrumah's approach to African unity. However, Tanzania's stand on this issue has been eloquently stated by President Nyerere on many occasions. In his article entitled "A United States of Africa," President Nyerere argues that while the goal toward a United States of Africa must remain firm, "this does not mean that we must—or that we could—achieve the goal tomorrow, in one step."[51] Dr. Nyerere goes on to say that "different areas may advance on the road to unity at different speeds, and that the methods of advance will vary according to the conditions now existing . . . many of us in East Africa believe that our best path to unity may be through a regional association."[52]

Uganda's stand in the talks for the establishment of an East African federation and Kenya's refusal to federate with Tanzania without Uganda seem to have caused considerable consternation among the leaders of the United Republic of Tanzania. While addressing the Annual Delegates' Conference of TANU on April 1, 1964, President Nyerere said that, judging from the pace things were moving at the moment, East African federation could not come about this year or even next year. President Nyerere said, "I would be deceiving you if I say there will be a federation this year; there may be one next year, but it is unexpected."[53] The President then revealed that East African leaders were now in the process of finding out what was to be done, having realized that the federation would not come about immediately.[54]

COLLAPSE OF HOPES FOR IMMEDIATE FEDERATION

Having failed to effect an immediate federation of East Africa, the United Republic of Tanzania turned its attention to the existing African federal arrangements and especially those concerning interstate trade. Economic cooperation and consultation among East African governments goes back many years. In 1917, free trade between Uganda and Kenya was established and extended subsequently to include Tanganyika and Zanzibar. Because of her unique political status—first as a League of Nations mandate territory, then as a United Nations trust territory—Tanganyika joined this embryonic common market only by stages. A common external tariff, free exchange of domestic products, a free transfer of imported goods, and a unified customs department were successfully added.[55]

On January 1948, the East African High Commission was inaugurated and assumed responsibility for the provision and supervision of many inter-

---

51 See the *Journal of Modern African Studies,* I (March 1963), 1–6.

52 *Ibid.*

53 *Tanganyika Standard,* April 2, 1964, p. 1.

54 *Loc. cit.*

55 *The Report of the Economic and Fiscal Commission,* p. 7.

territorial services. As Tanganyika approached independence, it was evident that it would be necessary to change the structure of the East African High Commission. Thus, in June 1961, discussions in London on the future of the High Commission services resulted in the formation of the present East African Common Services Organization. The headquarters of the High Commission was located in Nairobi. The location in Nairobi of the central offices of trans-territorial business and industrial companies added to Nairobi's disproportionate economic influence. These factors, when coupled with the existence in Kenya of large white and Asian populations, made Nairobi a "little London" in the heart of tropical Africa. Kenya became not only a magnet for outside capital but indeed a monopoly workshop for all goods produced in East Africa. Meanwhile both Tanganyika and Uganda were expected to pay their fair share to the maintenance of the common services. This imbalance helped to stimulate Kenya's economy at the expense of Uganda and Tanganyika. The consequences of this situation are clearly demonstrated by the direction and volume of trade passing between the three territories. (See Table 16–1.)

Table 16–1

Tanzania's Trade with Kenya and Uganda

	IMPORTS			EXPORTS		
Year	From Kenya	From Uganda	Total	To Kenya	To Uganda	Total
1959	6,513	1,587	8,100	1,848	726	2,574
1960	7,608	1,574	9,182	1,875	450	2,325
1961	8,901	1,704	10,605	1,844	390	2,234
1962	10,017	1,669	11,686	1,954	437	2,391
1963	10,365	1,993	12,358	2,915	508	3,423

SOURCE: East African Common Services Organization, *Economic and Statistical Review*, No. 12 (September 1964), 29. At the time of writing, the figures for 1964 were still provisional. Tanzania's value of imported goods from Kenya was estimated at around £3,299; from Uganda the value of imports for 1964 rose to £2,403. Tanzania exported goods worth £4,110 and £1,021 to Kenya and Uganda respectively during the same year. In other words, Tanzania's trade gap with Kenya and Uganda widened during 1964 to over £10.6 million. See Tanzania's *Budget Survey*, pp. 17–18.

NOTE: These figures appear in thousand £'s.

Regarding displacement of imports from overseas by those made in Kenya, the World Bank reported that "to the extent that Tanganyika's actual or potential imports from overseas are displaced by imports from Kenya, Tanganyika loses the revenue which it would otherwise obtain from import duties. In Kenya, on the other hand, the loss of revenue from import displacement will tend to be offset by increased revenue from income tax on companies and their employees."[56] The Tanganyika government has long been aware of this problem, but did not have the power to alter the situation until independence. However, in the words of Oscar Kambona, Minister for External Affairs, "with a federation in mind we remained within the East African Common Market in spite of its disadvantages for Tanganyika."[57]

Having been forced to give up hope for an immediate federation, Tanganyika could obviously ill afford to continue to support the inequitable Common Market arrangements. Thus at an inter-ministerial conference on March 19 called to coordinate development plans, Tanganyika's Minister for Economic Development and Planning, Nsilo Swai, reportedly told his colleagues that Tankanyika was considering withdrawing from the East African Common Market and establishing her own currency, unless something could be done about the ruinous imbalances of inter-territorial trade.[58] Tanganyika's attitude, surprisingly enough, dismayed the Kenya and Uganda governments. Tanganyika was accused by Uganda of threatening to disturb East African trade relations in order to speed up federation.[59] An emergency meeting of the heads of state was called in Nairobi in April 1964 to consider Tanganyika's proposals for reforming inter-territorial trade relations.[60] After subsequent ministerial meetings, the three governments finally agreed, in Kampala on April 29, on measures for reforming this economic relationship; and the three heads of government met in Nairobi, on May 15, to ratify the new trade agreement.[61]

Under these new arrangements, (1) the United Republic of Tanzania will have exclusive rights to supply the needs of the three countries in the assembly and manufacture of Land-Rovers, at least one type of lorry (truck), motor tires, tubes, and radio sets. Furthermore, new plants are to be established in Tanzania by firms now operating in Kenya to supply the local market with tobacco, footwear, and cement. Kenya and Uganda also agreed to increase their purchases and systematically to limit their exports to the United Republic. Reducing these arrangements is intended to reduce the existing Tanzanian trade deficit with Kenya by 24 per cent. (2) Uganda is to manufacture bicycles and nitrogenous fertilizers. (3) Kenya is to manufacture lamps, neon tubes, and pharmaceuticals.[62] Clyde Sanger, the *Man-*

[56] International Bank for Reconstruction and Development, *The Economic Development of Tanganyika* (Baltimore: Johns Hopkins Press, 1960), p. 133.

[57] *National Assembly, op. cit.*

[58] See *Manchester Guardian*, XC, April 9, 1964, 3.

[59] *Tanganyika Standard*, April 13, 1964, p. 1, and April 14, 1964, p. 1.

[60] *Ibid.*

[61] *Ibid.*, May 18, 1964, p. 1.

[62] Cited in *Africa Digest* (August 1964), p. 12. For a full report on the arrangement, see *Kampala Agreement*. The documents covering the discussion arrived at by the Kenya, Uganda, and Tanganyika governments in redressing the imbalance of trade between them, Information Service of the United Republic of Tanzania (Dar es Salaam: Mwananchi Publishing Co., Ltd. 1964).

chester Guardian's East African reporter, stated that Tanzania intends to balance her trade with the rest of East Africa within five or six years, one might add "within or without the Common Market."[63]

The proclamation of a union between Tanganyika and Zanzibar on April 22, 1964, is not irrelevant to an analysis of East African federation. At this writing, negotiations and arrangements leading to union are not publicly known. However, it is clear that the Tanganyika African National Union had long supported and assisted Zanzibar's Afro-Shirazi party.[64] It has been speculated that the Tanganyika government may have encouraged, if not materially supported, Zanzibar's January revolution, in order to place a sympathetic party in power, thus paving the way for union. One might argue that the fact that Presidents Nyerere and Karume decided to unify their two countries rather than wait for an East African federation is itself a manifestation of the impatience and frustration with the slow progress toward larger federation. That the union between Tanganyika and Zanzibar was negotiated in secrecy and did not involve consultation with Premiers Kenyatta and Obote was reflected by the swiftness with which the new union government dispatched its Foreign Minister, Oscar Kambona, to Nairobi and Entebbe to brief the neighboring heads of states about the new arrangements. Fortunately, the two leaders accepted and welcomed the union as one more step toward the ultimate goal of the Organization of African Unity.

CURRENT ALTERNATIVES

The new forces that are manifest in the wake of the breakdown of federation negotiations raise serious questions regarding the political and economic future of East Africa. What are the prospects, now, of forming an effective organic federation of all the East African countries? When might such a federation occur? There are a number of arguments that might be raised in response to those who maintain that hopes for federation have already been shattered by Uganda's position. The character of the international situation, especially with regard to world prices and investment resources, has not been altered by Uganda's decision. Export capital is still a scarce commodity, and an increase in the number of competitors for development capital is not

---

[63] *Manchester Guardian*, XII, August 1964, 3.

Early in June 1965, the three East African Ministers of Finance announced during their budget speeches that they intend to break up the East African Currency Board before the end of the year and that each country will set up its own state bank. Mr. James Aichuru, Kenya's Minister of Finance, is reported to have accused Tanzania for heading the developments which led to this action. See *The Standard*, June 11, 1965, p. 1.

[64] Hughes, *op. cit.*, pp. 209–210.

likely to increase the size of the available portions.[65] Until the Kampala agreement to redress trade inbalance in lieu of federation has been successfully implemented, there is no guarantee that even the present momentum of the East African Common Market can be maintained. Uganda, by rejecting federation and relying on EACSO and on the East African Common Market, may have jeopardized her economic security and chances for rapid development. Uganda's departure from the East African Tourist Travel Association and Tanganyika's near break with the Common Market in April 1964 are but two illustrations of the threat to existing cooperation. One might argue that the common danger is of sufficient magnitude that a worsening situation may auger well for the likelihood of a future federation.

Many observers point to the dangers posed to the existing level of cooperation by the three separate five-year development plans. If the Kampala agreements are implemented and taken into consideration, there is no automatic guarantee that successful fulfillment of the respective five-year plans will rule out a federation. Attainment of the goals of each plan within this framework could, in fact, overcome Kenya's fear of federation without Uganda, since current trade imbalances might be adjusted and there would be less cause to fear throwing in her lot with a significantly more highly developed Tanzania. In connection with this probability, one observer has remarked that, "Unless Tanganyika can create a formula which will overcome its relative backwardness and absolute economic disadvantages, it will continue to wait for a more favourable hearing."[66]

Still another factor that might lead to viewing federation more favorably is the fear that Tanzania's cooperation with the new states to the south might leave Kenya politically and economically isolated. Dr. Kaunda has long been a champion of federation, and recent events indicate that he has sustained this interest.[67] There is reason to believe that completion of a Tanzania–Zambia rail link would lead to Zambia's offering the same balance to federation as did Uganda. Alternatively, Uganda's attitude might change in response to new conditions in that country.[68] There is a strong likelihood that Dr. Obote will be able to consolidate his political position. In August 1964, his party's (UPC) alliance with Kabaka Yekka collapsed. However, he was able to employ the situation to strengthen his party and his

[65] Peter Newman, "East African Economic Growth," *East Africa Journal*, I (April 1964), pp. 16–17. See also T. W. Tyrrell, "The Case for Industrial Co-ordination," *East Africa Journal* (July 1964), pp. 3–5.

[66] Joseph S. Nye, Jr., "The Extent and Viability of East African Cooperation," papers on *Federation and Its Problems*, Nairobi; University of East Africa Conference on Public Policy 1963/64, p. 5.

[67] *Tanganyika Standard*, October 2, 1964, p. 1.

[68] *Ibid.*, April 14, 1964, p. 1.

position effectively. The UPC now has nearly four times as many members as the second-running Democratic party.[69]

The last possibility presented here involves a factor only recently appreciated in East Africa. There is evidence that there exists an increasingly powerful public opinion in support of federation. Nor has this support faded with the failure to implement the June 1963 agreement. It is not without significance that KANU and TANU backbenchers at a Nairobi meeting, ending May 8, demanded action on federation.[70] Such behavior—combined with the steady support given to federation by commercial, university, and other groups—is but a small measure of the wave of public opinion that is trying to make its presence felt as a force favoring federation.

In December 1963, Marco Surveys Ltd. of Nairobi conducted a poll throughout East Africa to try to ascertain the public's reaction to a number of questions pertaining to federation. It is interesting to note that in Uganda 88 per cent of those interviewed said they were in favor of a federation. The figure for Kenya was 96 per cent; and for Tanganyika, 82.5 per cent in favor.[71] In commenting on the results, Marco said that it had been asking similar questions for nearly four years, and the percentages of those interviewed had remained almost constant—with the exception of Uganda where the percentage of those approving had increased steadily over the years. Coupled with the known enthusiasm of many key political leaders in East Africa, this evidence of popular support provides some basis for hope that the prospects for an organic federation of East Africa are still within the realm of political possibility in the foreseeable future.

SELECTED BIBLIOGRAPHY

BOOKS

Altincham, Lord. *Kenya's Opportunity*. London: Faber and Faber, 1955.

Cameron, Sir Donald. *My Tanganyika Service and Some Nigeria*. London: Allen and Unwin, 1939.

Chidzero, B. T. G. *Tanganyika and International Trusteeship*. New York: Oxford University Press, 1961.

Cox, Richard. *Pan-Africanism in Practise*. London: Oxford University Press, 1964.

---

[69] *Reporter* (Nairobi), August 11, 1964, p. 11, and August 28, 1964, p. 15.

[70] *Daily Nation*, July 4, 1964, p. 6.
East Africa Journal, May 1964, p. 31.
The Nationalist, June 24, 1964, p. 6.
Tanganyika Standard, May 11, 1964, p. 1.

[71] Marco Surveys Ltd., *Public Opinion Poll Number 12*, Nairobi, December 1963, p. 1.

Frank, Thomas M. *East African Unity through Law*. New Haven: Yale University Press, 1964.

Hughes, A. J. *East Africa: The Search for Unity*. Baltimore: Penguin Books, 1963.

Ingham, Kenneth. *A History of East Africa*. London: Longmans, Green, and Company, 1962.

Mboya, Tom. *Freedom and After*. Boston: Little, Brown and Co., 1963.

Rothchild, Donald S. *Toward Unity in Africa*. Washington, D.C.: Public Affairs Press, 1960.

ARTICLES

Kibaki Mwai. "Federate How," *Spearhead,* Vol. I, No. 5 (March 1962).

Nkrumah, Kwame. "Why Africa Must Unite," *Africa and the World,* No. 1 (October 1964).

Nye, Joseph S., Jr. "East African Economic Integration," *The Journal of Modern African Studies,* Vol. I, No. 4 (December 1963).

Nyerere, Julius. "A United States of Africa," *The Journal of Modern African Studies,* Vol. I, No. 1 (March 1963).

Okondo, Peter J. H. "Prospects for Federation in East Africa," delivered at Symposium on Federation, Chicago University Law School, February 1–18, 1962.

Rosberg, Carl, Jr., and Aaron Segal, "An East African Federation," *International Conciliation.* No. 453 (May 1963).

Tyrrell, J. W. "The Case for Industrial Coordination," *East African Journal,* Vol. I, No. 4 (July 1964).

PAPERS AND DOCUMENTS

Birch, A. H. *Opportunities and Problems of Federation,* University of East Africa Conference on Public Policy 1963/64, "Federation and Its Problems," Nairobi, November 24–30, 1963.

Colonial Office, *East African Report of the Economic and Fiscal Commission,* Cmnd. 1279 (London: H.M.S.O., 1961).

The Future of the East African Common Services, Cmnd. 1433 (London: H.M.S.O., July 1961).

Kampala Agreement, Information Service of the United Republic of Tanganyika and Zanzibar (Dar es Salaam: Mwananchi Publishing Co., Ltd., 1964).

Macmahon, Arthur, W. *The Viability of Administrative Unions, Independent East Africa, and the Common Services Organization.* International Political Science Association, Oxford Round Table meeting, September 19–24, 1963.

Nyerere, Julius, *Memorandum on Federation and Self-Government,* Address to the PAFMECA Conference at Mbale, Uganda, October 24, 1960.

INDEX

DATE DUE

JUL 3 1969		
MAY 22 1970		
MT. UNION		
NOV 1 4 1977		
GAYLORD		PRINTED IN U.S.A.